JOURNAL

OF THE

CONSTITUTIONAL CONVENTION

OF THE

Commonwealth of Massachusetts,

BEGUN AND HELD

IN BOSTON, ON THE FOURTH DAY OF MAY,

1853.

PRINTED BY ORDER OF THE CONVENTION.

BOSTON:

WHITE & POTTER, PRINTERS TO THE CONVENTION.

1853.

JOURNAL.

Commonwealth of Massachusetts.

STATE HOUSE, CITY OF BOSTON,
WEDNESDAY, May 4, 1853.

Pursuant to the Act of the Legislature of this State, entitled "An Act relating to the calling a Convention of Delegates of the People, for the purpose of revising the Constitution," passed May 7, 1852, which is in the words and figures following, to wit:—

Be it Enacted by the Senate and House of Representatives, in General Court assembled, and by the authority of the same, as follows:—

SECTION 1. The inhabitants of the several cities, towns, districts, and places within this Commonwealth, qualified to vote for senators or representatives in the general court, shall, on the second Monday of November next, at the meeting to be then held in the several cities and towns in the Commonwealth, for the choice of governor, lieutenant-governor, senators and representatives in the general court, an article for this purpose being inserted in the warrants calling said meetings, give in their votes by ballot on this question: "Is it expedient that delegates should be chosen to meet in convention for the purpose of revising or altering the constitution of government of this Commonwealth?" And the vote upon said question shall be in open meeting, and the votes in the several cities and towns in the Commonwealth shall be received, sorted, counted, declared, and transmitted to the Secretary of the Commonwealth, in the same manner as the votes for governor, lieutenant-governor, and senators are now received, sorted, counted, declared and transmitted by the Constitution and laws of the Commonwealth; and all returns not thus made shall be rejected in the counting. And the Governor and Council shall open and examine the returns, made as aforesaid, and count the votes given on the said question; and the governor shall, by public proclamation, to be made on or before the first Wednesday in January next, make known the result, by declaring the number appearing in favor of choosing delegates for the purpose aforesaid, and the number of votes appearing against the same; and if it shall appear that a majority of the votes given in and returned as aforesaid are in favor of choosing delegates as aforesaid, the same shall be deemed and taken to be the will of the people of the Commonwealth, that a Convention should meet accordingly; and in case of such majority, the governor shall call upon the people to elect delegates to meet in Convention, in the manner hereinafter provided.

SECT. 2. If it shall be declared by the said proclamation, that the majority of votes, as aforesaid, is in favor of choosing delegates, as above-mentioned, the inhabitants of the several cities and towns within the Commonwealth, now entitled any one year to send one or more representatives to the general court, shall, on the first Monday of March, in the year one thousand eight hundred and fifty-three, assemble in their several meetings, to be duly notified by warrant from the selectmen of the several towns and the mayor and aldermen of the several cities, and shall elect one or more delegates, not exceeding the number of representatives to which each town or city was entitled last year, it being the year in which the valuation of estates in the Commonwealth was settled, to meet delegates from other towns and cities in Convention, for the purposes hereinafter expressed. And at such meetings of the inhabitants, every person entitled to vote for representatives in the general court, shall have a right to vote in the choice of delegates, and the same officers, in the several cities and towns in the Commonwealth, shall preside at such elections, as now preside in the choice of representatives to the general court; and the votes for said delegates shall be received, sorted, counted, declared, recorded, and copies thereof delivered to the delegates chosen, in the same manner as is now provided for in the case of representatives to the general court. And all laws now in force, regulating the duty and conduct of town and city officers, sheriffs, magistrates, and electors, in the election of governor, lieutenant-governor, senators and representatives, shall, as far as applicable, apply, and be in full force and operation, as to all meetings holden, and elections and returns made, under this Act, or which by this Act are required to be holden or made, and upon the like forfeitures and penalties.

SECT. 3. The persons so elected delegates shall meet in Convention in the State House, in Boston, on the first Wednesday in May, in the year one thousand eight hundred and fifty-three; and they shall be the judges of the returns and elections of their own members, and may adjourn from time to time; and one hundred of the persons elected shall constitute a quorum for the transaction of business; and they shall proceed, as soon as may be, to organize themselves in Convention, by choosing a president and such other officers as they may deem expedient, and by establishing proper rules of proceeding; and when organized, they may take into consideration the propriety and expediency of revising the present constitution of government of this Commonwealth, or the propriety and expediency of making any, and if any, what alterations or amendments, in the present constitution of government of this Commonwealth. And such alterations or amendments, when made and adopted by the said Convention, shall be submitted to the people for their ratification and adoption, in such manner as the said Convention shall direct; and if ratified by the people in the manner directed by the said Convention, the Constitution shall be deemed and taken to be altered or amended accordingly; and if not so ratified, the present Constitution shall be and remain the constitution of government of this Commonwealth.

SECT. 4. The said Convention shall establish the pay or compensation of its officers and members, and the expense of its session; and his excellency the Governor, by and with the advice and consent of the Council, is authorized to draw his warrant on the treasury therefor.

SECT. 5. The Secretary of the Commonwealth is hereby directed forthwith, after the passage thereof, to transmit printed copies of this Act to the selectmen of each town, and the mayor and aldermen of each city within the Commonwealth; and whenever the Governor shall issue his proclamation, calling upon the people to elect delegates, to meet in Convention as aforesaid, the said Secretary shall also, immediately thereafter, transmit printed copies of said proclamation, attested by himself, to the selectmen of each town, and the mayor and aldermen of each city, in the Commonwealth.

A Convention of Delegates, elected by the people, assembled at the State House in Boston on the first Wednesday, being the fourth day of May, A. D. one thousand eight hundred and fifty-three, and were called to order by the Hon. ROBERT RANTOUL, of Beverly, who appointed the following gentlemen a Committee to receive the Credentials of the Delegates, viz.:—

Messrs. Morton, of Taunton, Briggs, of Pittsfield, Bartlett, of Boston, De Witt, of Oxford, and Banks, of Waltham.

This committee afterwards reported that a quorum of Delegates was present.

Mr. CUSHMAN, of Bernardston, submitted the following Order, which was adopted:—

Whereas, It is wise and proper, at the commencement of any great and important work, to invoke the guidance and blessing of the Almighty Ruler of the nations, therefore,

Ordered, That the Chairman be requested to invite some clergyman, a member of this body, to commence the proceedings of the Convention with prayer.

The Rev. Dr. LOTHROP, of Boston, by request of the Chairman, then offered prayer.

Mr. HOOPER, of Fall River, moved that a committee be appointed to collect, sort and count the votes for Secretary of the Convention.

Mr. Williams, of Taunton, moved, as an amendment, that in the election of officers, the members vote *viva voce.* The amendment was rejected.

Mr. Nayson, of Amesbury, moved to amend, so as to provide for the choice of a President, instead of a Secretary. This amendment was also rejected.

The motion of Mr. Hooper was then agreed to.

The Chairman appointed Messrs. Griswold, member for Erving, Morey, of Boston, Allen, of Worcester, Upham, of Salem, and Graves, of Lowell, to constitute the committee.

Afterwards, the committee reported, as follows:—

The whole number of votes is	394
Necessary for a choice,	198
William S. Robinson, of Lowell, has	247
Charles W. Storey, of Roxbury, has	144
Lorenzo M. Gamwell, of Pittsfield, has	1
E. P. Hathaway, of Freetown, has	1
Ezra Wilkinson, of Dedham, has	1

The Report was accepted, and Messrs. Hood, of Lynn, Hale, of Bridgewater, and Gray, of Boston, were appointed a committee to notify Mr. Robinson of his election.

Mr. Keyes, member for Abington, moved that the Secretary be sworn to the faithful discharge of the duties of his office. This motion was agreed to, and the oath was administered by the Chairman.

Mr. Keyes, member for Abington, moved the appointment of a committee to receive, sort and count the votes for a second Secretary of the Convention; but afterwards withdrew the motion.

On motion of Mr. Hooper, of Fall River, the following gentlemen were appointed a committee to receive, sort and count the votes for President of the Convention, viz.: Messrs. Davis, of Worcester, Appleton, of Boston, Chapin, of Springfield, Walker, of North Brookfield, and Braman, of Danvers.

The committee afterwards reported, as follows:—

Whole number of ballots,	391
Necessary to a choice,	196
Hon. Nathaniel P. Banks, Jr., has	250
Hon. George N. Briggs, has	137
Hon. H. W. Bishop, has	1
Ezra Wilkinson, has	1
E. P. Hathaway, has	1
Bradford L. Wales, has	1

The Report was accepted, and the Chairman appointed Messrs. Choate, of Boston, Weston, of Duxbury, and Walcott, of Salem, a committee to notify Mr. BANKS of his election.

The PRESIDENT having been conducted to the chair, signified his acceptance of the office, and entered upon the discharge of its duties.

Mr. KEYES, member for Abington, renewed his motion for the appointment of a committee to receive, sort and count the votes for a second Secretary of the Convention.

The motion was agreed to, and Messrs. Griswold, member for Erving, Morey, of Boston, Allen, of Worcester, Upham, of Salem, and Graves, of Lowell, were appointed. They afterwards reported, as follows:—

Whole number of votes, ...	348
Necessary for a choice, ...	175
James T. Robinson, of Adams, has	235
W. E. P. Haskell, of Chelsea, has	83
Charles W. Storey, of Roxbury, has	29
Samuel B. Sumner, of Great Barrington, has . .	1

The Report was accepted, and upon motion of Mr. GOURGAS, of Concord, the Secretary was directed to notify Mr. J. T. ROBINSON of his election.

On motion of Mr. WILSON, of Natick,

Resolved, That a committee of one from each county be appointed by the President of the Convention, to consider and report as to the best mode of proceeding to the revision of the Constitution of the Commonwealth.

The President appointed the committee, as follows:—

Messrs.	Wilson, of Natick,	for Middlesex County.
	Choate, of Boston,	" Suffolk "
	Nayson, of Amesbury,	" Essex "
	Earle, of Worcester,	" Worcester "
	Beach, of Springfield,	" Hampden "
	Aspinwall, of Brookline,	" Norfolk "
	Gilbert, of Plainfield,	" Hampshire "
	Cushman, of Bernardston,	" Franklin "
	Dawes, of Adams,	" Berkshire "
	Hathaway, of Freetown,	" Bristol "
	Hale, of Bridgewater,	" Plymouth "
	Weeks, of Harwich,	" Barnstable "
	Meader, of Nantucket,	" Nantucket "
	Pease, of Edgartown,	" Dukes "

Mr. HALL, of Haverhill, offered an Order for the appointment of a committee of five to report Rules and Orders for the regulation of the Convention, and providing that in the mean time the Rules and Orders of the House of Representatives, as far as they are applicable, be the rules of the Convention.

The Order was adopted, and Messrs. Hall, of Haverhill, Crowninshield, of Boston, Whitney, of Conway, Gooch, of Melrose, and Lord, of Salem, were appointed upon the committee.

Mr. HALLETT, member for Wilbraham, offered the following Resolution, which was referred to the committee on reporting proper modes of proceeding to the revision of the Constitution.

Resolved, That the several distinct subjects and provisions embraced in the Constitution of this Commonwealth be referred each to a committee to take into consideration the propriety and expediency of making any, and if any, what alterations or amendments therein, with instructions to report thereon in printed form, at the adjourned meeting of this Convention, and with the power of conference between any or all of the committees herein appointed, namely:

1st. So much of the Constitution as is contained in the Preamble and Declaration of Rights.

2d. So much as relates to the General Court, in section 1 of chapter 1, and so much as relates to Settling Elections by the Legislature, in article 7 of section 3, chapter 2.

3d. So much as relates to the Senate in section 2 of chapter 1.

4th. So much as relates to the House of Representatives in section 3 of chapter 1.

5th. So much as relates to the Governor and the Militia, in section 1 of chapter 2.

6th. So much as relates to the Lieutenant-Governor, the Council, and the Secretary and Treasurer, in sections 2, 3 and 4 of chapter 2, except article 7 of section 3.

7th. So much as relates to the Judiciary Power in chapter 3, and the last two clauses of article 13, section 1 of chapter 2, relating to Salaries.

8th. So much as relates to the University at Cambridge, and Encouragement of Literature, in sections 1 and 2 of chapter 5.

9th. So much as relates to Oaths and Subscriptions, Incompatibility of Offices, Disqualifications, Commissions, Writs, Confirmation of Laws, Habeas Corpus, and the Enacting Style; including the first eight articles in chapter 6.

10th. So much as relates to the Qualifications of Voters, and

Manner of Voting, Amendments of the Constitution and its Enrolment, in articles 9, 10 and 11 of chapter 6.

Mr. MORTON, of Fairhaven, offered an Order for the appointment of a committee of seven, to take into consideration the course to be adopted for reporting the proceedings of the Convention, and for publishing the same; which Order was adopted.

Mr. WILSON, of Natick, offered the following Resolutions, which, upon his motion, were referred to the Committee on the proper mode of proceeding to the Revision of the Constitution:—

1. *Resolved*, That the Preamble and Bill of Rights, the Frame of Government and article 7 of chapter 6, concerning the writ of Habeas Corpus, be referred to a committee of nine, to consider and report thereon.

2. *Resolved*, That so much of the Constitution as relates to the Right of Suffrage, and also the subject of the Ballot, be referred to a committee of nine, to consider and report thereon.

3. *Resolved*, That so much of the Constitution as relates to the legislative power, the Senate and the House of Representatives, be referred to a committee of one from each county, to consider and report thereon.

4. *Resolved*, That so much of the Constitution as relates to the Governor, the Lieutenant-Governor, and the Council, be referred to a committee of nine, to consider and report thereon.

5. *Resolved*, That so much of the Constitution as relates to the Secretary of State, Treasurer, Attorney-General, Solicitor-General, Sheriffs, Coroners, Registers of Probate, and Notaries Public, be referred to a committee of nine, to consider and report thereon.

6. *Resolved*, That so much of the Constitution as relates to the Judiciary, be referred to a committee of nine, to consider and report thereon.

7. *Resolved*, That so much of the Constitution as relates to the University at Cambridge, and to the Encouragement of Literature, be referred to a committee of nine, to consider and report thereon.

8. *Resolved*, That so much of the Constitution as relates to Oaths and Subscriptions, Incompatibility of and Exclusion from Office, Pecuniary Qualifications, Commissions, Writs, Confirmation of Laws, the Enacting Style, and Amendments of the Constitution, be referred to a committee of nine, to consider and report thereon.

Mr. WALKER, of North Brookfield, offered an Order, which was adopted, for the appointment of a committee of five, to ascertain and report whether a suitable hall and committee-rooms can be obtained for the use of the Convention.

The PRESIDENT appointed the committee, as follows: Messrs. Walker, of North Brookfield, Bartlett, of Boston, Knowlton, of Worcester, Morton, of Andover, and Abbott, of Danvers.

Mr. HALLETT, member for Wilbraham, offered an Order, which was laid over under the rule of the Convention, until to-morrow, providing for the appointment of a committee of five, with authority to select and employ Reporters for the Convention.

On motion of Mr. EARLE, of Worcester,

Ordered, That when the Convention adjourn, it adjourn to meet again on Thursday, at ten o'clock in the forenoon.

Afterwards, Mr. HALE, of Bridgewater, moved a reconsideration of the vote adopting the Order, but the motion to reconsider was rejected.

Mr. KNOWLTON, of Worcester, presented the memorial of Leonard M. Parker, with a copy of the record of the town of Shirley, relating to the choice of Delegate in that town.

Laid upon the table.

Mr. WILSON, of Natick, offered an Order, that the Secretary of the Convention be directed to furnish, for the use of the members, five hundred copies of the Report of the Proceedings and Debates of the Constitutional Convention of 1820.

Laid over under the rule.

On motion of Mr. EARLE, of Worcester,

Ordered, That a Committee on Elections be appointed, consisting of seven members, to consider and report upon the qualifications of members of the Convention.

On motion of Mr. KEYES, member for Abington, the Secretary was directed to furnish to the several members of the Convention, during its sittings, such newspapers, published in the Commonwealth, as they may select, not exceeding three *per diem*.

On motion of Mr. CUSHMAN, of Bernardston, Thursday, at twelve o'clock, was assigned as the hour for the choice of a Chaplain.

On motion of Mr. BRONSON, of Fall River, the Convention adjourned.

THURSDAY, May 5, 1853.

Met according to adjournment. The Journal of yesterday was read. Prayer was offered by the Rev. Dr. BLAGDEN, of Boston, a member of the Convention.

On motion of Mr. GOURGAS, of Concord,

Ordered, That a committee of five be appointed, to consider and report what measures it is desirable for the Convention to adopt, to preserve and perpetuate its records.

On motion of Mr. BATES, of Plymouth,

Ordered, That the committee to whom was referred the credentials of members, be directed to ascertain what towns are represented, and report to the Convention the several towns where vacancies are known to exist, and the number of Delegates to which those towns are entitled.

The PRESIDENT read, for the information of the Convention, a communication which he had received from Benjamin Stevens, Esq., enclosing a joint Order of both branches of the legislature, by which he was directed to make all suitable provisions for the accommodation of the Convention, and to act in his capacity of Sergeant-at-Arms, until the Convention shall otherwise provide.

The PRESIDENT also read a communication from Hon. Henry Wilson, announcing that he had been elected a Delegate to the Convention from the town of Berlin, and also from the town of Natick, and asking leave to decline the position assigned to him by the town of Berlin.

On motion of Mr. HOOPER, of Fall River,

Ordered, That the members be authorized to select copies of the Reports of the Transactions of this Convention, in lieu of an equal number of papers authorized by the Order of yesterday, at the option of the members.

The PRESIDENT announced the appointment of the following gentlemen, to constitute the Committee upon Elections, viz. :—

Messrs. Abbott, of Lowell, Williams, of Taunton, Plunkett, of Adams, Dehon, of Boston, Simmons, of Hanover, White, of Quincy, and Ladd, of Cambridge.

The PRESIDENT also announced the appointment of the following gentlemen, to constitute the committee under the Order offered yesterday, by Mr. Morton, of Fairhaven, in relation to the proper course to be adopted for reporting and publishing the Proceedings of the Convention, viz.:—

Messrs. Hallett, member for Wilbraham, Hale, of Boston, Sleeper, of Roxbury, Schouler, of Boston, Gourgas, of Concord, Bates, of Plymouth, and Greene, of Brookfield.

The same gentlemen were appointed the committee under the Order offered by Mr. Hallett, upon the same subject, which Order was taken up and adopted.

On motion of Mr. KNOWLTON, of Worcester, the Memorial of Leonard M. Parker, concerning the election of Delegate in the town of Shirley, was taken from the table and referred to the Committee on Elections.

The Order offered yesterday by Mr. Wilson, of Natick, and laid over, directing the Secretary to furnish, for the use of the members, five hundred copies of the Report of the Proceedings and Debates of the Constitutional Convention of 1820, was adopted.

On motion of Mr. EARLE, of Worcester,

Ordered, That the Secretary of the Commonwealth be requested to send to the Convention the Credentials of the members thereof, with a list of the members, and that they be referred, when received, to the Committee on Elections.

The PRESIDENT appointed Mr. Brown, of Dracut, a member of the Committee upon Credentials, in place of Mr. Banks, of Waltham.

Mr. WALKER, of North Brookfield, from the committee appointed to ascertain whether a suitable hall and committee-rooms can be obtained for the use of the Convention, submitted a Report, closing with a recommendation that the hall of the Lowell Institute be occupied by the Convention, either temporarily or permanently, as may be deemed expedient.

Mr. HALLETT, member for Wilbraham, moved that the Report be laid upon the table, but the motion was rejected.

On motion of Mr. SIMMONS, of Hanover, the rule of the Convention was suspended so as to allow of the immediate consideration of the Report.

Pending the question upon the acceptance of the Report, Mr. THOMAS, of Weymouth, called for the special assignment, being the election of a Chaplain.

And the President appointed the following gentlemen a committee to receive, sort and count the votes, viz.:—

Messrs. Cushman, of Bernardston, Brinley, of Boston, Graves, of

Lowell, Walker, of Roxbury, Stacy, of Gloucester, and Mason, of Fitchburg.

Afterwards the committee reported as follows:—

The whole number of votes is,	385
Necessary for a choice,	193
Rev. Warren Burton, has	224
Rev. Lyman Beecher, has	129
Rev. James D. Farnsworth, has	17
Rev. Baron Stow, has	2
Rev. F. D. Huntington, has	2
Rev. Daniel Wise, has	2
Rev. Reuben Emerson, has	1
Father McIlroy, has	1
Rev. Charles H. Leonard, has	1
Rev. William H. Knapp, has	1
Rev. Pliny Wood, has	1
Rev. A. A. Miner, has	1
Rev. W. W. Ellis, has	1
Rev. George Richards, has	1
Rev. Joseph H. Clinch, has	1

The Report of the committee was accepted.

On motion of Mr. Morton, of Fairhaven, the Secretary was directed to inform the Rev. Warren Burton that he has been elected Chaplain of the Convention.

The Convention resumed the consideration of the Report on the subject of procuring a hall and committee-rooms; and the question being taken, two hundred and two members voted for the acceptance of the Report, and one hundred and twenty-five members against it. So the Report was accepted.

On motion of Mr. Earle, of Worcester,

Ordered, That when the Convention adjourn, it adjourn to meet to-morrow at ten o'clock in the forenoon.

Mr. Bartlett, of Boston, offered an Order, providing for the appointment of a committee of five to procure the temporary use of the hall of the Lowell Institute for the sittings of the Convention.

At the request of Mr. Hallett, member for Wilbraham, the Order was laid over, a motion made by Mr. Bartlett, of Boston, for a suspension of the rules, to allow of its immediate consideration, not being sustained by the Convention.

Mr. Thompson, of Charlestown, offered the following Order, which was laid over:—

Ordered, That the election of Messenger be specially assigned for to-morrow at the hour of eleven, and that the Messenger then elected shall have power to appoint Assistants.

Mr. Hallett, member for Wilbraham, offered an Order, which was laid over, providing for the appointment of a committee of five to concur with any committee the House of Representatives may appoint, upon an arrangement for alternate sessions on the same or succeeding days, of the House and of this Convention, and to report the result of such conference.

Mr. Thompson, of Charlestown, presented the Memorial of John Sanborn, of Charlestown, claiming a seat in the Convention; and it was referred to the Committee on Elections.

On motion of Mr. Earle, of Worcester, the Convention adjourned.

FRIDAY, May 6, 1853.

Met according to adjournment. Prayer was offered by the Chaplain of the Convention. The Journal of yesterday was read.

On motion of Mr. Briggs, of Pittsfield,

Ordered, That the law of the Commonwealth under which the Convention assembled, be recorded upon the first page of the Journal of the first day's proceedings.

The President read a communication from the Hon. Thomas G. Cary, in behalf of the Trustees of the Boston Athenæum, requesting him to tender to the members of the Convention an invitation to visit that institution, and make use of the Library and Reading-Room.

Mr. Morey, of Boston, in behalf of the Proprietors of the Boston Social Law Library, tendered to the members an invitation to visit that Library during the sittings of the Convention.

On motion of Mr. Allen, of Worcester,

Ordered, That the thanks of the Convention be tendered to the Proprietors of the Boston Athenæum and of the Boston Social Law Library.

Mr. Nayson, of Amesbury, presented the Memorial of Edwin Lawrence and Nehemiah Flanders, of Newburyport, in reference to the election of Delegates in that city; which was referred to the Committee on Elections.

The President read a letter from the Rev. Warren Burton, announcing his acceptance of the office of Chaplain.

Mr. Hall, of Haverhill, from the Committee appointed to prepare Rules and Orders for the regulation of the Convention, submitted a Report, which was read, and on motion of Mr. Livermore, of Cambridge, the rules were suspended, and the Report considered.

On motion of Mr. Hooper, of Fall River, the Report was laid upon the table, and was ordered to be printed.

Mr. Bartlett, of Boston, moved that the Act of the Commonwealth under which the Convention assembled be printed with the Rules and Orders; but afterwards withdrew the motion.

Mr. Morton, of Taunton, submitted a Report from the Committee on Credentials, recommending that the committee be discharged from the further consideration of the subject, and that the subject and papers be referred to the Committee on Elections; and the Report was accepted, and the papers so referred.

Mr. Bates, of Plymouth, offered an Order, that the President of the Convention be directed to issue a precept for the election of a member from the town of Berlin, in the place of Mr. Wilson.

Mr. Wilson, of Natick, from the Committee appointed to consider and report upon the best mode of proceeding to the revision of the Constitution, submitted a Report, recommending the adoption of the following Resolutions, viz.:—

1. *Resolved*, That so much of the Constitution as is contained in the Preamble and Declaration of Rights, be referred to a committee of thirteen, to take into consideration the expediency of making any, and if any, what alterations or amendments, and to report thereon.

2. *Resolved*, That so much of the Constitution as relates to the Frame of Government and the General Court, in section 1 of chapter 1, and also so much as relates to Settling Elections by the Legislature, in article 7 of section 3, chapter 2, be referred to a committee of thirteen, to take into consideration the expediency of making any, and if any, what alterations or amendments, and to report thereon.

3. *Resolved*, That so much of the Constitution as relates to the Senate, be referred to a committee of twenty-one, to take into consideration the expediency of making any, and if any, what alterations or amendments, and to report thereon.

4. *Resolved*, That so much of the Constitution as relates to the

House of Representatives, be referred to a committee of twenty-one, to take into consideration the expediency of making any, and if any, what alterations or amendments, and to report thereon.

5. *Resolved*, That so much of the Constitution as relates to the Governor, in section 1 of chapter 2, except so much as relates to the Militia, in section 10 of said chapter, and section 9 of said chapter, concerning appointments, be referred to a committee of thirteen, to take into consideration the expediency of making any, and if any, what alterations or amendments, and to report thereon.

6. *Resolved*, That so much of the Constitution as relates to the Militia, in section 1 of chapter 2, article 10, be referred to a committee of thirteen, to take into consideration the expediency of making any, and if any, what alterations or amendments, and to report thereon.

7. *Resolved*, That so much of the Constitution as relates to the Lieutenant-Governor, be referred to a committee of thirteen, to take into consideration the expediency of making any, and if any, what alterations or amendments, and to report thereon.

8. *Resolved*, That so much of the Constitution as relates to the Council, in sections 2, 3 and 4 of chapter 2, except article 7 of section 3, be referred to a committee of thirteen, to take into consideration the expediency of making any, and if any, what alterations or amendments, and to report thereon.

9. *Resolved*, That so much of the Constitution as relates to the Secretary and Treasurer, in section 4 of chapter 2, and the Attorney-General, Solicitor-General, Sheriffs, Coroners, Registers of Probate and Notaries Public, being article 9 of section 1, chapter 2, be referred to a committee of thirteen, to take into consideration the expediency of making any, and if any, what alterations or amendments, and to report thereon.

10. *Resolved*, That so much of the Constitution as relates to the Judiciary Power, chapter 3, and the two last clauses of article 13, section 1, chapter 2, relating to Salaries, be referred to a committee of thirteen, to take into consideration the expediency of making any, and if any, what alterations or amendments, and to report thereon.

11. *Resolved*, That so much of the Constitution as relates to the University at Cambridge, being chapter 5, section 2, be referred to a committee of thirteen, to take into consideration the expediency of making any, and if any, what alterations or amendments, and to report thereon.

12. *Resolved*, That so much of the Constitution as relates to the Encouragement of Literature, being chapter 5, section 2, be referred to a committee of thirteen, to take into consideration the expediency

of making any, and if any, what alterations or amendments, and to report thereon.

13. *Resolved*, That so much of the Constitution as relates to Oaths and Subscriptions, Incompatibility of, and Exclusion from Office, Pecuniary Qualifications, Commissions, Writs, Confirmation of Laws, Habeas Corpus, and the Enacting Style, including the eight first articles in chapter 6, be referred to a committee of thirteen, to take into consideration the expediency of making any, and if any, what alterations or amendments, and to report thereon.

14. *Resolved*, That so much of the Constitution as relates to the Qualifications of Voters, being article 9 of chapter 6, be referred to a committee of thirteen, to take into consideration the expediency of making any, and if any, what alterations or amendments, and to report thereon.

15. *Resolved*, That so much of the Constitution as relates to Amendments of the Constitution and Enrolment, being articles 10 and 11 of chapter 6, be referred to a committee of thirteen, to take into consideration the expediency of making any, and if any, what alterations or amendments, and to report thereon.

On motion of Mr. Wilson, the Report was laid upon the table, and ordered to be printed.

The President announced the appointment of the following gentlemen, to constitute the Committee under the Order offered yesterday by Mr. Gourgas, of Concord, to consider and report what measures it is desirable for the Convention to adopt, to preserve and perpetuate its records, viz. :—

Messrs. Gourgas, of Concord, Upham, of Salem, Frothingham, of Charlestown, Dana, member for Manchester, and Eames, of Washington.

The Order offered yesterday for the appointment of a committee to procure the Hall of the Lowell Institute for the sittings of the Convention, was taken up for consideration, and, on motion of Mr. Gardner, of Seekonk, it was laid upon the table.

Mr. Gardner then moved, that when the Convention adjourn on Monday next, it adjourn to meet on the 24th of this month at twelve o'clock. And the question being taken, one hundred and twenty-three members voted in favor of the motion, and two hundred and twenty-five members voted against it; so it was rejected.

On motion of Mr. Hallett, member for Wilbraham, the Order offered by him yesterday, for the appointment of a committee to confer with a committee of the House of Representatives, was taken up for consideration, and was adopted.

The PRESIDENT appointed the following gentlemen to constitute the Committee of Conference, viz.:—

Messrs. Hallett, member for Wilbraham, Briggs, of Pittsfield, Sumner, member for Marshfield, Sumner, member for Otis, and Gray, of Boston.

On motion of Mr. KNOWLTON, of Worcester, the Report of the Committee upon the Mode of Proceeding to the Revision of the Constitution, was taken from the table, and, on motion of the same gentleman, the vote by which the Convention ordered the Report to be printed, was reconsidered, and the Report, with the accompanying Resolutions, was adopted.

The Order offered yesterday by Mr. THOMPSON, of Charlestown, concerning the election of Messenger, was taken up, and having been modified so as to provide that the election shall take place at eleven o'clock on Saturday, was adopted.

On motion of Mr. LADD, of Cambridge,

Ordered, That the Report of Debates in the Convention, published by Messrs. White and Potter, be added to the list of weekly papers to be furnished to the members of the Convention.

On motion of Mr. THOMAS, of Weymouth, the rules were suspended for the purpose of considering the Order offered by Mr. Bates, of Plymouth, for the issuing of a precept to the town of Berlin; and the Order was then adopted.

Afterwards, on motion of Mr. BARTLETT, of Boston, the vote was reconsidered.

On motion of Mr. CROWNINSHIELD, of Boston, the Order was referred to a special committee, with instructions to report on Monday.

The PRESIDENT appointed the committee, consisting of the following gentlemen, viz.: Messrs. Allen, of Worcester, Bartlett, of Boston, Sumner, member for Otis, Crowninshield, of Boston, Butler, of Lowell, Huntington, of Northampton, and Walcott, of Salem.

An Order offered by Mr. THOMAS, of Weymouth, that the Secretary be directed to notify the town of Berlin, that Hon. Henry Wilson, Delegate elected from that town, has resigned his seat,

And an Order offered by Mr. KINSMAN, of Newburyport, instructing the committee under the Order concerning the vacancy in Berlin, to consider and report upon the expediency of filling such other vacancies as may exist in the Convention, from the different towns and cities in the Commonwealth, were considered, the rules being suspended for that purpose; and the Order offered by Mr. THOMAS was referred to the special committee, and the Order offered by Mr. KINSMAN was adopted.

On motion of Mr. MORTON, of Fairhaven,

Ordered, That when the Convention adjourn, it adjourn to meet to-morrow at ten o'clock in the forenoon.

And then, on motion of Mr. HALE, of Bridgewater, the Convention adjourned.

SATURDAY, May 7, 1853.

Met according to adjournment. Prayer was offered by the Chaplain. The Journal of yesterday was read.

Mr. LIVERMORE, of Cambridge, announced that he had been authorized by Edwin P. Whipple, the Superintendent of the Merchants' Exchange Reading-Room, to invite the members to visit that room at their pleasure, during the sittings of the Convention.

On motion of Mr. EARLE, of Worcester,

Ordered, That the thanks of the Convention be presented to Mr. Whipple, for the invitation.

The PRESIDENT read a communication from J. T. ROBINSON, announcing his acceptance of the office of Secretary; and, on motion of Mr. GOURGAS, of Concord, the oath of office was administered to him.

The PRESIDENT appointed Mr. Bishop, of Lenox, a member of the committee, to confer with a committee of the House of Representatives, in relation to the use of the hall of the House by the Convention, in place of Mr. Hallett, member for Wilbraham, who declined to serve.

Mr. BROWN, of Dracut, offered an Order, which was laid over, authorizing the Secretary to furnish each member with a copy of A. S. Barnes & Co.'s edition of the Constitutions of the several States.

Mr. NOYES, of Newbury, moved that when the Convention adjourn, it adjourn to meet at ten o'clock on Monday.

On motion of Mr. WESTON, of Duxbury, sustained by a vote of one hundred and thirty-nine in the affirmative, and ninety-three in the negative, the motion of Mr. Noyes was laid upon the table.

Mr. WESTON then moved to take from the table the Order offered by Mr. Bartlett, of Boston, for the appointment of a committee to procure the use of the hall of the Lowell Institute; and his motion was agreed to by a vote of one hundred and forty-two in the affirmative, to one hundred and four in the negative.

Mr. THOMPSON, of Charlestown, called for the special assignment, which was the election of Messenger; but on motion of Mr. GOURGAS, of Concord, the assignment was laid upon the table.

The question then being upon the adoption of the Order offered by Mr. Bartlett, it was rejected, by a vote of one hundred and eleven in the affirmative, to one hundred and seventy-five in the negative.

On motion of Mr. NOYES, of Newbury, his motion concerning the hour of adjournment was taken from the table. Mr. SIMONDS, of Bedford moved as an amendment, that when the Convention adjourn, it adjourn to meet at seven o'clock in the afternoon on Monday; but the amendment was rejected, and the motion of Mr. Noyes was then agreed to.

On motion of Mr. WOOD, of Fitchburg, the Order concerning the election of Messenger was taken from the table. Mr. CHURCHILL, of Milton, moved that the further consideration of the subject be postponed until Monday, at eleven o'clock; but the motion was rejected, by a vote of one hundred and seven in the affirmative, to one hundred and eighty-nine in the negative.

The PRESIDENT appointed the following gentlemen a committee to receive, sort and count the votes for Messenger, viz.: Messrs. Thompson, of Charlestown, Kuhn, of Boston, Churchill, of Milton, Oliver, of Lawrence, and Griswold, of Buckland. The committee afterwards reported as follows:—

Whole number of votes,	288
Necessary for a choice,	145
Benjamin Stevens, has	284
Albion M. Merrill, has	1
Timothy R. Page, has	1
John R. Bulkley, has	1
J. S. Poole, has	1

On motion of Mr. WILSON, of Natick,

Ordered, That the President be directed to notify the Speaker of the House of Representatives of the appointment of a committee on the part of the Convention, to confer with that body in regard to the occupancy of this hall by the Convention.

On motion of Mr. HOOPER, of Fall River, the Report of the Committee upon Rules and Orders was taken from the table, and amendments were adopted, as follow:—

On motion of Mr. HALL, of Haverhill, the word "House," in the first line of the forty-fifth rule was stricken out, and the word "Convention" substituted in its place;

On motion of Mr. SCHOULER, of Boston, the words "and such motion shall be placed first in the Orders of the Day succeeding that on which the motion is made," were inserted after the word "day," in the fourth line of the twenty-fourth rule;

On motion of Mr. GRAY, of Boston, the following was added to the seventh rule—"The names of members shall be called in alphabetical order";

On motion of the same gentleman, the words, "to suspend any rule," were inserted after the words "lay on the table," in the third line of the eleventh rule;

On motion of Mr. WILSON, of Natick, the words, "of the majority," were struck out of the second line of the twenty-fourth rule.

Pending the consideration of these amendments, Mr. HUBBARD, of Boston, moved to recommit the twenty-fourth rule to the committee; but the motion was rejected, by a vote of ninety-six in the affirmative to one hundred and thirty-one in the negative.

The Report was then adopted, as follows:—

Of the President.

1. The President shall take the chair every day at the hour to which the Convention shall have adjourned; shall call the members to order; and on the appearance of a quorum, shall cause the Journal of the preceding day to be read, and proceed to business.

2. He shall preserve decorum and order; may speak to points of order in preference to other members; and shall decide all questions of order, subject to an appeal to the Convention on motion regularly seconded; and no other business shall be in order till the question on the appeal shall have been decided.

3. He shall declare all votes; but if any member doubts a vote, the President shall order a return of the number voting in the affirmative, and in the negative, without any further debate upon the question. When a vote is doubted, the members for or against the question, when called by the President, shall rise and stand uncovered till they are counted.

4. He shall rise to put a question, or to address the Convention, but may read sitting.

5. In all cases the President may vote.

6. When the Convention shall determine to go into Committee of the Whole, the President shall appoint the member who shall take the chair.

7. On all questions and motions whatsoever, the President shall take the sense of the Convention by yeas and nays, provided one-fifth of

the members present shall so require. When the yeas and nays are taken, no member shall be allowed to vote, who shall have entered the Convention after the calling of the roll is finished. The names of members shall be called in alphabetical order.

8. He shall propound all questions, in the order in which they are moved, unless the subsequent motion be previous in its nature; except that, in naming sums and fixing times, the largest sum and the longest time shall be put first.

9. After a motion is stated or read by the President, it shall be deemed to be in possession of the Convention, and shall be disposed of by vote of the Convention; but the mover may withdraw it at any time before a decision or amendment, except a motion to reconsider, which shall not be withdrawn after the time has elapsed within which it could be originally made.

10. When a question is under debate the President shall receive no motion, but to adjourn, to lay on the table, for the previous question, to postpone to a day certain, to commit, to amend, or to postpone indefinitely; which several motions shall have precedence in the order in which they stand arranged.

11. He shall consider a motion to adjourn as always in order; and that motion, and the motions to lay on the table, to take up from the table, to suspend any rule, and for the yeas and nays, shall be decided without debate.

12. He shall put the previous question in the following form: "*Shall the main question be now put?*"—and all debate upon the main question shall be suspended until the previous question shall be decided. After the adoption of the previous question, the sense of the Convention shall forthwith be taken upon amendments reported by a committee, upon pending amendments, and then upon the main question.

13. On the previous question no member shall speak more than once without leave; and all incidental questions of order, arising after a motion is made for the previous question, shall be decided without debate, excepting on appeal, and on such appeal, no member shall be allowed to speak more than once without leave of the House.

14. When two or more members happen to rise at once, the President shall name the member who is first to speak.

15. All committees shall be appointed and announced by the President, unless otherwise specially directed by the Convention.

16. The President shall have the right to name any member to perform the duties of the Chair, but such substitution shall not extend beyond an adjournment.

17. The President shall have the general direction of the hall of the Convention, and of the galleries. No person excepting members, officers, and attendants of the Convention, and such persons as may be invited by the Convention, or by the President, shall be admitted within the bar of the Convention. The chairman of each Committee of the Whole, during the sitting of such committee, shall have the like power of preserving order in the hall and in the galleries.

Of Absence of President.

18. In case the President shall be absent at the hour to which the Convention was adjourned, the Secretary shall call the Convention to order, and shall preside until a President *pro tempore* shall be elected, which shall be the first business of the Convention.

Of Members.

19. A seat shall be assigned to each member in such manner as the Convention shall determine, which shall not be changed without leave of the President.

20. No member in debate shall mention a member then present by his name, but may describe him by the town he represents, the place he sits in, or such other designations as may be intelligible and respectful.

21. Every member when about to speak, shall rise and respectfully address the President, shall confine himself to the question under debate, and avoid personality, and shall sit down when he has finished. No member shall speak out of his place without leave of the President.

22. No member speaking shall be interrupted by another, but by rising up to call to order.

23. No member shall speak more than twice on one question, without first obtaining leave of the Convention; nor more than once, until other members, who have not spoken, shall speak, if they desire it.

Of Reconsideration.

24. When a vote has passed, it shall be in order for any member to move for a reconsideration thereof, on the same or the succeeding day, and such motion shall be placed first in the Orders of the Day for the day succeeding that on which the motion is made: a motion to reconsider being rejected shall not be renewed; nor shall any subject be a second time reconsidered: *provided, however*, that a motion to reconsider a vote, upon any collateral matter, shall not remove the main subject under consideration from before the Convention, but shall be considered at the time when it is made.

25. No member shall be obliged to be on more than two committees at the same time, nor chairman of more than one.

26. No member shall be permitted to stand up, to the interruption of another, while any member is speaking, or to pass unnecessarily between the President of the Convention and the person speaking; nor shall any member be permitted to stand in the alleys during the session of the Convention.

27. Every member shall keep an account of his own attendance and travel, and deliver the same to the committee appointed to make up the pay roll, and on his failure so to do, he shall be omitted from the roll; and no member shall receive pay for any weekday on which he has not actually attended, except in case of sickness.

28. Every member who shall neglect to give his attendance in the

Convention for more than six days after the session commences, shall, on making his appearance therein, be held to render the reason of such neglect; and in case the reason assigned shall be deemed by the Convention sufficient, such member shall be entitled to receive pay for his travel, and not otherwise; and no member shall be absent more than two days, without leave of the Convention; and a vote of leave of absence shall be inoperative, unless the member obtaining it shall avail himself of it within five days.

29. When any member shall be guilty of a breach of either of the Rules and Orders of the Convention, he may be required by the Convention, on motion, to make satisfaction therefor, and shall not be allowed to vote, or speak, except by way of excuse, till he has done so.

30. Every member, who shall be in the Convention when a question is put, shall give his vote, unless the Convention, for special reasons, shall excuse him. Any member desiring to be so excused on any question, shall make application to that effect before a division, or before the calling of the yeas and nays; and such application shall be accompanied by a brief statement of reasons, and shall be decided without debate.

31. Every motion shall be reduced to writing, if the President shall so direct.

32. Any member may call for the division of a question when the sense will admit of it. A motion to strike out and insert shall be deemed indivisible; but a motion to strike out being lost, shall neither preclude amendment, nor a motion to strike out and insert.

33. Motions and reports may be committed, or recommitted, at the pleasure of the Convention.

34. No motion or proposition of a subject different from that under consideration, shall be admitted under color of amendment.

35. The unfinished business in which the Convention was engaged at the time of the last adjournment, shall have the preference in the Orders of the Day.

36. No rule or order of the Convention shall be dispensed with, altered, or repealed, unless two-thirds of the members present shall consent thereto.

37. All questions relating to the priority of business to be acted upon, shall be decided without debate.

38. Every question of order shall be noted by the Secretary, with the decision thereon, and inscribed at large on the Journal.

39. It shall be the duty of each member who moves that any committee be instructed to inquire into the expediency of amending the existing Constitution, to point out the amendment which he deems expedient, in writing, to accompany his motion, or to furnish a written statement thereof to such committee. if by them required.

Of Monitors.

40. Two Monitors shall be appointed for each division, whose duty it shall be to see the due observance of the Rules and Orders of the

Convention, and on demand of the President, to return the number of votes and members in their respective divisions.

41. If any member shall transgress any of the Rules or Orders of the Convention, and persist therein after being notified thereof by any Monitor, it shall be the duty of such Monitor to give information thereof to the Convention.

Of Petitions, Memorials, &c.

42. All papers addressed to the Convention, except petitions, memorials and remonstrances, shall be presented by the President, or by a member in his place, and shall be read by the President, Secretary, or such other person as the President may request, and shall be taken up in the order in which they were presented, unless where the Convention shall otherwise direct.

43. Every member, presenting to the Convention a petition, memorial, or remonstrance, shall endorse his name thereon, with a brief statement of the nature and object of the instrument, and the reading of the same from the chair shall in all instances be dispensed with, unless specially ordered by the Convention.

44. All reports, petitions, memorials, remonstrances, and papers of a like nature, shall be presented during the first hour of each session, and at no other time, except by special leave of the Convention.

45. If any member of the Convention shall so request, any order, which shall be proposed for adoption, shall be passed over for that day without question; and the same shall be considered and disposed of, on the succeeding day, in the same manner as it would have been on the day on which it was offered, if no objection had been made.

Of Quorum.

46. Not less than one hundred members shall constitute a quorum for the transaction of business.

Of Committees, Reports, and Resolutions.

47. No committee shall sit during the sessions of the Convention, without special leave.

48. In all elections, by ballot, of the Convention, a time shall be assigned for such election at least one day previous thereto.

49. In all elections of committees of the Convention, by ballot, the person having the highest number of votes shall act as chairman, and when the committee is nominated by the Chair, the member first named shall be chairman.

50. All papers, relative to any business before the Convention, shall be left with the Secretary, by any member, who may obtain leave of absence, and may have any such papers in his possession.

51. The rules of proceeding in the Convention shall be observed in a Committee of the Whole, so far as they may be applicable, except the rule limiting the times of speaking: but no member shall speak twice upon any question, until every member, who shall not have spoken, shall speak, if he desires it. A motion to rise, report progress,

and ask leave to sit again, shall be always first in order, and shall be decided without debate.

52. Every order or resolution which proposes an alteration in the Constitution, and all reports of committees appointed to consider the propriety and expediency of making any alteration therein, shall be considered in Committee of the Whole before they are debated and finally acted upon in Convention.

53. Every resolution proposing any alteration in the Constitution, shall be read on two several days before it is finally acted upon and adopted by the Convention.

On motion of Mr. Lothrop, of Boston,

Ordered, That when the Convention adjourns, it adjourn to meet at the Music Hall, on Monday, at the hour agreed upon, and that the Messenger be directed to make the necessary arrangements for the meeting of the Convention.

Mr. Morton, of Fairhaven, offered an Order, which was amended upon motion of Mr. Hubbard, of Boston, and adopted in the following form, viz.:—

Ordered, That the Secretary cause the Act calling a Convention for revising the Constitution, to be printed and bound with the Rules and Orders of the Convention, and the Committees of the Convention; likewise the Constitution of this State as adopted in 1780, with the several amendments since adopted, specifying the dates thereof, in the form printed in the Revised Statutes; and the Constitution of the United States; also the names of the members of the Convention, with their boarding places or residences, substantially in the manner in which the Rules and Orders of the present House of Representatives are printed and bound.

On motion of Mr. Thompson, of Charlestown, the Secretary was directed to notify Benjamin Stevens, Esq., of his election to the office of Messenger.

On motion of Mr. Morton, of Quincy, the Convention adjourned.

MONDAY, May 9, 1853.

Met according to adjournment, in the Music Hall. Prayer was offered by the Chaplain. The Journal of Saturday was read.

The President read a communication from Benjamin Stevens, Esq., signifying his acceptance of the office of Messenger of the Convention.

The committee appointed to confer with any committee of the House of Representatives, upon an arrangement for alternate sessions of that body and of the Convention, reported, as the result of the conference, that the House of Representatives occupy their hall from nine o'clock in the forenoon to three o'clock in the afternoon, and that the Convention occupy the same from three o'clock in the afternoon on each day till further ordered.

The rules being suspended, on motion of Mr. THOMPSON, of Charlestown, the Report was considered.

Mr. KEYES, member for Abington, moved that the Report be laid upon the table; but the motion was rejected, by a vote of fifty-six in the affirmative to one hundred and eighty in the negative. The Report was then accepted.

Mr. ALLEN, of Worcester, from the Special Committee to which was referred the several Orders respecting the choice of a Delegate to the Convention from the town of Berlin, in the place of Hon. Henry Wilson, who was elected, but declines to act as such Delegate, and the Order of the same date concerning such vacancies as may exist in the delegations from other towns in the Commonwealth, in part performance of said duty, reported the following Order:—

Ordered, That the Secretary of this Convention give notice to the town of Berlin, that the Hon. Henry Wilson, returned as the Delegate from said town, declines to act in that capacity.

Pending the question upon the acceptance of the Report, Mr. PARKER, of Cambridge, moved that its further consideration be postponed until to-morrow, at four o'clock in the afternoon; but the motion was rejected.

After some further discussion, Mr. LIVERMORE, of Cambridge, moved that the Report be laid upon the table; but the motion was rejected; and the Report, with the accompanying Order, was adopted.

On motion of Mr. LIVERMORE, of Cambridge,

Ordered, That on and after to-morrow, the Convention will meet daily at the State House, at three o'clock in the afternoon, until otherwise ordered.

The PRESIDENT appointed Mr. Hathaway, of Freetown, upon the committee to consider the subject of the vacancies in the Convention, in place of Mr. Sumner, member for Otis, who was absent.

Mr. BUTLER, of Lowell, offered the following Order, which was laid over:—

Ordered, That the Secretary of this Convention, be directed, in notifying the town of Berlin, to use substantially the form herewith submitted:—

HALL OF THE CONSTITUTIONAL CONVENTION,
Boston, May —, 1853.

To the Selectmen of the Town of Berlin,—

GENTLEMEN: The Hon. Henry Wilson, late Delegate for Berlin in the Convention for revising the Constitution, having tendered his resignation as such Delegate, which has been accepted by the Convention, and his seat being thereby vacated, I am directed, by a vote of the Convention, to request you to convene the qualified electors of your town, as soon as may be with a due regard to notice, in order to their electing and deputing a Delegate to represent them in this Convention, in the manner prescribed by the second section of the Act calling the Convention, adopted by the people on the second Monday in November, A. D. 1852.

I am, very respectfully,
Your obedient servant,
——— ———, Secretary.

The Order offered by Mr. Brown, of Dracut, on Saturday, for supplying the members of the Convention with A. S. Barnes & Co.'s edition of the Constitutions of the several States, was taken up and adopted.

Mr. HOOPER, of Fall River, offered the following Resolution, and moved that it be referred to a special committee.

Resolved, That it is expedient so to revise the Constitution that in all elections by the people under it, the person having the highest number of votes shall be deemed and declared to be elected.

On motion of Mr. BRIGGS, of Pittsfield, the Resolution was laid upon the table,

And then, on motion of Mr. THOMPSON, of Charlestown, the Convention adjourned.

TUESDAY, May 10, 1853.

Met according to adjournment. Prayer was offered by the Chaplain. The Journal of yesterday was read.

Mr. EARLE, of Worcester, presented the Credentials of George A. Vinton, Delegate from Southbridge.

Referred to the Committee on Elections.

On motion of Mr. BATES, of Plymouth,

Ordered, That a committee of five be appointed, in connection with the Messenger, to assign seats to members of the Convention, as contemplated by the nineteenth rule.

The PRESIDENT read a communication from the Speaker of the House of Representatives, enclosing the following Order, adopted by that body:—

Ordered, That the members of the Constitutional Convention be invited, during its session, to avail themselves of such privileges of the Library of the Commonwealth, as the members of the legislature are entitled to.

Mr. ABBOTT, of Lowell, presented the Memorial of James Russell, of West Cambridge, claiming a seat in the Convention; which was referred to the Committee on Elections.

The PRESIDENT announced the Standing Committees, as follows:

On so much of the Constitution as is contained in the Preamble and Declaration of Rights.

Messrs. Sumner, member for Marshfield, Parker, of Cambridge, Hallett, member for Wilbraham, Hillard, of Boston, Allen, of Worcester, Gray, of Boston, Huntington, of Salem, Rockwell, of Pittsfield, Dana, member for Manchester, Bell, of Somerville, Williams, of Taunton, Burlingame, member for Northborough, Marcy, of Greenwich.

On so much of the Constitution as relates to the Frame of Government, Elections by the Legislature, &c.

Messrs. Allen, of Worcester, Upham, of Salem, Wilkinson, of Dedham, Appleton, of Boston, Gourgas, of Concord, Hale, of Bridgewater, Morton, of Fairhaven, Plunkett, of Adams, Davis, of Plymouth, Livermore, of Cambridge, Bliss, of Longmeadow, Nash, of Williamsburg, Hoyt, of Deerfield.

On so much of the Constitution as relates to the Senate.

Messrs. Wilson, of Natick, Beach, of Springfield, Stevenson, of Boston, Morton, of Andover, Thompson, of Charlestown, Morey, of Boston, Keyes, member for Abington, Hobart, of Foxborough, Howland, of New Bedford, Whitney, of Conway, Hooper, of Fall River, Conkey, of Amherst, Dawes, of Adams, Alley, of Lynn, Pomroy, of Rowe, Waters, of Millbury, James, of South Scituate, French, of Canton, Tilton, of Chilmark, Crowell, of Dennis, Easton, of Nantucket.

On so much of the Constitution as relates to the House of Representatives.

Messrs. Griswold, member for Erving, Butler, of Lowell, Hale, of Boston, Burlingame, member for Northborough, Alvord, member for Montague, Schouler, of Boston, Earle, of Worcester, Bullock, of Royalston, Sargent, of Cambridge, Warner, of Wrentham, Kinsman, of Newburyport, Ide, of Attleborough, Eaton, of Pelham, Parsons, of Sandisfield, Hurlburt, of Lee, Wood, of Middleborough, Aspinwall, of Brookline, Weeks, of Harwich, Carter, of Chicopee, Meader, of Nantucket, Norton, of Tisbury.

On so much of the Constitution as relates to the Governor, &c.

Messrs. Davis, of Worcester, Crowninshield, of Boston, Brown, of Dracut, Hopkinson, of Boston, Tyler, of Pawtucket, Loud, of Dorchester, Denison, of Coleraine, Bradbury, of Newton, Boutwell, of Lunenburg, Huntington, of Becket, Stephens, of Gloucester, Miller, of Wareham, Langdon, of Monterey.

On so much of the Constitution as relates to the Militia, &c.

Messrs. Oliver, of Lawrence, Chapin, of Springfield, Underwood, of Milford, Tyler, of Boston, Churchill, of Milton, Prince, of Winchester, Abbott, of Danvers, Strong, of Easthampton, Bumpus, of Plympton, Stacy, of Gloucester, Fellows, of Lowell, Winn, of Woburn, Swain, of Nantucket.

On so much of the Constitution as relates to the Lieutenant-Governor, &c.

Messrs. Cushman, of Bernardston, Wilkins, of Boston, Graves, of Lowell, Storrow, of Lawrence, Gardner, of Seekonk, Cole, of Cheshire, Tileston, of Dorchester, Bullen, of Northampton, Cooledge, of North Chelsea, Bigelow, of Grafton, Eames, of Washington, Crosby, of Orleans, Perkins, of North Bridgewater.

On so much of the Constitution as relates to the Council, &c.

Messrs. Hallett, member for Wilbraham, Giles, of Boston, De Witt, of Oxford, Walcott, of Salem, Wales, of Randolph, Adams, of Lowell, Brown, of Medway, Buck, of Lanesborough, Kuhn, of Boston, Hobart, of East Bridgewater, Packer, of Leyden, Curtis, of Egremont, Durgin, of Wilmington.

On so much of the Constitution as relates to the Secretary and Treasurer, and the Attorney-General, Solicitor-General, Sheriffs, Coroners, Registers of Probate, and Notaries Public, &c.

Messrs. Bishop, of Lenox, Weston, of Duxbury, Eliot, of Boston, Hall, of Haverhill, Bates, of Plymouth, Perkins, of Malden, Brinley, of Boston, Paine, of Brewster, Walker, of Roxbury, Eaton, of South Reading, Orne, of Marblehead, Penniman, of Chelsea, Knight, of Peru.

On so much of the Constitution as relates to the Judiciary, &c.

Messrs. Morton, of Taunton, Choate, of Boston, Huntington, of Northampton, Bartlett, of Boston, Bishop, of Lenox, Greenleaf, of Cambridge, Sumner, member for Otis, Lord, of Salem, Abbott, of Lowell, Chapin, of Worcester, Hathaway, of Freetown, Lowell, of Roxbury, Leland, of Holliston.

On so much of the Constitution as relates to the University at Cambridge, &c.

Messrs. Knowlton, of Worcester, Sprague, of Boston, Sumner, member for Otis, Briggs, of Pittsfield, Huntington, of Northampton, Beach, of Springfield, Putnam, of Roxbury, Braman, of Danvers, Train, of Framingham, Greene, of Brookfield, Ward, of Newton, Marvin, of Winchendon.

On so much of the Constitution as relates to the Encouragement of Literature.

Messrs. Briggs, of Pittsfield, Frothingham, of Charlestown, Blagden, of Boston, Lothrop, of Boston, Perkins, of Salem, Mason, of Fitchburg, Chandler, of Greenfield, Copeland, of Roxbury, Foster, of Charlemont, Thayer, of Uxbridge, Cogswell, of Yarmouth, Coggin, of Tewksbury, Wilbur, of Taunton.

On so much of the Constitution as relates to Oaths and Subscriptions, Incompatibility and Exclusion from Office, Pecuniary Qualifications, &c.

Messrs. Butler, of Lowell, Parker, of Boston, Simmons, of Hanover, Payson, of Rowley, Lawton, of Fall River, Eustis, of Boston, Gooch, of Melrose, Denton, of Chelsea, Goulding, of Phillipston, Kingman, of West Bridgewater, Wallace, of Palmer, Hurd, of Brighton, Knight, of Marblehead.

On so much of the Constitution as relates to the Qualifications of Voters, &c.

Messrs. Walker, of North Brookfield, Hubbard, of Boston, Hood, of Lynn, Morss, of Newburyport, French, of New Bedford, Phinney, of Barnstable, Thomas, of Weymouth, Cook, of Boston, Aldrich, of Barre, Morton, of Quincy, Warner, of Stockbridge, Phelps, of Monroe, Clarke, of Holyoke.

On so much of the Constitution as relates to Amendments and Enrolment.

Messrs. Nayson, of Amesbury, Stetson, of Braintree, Upton, of Boston, Wood, of Fitchburg, Paige, of Boston, Duncan, of Williamstown, Allen, of Brimfield, Wheeler, of Lincoln, Sherman, of Chicopee, Viles, of Lexington, Kellogg, of Hadley, Paine, of Brewster, Nute, of Lowell.

Mr. RANTOUL, of Beverly, submitted an Order concerning the Senate, and an Order concerning the House of Representatives, which were referred to the committees having those subjects in charge, and were ordered to be printed.

The Order offered by Mr. HOOPER, of Fall River, on Monday, relative to the number of votes required for an election, was referred to a special committee.

On motion of Mr. WILSON, of Natick,

Ordered, That the committees to which have been referred the several parts of the Constitution, be instructed to meet at ten o'clock, on and after to-morrow, until they make their final reports, or until otherwise ordered by the Convention.

The Order offered by Mr. BUTLER, of Lowell, yesterday, prescribing a form of notification to the town of Berlin, came up for consideration.

Mr. BARTLETT, of Boston, moved to amend by substituting the following:—

Ordered, That the Secretary, in notifying the town of Berlin of the vacancy in the Convention, be directed to forward to that town an attested copy of the Order adopted by the Convention upon that subject.

On motion of Mr. KEYES, member for Abington, the consideration of the subject was postponed until to-morrow.

On motion of Mr. WILKINS, of Boston, the Committee on Elections were instructed to inquire if any vacancy or vacancies exist in the Boston delegation; and if any, to consider and report what measures it is proper to adopt in relation thereto.

On motion of Mr. WILSON, of Natick,

Ordered, That the Committee on the Bill of Rights be instructed to consider the expediency of providing that—

No distinction shall ever be made by law between resident aliens and citizens in reference to the possession, enjoyment, or descent of property; and that—

No person shall be imprisoned for debt arising out of, or founded upon, any contract, expressed or implied.

On motion of Mr. THOMPSON, of Charlestown,

Ordered, That the Secretary of State be requested to furnish to the Convention such statistics as may be upon the records of his office, relating to the population, ratable polls, and valuation of the several towns and cities in the Commonwealth.

On motion of Mr. EARLE, of Worcester, the list of Standing Committees, with the places of their meeting, were ordered to be printed.

The PRESIDENT announced the appointment of the following gentlemen as Monitors:—

First Division—Messrs. Cushman, of Bernardston, and Prince, of Winchester.

Second Division—Messrs. Hall, of Haverhill, and Train, of Framingham.

Third Division—Messrs. Morton, of Fairhaven, and Bumpus, of Plympton.

Fourth Division—Messrs. Bates, of Plymouth, and Gilbert, of Plainfield.

Fifth Division—Messrs. Churchill, of Milton, and Dawes, of Adams.

Sixth Division—Messrs. Greene, of Brookfield, and Schouler, of Boston.

On motion of Mr. LIVERMORE, of Cambridge, the President was authorized to appoint a Committee on the Pay Roll, and a Committee on Leave of Absence.

Mr. ABBOTT, of Lowell, from the Committee on Elections, submitted a Report on the subject of vacancies, which was placed in the Orders of the Day, and ordered to be printed.

Mr. TYLER, of Pawtucket, moved that when the Convention adjourn, it adjourn to meet at half-past three o'clock to-morrow, but the motion was rejected; and then, upon motion of Mr. LELAND, of Holliston,

The Convention adjourned.

WEDNESDAY, May 11, 1853.

Met according to adjournment. Prayer was offered by the Chaplain. The Journal of yesterday was read.

On motion of Mr. Strong, of Easthampton,

Ordered, That the Committee under the 13th Resolution, be instructed to consider the expediency of so amending the Constitution as to exempt from attachment on mesne process so much of the freehold estate of every citizen of this Commonwealth as shall amount to the sum of five hundred dollars; and report thereon.

On motion of Mr. Earle, of Worcester,

Ordered, That the Committee under the 9th Resolution, consider and report on the expediency of so amending the Constitution as to provide that all officers recognized by the portions of the Constitution referred to them shall be elected by direct vote of the people.

On motion of Mr. Cushman, of Bernardston,

Ordered, That the Standing Committee to whom was referred so much of the Constitution as relates to the General Court, be directed to consider the expediency of so amending the Constitution that no session of the legislature shall continue a longer time than one hundred days, and that each member of the Senate and House of Representatives shall receive for his compensation a sum not exceeding two hundred dollars per annum.

On motion of Mr. Wilson, of Natick,

Ordered, That the Committee on the Frame of Government and the Legislative Power, be instructed to consider the expediency of incorporating into the section on the Legislative Powers, the following provisions:—

The members of the legislature shall receive for their services a compensation to be fixed by law, and paid out of the public treasury; but no increase of compensation shall take effect during the term for which the members of either House shall have been elected.

No senator or representative shall, during the term for which he shall have been elected, be appointed to any civil office, by the governor or the legislature; nor shall any senator or representative be appointed, by the governor or the legislature, within one year after his term shall have expired, to any office which shall have been created, or the emoluments of which shall have been increased during such term.

A majority of each House shall constitute a quorum to do business, but a smaller number may adjourn from day to day, and may compel the attendance of absent members, in such manner, and under such penalties, as each House may provide.

No private or local bill which may be passed by the legislature, shall embrace more than one subject, and that shall be expressed in the title; and no law shall be revised or amended by reference to its title; but, in such case, the act revised, or the section amended, shall be re-enacted and published at length.

On motion of Mr. CHURCHILL, of Milton,

Ordered, That the Committee on the Qualifications of Voters, be instructed to inquire into the expediency of so amending the Constitution as to provide for the freedom of the ballot, in conformity with the provisions of the Act entitled "An Act for the better security of the Ballot," passed in 1851, and the Act in addition thereto, passed in 1852.

On motion of Mr. HALL, of Haverhill,

Ordered, That the Committee on the Secretary, Treasurer, &c., be instructed to inquire into the expediency of recognizing, in the Constitution, an additional officer, to be designated as Auditor or Comptroller, and report thereon.

On motion of Mr. ELY, of Westfield,

Ordered, That the Committee under the 14th Resolution, relating to the Qualifications of Voters, be instructed to consider the expediency of so amending the Constitution as to require no tax qualification to constitute a legal voter in this Commonwealth, and report thereon.

On motion of Mr. BROWN, of Dracut,

Ordered, That a special committee of thirteen be appointed, to inquire and report to the Convention upon the expediency of so amending the Constitution that the legislature shall have no right to loan the credit of the State to any individual or corporation, or to contract any debt, for any purpose except to carry on the government and defray its necessary expenses, or to repel invasion, or to suppress insurrection.

On motion of Mr. GOURGAS, of Concord,

Ordered, That the Committee who have under consideration so much of the Constitution as relates to the amendment thereof, consider the expediency of providing, that in the general election which shall be held in the year 1866, and every fifteenth year thereafter, and also at such other times as the legislature may by law provide, the question—"Shall there be a Convention to revise the Constitution and amend the same?" shall be submitted to the electors qualified to vote for members of the legislature; and, in the event that a majority of the electors so qualified, voting at such election, shall decide in favor of a Convention for such purpose, the legislature, at its session next ensuing after such decision, shall provide by law for the election of delegates to such Convention.

Mr. EARLE, of Worcester, offered the following Resolutions, which were referred to the appropriate committees.

Resolved, That in the apportionment of senators in the general court, the distribution should be made in proportion to the number of qualified voters in the several sections of the Commonwealth.

Resolved, That in the organization of the House of Representatives, the apportionment should be made according to the number of qualified voters in the several cities and towns of the Commonwealth.

Mr. WARD, of Newton, asked to be excused from serving upon the Committee upon the University at Cambridge, and Mr. PAINE, of Brewster, asked to be excused from serving upon the Committee upon the Secretary, Treasurer, &c., and upon the Committee on Amendments of the Constitution; and their requests were granted.

Mr. Morton, of Fairhaven, was appointed Monitor of the Fourth Division, in place of Mr. French, of Stoughton, who declined to serve.

On motion of Mr. GARDNER, of Seekonk, the Order offered by Mr. Butler, of Lowell, prescribing a form of notification to the town of Berlin, was taken up, and after debate, the amendment offered by Mr. Bartlett, of Boston, was rejected, and the Order was adopted.

The Orders of the Day were taken up, the first matter being the Report of the Committee on Elections on the subject of vacancies.

Mr. LADD, of Cambridge, moved to recommit the Report to the Committee, with instructions to report a vacancy in the delegation from the town of Walpole.

Pending the question upon this motion, on motion of Mr. BROWN, of Dracut, the subject was postponed until to-morrow.

Mr. TRAIN, of Framingham, moved a reconsideration of the vote by which the Convention adopted the Order of Mr. Butler, of Lowell, prescribing a form of notice to the town of Berlin.

Mr. Thomas, of Weymouth, moved a suspension of the rule of the Convention, that the subject might be immediately considered; but the motion was rejected by a vote of one hundred and forty-five in the affirmative to eighty-eight in the negative; two-thirds of the members not voting in the affirmative.

On motion of Mr. Wilson, of Natick, the Order of the 10th inst., concerning the time of meeting of the committees, was so far modified as to allow the said committees to arrange the hour of meeting.

Mr. Appleton, of Boston, presented a communication from Henry B. Rogers, a Delegate from the city of Boston; which was referred to the Committee on Elections.

The President announced the following gentlemen as the committee on procuring seats for the members. Messrs. Bates, of Plymouth, Gardner, of Boston, Earle, of Worcester, Bennett, of Hubbardston, Peabody, of Salem, Jackson, of Roxbury, and Case, of New Bedford.

On motion of Mr. Butler, of Lowell, the Convention adjourned.

THURSDAY, May 12, 1853.

Met according to adjournment. Prayer was offered by the Chaplain. The Journal of yesterday was read.

Mr. Schouler, of Boston, presented the Petition and Memorial of John W. Le Barnes, and four hundred others, citizens of Boston, asking that the doctrines of no religion shall be established or recommended in the Constitution, and that no religious or ecclesiastical interference with the laws of the State, its official institutions, or its public schools, shall be hereafter possible in this Commonwealth.

Mr. French, of New Bedford, presented the Petition of Francis Jackson, and fourteen hundred and seven others, asking to have the word "male" struck out of the Constitution.

Mr. Keyes, member for Abington, presented the Petition of Harriet L. Randall, and two hundred and three others, women and men of Abington, making the same request.

Mr. Wilson, of Natick, presented the Petition of James B. Allen, and others, citizens of Boston, for the abolition of imprisonment for debt.

These Petitions were severally referred to the Committee on the Bill of Rights.

On motion of Mr. Davis, of Plymouth, the Committee upon the Bill of Rights were instructed to consider the expediency of declaring that the legislature shall pass no law recognizing a distinction in the rights of citizens solely on account of color or caste, and that no rule or regulation made by inn-keepers, common carriers, municipal or other public institutions, or made for public schools, lectures, exhibiions or amusements, founded solely upon color or birth, shall be recognized in this Commonwealth.

On motion of Mr. FRENCH, of New Bedford,

Ordered, That the Committee on the Judiciary Power be instructed to inquire into the expediency of electing all our judges by the people, and report thereon.

On motion of the same gentleman,

Ordered, That the Committee on the Qualifications of Voters, be instructed to inquire into the expediency of having the same manner of voting apply to the election of county, town and city officers, who are elected by ballot, as by the Acts of 1851 and 1852, apply to the election of State and United States officers, and report thereon.

On motion of Mr. ALVORD, member for Montague,

Ordered, That the Committee on Attorney-General, Solicitor-General, Sheriffs, Coroners, Registers of Probate and Notaries Public, be instructed to consider the expediency of incorporating into the Constitution provisions for the election by the people, of Judges of Probate, Commissioners of Insolvency, Clerks of the Courts, District-Attorneys, and all other county and district officers, and report thereon.

On motion of Mr. DUNCAN, of Williamstown,

Ordered, That the Committee on the Qualifications of Voters, be instructed to consider the expediency of amending article 9 of chapter 6, by the addition of the following clause:—

"*Provided, however*, That for the purpose of voting, no person shall be deemed to have gained or lost a residence by reason of his presence or absence while employed in the army or navy of the United States, nor while engaged in navigating the waters of this State, or of the United States, or of the high seas, nor while a member of any seminary of learning."

On motion of Mr. MORTON, of Quincy,

Ordered, That the Messenger be directed to furnish to each member of the Convention a regular file of all the documents which have been or may be printed by order of this body.

Mr. ALLEN, of Worcester, from the special committee on the subject of filling vacancies in the Convention, submitted a Report, concluding with a recommendation, that no action be taken upon the subject by the Convention at the present time.

The same gentleman, from the Committee on the Frame of Government, submitted a Report on the subject of the name—"The Commonwealth of Massachusetts," recommending that it be retained in the Constitution; which Reports were read, and placed in the Orders of the Day for to-morrow.

Mr. SIMONDS, of Bedford, presented a series of Resolutions relating to election returns.

Referred to the Committee on Elections.

On motion of Mr. BROWN, of Dracut, the Convention proceeded to the consideration of the Report of the Committee on Elections, the pending question being the motion of Mr. LADD, of Cambridge, to recommit the Report, with instructions to report a vacancy in the delegation from the town of Walpole.

After debate, the motion was rejected, and the Report was then accepted.

On motion of Mr. LIVERMORE, of Cambridge, the Convention proceeded to the consideration of the Orders of the Day; the first matter being the motion of Mr. TRAIN, of Framingham, that the vote by which the form of notice to the town of Berlin was adopted, be reconsidered.

Without disposing of the subject, upon motion of Mr. DURGIN, of Wilmington,

The Convention adjourned.

FRIDAY, May 13, 1853.

Met according to adjournment. Prayer was offered by the Chaplain. The Journal of yesterday was read.

Mr. BATES, of Plymouth, from the committee to whom was referred the subject of assigning seats to the members, submitted the following Report:—

They recommend that after reserving twelve seats to be given to those who were members of the Convention of 1820, and those who are aged and infirm, the remainder be distributed by lot, in the manner now provided for seating members of the House of Representatives.

On motion of Mr. LIVERMORE, of Cambridge, the rules were suspended, and the Report considered and accepted.

Afterwards, Mr. Bates, from the same committee, offered an Order for the appointment of a committee to proceed to the drawing of seats.

Mr. Thompson, of Charlestown, offered an amendment, and then, upon motion of Mr. Hooper, of Fall River, the Order was recommitted to the committee.

On motion of Mr. Cole, of Cheshire,

Ordered, That the Committee on the General Court be instructed to consider the expediency of so amending the Constitution that no bill or resolve of the Senate and House of Representatives shall become a law or have force as such, until it shall have received a majority of the votes of all the members of both branches of the legislature elected by the people.

On motion of Mr. French, of New Bedford,

Ordered, That the Committee on the Bill of Rights be instructed to inquire into the justice of incorporating into that instrument provisions which shall effectually secure to all persons on Massachusetts soil their inherent and inalienable rights to liberty, in all cases whatsoever, except as a punishment for crime, and that they shall not be deprived of that liberty without trial by jury and the application of all the forms and safeguards included in what is called "due process of law," and report thereon.

On motion of Mr. Hathaway, of Freetown,

Ordered, That the Committee on the Bill of Rights be instructed to consider the expediency of incorporating therein a declaration that in all criminal proceedings for libel, the truth may be given in evidence to the jury; and if it shall appear to the jury that the matter charged as libellous is true, and was published with good motives, and for justifiable ends, the party shall be acquitted.

On motion of Mr. Rice, of Leverett,

Ordered, That the Committee on the Senate and House of Representatives be directed to consider the expediency of so amending the Constitution that those bodies shall convene not over ninety days at one time, under pay of the State; that their compensation shall not exceed two dollars and fifty cents per day, and that after the ninety days shall have expired, if the session is continued, their services shall be gratuitous.

On motion of Mr. Edwards, of Southampton,

Ordered, That the Committee on the House of Representatives be directed to consider the expediency of so amending the Constitution that each and every incorporated town shall be entitled to at least one representative annually.

On motion of Mr. BRADFORD, of Essex,

Ordered, That the Committee on the Governor be instructed to consider the expediency of so amending the Constitution that every citizen of the Commonwealth, being a legal voter therein, shall be eligible to the office of governor thereof.

Ordered, That the Committee on Amendments and Enrolment be instructed to consider the expediency of adding to article 10, chapter 6, part 2, the words—" Provided, that the people of the Commonwealth shall at all times have the right inalienable of making any revision and alteration of this Constitution, by delegates to be by them chosen for this purpose, in convention assembled."

On motion of Mr. TRAIN, of Framingham,

Ordered, That the Committee on the University at Cambridge be directed to consider the propriety and expediency of expunging from the Constitution, so much thereof as relates to the University at Cambridge.

On motion of Mr. WALLACE, of Palmer,

Ordered, That the Committee on the Judiciary be instructed to consider the expediency of providing in the Constitution that the judges of the several courts of the Commonwealth shall receive ample and honorable salaries; which shall not be diminished during their continuance in office; and report thereon.

On motion of Mr. DUNCAN, of Williamstown,

Ordered, That the Committee on the Judiciary be directed to consider the expediency of providing for the election of justices of the Supreme Court, and the judges of the Court of Common Pleas by the legislature upon joint ballot for the term of seven years, in such order as may be hereafter determined: *provided,* that no person shall be deemed eligible to, or continued in such office, who shall have passed the age of seventy.

On motion of Mr. BROWN, of Dracut,

Ordered, That the Committee on the Encouragement of Literature be instructed to inquire into the expediency of so amending the Constitution, that all the proceeds of the sales of the public lands in the State of Maine, owned by this State, and not now otherwise appropriated, shall be appropriated to the support of common schools.

On motion of Mr. Leland, of Holliston,

Ordered, That the Secretaries of the Convention be authorized to employ the present contractors for legislative printing, to execute the printing for the Convention, at the same rate of compensation fixed by their contract for legislative printing.

Mr. Greene, of Brookfield, offered Resolutions concerning the organization of, and mode of electing the Senate. Referred to the committee on that subject.

The President announced the appointment of the following Committees, viz.:—

On the Pay Roll.

Messrs. Livermore, of Cambridge, Ely, of Westfield, Preston, of Boston, Pool, of Abington, Hunt, of Weymouth, Davis, of Methuen, and Carruthers, of Salisbury.

On Leave of Absence.

Messrs. Fay, of Southborough, Fowler, of Danvers, Dean, of Stoneham, Crockett, of Boston, Brown, of Tolland, Adams, of Topsfield, and Clarke, of Townsend.

On the Order offered by Mr. Hooper, of Fall River, concerning Elections by Plurality.

Messrs. Hooper, of Fall River, Osgood, of Northfield, Beebe, of Boston, Hyde, of Sturbridge, Parsons, of Lawrence, Edwards, of Southampton, Davis, of Truro, Winslow, of Windsor, Simonds, of Bedford, Breed, of Lynn, Parker, of Chicopee, Beal, of Scituate, and Andrews, of New Salem.

The President appointed Mr. Bird, of Walpole, to serve upon the Committee on the University at Cambridge, in place of Mr. Ward, of Newton, excused. Also, Mr. Lincoln, of Raynham, to serve upon the Committee on Secretary, Treasurer, &c., in place of Mr. Paine, of Brewster, excused.

Mr. Wilson, of Natick, from the Committee on the Senate, submitted a Report on that subject, which was referred to the Committee of the Whole, and ordered to be printed.

Mr. Abbott, of Lowell, from the Committee on Elections, submitted a Report on the subject of the vacancy in Boston, which was considered and accepted, as follows:—

That from the examination of a letter from Henry B. Rogers, one of the persons chosen as a Delegate to this Convention from the city of Boston, to Hon. William Appleton, a Delegate from said city, the committee are satisfied that Mr. Rogers intended to decline serving as a Delegate in this Convention; they therefore report, that one vacancy exists in the delegation from the city of Boston, and that a notice of such vacancy be given from the Convention to the authorities of the said city of Boston, in the form to be determined upon by the Convention.

Ordered, That when the Convention adjourn, it adjourn to meet on Monday next, at three o'clock in the afternoon.

The Convention proceeded to the Orders of the Day, the first matter being the motion of Mr. TRAIN, of Framingham, to reconsider the vote by which the form of notice to the town of Berlin was adopted.

Without taking the question,

On motion of Mr. WILSON, of Natick, the Convention adjourned.

MONDAY, May 16, 1853.

Met according to adjournment. Prayer was offered by the Chaplain. The Journal of Saturday was read.

Mr. GOURGAS, of Concord, submitted a Report from the Committee appointed to consider the subject of reporting and printing the Proceedings and Debates of the Convention, accompanied by several Orders, and on his motion, the subject was considered at the present time.

After debate, upon motion of Mr. SCHOULER, of Boston, the subject was assigned for consideration at a quarter past three o'clock, and the Report and Orders were ordered to be printed.

The PRESIDENT read a communication from Hon. Peleg Sprague, one of the Delegates elected from the city of Boston, resigning his seat in the Convention, on account of the state of his health.

On motion of Mr. BARTLETT, of Boston, his resignation was accepted by the Convention. Mr. Bartlett further moved, that the Secretary give notice to the city of Boston of the existing vacancy.

This proposition was amended, upon motion of Mr. FROTHINGHAM, of Charlestown, so as to direct the Secretary to notify, "in such manner and form as the Convention shall hereafter adopt;" and the motion thus amended was adopted.

On motion of Mr. Wilson, of Natick,

Ordered, That the Committee on the University at Cambridge, be instructed to consider the expediency of so amending the Constitution as to provide, that the Corporation of the University shall consist (exclusive of the President, who shall be, *ex officio*, a member of the Corporation,) of seven persons, to be chosen by the legislature in joint ballot, for the term of seven years, in such a manner that one shall retire and the vacancy be filled each year; and to provide, also, that a majority of the members of said Corporation shall not belong to any one religious sect or denomination.

On motion of Mr. Hooper, of Fall River,

Ordered, That the Committee on the Bill of Rights inquire into the expediency of so amending that part of the Constitution, as to declare therein, that in criminal prosecutions the jury shall be judges of the law as well as the fact; also so to amend the twentieth article, as to insert in the fourth line, after "it," the words, "or by the people;" also so to amend the twenty-ninth article as to strike out after the word "should" in the tenth line, the words "hold their offices as long as they behave themselves well, and that they should;" and report thereon.

On motion of Mr. Churchill, of Milton,

Ordered, That the Committee on the Judiciary consider the expediency of making the clerks of all courts, except in case of the death or absence of the standing clerk, periodically elected by the members of the Bar, having their places of business within the county where such courts are situated; subject, however, to the approval of the justices of the several courts respectively.

On motion of Mr. Kellogg, of Hadley,

Ordered, That the Committee on the Qualifications of Voters consider the expediency of making a constitutional provision, that voters, in the election of state, county, city, town, district and parish officers, and in the transaction of all city, town, district and parish affairs, shall have the same qualifications.

Also, that the Committee on the House of Representatives consider the expediency of so amending the Constitution, that the forty districts into which it is proposed to divide the Commonwealth for the choice of senators, be called Legislative Districts; that each of said districts shall annually elect eight representatives to the general court, and that it shall be the duty of the legislature to form said districts anew at the expiration of every period of ten years from and after the first formation thereof.

On motion of Mr. GARDNER, of Seekonk,

Ordered, That the Committee on the Frame of Government inquire into the expediency of so amending the Constitution, as that no petitions shall be received and acted upon by the legislature, unless they shall be presented within two weeks from the commencement of each session thereof.

On motion of Mr. WHITNEY, of Conway,

Ordered, That a committee of thirteen be appointed, to consider the expediency of making a constitutional provision, requiring that corporations shall not be created by special act, except for municipal purposes, and in cases where the objects of the corporation cannot be obtained under general laws.

On motion of Mr. FROTHINGHAM, of Charlestown,

Ordered, That a special committee be appointed, to consider the expediency of incorporating into the Constitution, articles providing that the legislature shall have no power to pass any act granting any special charter for banking purposes, but requiring corporations for such purposes, to form under general laws; that the legislature shall provide, by law, for the registry of all bills or notes now issued or put in circulation as money; and shall require ample security from such corporations as form under general laws, for the redemption of their notes in specie; that in case of the insolvency of any banking corporation, the bill-holders thereof shall be entitled to preference over all other creditors of such bank.

On motion of Mr. GRAY, of Boston,

Ordered, That the Secretary of the Convention cause to be printed, for the use of this Convention, the census last taken by the authority of the Commonwealth, together with the representation in the Senate and House, to which the several districts and towns are entitled according to such census.

On motion of Mr. BIRD, of Walpole, the Orders of the Day were taken up, the first matter being the motion to reconsider the vote by which the Convention agreed to the Order of Mr. Butler, of Lowell, prescribing the form of notice to the town of Berlin.

Without disposing of the question,

On motion of Mr. EAMES, of Washington, the Convention adjourned.

TUESDAY, May 17, 1853.

Met according to adjournment. Prayer was offered by the Chaplain. The Journal of yesterday was read.

The following Petitions were presented:—

By Mr. Wilson, of Natick,

The Petition of Thomas Wentworth Higginson, of Worcester, and two hundred and forty-nine others, asking that the word "male" may be stricken from the Constitution wherever it occurs.

Referred to the Committee on the Qualifications of Voters.

By Mr. French, of New Bedford,

The Petition of Harriet K. Hunt, to be allowed to vote, or be excused from paying taxes.

Referred to the same committee.

Also, the Petition of Harriet K. Hunt, that females may have the same advantages of education with males.

Referred to the Committee on the Encouragement of Literature.

By Mr. Cole, of Cheshire,

The Petitions of M. McIntosh, and fifty others, citizens of Roxbury; Luther Shove and forty-six others, citizens of Uxbridge; and Mark Kline and fifty-six others, citizens of Egremont, severally in aid of the Petition of John W. Le Barnes and others.

Referred to the Committee on the Bill of Rights.

On motion of Mr. Marvin, of Winchendon,

Ordered, That the Committee on the University at Cambridge inquire into the expediency of so amending the Constitution, as to require that the Board of Overseers of Harvard College shall be hereafter constituted in accordance with the third article of the first section of chapter fifth of the Constitution of 1820.

On motion of Mr. Davis, of Worcester,

Ordered, That the Committee on Settling Elections by the Legislature inquire into the expediency of providing for the *viva voce* selection of all officers which may devolve on either branch of the legislature.

On motion of Mr. Mason, of Fitchburg,

Ordered, That the Committee on the Frame of Government, consider the expediency of providing that it shall be incompetent for the legislature to refer to the people for their approval or ratification, any legislative act other than such as have reference to amending or altering the Constitution.

On motion of Mr. Wheeler, of Lincoln,

Ordered, That the Committee on the Frame of Government consider the expediency of so altering or amending the Constitution as to provide that all bills and resolves authorizing the expenditure of money, or the payment of money from the treasury of the Commonwealth, shall originate in the House of Representatives; and also of providing that all bills and resolves shall originate and be first acted upon in the House of Representatives.

On motion of Mr. Leland, of Holliston,

Ordered, That the Committee on the Frame of Government consider the expediency of limiting the power of the legislature for loaning the credit of the State, or contracting debts, except for paying its own expenses, or for the public safety, unless the question is submitted to the qualified voters, and is approved by a majority of those voting thereon.

On motion of Mr. Harmon, of New Ashford,

Ordered, That the Committee on the House of Representatives consider the expediency of providing for continuing, in some form, the representation by towns, according to their present boundaries.

On motion of Mr. Wilson, of Natick,

Ordered, That the Committee on the Judiciary Power be instructed to inquire into the expediency of so amending the Constitution as to provide that the justices of the Supreme Judicial Court, and the Court of Common Pleas, shall be appointed by the governor, for the term of ten years, subject to the confirmation of the Senate in executive session; that they shall be eligible to reappointment, at the expiration of their term, and that they shall not, in any case, remain in office after they have attained the age of seventy years.

On motion of Mr. Morton, of Andover,

Ordered, That the Committee on the Judiciary Power be directed to inquire into the expediency of expunging or amending that part of the Constitution which provides that "each branch of the legislature, as well as the Governor and Council, shall have authority to require the opinions of the justices of the Supreme Judicial Court upon important questions of law, and upon solemn occasions."

On motion of Mr. Frothingham, of Charlestown,

Ordered, That the Committee on the Pay Roll be instructed to consider what compensation should be allowed to the members of this Convention, and report thereon.

Mr. Cole, of Cheshire, submitted the following Resolution, which was referred to the Committee on Amendments of the Constitution :—

Resolved, That the Constitution be so amended that at the general election to be held in the year one thousand eight hundred and seventy-three, and in each twentieth year thereafter, and also at such other times as the legislature may by law provide, the question— "Shall there be a Convention to revise the Constitution and amend the same?" shall be decided by the electors qualified to vote for members of the legislature; and in case a majority of the electors so qualified, voting at such elections, shall decide in favor of a Convention for such purpose, the legislature, at its next session, shall provide by law for the election of delegates to such Convention.

Mr. Hooper, of Fall River, from the Special Committee on Elections by Plurality of Votes, submitted a Report, accompanied by the following Resolution :—

Resolved, That it is expedient so to amend the Constitution, that in all elections the person having the highest number of votes shall be deemed and declared to be elected.

Referred to the Committee of the Whole, and ordered to be printed.

Mr. Davis, of Worcester, from the Committee on the Governor, submitted a Report and Resolutions on that subject.

Referred to the Committee of the Whole, and ordered to be printed.

Mr. Frothingham, of Charlestown, called for the special assignment for a quarter past three o'clock, which was the Report and Orders on the subject of reporting and printing the Proceedings and Debates of the Convention.

On motion of Mr. Schouler, of Boston, the third of the Orders was amended by striking out all after the words "such prices as," and inserting instead, the words "have been proposed therefor by Mr. Henry M. Parkhurst;" and the Orders were then adopted, as follow :—

Ordered, That a committee of be appointed, with authority to contract with Harvey Fowler, to report the Proceedings and Debates of this Convention, on certain terms which he has proposed, and which have been this day communicated to the Convention in the Report of a committee to whom the subject had been referred; and that said committee be further authorized to exercise such general supervision over said reporter as they may deem necessary, subject at all times to such directions as the Convention may see fit to give.

Ordered, That the same committee have like authority to contract with White & Potter for the printing and publishing of said Reports, upon the terms they have proposed, and which have been communicated to this Convention this day in a Report of a committee to whom the subject had been referred; and that said committee be further authorized to exercise such general supervision over the printing of the Reports referred to, as will secure the faithful and prompt performance of the terms and conditions of the contract for the same, subject at all times to such directions as the Convention may consider proper to give them.

Ordered, That the same committee have authority to procure correct reports of the Debates and Proceedings had in this Convention up to the time of the execution of the contracts provided for in the two preceding Orders, and to pay for the same, and the printing thereof, if necessary, such prices as have been proposed therefor by Mr. Henry M. Parkhurst.

The PRESIDENT appointed the following gentlemen as the committee under the preceding Orders, viz.: Messrs. Hallett, member for Wilbraham, Hale, of Boston, Sleeper, of Roxbury, Schouler, of Boston, Gourgas, of Concord, Bates, of Plymouth, and Greene, of Brookfield.

On motion of Mr. NAYSON, of Amesbury, the Orders of the Day were taken up, and the first subject, being the motion to reconsider the vote by which the Convention agreed to the Order of Mr. Butler, of Lowell, prescribing a form of notice to the town of Berlin, was considered, but not disposed of.

On motion of Mr. GRISWOLD, member for Erving,

The Convention adjourned.

WEDNESDAY, May 18, 1853.

Met according to adjournment. Prayer was offered by the Chaplain. The Journal of yesterday was read.

On motion of Mr. GOURGAS, of Concord,

Ordered, That fifteen hundred copies of the reports of the Debates of this Convention be printed, and bound in a durable manner, for distribution as follows: one copy to each member of the Convention, and to each town and city in the Commonwealth, and the remainder to be placed in the office of the Secretary of the Commonwealth for such gratuitous distribution as is usually made of books published by the State; and that an additional fifteen hundred copies of the same edition be placed in the hands of the Secretary of the Commonwealth, on sale, at such price as may be hereafter determined upon by the Convention, the proceeds of such sales to be paid into the public treasury.

Ordered, That the Messenger, under the direction of the President, provide all necessary accommodations for the official Reporter of the Convention.

On motion of Mr. IDE, of Attleborough,

Ordered, That the Committee on the Frame of Government and mode of Settling Elections in the Legislature, consider the expediency of so amending the Constitution as to provide therein for elections to fill all vacancies which may occur in both branches of the legislature, by reason of death or resignation of members thereof, or from any other cause, not otherwise provided for.

On motion of Mr. SUMNER, member for Otis,

Ordered, That the Committee on the Frame of Government be instructed to consider the expediency of permanently establishing the seat of government at the city of Boston.

On motion of Mr. MORSS, of Newburyport,

Ordered, That the Committee on the Frame of Government consider the expediency of so amending the Constitution, that the governor and all state officers, and the members of the general court, be chosen for a term of two years. Also, the expediency of biennial sessions of the general court.

On motion of Mr. BIRD, of Walpole,

Ordered, That the Committee on the Frame of Government be instructed to inquire into the expediency of so amending the Constitution, that all elections for state and county officers shall be held on the Tuesday next following the first Monday of November of each year, and to report thereon.

On motion of Mr. COLE, of Cheshire,

Ordered, That the Committee on the Frame of Government be instructed to consider the propriety of so amending the Constitution, that no private or local bill, making appropriations of the public funds, shall be passed without the assent of three-fifths of all the members elected to both branches of the legislature.

On motion of Mr. CADY, of Monson,

Ordered, That the Committee on the Bill of Rights be instructed to consider the expediency of so amending article 11, as to make compensation for sacrifice of time and expense of counsel to the injured party in case of unjust prosecution.

On motion of Mr. IDE, of Attleborough,

Ordered, That the Committee on the Qualifications of Voters consider the expediency of so amending the Constitution, as to provide that the payment of any poll or registry tax, exceeding in amount the sum of one dollar, shall not be required to constitute any part of the qualifications of voters in this Commonwealth.

On motion of Mr. SUMNER, member for Otis,

Ordered, That each of the committees appointed under the fifteen Resolutions adopted by this Convention be authorized to consider any proposition they may deem compatible with the objects or purposes of their appointment, though not expressly or impliedly embodied in the Resolutions submitted to them; and report thereon.

On motion of Mr. HOOD, of Lynn,

Ordered, That ——— be a committee to consider and report upon the order of business which it may be expedient or necessary for the Convention to adopt, in order to bring the session to a close on or before the first day of July next.

On motion of Mr. WALKER, of North Brookfield,

Ordered, That the Secretary of the Commonwealth be requested to furnish, for the use of this Convention, an alphabetical list of all the towns in the State entitled to only a fractional representation, or less than one each year; also, of all towns having a representation of one each year; also, of all having each two, three, four, five, six, ten, and over ten representatives annually.

Mr. ALVORD, member for Montague, presented the Credentials of Amariah Chandler, the Delegate elected from Greenfield; which were read and placed on file.

Mr. CUSHMAN, of Bernardston, from the Committee on so much of the Constitution as relates to the Lieutenant-Governor, submitted a Report on that subject, which was referred to the Committee of the Whole, and ordered to be printed.

On motion of Mr. French, of New Bedford,

Ordered, That four o'clock this day be assigned as the time for taking the question on the motion to reconsider the vote by which the Convention agreed to the Order concerning the election in Berlin.

Mr. Bates, of Plymouth, moved that the Convention proceed to the consideration of the Orders of the Day; and the motion was agreed to by a vote of one hundred and twenty-eight in the affirmative, to ninety-eight in the negative.

The Orders of the Day were accordingly taken up and considered.

The hour of four having arrived, Mr Parker, of Cambridge, moved that the time of taking the question be postponed until Friday at four o'clock; but the motion was rejected.

Mr. Schouler, of Boston, moved that the time of taking the question be postponed until six o'clock to-day; but the motion was rejected.

On motion of Mr Bates, of Plymouth,

Ordered, That when the question is taken, it be taken by yeas and nays.

And the roll being called, one hundred and eighteen members voted for the reconsideration, and two hundred and nineteen members against it; so the motion to reconsider was rejected.

Those who voted in the affirmative are:—

Messrs. Benjamin P. Adams,
Robert Andrews,
William Appleton,
William Aspinwall,
David C. Atwood,
Samuel Ayres,
Joseph Barrows,
Russell Bartlett,
Sidney Bartlett,
James M. Beebe,
Luther V. Bell,
Jacob Bigelow,
George W. Blagden,
William C. Bliss,
Ebenezer Bradbury,
Milton P. Braman,
Osmyn Brewster,
Francis Brinley,
Rufus Bullock,
Cephas C. Bumpus,
Henry Cady,
Timothy W. Carter,
Rufus Choate,
Salah Clark,
Nathaniel Cogswell,

Messrs. Ithamar Conkey,
Charles E. Cook,
Henry F. Cooledge,
Simeon Crittenden,
Leander Crosby,
Seth Crowell,
Joseph Cummings,
Wilber Curtis,
John Davis,
Solomon Davis,
Henry L. Dawes,
William Dehon,
James C. Doane,
Moses Dorman,
Philip Eames,
James Easton, 2d,
Lilley Eaton,
Homer Ely,
William T. Eustis,
A. G. Farwell,
Aaron Foster,
Samuel P. Fowler,
Wanton C. Gilbert,
Joel Giles,
Jason Goulding,

Messrs. John C. Gray,
Artemas Hale,
A. B. Hammond,
George Hayward,
Charles Heard,
Samuel Henry,
Henry Hersey,
George S. Hillard,
William Hinsdale,
Samuel Houghton,
William J. Hubbard,
William Hunt,
Asahel Huntington,
Samuel A. Hurlburt,
Samuel Jackson,
William James,
John Jenkins,
Samuel H. Jenks,
Giles C. Kellogg,
Martin R. Kellogg,
Joseph Knight,
George H. Kuhn,
John S. Ladd,
Frederic W. Lincoln, Jr.,
Isaac Livermore,
Otis P. Lord,
Samuel K. Lothrop,
Samuel P. Loud,
William P. Marble,
Seth Miller, Jr.,
Samuel Mixter,
Joseph B. Morss,
Daniel Noyes,
Nathan Orcutt,

Messrs. James W. Paige,
John G. Park,
Adolphus G. Parker,
Joel Parker,
Samuel D. Parker,
Thomas A. Parsons,
George Peabody,
William C. Plunkett,
Jeremiah Pomroy,
James Read,
Sampson Reed,
George R. Sampson,
John Sargent,
William Schouler,
Charles Sherman,
John Sherrill,
John S. Sleeper,
John Souther,
Charles G. Stevens,
J. Thomas Stevenson,
William Stutson,
Thomas Talbot,
Ralph Taylor,
Charles W. Upham,
George B. Upton,
Samuel B. Walcott,
Samuel Walker,
Cyrus Weeks,
William F. Wheeler,
Benjamin White,
Joel Wilder,
John H. Wilkins,
Milo Wilson,
Josiah B. Woods.

Those who voted in the negative are:—

Messrs. Alfred A. Abbott,
Shubael P. Adams,
James B. Allen,
Joel C. Allen,
Parsons Allen,
John B. Alley,
D. W. Alvord,
George Austin,
Hillel Baker,
Alvah Ballard,
George S. Ball,
Alpheus Bancroft,
Marcus Barrett,
Eliakim A. Bates,
Moses Bates, Jr.,
Erasmus D. Beach,
John Beal,

Messrs. William Bennett, Jr.,
Zephaniah Bennett,
Edward B. Bigelow,
Francis W. Bird,
Gad O. Bliss,
William S. Booth,
Sewell Boutwell,
William J. A. Bradford,
Hiram N. Breed,
Asa Bronson,
Adolphus F. Brown,
Alpheus R. Brown,
Artemas Brown,
Hammond Brown,
Hiram C. Brown,
Joseph Brownell,
Patrick Bryant,

Messrs. Asahel Buck,
Anson Burlingame,
Benjamin F. Butler,
William Carruthers,
Isaac Case,
Amariah Chandler,
Chester W. Chapin,
Daniel E. Chapin,
Josiah Childs,
J. McKean Churchill,
Henry Clark,
Ransom Clark,
Alpheus B. Clarke,
William Cleverly,
Lansing J. Cole,
Sumner Cole,
George B. Crane,
Oliver S. Cressy,
Joseph W. Cross,
Henry W. Cushman,
Thomas Cushman,
Simeon N. Cutler,
Richard H. Dana, Jr.,
Ebenezer Davis,
Isaac Davis,
Robert T. Davis,
Gilman Day,
Silas Dean,
Elijah S. Deming,
Augustus Denton,
Alexander De Witt,
Samuel Duncan,
Bradish Dunham,
John M. Durgin,
Peter Easland,
Calvin D. Eaton,
Elisha Edwards,
Samuel Edwards,
Joseph M. Ely,
Sullivan Fay,
Lyman Fisk,
Emery Fiske,
Ezekiel W. Fitch,
Samuel Fowle,
Charles A. French,
Charles H. French,
Samuel French,
Richard Frothingham, Jr.,
Luther Gale,
Johnson Gardner,
Elbridge Gates,
Charles G. Giles,
Daniel W. Gooch,
F. R. Gourgas,

Messrs. John W. Graves,
Jabez Green,
William B. Greene,
Josiah W. Griswold,
Whiting Griswold,
Samuel P. Hadley,
Charles B. Hall,
B. F. Hallett,
Lyman W. Hapgood,
Seth Hapgood,
Phineas Harmon,
William Haskins,
Elnathan P. Hathaway,
Stephen E. Hawkes,
Ezra Heath, 2d,
James Hewes,
William H. Hewes,
Aaron Hobart,
Henry Hobart,
Nathaniel Holder,
George Hood,
Martin Howard,
Abraham H. Howland,
Henry K. Hoyt,
Charles E. Hunt,
Charles P. Huntington,
Abijah M. Ide, Jr.,
John Jacobs,
John Johnson,
Isaac Kendall,
Edward L. Keyes,
Joseph Kimball,
Joseph Kingman,
Hiram Knight,
Jefferson Knight,
J. S. C. Knowlton,
William H. Knowlton,
Albert Knox,
Gardner P. Ladd,
Wilber C. Langdon,
Job G. Lawton, Jr.,
Alden Leland,
Otis Little,
Tristram Littlefield,
Abijah P. Marvin,
Charles Mason,
Simeon Merritt,
James L. Monroe,
James M. Moore,
Elbridge G. Morton,
Marcus Morton, Jr.,
William S. Morton,
Jonathan Nayson,
Charles Newman,

Messrs. William Nichols,
Alfred Norton,
Andrew T. Nute,
Joseph E. Ober,
Benjamin S. Orne,
Charles Osgood,
E. Wing Packer,
Benjamin Paine,
Samuel C. Parsons,
John Partridge,
Nathaniel Peabody,
Jeremiah Pease, Jr.,
John Penniman,
Daniel A. Perkins,
Jesse Perkins,
Charles Phelps,
Silvanus B. Phinney,
Henry Pierce,
James M. Pool,
John A. Putnam,
Robert Rantoul,
Silas Rawson,
David Rice,
Luther Richards,
Daniel Richardson,
Nathan Richardson,
Samuel H. Richardson,
Elkanah Ring, Jr.,
Joseph M. Rockwood,
John Rogers,
David S. Ross,
James C. Royce,
Amasa Sanderson,
Chester Sanderson,
Luther Sheldon,
Chester Sikes,
Perez Simmons,
John W. Simonds,
Melzar Sprague,

Messrs. Samuel W. Spooner,
Caleb Stetson,
Granville Stevens,
Joseph L. Stevens, Jr.,
William Stevens,
Gideon Stiles,
Alfred L. Strong,
Charles Sumner,
Increase Sumner,
Alanson Swain,
Isaac C. Taber,
Arnold Taft,
Willard Thayer, 2d,
John W. Thomas,
Charles Thompson,
Abraham Tilton,
Horatio W. Tilton,
David P. Turner,
William Tyler,
Orison Underwood,
George A. Vinton,
Bradford L. Wales,
Frederic T. Wallace,
Freeland Wallis,
Amasa Walker,
Marshal Warner,
Samuel Warner, Jr.,
Gershom B. Weston,
Daniel S. Whitney,
James S. Whitney,
J. B. Williams,
Henry Wilson,
Willard Wilson,
Jonathan B. Winn,
Charles C. Wood,
Nathaniel Wood,
Otis Wood,
Ezekiel Wright.

The Order, as adopted, is as follows:—

In Convention, May, 9, 1853.

Ordered, That the Secretary be directed, in notifying the town of Berlin, to use substantially the form herewith submitted:—

HALL OF THE CONSTITUTIONAL CONVENTION,
Boston, May —, 1853.

To the Selectmen of Berlin:—

GENTLEMEN:—The Hon. Henry Wilson, late Delegate for Berlin, in the Convention for revising the Constitution, having tendered his resignation as such Delegate, which has been accepted by the Convention, and his seat thereby vacated, I am directed by a vote of the Convention to request you, Gentlemen, to convene the qualified electors of your town as soon as may be with a due regard to notice, in order to their electing and deputing a Delegate to represent them in this Convention in the manner prescribed by the second section of the Act calling the Convention, adopted by the people on the second Monday of November, A. D. 1852.

I am, very respectfully,

Your obedient servant,

——— ———, *Secretary.*

The Report, inexpedient to take action upon the subject of filling such vacancies as may exist in this Convention from the different cities and towns in the Commonwealth, was accepted.

The Report on the subject of the name—"The Commonwealth of Massachusetts," was passed over.

On motion of Mr. FROTHINGHAM, of Charlestown,

Ordered, That in all cases where notice is issued to the towns or cities in which vacancies exist, or shall hereafter exist, the Secretary be instructed to follow the form of notice issued to the town of Berlin.

On motion of Mr. FRENCH, of New Bedford,

The Convention adjourned.

THURSDAY, May 19, 1853.

Met according to adjournment. Prayer was offered by the Chaplain. The Journal of yesterday was read.

Mr. BUTLER, of Lowell, presented the Petitions of Benjamin King Brown, and others, of Watertown; Solomon Howe, and others, of Ware; B. G. Veazie, and others, of Randolph; and James S. Olcott, and others, of Lowell; severally in aid of the Petition of John W. Le Barnes, and others.

Referred to the Committee on the Bill of Rights.

On motion of Mr. CHURCHILL, of Milton,

Ordered, That the Committee on Qualifications of Voters, be instructed to inquire into the expediency of so amending the Constitution as to provide that no person, who shall make, or become directly or indirectly interested in any bet or wager depending upon the result of any election, shall have a right to vote at such election, or be qualified to hold any office for which he shall be a candidate at such election.

Ordered, That the same committee consider the expediency of excluding from the right of suffrage, and the right to hold any office of profit or trust, all persons who may be convicted of bribery, larceny, or any infamous crime; all persons who forcibly, or by promises of reward, shall attempt to induce any voter to refrain from casting his vote, or shall attempt, in either of such ways, to procure votes for any candidate for office at any election hereafter to be held in this State; and all persons who shall give, or cause to be given, any illegal vote, knowing it to be such, at any election to be held in this State.

On motion of Mr. THOMPSON, of Charlestown,

Ordered, That the Committee on the House of Representatives consider the expediency of providing that the House consist of two hundred and eighty members, based upon ratable polls, to be elected in single districts, composed of contiguous territory, and of as nearly equal number of ratable polls as is practicable.

On motion of Mr. LOTHROP, of Boston,

Ordered, That the Committee to whom was referred so much of the Constitution as relates to Harvard College, inquire whether there are any reasons for having the members of the corporation of that college chosen by the legislature, which do not appertain in principle to the two other colleges in the Commonwealth; and whether it would not be expedient to provide that the members of the Boards of Trustees of these two other colleges, should also be chosen by the legislature, and that no one religious denomination, and no one political party, should have a majority in either of those Boards.

Ordered, That the same committee inquire how much of the present property and available instrumentalities of education, possessed by Harvard College, may be traced to direct grants from the legislature, and how much has been received from private donations and benefactions; and to what extent, comparatively, in this respect, Harvard College differs from the two other colleges in the Commonwealth.

Ordered, That the same committee consider the expediency of providing for the separation of all the colleges, now established in the Commonwealth, from any direct connection with the State, so that the legislature shall not elect all or any of the members of any of their Board of Corporation, Trustees, or Overseers, and so that these institutions shall only be so far connected with the State, as to be subject to the same general laws, duties, liabilities and penalties that attach to all other corporate franchises.

Ordered, That the same committee consider whether it be expedient or practicable to provide that Harvard College, and all other colleges now existing, or that may hereafter be established in this Commonwealth, shall be so incorporated with the general system of public instruction, through primary, grammar and high schools, now sustained by the State, as that the annual expenses of these colleges, so far as those expenses exceed the income of the funds and endowments now possessed and held by them, or that may be hereafter possessed and held by them, shall be met by a general tax, and by such appropriations as the legislature may see fit from time to time to make—and that every male child throughout the Commonwealth, who, upon examination, shall be found duly qualified, shall be at liberty, at any time between the ages of fourteen and twenty-one years, to enter either of these colleges, and enjoy their advantages and receive their honors or degrees, without any charge for tuition, lectures, use of library, college-rooms or text-books.

On motion of Mr. HOOPER, of Fall River,

Ordered, That the Committee on the Judiciary inquire into and report upon the expediency of so amending the Constitution, as to provide, that whenever a vacancy shall occur on the Bench of the Supreme Court, such vacancy shall be filled by an election at large, by the qualified voters in the State, for a term of years equal to the whole number of judges in said court, unless two or more vacancies shall occur in one and the same year; in that case the term of service for which each shall be elected shall be specified by the governor when ordering the election, so that the term of service of no two shall expire in any one year, but that one shall be elected every year when the seats of the present incumbents shall have been vacated.

Also, that said committee consider and report upon the expediency of electing the chief justice of the Court of Common Pleas by an election at large, by the qualified voters of the State, for a term of five years, and that the other judges of the same court be elected by districts, into which the State shall be divided for that purpose, and for the election of councillors; each judge so elected to hold his office for five years, and no two to be elected in any one year unless it shall be for the purpose of filling a vacancy.

On motion of Mr. BUTLER, of Lowell,

Ordered, That the Secretary of the Commonwealth be requested to furnish, for the use of the Convention, a table containing the names of all the cities and towns of the Commonwealth, arranged in the order of the number of their population by the census of 1840, and also of 1850, with the population of each, with the aggregate number of votes cast at the gubernatorial election of 1850 by each, and the aggregate number of voters on the voting list of each, and the number of Delegates to which each city and town is entitled in this Convention.

On motion of Mr. Cushman, of Bernardston,

Ordered, That the Committee on the Council consider the expediency of so amending the Constitution, that the Council shall consist of five persons, to be elected by the people in single Councillor Districts; and that eight contiguous Senatorial Districts shall constitute one Councillor District.

The President presented the Credentials of Mr. Deming, of Sheffield, and Mr. Stutson, of Sandwich, which were ordered to be placed on file.

Mr. Walker, of North Brookfield, from the Committee on the Qualifications of Voters, submitted a Report on that subject.

Referred to the Committee of the Whole, and ordered to be printed.

Mr. Hale, of Boston, at his request, and by reason of his engagements upon another committee, was excused from serving upon the Committee upon the subject of Reporting and Publishing the Proceedings and Debates of the Convention.

On motion of Mr. Gourgas, of Concord, the Convention proceeded to the consideration of the Orders of the Day.

The first subject, being the Report of the Committee on the Frame of Government, on the name—"The Commonwealth of Massachusetts," was referred to the Committee of the Whole.

On motion of Mr. Thompson, of Charlestown, the Convention resolved itself into Committee of the Whole, for the purpose of considering the Resolves on the subject of the Senate, and the President requested Mr. Morton, of Taunton, to take the chair.

Afterwards, Mr. Morton reported to the Convention that the Committee of the Whole had had under consideration the subject referred to them, had made some progress therein, but had come to no conclusion, and had instructed him to ask leave to sit again.

And leave was accordingly granted.

On motion of Mr. Schouler, of Boston, the amendments offered to the Report on the Senate in Committee of the Whole, by Mr. Bradford, of Essex, were ordered to be printed.

And, at ten minutes before six o'clock,

On motion of Mr. Bumpus, of Plympton,

The Convention adjourned.

FRIDAY, May 20, 1853.

Met according to adjournment. Prayer was offered by the Chaplain. The Journal of yesterday was read.

On motion of Mr. Foster, of Charlemont,

Ordered, That the Committee on the Frame of Government be instructed to inquire into the expediency of adding to the Constitution a provision, that the marriage contract shall not change the legal relation which the wife sustains to the ownership and disposal of the property which she possessed before marriage, or may legally acquire afterwards, by inheritance or otherwise.

Ordered, That the Committee on the Encouragement of Literature be instructed to consider the expediency of so amending the Constitution, that the State shall provide, or know that provision is made by private bounty, as liberally for the education of her daughters as for her sons, so far as the female character and condition require; that physical, moral, literary, and scientific education be made as accessible and as cheap to our daughters as to our sons, so far as the thirst and capacity of our daughters for education, the true interests and glory of Massachusetts, and the supply of that rapidly increasing demand for educated and highly educated females, requires; that such provision be made within the following ten years, and after, and be made in connection with and in some proportion to private endowments, since there is a reasonable expectation that private bounty will be directed, in an eminent degree, more than it has been to the superior education of the daughters of Massachusetts.

On motion of Mr. Knight, of Leicester,

Ordered, That the Committee on the Bill of Rights be instructed to consider the expediency of so amending that part of the Constitution, as to provide that every citizen of this Commonwealth be at liberty to pursue any business, trade, or employment for a livelihood, being responsible for the abuse of that privilege, and that no law shall impair that right.

On motion of Mr. WATERS, of Millbury,

Ordered, That the Committee on so much of the Constitution as relates to Sheriffs, Registers of Probate, and other County Officers, be instructed to inquire into the expediency of so amending the Constitution as to provide for the election of justices of the peace by the people, for a term not exceeding five years, and in a proportion not exceeding one to every five hundred inhabitants in the several cities and towns of this Commonwealth.

On motion of Mr. WILSON, of Natick,

Ordered, That the Committee on the Encouragement of Literature be instructed to consider the expediency of so amending the Constitution as to provide that all moneys to be derived from the sale of the public lands in Maine; and from that portion of the shares owned by the Commonwealth in the Western Railroad, paid for by the proceeds of sales of lands in Maine; and also the moneys to be derived from the claim of the State on the general government for military services, shall be added to the School Fund, until said fund shall amount to the sum of two millions of dollars; said fund to be preserved inviolate, and the income of the same to be applied only to the aid of common schools and for other educational purposes.

On motion of Mr. GILBERT, of Harvard,

Ordered, That the Committee on Oaths and Subscriptions be instructed so to amend the Constitution that the provision made in favor of the "Quakers" shall be extended to all who have conscientious scruples in regard to taking an oath.

On motion of Mr. BIRD, of Walpole,

Ordered, That the Committee on the Frame of Government be instructed to inquire into the expediency of a constitutional provision that no special privileges or immunities shall ever be granted that may not be altered, revoked, or repealed by the legislature, and to report thereon.

On motion of Mr. DURGIN, of Wilmington,

Ordered, That the Committee on the Qualifications of Voters consider the propriety of so altering the Constitution as to provide that no individual shall be deprived of the privilege of voting for State and United States officers in consequence of having changed his residence to another portion of the State, or lose his residence for the above purpose, until he shall have gained it in another.

Mr. Cole, of Cheshire, offered the following Resolution, which was referred to the Committee on the Frame of Government.

Resolved, That the legislature shall have no power to pass an act, the provisions of which release or discharge debtors from the payment of just liabilities.

On motion of Mr. French, of New Bedford,

Ordered, That when the Convention adjourn, it adjourn until Tuesday next at three o'clock.

Mr. Allen, of Worcester, from the Committee on the Frame of Government, submitted a Report on the subject of the time of holding elections of state and county officers, which was referred to the Committee of the Whole.

On motion of Mr. Wilson, of Natick, the Convention resolved itself into Committee of the Whole, for the purpose of further considering the Report on the subject of the Senate; and the President requested Mr. Morton, of Taunton, to take the chair.

Afterwards, Mr. Morton reported, that the committee had further considered the Resolves referred to them, and had instructed him to report them to the Convention without amendment.

The Resolves were then ordered to a second reading.

The President announced the appointment of Monitors for the galleries, as follows:—

For the Eastern Gallery—Messrs. Ober, of Beverly, and Bliss, of Hatfield.

For the Western Gallery—Messrs. Cleverly, of Wellfleet, and Woods, of Enfield.

Mr. Butler, of Lowell, moved a reconsideration of the vote by which the Convention agreed to adjourn until Tuesday; and the question being taken, one hundred and thirty-nine members voted in the affirmative, and seventy in the negative; so the vote was reconsidered.

On motion of Mr. Wilson, of Natick, the motion to adjourn until Tuesday was laid upon the table.

Whereupon, on motion of Mr. Butler, of Lowell,

Ordered, That when the Convention adjourn, it adjourn until Monday next at three o'clock, P. M.

On motion of Mr. Noyes, of Newbury, at six o'clock, P. M.,

The Convention adjourned.

MONDAY, May 23, 1853.

Met according to adjournment. Prayer was offered by the Chaplain. The Journal of Saturday was read.

Mr. Greene, of Brookfield, presented the Petition of Mrs. Abby B. Alcott and seventy-three others, women of Massachusetts, that they may be permitted to vote on the amendments and alterations of the Constitution that are to be submitted to the people.

Referred to the Committee on the Qualifications of Voters.

Mr. Keyes, member for Abington, presented the Petition of Wendell Phillips and nine hundred and thirty others, asking that the word "male" may be stricken from the Constitution, wherever it occurs.

Laid upon the table, but afterwards referred to the Committee on the Qualifications of Voters.

On motion of Mr. Bates, of Plymouth,

Ordered, That the Committee on the Pay Roll consider the expediency of providing for the pay of the members of this Convention, at the rate of three dollars per diem, for the term of sixty days, and that no pay shall be allowed beyond that period of time.

On motion of Mr. Cushman, of Bernardston,

Ordered, That the Committee on the Encouragement of Literature, be requested to consider the expediency of so amending the Constitution as to provide that the Board of Education and the Board of Agriculture shall be established as permanent departments of the government.

On motion of Mr. Hobart, of East Bridgewater,

Ordered, That the Committee on the Governor, consider the expediency of amending the Constitution, by striking out such parts thereof as provide that the governor shall have the title of "His Excellency," the lieutenant-governor the title of "His Honor," and that the councillors, in the civil arrangements of the Commonwealth, shall have rank next after the lieutenant-governor.

The President read a communication from Hon. Samuel A. Eliot, Delegate from Boston, resigning his seat in the Convention on account of the state of his health; which was placed on file.

Mr. Hale, of Boston, submitted a Resolution on the subject of the House of Representatives.

Referred to the committee on that subject, and ordered to be printed.

The PRESIDENT announced the appointment of the following Committees, viz.:—

On the Order offered by Mr. HOOD, of Lynn, concerning the mode of business which may be necessary or expedient, to bring the session to a close on or before July 1st:

Messrs. Hood, of Lynn, Walker, of North Brookfield, Gray, of Boston, Fowler, of Danvers, Reed, of Boston, Brownell, of New Bedford, Hewes, of Lynnfield, Clark, of Clarksburg, Griswold, of Buckland, Davis, of Fall River, Pease, of Edgartown, Woods, of Enfield, and Wilson, of Blackstone.

On the Order offered by Mr. WHITNEY, of Conway, concerning general laws for corporations:

Messrs. Whitney, of Conway, Beach, of Springfield, Brewster, of Boston, Ely, of West Springfield, Hapgood, of Athol, Knox, of Blandford, Bradford, of Essex, Cross, of West Boylston, Bartlett, of Worthington, Hewes, of Haverhill, Haskins, of Medford, Hersey, of Hingham, and Nichols, of Burlington.

On the Order offered by Mr. FROTHINGHAM, of Charlestown, concerning banking corporations:

Messrs. Frothingham, of Charlestown, Chapin, of Springfield, Jenks, of Boston, De Witt, of Oxford, Allis, of Whately, Sampson, of Boston, Day, of Templeton, Taber, of New Bedford, Bennett, of Hubbardston, Noyes, of Newbury, Wilder, of Lancaster, Richardson, of Middleton, and Turner, of South Hadley.

Mr. Marvin, of Boston, was appointed one of the Committee on the publication of Reports, in place of Mr. Hale, excused.

Mr. Giles, of Boston, was appointed one of the Committee on the University at Cambridge, in place of Mr. Sprague, excused.

On motion of Mr. NAYSON, of Amesbury, the Convention proceeded to the consideration of the Orders of the Day, the first subject being the Resolves concerning the Senate.

On motion of Mr. GOURGAS, of Concord,

Ordered, That when the question is taken on the passage of the Resolves, it be taken by yeas and nays.

Mr. HATHAWAY, of Freetown, moved to amend the Resolves, by substituting the words "number of qualified voters" for the word "population."

And further moved that when the question is taken on the amendment, it be taken by yeas and nays; and that the vote be taken at four o'clock on Tuesday.

He afterwards withdrew the motion to postpone the taking of the question; and the question being put upon his demand for the yeas and nays upon the amendment, it was rejected, one-fifth not voting in the affirmative.

The amendment was then rejected.

The Resolves were then taken up separately and passed, and the question being upon the final passage, the roll was called, and one hundred and sixty-five members voted in the affirmative, and five in the negative.

Those who voted in the affirmative are:—

Messrs. Benjamin P. Adams,
Josiah Allis,
D. W. Alvord,
Hillel Baker,
Alvah Ballard,
George S. Ball,
Alpheus Bancroft,
Erasmus D. Beach,
John Beal,
William C. Bliss,
Ebenezer Bradbury,
Hiram N. Breed,
Francis Brinley,
Adolphus F. Brown,
Alpheus R. Brown,
Hammond Brown,
Hiram C. Brown,
Frederick Brownell,
Rufus Bullock,
Anson Burlingame,
William Carruthers,
Isaac Case,
Amariah Chandler,
Henry Chapin,
Josiah Childs,
Rufus Choate,
J. McKean Churchill,
Ransom Clark,
Salah Clark,
Nathaniel Cogswell,
Lansing J. Cole,
Sumner Cole,
Henry F. Cooledge,
George W. Crockett,
Leander Crosby,
Joseph W. Cross,
Seth Crowell,
Henry W. Cushman,
Solomon Davis,
Silas Dean,
William Dehon,

Messrs. Augustus Denton,
James C. Doane,
Samuel Duncan,
John M. Durgin,
Peter Easland,
Calvin D. Eaton,
A. G. Farwell,
Ezekiel W. Fitch,
Aaron Foster,
Abram Foster,
James M. Freeman,
Samuel French,
Luther Gale,
Wanton C. Gilbert,
Joel Giles,
F. R. Gourgas,
Jabez Green,
William B. Greene,
Josiah W. Griswold,
Whiting Griswold,
Artemas Hale,
Nathan Hale,
B. F. Hallett,
Lyman W. Hapgood,
Elnathan P. Hathaway,
Stephen E. Hawkes,
George Hayward,
Charles Heard,
Henry Hersey,
James Hewes,
Edwin Hobbs,
Nathaniel Holder,
George Hood,
Thomas Hopkinson,
Samuel Houghton,
Abraham H. Howland,
William J. Hubbard,
Charles E. Hunt,
William Hunt,
Charles P. Huntington,
Abijah M. Ide, Jr.,

Messrs. Samuel Jackson,
John Jacobs,
John Jenkins,
Samuel H. Jenks,
Giles C. Kellogg,
Isaac Kendall,
Edward L. Keyes,
Hiram Knight,
Albert Knox,
George H. Kuhn,
Gardner P. Ladd,
Tristram Littlefield,
Justin E. Loomis,
Samuel K. Lothrop,
Samuel P. Loud,
John A. Lowell,
Abijah P. Marvin,
Theophilus R. Marvin,
Charles Mason,
Simeon Merritt,
Seth Miller, Jr.,
James M. Moore,
George Morey,
Marcus Morton,
Marcus Morton, Jr.,
Jonathan Nayson,
Charles Newman,
Andrew T. Nute,
Nathan Orcutt,
James W. Paige,
Benjamin Paine,
Henry Paine,
John G. Park,
Samuel D. Parker,
Samuel C. Parsons,
John Partridge,
Daniel A. Perkins,
Charles Phelps,
Jeremiah Pomroy,
George Putnam,
Robert Rantoul,
Daniel Richardson,

Messrs. Nathan Richardson,
Joseph M. Rockwood,
David S. Ross,
Amasa Sanderson,
Chester Sanderson,
William Schouler,
Luther Sheldon,
Charles Sherman,
John Souther,
Samuel W. Spooner,
Eben H. Stacy,
Charles G. Stevens,
Gideon Stiles,
Charles Sumner,
Willard Thayer, 2d,
John W. Thomas,
Horatio W. Tilton,
David Turner,
William Tyler,
Orison Underwood,
Freeland Wallis,
Amasa Walker,
Samuel Walker,
Andrew H. Ward,
Marshal Warner,
Samuel Warner, Jr.,
Gershom B. Weston,
Thomas Wetmore,
William F. Wheeler,
Benjamin White,
George White,
James S. Whitney,
John H. Wilkins,
Ezra Wilkinson,
J. B. Williams,
Henry Wilson,
Milo Wilson,
Willard Wilson,
Jonathan B. Winn,
Charles C. Wood,
Josiah B. Woods.

Those who voted in the negative are:—

Messrs. William J. A. Bradford,
William Haskins,
Silas Rawson,

Messrs. Luther Richards,
John W. Simonds.

So the Resolves were passed, as follow:—

1. *Resolved,* That it is expedient to alter and amend the Constitution of this Commonwealth so that it shall provide that the Senate

shall consist of forty members, to be elected annually, in single districts, composed of contiguous territory, and of as equal population as is practicable.

2. *Resolved*, That it is expedient to alter and amend the Constitution of this Commonwealth so that it shall provide that the meetings for the choice of senators shall be held on the Tuesday next after the first Monday of November annually.

3. *Resolved*, That it is expedient to alter and amend the Constitution of the Commonwealth so that it shall provide that the Senate shall have power to adjourn, provided such adjournments do not exceed three days at a time.

4. *Resolved*, That it is expedient to alter and amend the Constitution of the Commonwealth so that it shall provide that not less than a majority of the Senate shall constitute a quorum for doing business; but a smaller number may organize, adjourn from day to day, and may compel the attendance of absent members in such manner as the Senate may provide.

5. *Resolved*, That it is not expedient to alter or amend that part of the Constitution of the Commonwealth which provides that no person shall be capable of being elected as a senator, who has not been an inhabitant of this Commonwealth for the space of five years immediately preceding his election, and which also provides that he shall be, at the time of his election, an inhabitant of the district for which he shall be chosen.

6. *Resolved*, That it is not expedient to alter or amend the provisions of the Constitution of the Commonwealth which are contained in the eighth article of the second section of the first chapter of the Constitution.

Mr. Churchill, of Milton, moved that when the Convention adjourn, it adjourn to meet on Wednesday next, at three o'clock; but the motion was rejected.

The President read a communication from the Secretary of State, covering a statement of the population and representation of the several towns and cities of the Commonwealth. Laid upon the table and ordered to be printed.

At half-past six o'clock, on motion of Mr. Brown, of Douglas,

The Convention adjourned.

TUESDAY, May 24, 1853.

Met according to adjournment. Prayer was offered by the Chaplain. The Journal of yesterday was read.

Mr. SUMNER, member for Otis, offered an Order providing for the printing of the various Orders and Resolves which had been adopted.

Laid upon the table.

On motion of Mr. COLE, of Cheshire,

Ordered, That the Committee of Ways and Means to expedite the business of the Convention, be instructed to consider the expediency of reporting that from and after the present week, the Convention hold two sessions per day, commencing at nine, A. M., and three, P. M.

Mr. CHURCHILL, of Milton, offered an Order on the subject of the purchase of books for the use of members of the legislature.

Laid over under the rule.

The PRESIDENT presented the Credentials of Charles L. Knowlton, Delegate from Holden, which were ordered to be placed on file.

Leave of absence until Thursday, of this week, was granted to Mr. Taft, of Mendon, on account of the death of a son.

Mr. BUTLER, of Lowell, from the Committee on Oaths and Subscriptions, &c., presented a Report on that subject.

Referred to the Committee of the Whole and ordered to be printed.

Mr. WALKER, of North Brookfield, moved that the Committee of the Whole on the subject of elections by plurality of votes, be discharged from the further consideration of that subject; which motion was adopted.

Mr. WALKER further moved to assign the consideration of the subject, in Committee of the Whole, for three o'clock on Friday.

He afterwards withdrew this motion, and the Report, upon motion of Mr. HOOPER, of Fall River, was again placed first in the order of subjects referred to the Committee of the Whole.

On motion of Mr. WILSON, of Natick, the Convention resolved itself into Committee of the Whole, for the purpose of considering the Resolve on the subject of elections by plurality; and the President requested Mr. Sumner, member for Marshfield, to take the chair.

Afterwards, Mr. SUMNER reported that the Committee of the Whole had made progress in the consideration of the subject, but had come to no conclusion, and had directed him to ask leave to sit again.

And leave was accordingly granted.

On motion of Mr. WILSON, of Natick,

Ordered, That when the Convention adjourn, it adjourn to meet on Thursday at ten o'clock in the forenoon.

The PRESIDENT appointed the following gentlemen to constitute the committee upon the Order offered by Mr. Brown, of Dracut, concerning the loan of the credit of the State, viz.:—

Messrs. Brown, of Dracut, Warner, of Wrentham, Farwell, of Boston, Wilson, of Shelburne, Tower, of Florida, Little, of Pembroke, Hobbs, of Weston, Dorman, of Boxford, Powers, of Lowell, Freeman, of Franklin, Jacobs, of Carlisle, Loomis, of Russell, Cummings, of Ware, and Hurlbut, of Sudbury.

At five minutes before six o'clock, on motion of Mr. THOMPSON, of Charlestown,

The Convention adjourned.

THURSDAY, May 26, 1853.

Met according to adjournment. Prayer was offered by the Chaplain. The Journal of Tuesday was read.

The Order offered on Tuesday by Mr. Churchill, of Milton, and laid over, was taken up and adopted; as follows:—

Ordered, That the Committee on the Frame of Government be instructed to consider and report on the expediency of providing that no book or other printed matter, not strictly appertaining to the business of the session, thereafter to be transacted, shall be purchased or subscribed for, for the use of the members of the legislature, or be distributed among them at the public expense.

The Order offered on Tuesday, by Mr. Sumner, member for Otis, was taken from the table and adopted, as follows:—

Ordered, That all Resolves and Orders, referring subjects to the several committees of this Convention, prior to and including this date, be printed for the use of the Convention.

On motion of Mr. WILSON, of Natick,

Ordered, That the Secretary of the Commonwealth be requested to furnish, for the use of the Convention, a statement showing the number of business corporations that have been created by the legislature, since the last abstract upon this subject, furnished from the secretary's office for the use of the legislature, the purposes for which they have been created, the capital granted to each, the aggregate capital of each class, and the aggregate capital of all; also, a similar statement of corporations created the present year; and acts for the increase of the capital of existing corporations.

Also, a statement of the acts increasing the capital of existing corporations since the abstract referred to up to the present year.

Also, the aggregate number of the different classes of corporations, and the aggregate capital of the same, as contained in the two statements heretofore furnished from his office for the use of the legislature.

Mr. Earle, of Worcester, offered the following Resolution:—

Resolved, That the Constitution of the State ought to be so amended as to provide that the next census of the State shall be taken in the year 1855, and in each subsequent decennial period thereafter, so as to make the State census intermediate between the periods of the National census.

Referred to the Committee on the Frame of Government.

On motion of Mr. Hall, of Haverhill, the Convention resolved itself into Committee of the Whole, for the purpose of considering the Resolves on the subject of elections by plurality, and the President requested Mr. Sumner, member for Marshfield, to take the chair.

Afterwards Mr. Sumner reported to the Convention, that the committee had made further progress in the consideration of the subject but had come to no conclusion, and had instructed him to ask leave to sit again.

And leave was accordingly granted.

A communication was received from the Secretary of State, covering an Abstract of the Returns of the population of the State in 1840 and 1850, &c.

Laid upon the table, and ordered to be printed.

Mr. Crowell, of Dennis, moved that when the Convention adjourn, it adjourn to meet this afternoon at three o'clock.

Mr. Gray, of Boston, moved to substitute the hour of ten tomorrow.

The question being upon the motion of Mr. Gray, it was adopted by a vote of one hundred and thirty-seven in the affirmative, and one hundred and thirty-one in the negative.

And then, on motion of Mr. Hale, of Bridgewater, at two o'clock,
The Convention adjourned.

FRIDAY, May 27, 1853.

Met according to adjournment. Prayer was offered by the Chaplain. The Journal of yesterday was read.

On motion of Mr. DANA, member for Manchester,

Ordered, That the Committee on the Bill of Rights consider the expediency of declaring the right of every person having a claim against the Commonwealth, to a judicial remedy therefor.

On motion of Mr. BUTLER, of Lowell,

Ordered, That the Committee on the Loan of State Credit inquire into the expediency of providing that the credit or moneys of the State be not loaned to the prosecution of any private enterprise after the first day of July, which will be in the year one thousand eight hundred and fifty-five.

On motion of Mr. SCHOULER, of Boston,

Ordered, That the Secretary of the Commonwealth be requested to transmit to this Convention the number of new towns that have been formed since the year 1820—the names of the same, the counties in which they are, and the years in which they were severally created.

Mr. CRESSY, of Hamilton, offered the following Resolution:—

Resolved, That it is expedient to insert into the Constitution (in the legislative department) the following, viz.: Each member of the legislature shall receive from the public treasury a compensation for his services, which may be increased or diminished by law; but no increase of compensation shall take effect during the session at which such increase shall have been made.

Referred to the Committee on the Frame of Government.

Mr. GRISWOLD, member for Erving, from the Committee on the House of Representatives, submitted a Report on that subject; also, a Report from a Minority of the same Committee.

Referred to the Committee of the Whole and ordered to be printed.

Mr. WARNER, of Wrentham, requested to be excused from serving upon the Committee to whom was referred the subject of Loaning the Credit of the State.

Mr. Hall, of Haverhill, was appointed a member of the Committee upon the University at Cambridge, to fill a vacancy.

On motion of Mr. BUTLER, of Lowell, the Convention resolved itself into Committee of the Whole, for the purpose of considering the Resolve on the subject of elections by plurality; and the

President requested Mr. Sumner, member for Marshfield, to take the chair.

Afterwards, Mr. SUMNER reported that the committee had made further progress in the consideration of the subject referred to them, but had come to no conclusion, and had instructed him to ask leave to sit again.

And leave was accordingly granted.

Mr. HOOD, of Lynn, from the special committee to whom was referred an Order concerning the order of business; also an Order concerning the hour of meeting, and holding two sessions a day, submitted a Report, concluding with the following Order, which, under a suspension of the rules, was considered and adopted :—

Ordered, That on and after Monday next the Convention will hold two sessions per day, commencing at ten o'clock, A. M., and three o'clock, P. M.

Mr. BATES, of Plymouth, moved that when the Convention adjourn, it adjourn to meet at half-past three o'clock this afternoon.

Mr. THOMPSON, of Charlestown, moved to substitute the hour of ten to-morrow.

The question being upon Mr. Thompson's motion, it was rejected by a vote of one hundred and twenty-one in the affirmative, to one hundred and sixty-eight in the negative.

The motion of Mr. Bates was then agreed to.

On motion of Mr. CASE, of New Bedford, at a quarter past two o'clock,

The Convention adjourned.

AFTERNOON SESSION.

Met according to adjournment.

Mr. TOWER, of Florida, presented the Petitions of Charles Phelps and others, of Monroe; Joseph Proctor and others, of Gloucester; Jacob W. Hinckley and others, of Fall River; George W. Todd and others, of Acton; and Frederick W. Folger and others, of Nantucket, severally in aid of the Petition of John W. Le Barnes and others.

Referred to the Committee on the Bill of Rights.

Mr. KNOWLTON, of Worcester, moved that debate in Committee of the Whole upon the Resolve relating to elections by plurality, cease at half-past four o'clock to-day.

Mr. HOOPER, of Fall River, moved that the debate cease at twelve o'clock on Tuesday next.

The question being on Mr. Hooper's motion, it was rejected. The motion of Mr. Knowlton was then also rejected by a vote of ninety-four in the affirmative, to one hundred and thirteen in the negative.

Mr. BATES, of Plymouth, then moved that debate cease on Monday next at twelve o'clock; but the motion was rejected.

On motion of Mr. HOOPER, of Fall River, the Convention resolved itself into Committee of the Whole, for the purpose of considering the Resolve on the subject of elections by plurality; and the President requested Mr. Sumner, member for Marshfield, to take the chair.

Afterwards, Mr. SUMNER reported that the committee had made further progress in the consideration of the subject referred to them, but had come to no conclusion, and had instructed him to ask leave to sit again.

And leave was accordingly granted.

On motion of Mr. SHELDON, of Easton,

Ordered, That when the Convention adjourn, it adjourn to meet at ten o'clock to-morrow.

And then, on motion of Mr. EAMES, of Washington, at twenty minutes before seven o'clock,

The Convention adjourned.

SATURDAY, May 28, 1853.

Met according to adjournment. Prayer was offered by the Chaplain. The Journal of yesterday was read.

Mr. DAVIS, of Worcester, moved that the Convention resolve itself into Committee of the Whole, for the purpose of considering the Resolve in relation to the office of governor.

After some debate, the motion was agreed to, by a vote of one hundred and fifty-three in the affirmative, and sixty-two in the negative; and the President requested Mr. Hooper, of Fall River, to take the chair.

Afterwards, Mr. HOOPER reported that the Committee of the Whole had considered the subject, and recommended the passage of the resolves referred to them, with the following amendments, viz.:—

In the first Resolution, striking out the words "the United States," and inserting instead thereof, the word "Massachusetts."

In the same Resolution, striking out all after the word "governor."

The amendments were agreed to by the Convention, and the Resolves were ordered to a second reading.

On motion of Mr. Waters, of Millbury,

Ordered, That the Committee on the Judiciary be instructed to consider the expediency of defining more clearly the power and the manner of removing justices of the peace for sufficient cause, the same being now involved in doubt and wholly impracticable.

On motion of Mr. Davis, of Acton,

Ordered, That the Committee on the Bill of Rights be instructed to inquire into the expediency of so amending the same, that no person, by act of government, shall be released from paying his honest debts, whenever he has the ability so to do; and report thereon.

Mr. Hallett, member for Wilbraham, from the Committee on the subject of the Council, submitted a Report and Resolves on that subject.

Referred to the Committee of the Whole and ordered to be printed.

Mr. Brown, of Douglas, moved that when the Convention adjourn, it adjourn to meet on Monday at three o'clock, P. M.

Mr. Austin, of Swanzey, moved to substitute the hour of ten o'clock on Tuesday.

The question being on the motion of Mr. Austin, it was rejected.

The motion of Mr. Brown was agreed to by a vote of one hundred and thirty-seven in the affirmative, and thirty-two in the negative.

And then, on motion of Mr. Oliver, of Lawrence, at half past one o'clock,

The Convention adjourned.

MONDAY, May 30, 1853.

Met according to adjournment. Prayer was offered by the Chaplain. The Journal of Saturday was read.

A communication was received from the Secretary of State, enclosing a list of the towns formed in this State since the year 1820.

Laid on the table and ordered to be printed.

Mr. Gourgas, of Concord, presented the Credentials of George S. Boutwell, elected a Delegate to the Convention from the town of Berlin.

Ordered to be placed on file.

On motion of Mr. Wilson, of Natick,

Ordered, That the Committee on the Secretary, Treasurer, &c., be instructed to consider the expediency of amending the Constitution, so as to provide for the election by the people of the Commonwealth of a Prison Inspector.

On motion of Mr. LOTHROP, of Boston,

Ordered, That the Committee on the Qualifications of Voters, consider the expediency of providing that ability to read and write shall be an indispensable requisite for the exercise of the elective franchise in all elections held for the choice of town, city, county, and state officers.

Ordered, That the same committee consider the expediency of regarding the power to vote as a sacred trust, as well as a civil right, and of therefore providing that the neglect of this trust,—that is, the neglect to vote,—when not caused by sickness, or absence from the State, shall be an offence punishable by fine, and if persevered in for a given term of years, shall work a forfeiture of the right to vote.

The following Order, offered by Mr. FRENCH, of Berkley, was referred to the Committee of the Whole.

Ordered, That the Committee on the Lieutenant-Governor inquire into the expediency of abolishing that office in this Commonwealth.

On motion of Mr. WARNER, of Wrentham, the Convention proceeded to the consideration of the Orders of the Day, the first matter being the Resolves on the subject of the governor.

On motion of Mr. THOMPSON, of Charlestown,

Ordered, That when the question is taken on the final passage of the Resolves, it be taken by yeas and nays.

And the roll being called, two hundred and eighty-nine members voted for the Resolves, and six members against them.

Those who voted in the affirmative are:—

Messrs. Benjamin P. Adams,
Shubael P. Adams,
P. Emory Aldrich,
Charles Allen,
James B. Allen,
Joel C. Allen,
Parsons Allen,
John B. Alley,
Robert Andrews,
William Appleton,
Samuel Ayres,
Alvah Ballard,
George S. Ball,
Russell Bartlett,
Sidney Bartlett,

Messrs. Marcus Barrett,
Moses Bates, Jr.,
Erasmus D. Beach,
John Beal,
James M. Beebe,
Zephaniah Bennett,
Edward B. Bigelow,
Francis W. Bird,
George W. Blagden,
Gad O. Bliss,
George S. Boutwell,
Sewell Boutwell,
William J. A. Bradford,
Hiram N. Breed,
George N. Briggs,

Messrs. Adolphus F. Brown,
Alpheus R. Brown,
Artemas Brown,
Hammond Brown,
Joseph Brownell,
Amos H. Bullen,
Rufus Bullock,
Cephas C. Bumpus,
Anson Burlingame,
Benjamin F. Butler,
Henry Cady,
William Carruthers,
Isaac Case,
Amariah Chandler,
Daniel E. Chapin,
Josiah Childs,
Rufus Choate,
J. McKean Churchill,
Salah Clark,
Alpheus B. Clarke,
Stillman Clarke,
William Cleverly,
Jacob Coggin,
Nathaniel Cogswell,
Sumner Cole,
Ithamar Conkey,
Henry F. Cooledge,
George B. Crane,
Oliver S. Cressy,
Simeon Crittenden,
George W. Crockett,
Leander Crosby,
Joseph W. Cross,
Francis B. Crowninshield,
Joseph Cummings,
Thomas Cushman,
Simeon N. Cutler,
Richard H. Dana, Jr.,
Ebenezer Davis,
John Davis,
Robert T. Davis,
Solomon Davis,
Silas Dean,
William Dehon,
Elijah S. Deming,
Augustus Denton,
Alexander De Witt,
James C. Doane,
Samuel Duncan,
Bradish Dunham,
John M. Durgin,
Philip Eames,
John M. Earle,

Messrs. Peter Easland,
James Easton, 2d,
Lilley Eaton,
Elisha Edwards,
Homer Ely,
William T. Eustis,
A. G. Farwell,
James K. Fellows,
Lyman Fisk,
Emery Fiske,
Ezekiel W. Fitch,
Aaron Foster,
Abram Foster,
Samuel Fowle,
Samuel P. Fowler,
James M. Freeman,
Charles A. French,
Samuel French,
Richard Frothingham, Jr.,
Luther Gale,
Elbridge Gates,
Washington Gilbert,
Charles G. Giles,
Joel Giles,
Daniel W. Gooch,
Leonard Gooding,
Robert Gould,
Jason Goulding,
Francis R. Gourgas,
John W. Graves,
John C. Gray,
Jabez Green,
William B. Greene,
Samuel P. Hadley,
Artemas Hale,
Charles B. Hall,
Benjamin F. Hallett,
A. B. Hammond,
Lyman W. Hapgood,
Seth Hapgood,
Phineas Harmon,
William Haskins,
Elnathan P. Hathaway,
Stephen E. Hawkes,
Isaac Hayden,
Charles Heard,
Ezra Heath, 2d,
Samuel Henry,
Henry Hersey,
James Hewes,
William H. Hewes,
Levi Heywood,
William Hinsdale,

Messrs. Aaron Hobart,
Henry Hobart,
Edwin Hobbs,
Nathaniel Holder,
George Hood,
Thomas Hopkinson,
Samuel Houghton,
Martin Howard,
William J. Hubbard,
William Hunt,
Charles P. Huntington,
George H. Huntington,
Moses C. Hurlbut,
Benjamin D. Hyde,
John Jacobs,
Samuel H. Jenks,
John Johnson,
Giles C. Kellogg,
Isaac Kendall,
Edward L. Keyes,
Joseph Kimball,
Joseph Kingman,
Henry W. Kinsman,
Jefferson Knight,
Joseph Knight,
J. S. C. Knowlton,
William H. Knowlton,
George H. Kuhn,
Gardner P. Ladd,
John S. Ladd,
Job G. Lawton, Jr.,
Alden Leland,
Abishai Lincoln,
Frederic W. Lincoln, Jr.,
Tristram Littlefield,
Isaac Livermore,
Samuel K. Lothrop,
Samuel P. Loud,
John A. Lowell,
William P. Marble,
Laban Marcy,
Abijah P. Marvin,
Reuben Meader,
Simeon Merritt,
Samuel Mixter,
James L. Monroe,
Joseph B. Morss,
Marcus Morton,
Marcus Morton, Jr.,
William S. Morton,
Hiram Nash,
Jonathan Nayson,
Charles Newman,

Messrs. William Nichols,
Daniel Noyes,
Andrew T. Nute,
Henry K. Oliver,
Nathan Orcutt,
Benjamin S. Orne,
Charles Osgood,
E. Wing Packer,
Benjamin Paine,
Henry Paine,
John G. Park,
Adolphus G. Parker,
Joel Parker,
Samuel D. Parker,
Jonathan Parris,
John Partridge,
Thomas E. Payson,
Nathaniel Peabody,
John Penniman,
Daniel A. Perkins,
Noah C. Perkins,
Charles Phelps,
Henry Pierce,
James M. Pool,
Peter Powers,
George Putnam,
John A. Putnam,
Robert Rantoul,
Silas Rawson,
James Read,
Sampson Reed,
David Rice,
Luther Richards,
Samuel H. Richardson,
Elkanah Ring, Jr.,
John Rogers,
James C. Royce,
George R. Sampson,
Chester Sanderson,
John Sargent,
William Schouler,
John Sherril,
Chester Sikes,
John S. Sleeper,
Matthew Smith,
John Souther,
Melzar Sprague,
Samuel W. Spooner,
Charles G. Stevens,
Granville Stevens,
Joseph L. Stevens, Jr.,
William Stevens,
Alfred L. Strong,

Messrs. Charles Sumner,
Increase Sumner,
Alanson Swain,
Arnold Taft,
Thomas Talbot,
Ralph Taylor,
Joseph Thayer,
Willard Thayer, 2d,
John W. Thomas,
Charles Thompson,
Edmund P. Tileston,
Abraham Tilton,
Horatio W. Tilton,
Ephraim Tower,
Charles R. Train,
David Turner,
William Tyler,
Orison Underwood,
Charles W. Upham,
George B. Upton,
Joel Viles,
Freeland Wallis,
Samuel Walker,
Andrew H. Ward,

Messrs. Marshal Warner,
Samuel Warner, Jr.,
Cyrus Weeks,
Gershom B. Weston,
William F. Wheeler,
Benjamin White,
George White,
Daniel S. Whitney,
Daniel Wilbur,
Joel Wilder,
John H. Wilkins,
Henry Williams,
J. B. Williams,
Henry Wilson,
Milo Wilson,
Willard Wilson,
Jonathan B. Winn,
Levi M. Winslow,
Nathaniel Wood,
Otis Wood,
William H. Wood,
Josiah B. Woods,
Ezekiel Wright.

Those who voted in the negative are:—

Messrs. William Aspinwall,
David C. Atwood,
Benjamin F. Copeland,

Messrs. Samuel Edwards,
Dalton Goulding,
Samuel B. Walcott.

So the Resolves were finally passed, as follow:—

Resolved, That it is expedient, to alter and amend the Constitution, so as to provide that no person except a citizen of Massachusetts, shall be eligible to the office of governor.

Resolved, That it is expedient to alter and amend the Constitution, by abolishing the property qualification for governor.

Resolved, That it is expedient to alter and amend the Constitution, so as to provide for the election of governor, on the Tuesday next after the first Monday in the month of November, annually.

Resolved, That it is expedient to alter and amend the Constitution, so as to provide that in case of the failure of an election of governor by the people, he shall be elected by the Senate and House of Representatives, by joint ballot.

On motion of Mr. Wilson, of Natick, the Convention resolved itself into Committee of the Whole, for the purpose of considering the Report of the Committee on the Frame of Government, on the subject of the name—"The Commonwealth of Massachusetts," and the President requested Mr. Thompson, of Charlestown, to take the chair.

Afterwards, Mr. THOMPSON reported, that the committee had considered the subject referred to them, and recommended the acceptance of the Report.

The Resolve was accordingly ordered to a second reading, and afterwards, under a suspension of the rules, was accepted, as follows:

They recommend that the name—" The Commonwealth of Massachusetts," be retained, and that no amendment is needed in the introductory portion of " part the second " of said Constitution.

On motion of Mr. HALL, of Haverhill, the Convention resolved itself into Committee of the Whole, for the purpose of considering the Report of the Committee on the Frame of Government, on the subject of the time of holding elections, and the President requested Mr. Butler, of Lowell, to take the chair.

Afterwards, Mr. BUTLER reported, that the committee had considered the subject referred to them, and recommended the passage of the Resolve.

The Resolve was accordingly ordered to a second reading, and then, under a suspension of the rules, was finally passed, as follows:—

Resolved, That the Constitution be so amended, as to provide that all popular elections of state and county officers, recurring at stated periods, be held, hereafter, on the Tuesday next succeeding the first Monday in November.

On motion of Mr. WILSON, of Natick, the Convention resolved itself into Committee of the Whole, for the purpose of considering the Resolves relating to the lieutenant-governor, and the President requested Mr. Crowninshield, of Boston, to take the chair.

Afterwards, Mr. CROWNINSHIELD reported, that the committee had had under consideration the articles referred to them, and had instructed him to report them to the Convention, with certain amendments to the first article.

The amendments were agreed to by the Convention, as follows:—

In the second and third lines, (printed copy,) strike out the words, " whose title shall be His Honor, and ".

In the ninth and tenth lines, strike out the words, " have a majority of all the votes returned," and insert instead thereof, the words, " be elected."

In the thirteenth line, strike out the words, " a majority of " and insert instead thereof, the words, " been elected by."

On motion of Mr. BUTLER, of Lowell, the articles were recommitted to the Committee of the Whole, to take their place in the Calendar with the Report on the subject of the Council.

On motion of Mr. BUTLER, of Lowell, the Convention resolved itself into Committee of the Whole, for the purpose of considering the Report of the Committee on the subject of Oaths and Subscriptions, &c., and the President requested Mr. Gray, of Boston, to take the chair.

Afterwards, Mr. GRAY reported, that the Committee of the Whole had made progress in the consideration of the subject referred to them, but had come to no conclusion, and had instructed him to ask leave to sit again.

And leave was accordingly granted.

And then, at twenty minutes past six o'clock, on motion of Mr. CHURCHILL, of Milton,

The Convention adjourned.

TUESDAY, May 31, 1853.

Met according to adjournment. Prayer was offered by the Chaplain. The Journal of yesterday was read.

Mr. GREENE, of Brookfield, presented the Petition of Josiah Henshaw and eighty others, of West Brookfield, to have the word "male" stricken from the Constitution.

On motion of Mr. MARVIN, of Winchendon,

Ordered, That the Committee on the Encouragement of Literature be instructed to inquire into the expediency of so amending the Constitution as to require that all persons who may be admitted to the right of suffrage after the year 1856, shall be able to read the Constitution of this Commonwealth, printed in the English language.

On motion of Mr. POWERS, of Lowell,

Ordered, That the Committee on the Encouragement of Literature be instructed to inquire into the expediency of so amending the Constitution, that the School Fund belonging to the Commonwealth, shall never be appropriated or applied to the support of any sectarian schools, or schools founded upon sectarian principles.

On motion of Mr. DANA, member for Manchester,

Ordered, That the Committee on the Judiciary consider the expediency, in the event of the Council being abolished, of amending the provision for the removal of judicial officers by address, so as to require a vote of two-thirds of one or both branches of the legislature.

On motion of Mr. BUTLER, of Lowell, the Convention resolved itself into Committee of the Whole, for the purpose of considering further, the Resolves reported by the Committee on Oaths and Subscriptions, &c., and the President requested Mr. Gray, of Boston, to take the chair.

Afterwards, Mr. GRAY reported the Resolves to the Convention without amendment, and they were ordered to a second reading.

On motion of Mr. HOOPER, of Fall River, the Convention resolved itself into Committee of the Whole for the purpose of considering the Resolve on the subject of elections by plurality of votes, and the President requested Mr. Sumner, member for Marshfield, to take the chair.

Afterwards, Mr. SUMNER reported, that the Committee of the Whole had had under consideration the Resolve which was referred to them, had made some progress therein, but had come to no conclusion, and had instructed him to ask leave to sit again.

And leave was accordingly granted.

At half past one o'clock, on motion of Mr. EARLE, of Worcester,

The Convention adjourned.

AFTERNOON SESSION.

Met according to adjournment.

On motion of Mr. WHEELER, of Lincoln,

Ordered, That the Committee on the Frame of Government consider the expediency of incorporating into the Constitution a provision that senators in congress shall be chosen by joint ballot of both branches of the legislature, assembled in convention.

On motion of Mr. WILSON, of Natick,

Ordered, That the Committee on the Governor, be instructed to consider the expediency of amending article 7, of section 1, chapter 2, of the Constitution, by substituting therefor the following words, to wit: The governor shall be commander-in-chief of the militia of the Commonwealth, and of the army and navy.

Mr. BRIGGS, of Pittsfield, submitted the following Resolution:—

Resolved, That the Committee on the House of Representatives be intructed to inquire into the expediency of so altering that part of the Constitution which relates to the time of choosing representatives to the general court, as to provide that representatives may be elected at any time before the day of the final adjournment of the legislature to which they are to be elected.

Referred to the Committee of the Whole.

Mr. SHELDON, of Easton, moved that when the Convention adjourn, it adjourn to meet at nine o'clock to-morrow morning, but afterwards withdrew the motion.

On motion of Mr. BROWN, of Douglas, the Convention resolved itself into Committee of the Whole for the purpose of considering the Resolve concerning elections by plurality of votes, and the President requested Mr. Sumner, member for Marshfield, to take the chair.

Afterwards, Mr. SUMNER reported to the Convention that the committee had made further progress in the consideration of the subject, but had come to no conclusion, and had instructed him to ask leave to sit again.

And leave was accordingly granted.

Mr. BUTLER, of Lowell, moved that the debate on this subject, in Committee of the Whole, shall close at eleven o'clock to-morrow.

At the suggestion of Mr. DURGIN, of Wilmington, he afterwards modified his motion by substituting the hour of twelve, and then the motion was adopted.

At a quarter past six o'clock, upon motion of Mr. UNDERWOOD, of Milford,

The Convention adjourned.

WEDNESDAY, June 1, 1853.

Met according to adjournment. Prayer was offered by the Chaplain. The Journal of yesterday was read.

Mr. FAY, of Southborough, from the Committee on Leave of Absence, submitted a Report, granting leave of absence to Mr. Aldrich, of Barre, for two weeks, commencing May 31st; and to Mr. Sampson Reed, of Boston, for twenty days, commencing on Friday next; which Report was accepted, and leave granted accordingly.

On motion of Mr. BUTLER, of Lowell, the Convention proceeded to the consideration of the Orders of the Day, the first matter being the Resolves reported by the Committee on the subject of Oaths and Subscriptions, &c.

And the Resolves were read a second time, and finally passed, as follow:—

1. *Resolved*, That it is expedient to amend and alter the existing Constitution in this article, by incorporating the oath of allegiance and the oath of office into one formula.

2. *Resolved*, That it is expedient to alter and amend this part of the Constitution, as follows, namely: Strike out the words, "So help me God," where they first occur, and in lieu thereof insert the word "and." Also, strike out in the official oath the words, "I, A. B., do solemnly swear and affirm." So that there shall be but one oath taken and subscribed, which, as amended, shall read as follows:—

"I, A. B., do solemnly swear that I will bear true faith and allegiance to the Commonwealth of Massachusetts, and will support the Constitution thereof; and that I will faithfully and impartially discharge and perform all the duties incumbent on me as [here insert the office,] according to the best of my abilities and understanding, agreeably to the rules and regulations of the Constitution and the laws of the Commonwealth. So help me God."

3. *Resolved*, That it is expedient to amend and alter the proviso in this article as follows:—

1. Strike out the words, "of the denomination of the people called Quakers," and insert the words "conscientiously scrupulous of taking and subscribing an oath."

2. Strike out the letter "s" in the word "oaths," which follows the words "taking the said;" and strike out the words "in the foregoing form."

3. Strike out the words "in the first oath." Also, the words "in the second oath," and in each of them the words—So help me God.

4. Strike out the words, "instead thereof," where they first occur in said proviso, so that the proviso, as amended, shall read as follows:—

"*Provided, always*, that when any person, chosen or appointed as aforesaid, shall be conscientiously scrupulous of taking and subscribe ing an oath, and shall decline taking the said oath, he shall make his affirmation, and subscribe the same, omitting the word 'swear,' and inserting the word 'affirm' instead thereof, and subjoining—This I do under the pains and penalties of perjury."

4. *Resolved*, That the third article of the sixth chapter be stricken out of the Constitution.

5. *Resolved*, That it is not expedient to alter, revise, or amend the fourth and sixth articles of the sixth chapter, but that the same stand as they and each of them now are.

6. *Resolved*, That it is expedient to alter and amend the fifth article of the sixth chapter, by striking out the words "they shall bear test of the first justice of the court to which they shall be returnable, who is not a party." So that the article, as amended, shall read thus:—

"ARTICLE 5. All writs issuing out of the clerk's office in any of the courts of law, shall be in the name of the Commonwealth of Massachusetts; they shall be under the seal of the court from whence they issue, and be signed by the clerk of such court."

On motion of Mr. WILSON, of Natick, the Convention resolved itself into Committee of the Whole, for the purpose of considering the Resolve on the subject of elections by plurality; and the President requested Mr. Sumner, member for Marshfield, to take the chair.

Afterwards, Mr. SUMNER reported, that the committee had made further progress in the consideration of the Resolve referred to them, and had instructed him to report that it ought not to pass.

Mr. MORTON, of Taunton, offered a substitute for the Resolve; pending the consideration of which,

At a quarter past two o'clock, on motion of Mr. BUTLER, of Lowell,

The Convention adjourned.

AFTERNOON SESSION.

Met according to adjournment.

Mr. HOYT, of Deerfield, presented the Petition of J. A. Saxton, and thirty-two others, of Deerfield, for a declaration in favor of protection to fugitive slaves.

Referred to the Committee on the Bill of Rights.

Mr. PENNIMAN, of Chelsea, presented the Petition of John P. Coburn, and one hundred others, for a modification of the laws, so that no able-bodied citizen shall be prevented from serving or holding office or commission in the militia, on account of his color.

Referred to the same committee.

Mr. ALLEN, of Worcester, from the Committee on the Frame of Government, submitted a Report upon an Order of May 17th, concerning the loan of the credit of the State, recommending that it be referred to the committee having that subject in charge.

The Report was accepted, and the Order so referred.

The same gentleman, from the same committee, submitted a Report, inexpedient to act upon the subject of an Order of the 16th of

May, concerning a limitation of the time for the reception of petitions by the legislature.

Also, inexpedient to act upon the subject of an Order of the 17th of May, respecting the originating of bills and resolves in the House of Representatives.

Also, inexpedient to act upon the subject of an Order of the 18th of May, relating to the permanent establishment of the seat of government at Boston.

Also, a Resolve on the subject of an Order of the 16th of May, relative to *viva voce* elections by the legislature.

Mr. WHITNEY, of Conway, from the special committee on the subject of making constitutional provisions for the creation of corporations, submitted a Report and Resolve on that subject.

These Reports were severally referred to the Committee of the Whole, and were ordered to be printed.

Mr. KEYES, member for Abington, moved that the Resolve on the subject of elections by plurality of votes, and the substitute offered by Mr. Morton, of Taunton, be recommitted to the special committee on that subject.

On motion of Mr. SCHOULER, of Boston, the Convention proceeded to the consideration of the Orders of the Day.

Mr. BUTLER, of Lowell, then renewed the motion for recommitment, previously made by Mr. Keyes, but afterwards, at the suggestion of Mr. Cady, of Monson, moved to commit the subject to a special committee of one from each county, which motion was agreed to.

Mr. HALLETT, member for Wilbraham, offered a Resolution on the subject of elections.

Referred to the special committee.

Mr. GRAY, of Boston, offered an Order, instructing the Committee on the House of Representatives to prepare a table of population and representation, &c.

Laid over, under the rule.

On motion of the same gentleman, the Convention resolved itself into Committee of the Whole, for the purpose of considering the Resolves on the subject of the Council; and the President requested Mr. Briggs, of Pittsfield, to take the chair.

Afterwards, Mr. BRIGGS reported, that the committee had made progress in the consideration of the subject referred to them, but had come to no conclusion, and had instructed him to ask leave to sit again.

And leave was accordingly granted.

At six o'clock, on motion of Mr. WEEKS, of Harwich,

The Convention adjourned.

THURSDAY, June 2, 1853.

Met according to adjournment. Prayer was offered by the Chaplain. The Journal of yesterday was read.

On motion of Mr. Wilson, of Natick,

Ordered, That the Special Committee on Elections by Plurality be instructed to inquire into the expediency of so amending the Constitution that all vacancies occasioned by failures to elect senators and representatives by a majority on the day of the annual election, shall be filled by elections to be held on the second Tuesday of December, by a plurality of votes; also, so as to give the legislature authority to provide by law that county and municipal officers may be chosen by a plurality of votes—such law not to take effect until two years after its passage.

On motion of Mr. Cole, of Cheshire,

Ordered, That the Committee on Enrolment be directed to consider the propriety of reporting to the Convention that it is expedient and proper to submit to the people, for adoption or rejection, so much of the amended Constitution as relates to the number of representatives and the basis of their apportionment, elections by plurality or majority, and granting the loan of State credit, in questions distinct from each other and from the Constitution as a whole.

Mr. Underwood, of Milford, submitted the following Resolutions:—

Resolved, That the House of Representatives shall be composed of members chosen as follows:—

Every town or city containing less than one thousand inhabitants shall be entitled to one representative every third year. Said towns to be divided, as equally as may be, into three classes; the first class to elect the first year, the second class the second year, and the third class the third year.

Every town or city containing over one thousand and less than two thousand inhabitants shall be entitled to one representative every second year. Said towns to be divided, as equally as may be, into two classes; the first class to elect the first year, and the second class the second year.

Every town or city of two thousand inhabitants shall have one representative annually.

Every town or city of six thousand, shall have two.

Every town or city of twelve thousand, shall have three.

Every town or city of twenty thousand, shall have four.

Resolved, further, That the rate of increase above twenty thousand inhabitants, to entitle any town or city to an additional representative, shall be ten thousand, but no town or city shall in any case have over twenty-five representatives.

The Order offered yesterday, instructing the Committee on the House of Representatives to prepare a table of population and representation, &c., was considered and rejected.

Mr. Morton, of Taunton, from the Committee on the Judiciary Power, submitted a Report and Resolves on that subject.

Referred to the Committee of the Whole and ordered to be printed.

Mr. Cole, of Cheshire, offered the following Order, which was adopted by a vote of one hundred and sixty-five in the affirmative, and sixty-one in the negative:—

Ordered, That the Convention hereafter adjourn at one o'clock, P. M., until otherwise determined.

Afterwards, Mr. Miller, of Wareham, moved a reconsideration of the vote by which the Order was adopted; and the motion was placed in the Orders of the Day.

On motion of Mr. Cushman, of Bernardston, the Convention resolved itself into Committee of the Whole, for the purpose of further considering the Resolves relating to the Council, and the Resolves relating to the Lieutenant-Governor; and the President requested Mr. Briggs, of Pittsfield, to take the chair.

Afterwards, Mr. Briggs reported, that the committee had made progress in the consideration of the Resolves, but had come to no conclusion, and had instructed him to ask leave to sit again.

And leave was accordingly granted.

At one o'clock, on motion of Mr. Morton, of Quincy,

The Convention adjourned.

AFTERNOON SESSION.

Met according to adjournment.

The President appointed the Committee ordered by the Convention, on the subject of Elections by Plurality and Majority, consisting of the following members, viz.:—

Messrs. Butler, of Lowell, Keyes, member for Abington, Stevenson, of Boston, Rockwell, of Pittsfield, Williams, of Taunton, De Witt, of Oxford, Phinney, member for Chatham, White, of Quincy, Griswold, of Buckland, Morss, of Newburyport, Parker, of Chicopee, Gilbert, of Plainfield, Pease, of Edgartown, and Easton, of Nantucket.

On motion of Mr. NAYSON, of Amesbury, the Convention resolved itself into Committee of the Whole, for the purpose of further considering the Resolves relating to the Council and the Lieutenant-Governor, and the President requested Mr. Briggs, of Pittsfield, to take the chair.

Afterwards, Mr. BRIGGS reported, that the committee had made further progress in the consideration of the subject, but had come to no conclusion, and had instructed him to ask leave to sit again.

And leave was accordingly granted.

At twenty minutes past six o'clock, on motion of Mr. DUNCAN, of Williamstown,

The Convention adjourned.

FRIDAY, June 3, 1853.

Met according to adjournment. Prayer was offered by the Chaplain. The Journal of yesterday was read.

Mr. GREENE, of Brookfield, presented the Petition of Zilpha W. H. Spooner and forty-three others, women of Massachusetts, that they may be permitted to vote on the proposed amendments of the Constitution.

Referred to the Committee on the Qualifications of Voters.

On motion of Mr. CHURCHILL, of Milton,

Ordered, That the Committee on the Governor be requested to consider and report upon the expediency of so amending the Constitution as to provide that in all applications to the executive of this Commonwealth for the exercise of the power to pardon or commute, public notice thereof and of the time and place of hearing the same shall be given, both in the county where the person in whose behalf such application is made, was tried and convicted, and in some newspaper published in the city of Boston; and that it shall likewise be the duty of the said Governor and Council to consult and advise with the attorney of the Commonwealth who was engaged in the trial and conviction of such applicant for executive clemency, as to the propriety of granting the same, or to require the presence of said attorney at the hearing of such application.

On motion of Mr. PHELPS, of Monroe,

Ordered, That the Committee on Plurality in Elections, take into consideration the expediency of so altering or amending the Constitution, that whenever there shall be a failure to elect any state, county, district, or municipal officer, at the first election which shall be held therefor, at a subsequent meeting held for that purpose, the person receiving the highest number of votes at any such subsequent meeting, shall be declared elected.

On motion of Mr. MORTON, of Quincy,

Ordered, That the Committee on the Frame of Government, take into consideration the expediency of so amending the Constitution, that, by that instrument, the rights of women to their property, acquired by devise, inheritance, their own labor, or otherwise, shall be so secured to them as not to be subject to be alienated except by their own act and consent.

On motion of Mr. CUSHMAN, of Bernardston,

Ordered, That the Committee on the Secretary, Treasurer, &c., be directed to consider the expediency of so amending the Constitution, that there shall be two classes of justices of the peace, viz. :—

1st. Police or trial justices, consisting of such a number as may be necessary, but not less than one in each town, who shall be elected by the people for five years, and who shall have all the powers, and shall perform all the duties that are now exercised by justices of the peace, justices of the quorum, and by qualifying officers; and

2d. Justices of the peace, whose authority shall extend only to the acknowledgment of deeds, and to the administration of oaths.

Mr. BISHOP, of Lenox, from the Committee on the subject of the Secretary, Treasurer, Attorney-General, &c., submitted a Report and Resolutions on that subject.

Referred to the Committee of the Whole and ordered to be printed.

The same gentleman, from the same committee, submitted a Report on an Order of inquiry as to the expediency of electing justices of the peace by the people; recommending that the committee be discharged from the further consideration of the Order, and that it be referred to the Committee on the Judiciary Power.

After debate, on motion of Mr. WATERS, of Millbury, the Report was recommitted to the Committee on the Secretary, Treasurer, &c.

Mr. LIVERMORE, of Cambridge, from the Committee on the Pay Roll, submitted a Report on the subject of the compensation of the members of the Convention.

Laid upon the table, and ordered to be printed.

On motion of Mr. BIRD, of Walpole, the Secretary was directed to give notice to the city of Boston, of a vacancy existing in the delegation from that city, occasioned by the resignation of Hon. Samuel A. Eliot.

On motion of Mr. CHANDLER, of Greenfield, the Convention proceeded to the consideration of the Orders of the Day.

The first subject was the motion of Mr. Miller, of Wareham, that the vote by which the Convention agreed to adjourn each day at one o'clock, P. M., be reconsidered.

After debate, the motion to reconsider was rejected by a vote of seventy-four in the affirmative, and one hundred and twenty-four in the negative.

On motion of Mr. PHINNEY, member for Chatham, the Convention resolved itself into Committee of the Whole, for the purpose of considering the Resolves on the subject of the Council and the Lieutenant-Governer; and the President requested Mr. Briggs, of Pittsfield, to take the chair.

Afterwards, Mr. BRIGGS reported that the committee had made further progress in the consideration of the Resolves, but had come to no conclusion, and had instructed him to ask leave to sit again.

And leave was accordingly granted.

At one o'clock, on motion of Mr. EARLE, of Worcester,

The Convention adjourned.

AFTERNOON SESSION.

Met according to adjournment.

A communication was read from Mr. Storrow, member from Lawrence, asking leave of absence for ten days, on account of ill health.

Referred to the Committee on Leave of Absence.

On motion of Mr. WILSON, of Natick,

Ordered, That the Committee on the Frame of Government be instructed to consider the expediency of providing that all Acts or Resolves for the appointment of Commissioners, shall specify the compensation for the services to be performed, and that in no case shall any extra compensation be allowed after the services have been performed.

On motion of Mr. HALL, of Haverhill, sustained by a vote of ninety-two in the affirmative to seventy-seven in the negative,

Ordered, That debate in Committee of the Whole upon the Resolves concerning the Council, shall cease at four o'clock this afternoon.

On motion of Mr. Edwards, of Southampton, the Convention resolved itself into Committee of the Whole, for the purpose of considering the Resolve on the subject of the Council and the Lieutenant-Governor; and the President requested Mr. Briggs, of Pittsfield, to take the chair.

Afterwards, Mr. Briggs reported, that the Committee had considered the Resolves on the subject of the Council, and had instructed him to report them to the Convention, as amended;

Also, that they had made progress in the consideration of the Resolves on the subject of the lieutenant-governor, but had come to no conclusion, and had instructed him to ask leave to sit again.

The question being upon granting leave to the Committee to sit again for the further consideration of the Resolves on the subject of the lieutenant-governor,

Leave was granted.

Pending the consideration of the 'Resolves on the subject of the Council,

At six o'clock, on motion of Mr. Kingman, of West Bridgewater,

The Convention adjourned.

SATURDAY, June 4, 1853.

Met according to adjournment. Prayer was offered by the Chaplain. The Journal of yesterday was read.

Mr. Allen, of Worcester, from the Committee on the Frame of Government, submitted Reports, as follow:—

Inexpedient to act upon the subject of an Order of May 20th, concerning special privileges and immunities.

Also, inexpedient to act upon the subject of an Order of May 24th, concerning the purchase of books by the legislature.

Also, inexpedient to act upon the subject of an Order of May 18th, concerning biennial elections and biennial sessions of the legislature.

Also, inexpedient to act upon the subject of an Order of May 13th, concerning the expediency of requiring the votes of a majority of all the members elected to the legislature, to the enactment of a law or the passage of a resolve.

These Reports were severally referred to the Committee of the Whole and ordered to be printed.

Mr. SUMNER, member for Marshfield, from the Committee on the Bill of Rights, submitted a Report:—

That the Committee have had under consideration the Petition of John P. Coburn and others, praying that the laws of the Commonwealth be so modified that no able-bodied male citizen be prevented from serving or holding a commission in the militia on account of his color; and that they ask to be discharged from the same, and recommend that it be referred to the Committee on the Militia.

And the Report was accepted, and the Petition so referred.

On motion of Mr. WHITNEY, of Conway, sustained by a vote of one hundred and twelve in the affirmative to fifty in the negative,

Ordered, That the question upon the Resolve relating to the Council, be taken at eleven o'clock to-day.

On motion of Mr. WILSON, of Natick, the Convention proceeded to the consideration of the Orders of the Day.

The first subject was the Resolves on the subject of the Council, as amended in Committee of the Whole.

Mr. DANA, member for Manchester, moved to strike out all after the word "Resolved," and substitute therefor the following:—

That the Constitution should be so altered as to strike out the third section of chapter 2, relating to "the Council for advising the governor in the executive part of the government," and substitute therefor a distribution of its powers and duties to other branches and officers of the government.

Being the first Resolution of the series reported by the standing committee of the Convention.

On motion of Mr. DE WITT, of Oxford,

Ordered, That when the question is taken on the proposed amendment, it be taken by yeas and nays.

And the roll being called, one hundred and twenty-two members voted for the amendment, and one hundred and eighty-four against it.

So the amendment was rejected.

Those who voted in the affirmative are:—

Messrs. Josiah G. Abbott,
Shubael P. Adams,
Charles Allen,
James B. Allen,
Parsons Allen,
Josiah Allis,
George Austin,
Hillel Baker,
Messrs. Alvah Ballard,
Alpheus Bancroft,
Eliakim A. Bates,
Erasmus D. Beach,
Henry W. Bishop,
William S. Booth,
William J. A. Bradford,
Hiram N. Breed,

Messrs. Adolphus F. Brown,
Hammond Brown,
Hiram C. Brown,
Frederick Brownell,
Amos H. Bullen,
Anson Burlingame,
Benjamin F. Butler,
Isaac Case,
Amariah Chandler,
Chester W. Chapin,
Josiah Childs,
J. McKean Churchill,
Henry Clark,
Ransom Clark,
Alpheus B. Clarke,
Stillman Clarke,
Lansing J. Cole,
George B. Crane,
Joseph W. Cross,
F. B. Crowninshield,
Henry W. Cushman,
Richard H. Dana, Jr.,
Charles G. Davis,
Isaac Davis,
Gilman Day,
Elijah S. Deming,
Augustus Denton,
Alexander De Witt,
Samuel Duncan,
Bradish Dunham,
James Easton, 2d,
Lyman Fisk,
Emery Fiske,
Ezekiel W. Fitch,
James M. Freeman,
Charles A. French,
Luther Gale,
Elbridge Gates,
Joel Giles,
Leonard Gooding,
William B. Greene,
Josiah W. Griswold,
Whiting Griswold,
B. F. Hallett,
Seth Hapgood,
Phineas Harmon,
William Haskins,
Stephen E. Hawkes,
Aaron Hobart,
George Hood,
Charles P. Huntington,
Moses C. Hurlbut,
Abijah M. Ide, Jr.,

Messrs. John Jacobs,
Joseph Kimball,
Jefferson Knight,
J. S. C. Knowlton,
George H. Kuhn,
Gardner P. Ladd,
Abishai Lincoln,
Otis Little,
William P. Marble,
Abijah P. Marvin,
Simeon Merritt,
James L. Monroe,
James M. Moore,
Marcus Morton,
Hiram Nash,
William Nichols,
Alfred Norton,
Andrew T. Nute,
Charles Osgood,
John G. Park,
Samuel C. Parsons,
John Penniman,
Charles Phelps,
Henry Pierce,
John A. Putnam,
Robert Rantoul,
John Rogers,
Chester Sanderson,
Luther Sheldon,
John Sherril,
Melzar Sprague,
Samuel W. Spooner,
Caleb Stetson,
William Stevens,
Charles Sumner,
Arnold Taft,
Joseph Thayer,
Willard Thayer, 2d,
Horatio W. Tilton,
Charles R. Train,
David P. Turner,
Orison Underwood,
Bradford L. Wales,
Freeland Wallis,
Samuel Warner, Jr.,
James S. Whitney,
Joseph Wilbur,
Henry Williams,
Henry Wilson,
Willard Wilson,
Levi M. Winslow,
Otis Wood,
Ezekiel Wright.

Those who voted in the negative are :—

Messrs. Alfred A. Abbott,
Benjamin P. Adams,
Joel C. Allen,
Robert Andrews,
William Appleton,
William Aspinwall,
David C. Atwood,
Samuel Ayres,
Russel Bartlett,
Sidney Bartlett,
Marcus Barrett,
Moses Bates, Jr.,
John Beal,
James M. Beebe,
William Bennett, Jr.,
Zephaniah Bennett,
Jacob Bigelow,
Francis W. Bird,
Gad O. Bliss,
William C. Bliss,
George S. Boutwell,
Sewell Boutwell,
Ebenezer Bradbury,
Milton P. Braman,
Osmyn Brewster,
Francis Brinley,
Asa Bronson,
Artemas Brown,
Rufus Bullock,
Cephas C. Bumpus,
Henry Cady,
Timothy W. Carter,
Daniel E. Chapin,
Rufus Choate,
Salah Clark,
William Cleverly,
Jacob Coggin,
Nathaniel Cogswell,
Ithamar Conkey,
Charles E. Cook,
Henry F. Cooledge,
Oliver S. Cressy,
Leander Crosby,
Seth Crowell,
Joseph Cummings,
Wilber Curtis,
Thomas Cushman,
Simeon N. Cutler,
Ebenezer Davis,
John Davis,
Robert T. Davis,

Messrs. Solomon Davis,
Henry L. Dawes,
Silas Dean,
William Dehon,
John M. Durgin,
Philip Eames,
Lilley Eaton,
Elisha Edwards,
Samuel Edwards,
A. G. Farwell,
Sullivan Fay,
Samuel Fowle,
Samuel P. Fowler,
Wanton C. Gilbert,
Charles G. Giles,
Daniel W. Gooch,
Robert Gould,
Dalton Goulding,
F. R. Gourgas,
John W. Graves,
John C. Gray,
Jabez Green,
Samuel P. Hadley,
Artemas Hale,
Nathan Hale,
A. B. Hammond,
Elnathan P. Hathaway,
Isaac Hayden,
George Hayward,
Ezra Heath, 2d,
Samuel Henry,
Henry Hersey,
James Hewes,
William H. Hewes,
George S. Hillard,
William Hinsdale,
Henry Hobart,
Edwin Hobbs,
Nathaniel Holder,
Foster Hooper,
Thomas Hopkinson,
Samuel Houghton,
Henry K. Hoyt,
William J. Hubbard,
Charles E. Hunt,
William Hunt,
William James,
John Jenkins,
John Johnson,
Giles C. Kellogg,
Martin R. Kellogg,

Messrs. Isaac Kendall,
Joseph Kingman,
Henry W. Kinsman,
Joseph Knight,
William H. Knowlton,
John S. Ladd,
Luther Lawrence,
F. W. Lincoln, Jr.,
Tristram Littlefield,
Isaac Livermore,
Samuel K. Lothrop,
Samuel P. Loud,
John A. Lowell,
Theophilus R. Marvin,
Reuben Meader,
Seth Miller, Jr.,
Samuel Mixter,
George Morey,
Marcus Morton, Jr.,
William S. Morton,
Jonathan Nayson,
Charles Newman,
Daniel Noyes,
Henry K. Oliver,
Nathan Orcutt,
Benjamin S. Orne,
James W. Paige,
Benjamin Paine,
Henry Paine,
Jonathan Parris,
Thomas A. Parsons,
George Peabody,
Nathaniel Peabody,
Daniel A. Perkins,
Jesse Perkins,
Noah C. Perkins,
F. O. Prince,
George Putnam,
Silas Rawson,
James Read,
David Rice,

Messrs. Luther Richards,
Daniel Richardson,
Samuel H. Richardson,
George R. Sampson,
Amasa Sanderson,
John Sargent,
William Schouler,
Charles Sherman,
Chester Sikes,
John W. Simonds,
John S. Sleeper,
Matthew Smith,
John Souther,
Eben H. Stacy,
Granville Stevens,
Joseph L. Stevens, Jr.,
Alfred L. Strong,
Alanson Swain,
Ralph Taylor,
Charles Thompson,
Edmund P. Tileston,
Ephraim Tower,
William Tyler,
Charles W. Upham,
George B. Upton,
Joel Viles,
Samuel B. Walcott,
Amasa Walker,
Samuel Walker,
Asa H. Waters,
Cyrus Weeks,
Gershom B. Weston,
Thomas Wetmore,
William F. Wheeler,
Daniel S. Whitney,
Daniel Wilbur,
Joel Wilder,
Milo Wilson,
Jonathan B. Winn,
Nathaniel Wood,
William H. Wood.

Mr. Walker, of North Brookfield, moved that the word "eight" be struck out of the first line, and the word "five" inserted instead.

Also, that the word "five" be struck out of the fourth line, and the word "eight" inserted instead.

But the amendment was rejected.

Mr. Bartlett, of Boston, moved to amend by striking out all after the word "people," in the second line of the first Resolve, and inserting instead thereof the words "by general ticket;" also, by inserting the word "annually" after the word "elected," in the second line.

But the amendment was rejected by a vote of ninety-five in the affirmative, and one hundred and forty-eight in the negative.

The Resolves were then ordered to a second reading.

On motion of Mr. WESTON, of Duxbury,

Ordered, That debate in Committee of the Whole upon the Resolves on the subject of the lieutenant-governor shall cease at half-past twelve o'clock to-day.

On motion of Mr. CUSHMAN, of Bernardston, the Convention resolved itself into Committee of the Whole, for the purpose of considering the Resolves on the subject of the lieutenant-governor; and the President requested Mr. Griswold, member for Erving, to take the chair.

Afterwards, Mr. GRISWOLD reported the Resolves to the Convention, amended by the Committee of the Whole, with a recommendation that they ought to pass.

Pending the question upon the Resolves, on motion of Mr. MORTON, of Quincy, they were laid upon the table.

On motion of Mr. BUTLER, of Lowell, sustained by a vote of one hundred and thirty-nine in the affirmative to twenty-eight in the negative, the Order of the Convention providing for an adjournment each day at one o'clock, was so far modified that the adjournment this day shall not take place until two o'clock.

Mr. WESTON, of Duxbury, offered an Order, providing for an adjournment of the forenoon session each day at two o'clock, which, on motion of Mr. EAMES, of Washington, was

Laid upon the table.

On motion of Mr. BUTLER, of Lowell, the Orders of the Day were taken up, and the Convention resumed the consideration of the Resolves on the subject of the lieutenant-governor.

On motion of Mr. KELLOGG, of Hadley, sustained by a vote of fifty-nine in the affirmative to fifty-eight in the negative,

The Resolve was amended by striking out article third, and inserting instead thereof the following:—

When by reason of sickness or temporary absence from the Commonwealth, the governor shall be unable to perform his official duties, the lieutenant-governor shall have the powers, and perform the duties, of the governor; and in case of the removal from office, resignation or death of the governor, the lieutenant-governor shall succeed to the office, and be the governor of the Commonwealth.

The Resolves, as amended, were then ordered to a second reading.

On motion of Mr. Eames, of Washington, at half-past one o'clock,

The Convention adjourned.

MONDAY, June 6, 1853.

Met according to adjournment. Prayer was offered by the Chaplain. The Journal of Saturday was read.

Mr. Keyes, member for Abington, presented the Petition of Robert L. Killam, and forty other legal voters, and sixteen women of Hanover, that the word "male" be stricken from the Constitution.

Referred to the Committee on the Qualifications of Voters.

Mr. Duncan, of Williamstown, offered the following Resolution :—

Resolved, That it is expedient to amend so much of article 3, chapter 2, as relates to the assorting, counting, and recording of votes in elections, so as to make it correspond with the provision of section 3, chapter 1.

Referred to the Committee on Elections.

On motion of Mr. Sumner, member for Marshfield,

Ordered, That the Committee on the Judiciary be directed to consider the expediency of so amending the Constitution as to provide that the legislature, at its first session after the adoption of the Constitution, shall constitute two several commissions, whose duties shall be respectively as follow :—

1. To reduce into a written and systematic code the whole body of the law of this Commonwealth, or so much and such parts thereof as to the said commission shall seem practicable and expedient.

2. To revise, reform, simplify and abridge the rules, practice, pleadings and forms of the courts of this Commonwealth, and to provide, so far as practicable and expedient, that justice shall be administered by intelligible and uniform proceedings, without any distinction between law and equity.

On motion of Mr. Boutwell, member for Berlin, the Convention proceeded to the consideration of the Orders of the Day; and

The Resolves on the subject of the Council, and

The Resolves on the subject of the lieutenant-governor, were

Read a second time, and then, on motion of Mr. Boutwell, were laid upon the table.

On motion of Mr. Wilson, of Natick, the Convention resolved itself into Committee of the Whole, for the purpose of considering the Report of the Committee on the Frame of Government, inexpedient to act upon the subject of an Order of May 17th, respecting the originating of Bills and Resolves in the House of Representatives; and the President requested Mr. Hood, of Lynn, to take the chair.

Afterwards, Mr. Hood reported, that it was the opinion of the committee that the Report ought to be accepted.

And it was accordingly accepted.

On motion of Mr. Allen, of Worcester, the Convention resolved itself into Committee of the Whole, for the purpose of considering the Resolve reported by the Committee on the Frame of Government, in favor of the *viva voce* mode of elections in the legislature; and the President requested Mr. Frothingham, of Charlestown, to take the chair.

Afterwards, Mr. Frothingham reported, that it was the opinion of the committee that the Resolve ought to pass.

And it was accordingly ordered to a second reading.

On motion of Mr. Butler, of Lowell, the Convention resolved itself into Committee of the Whole, for the purpose of considering the Report of the Committee on the Frame of Government, inexpedient to act upon the subject of an Order of May 18th, relating to the permanent establishment of the seat of government in Boston; and the President requested Mr. Bates, of Plymouth, to take the chair.

Afterwards, Mr. Bates reported, that it was the opinion of the committee that the Report ought to be accepted.

And it was accordingly accepted.

On motion of Mr. Allen, of Worcester, the Convention resolved itself into Committee of the Whole, for the purpose of considering the Report of the Committee on the Frame of Government, inexpedient to act upon the subject of an Order of May 16th, concerning a limitation of the time for the reception of petitions by the legislature; and the President requested Mr. Whitney, of Conway, to take the chair.

Afterwards, Mr. Whitney reported, that it was the opinion of the committee that the Report ought to be accepted.

And it was accordingly accepted.

On motion of Mr. Butler, of Lowell, the Convention resolved itself into Committee of the Whole, for the consideration of the Report of the Committee on the Qualifications of Voters; and the

President requested Mr. Dana, member for Manchester, to take the chair.

Afterwards, Mr. DANA reported, that the committee had made progress in the consideration of the subject, but had come to no conclusion, and had instructed him to ask leave to sit again.

And leave was accordingly granted.

Mr. THOMPSON, of Charlestown, moved that when the Convention adjourn, it adjourn to meet at ten o'clock, to-morrow.

Mr. BUTLER, of Lowell, moved an adjournment; but the motion was rejected.

Mr. HOOPER, of Fall River, moved to amend the motion of Mr. Thompson, by substituting the hour of half past two this afternoon,

Pending this question, the hour fixed for adjournment arrived.

And at one o'clock, the Convention adjourned.

AFTERNOON SESSION.

Met according to adjournment.

On motion of Mr. STRONG, of Easthampton,

Ordered, That the Committee on the Bill of Rights be requested to take into consideration the expediency of so amending the Constitution, that the poor debtor's oath shall be administered by the magistrates of the several towns where the debtors reside, and that no citizen of this Commonwealth shall be imprisoned for debt.

On motion of Mr. HARMON, of New Ashford,

Ordered, That the Committee on the Judiciary consider the expediency of so revising the Constitution, as to give efficacy to the eleventh article of the Declaration of Rights, granting the subject a certain remedy in law, promptly and without delay.

On motion of Mr. WILSON, of Natick, the Convention resolved itself into Committee of the Whole, for the purpose of considering the Resolves on the subject of the qualifications of voters, and the President requested Mr. Dana, member for Manchester, to take the chair.

Afterwards, Mr. DANA reported, that the committee had made further progress in the consideration of the subject, but had come to no conclusion, and had instructed him to ask leave to sit again.

And leave was accordingly granted.

At a quarter past five o'clock, on motion of Mr. TYLER, of Pawtucket,

The Convention adjourned.

TUESDAY, June 7, 1853.

Met according to adjournment. Prayer was offered by the Chaplain. The Journal of yesterday was read.

On motion of Mr. Buck, of Lanesborough, the Convention proceeded to the consideration of the Orders of the Day.

The Resolve upon the subject of *viva voce* voting, was read a second time, and finally passed, as follows:—

Resolved, That it is expedient to provide in the Constitution, that in all elections made directly by the legislature, or either branch thereof, the *viva voce* mode be adopted.

On motion of Mr. Brown, of Douglas, the Convention resolved itself into Committee of the Whole, for the consideration of the Resolves on the subject of the qualifications of voters, and the President requested Mr. Dana, member for Manchester, to take the chair.

At one o'clock, the Convention adjourned.

AFTERNOON SESSION.

Met according to adjournment.

On motion of Mr. Tyler, of Pawtucket,

Ordered, That the Committee on so much of the Constitution as relates to county and town officers, and the registry of deeds, be directed to inquire into the expediency of so amending the Constitution, that all deeds of real estate, instead of being recorded as now, in one or more towns in the county specially designated for that purpose, shall be recorded in the several towns where such real estate is situated; that the town clerks of the several towns shall be the registers of deeds, and that good and sufficient safes shall be provided, at the expense of the towns, for the safe keeping of the records.

Mr. Earle, of Worcester, offered a paper, containing a plan of representation in the House of Representatives.

Referred to the Committee of the Whole and ordered to be printed.

Mr. Greene, of Brookfield, presented the Petition of Mary Osgood and twelve others, women of Medford, in aid of the Petition of Mrs. Abby Alcott and others, that women may be allowed to vote on the proposed alterations and amendments of the Constitution.

Referred to the Committee on the Qualifications of Voters.

Mr. Fay, of Southborough, from the Committee on Leave of Absence, submitted a Report, granting leave of absence to Mr. Storrow, of Lawrence, for two weeks, and to Mr. Cushman, of Kingston, for four days.

The Report was considered and accepted.

Mr. Dana, member for Manchester, reported that the Committee of the Whole had made progress in the consideration of the Resolves on the subject of the qualifications of voters, but had come to no conclusion, and had instructed him to ask leave to sit again.

And leave was accordingly granted.

And then, on motion of Mr. Hooper, of Fall River, the Convention again resolved itself into Committee of the Whole, for the purpose of further considering the same subject, and the President requested Mr. Dana, member for Manchester, to take the chair.

Afterwards, Mr. Dana reported, that the committee had made further progress in the consideration of the subject, but had come to no conclusion, and had instructed him to ask leave to sit again.

And leave was accordingly granted.

At six o'clock, on motion of Mr. Freeman, of Franklin,

The Convention adjourned.

WEDNESDAY, June 8, 1853.

Met according to adjournment. Prayer was offered by the Chaplain. The Journal of yesterday was read.

Mr. Briggs, of Pittsfield, presented the Petition of Jonathan E. Field, and forty-seven others, citizens of Stockbridge, suggesting certain amendments of the Constitution on the subjects of the pay of members of the legislature, the plurality rule in elections, the mode of electing senators and representatives, and the power of the legislature to make permanent loans.

Referred to the Committee of the Whole, and to the several standing committees having those subjects in charge.

A communication was read from Mr. Taft, of Mendon, asking leave of absence on account of the death of a sister; which was considered, and leave of absence granted.

A communication was received from the Secretary of State, enclosing lists of the business corporations authorized since the adoption of the Constitution to the present time.

On motion of Mr. Thompson, of Charlestown,

Ordered, That the debate in Committee of the Whole on the subject of the qualifications of voters, shall cease at twelve o'clock.

On motion of Mr. Schouler, of Boston, the Convention resolved itself into Committee of the Whole, for the purpose of further considering the Resolves on the qualifications of voters; and the President requested Mr. Dana, member for Manchester, to take the chair.

Afterwards, Mr. Dana reported, that the committee had considered the Resolves, and had instructed him to report,

That the first Resolve ought to pass;

That the second Resolve ought not to pass;

That the third Resolve ought to be amended by substituting the word "student" for the word "member" in the fifth line, (of the printed copy);

And that the fourth Resolve ought to pass.

The amendment to the third Resolve, recommended by the committee, was agreed to, and,

Pending the question on the adoption of the Resolves,

At one o'clock, the Convention adjourned.

AFTERNOON SESSION.

Met according to adjournment.

The communication from the Secretary of State, received in the morning, with the enclosed list of corporations, was ordered to be printed.

Mr. Fay, of Southborough, from the Committee on Leave of Absence, submitted a Report, granting leave of absence to Mr. Knight, of Peru, for five days.

The Report was considered, and leave of absence granted.

On motion of Mr. Lord, of Salem, the Convention proceeded to the consideration of the Orders of the Day; the first subject being the Resolves on the qualifications of voters.

Mr. Schouler, of Boston, moved that the fourth Resolve be amended by striking out all after the words "shall be," at the close of the second line, (printed copy,) and inserting instead thereof the words, "by secret ballot;" but the amendment was rejected.

Mr. Briggs, of Pittsfield, moved that the first Resolve be amended by striking out all after the word "vote" in the second line, (printed copy);

And further moved that when the question is taken on the amendment, it be taken by yeas and nays.

Pending this question,

At twenty minutes past six o'clock, on motion of Mr. BRADFORD, of Essex,

The Convention adjourned.

THURSDAY, June 9, 1853.

Met according to adjournment. Prayer was offered by the Chaplain. The Journal of yesterday was read.

On motion of Mr. KINGMAN, of West Bridgewater,

Ordered, That the Committee on the Frame of Government be instructed to inquire into the expediency of incorporating into the Constitution the principle, that when any person shall be arrested in behalf of the Commonwealth, on suspicion of crime, and tried and not found guilty, such person shall be remunerated for loss of time and the cost he is thus subjected to.

Mr. ALLEN, of Worcester, from the Committee on the Frame of Government, submitted Reports as follow:—

Inexpedient to act on the subject of an Order of May 31st, concerning the election of senators in the congress of the United States by joint ballot of the two Houses of the legislature.

Also, inexpedient to act upon the subject of an Order of June 3d, concerning extra payment to commissioners.

Also, a Resolve on the subject of the legislative department of the government.

Severally referred to the Committee of the Whole and ordered to be printed.

On motion of Mr. ALLEN, of Worcester, the Convention resolved itself into Committee of the Whole, for the purpose of considering the Report of the Committee on the Frame of Government, inexpedient to act on the subject of an Order of May 20th, concerning special privileges and immunities; and the President requested Mr. Thompson, of Charlestown, to take the chair.

Afterwards, Mr. THOMPSON reported, that it was the opinion of the committee that the Report ought to be accepted.

And it was accordingly accepted.

On motion of Mr. ALLEN, of Worcester, the Convention resolved itself into Committee of the Whole, for the purpose of considering the Report of the Committee on the Frame of Government, inexpedient to act on the subject of an Order of May 24th, concerning the purchase of books by the legislature, and the President requested Mr. Morton, of Fairhaven, to take the chair.

Afterwards, Mr. MORTON reported, that it was the opinion of the committee that the Report ought to be accepted.

And it was accordingly accepted.

On motion of Mr. ALLEN, of Worcester, the Convention resolved itself into Committee of the Whole, for the purpose of considering the Report of the Committee on the Frame of Government, inexpedient to act on the subject of an Order of May 18th, concerning biennial elections and biennial sessions of the legislature; and the President requested Mr. Hall, of Haverhill, to take the chair.

Afterwards, Mr. HALL reported that it was the opinion of the committee that the Report ought to be accepted.

And it was accordingly accepted.

On motion of Mr. ALLEN, of Worcester, the Convention resolved itself into Committee of the Whole, for the purpose of considering the Report of the Committee on the Frame of Government, inexpedient to act on the subject of an Order of May 13th, concerning the expediency of requiring the votes of a majority of all the members elected to the legislature, to the enactment of a law or passage of a resolve; and the President requested Mr. Alvord, member for Montague, to take the chair.

Afterwards, Mr. ALVORD reported, that it was the opinion of the committee that the Report ought to be accepted.

And it was accordingly accepted.

On motion of Mr. THOMPSON, of Charlestown, the Convention proceeded to the consideration of the Orders of the Day; the first subject being the Resolves on the qualifications of voters.

Mr. BRIGGS, of Pittsfield, modified his amendment offered yesterday, so as to insert, in place of the words proposed to be struck out, the words following, viz.:—

"For any national, state, county, district, city, or town officers, or in town affairs."

The yeas and nays were ordered upon the question of adopting the amendment.

Mr. WESTON, of Duxbury, moved to amend the amendment so as to insert parish officers and parish affairs after the word "town" in both cases.

Without taking the question,

At one o'clock, the Convention adjourned.

AFTERNOON SESSION.

Met according to adjournment.

On motion of Mr. Buck, of Lanesborough, the Convention proceeded to the consideration of the Orders of the Day.

Mr. Weston, of Duxbury, withdrew his proposed amendment to the amendment of Mr. Briggs.

Mr. Boutwell, member for Berlin, then moved to amend the amendment of Mr. Briggs by striking out all after the word "national," and inserting instead thereof the words, "or state officers whose election by the people is provided for in this Constitution."

Mr. Chapin, of Worcester, moved the Previous Question; which was ordered by the Convention.

On motion of Mr. Dawes, of Adams,

Ordered, That when the question is taken upon the amendment of Mr. Boutwell, it be taken by yeas and nays.

And the roll being called, two hundred and ten members voted for the amendment, and one hundred and twenty-seven against it.

So the amendment was adopted.

Those who voted in the affirmative are:—

Messrs. Shubael P. Adams,
Charles Allen,
James B. Allen,
Joel C. Allen,
Parsons Allen,
John B. Alley,
Josiah Allis,
D. W. Alvord,
Hillel Baker,
Alvah Ballard,
George S. Ball,
Alpheus Bancroft,
Marcus Barrett,
Moses Bates, Jr.,
Erasmus D. Beach,
John Beal,
William Bennett, Jr.,
Zephaniah Bennett,
Francis W. Bird,
Henry W. Bishop,
William S. Booth,
George S. Boutwell,
Sewell Boutwell,
William J. A. Bradford,
Hiram N. Breed,

Messrs. Asa Bronson,
Adolphus F. Brown,
Alpheus R. Brown,
Hammond Brown,
Hiram C. Brown,
Frederick Brownell,
Joseph Brownell,
Patrick Bryant,
Anson Burlingame,
Henry Cady,
William Carruthers,
Isaac Case,
Amariah Chandler,
Chester W. Chapin,
Daniel E. Chapin,
Henry Chapin,
Josiah Childs,
J. McKean Churchill,
Henry Clark,
Ransom Clark,
Alpheus B. Clarke,
William Cleverly,
Lansing J. Cole,
Sumner Cole,
George B. Crane,

Messrs. Simeon Crittenden,
Joseph W. Cross,
Henry W. Cushman,
Simeon N. Cutler,
Richard H. Dana, Jr.,
Charles G. Davis,
Ebenezer Davis,
Isaac Davis,
Robert T. Davis,
Gilman Day,
Silas Dean,
Elijah S. Deming,
Samuel Duncan,
Bradish Dunham,
John M. Durgin,
John M. Earle,
James Easton, 2d,
Calvin D. Eaton,
Elisha Edwards,
Joseph M. Ely,
Sullivan Fay,
James K. Fellows,
Lyman Fisk,
Ezekiel W. Fitch,
Aaron Foster,
Samuel Fowle,
James M. Freeman,
Luther Gale,
Elbridge Gates,
Washington Gilbert,
Daniel W. Gooch,
Dalton Goulding,
F. R. Gourgas,
John W. Graves,
Jabez Green,
William B. Greene,
Josiah W. Griswold,
Whiting Griswold,
Samuel P. Hadley,
Charles B. Hall,
B. F. Hallett,
Lyman W. Hapgood,
Seth Hapgood,
Phineas Harmon,
William Haskins,
Stephen E. Hawkes,
Ezra Heath, 2d,
James Hewes,
William H. Hewes,
Henry Hobart,
Nathaniel Holder,
George Hood,
Foster Hooper,

Messrs. Martin Howard,
Abraham H. Howland,
Henry K. Hoyt,
Charles E. Hunt,
George E. Huntington,
Moses C. Hurlbut,
Benjamin D. Hyde,
Abijah M. Ide, Jr.,
John Jacobs,
Isaac Kendall,
Joseph Kimball,
Joseph Kingman,
Jefferson Knight,
J. S. C. Knowlton,
William H. Knowlton,
Gardner P. Ladd,
Wilber C. Langdon,
Alden Leland,
Abishai Lincoln,
Otis Little,
Tristram Littlefield,
Justin E. Loomis,
William P. Marble,
Laban Marcy,
Charles Mason,
Reuben Meader,
Simeon Merritt,
James L. Monroe,
James M. Moore,
William S. Morton,
Hiram Nash,
Jonathan Nayson,
Charles Newman,
Alfred Norton,
Andrew T. Nute,
Joseph E. Ober,
Benjamin S. Orne,
Charles Osgood,
E. Wing Packer,
Benjamin Paine,
Henry Paine,
Jonathan Parris,
Samuel C. Parsons,
John Partridge,
Nathaniel Peabody,
Jeremiah Pease, Jr.,
John Penniman,
Daniel A. Perkins,
Jesse Perkins,
Charles Phelps,
Silvanus B. Phinney,
Henry Pierce,
James M. Pool,

Messrs. Peter Powers,
Robert Rantoul,
Silas Rawson,
David Rice,
Luther Richards,
Daniel Richardson,
Nathan Richardson,
Samuel H. Richardson,
Joseph M. Rockwood,
John Rogers,
James C. Royce,
Amasa Sanderson,
Chester Sanderson,
Luther Sheldon,
Perez Simmons,
John W. Simonds,
Melzar Sprague,
Samuel W. Spooner,
Granville Stevens,
Joseph L. Stevens, Jr.,
William Stevens,
Gideon Stiles,
Alfred L. Strong,
Charles Sumner,
Alanson Swain,
Willard Thayer, 2d,
John W. Thomas,

Messrs. Abraham Tilton,
Horatio W. Tilton,
David P. Turner,
Orison Underwood,
Joel Viles,
George A. Vinton,
Bradford L. Wales,
Frederick T. Wallace,
Freeland Wallis,
Amasa Walker,
Andrew H. Ward,
Samuel Warner, Jr.,
Asa H. Waters,
Gershom B. Weston,
George White,
Daniel S. Whitney,
James S. Whitney,
Daniel Wilbur,
J. B. Williams,
Henry Wilson,
Willard Wilson,
Levi M. Winslow,
Charles C. Wood,
Nathaniel Wood,
Otis Wood,
William H. Wood,
Ezekiel Wright.

Those who voted in the negative are:—

Messrs. P. Emory Aldrich,
Robert Andrews,
William Appleton,
William Aspinwall,
David C. Atwood,
George Austin,
Samuel Ayres,
Joseph Barrows,
Russel Bartlett,
Sidney Bartlett,
Jacob Bigelow,
George W. Blagden,
Gad O. Bliss,
William C. Bliss,
Ebenezer Bradbury,
Milton P. Braman,
Osmyn Brewster,
Francis Brinley,
George N. Briggs,
Asahel Buck,
Rufus Bullock,
Timothy W. Carter,
Rufus Choate,
Nathaniel Cogswell,

Messrs. Ithamar Conkey,
Charles E. Cook,
Henry F. Cooledge,
Benjamin F. Copeland,
George W. Crockett,
Leander Crosby,
Seth Crowell,
Joseph Cummings,
Wilber Curtis,
John Davis,
Solomon Davis,
Henry L. Dawes,
William Dehon,
Hiram S. Denison,
Moses Dorman,
Philip Eames,
Lilley Eaton,
Samuel Edwards,
Homer Ely,
A. G. Farwell,
Samuel P. Fowler,
Samuel French,
Henry J. Gardner,
Wanton C. Gilbert,

Messrs. Jason Goulding,
John C. Gray,
Artemas Hale,
Nathan Hale,
A. B. Hammond,
George Hayward,
Charles Heard,
Samuel Henry,
Henry Hersey,
George S. Hillard,
William Hinsdale,
Thomas Hopkinson,
Samuel Houghton,
William J. Hubbard,
William Hunt,
Samuel Jackson,
William James,
John Jenkins,
Samuel H. Jenks,
John Johnson,
Giles C. Kellogg,
Martin R. Kellogg,
Henry W. Kinsman,
Hiram Knight,
George H. Kuhn,
John S. Ladd,
Job G. Lawton, Jr.,
Isaac Livermore,
Samuel K. Lothrop,
Samuel P. Loud,
John A. Lowell,
Abijah P. Marvin,
Theophilus R. Marvin,
Seth Miller, Jr.,
Samuel Mixter,
George Morey,
Joseph B. Morss,
Marcus Morton,
William Nichols,
Daniel Noyes,

Messrs. Henry K. Oliver,
Nathan Orcutt,
James W. Paige,
Adolphus G. Parker,
Joel Parker,
Samuel D. Parker,
Thomas A. Parsons,
George Peabody,
Jonathan Preston,
George Putnam,
John A. Putnam,
James Read,
John Sargent,
William Schouler,
Charles Sherman,
John Sherril,
Chester Sikes,
John S. Sleeper,
Matthew Smith,
John Souther,
J. Thomas Stevenson,
Thomas Talbot,
Ralph Taylor,
Edmund P. Tileston,
Ephraim Tower,
David Turner,
John S. Tyler,
William Tyler,
Charles W. Upham,
George B. Upton,
Samuel B. Walcott,
Samuel Walker,
Cyrus Weeks,
Thomas Wetmore,
Benjamin White,
Joel Wilder,
John H. Wilkins,
Milo Wilson,
Jonathan B. Winn.

The amendment of Mr. Briggs, as amended, was then agreed to, and the Resolve, as amended, was adopted.

The second Resolve was rejected

On motion of Mr. Davis, of Plymouth, sustained by a vote of one hundred and thirty-eight in the affirmative to fifty-three in the negative.

The third Resolve was amended by the addition of the following: "And no person removing his domicile from one town or city to another within this Commonwealth shall, by reason of such removal, be deemed to have lost his residence in the former for the purpose aforesaid, until six months after his removal."

On motion of Mr. Griswold, member for Erving, the Resolve was then recommitted to the committee.

The question being upon the adoption of the fourth Resolve,

Mr. Bates, of Plymouth, moved to amend it by striking out the words "or municipal," in the second line, (printed copy,) and inserting the word "or" before the word "county" in the same line.

Mr. Walker, of North Brookfield, moved to amend the amendment by substituting the word "city" for the word "municipal."

Pending this question,

At half past six o'clock, on motion of Mr. Duncan, of Williamstown,

The Convention adjourned.

FRIDAY, June 10, 1853.

Met according to adjournment. Prayer was offered by the Chaplain. The Journal of yesterday was read.

On motion of Mr. Stetson, of Braintree,

Ordered, That the Committee to whom was referred that part of the Constitution included in the first eight articles in chapter 6, consider the expediency of providing in the Constitution, that no president, director, cashier, or other officer of any banking institution of this State shall be eligible to the office of governor, lieutenant-governor, senator, or representative to the general court, so long as he shall be such president, director, cashier, or other officer.

On motion of Mr. Phinney, member for Chatham, the Convention proceeded to the consideration of the Orders of the Day; the first subject being the Resolves on the qualifications of voters.

After debate, Mr. Bird, of Walpole, moved the Previous Question; which was ordered by a vote of two hundred in the affirmative, and nineteen in the negative.

The first question being upon Mr. Walker's proposition, substituting the word "city" for the word "municipal" in the second line of the fourth Resolve, it was agreed to by a vote of one hundred and eighty-three in the affirmative, and eighty-two in the negative.

The amendment as amended was then agreed to, and the Resolve was thus amended so as to apply to all ballots required by law to be given, "at any national, state, county, or city election."

On motion of Mr. THOMPSON, of Charlestown,

Ordered, That when the question is taken upon the adoption of the Resolve, it be taken by yeas and nays.

And the roll being called, two hundred and thirty-three members voted for the Resolve, and ninety-four against it.

Those who voted in the affirmative are:—

Messrs. Josiah G. Abbott,
Shubael P. Adams,
Charles Allen,
James B. Allen,
Joel C. Allen,
Parsons Allen,
John B. Alley,
Josiah Allis,
D. W. Alvord,
George Austin,
Hillel Baker,
Alvah Ballard,
George S. Ball,
Alpheus Bancroft,
Marcus Barrett,
Moses Bates, Jr.,
Erasmus D. Beach,
John Beal,
William Bennett, Jr.,
Zephaniah Bennett,
Edward B. Bigelow,
Francis W. Bird,
Henry W. Bishop,
Gad O. Bliss,
William S. Booth,
George S. Boutwell,
Sewell Boutwell,
William J. A. Bradford,
Hiram N. Breed,
Asa Bronson,
Adolphus F. Brown,
Alpheus R. Brown,
Artemas Brown,
Hammond Brown,
Hiram C. Brown,
Frederick Brownell,
Joseph Brownell,
Patrick Bryant,
Asahel Buck,
Amos H. Bullen,
Anson Burlingame,
Henry Cady,
Timothy W. Carter,

Messrs. William Carruthers,
Isaac Case,
Daniel E. Chapin,
Josiah Childs,
J. McKean Churchill,
Henry Clark,
Ransom Clark,
Stillman Clarke,
William Cleverly,
Lansing J. Cole,
Sumner Cole,
George B. Crane,
Oliver S. Cressy,
Joseph W. Cross,
Henry W. Cushman,
Simeon N. Cutler,
Charles G. Davis,
Ebenezer Davis,
Isaac Davis,
Robert T. Davis,
Gilman Day,
Silas Dean,
Elijah S. Deming,
Augustus Denton,
Alexander De Witt,
Samuel Duncan,
Bradish Dunham,
John M. Durgin,
John M. Earle,
James Easton, 2d,
Calvin D. Eaton,
Elisha Edwards,
Joseph M. Ely,
Lyman Fisk,
Emery Fiske,
Ezekiel W. Fitch,
Aaron Foster,
Abram Foster,
Samuel Fowle,
James M. Freeman,
Charles A. French,
Samuel French,
Luther Gale,

Messrs. Johnson Gardner,
Elbridge Gates,
Washington Gilbert,
Charles G. Giles,
Daniel W. Gooch,
Leonard Gooding,
F. R. Gourgas,
John W. Graves,
Jabez Green,
William B. Greene,
Josiah W. Griswold,
Whiting Griswold,
Samuel P. Hadley,
Lyman W. Hapgood,
Seth Hapgood,
George Haskell,
William Haskins,
Stephen E. Hawkes,
Isaac Hayden,
Ezra Heath, 2d,
James Hewes,
William H. Hewes,
Levi Heywood,
Henry Hobart,
Edwin Hobbs,
Nathaniel Holder,
George Hood,
Foster Hooper,
Martin Howard,
Abraham H. Howland,
Henry K. Hoyt,
Charles E. Hunt,
Charles P. Huntington,
George H. Huntington,
Moses C. Hurlbut,
Benjamin D. Hyde,
Abijah M. Ide, Jr.,
John Jacobs,
John Johnson,
Isaac Kendall,
Joseph Kimball,
Joseph Kingman,
Hiram Knight,
Jefferson Knight,
Charles L. Knowlton,
J. S. C. Knowlton,
William H. Knowlton,
Albert Knox,
George H. Kuhn,
Gardner P. Ladd,
Wilber C. Langdon,
Luther Lawrence,
Job G. Lawton, Jr.,

Messrs. Abishai Lincoln,
Otis Little,
Justin E. Loomis,
William P. Marble,
Abijah P. Marvin,
Charles Mason,
Reuben Meader,
Simeon Merritt,
James L. Monroe,
James M. Moore,
Marcus Morton,
Marcus Morton, Jr.,
William S. Morton,
Hiram Nash,
Jonathan Nayson,
Charles Newman,
William Nichols,
Alfred Norton,
Andrew T. Nute,
Benjamin S. Orne,
Charles Osgood,
E. Wing Packer,
Benjamin Paine,
Henry Paine,
Samuel C. Parsons,
John Partridge,
Jeremiah Pease, Jr.,
John Penniman,
Daniel A. Perkins,
Jesse Perkins,
Noah C. Perkins,
Charles Phelps,
Silvanus B. Phinney,
Henry Pierce,
James M. Pool,
Peter Powers,
John A. Putnam,
Robert Rantoul,
Silas Rawson,
Luther Richards,
Daniel Richardson,
Nathan Richardson,
Samuel H. Richardson,
Joseph M. Rockwood,
John Rogers,
David S. Ross,
James C. Royce,
Chester Sanderson,
Luther Sheldon,
John Sherril,
Perez Simmons,
John W. Simonds,
Matthew Smith,

Messrs. Melzar Sprague,
Samuel W. Spooner,
Eben H. Stacy,
Caleb Stetson,
Granville Stevens,
Joseph L. Stevens, Jr.,
William Stevens,
Gideon Stiles,
Alfred L. Strong,
Charles Sumner,
Alanson Swain,
Willard Thayer, 2d,
Charles Thompson,
Abraham Tilton,
Horatio W. Tilton,
David P. Turner,
William Tyler,
Orison Underwood,
Joel Viles,
George A. Vinton,
Freeland Wallis,

Messrs. Amasa Walker,
Andrew H. Ward,
Samuel Warner, Jr.,
Gershom B. Weston,
George White,
Daniel S. Whitney,
James S. Whitney,
Daniel Wilbur,
John H. Wilkins,
Henry Williams,
J. B. Williams,
Henry Wilson,
Willard Wilson,
Jonathan B. Winn,
Levi M. Winslow,
Charles C. Wood,
Nathaniel Wood,
Otis Wood,
William H. Wood,
Ezekiel Wright.

Those who voted in the negative are:—

Messrs. Benjamin P. Adams,
P. Emory Aldrich,
Robert Andrews,
William Appleton,
William Aspinwall,
David C. Atwood,
Samuel Ayres,
Joseph Barrows,
Russel Bartlett,
Luther V. Bell,
George W. Blagden,
William C. Bliss,
Milton P. Braman,
Osmyn Brewster,
Francis Brinley,
George N. Briggs,
Rufus Bullock,
Jacob Coggin,
Nathaniel Cogswell,
Ithamar Conkey,
Charles E. Cook,
Henry F. Cooledge,
Benjamin F. Copeland,
Simeon Crittenden,
George W. Crockett,
Leander Crosby,
Seth Crowell,
Joseph Cummings,
Wilber Curtis,
John Davis,

Messrs. Solomon Davis,
Henry L. Dawes,
Hiram S. Denison,
Moses Dorman,
Philip Eames,
Lilley Eaton,
Samuel Edwards,
Homer Ely,
A. G. Farwell,
Samuel P. Fowler,
Charles H. French,
Wanton C. Gilbert,
Robert Gould,
Jason Goulding,
John C. Gray,
Artemas Hale,
A. B. Hammond,
Phineas Harmon,
George Hayward,
Samuel Henry,
Henry Hersey,
William Hinsdale,
Aaron Hobart,
Samuel Houghton,
William Hunt,
Samuel A. Hurlburt,
Samuel Jackson,
William James,
John Jenkins,
Giles C. Kellogg,

Messrs. Henry W. Kinsman,
Frederic W. Lincoln, Jr.,
Tristram Littlefield,
Isaac Livermore,
Samuel K. Lothrop,
Samuel P. Loud,
John A. Lowell,
Seth Miller, Jr.,
George Morey,
Daniel Noyes,
Henry K. Oliver,
Nathan Orcutt,
John G. Park,
Adolphus G. Parker,
Thomas A. Parsons,
George Peabody,
John Sargent,

Messrs. William Schouler,
John S. Sleeper,
Charles G. Stevens,
Thomas Talbot,
Ralph Taylor,
Edmund P. Tileston,
David Turner,
Charles W. Upham,
George B. Upton,
Samuel B. Walcott,
Samuel Walker,
Cyrus Weeks,
Thomas Wetmore,
William F. Wheeler,
Benjamin White,
Joel Wilder,
Milo Wilson.

The Resolve was ordered to a second reading, and placed in the Orders of the Day for to-morrow.

On motion of Mr. Wilson, of Natick, the Convention resolved itself into Committee of the Whole, for the purpose of considering the Resolves reported by the Committee on the subject of the Secretary, Treasurer, &c.; and the President requested Mr. Griswold, member for Erving, to take the chair.

Afterwards, Mr. Griswold reported, that the committee had made progress in the consideration of the subject, but had come to no conclusion, and had instructed him to ask leave to sit again.

And leave was accordingly granted.

At one o'clock the Convention adjourned.

AFTERNOON SESSION.

Met according to adjournment.

Mr. Griswold, member for Erving, offered the following Order:—

Ordered, That on and after Tuesday next, the Convention meet at nine o'clock in the forenoon.

Laid over, under the rule.

Mr. Dana, member for Manchester, offered the following Resolution:—

Resolved, That the Constitution be so amended, as to require a voting list or registry, and to protect presiding officers in adhering thereto.

Referred to the Committee on the Qualifications of Voters.

On motion of Mr. Phinney, member for Chatham, the Convention resolved itself into Committee of the Whole, for the purpose of further considering the Resolves on the subject of the secretary, treasurer, &c., and the President requested Mr. Griswold, member for ke the chair.

Afterwards, Mr. GRISWOLD reported the Resolves to the Convention, with amendments, as follow:—

In the first line of the third Resolve, after the words "judges of probate," insert the words, "shall be elected once in six years, and."

In the third line of the same Resolve, strike out the words "county treasurers," and in the fourth line, after the word "triennially," insert the words, "and county treasurers annually."

The first amendment was agreed to.

The second amendment was rejected, by a vote of fifty-eight in the affirmative and one hundred and five in the negative.

Mr. WILKINS, of Boston, moved further to amend the third Resolve, by adding, after the words "county treasurers" in the third line, the words, "except the treasurers of the counties of Suffolk and Nantucket."

The amendment was agreed to, by a vote of sixty-six in the affirmative and fifty-nine in the negative.

The Resolves were then ordered to a second reading.

On motion of Mr. GRISWOLD, member for Erving,

Ordered, That Tuesday next, at ten o'clock in the forenoon, be assigned for the consideration of the Majority and Minority Reports on the subject of the House of Representatives.

Mr. FAY, of Southborough, from the Committee on Leave of Absence, submitted a Report, granting leave of absence to Mr. Cummings, of Ware, for ten days.

The Report was accepted, and leave of absence granted.

At twenty minutes past six o'clock, on motion of Mr. OLIVER, of Lawrence,

The Convention adjourned.

SATURDAY, June 11, 1853.

Met according to adjournment. Prayer was offered by the Chaplain. The Journal of yesterday was read.

On motion of Mr. WHITNEY, of Boylston,

Ordered, That the Committee on Oaths and Subscriptions, &c., consider the propriety of permitting persons who have conscientious scruples against the taking of human life, either as punishment for crime, in war, or self-defence, to act under the Constitution without taking the oath or affirmation ordinarily required.

On motion of Mr. BRADFORD, of Essex,

Ordered, That the Committee on the subject of the Secretary, Treasurer, &c., inquire into the expediency of incorporating into the Constitution a provision that every person holding office in or under the State government, shall retire therefrom at the expiration of six years of service, and shall be ineligible thereto for a like period of six years.

Mr. WILSON, of Natick, offered the following Order:

Ordered, That the several committees be instructed to make their final reports on or before Wednesday, the twenty-second instant.

Laid over, under the rule.

On motion of Mr. JAMES, of South Scituate, the Special Committee on the subject of Elections by Plurality, were directed to report on or before Wednesday next.

The Order offered yesterday, by Mr. Griswold, concerning the time of meeting in the morning, was taken up.

Mr. BLISS, of Hatfield, demanded the yeas and nays on the question of adopting the Order, but the demand was not sustained by one-fifth of the members.

Mr. HOOPER, of Fall River, moved to amend the Order by substituting the hour of half past nine for the hour of nine.

A motion to lay the Order on the table, was rejected.

Mr. SCHOULER, of Boston, moved the Previous Question, which was ordered.

The amendment of Mr. Hooper was then rejected, and

The Order was adopted.

On motion of Mr. HALE, of Bridgewater,

Ordered, That when the Convention adjourns this forenoon, it adjourn to meet again on Monday, at ten o'clock in the forenoon.

Mr. OLIVER, of Lawrence, moved that the Standing Order of the Convention, providing for an adjournment of the forenoon session at one o'clock, be modified by substituting half past one o'clock.

On motion of Mr. STETSON, of Braintree, the motion was laid on the table.

On motion of Mr. PHINNEY, member for Chatham, the Convention proceeded to the consideration of the Orders of the Day, and

The Resolves on the subject of the qualifications of voters, were read a second time.

The question being upon their final passage,

Mr. ALDRICH, of Barre, moved that the first Resolve be amended, by striking out the words, "the payment of a tax shall not be required as a qualification," and inserting instead thereof, the words, "all persons exempted by law, or under any provisions of law, from taxation, and who are, in all other respects, qualified as the Constitution requires, shall be entitled."

After debate, the Previous Question was moved by Mr. HOOD, of Lynn, and ordered by the Convention.

The amendment was rejected.

The question being upon the final passage of the first Resolve,

On motion of Mr. BIRD, of Walpole,

Ordered, That when the question is taken, it be taken by yeas and nays.

And the roll being called,

Two hundred and six members voted for the Resolve, and sixty-five against it.

Those who voted in the affirmative are :—

Messrs. Shubael P. Adams,
James B. Allen,
Parsons Allen,
John B. Alley,
D. W. Alvord,
Robert Andrews,
William Aspinwall,
George Austin,
Hillel Baker,
Alvah Ballard,
Alpheus Bancroft,
Marcus Barrett,
Eliakim A. Bates,
Moses Bates, Jr.,
Erasmus D. Beach,
John Beal,
William Bennett, Jr.,
Zephaniah Bennett,
Edward B. Bigelow,
Francis W. Bird,
Henry W. Bishop,
Gad O. Bliss,
William S. Booth,
George S. Boutwell,
Sewell Boutwell,
William J. A. Bradford,

Messrs. Hiram N. Breed,
George N. Briggs,
Asa Bronson,
Adolphus F. Brown,
Artemas Brown,
Hiram C. Brown,
Joseph Brownell,
Asahel Buck,
Amos H. Bullen,
Anson Burlingame,
Timothy W. Carter,
Isaac Case,
J. McKean Churchill,
Henry Clark,
Ransom Clark,
Stillman Clarke,
William Cleverly,
Lansing J. Cole,
Sumner Cole,
Henry F. Cooledge,
George B. Crane,
Oliver S. Cressy,
Joseph W. Cross,
Joseph Cummings,
Simeon N. Cutler,
Ebenezer Davis,

Messrs. Silas Dean,
Augustus Denton,
Alexander De Witt,
Samuel Duncan,
Bradish Dunham,
John M. Durgin,
James Easton, 2d,
Calvin D. Eaton,
Lilley Eaton,
Elisha Edwards,
Samuel Edwards,
Joseph M. Ely,
Sullivan Fay,
James K. Fellows,
Lyman Fisk,
Abram Foster,
Samuel Fowle,
James M. Freeman,
Charles A. French,
Richard Frothingham, Jr.,
Luther Gale,
Elbridge Gates,
Wanton C. Gilbert,
Charles G. Giles,
Daniel W. Gooch,
Leonard Gooding,
F. R. Gourgas,
Jabez Green,
William B. Greene,
Josiah W. Griswold,
Whiting Griswold,
Samuel P. Hadley,
Charles B. Hall,
Lyman W. Hapgood,
Phineas Harmon,
George Haskell,
William Haskins,
Stephen E. Hawkes,
Isaac Hayden,
Ezra Heath, 2d,
James Hewes,
William H. Hewes,
Henry Hobart,
Edwin Hobbs,
Nathaniel Holder,
George Hood,
Foster Hooper,
Martin Howard,
Abraham H. Howland,
Charles E. Hunt,
Charles P. Huntington,
George H. Huntington,
Moses C. Hurlbut,

Messrs. John Jacobs,
Giles C. Kellogg,
Isaac Kendall,
Joseph Kingman,
Jefferson Knight,
William H. Knowlton,
George H. Kuhn,
John S. Ladd,
Wilber C. Langdon,
Alden Leland,
Abishai Lincoln,
Frederic W. Lincoln, Jr.,
Otis Little,
Tristram Littlefield,
William P. Marble,
Laban Marcy,
Reuben Meader,
Simeon Merritt,
James L. Monroe,
James M. Moore,
Elbridge G. Morton,
Marcus Morton,
Marcus Morton, Jr.,
William S. Morton,
Jonathan Nayson,
Charles Newman,
Joseph E. Ober,
Henry K. Oliver,
Nathan Orcutt,
Benjamin S. Orne,
E. Wing Packer,
Benjamin Paine,
Henry Paine,
Adolphus G. Parker,
Joel Parker,
Jonathan Parris,
Samuel C. Parsons,
John Partridge,
Nathaniel Peabody,
John Penniman,
Daniel A. Perkins,
Jesse Perkins,
Noah C. Perkins,
Charles Phelps,
Silvanus B. Phinney,
Henry Pierce,
James M. Pool,
Peter Powers,
John A. Putnam,
Robert Rantoul,
Silas Rawson,
Luther Richards,
Daniel Richardson,

Messrs. Samuel H. Richardson,
Joseph M. Rockwood,
John Rogers,
David S. Ross,
Amasa Sanderson,
Chester Sanderson,
William Schouler,
Luther Sheldon,
Charles Sherman,
John Sherril,
John W. Simonds.
Samuel W. Spooner,
Eben H. Stacy,
Caleb Stetson,
Granville Stevens,
Joseph L. Stevens, Jr.,
William Stevens,
Gideon Stiles,
Charles Sumner,
Joseph Thayer,
Willard Thayer, 2d,
John W. Thomas,
Horatio W. Tilton,
David Turner,

Messrs. David P. Turner,
Orison Underwood,
Charles W. Upham,
Joel Viles,
Bradford L. Wales,
Freeland Wallis,
Andrew H. Ward,
Samuel Warner, Jr.,
Asa H. Waters,
Gershom B. Weston,
Benjamin White,
George White,
Daniel S. Whitney,
James S. Whitney,
Daniel Wilbur,
Joseph Wilbur,
Henry Williams,
J. B. Williams,
Henry Wilson,
Levi M. Winslow,
Charles C. Wood,
Otis Wood,
William H. Wood,
Ezekiel Wright.

Those who voted in the negative are:—

Messrs. Alfred A. Abbott,
Benjamin P. Adams,
P. Emory Aldrich,
William Appleton,
David C. Atwood,
Samuel Ayres,
Joseph Barrows,
Sidney Bartlett,
Milton P. Braman,
Osmyn Brewster,
Francis Brinley,
Rufus Bullock,
Daniel E. Chapin,
Josiah Childs,
Rufus Choate,
Ithamar Conkey,
Charles E. Cook,
Simeon Crittenden,
Leander Crosby,
Seth Crowell,
F. B. Crowninshield,
Solomon Davis,
William Dehon,
Hiram S. Denison,
Philip Eames,
Homer Ely,

Messrs. Robert Gould,
Dalton Goulding,
Jason Goulding,
John C. Gray,
Artemas Hale,
George Hayward,
Charles Heard,
William Hinsdale,
Samuel Houghton,
William J. Hubbard,
William Hunt,
Samuel Jackson,
John Johnson,
Isaac Livermore,
Samuel K. Lothrop,
Samuel P. Loud,
John A. Lowell,
Theophilus R. Marvin,
Seth Miller, Jr.,
George Morey,
William Nichols,
Daniel Noyes,
George Peabody,
George R. Sampson,
John Sargent,
John S. Sleeper,

Messrs. Matthew Smith,
John Souther,
Charles G. Stevens,
Edmund P. Tileston,
Samuel B. Walcott,
Samuel Walker,
Cyrus Weeks,

Messrs. Thomas Wetmore,
William F. Wheeler,
Joel Wilder,
Willard Wilson,
Jonathan B. Winn,
Josiah B. Woods.

Mr. Foster, of Charlemont, at his own request, was excused from voting on the Resolve.

The question then being upon the passage of the second Resolve,

Mr. Oliver, of Lawrence, moved that it be amended by adding after the woids, "city election," the words "or for town clerk, or selectmen."

On motion of Mr. Wilson, of Natick, the Orders of the Day being laid upon the table,

The Standing Order providing for adjournment at one o'clock, was modified so as to extend the time, for this day, until two o'clock.

Afterwards, on motion of Mr. Greene, of Brookfield, the Orders of the Day were again laid upon the table, and the time extended until quarter past two.

The Orders of the Day were again taken up.

Mr. Crane, of Norton, moved the Previous Question, but the motion was not sustained; sixty-six members voting for it, and seventy-six against it.

Mr. Aspinwall, of Brookline, moved that the question on Mr. Oliver's amendment be taken by yeas and nays; but the motion was rejected, one-fifth of the members not voting in its favor.

Mr. Oliver's amendment was then rejected by a vote of thirty-five in the affirmative, to one hundred and nine in the negative.

The Resolve was then finally passed, and at quarter past two o'clock,

On motion of Mr. Wilson, of Natick,

The Convention adjourned.

MONDAY, June 13, 1853.

Met according to adjournment. Prayer was offered by the Chaplain. The Journal of Saturday was read.

Mr. Frothingham, of Charlestown, presented the Petition of Timothy Fletcher and ninety-four others, citizens of Charlestown, in aid of the Petition of John W. Le Barnes and others.

Referred to the committee having that subject in charge.

The Order offered by Mr. WILSON, of Natick, on Saturday, directing the committees to make their final Reports on Wednesday, the 22d inst., was, on motion of Mr. WILSON,

Laid upon the table.

On motion of Mr. FREEMAN, of Franklin, the Convention proceeded to the consideration of the Orders of the Day;

And the Resolves from the Committee on the subject of the Secretary, Treasurer, &c., were read a second time.

On motion of Mr. FREEMAN, of Franklin, the first Resolve was amended by striking out the word "coroners" from the fourth line, (printed copy).

The Resolve was then finally passed.

On motion of Mr. SCHOULER, of Boston, the second Resolve was amended by striking from the ninth line, (printed copy,) the words, "and receiver-general."

On motion of Mr. BIRD, of Walpole, the Resolve was further amended by the addition of the following words, viz.: "And that the Constitution be further amended by striking out from the last line of article 1, section 4, chapter 2, of the Constitution, the words, "and receiver-general."

The Resolve was then finally passed.

Mr. WILKINS, of Boston, moved that the third Resolve be amended by inserting after the words "county commissioners," the words "excepting in the counties of Suffolk and Nantucket";

But the amendment was rejected.

On motion of Mr. DENTON, of Chelsea, the third Resolve was amended by striking from it the words, "except the treasurers of the counties of Suffolk and Nantucket."

Mr. BATES, of Plymouth, moved that the Resolve be further amended by striking out the words, "be elected once in six years," and,

Pending this question,

At one o'clock, the Convention adjourned.

AFTERNOON SESSION.

Met according to adjournment.

Mr. BRINLEY, of Boston, submitted a paper containing a proposed substitute for the plan of representation reported by the Committee on the House of Representatives; which was ordered to be printed.

Mr. GOURGAS, of Concord, from the Committee on Reporting and

Publishing the Debates, submitted a Report, accompanied by a Resolve, which was considered and adopted, as follows :—

Resolved, That there be paid to Henry M. Parkhurst, the sum of six hundred and twenty-seven dollars, being the amount due him for reporting the Debates of the Convention from May 4th to 17th, inclusive; and that the governor of the Commonwealth be requested to draw his warrant on the treasury for the same.

On motion of Mr. UNDERWOOD, of Milford, the Convention proceeded to the consideration of the Orders of the Day; the first question being upon the amendment offered by Mr. Bates, of Plymouth, to the third Resolve reported by the Committee on the subject of the Secretary, Treasurer, &c.

Mr. KINGMAN, of West Bridgewater, moved the Previous Question, which was ordered by the Convention.

The amendment was then adopted by a vote of one hundred and thirteen in the affirmative, to fifty-eight in the negative.

On motion of Mr. BIRD, of Walpole,

Ordered, That when the question is taken on the final passage of the Resolve, it be taken by yeas and nays.

And the roll being called,

One hundred and ninety-two members voted for the Resolve, and forty-seven against it.

Those who voted in the affirmative are :—

Messrs. Shubael P. Adams,
Charles Allen,
Josiah Allis,
D. W. Alvord,
Hillel Baker,
Alvah Ballard,
Alpheus Bancroft,
Marcus Barrett,
Moses Bates, Jr.,
Erasmus D. Beach,
John Beal,
Zephaniah Bennett,
Francis W. Bird,
Henry W. Bishop,
Gad O. Bliss,
William S. Booth,
George S. Boutwell,
Sewell Boutwell,
William J. A. Bradford,
Hiram N. Breed,
Asa Bronson,

Messrs. Adolphus F. Brown,
Alpheus R. Brown,
Hiram C. Brown,
Joseph Brownell,
Patrick Bryant,
Asahel Buck,
Anson Burlingame,
William Carruthers,
Daniel E. Chapin,
Henry Chapin,
Josiah Childs,
J. McKean Churchill,
Stillman Clarke,
William Cleverly,
Jacob Coggin,
Lansing J. Cole,
Sumner Cole,
George B. Crane,
Oliver S. Cressy,
Simeon Crittenden,
Joseph W. Cross,

Messrs. Thomas Cushman,
Simeon N. Cutler,
Ebenezer Davis,
Isaac Davis,
Silas Dean,
Augustus Denton,
Bradish Dunham,
John M. Durgin,
James Easton, 2d,
Calvin D. Eaton,
Lilley Eaton,
Elisha Edwards,
James K. Fellows,
Lyman Fisk,
Emery Fiske,
Aaron Foster,
Abram Foster,
Samuel Fowle,
James M. Freeman,
Charles A. French,
Samuel French,
Luther Gale,
Elbridge Gates,
Washington Gilbert,
Charles G. Giles,
Leonard Gooding,
F. R. Gourgas,
Jabez Green,
Josiah W. Griswold,
Samuel P. Hadley,
Charles B. Hall,
B. F. Hallett,
Phineas Harmon,
George Haskell,
Elnathan P. Hathaway
Stephen E. Hawkes,
Isaac Hayden,
Ezra Heath, 2d,
James Hewes,
William H. Hewes,
Aaron Hobart,
Henry Hobart,
Edwin Hobbs,
Nathaniel Holder,
George Hood,
Foster Hooper,
Martin Howard,
Charles P. Huntington,
George H. Huntington,
Moses C. Hurlbut,
John Jacobs,
John Johnson,
Isaac Kendall,

Messrs. Joseph Kingman,
Hiram Knight,
Jefferson Knight,
Charles L. Knowlton,
J. S. C. Knowlton,
William H. Knowlton,
Albert Knox,
George H. Kuhn,
Gardner P. Ladd,
Wilber C. Langdon,
Job G. Lawton, Jr.,
Alden Leland,
Abishai Lincoln,
E. Justin Loomis,
William P. Marble,
Abijah P. Marvin,
Charles Mason,
Reuben Meader,
Simeon Merritt,
James M. Moore,
Elbridge G. Morton,
Marcus Morton,
Marcus Morton, Jr.,
Charles Newman,
William Nichols,
Andrew T. Nute,
Joseph E. Ober,
Henry K. Oliver,
Benjamin S. Orne,
E. Wing Packer,
Adolphus G. Parker,
Jonathan Parris,
Samuel C. Parsons,
Thomas A. Parsons,
John Partridge,
Nathaniel Peabody,
Jeremiah Pease, Jr.,
John Penniman,
Daniel A. Perkins,
Jesse Perkins,
Noah C. Perkins,
Charles Phelps,
Henry Pierce,
James M. Pool,
Robert Rantoul,
Silas Rawson,
James Read,
Daniel Richardson,
Samuel H. Richardson,
Joseph M. Rockwood,
John Rogers,
David S. Ross,
Amasa Sanderson,

Messrs. Chester Sanderson,
William Schouler,
Luther Sheldon,
John Sherril,
John W. Simonds,
Matthew Smith,
John Souther,
Melzar Sprague,
Samuel W. Spooner,
Eben H. Stacy,
Granville Stevens,
Joseph L. Stevens, Jr.,
William Stevens,
Gideon Stiles,
Charles Sumner,
Joseph Thayer,
Willard Thayer, 2d,
John W. Thomas,
Abraham Tilton,
Horatio W. Tilton,
David Turner,
David P. Turner,

Messrs. William Tyler,
Orison Underwood,
Joel Viles,
Bradford L. Wales,
Amasa Walker,
Andrew H. Ward,
Samuel Warner, Jr.,
Gershom B. Weston,
Benjamin White,
George White,
Daniel S. Whitney,
James S. Whitney,
Joseph Wilbur,
Henry Williams,
Henry Wilson,
Willard Wilson,
Jonathan B. Winn,
Levi M. Winslow,
Charles C. Wood,
Nathaniel Wood,
Otis Wood,
Ezekiel Wright.

ho'voted in the negative are :—

Messrs. William Aspinwall,
David C. Atwood,
Joseph Barrows,
Luther V. Bell,
Ebenezer Bradbury,
Francis Brinley,
George N. Briggs,
Rufus Bullock,
Cephas C. Bumpus,
Nathaniel Cogswell,
Henry F. Cooledge,
Leander Crosby,
Solomon Davis,
Philip Eames,
William T. Eustis,
Samuel P. Fowler,
Wanton C. Gilbert,
Robert Gould,
Dalton Goulding,
Artemas Hale,
A. B. Hammond,
Charles Heard,
Henry Hersey,
William Hindsdale,

Messrs. Thomas Hopkinson,
Samuel Houghton,
William Hunt,
Samuel Jackson,
Giles C. Kellogg,
John S. Ladd,
Frederic W. Lincoln, Jr.,
Isaac Livermore,
Samuel P. Loud,
John A. Lowell,
Seth Miller, Jr.,
Samuel Mixter,
Daniel Noyes,
Nathan Orcutt,
John G. Park,
Samuel D. Parker,
John Sargent,
Charles G. Stevens,
Samuel B. Walcott,
Cyrus Weeks,
John H. Wilkins,
Milo Wilson,
Josiah B. Woods.

So the Resolve was passed.

The fourth Resolve was also finally passed, making the series in the following form:—

Resolved, That the words, "solicitor-general" be stricken from article 9, section 1, chapter 2, of the Constitution, and that said article be so amended as to require that all sheriffs and registers of probate be elected triennially by the people in their respective counties, and that the attorney-general be elected annually by the people of the Commonwealth.

Resolved, That article 1, section 4, chapter 2, be amended by striking out the word "and" after the word "secretary" in the first line, and inserting after the words "receiver-general" in the second line, the words, "and auditor of accounts," and also, by substituting for the words "by joint ballot of the senators and representatives in one room," the words "by the people of the Commonwealth," so that said article, as far as, and including the word "room," may read thus: "The secretary, treasurer, and auditor of accounts, shall be chosen annually by the people of the Commonwealth." And that the Constitution be further amended by striking out from the last line of article 1, section 4, chapter 2, of the Constitution, the words, "and receiver-general."

Resolved, That judges of probate, clerks of the courts, commissioners of insolvency, district-attorneys, registers of deeds, county treasurers, and county commissioners, be elected triennially by the people of their respective counties and districts.

Resolved, That it is not expedient so to amend the Constitution as to provide for the election by the people of the Commonwealth of a prison inspector.

Mr. Hall, of Haverhill, at his request, was excused from serving upon the Committee on the University at Cambridge.

On motion of Mr. Wilson, of Natick, the Convention resolved itself into Committee of the Whole, for the purpose of considering the Resolves reported by the Committee on the Frame of Government on the subject of the legislative department of the government; and the President requested Mr. Livermore, of Cambridge, to take the chair.

Afterwards, Mr. Livermore reported, that the committee had made progress in the consideration of the subject, but had come to no conclusion, and had instructed him to ask leave to sit again.

And leave was accordingly granted.

At half past six o'clock, on motion of Mr. Churchill, of Milton,

The Convention adjourned.

TUESDAY, June 14, 1853.

Met according to adjournment. Prayer was offered by the Chaplain. The Journal of yesterday was read.

On motion of Mr. Phelps, of Monroe,

Ordered, That the roll of the members be called.

And, on motion of Mr. Breed, of Lynn,

Ordered, That the doors be closed during the calling of the roll.

The roll was then called, and it was ascertained that a quorum of the members was present.

The doors were then opened.

Mr. Sumner, member for Otis, moved that the Order of the Convention, providing that the morning session shall commence at nine o'clock, be rescinded.

Mr. Allen, of Worcester, moved the Previous Question, which was ordered,

And the motion of Mr. Sumner was agreed to.

On motion of Mr. Allen, of Worcester, the Convention resolved itself into Committee of the Whole, for the purpose of further considering the Resolve on the subject of the legislative department of the government; and the President requested Mr. Livermore, of Cambridge, to take the chair.

Afterwards, Mr. Livermore reported, that the committee had considered the Resolve, and had instructed him to report, that it ought to pass, with an amendment, as follows:—

Striking out the last paragraph of the proposed article of amendment, and substituting therefor the following:—

The legislature which shall assemble next after the adoption of this article in the Constitution, shall fix the compensation of members, which may be changed at any subsequent session; but no act affecting the pay of members, passed after the year 1854, shall take effect until the session next after its passage. And no compensation or pay shall hereafter be allowed for the attendance of members longer than one hundred days at any one session.

The question being upon agreeing to the proposed amendment,

Mr. Morton, of Taunton, moved to amend it by striking out the first part, as far as, and including the word "passage," and inserting instead thereof the words, "the legislature shall by law establish the compensation of the members thereof, which shall in no case be increased or diminished during their continuance in office."

The amendment to the amendment was adopted, and then,

On motion of Mr. Morton, the amendment was further amended by striking out the last part, after the word "passage," and inserting instead thereof the words, "but shall never, except in case of insurrection or invasion, continue in session longer than ninety days, nor sit during any year more than one hundred days."

On motion of Mr. Kellogg, of Hadley, the second paragraph of the proposed article of the Constitution was amended by striking out the word "said" in the third line, (printed copy,) and inserting the word "following" after the word "January" in the same line.

Mr. Kingman, of West Bridgewater, moved that the question on the adoption of the Resolve be taken by yeas and nays; but the motion was rejected; one-fifth of the members not voting in its favor.

The Resolve was then ordered to a second reading.

On motion of Mr. Cushman, of Bernardston, the Convention resolved itself into Committee of the Whole, for the purpose of considering the Resolves reported by the Committee on the subject of the House of Representatives; and the Resolves reported by a minority of the same committee; and the President requested Mr. Wilson, of Natick, to take the chair.

Afterwards, Mr. Wilson reported, that the committee had made progress in the consideration of the subject, but had come to no conclusion, and had instructed him to ask leave to sit again.

And leave was accordingly granted.

Mr. Greene, of Brookfield, presented the Petition of Lucretia Upham and twenty-two others, women of Brookfield, that women may be permitted to vote on the proposed alterations and amendments of the Constitution.

Also, the Petition of Wendell Phillips and thirty-three others, that woman may be heard at the bar of the Convention, in support of her rights.

Severally referred to the Committee on the Qualifications of Voters.

Mr. Allen, of Worcester, from the Committee on the Frame of Government, submitted a Report upon an Order of May 18th, concerning the appropriation of public funds for local or private purposes; recommending that it be referred to the special committee having under consideration the subject of loans of the credit of the State.

The Report was accepted, and the Order so referred.

At one o'clock, the Convention adjourned.

AFTERNOON SESSION.

Met according to adjournment.

Mr. Davis, of Worcester, from the Committee on the Governor, submitted Reports, as follow:—

Inexpedient to act upon the subject of an Order of June 3d, relative to the pardoning power.

Also, inexpedient to act upon the subject of an Order of May 30th, relative to the governor's command of the militia, &c.

Also, a Resolve on the subject of the title of the governor.

Severally referred to the Committee of the Whole and ordered to be printed.

Mr. Oliver, of Lawrence, from the Committee on the Militia, submitted a Report and articles of amendment on that subject.

Referred to the Committee of the Whole and ordered to be printed.

Mr. Dana, member for Manchester, moved a reconsideration of the vote by which the third of the Resolves reported by the Committee on Secretary, Treasurer, &c., was finally passed.

Placed in the Orders of the Day for to-morrow.

On motion of Mr. Morton, of Andover, the Convention resolved itself into Committee of the Whole, for the purpose of considering the Resolves on the subject of the House of Representatives; and the President requested Mr. Wilson, of Natick, to take the chair.

Afterwards, Mr. Wilson reported, that the committee had made further progress in the consideration of the subject, but had come to no conclusion, and had instructed him to ask leave to sit again.

And leave was accordingly granted.

At ten minutes past six o'clock, on motion of Mr. Ball, of Upton,

The Convention adjourned.

WEDNESDAY, June 15, 1853.

Met according to adjournment. Prayer was offered by the Chaplain. The Journal of yesterday was read.

Mr. Greene, of Brookfield, presented the Petition of Mary C. Higginson and forty-one others, women of Worcester, in aid of the Petion of Mrs. Abby C. Alcott and others, that women may be allowed to vote upon the proposed amendments of the Constitution.

Referred to the Committee on the Qualifications of Voters.

On motion of Mr. WHITNEY, of Boylston,

Ordered, That the Committee on the Militia be instructed to consider the expediency of so amending the Constitution as to strike out whatever in it relates to the militia; and instead thereof, provide for the registration of all citizens, between twenty-one and fifty years of age, as a standing police of the Commonwealth, to render such assistance as may at any time be necessary for the preservation of the peace, and the faithful and efficient execution of the laws of the Commonwealth.

On motion of Mr. AUSTIN, of Swanzey, the Convention resolved itself into Committee of the Whole, for the purpose of considering the Resolves on the subject of the House of Representatives; and the President requested Mr. Wilson, of Natick, to take the chair.

Afterwards, Mr. WILSON reported, that the committee had made further progress in the consideration of the subject, but had come to no conclusion, and had instructed him to ask leave to sit again.

And leave was accordingly granted.

At one o'clock, the Convention adjourned.

AFTERNOON SESSION.

Met according to adjournment.

Mr. BROWN, of Dracut, from the Special Committee on the subject of Loaning the Credit of the State, submitted a Report, inexpedient to act on that subject.

Referred to the Committee of the Whole and ordered to be printed.

Mr. WHITE, of Quincy, offered a series of Resolves, as a substitute for the Report of the Majority of the Committee on the House of Representatives.

Referred to the Committee of the Whole and ordered to be printed.

Mr. STEVENSON, of Boston, from the Special Committee on the subject of Elections by Plurality of Votes, stated, that on account of the unavoidable absence of the chairman and other members, the committee were not able to comply with the Order of the Convention, directing them to report to-day; and on his motion, further time was granted to the committee for the consideration of the subject.

The PRESIDENT appointed Mr. Boutwell, member for Berlin, one of the Committee on the University at Cambridge, in place of Mr. Hall, of Haverhill, excused from serving.

On motion of Mr. BRIGGS, of Pittsfield, the Convention resolved itself into Committee of the Whole, for the purpose of considering the Resolves on the subject of the House of Representatives; and the President requested Mr. Wilson, of Natick, to take the chair.

Afterwards, Mr. Wilson reported, that the committee had made further progress in the consideration of the subject, but had come to no conclusion, and had instructed him to ask leave to sit again.

And leave was accordingly granted.

On motion of Mr. Bird, of Walpole, the Convention proceeded to the consideration of the Orders of the Day.

The first subject being the motion to reconsider the vote on the passage of the third Resolve, reported by the Committee on the Secretary, Treasurer, &c., was passed over.

At a quarter past five o'clock, on motion of Mr. Thompson, of Charlestown,

The Convention adjourned.

THURSDAY, June 16, 1853.

Met according to adjournment. Prayer was offered by the Chaplain. The Journal of yesterday was read.

Mr. Rockwood, of Belchertown, presented a plan of representation in the House of Representatives.

Referred to the Committee of the Whole and ordered to be printed.

On motion of Mr. Hurlbut, of Sudbury, the Convention resolved itself into Committee of the Whole, for the purpose of considering the Resolves on the subject of the House of Representatives; and the President requested Mr. Wilson, of Natick, to take the chair.

Afterwards, Mr. Wilson reported, that the committee had made further progress in the consideration of the subject, but had come to no conclusion, and had instructed him to ask leave to sit again.

And leave was accordingly granted.

On motion of Mr. Morton, of Quincy, the Convention proceeded to the consideration of the Orders of the Day.

The first subject, being the motion to reconsider the vote on the passage of the third Resolve reported by the Committee on Secretary, Treasurer, &c., was passed over.

At half-past twelve o'clock, on motion of Mr. Hale, of Bridgewater,

The Convention adjourned.

AFTERNOON SESSION.

Met according to adjournment.

On motion of Mr. Wilson, of Natick,

Ordered, That the Committee on the Qualifications of Voters, be instructed to consider the expediency of incorporating into the Constitution the following provisions, to wit:—

1. No person shall be deemed to have lost his residence in the Commonwealth, by reason of his absence, either on business of this State or of the United States.

2. No idiot, or insane person, or persons convicted of any infamous crime, shall be entitled to vote in any election.

Mr. Walker, of North Brookfield, offered a Resolution, containing a plan of representation in the House of Representatives.

Referred to the Committee of the Whole and ordered to be printed.

On motion of Mr. Phinney, member for Chatham, the Convention resolved itself into Committee of the Whole, for the purpose of considering the Resolves on the subject of the House of Representatives; and the President requested Mr. Wilson, of Natick, to take the chair.

Afterwards, Mr. Wilson reported, that the committee had made further progress in the consideration of the subject, but had come to no conclusion, and had instructed him to ask leave to sit again.

And leave was accordingly granted.

On motion of Mr. Warner, of Wrentham, the Convention proceeded to the consideration of the Orders of the Day.

The first subject, being the motion to reconsider the vote on the passage of the third Resolve reported by the Committee on Secretary, Treasurer, &c., was, on motion of Mr. Eames, of Washington, laid upon the table.

And then, at half-past five o'clock, on motion of Mr. Churchill, of Milton,

The Convention adjourned.

FRIDAY, June 17, 1853.

Met according to adjournment. Prayer was offered by the Chaplain. The Journal of yesterday was read.

Mr. HOYT, of Deerfield, presented the Petition of N. T. Johnson and ninety-seven others, inhabitants of Deerfield, asking for a declaration in the Bill of Rights in favor of protection to fugitive slaves.

Referred to the Committee on the Bill of Rights.

On motion of Mr. WOOD, of Fitchburg, the Convention resolved itself into Committee of the Whole, for the purpose of considering the Resolves on the subject of the House of Representatives; and the President requested Mr. Wilson, of Natick, to take the chair.

Afterwards, Mr. WILSON reported, that the committee had made further progress in the consideration of the subject, but had come to no conclusion, and had instructed him to ask leave to sit again.

And leave was accordingly granted.

At one o'clock, on motion of Mr. GRISWOLD, member for Erving,

The Convention adjourned.

AFTERNOON SESSION.

Met according to adjournment.

Mr. OLIVER, of Lawrence, from the Committee on the Militia, submitted a Report, inexpedient to act upon the Petition of John P. Coburn and others.

Referred to the Committee of the Whole and ordered to be printed.

Mr. ABBOTT, of Lowell, from the Committee on Elections, to whom was referred the Memorials of Leonard M. Parker and James Russell, claiming seats in the Convention, submitted a Report on that subject.

Also, a Report, leave to withdraw, on the Memorial of John Sanborn, claiming a seat in the Convention.

Laid on the table and ordered to be printed.

Mr. WEEKS, of Harwich, presented the Petition of Silas Lamson and forty-four others, praying that the fundamental changes in government may be in accordance with the polity instituted by the Holy Apostles.

Referred to the Committee on the Bill of Rights.

On motion of Mr. BREED, of Lynn, the Convention resolved itself into Committee of the Whole, for the purpose of considering the Resolves on the subject of the House of Representatives; and the President requested Mr. Wilson, of Natick, to take the chair.

Afterwards, Mr. Wilson reported, that the committee had made further progress in the consideration of the subject, but had come to no conclusion, and had instructed him to ask leave to sit again.

And leave was accordingly granted.

Mr. Kinsman, of Newburyport, moved that the Convention resolve itself into Committee of the Whole, for the purpose of considering the Resolves on the subject of the House of Representatives, on Tuesday next, at ten o'clock; but the motion was rejected.

At a quarter before six o'clock, on motion of Mr. Putnam, of Wenham,

The Convention adjourned.

SATURDAY, June 18, 1853.

Met according to adjournment. Prayer was offered by the Chaplain. The Journal of yesterday was read.

On motion of Mr. Aldrich, of Barre,

Ordered, That the Committee on the Qualifications of Voters inquire into the expediency of providing in the Constitution, that no voter, during the time for holding any election at which he is entitled to vote, shall be compelled to perform military service, except in time of war or public danger, or to attend any court as suitor, juror, or witness; and no voter shall be subject to arrest under any civil process during his attendance at elections, or in going to and returning from them.

Mr. Butler, of Lowell, offered an Order, which was amended, on motion of Mr. Keyes, member for Abington, and adopted, as follows:

That the Secretary of the Commonwealth be requested to furnish a statement of the number of criminals pardoned by the executive annually for the last ten years, and the classes of crimes with which the persons pardoned were charged, and also a statement of the number of applications for pardon that have not been granted; and also, in each case where pardon has been granted, a statement of the original sentence, and the portion of the sentence that has been remitted.

Mr. Walker, of North Brookfield, from the Committee on the Qualifications of Voters, to whom was recommitted the third Resolve of the first series reported by that committee, with an amendment proposed thereto, submitted a Report, accompanied by Resolves on that subject.

Referred to the Committee of the Whole and ordered to be printed.

On motion of Mr. BUTLER, of Lowell, the Convention proceeded to the consideration of the Orders of the Day; the first subject being the final passage of the Resolves on the subject of the legislative department of the government.

Mr. HALLETT, member for Wilbraham, moved to amend the Resolves by substituting for the last paragraph of the proposed article of amendment, the following:—

The legislature shall by law establish the compensation of the members thereof, but no increase of such compensation which may be thereafter made, shall take effect during the term for which the members, at the time of such increase, shall have been elected; and no compensation shall be allowed for the attendance of members onger than for one hundred days at any one session.

After debate, Mr. KINGMAN, of West Bridgewater, moved the Previous Question; which was ordered, and

The amendment was adopted.

On motion of Mr. MORTON, of Andover,

Ordered, That when the question is taken on the final passage of the Resolves, it be taken by yeas and nays.

Mr. KEYES, member for Abington, called for a division of the question, and no objection being made, the question was put upon the adoption of the first two paragraphs of the article of amendment, and they were agreed to.

The question then being upon the adoption of the last paragraph,

The roll was called, and two hundred and forty-one members voted in the affirmative, and forty in the negative.

Those who voted in the affirmative are:—

Messrs. Josiah G. Abbott,
Benjamin P. Adams,
P. Emory Aldrich,
James B. Allen,
Parsons Allen,
John B. Alley,
Josiah Allis,
D. W. Alvord,
George Austin,
Samuel Ayres,
George S. Ball,
Sidney Bartlett,
Eliakim A. Bates,
Moses Bates, Jr.,
John Beal,
William Bennett, Jr.,

Messrs. Zephaniah Bennett,
Edward B. Bigelow,
Jacob Bigelow,
Francis W. Bird,
Gad O. Bliss,
William C. Bliss,
William S. Booth,
George S. Boutwell,
Ebenezer Bradbury,
William J. A. Bradford,
Hiram N. Breed,
Osmyn Brewster,
George N. Briggs,
Asa Bronson,
Artemas Brown,
Hammond Brown,

Messrs. Hiram C. Brown,
Frederick Brownell,
Patrick Bryant,
Asahel Buck,
Amos H. Bullen,
Anson Burlingame,
Benjamin F. Butler,
Henry Cady,
Timothy W. Carter,
Isaac Case,
Amariah Chandler,
Daniel E. Chapin,
J. McKean Churchill,
Ransom Clark,
Alpheus B. Clarke,
Stillman Clarke,
Jacob Coggin,
Nathaniel Cogswell,
Lansing J. Cole,
Sumner Cole,
Henry F. Cooledge,
George B. Crane,
Oliver S. Cressy,
Simeon Crittenden,
Joseph W. Cross,
Henry W. Cushman,
Thomas Cushman,
Simeon N. Cutler,
Isaac Davis,
Robert T. Davis,
Solomon Davis,
Henry L. Dawes,
Gilman Day,
Silas Dean,
Elijah S. Deming,
Hiram S. Denison,
Augustus Denton,
Samuel Duncan,
Bradish Dunham,
Philip Eames,
John M. Earle,
Peter Easland,
Elisha Edwards,
Samuel Edwards,
A. G. Farwell,
Sullivan Fay,
Lyman Fisk,
Ezekiel W. Fitch,
Aaron Foster,
Abram Foster,
Samuel Fowle,
James M. Freeman,
Charles A. French,

Messrs. Rodney French,
Samuel French,
Richard Frothingham, Jr.,
Luther Gale,
Johnson Gardner,
Elbridge Gates,
Wanton C. Gilbert,
Leonard Gooding,
Robert Gould,
Jason Goulding,
John W. Graves,
Jabez Green,
Josiah W. Griswold,
Whiting Griswold,
Charles B. Hall,
Benjamin F. Hallett,
A. B. Hammond,
Lyman W. Hapgood,
Seth Hapgood,
William Haskins,
Stephen E. Hawkes,
Isaac Hayden,
Ezra Heath, 2d,
Henry Hersey,
James Hewes,
William H. Hewes,
William Hinsdale,
Aaron Hobart,
Henry Hobart,
Edwin Hobbs,
Nathaniel Holder,
George Hood,
Foster Hooper,
Thomas Hopkinson,
William J. Hubbard,
Charles E. Hunt,
Charles P. Huntington,
Moses C. Hurlbut,
Abijah M. Ide, Jr.,
Samuel Jackson,
John Jacobs,
John Jenkins,
John Johnson,
Joseph Kingman,
Hiram Knight,
Jefferson Knight,
Joseph Knight,
William H. Knowlton,
Albert Knox,
John S. Ladd,
Luther Lawrence,
Job G. Lawton, Jr.,
Alden Leland,

Messrs. Abishai Lincoln,
Otis Little,
Tristram Littlefield,
Samuel K. Lothrop,
Samuel P. Loud,
John A. Lowell,
William P. Marble,
Laban Marcy,
Theophilus R. Marvin,
Reuben Meader,
Samuel Mixter,
James L. Monroe,
George Morey,
Marcus Morton, Jr.,
Hiram Nash,
Jonathan Nayson,
Charles Newman,
William Nichols,
Alfred Norton,
Nathan Orcutt,
Benjamin S. Orne,
E. Wing Packer,
Benjamin Paine,
Henry Paine,
Joel Parker,
Jonathan Parris,
Samuel C. Parsons,
John Partridge,
Nathaniel Peabody,
Jeremiah Pease, Jr.,
John Penniman,
Daniel A. Perkins,
Jesse Perkins,
Noah C. Perkins,
Charles Phelps,
Silvanus B. Phinney,
Jeremiah Pomroy,
James M. Pool,
Jonathan Preston,
Robert Rantoul,
Silas Rawson,
David Rice,
Daniel Richardson,
Nathan Richardson,
Samuel H. Richardson,
Elkanah Ring, Jr.,
Joseph M. Rockwood,
John Rogers,
David S. Ross,
James C. Royce,
George R. Sampson,
Amasa Sanderson,

Messrs. Luther Sheldon,
John Sherril,
Chester Sikes,
John W. Simonds,
Matthew Smith,
John Souther,
Samuel W. Spooner,
Eben H. Stacy,
Caleb Stetson,
Joseph L. Stevens, Jr.,
William Stevens,
Gideon Styles,
Charles Sumner,
Alanson Swain,
Thomas Talbot,
Ralph Taylor,
John W. Thomas,
Edmund P. Tileston,
Horatio W. Tilton,
Ephraim Tower,
David Turner,
David P. Turner,
William Tyler,
Orison Underwood,
Charles W. Upham,
Joel Viles,
Samuel B. Walcott,
Freeland Wallis,
Amasa Walker,
Andrew H. Ward,
Marshal Warner,
Samuel Warner, Jr.,
Gershom B. Weston,
William F. Wheeler,
Benjamin White,
George White,
Daniel S. Whitney,
Daniel Wilbur,
Joseph Wilbur,
Joel Wilder,
John H. Wilkins,
Henry Williams,
Henry Wilson,
Milo Wilson,
Willard Wilson,
Jonathan B. Winn,
Levi M. Winslow,
Charles C. Wood,
Otis Wood,
William H. Wood,
Ezekiel Wright.

Those who voted in the negative are:—

Messrs. Charles Allen, William Appleton, Joseph Barrows, Marcus Barrett, James M. Beebe, Francis Brinley, Josiah Childs, Rufus Choate, Benjamin F. Copeland, Leander Crosby, Francis B. Crowninshield, William Dehon, James C. Doane, James Easton, 2d, Joel Giles, John C. Gray, Artemas Hale, Nathan Hale, Elnathan P. Hathaway, George Hayward,

Messrs. Charles Heard, Samuel Houghton, Henry K. Hoyt, Giles C. Kellogg, Isaac Kendall, Edward L. Keyes, George H. Kuhn, Elbridge G. Morton, Andrew T. Nute, James W. Paige, Luther Richards, William Schouler, Charles Sherman, Increase Sumner, Arnold Taft, Charles R. Train, George B. Upton, Cyrus Weeks, Thomas Wetmore, J. B. Williams.

So the Resolve was finally passed, as follows:—

Resolved, That the Constitution be amended by striking out the first article in the first section of the first chapter of "Part the Second," and substituting therefor the following article:—

Article 1. The department of legislation shall be styled the General Court of Massachusetts. It shall consist of two branches, a Senate and a House of Representatives, each of which shall have a negative upon the other.

The legislature shall assemble every year, on the first Wednesday in January; and shall be dissolved on the day next preceding the first Wednesday in January following, without any proclamation or other act of the governor.

The legislature shall by law establish the compensation of the members thereof, but no increase of such compensation which may be thereafter made shall take effect during the term for which the members, at the time of such increase, shall have been elected; and no compensation shall be allowed for the attendance of members longer than for one hundred days at any one session.

On motion of Mr. Weston, of Duxbury, the hour for the adjournment of the forenoon session was extended, for this day, until two o'clock.

On motion of Mr. Bates, of Plymouth,

Ordered, That when the Convention adjourn, it adjourn to meet on Monday, at ten o'clock.

On motion of Mr. Bird, of Walpole, the Convention resolved itself into Committee of the Whole, for the purpose of considering the Report of the Committee on the Frame of Government, inexpedient to act upon the subject of an Order of June 3d, concerning the compensation of commissioners; and the President requested Mr. Nayson, of Amesbury, to take the chair.

Afterwards, Mr. Nayson reported, that it was the opinion of the committee that the Report ought to be accepted.

And it was accordingly accepted.

On motion of Mr. Wilson, of Natick, the Convention resolved itself into Committee of the Whole, for the purpose of considering the Report of the Committee on the Governor, inexpedient to act upon the subject of an Order of June 3d, relative to the pardoning power; and the President requested Mr. Bradbury, of Newton, to take the chair.

Afterwards, Mr. Bradbury reported, that the committee had made progress in the consideration of the subject, but had come to no conclusion, and had instructed him to ask leave to sit again.

And leave was accordingly granted.

At two o'clock, on motion of Mr. Wilson, of Natick,

The Convention adjourned.

MONDAY, June 20, 1853.

Met according to adjournment. Prayer was offered by the Chaplain. The Journal of Saturday was read.

Mr. Hooper, of Fall River, offered the following Resolutions:—

Resolved, That it is expedient so to revise the Constitution, that all vacancies occasioned by death, resignation, or other cause, among the judges of the supreme judicial court, shall be filled by an election at large throughout the State, for a term of ——— years, so arranged that two shall not be elected at the same time for the same term of years.

Resolved, That it is expedient so to revise the Constitution, as to require that provision shall be made, by law, for the election of all the judges and justices of inferior courts, in districts, for a term of years; and that so long as the court of common pleas shall continue as at present constituted, the judges thereof shall be elected in districts for a term of ——— years, so arranged that only one shall be elected in any one year, unless it shall be to fill a vacancy in an unexpired term, and the judge whose term of service is first to expire, shall be the chief justice of said court, till such expiration, so that each shall in turn be, successively, the chief justice.

Referred to the Committee of the Whole and ordered to be printed.

On motion of Mr. WILLIAMS, of Taunton,

Ordered, That the Special Committee appointed to consider the expediency of providing that the legislature hereafter shall issue no special act of incorporation for banking purposes, also consider the expediency of providing that the legislature shall have no power to authorize nor pass any law sanctioning the suspension of specie payment by any association or corporation issuing bank notes.

A communication was read from Mr. Kellogg, of West Stockbridge, asking leave of absence, to enable him to attend the funeral obsequies of his father-in-law, in a neighboring State.

Considered, and leave granted.

On motion of Mr. WILSON, of Natick, the Convention resolved itself into Committee of the Whole, for the purpose of considering the Report of the Committee on the Governor, inexpedient to act upon the subject of an Order of June 3d, relative to the pardoning power; and the President requested Mr. Bradbury, of Newton, to take the chair.

Afterwards, Mr. BRADBURY reported, that it was the opinion of the committee, that the Report ought to be accepted.

And it was acordingly accepted.

On motion of Mr. WILSON, of Natick, the Convention resolved itself into Committee of the Whole, for the purpose of considering the Resolve on the subject of the title of the governor; and the President requested Mr. WOOD, of Fitchburg, to take the chair.

Afterwards, Mr. WOOD reported, that it was the opinion of the committee, that the Resolve ought to pass.

And it was accordingly ordered to a second reading.

On motion of Mr. WILSON, of Natick, the Convention resolved itself into Committee of the Whole, for the purpose of considering the Resolve, and proposed part of the Constitution relative to the militia; and also the Report of the Committee on the Governor, inexpedient to act upon the subject of an Order of May 30th, relative to the governor's command of the militia; and the President requested Mr. Allen, of Worcester, to take the chair.

Afterwards, Mr. ALLEN reported, that the committee had made progress in the consideration of the subjects referred to them, but had come to no conclusion, and had instructed him to ask leave to sit again.

And leave was accordingly granted.

At one o'clock, the Convention adjourned.

AFTERNOON SESSION.

Met according to adjournment.

Mr. Wright, of Westford, presented the Petition of J. F. Evans and eighteen others, in aid of the Petition of John W. Le Barnes and others.

Referred to the Committee on the Bill of Rights.

The Order offered by Mr. Wilson, of Natick, instructing the committees to make their final Reports, was taken from the table, modified, and adopted, as follows:—

Ordered, That the several committees be instructed to make their final Reports on or before Monday next, the 27th instant.

Mr. Eames, of Washington, offered the following Order:—

Ordered, That on and after Wednesday next, the Convention meet at nine o'clock, A. M., until otherwise determined.

Laid over, under the rule.

Mr. Walker, of North Brookfield, from the Committee on the Qualifications of Voters, submitted a Report on the subject of an Order of June 10th, concerning a voting list or registry.

Referred to the Committee of the Whole and ordered to be printed.

On motion of Mr. Wilson, of Natick, the Convention resolved itself into Committee of the Whole, for the purpose of considering the Resolve on the subject of the militia, &c.; and the President requested Mr. Allen, of Worcester, to take the chair.

Afterwards, Mr. Boutwell, member for Berlin, chairman of the committee in the absence of Mr. Allen, reported, that the committee had considered the subject, and had instructed him to report as follows:—

That the first, second, third, fourth, fifth, seventh, eighth, ninth, eleventh, thirteenth, fourteenth, and fifteenth articles ought to pass without amendment.

That the sixth article ought to be amended by inserting the words, "a majority of" after the word "by" in the first line, (printed copy).

That the tenth article ought to be amended by inserting after the word "appoint" in the first line, the words, "and commission for one year, or until their successors shall be commissioned and qualified;" and by substituting the word "the" for the word "and" in the third line.

And that the twelfth article ought to be amended, by inserting the word "elective" after the word "several" in the first line, and by striking out all after the word "qualified" in the fourth line.

The amendments recommended by the committee, were concurred in, and the Resolve ordered to a second reading.

At seven o'clock, on motion of Mr. Briggs, of Pittsfield,

The Convention adjourned.

TUESDAY, June 21, 1853.

Met according to adjournment. Prayer was offered by the Chaplain. The Journal of yesterday was read.

On motion of Mr. Brinley, of Boston, the paper presented by him on the 13th inst., containing a plan of representation in the House of Representatives, was

Referred to the Committee of the Whole.

On motion of Mr. Boutwell, member for Berlin, the Resolves on the subject of the Council, and the Resolves on the subject of the lieutenant-governor, were

Taken from the table, and placed in the Orders of the Day.

On motion of Mr. Boutwell, member for Berlin,

Ordered, That a committee of —— members be appointed to reduce such amendments as have been, or may be, agreed upon, to the form in which it will be proper to submit the same to the people for ratification.

Mr. Jenks, of Boston, submitted a plan of representation in the House of Representatives.

Referred to the Committee of the Whole and ordered to be printed.

Mr. Oliver, of Lawrence, from the Committee on the Militia, submitted a Report, inexpedient to act upon the subject of an Order of June 15th, concerning the registration of citizens as a standing police.

Referred to the Committee of the Whole and ordered to be printed.

The Order offered yesterday, by Mr. Eames, of Washington, and laid over, was taken up, and adopted by a vote of eighty-nine in the affirmative, and sixty-five in the negative.

Mr. Wilson, of Natick, moved that in Committee of the Whole on the subject of the House of Representatives, debate on the pending question, viz.: the substitution of the Report of the Minority for the Report of the Majority, shall cease on Friday next, at eleven o'clock; but afterwards withdrew the motion.

On motion of Mr. Schouler, of Boston, the Convention resolved itself into Committee of the Whole, for the purpose of considering the Resolves on the subject of the House of Representatives; and the President requested Mr. Wilson, of Natick, to take the chair.

Afterwards, Mr. Wilson reported that the committee had made further progress in the consideration of the subject, but had come to no conclusion, and had instructed him to ask leave to sit again.

And leave was accordingly granted.

At one o'clock, on motion of Mr. Briggs, of Pittsfield,

The Convention adjourned.

AFTERNOON SESSION.

Met according to adjournment.

On motion of Mr. Morton, of Andover, the Convention resolved itself into Committee of the Whole, for the purpose of considering the Resolves on the subject of the House of Representatives; and the President requested Mr. Wilson, of Natick, to take the chair.

Afterwards, Mr. Wilson reported, that the committee had made further progress in the consideration of the subject, but had come to no conclusion, and had instructed him to ask leave to sit again.

And leave was accordingly granted.

On motion of Mr. Boutwell, member for Berlin, the Convention proceeded to the consideration of the Orders of the Day.

The Resolve on the subject of the title of the governor was finally passed, by a vote of one hundred and sixty-two in the affirmative, to eight in the negative, as follows:—

Resolved, That it is expedient to amend the Constitution, by abolishing the title of "His Excellency."

Mr. Hallett, member for Wilbraham, moved a reconsideration of the vote by which the Resolve was passed.

No objection being made, the motion was immediately considered, and rejected.

The Resolve and articles of amendment on the subject of the militia were next taken up.

Mr. SUMNER, member for Marshfield, offered the two following articles as a substitute for the series, viz.:—

1. The governor shall be commander-in-chief of the army and navy of the Commonwealth, and of the militia thereof, excepting when these forces shall be actually in the service of the United States; and shall have power to call out the same to aid in the execution of the laws, to suppress insurrection, and to repel invasion.

2. The appointment of the officers, and the training of the militia, shall be regulated in such manner as may hereafter be deemed expedient by the legislature; and all persons, who, from scruples of conscience, may be averse to bearing arms, shall be excused therefrom upon conditions prescribed by law.

Pending the question upon the adoption of the amendment,

At six o'clock, on motion of Mr. CHURCHILL, of Milton,

The Convention adjourned.

WEDNESDAY, June 22, 1853.

Met according to adjournment. Prayer was offered by the Chaplain. The Journal of yesterday was read.

Mr. DENTON, of Chelsea, presented the Petition of A. T. Willard and thirty-three others, legal voters of Chelsea, asking that all corporate bodies shall come under general laws.

Referred to the Committee of the Whole to which was referred the Report of the committee on that subject.

Mr. ROCKWELL, of Pittsfield, presented the Petition of Edward A. Newton and one hundred and fifteen others, citizens of Pittsfield, asking for certain amendments of the Constitution.

Referred to the several committees having the various subjects in charge.

Mr. SUMNER, member for Otis, offered the following Resolve:—

Resolved, That it is expedient to amend the Constitution, as follows:—

The tenure that all judicial officers shall have by law in their offices, excepting those concerning whom there is a different provision made in the Constitution, shall be ten years: *provided, however*, they may be removed from office by the executive, upon the address of a majority of the members present of each House of the legislature; but no address for the removal of any judicial officer shall pass either

House of the legislature until the causes of such removal are first stated, and entered on the journal of the House in which it shall originate, and a copy thereof served on the person in office, so that he may be admitted to a hearing in his defence before each of said Houses.

The present justices of the supreme judicial court and court of common pleas, shall hold their offices according to their respective commissions; but hereafter, when any vacancy in said offices shall occur, it shall be filled by election by the qualified voters of the Commonwealth, and the person elected shall be commissioned by the executive.

The legislature shall, by law, regulate the mode of elections for filling said offices, and of ascertaining who is chosen.

Former incumbents of either of said offices shall be eligible to re-election.

Mr. WILSON, of Natick, offered the following Resolve:—

Resolved, That it is proper and expedient so to amend the Constitution, as to provide that the justices of the supreme judicial court shall be appointed for the term of ten years, and the justices of such inferior courts as are, or may be established by law, for the term of seven years; said justices to be eligible to reappointment, but in no case to continue in office after attaining seventy years of age.

Severally referred to the Committee of the Whole to which was referred the Resolves on the subject of the judiciary, and ordered to be printed.

Mr. WALKER, of North Brookfield, from the Committee on the Qualifications of Voters, submitted a Report and Resolves on the subject of the loss of residence by absence on the business of the State, &c.

Referred to the Committee of the Whole and ordered to be printed.

On motion of Mr. WILSON, of Natick, the Convention resolved itself into Committee of the Whole, for the purpose of considering the Report of the Committee on the Militia, inexpedient to act upon the subject of the Petition of John P. Coburn and others; and the President requested Mr. Schouler, of Boston, to take the chair.

Afterwards, Mr. SCHOULER reported, that it was the opinion of the committee that the Report ought to be accepted.

The question being upon the acceptance of the Report,

Mr. WILSON, of Natick, moved that the Report be amended by striking out all after the word "Report," and inserting the following Resolution:—

Resolved, That no distinction shall ever be made, in the organization of the voluntary military companies of this Commonwealth, on account of color or race.

On motion of Mr. Wilson, the yeas and nays were ordered on the adoption of the amendment.

Without taking the question, the whole subject, on motion of Mr. Abbott, of Lowell, was

Laid upon the table.

On motion of Mr. Train, of Framingham, leave was granted to the Committee on the University at Cambridge, to sit during the morning session of the Convention.

On motion of Mr. Churchill, of Milton, the Convention proceeded to the consideration of the Orders of the Day.

The first subject was the Resolve on the subject of the militia.

The substitute offered yesterday by Mr. Sumner, member for Marshfield, was rejected by a vote of seventy-eight in the affirmative, to one hundred and twelve in the negative.

Mr. Hathaway, of Freetown, moved to amend the first of the proposed articles by striking from the second and third lines, (printed copy,) the words, "the laws of the Commonwealth may exempt," and inserting instead thereof the words, "may by law be exempted."

Also, by striking out in the fourth line the words, "the legislature may prescribe," and inserting instead thereof the words, "by law may be required."

Mr. Dana, member for Manchester, moved to recommit the Resolve to the Committee on the Militia.

Pending this question,

At one o'clock, the Convention adjourned.

AFTERNOON SESSION.

Met according to adjournment.

Mr. Greene, of Brookfield, presented the Petition of J. G. Forman and one hundred and one others, of Nantucket and Dukes Counties, in aid of the Petition of Mrs. Alcott, that women may be permitted to vote on the proposed amendments of the Constitution.

Referred to the Committee on the Qualifications of Voters.

Mr. Adams, of Lowell, offered an Order, providing that hereafter no member shall speak more than one hour on any question either in Committee of the Whole or in Convention, without leave.

Laid over, under the rule

The PRESIDENT appointed the following gentlemen as the committee under the Order offered by Mr. Boutwell, member for Berlin, providing for the appointment of a committee to reduce the amendments of the Constitution to the form in which it will be proper to submit the same to the people for ratification, viz. :—

Messrs. Boutwell, member for Berlin, Allen, of Worcester, Choate, of Boston, Hallett, member for Wilbraham, Morton, of Taunton, Abbott, of Lowell, Briggs, of Pittsfield, Dana, member for Manchester, Griswold, member for Erving, Parker, of Cambridge, Lord, of Salem, Oliver, of Lawrence, and Knowlton, of Worcester.

On motion of Mr. STETSON, of Braintree, the Orders of the Day were taken up; the first subject being the Resolve on the subject of the militia.

The motion of Mr. Dana, member for Manchester, to recommit the Resolve to the standing committee, was rejected.

The amendment offered by Mr. Hathaway, of Freetown, in the morning session, was adopted.

The Resolve was further amended, on motion of Mr. HATHAWAY, as follows:—

In the eleventh of the proposed articles, by striking from the third line, (printed copy,) the words "the legislature," and inserting instead thereof the word "law."

In the thirteenth article, by striking from the last line the words "the legislature may prescribe," and inserting instead thereof the words "may be prescribed by law."

In the fifteenth article, by striking from the fourth line the words "the legislature may by law prescribe," and inserting instead thereof the words "may be by law prescribed."

Mr. CHURCHILL, of Milton, moved the Previous Question, which was ordered;

And the Resolves were finally passed, by a vote of one hundred and seventy-three in the affirmative, and thirty-five in the negative, as follows:—

Resolved, That the following be adopted as part of the Constitution relating to the militia.

1. All citizens of this Commonwealth, liable to military service, except such as may by law be exempted, shall be enrolled in the militia, and held to perform such military duty as by law may be required.

2. The militia shall be divided into convenient divisions, brigades, regiments, squadrons, battalions and companies, and officers of appropriate rank and titles shall be elected to command them; and said

militia shall be made to conform, as nearly as practicable, to the discipline of the army of the United States.

3. The captains and subalterns of the militia shall be elected by a majority of the written votes of the members present and voting, of the respective companies, at a meeting legally convened therefor.

4. The field-officers of regiments, squadrons, and battalions, shall be elected by a majority of the written votes of the captains and subalterns present and voting, of the companies of the respective regiments, squadrons and battalions, at a meeting legally convened therefor.

5. The brigadier-generals shall be elected by a majority of the written votes of the field-officers and captains of companies present and voting, of the regiments, squadrons and battalions of the respective brigades, at a meeting legally convened therefor.

6. The major-generals shall be elected by a majority of the written votes of the brigadier-generals and field-officers, present and voting, of the brigades, regiments, squadrons and battalions of the respective divisions, at a meeting legally convened therefor.

7. The governor shall be the commander-in-chief of the army and navy of the State, and of the militia thereof, excepting when these forces shall be actually in the service of the United States; and shall have power to call out the same to aid in the execution of the laws, to suppress insurrection, and to repel invasion.

8. In all elections of military officers, no person entitled to vote as hereinbefore provided, shall be disqualified by reason of his being under twenty-one years of age.

9. If the electors of the several officers of the militia, hereinbefore named, shall refuse or neglect, for the space of three months after having been legally notified, to make elections, the governor shall appoint suitable persons to fill the vacant offices, advising with the Council, if the vacancy be that of a major-general; and with the major-general of the division in which the appointment is to be made, if the vacancy be of an officer of inferior grade.

10. The governor shall appoint and commission for one year, or until their successors shall be commissioned and qualified, the adjutant-general, the quartermaster-general, and such other general staff officers as shall be provided for by law. The major-generals, and brigadier-generals, and commandants of regiments, squadrons, and battalions, shall severally appoint such staff officers as shall be provided for by law for their respective commands.

11. The salary of the adjutant-general, of the quartermaster-general, and of such other general staff officers as may be provided

for by law, shall be fixed by law, and shall be in full for all services rendered by them in their several offices.

12. The several officers elective, hereinbefore named, shall be commissioned by the governor for the term of three years from the date of their commissions, and until their successors shall have been commissioned and qualified.

13. All non-commissioned officers, whether of staff or company, and all musicians, shall be appointed and warranted in such manner as may be prescribed by law.

14. The legislature shall prescribe the time and manner of convening the electors hereinbefore named, of conducting the elections, and of certifying to the governor the officers elect.

15. All officers commissioned or appointed to command in the militia, as well as all staff officers and musicians, may be removed from office by trial by court martial, or by such other modes as may be by law prescribed.

The Resolves on the subject of the Council, were, on motion of Mr. Boutwell, member for Berlin,

Laid upon the table.

On motion of Mr. Wilson, of Natick, the Committee of the Whole was discharged from the consideration of the Report, inexpedient to act upon the subject of an Order concerning the governor's command of the militia.

And the Report was recommitted to the Standing Committee on the Governor.

Mr. Wilson offered the following Resolution, which was referred to the same committee.

Resolved, That it is expedient to alter the Constitution of the Commonwealth by striking out the whole of article 7 of section 1, chapter 2.

On motion of Mr. Boutwell, member for Berlin, the Convention resolved itself into Committee of the Whole, for the purpose of considering the Report of the Special Committee, inexpedient to act upon the subject of loaning the credit of the State, and the President requested Mr. Boutwell, member for Berlin, to take the chair.

Afterwards, Mr. Boutwell reported, that the committee had made progress in the consideration of the subject, but had come to no conclusion, and had instructed him to ask leave to sit again.

And leave was accordingly granted.

Mr. Waters, of Millbury, moved an adjournment, but the motion was rejected by a vote of eighty-one in the affirmative, to ninety in the negative.

On motion of Mr. WILSON, of Natick, the Convention resolved itself into Committee of the Whole, for the purpose of considering the Report, inexpedient to act upon the subject of an Order of May 31st, concerning the election of senators in the congress of the United States by joint ballot of the two Houses of the legislature, and the President requested Mr. Cushman, of Bernardston, to take the chair.

Afterwards, Mr. CUSHMAN reported, that it was the opinion of the committee that the Report ought to be accepted.

And it was accordingly accepted.

On motion of Mr. WILSON, of Natick, the Convention resolved itself into Committee of the Whole, for the purpose of considering the Resolves reported by the Committee on the Qualifications of Voters, on the subject of the loss of residence by voters, and the President requested Mr. Briggs, of Pittsfield, to take the chair.

Afterwards, Mr. BRIGGS reported, that the committee had made progress in the consideration of the subject, but had come to no conclusion, and had instructed him to ask leave to sit again.

And leave was accordingly granted.

At a quarter past six o'clock, on motion of Mr. DUNCAN, of Williamstown,

The Convention adjourned.

THURSDAY, June 23, 1853.

Met according to adjournment. Prayer was offered by the Chaplain. The Journal of yesterday was read.

The Order offered yesterday by Mr. Adams, of Lowell, and laid over, was taken up and adopted, by a vote of one hundred and fourteen in the affirmative to forty in the negative.

Mr. BRIGGS, of Pittsfield, from the Committee on the Encouragement of Literature, having under consideration an Order concerning the propriety of requiring that voters shall be able to read the Constitution in the English language, submitted a Report, asking to be discharged from the consideration of the Order, and recommending that it be referred to the Committee on the Qualifications of Voters.

The Report was accepted, and the Order so referred.

On motion of Mr. WILSON, of Natick, the Convention resolved itself into Committee of the Whole, for the purpose of considering the Resolve reported by the Special Committee on the subject of general laws for corporations, and the President requested Mr. Sumner, member for Otis, to take the chair.

Afterwards, Mr. SUMNER reported, that the committee had made progress in the consideration of the subject, but had come to no conclusion, and had instructed him to ask leave to sit again.

And leave was accordingly granted.

On motion of Mr. WILSON, of Natick, the Convention resolved itself into Committee of the Whole, for the purpose of considering the Resolves on the subject of the House of Representatives, and the President requested Mr. Wilson, of Natick, to take the chair.

Afterwards, Mr. WILSON reported, that the committee had made further progress in the consideration of the subject, but had come to no conclusion, and had instructed him to ask leave to sit again.

And leave was accordingly granted.

At twenty minutes before one o'clock, on motion of Mr. BREED, of Lynn,

The Convention adjourned.

AFTERNOON SESSION.

Met according to adjournment.

On motion of Mr. EARLE, of Worcester,

Ordered, That the Committee on the Secretary, Treasurer, &c., consider the expediency of a constitutional provision for the limitation of the terms of service of justices and clerks of police courts, and for their election by the voters of the towns or cities respectively in which they may be located.

On motion of Mr. WILSON, of Natick,

Ordered, That the Secretary of the Commonwealth be requested to furnish a list of the justices of the supreme court, and also of the court of common pleas, since the adoption of the Constitution, specifying in each case the time of the appointment, the length of the time in office, and whether the incumbent resigned or died in office.

Mr. WALKER, of North Brookfield, from the Committee on the Qualifications of Voters, submitted a Report, inexpedient to act upon the subject of an Order providing that voters shall have the ability to read and write, and an Order concerning the forfeiture of the right to vote in case of voluntary neglect.

Referred to the Committee of the Whole and ordered to be printed.

Mr. GARDNER, of Seekonk, and Mr. HUNTINGTON, of Northampton, severally submitted Resolves containing each a plan of representation in the House of Representatives.

Referred to the Committee of the Whole having that subject in charge, and ordered to be printed.

Mr. SCHOULER, of Boston, submitted a Resolve on the same subject.

Referred to the same committee and ordered to be printed.

On motion of Mr. KNOWLTON, of Worcester, the Convention resolved itself into Committee of the Whole, for the purpose of considering the Resolves on the subject of the House of Representatives, and the President requested Mr. Wilson, of Natick, to take the chair.

Afterwards, Mr. WILSON reported, that the committee had made further progress in the consideration of the subject, but had come to no conclusion, and had instructed him to ask leave to sit again.

And leave was accordingly granted.

An amendment to the Resolves on the subject of the House of Representatives, submitted in Committee of the Whole by Mr. Butler, of Lowell, was ordered to be printed.

At six o'clock, on motion of Mr. BRIGGS, of Pittsfield,

The Convention adjourned.

FRIDAY, June 24, 1853.

Met according to adjournment. Prayer was offered by the Chaplain. The Journal of yesterday was read.

Mr. HOUGHTON, of Sterling, offered the following Order:—

Ordered, That the pay roll for travel and attendance of members be made up and paid, and that the Convention adjourn to meet again on the second Tuesday of September next, at ten o'clock, A. M., and no member shall be entitled to be paid for more than one travel, during the whole term of the Convention.

Laid over, under the rule.

Mr. FAY, of Southborough, from the Committee on Leave of Absence, submitted a Report granting leave of absence to Mr. Train, of Framingham, for two weeks, and to Mr. Hoyt, of Deerfield, for four days.

The Report was accepted, and leave of absence granted.

Mr. Earle, of Worcester, presented a plan of representation in the House of Representatives.

Referred to the Committee of the Whole and ordered to be printed.

On motion of Mr. Breed, of Lynn, the Convention resolved itself into Committee of the Whole, for the purpose of considering the Resolves on the subject of the House of Representatives; and in the absence of Mr. Wilson, of Natick, the President requested Mr. Walker, of North Brookfield, to take the chair.

Afterwards, Mr. Wilson, who had resumed his place as chairman of the committee, reported, that the committee had made further progress in the consideration of the subject, but had come to no conclusion, and had instructed him to ask leave to sit again.

And leave was accordingly granted.

A plan of representation in the House of Representatives, submitted in Committee of the Whole by Mr. Stetson, of Braintree, was ordered to be printed.

At one o'clock, the Convention adjourned.

AFTERNOON SESSION.

Met according to adjournment.

On motion of Mr. Hurlbut, of Sudbury, the Convention resolved itself into Committee of the Whole, for the purpose of considering the Resolves on the subject of the House of Representatives, and the President requested Mr. Wilson, of Natick, to take the chair.

Afterwards, Mr. Wilson reported, that the committee had made further progress in the consideration of the subject, but had come to no conclusion, and had instructed him to ask leave to sit again.

And leave was accordingly granted.

At a quarter past six o'clock, on motion of Mr. Knight, of Peru,

The Convention adjourned.

SATURDAY, June 25, 1853.

Met according to adjournment. Prayer was offered by the Chaplain. The Journal of yesterday was read.

On motion of Mr. Stevens, of Gloucester,

Ordered, That the Committee on the House of Representatives be requested to consider the expediency of so modifying article 3 of section 3, chapter 1, of the Constitution, that towns and districts may have the right to be represented by any citizens of the Commonwealth.

Mr. Chapin, of Springfield, and Mr. Thompson, of Charlestown, severally offered Resolves, containing each a plan of representation in the House of Representatives.

Referred to the Committee of the Whole and ordered to be printed.

Mr. Knowlton, of Worcester, from the Committee on the University at Cambridge, submitted a Report and Resolutions on that subject.

Referred to the Committee of the Whole and ordered to be printed.

The Order offered yesterday by Mr. Houghton, of Sterling, providing for an adjournment until September, was taken up for consideration.

Mr. Houghton moved that the consideration of the subject be postponed until Wednesday next, at eleven o'clock.

Mr. Eames, of Washington, moved that the motion be laid upon the table.

The motion of Mr. Eames was rejected, and,

The Previous Question having been moved, by Mr. Adams, of Lowell, and ordered by the Convention,

The Order was rejected, by a vote of thirteen in the affirmative to one hundred and fifty-four in the negative.

Mr. Wheeler, of Lincoln, moved that when the Convention adjourn, it adjourn to meet on Monday, at ten o'clock.

Mr. Eames, of Washington, moved to amend by substituting the hour of nine.

The amendment was adopted; but the vote was afterwards reconsidered, and the amendment was rejected.

The motion of Mr. Wheeler was then agreed to.

On motion of Mr. Earle, of Worcester,

Ordered, That the rule requiring an adjournment of the forenoon sessions at one o'clock, be rescinded for this day.

On motion of Mr. Cushman, of Bernardston, the Convention resolved itself into Committee of the Whole, for the purpose of considering the Resolves on the subject of the House of Representatives; and the President requested Mr. Wilson, of Natick, to take the chair.

Afterwards, Mr. Wilson reported, that the committee had made further progress in the consideration of the subject, but had come to no conclusion, and had instructed him to ask leave to sit again.

And leave was accordingly granted.

Mr. BUTLER, of Lowell, moved that in Committee of the Whole on the subject of the House of Representatives, debate shall cease on the various propositions, at eleven o'clock on Tuesday next.

But the motion was rejected by a vote of seventy-two in the affirmative to one hundred and four in the negative.

Mr. BEACH, of Springfield, moved that the Committee of the Whole having in charge the subject of the House of Representatives, be discharged from its further consideration.

Mr. THOMPSON, of Charlestown, moved to lay this motion upon the table.

Pending this question,

At half past one o'clock, on motion of Mr. WHITE, of Quincy,

The Convention adjourned.

MONDAY, June 27, 1853.

Met according to adjournment. Prayer was offered by the Chaplain. The Journal of Saturday was read.

Mr. THOMPSON, of Charlestown, presented a paper containing a table designed to accompany the Resolve offered by him on the subject of the House of Representatives.

Ordered to be printed.

Mr. EAMES, of Washington, presented the Petition of Josiah Francis and one hundred and ten others, citizens of Pittsfield, in aid of town representation.

Referred to the Committee of the Whole and ordered to be printed.

On motion of Mr. CUSHMAN, of Bernardston,

Ordered, That the Committee on the Pay Roll be requested to report a Resolve for the payment of the Chaplain, and other officers of the Convention.

Mr. HALL, of Haverhill, from the Committee on the Secretary, Treasurer, &c., submitted a request for further time for the consideration of the subject of electing justices of the peace by the people.

The request was considered, and further time granted.

The same gentleman, from the same committee, submitted a Report and Resolve, inexpedient to amend the Constitution so as to require that every person holding an office in or under the State government, shall retire therefrom at the expiration of six years' service.

Referred to the Committee of the Whole and ordered to be printed.

On motion of Mr. LIVERMORE, of Cambridge, the Convention proceeded to the consideration of the Orders of the Day; the first subject being the motion of Mr. Beach, of Springfield, that the Committee of the Whole on the House of Representatives be discharged from the further consideration of that subject.

The motion of Mr. Thompson, that the proposition of Mr. Beach be laid upon the table, was agreed to.

On motion of Mr. HALL, of Haverhill, the Convention resolved itself into Committee of the Whole, for the purpose of considering the Report of the Committee on the Militia, inexpedient to act upon the subject of an Order of June 15th, providing for the registration of citizens as a police force; and the President requested Mr. Huntington, of Northampton, to take the chair.

Afterwards, Mr. HUNTINGTON reported, that it was the opinion of the committee that the Report ought to be accepted.

And it was accordingly accepted.

On motion of Mr. WILSON, of Natick, the Convention resolved itself into Committee of the Whole, for the purpose of considering the Report of the Committee on the Qualifications of Voters, inexpedient to act upon the subject of an Order of May 30th, concerning the expediency of requiring, that ability to read and write shall be a requisite for the exercise of the elective franchise, and of the forfeiture of the right to vote in case of voluntary neglect to exercise that right, and the President requested Mr. Griswold, member for Erving, to take the chair.

Afterwards, Mr. GRISWOLD reported, that it was the opinion of the committee that the Report ought to be accepted.

And it was accordingly accepted.

On motion of Mr. WILSON, of Natick, the Convention resolved itself into Committee of the Whole, for the purpose of considering the Resolve reported by the Committee on the Qualifications of Voters, on the subject of a voting list or registry, and the President requested Mr. Stetson, of Braintree, to take the chair.

Afterwards, Mr. STETSON reported, that it was the opinion of the committee that the Resolve ought to pass.

And it was accordingly ordered to a second reading.

On motion of Mr. CUSHMAN, of Bernardston, the Convention resolved itself into Committee of the Whole, for the purpose of considering the Resolves reported by the Special Committee on the subject of a general constitutional provision for the government of corporations, and in the absence of Mr. Sumner, member for Otis, the

President requested Mr. Keyes, member for Abington, to take the chair.

Afterwards, Mr. Keyes reported, that the committee had made progress in the consideration of the subject, but had come to no conclusion, and had instructed him to ask leave to sit again.

And leave was accordingly granted.

At one o'clock, on motion of Mr. Whitney, of Conway,

The Convention adjourned.

AFTERNOON SESSION.

Met according to adjournment.

Mr. Allen, of Worcester, from the Committee on the Frame of Government, submitted a Report and Resolve on the subject of taking the census of the State in the year 1855, and every tenth year thereafter.

Also, a Report, inexpedient to act on the subject of remuneration to persons tried for offences against the State, and acquitted.

Also, a Report, inexpedient to act on the subject of an Order of June 3d, on the expediency of securing to women, by constitutional provision, their property acquired by devise, inheritance, or otherwise.

Also, a Report, inexpedient to act on the subject of an Order of May 17th, respecting the reference, by the legislature to the people, of legislative acts, for approval or rejection.

Also, a Report, inexpedient to act upon the subject of the Petition of Silas Lamson and others.

Mr. Morton, of Taunton, from the Committee on the Judiciary Power, submitted a Report, inexpedient to act upon the subject of an Order of June 6th, relating to granting the subject "a certain remedy in law, prompt and without delay;" and on an Order of June 6th, relating to the codification of the laws.

Mr. Butler, of Lowell, from the Special Committee on Elections by Plurality, submitted a Report on that subject.

Mr. Butler, of Lowell, from the Committee on Oaths and Subscriptions, submitted a Report and Resolves on that subject.

Also, a Resolve on the subject of the incompatibility of offices.

Also, a Resolve on the subject of the enacting style.

Also, a Resolve, inexpedient to act on the subject of a constitutional provision relative to exempting a certain amount of property on *mesne* process.

Also, a Resolve, inexpedient to act on the subject of an Order concerning the propriety of exempting certain persons from taking the oath or affirmation ordinarily required.

Also, a Resolve, inexpedient to act on the subject of an Order concerning the election of officers of banks to office.

Mr. NAYSON, of Amesbury, from the Committee on Amendments of the Constitution and Enrolment, submitted a Report and Resolves on the subject of future amendments of the Constitution.

These Reports and Resolves were severally referred to the Committee of the Whole, and ordered to be printed.

Mr. BUTLER, of Lowell, presented a paper, containing a table designed to accompany his plan of representation, which was ordered to be printed.

On motion of Mr. ALLEN, of Worcester, the Committee on the Frame of Government were granted further time to enable them to report on the subjects remaining in their hands.

On motion of Mr. BUTLER, of Lowell, the Convention resolved itself into Committee of the Whole, for the purpose of considering the Resolves on the subject of the House of Representatives, and the President requested Mr. Wilson, of Natick, to take the chair.

Afterwards, Mr. WILSON reported, that the committee had made further progress in the consideration of the subject, but had come to no conclusion, and had instructed him to ask leave to sit again.

And leave was accordingly granted.

On motion of Mr. KEYES, member for Abington, the Convention resolved itself into Committee of the Whole, for the purpose of considering the Resolves reported by a Special Committee, in favor of a constitutional provision for the creation of corporations, and the President requested Mr. Keyes, member for Abington, to take the chair.

Afterwards, Mr. KEYES reported the Resolve to the Convention, with the following amendment:—

Striking out all after the word "laws," in the third line, and inserting instead thereof, the words, "in all cases when the object of such corporation is attainable under the same, and where provision is thus made by general laws, no corporation shall be formed by special act."

The amendment was agreed to.

On motion of Mr. BUTLER, of Lowell, the yeas and nays were ordered on the question of passing the Resolve to a second reading.

Afterwards, on motion of Mr. WHITNEY, of Conway, the vote ordering the yeas and nays was reconsidered; and

On motion of Mr. BUTLER, the further consideration of the subject was postponed until to-morrow.

Mr. DAVIS, of Worcester, offered the following Resolution, as a substitute for the one just previously under consideration, and it was ordered to be printed, as follows:—

Resolved, That it is expedient to incorporate into the Constitution a provision, that corporations shall not be created by special act when the object of the incorporation shall be attainable under general laws.

On motion of Mr. WILSON, of Natick, the Convention resolved itself into Committee of the Whole, for the purpose of considering the Resolves reported by the Committee on the Qualifications of Voters, viz.: 1st, that the Constitution be so amended as to provide, that no person shall be deemed to have lost his residence in this Commonwealth, by reason of his absence while on the business of this State, or of the United States; and 2d, that no idiot or insane person, or person convicted of a felony, unless pardoned and restored to the right of suffrage, shall be entitled to vote in any election, and the President requested Mr. Frothingham, of Charlestown, to take the chair.

Afterwards, Mr. FROTHINGHAM reported, that it was the opinion of the committee that the Resolves ought not to pass.

A division of the question was called for, and the question being taken upon the first resolution, it was rejected.

Mr. HATHAWAY, of Freetown, moved that the second resolution be amended, by striking out the words "idiot or insane person," and inserting instead thereof, the words, "pauper or person under guardianship;" but afterwards withdrew the amendment.

A motion to postpone the subject until to-morrow, was also made, but withdrawn; and

The Previous Question having been moved by Mr. WEEKS, of Harwich, and ordered by the Convention,

The second Resolution was also rejected.

On motion of Mr. WILSON, of Natick, the Convention resolved itself into Committee of the Whole, for the purpose of considering the Report of the Special Committee, inexpedient to act upon the subject of loaning the credit of the State, and the President requested Mr. Boutwell, member for Berlin, to take the chair.

Afterwards, Mr. BOUTWELL reported, that the committee had made further progress in the consideration of the subject, but had come to no conclusion, and had instructed him to ask leave to sit again.

And leave was accordingly granted.

At ten minutes past six o'clock, on motion of Mr. UNDERWOOD, of Milford,

The Convention adjourned.

TUESDAY, June 28, 1853.

Met according to adjournment. Prayer was offered by the Chaplain. The Journal of yesterday was read.

Mr. Greene, of Brookfield, presented the Petitions of Betsey T. Heywood and ninety-two others, women of Milford, and Abby H. Price and forty-five others, women of Hopedale, in aid of the Petition of Mrs. Alcott, that women may be permitted to vote on the proposed alterations of the Constitution.

Referred to the Committee on the Qualifications of Voters.

Mr. Davis, of Worcester, from the Committee on the subject of the Governor, submitted a Report and Resolve, in favor of amending the Constitution by striking out the whole of article 7, in section 1, chapter 2.

Referred to the Committee of the Whole and ordered to be printed.

On motion of Mr. Walker, of North Brookfield, the Convention proceeded to the consideration of the Orders of the Day.

The Resolve on the subject of a voting list was read a second time, and finally passed, as follows:—

Resolved, That the Constitution be so amended, as to require a voting list or registry, and to protect presiding officers in adhering thereto.

The second subject in the Orders of the Day, viz.: the Resolve on the subject of general laws for corporations, was passed over.

On motion of Mr. Wilson, of Natick, the Convention resolved itself into Committee of the Whole, for the purpose of considering the Report, inexpedient to act on the subject of loaning the credit of the State, and the President requested Mr. Boutwell, member for Berlin, to take the chair.

Afterwards, Mr. Boutwell reported, that the committee had made further progress in the consideration of the subject, but had come to no conclusion, and had instructed him to ask leave to sit again.

And leave was accordingly granted.

Mr. Morton, of Taunton, offered the following Resolution:—

Resolved, That the Committee of the Whole be discharged from the further consideration of the Report of the Committee, and that the same be recommitted, with instructions to report a Resolve limiting the power of the legislature to create debt and incur liabilities on behalf of the State.

At one o'clock, the Convention adjourned.

AFTERNOON SESSION.

Met according to adjournment.

Mr. MORTON, of Taunton, modified his Resolution offered in the morning session, so as to read as follows:—

Resolved, That the Committee of the Whole to whom was referred the Report of the Committee on the State Credit, be discharged from the further consideration of that subject, and that the same be referred to a select committee, with instructions to report a Resolve limiting the power of the legislature to incur debts and create liabilities in behalf of the State.

On motion of Mr. WHITNEY, of Boylston, sustained by a vote of one hundred and four in the affirmative to fifty-one in the negative,

The Resolution was laid upon the table.

The Orders of the Day were then laid upon the table, and

On motion of Mr. BUTLER, of Lowell, the Convention resolved itself into Committee of the Whole, for the purpose of considering the Resolves on the subject of the House of Representatives, and the President requested Mr. Wilson, of Natick, to take the chair.

Afterwards, Mr. WILSON reported the Resolves to the Convention, with an amendment, as follows:—

Striking out all after the word "Resolved," and substituting therefor, the following, viz.:—

That the Constitution be so revised and altered, that the representation of the Commonwealth be apportioned as follows:—

Every town of a less number than one thousand inhabitants, shall be entitled to five representatives, in each ten years, with an additional representative for the year when the valuation of estates shall be settled.

Any two of such towns may, by a vote of a major part of the legal voters of each, at legal meetings thereof, unite together in a district, which shall be entitled to a representative each year, and which shall continue for a period of not less than five years, excepting the year in which the valuation of estates is settled.

Every town of one thousand inhabitants, and of less than four thousand, shall be entitled to one representative each year.

Every town of four thousand inhabitants, and of less than eight thousand, shall be entitled to two representatives each year.

Every town of eight thousand inhabitants, and of less than twelve thousand, shall be entitled to three representatives each year.

Every city or town of twelve thousand inhabitants, shall be entitled to four representatives each year.

Every city or town of over twelve thousand inhabitants, shall be entitled to as many additional representatives in each year as the number of times five thousand may be contained in the additional number of the inhabitants thereof.

Resolved, That this apportionment be based upon the census of 1850, until a new census be taken.

Resolved, That the Senate, at its first session after this Constitution shall have been adopted, and at its first session after the next State census shall have been taken, and at its first session next after each decennial State census thereafterwards, shall apportion the number of representatives to which each town and city shall be entitled, and shall cause the same to be seasonably published; and in all apportionments after the first, the numbers which shall entitle any city or town to two, three, four or more representatives, shall be so adjusted, in proportion, as hereinbefore provided, that the whole number of representatives, exclusive of those which may be returned by towns of less than one thousand inhabitants, and of the towns which shall hereafter be created with power to send one representative, shall never exceed three hundred and seventy.

Resolved, That no town hereafter be incorporated with a privilege of representation as such, containing less than fifteen hundred inhabitants.

Resolved, That each city in this Commonwealth shall be divided, by such means as the legislature may provide, into districts of contiguous territory, as nearly equal in population as may be, for the election of representatives, which districts shall not be changed oftener than once in five years: *provided, however*, that no one district shall be entitled to elect more than three representatives.

Mr. Huntington, of Northampton, moved to amend the amendment of the Committee of the Whole, by striking from the first paragraph the words "one thousand," and inserting instead thereof, the words "twelve hundred."

And also, by making the same alteration in the third paragraph.

And, pending the question upon this proposition,

On motion of Mr. Huntington, the subject was postponed until to-morrow.

On motion of Mr. Livermore, of Cambridge, the Resolve reported by the Committee on the Pay Roll, on the subject of the compensation of the members of the Convention, was taken from the table and considered.

On motion of Mr. LIVERMORE, the Resolve was amended by substituting the word "requested" for the word "authorized," in the twelfth line.

On motion of Mr. MORTON, of Fairhaven, the Resolve was further amended, by striking out the words, "*provided*, that in no case shall any member receive more than two hundred dollars for attendance."

Mr. HOOD, of Lynn, moved further to amend the Resolve, by substituting the word "two" for the word "three," in the third line.

And also moved, that when the question is taken upon the amendment, it be taken by yeas and nays.

But one-fifth of the members not voting in the affirmative, the yeas and nays were not ordered.

Afterwards, Mr. DANA, member for Manchester, again moved for the yeas and nays on the amendment, and they were ordered.

Mr. HOOD then withdrew his amendment,

Which was renewed by Mr. BIRD, of Walpole,

And, upon his motion, the yeas and nays were again ordered.

Mr. THOMAS, of Weymouth, moved an adjournment; but the motion was rejected.

The roll being called, fifty-four members voted for the amendment, and one hundred and ninety-two against it.

So it was rejected.

Those who voted in the affirmative are:—

Messrs. Parsons Allen,
John B. Alley,
D. W. Alvord,
Samuel Ayres,
Moses Bates, Jr.,
William Bennett, Jr.,
Francis W. Bird,
George S. Boutwell,
Sewell Boutwell,
Hiram N. Breed,
Hammond Brown,
Hiram C. Brown,
Rufus Bullock,
Benjamin F. Butler,
Chester W. Chapin,
Charles E. Cook,
George W. Crockett,
F. B. Crowninshield,
Henry W. Cushman,
Isaac Davis,
Elijah S. Deming,

Messrs. Lyman Fisk,
James M. Freeman,
Elbridge Gates,
Wanton C. Gilbert,
Joel Giles,
Whiting Griswold,
Nathan Hale,
Seth Hapgood,
George Hood,
Martin Howard,
Moses C. Hurlbut,
William James,
William P. Marble,
Simeon Merritt,
Marcus Morton, Jr.,
Charles Newman,
E. Wing Packer,
Sylvanus B. Phinney,
Luther Richards,
Samuel H. Richardson,
John W. Simonds,

Messrs. Samuel W. Spooner,
William Stevens,
John W. Thomas,
Orison Underwood,
Amasa Walker,
Samuel Warner, Jr.,
Messrs. Gershom B. Weston,
William F. Wheeler,
James S. Whitney,
Charles C. Wood,
Nathaniel Wood,
Otis Wood.

Those who voted in the negative are :—

Messrs. Benjamin P. Adams,
P. Emory Aldrich,
James B. Allen,
Josiah Allis,
Robert Andrews,
William Aspinwall,
David C. Atwood,
George Austin,
Hillel Baker,
Alvah Ballard,
Alpheus Bancroft,
Joseph Barrows,
Russel Bartlett,
Erasmus D. Beach,
John Beal,
Jacob Bigelow,
Gad O. Bliss,
William C. Bliss,
William S. Booth,
William J. A. Bradford,
Milton P. Braman,
Osmyn Brewster,
Francis Brinley,
George N. Briggs,
Adolphus F. Brown,
Joseph Brownell,
Patrick Bryant,
Cephas C. Bumpus,
Anson Burlingame,
Henry Cady,
Timothy W. Carter,
Isaac Case,
Amariah Chandler,
J. McKean Churchill,
Ransom Clark,
Alpheus B. Clarke,
William Cleverly,
Nathaniel Cogswell,
Lansing J. Cole,
Sumner Cole,
Ithamar Conkey,
Henry F. Cooledge,
Benjamin F. Copeland,
Simeon Crittenden,
Messrs. Joseph W. Cross,
Wilber Curtis,
Richard H. Dana, Jr.,
Ebenezer Davis,
Solomon Davis,
Gilman Day,
Hiram S. Denison,
Augustus Denton,
Alexander De Witt,
James C. Doane,
Moses Dorman,
Samuel Duncan,
Bradish Dunham,
John M. Durgin,
Philip Eames,
Peter Easland,
Calvin D. Eaton,
Elisha Edwards,
Samuel Edwards,
Homer Ely,
Joseph M. Ely,
Sullivan Fay,
Ezekiel W. Fitch,
Aaron Foster,
Abram Foster,
Samuel Fowle,
Samuel French,
Luther Gale,
Washington Gilbert,
Jason Goulding,
John C. Gray,
Jabez Green,
Josiah W. Griswold,
B. F. Hallett,
A. B. Hammond,
Lyman W. Hapgood,
Phineas Harmon,
George Hayward,
Charles Heard,
Ezra Heath, 2d,
Samuel Henry,
George S. Hillard,
Edwin Hobbs,
Nathaniel Holder,

Messrs. Samuel Houghton,
Abraham H. Howland,
William J. Hubbard,
Charles E. Hunt,
William Hunt,
Asahel Huntington,
Charles P. Huntington,
George H. Huntington,
Samuel A. Hurlburt,
Benjamin D. Hyde,
Samuel Jackson,
John Jenkins,
Samuel H. Jenks,
John Johnson,
Giles C. Kellogg,
Martin R. Kellogg,
Isaac Kendall,
Edward L. Keyes,
Joseph Kingman,
Hiram Knight,
Joseph Knight,
Charles L. Knowlton,
William H. Knowlton,
Otis Little,
Tristram Littlefield,
Isaac Livermore,
Justin E. Loomis,
Samuel P. Loud,
John A. Lowell,
Laban Marcy,
Abijah P. Marvin,
Theophilus R. Marvin,
Seth Miller, Jr.,
Samuel Mixter,
James L. Monroe,
George Morey,
Elbridge G. Morton,
William S. Morton,
Hiram Nash,
William Nichols,
Daniel Noyes,
Andrew T. Nute,
Nathan Orcutt,
Charles Osgood,
Benjamin Paine,
Henry Paine,
Adolphus G. Parker,
Samuel D. Parker,
Samuel C. Parsons,
John Partridge,
John Penniman,
Daniel A. Perkins,

Messrs. Charles Phelps,
Henry Pierce,
William C. Plunkett,
Jeremiah Pomroy,
Silas Rawson,
Sampson Reed,
David Rice,
Elkanah Ring, Jr.,
Joseph M. Rockwood,
David S. Ross,
James C. Royce,
Chester Sanderson,
John Sargent,
Charles Sherman,
John Sherril,
Chester Sikes,
John S. Sleeper,
Matthew Smith,
Melzar Sprague,
Caleb Stetson,
Charles G. Stevens,
Granville Stevens,
Alfred L. Strong,
Charles Sumner,
Alanson Swain,
Ralph Taylor,
Joseph Thayer,
Charles Thompson,
Edmund P. Tileston,
Horatio W. Tilton,
Ephraim Tower,
David Turner,
David P. Turner,
William Tyler,
Freeland Wallis,
Samuel Walker,
Andrew H. Ward,
Marshal Warner,
Asa H. Waters,
Cyrus Weeks,
Thomas Wetmore,
Benjamin White,
George White,
Joel Wilder,
Ezra Wilkinson,
J. B. Williams,
Henry Wilson,
Milo Wilson,
Jonathan B. Winn,
Levi M. Winslow,
Josiah B. Woods,
Ezekiel Wright.

Mr. Spooner, of Warwick, moved to amend by substituting two dollars and a half for three dollars a day, but the motion was rejected.

On motion of Mr. Thompson, of Charlestown, the yeas and nays had been ordered upon the question of the final passage of the Resolve; but no objection being made,

The calling of the roll was dispensed with, and the Resolve was finally passed, as follows:—

Resolved, That there be paid out of the treasury of this Commonwealth, to the members of this Convention, respectively, three dollars for each and every day's attendance, and two dollars for every ten miles' travel from their respective places of abode, once during the session; and to the President three dollars a day, in addition to his pay as a member; and the governor is hereby requested to draw his warrant accordingly, on the treasurer, on an order of this Convention.

At half past six o'clock, on motion of Mr. Fay, of Southborough,
The Convention adjourned.

WEDNESDAY, June 29, 1853.

Met according to adjournment. Prayer was offered by the Chaplain. The Journal of yesterday was read.

Mr. Bates, of Plymouth, from the Committee on the subject of reporting and publishing the Debates and Proceedings of the Convention, submitted the following Resolution, which was adopted:—

Resolved, That there be paid to Harvey Fowler, the official Reporter of this Convention, the sum of $1,000 dollars, in part payment for his services, and that the governor of the Commonwealth be requested to draw his warrant on the treasury for the same.

On motion of Mr. Breed, of Lynn, the Convention proceeded to the consideration of the Orders of the Day.

The first subject was the Resolve upon the basis of the House of Representatives, with the amendment proposed by the Committee of the Whole;

The pending question being upon the amendment to the amendment, moved yesterday by Mr. Huntington, of Northampton.

After debate, Mr. Huntington withdrew his amendment.

Mr. French, of New Bedford, moved that the whole subject be committed to a select committee of one from each congressional district.

Pending this question, at one o'clock,

The Convention adjourned.

AFTERNOON SESSION.

Met according to adjournment.

On motion of Mr. Wheeler, of Lincoln, a paper read by Mr. Giles, of Boston, containing a list of towns unrepresented during the last thirteen years, was ordered to be printed.

On motion of Mr. Underwood, of Milford, the Convention proceeded to the consideration of the Orders of the Day; the first subject being the unfinished business of the morning session, and the pending question being the motion of Mr. French, of New Bedford, to commit the whole subject to a select committee of one from each congressional district.

The motion was rejected, by a vote of one hundred and sixteen in the affirmative, to one hundred and seventy-eight in the negative.

On motion of Mr. Boutwell, member for Berlin, the amendment of the Committee of the Whole was amended by striking out all after the word "inhabitants," in the last line but one of the third Resolution, and inserting the words "shall not exceed three hundred and seventy-five in one thousand eight hundred and sixty, or be increased more than ten in any one decennial period thereafter."

Mr. Thompson, of Charlestown, moved to amend the amendment of the Committee of the Whole, by substituting the following:—

That the Constitution be so amended as to provide for an apportionment of the House of Representatives, as follows:—

1. Every town having less than fifteen hundred inhabitants, may elect one representative every alternate year, or any five years in ten years; also each of said towns may elect one representative on the decennial or valuation year.

2. Any two of such towns may, by a vote of a major part of the legal voters of each, at legal meetings thereof, unite together in a district, which shall be entitled to a representative each year, and which shall continue for a period of not less than five years, excepting the year in which the valuation of estates is settled.

3. Every town having fifteen hundred, and less than four thousand inhabitants, may elect one representative annually.

4. Every town having four thousand inhabitants, may elect two representatives annually; the mean increasing ratio shall be four thousand.

The foregoing apportionment to be made upon the census of 1850, and at, or after each succeeding decennial census, the ratio of towns, and the mean increasing ratio, shall be so increased as to retain the same number of members of the House of Representatives as herein proposed.

Resolved, That each city entitled to more than three representatives, shall be divided into districts of as nearly equal number of inhabitants as may be practicable; *provided*, *however*, that no district shall elect more than three representatives.

The PRESIDENT said the amendment proposed by the gentleman from Charlestown, being a substitute for the amendment moved by the gentleman from Lowell (Mr. Butler), which was in itself a substitute for the original proposition, was not in order. It could be admitted only by unanimous consent of the Convention, as two substitutes could not be pending at the same time.

Unanimous consent being given, the question was stated on the amendment of Mr. Thompson.

On motion of Mr. FRENCH, of New Bedford, the yeas and nays were ordered upon the question of adopting the amendment.

Mr. CADY, of Monson, moved to amend the amendment by substituting the word "five" for the word "four" in the first line of the third paragraph, (printed copy,) and also by making the same alteration in the first and third lines of the fourth paragraph.

Mr. BRIGGS, of Pittsfield, inquired of the Chair if that amendment was in order, inasmuch as it was an amendment in the third degree, which was not admissible.

The PRESIDENT said that it was competent for the Convention to perfect the amendment, before the question should be taken on striking out and inserting. An amendment in the third degree was not admissible; but the proposition before the Convention did not present that question. The Committee of the Whole had reported an amendment to the original proposition, which was in the nature of a substitute, striking out all after the enacting clause, and inserting another proposition. It was in order to amend either the part proposed to be stricken out, or the part to be inserted, and the rule as to amendments in the third degree, did not apply. But the gentleman from Charlestown had moved, not an amendment to an amendment, but an original proposition, striking out every word of the amendment. The Chair, regarding it as in the nature of a substitute, and not as an amendment, ruled it not in order, as two substitutes for an original proposition could not be pending at the same time. The Convention admitted the amendment by unanimous consent, and the proposition of the gentleman from Charlestown stood before the Convention, for the time being, as if the proposition of the Committee of the Whole had been disposed of, and, under these circumstances, the parliamentary rule admitting the right to perfect by amendments, a part to be stricken out or inserted, was applicable. The amendment of the gentleman from Monson, the Chair held to be in order. The Convention acquiesced in the decision of the Chair.

The question being stated on the amendment of the gentleman from Monson, it was decided in the negative.

Mr. KEYES, member for Abington, moved to amend by substituting the word "twelve" for the word "fifteen" in the first line of the first paragraph; but the motion was rejected.

Mr. GARDNER, of Seekonk, moved to strike out of the first and second paragraphs the words "fifteen hundred," and insert instead thereof the words, "one thousand"; but the motion was rejected.

On motion of Mr. BOUTWELL, member for Berlin, the Orders of the Day were laid upon the table, and

At six o'clock, on motion of Mr. WILSON, of Natick,

The Convention adjourned.

THURSDAY, June 30, 1853.

Met according to adjournment. Prayer was offered by the Chaplain. The Journal of yesterday was read.

Mr. VILES, of Lexington, presented a paper, containing a plan of representation in the House of Representatives; which was ordered to be printed.

Mr. BRIGGS, of Pittsfield, from the Committee on the Encouragement of Literature, submitted a Report, in favor of amending the Constitution, so as to provide, that no public money in this Commonwealth, whether accruing from funds or raised by taxation, shall ever be appropriated for the support of sectarian or denominational schools.

Also, a Report, inexpedient to act upon the subject of an Order of May 20th, and the Petition of Harriet K. Hunt, on the subject of securing to females greater educational rights.

Also, a Report, inexpedient to act upon the subject of an Order of

May 23d, concerning the propriety of establishing the Board of Education, and the Board of Agriculture, as permanent departments of the government.

These Reports were severally referred to the Committee of the Whole, and ordered to be printed.

On motion of Mr. WILSON, of Natick, the Convention resolved itself into Committee of the Whole, for the purpose of considering the Report of the Committee on the Frame of Government, inexpedient to act upon the subject of an Order of May 17th, respecting the reference by the legislature to the people, of legislative acts for approval or rejection; and the President requested Mr. Lord, of Salem, to take the chair.

Afterwards, Mr. LORD reported, that it was the opinion of the committee, that the Report ought to be accepted.

And it was accordingly accepted.

On motion of Mr. ALLEN, of Worcester, the Convention resolved itself into Committee of the Whole, for the purpose of considering the Report of the Committee on the Frame of Government, inexpedient to act upon the subject of an Order of June 3d, on the expediency of securing to women, by constitutional provision, their property acquired by devise, inheritance or otherwise, and the President requested Mr. Earle, of Worcester, to take the chair.

Afterwards, Mr. EARLE reported, that it was the opinion of the committee that the Report ought to be accepted.

And it was accordingly accepted.

On motion of Mr. ALLEN, of Worcester, the Convention resolved itself into Committee of the Whole, for the purpose of considering the Report of the Committee on the Frame of Government, inexpedient to act upon the subject of an Order of June 9th, relative to the remuneration of persons tried for offences against the State and acquitted, and the President requested Mr. Whitney, of Boylston, to take the chair.

Afterwards, Mr. WHITNEY reported, that it was the opinion of the committee that the Report ought to be accepted.

And it was accordingly accepted.

On motion of Mr. ALLEN, of Worcester, the Convention resolved itself into Committee of the Whole, for the purpose of considering the Report of the Committee on the Frame of Government, inexpedient to act upon the subject of the Petition of Silas Lamson and others, and the President requested Mr. Wood, of Middleborough, to take the chair.

Afterwards, Mr. Wood reported, that it was the opinion of the committee that the Report ought to be accepted.

And it was accordingly accepted.

On motion of Mr. Wilson, of Natick, the Convention resolved itself into Committee of the Whole, for the purpose of considering the Report of the Committee on the Judiciary, inexpedient to act upon the subject of Orders of June 6th, relating to granting the subject "a certain remedy in law, prompt and without delay," and relating to the codification of the laws; and the President requested Mr. James, of South Scituate, to take the chair.

Afterwards, Mr. James reported, that it was the opinion of the committee that the Report ought to be accepted.

And it was accordingly accepted.

On motion of Mr. Wilson, of Natick, the Convention resolved itself into Committee of the Whole, for the purpose of considering the Report of the Committee on the Secretary, Treasurer, &c., inexpedient to act upon the subject of an Order of June 11th, relating to the expediency of requiring that every person holding an office in or under the State government, shall retire therefrom at the expiration of six years service; and the President requested Mr. Davis, of Plymouth, to take the chair.

Afterwards, Mr. Davis reported, that it was the opinion of the committee that the Report ought to be accepted.

And it was accordingly accepted.

On motion of Mr. Wilson, of Natick, the Convention resolved itself into Committee of the Whole, for the purpose of considering the Resolve reported by the Committee on the Governor, in favor of amending the Constitution by striking out the whole of article 7, section 1, chapter 2; and the President requested Mr. Sargent, of Cambridge, to take the chair.

Afterwards, Mr. Sargent reported, that it was the opinion of the committee that the Resolve ought to pass.

And it was accordingly read a second time, and finally passed, as follows:—

Resolved, That it is expedient to amend the Constitution, by striking out the whole of article 7, in section 1, chapter 2.

On motion of Mr. Earle, of Worcester, the Convention resolved itself into Committee of the Whole, for the purpose of considering the Report of the Committee on the Frame of Government, being a Resolve on the subject of the census; and the President requested Mr. Hooper, of Fall River, to take the chair.

Afterwards, Mr. Hooper reported the Resolve to the Convention, with amendments, viz.:—

Inserting after the word "the," in the second line, (printed copy,) the words, "whole population of the."

And also adding at the close, the words, "instead of the decennial census now required by the Constitution."

On motion of Mr. Briggs, of Pittsfield, the first of the proposed amendments was amended, by striking out the words "whole population of the," and inserting instead thereof, the words, "inhabitants of each city and town in the," and also by inserting the word "all" before the word "the."

The amendment was agreed to, and the amendments of the committee, thus amended, were agreed to.

The Resolve was then read a second time, and finally passed, as follows:—

Resolved, That the Constitution be so amended as to require that a census of all the inhabitants of each city and town in the State be taken in the year 1855, and on every tenth year from and after that period, instead of the decennial census now required by the Constitution.

On motion of Mr. Wilson, of Natick, the Convention proceeded to the consideration of the Orders of the Day.

The first subject was the Resolve on the basis of the House of Representatives, the pending question being upon the amendment of Mr. Thompson, of Charlestown, to the amendment of the Committee of the Whole.

Mr. Davis, of Plymouth, moved to amend the amendment of the Committee of the Whole, by striking out the first paragraph, and substituting therefor the following:—

"Each town having five hundred inhabitants or less, shall be entitled to five representatives in ten years.

"Each town having between five hundred and fifteen hundred inhabitants, shall be entitled to an additional representative in ten years for every two hundred additional inhabitants, and each town having less than fifteen hundred inhabitants, shall have an additional representative in every ten years, for valuation year, provided that no more than one representative shall be sent in any one year."

A question was raised, as to the propriety of admitting the amendment, but the President decided to put the question, upon the principle stated by him yesterday, at the time the amendment was offered by Mr. Cady, of Monson.

Mr. BRIGGS, of Pittsfield, appealed from the decision of the Chair, but afterwards withdrew his appeal, and the decision was acquiesced in by the Convention.

At one o'clock, the Convention adjourned.

AFTERNOON SESSION.

Met according to adjournment.

The Convention resumed the consideration of the Orders of the Day; the pending question being the amendment of Mr. Davis, of Plymouth, to the amendment of the Committee of the Whole.

Mr. ALLEN, of Worcester, moved the Previous Question; but afterwards withdrew the motion.

The amendment of Mr. Davis was then rejected.

On motion of Mr. ALLEY, of Lynn, sustained by a vote of one hundred and eighty-eight in the affirmative to eighty in the negative, the vote by which the yeas and nays were ordered upon the amendment of Mr. Thompson, of Charlestown, was reconsidered;

And the question recurring upon the demand for the yeas and nays, it was sustained by one-fifth of the members.

And the roll being called, one hundred and twenty-nine members voted for the amendment, and two hundred against it; so it was rejected.

Those who voted in the affirmative are:—

Messrs. Alfred A. Abbott,
P. Emory Aldrich,
James B. Allen,
Joel C. Allen,
William Aspinwall,
David C. Atwood,
George Austin,
Joseph Barrows,
Erasmus D. Beach,
John Beal,
George W. Blagden,
William J. A. Bradford,
Osmyn Brewster,
Francis Brinley,
George N. Briggs,
Asa Bronson,
Rufus Bullock,
Cephas C. Bumpus,
Timothy W. Carter,
Chester W. Chapin,

Messrs. Josiah Childs,
J. McKean Churchill,
Sumner Cole,
Ithamar Conkey,
George W. Crockett,
Leander Crosby,
Seth Crowell,
Joseph Cummings,
Charles G. Davis,
John Davis,
Robert T. Davis,
Solomon Davis,
Silas Dean,
William Dehon,
Hiram S. Denison,
Samuel Duncan,
James Easton, 2d,
Homer Ely,
A. G. Farwell,
Samuel P. Fowler,

Messrs. Rodney French,
Henry J. Gardner,
Robert Gould,
Dalton Goulding,
Jason Goulding,
John C. Gray,
Artemas Hale,
Nathan Hale,
A. B. Hammond,
William Haskins,
Elnathan P. Hathaway,
George Hayward,
Charles Heard,
Henry Hersey,
William H. Hewes,
George S. Hillard,
Foster Hooper,
Samuel Houghton,
Abraham H. Howland,
William J. Hubbard,
William Hunt,
Asahel Huntington,
Charles P. Huntington,
Samuel A. Hurlburt,
Samuel Jackson,
William James,
John Johnson,
Giles C. Kellogg,
Martin R. Kellogg,
Henry W. Kinsman,
George H. Kuhn,
John S. Ladd,
Tristram Littlefield,
Isaac Livermore,
Samuel K. Lothrop,
Samuel P. Loud,
John A. Lowell,
Theophilus R. Marvin,
Seth Miller, Jr.,
Samuel Mixter,
George Morey,
Elbridge G. Morton,
Marcus Morton,
Marcus Morton, Jr.,
Daniel Noyes,

Messrs. Joseph E. Ober,
Henry K. Oliver,
Benjamin S. Orne,
Adolphus G. Parker,
Joel Parker,
Thomas A. Parsons,
Daniel A. Perkins,
Jonathan C. Perkins,
William C. Plunkett,
Jonathan Preston,
Robert Rantoul,
James Read,
Sampson Reed,
John Sargent,
William Schouler,
Charles Sherman,
John S. Sleeper,
John Souther,
Caleb Stetson,
Charles G. Stevens,
Charles S. Storrow,
Charles Sumner,
Thomas Talbot,
Ralph Taylor,
Joseph Thayer,
Charles Thompson,
Edmund P. Tileston,
David Turner,
William Tyler,
Charles W. Upham,
Samuel B. Walcott,
Bradford L. Wales,
Frederic T. Wallace,
Samuel Walker,
Asa H. Waters,
Cyrus Weeks,
Thomas Wetmore,
Joseph Wilbur,
Joel Wilder,
John H. Wilkins,
Ezra Wilkinson,
Henry Williams,
Jonathan B. Winn,
Josiah B. Woods.

Those who voted in the negative are:—

Messrs. Josiah G. Abbott,
Benjamin P. Adams,
Shubael P. Adams,
Charles Allen,

Messrs. Parsons Allen,
John B. Alley,
Josiah Allis,
D. W. Alvord,

Messrs. Robert Andrews,
Samuel Ayres,
Alvah Ballard,
George S. Ball,
Alpheus Bancroft,
Russel Bartlett,
Marcus Barrett,
Eliakim A. Bates,
Moses Bates, Jr.,
William Bennett, Jr.,
Zephaniah Bennett,
Edward B. Bigelow,
Francis W. Bird,
Henry W. Bishop,
William C. Bliss,
William S. Booth,
George S. Boutwell,
Sewell Boutwell,
Hiram N. Breed,
Adolphus F. Brown,
Alpheus R. Brown,
Artemas Brown,
Hammond Brown,
Joseph Brownell,
Patrick Bryant,
Asahel Buck,
Anson Burlingame,
Benjamin F. Butler,
Henry Cady,
William Carruthers,
Isaac Case,
Amariah Chandler,
Daniel E. Chapin,
Henry Chapin,
Ransom Clark,
Alpheus B. Clarke,
William Cleverly,
Lansing J. Cole,
Henry F. Cooledge,
George B. Crane,
Oliver S. Cressy,
Simeon Crittenden,
Joseph W. Cross,
Wilber Curtis,
Henry W. Cushman,
Thomas Cushman,
Richard H. Dana, Jr.,
Ebenezer Davis,
Isaac Davis,
Gilman Day,
Elijah S. Deming,
Augustus Denton,
Moses Dorman,

Messrs. Bradish Dunham,
John M. Durgin,
Philip Eames,
John M. Earle,
Elisha Edwards,
Samuel Edwards,
Joseph M. Ely,
Sullivan Fay,
Lyman Fisk,
Emery Fiske,
Ezekiel W. Fitch,
Aaron Foster,
Samuel Fowle,
James M. Freeman,
Charles A. French,
Samuel French,
Luther Gale,
Johnson Gardner,
Elbridge Gates,
Wanton C. Gilbert,
Joel Giles,
Daniel W. Gooch,
Leonard Gooding,
John W. Graves,
Jabez Green,
William B. Greene,
Josiah W. Griswold,
Whiting Griswold,
Samuel P. Hadley,
B. F. Hallett,
Lyman W. Hapgood,
Seth Hapgood,
Phineas Harmon,
Stephen E. Hawkes,
Ezra Heath, 2d,
Samuel Henry,
James Hewes,
William Hinsdale,
Henry Hobart,
Edwin Hobbs,
George Hood,
George H. Huntington,
Moses C. Hurlbut,
John Jacobs,
Isaac Kendall,
Joseph Kimball,
Joseph Kingman,
Hiram Knight,
Jefferson Knight,
Joseph Knight,
Charles L. Knowlton,
J. S. C. Knowlton,
William H. Knowlton,

Messrs. Albert Knox,
Gardner P. Ladd,
Alden Leland,
Abishai Lincoln,
Otis Little,
Justin E. Loomis,
William P. Marble,
Laban Marcy,
Abijah P. Marvin,
Reuben Meader,
Simeon Merritt,
James L. Monroe,
James M. Moore,
William S. Morton,
Hiram Nash,
Charles Newman,
William Nichols,
Andrew T. Nute,
Nathan Orcutt,
E. Wing Packer,
Benjamin Paine,
Henry Paine,
John Partridge,
Nathaniel Peabody,
Jeremiah Pease, Jr.,
John Penniman,
Jesse Perkins,
Charles Phelps,
Silvanus B. Phinney,
Henry Pierce,
Jeremiah Pomroy,
James M. Pool,
Peter Powers,
John A. Putnam,
Silas Rawson,
David Rice,
Luther Richards,
Daniel Richardson,
Nathan Richardson,
Samuel H. Richardson,
Elkanah Ring, Jr.,
Joseph M. Rockwood,
David S. Ross,

Messrs. James C. Royce,
Amasa Sanderson,
Chester Sanderson,
Luther Sheldon,
John Sherril,
Chester Sikes,
Perez Simmons,
John W. Simonds,
Matthew Smith,
Melzar Sprague,
Samuel W. Spooner,
Eben H. Stacy,
Granville Stevens,
William Stevens,
Alfred L. Strong,
Alanson Swain,
Arnold Taft,
Willard Thayer, 2d,
Abraham Tilton,
Horatio W. Tilton,
Ephraim Tower,
Orison Underwood,
Joel Viles,
George A. Vinton,
Freeland Wallis,
Amasa Walker,
Andrew H. Ward,
Marshal Warner,
Samuel Warner, Jr.,
Gershom B. Weston,
William F. Wheeler,
Benjamin White,
George White,
James S. Whitney,
J. B. Williams,
Henry Wilson,
Milo Wilson,
Willard Wilson,
Levi M. Winslow,
Charles C. Wood,
Nathaniel Wood,
Otis Wood,
Ezekiel Wright.

Mr. Wilson, of Natick, moved to amend the amendment of the Committee of the Whole, by adding, at the close of the fourth paragraph, the words, "and the mean increasing ratio for an additional representative for each city and town shall be four thousand," and also by striking out the remainder of the first Resolve.

He afterwards withdrew his amendment.

Mr. Schouler, of Boston, moved to amend the amendment of the

Committee of the Whole, by striking out all after the word "Resolved," and inserting the following:—

That whereas, by the theory of our institutions, and the Declaration of Independence, all men are created equal, and have an inherent and inalienable right to an equal voice in electing their rulers, and in making the laws by which they are governed: and whereas, these are the fundamental maxims upon which every truly democratic government is founded, and by which a genuine democracy alone can be maintained: therefore, be it

Resolved, That it is expedient so to amend the Constitution of Massachusetts, that the popular branch of the government—the House of Representatives—like the Senate, shall be so constituted that all men shall be equal in political power, and be equally represented, as near as may be, man for man, by districts based upon population or legal voters, in the State government.

No objection being made, the amendment was admitted, and the question was first stated upon the adoption of the second paragraph, beginning at the word "Resolved."

On motion of Mr. SCHOULER, the yeas and nays were ordered upon the question of adopting the amendment.

Without taking the question,

On motion of Mr. CHURCHILL, of Milton, by a vote of one hundred and thirty-five in the affirmative, to seventy-one in the negative,

The Convention adjourned.

FRIDAY, July 1, 1853.

Met according to adjournment. Prayer was offered by the Chaplain. The Journal of yesterday was read.

Mr. STETSON, of Braintree, offered the following Resolution:—

Resolved, That the Constitution be so amended that hereafter no town shall be incorporated with less than fifteen hundred inhabitants.

Referred to the Committee of the Whole.

Mr. BRIGGS, of Pittsfield, from the Committee on the Encouragement of Literature, submitted a Report and Resolve on the subject of the enlargement and preservation of the School Fund.

Also a Resolve in favor of striking out of the fifth chapter of the Constitution, the words "University of Cambridge."

Mr. WALKER, of North Brookfield, from the Committee on the Qualifications of Voters, submitted a Report, inexpedient to act upon the subject of the Petition of Francis Jackson and others, that the word "male" may be struck out of the Constitution; and the Petition of Mrs. Abby B. Alcott and other women of Massachusetts, that they may be allowed to vote upon the amendments of the Constitution that may be proposed.

On motion of Mr. BOUTWELL, member for Berlin,

Ordered, That debate upon the Report of the Committee on the basis of the House of Representatives, and all pending questions thereon, cease at eleven o'clock to-day; but amendments shall be admitted after debate upon the main question shall cease, and the mover of each amendment shall be allowed ten minutes to explain his amendment; and the same time shall be allowed to members of the Convention who shall obtain the floor, to oppose such amendment, when the question thereon shall be taken, without further debate.

On motion of Mr. BRIGGS, of Pittsfield, the Convention proceeded to the consideration of the Orders of the Day.

The first subject was the unfinished business of yesterday, viz.: the Resolve on the subject of the House of Representatives; and the pending question was upon the amendment of Mr. Schouler, of Boston, to the amendment of the Committee of the Whole.

Mr. SCHOULER withdrew his amendment, and offered instead thereof, the two following Resolutions:—

Resolved, 1st. That by the theory of our government and the Declaration of Independence, all men are created equal, and have a right to an equal voice in electing their rulers, and in making the laws by which they are governed: and that these are fundamental maxims upon which every truly democratic government is founded, particularly where the people, as in Massachusetts, are kindred and homogeneous, and by which alone a genuine democracy can permanently be maintained.

Resolved, 2d. That it is expedient so to amend the Constitution of Massachusetts, that the popular branch of the government, the House of Representatives, shall be based upon population, ratable polls, or upon legal voters, to the end that all men shall be equal in power and be equally represented, as near as may be, man for man, in the State government.

On motion of Mr. HALLETT, member for Wilbraham, sustained by a vote of one hundred and forty-nine in the affirmative to sixty-seven in the negative, the amendment of the Committee of the Whole was amended by striking out the last paragraph of the first Resolution, and inserting instead thereof, the following :—

Every city or town containing over twelve thousand inhabitants, shall be entitled to elect one additional representative for every four thousand inhabitants it may contain over twelve thousand.

Mr. MORTON, of Taunton, offered an amendment to the amendment of Mr. Schouler, but afterwards withdrew it.

Mr. BURLINGAME, member for Northborough, moved to amend the proposition of Mr. Schouler, by substituting the following for the first Resolution, viz. :—

Resolved, That by the theory of government, and the Declaration of Independence, all men are created equal, and are endowed by their Creator with certain inalienable rights; that among these are life, liberty, and the pursuit of happiness; that to secure these rights, governments are instituted among men, deriving their just powers from the consent of the governed, and that these are fundamental maxims, upon which every truly democratic government is founded, and by which alone genuine democracy can be permanently maintained.

The amendment was accepted by Mr. Schouler; but the first Resolution, as above amended, was afterwards withdrawn.

Mr. DANA, member for Manchester, moved to amend the second Resolution, by inserting, after the words "man for man," the words "woman by woman, child by child, and irrespective of citizenship or residence"; but afterwards withdrew the amendment.

Mr. GRISWOLD, member for Erving, moved to amend the second Resolve, by striking out the words "ratable polls, or upon legal voters," and inserting, instead thereof, the words "as near as may be, by a system of town representation, adjusted in a manner as equal and just as is practicable"; but afterwards withdrew the amendment.

On motion of Mr. SCHOULER, the yeas and nays were ordered upon the question of adopting his amendment.

And the roll being called, one hundred and thirty-three members voted in the affirmative, and two hundred and twenty-three in the negative.

So the amendment was rejected.

Those who voted in the affirmative are :—

Messrs. Alfred A. Abbott,
Benjamin P. Adams,
P. Emory Aldrich,
Robert Andrews,
William Appleton,
William Aspinwall,
David C. Atwood,
George Austin,
Joseph Barrows,
Sidney Bartlett,
Erasmus D. Beach,
James M. Beebe,
William J. A. Bradford,
Milton P. Braman,
Osmyn Brewster,
Francis Brinley,
George N. Briggs,
Rufus Bullock,
Cephas C. Bumpus,
Timothy W. Carter,
Josiah Childs,
J. McKean Churchill,
Jacob Coggin,
Nathaniel Cogswell,
Ithamar Conkey,
Charles E. Cook,
Henry F. Cooledge,
Seth Crowell,
F. B. Crowninshield,
Joseph Cummings,
Wilber Curtis,
John Davis,
Robert T. Davis,
Solomon Davis,
William Dehon,
Hiram S. Denison,
James C. Doane,
Moses Dorman,
Lilley Eaton,
Homer Ely,
A. G. Farwell,
Samuel P. Fowler,
Charles H. French,
Henry J. Gardner,
Joel Giles,
Robert Gould,
Dalton Goulding,
Jason Goulding,
John C. Gray,
Simon Greenleaf,
Artemas Hale,

Messrs. Nathan Hale,
A. B. Hammond,
George Haskell,
Elnathan P. Hathaway,
George Hayward,
Henry Hersey,
George S. Hillard,
Samuel Houghton,
Abraham H. Howland,
William J. Hubbard,
William Hunt,
Samuel A. Hurlburt,
Samuel Jackson,
William James,
Samuel H. Jenks,
Giles C. Kellogg,
Martin R. Kellogg,
Henry W. Kinsman,
George H. Kuhn,
John S. Ladd,
Job G. Lawton, Jr.,
Frederic W. Lincoln, Jr.,
Tristram Littlefield,
Isaac Livermore,
Samuel K. Lothrop,
Samuel P. Loud,
Theophilus R. Marvin,
Seth Miller, Jr.,
Samuel Mixter,
George Morey,
Joseph B. Morss,
Elbridge G. Morton,
Marcus Morton,
Daniel Noyes,
Joseph E. Ober,
Henry K. Oliver,
Nathan Orcutt,
James W. Paige,
John G. Park,
Adolphus G. Parker,
Joel Parker,
Samuel D. Parker,
Thomas A. Parsons,
Jonathan C. Perkins,
William C. Plunkett,
Jonathan Preston,
Robert Rantoul,
James Read,
Sampson Reed,
George R. Sampson,
John Sargent,

Messrs. William Schouler,
Charles Sherman,
John S. Sleeper,
John Souther,
Caleb Stetson,
Charles G. Stevens,
J. Thomas Stevenson,
Charles Sumner,
Increase Sumner,
Alanson Swain,
Ralph Taylor,
Joseph Thayer,
Charles Thompson,
Edmund P. Tileston,
John S. Tyler,
Charles W. Upham,

Messrs. George B. Upton,
Samuel B. Walcott,
Bradford L. Wales,
Samuel Walker,
Cyrus Weeks,
Thomas Wetmore,
Daniel Wilbur,
Joseph Wilbur,
Joel Wilder,
John H. Wilkins,
Ezra Wilkinson,
Henry Williams,
Milo Wilson,
Jonathan B. Winn,
Josiah B. Woods.

Those who voted in the negative are :—

Messrs. Josiah G. Abbott,
Shubael P. Adams,
Charles Allen,
Joel C. Allen,
Parsons Allen,
John B. Alley,
Josiah Allis,
D. W. Alvord,
Samuel Ayres,
Alvah Ballard,
George S. Ball,
Alpheus Bancroft,
Russel Bartlett,
Eliakim A. Bates,
Moses Bates, Jr.,
William Bennett, Jr.,
Zephaniah Bennett,
Edward B. Bigelow,
Francis W. Bird,
Henry W. Bishop,
Gad O. Bliss,
William C. Bliss,
William S. Booth,
George S. Boutwell,
Sewell Boutwell,
Hiram N. Breed,
Asa Bronson,
Adolphus F. Brown,
Alpheus R. Brown,
Artemas Brown,
Hammond Brown,
Joseph Brownell,
Anson Burlingame,
Benjamin F. Butler,

Messrs. Henry Cady,
William Carruthers,
Isaac Case,
Amariah Chandler,
Chester W. Chapin,
Daniel E. Chapin,
Henry Chapin,
Henry Clark,
Ransom Clark,
Alpheus B. Clarke,
Stillman Clarke,
William Cleverly,
Lansing J. Cole,
George B. Crane,
Oliver S. Cressy,
Simeon Crittenden,
Joseph W. Cross,
Henry W. Cushman,
Thomas Cushman,
Simeon N. Cutler,
Richard H. Dana, Jr.,
Charles G. Davis,
Ebenezer Davis,
Isaac Davis,
Gilman Day,
Silas Dean,
Elijah S. Deming,
Augustus Denton,
Alexander De Witt,
Samuel Duncan,
Bradish Dunham,
John M. Durgin,
Philip Eames,
John M. Earle,

Messrs. Elisha Edwards,
Samuel Edwards,
Sullivan Fay,
James K. Fellows,
Lyman Fisk,
Emery Fiske,
Ezekiel W. Fitch,
Aaron Foster,
Abram Foster,
Samuel Fowle,
Charles A. French,
Rodney French,
Samuel French,
Luther Gale,
Elbridge Gates,
Wanton C. Gilbert,
Washington Gilbert,
Charles G. Giles,
Daniel W. Gooch,
Leonard Gooding,
John W. Graves,
Jabez Green,
Josiah W. Griswold,
Whiting Griswold,
Samuel P. Hadley,
Charles B. Hall,
B. F. Hallett,
Lyman W. Hapgood,
Phineas Harmon,
William Haskins,
Stephen E. Hawkes,
Isaac Hayden,
Ezra Heath, 2d,
Samuel Henry,
James Hewes,
William H. Hewes,
William Hinsdale,
Henry Hobart,
Edwin Hobbs,
Nathaniel Holder,
George Hood,
Martin Howard,
Charles E. Hunt,
Charles P. Huntington,
George H. Huntington,
Moses C. Hurlbut,
Abijah M. Ide, Jr.,
John Jacobs,
John Johnson,
Isaac Kendall,
Joseph Kimball,
Joseph Kingman,
Hiram Knight,

Messrs. Jefferson Knight,
Charles L. Knowlton,
J. S. C. Knowlton,
William H. Knowlton,
Albert Knox,
Gardner P. Ladd,
Wilber C. Langdon,
Luther Lawrence,
Alden Leland,
Abishai Lincoln,
Otis Little,
Justin E. Loomis,
William P. Marble,
Laban Marcy,
Charles Mason,
Reuben Meader,
Simeon Merritt,
James L. Monroe,
James M. Moore,
Marcus Morton, Jr.,
William S. Morton,
Hiram Nash,
Jonathan Nayson,
Charles Newman,
William Nichols,
Alfred Norton,
Andrew T. Nute,
Benjamin S. Orne,
E. Wing Packer,
Benjamin Paine,
Henry Paine,
Jonathan Parris,
John Partridge,
Nathaniel Peabody,
Jeremiah Pease, Jr.,
John Penniman,
Daniel A. Perkins,
Jesse Perkins,
Noah C. Perkins,
Charles Phelps,
Silvanus B. Phinney,
Henry Pierce,
James M. Pool,
Peter Powers,
John A. Putnam,
Luther Richards,
Daniel Richardson,
Nathan Richardson,
Samuel H. Richardson,
Elkanah Ring, Jr.,
Joseph M. Rockwood,
John Rogers,
David S. Ross,

Messrs. James C. Royce,
Amasa Sanderson,
Chester Sanderson,
John Sherril,
Chester Sikes,
Perez Simmons,
John W. Simonds,
Matthew Smith,
Melzar Sprague,
Samuel W. Spooner,
Eben H. Stacy,
Granville Stevens,
William Stevens,
Gideon Stiles,
Alfred L. Strong,
Isaac C. Taber,
Arnold Taft,
Thomas Talbot,
Willard Thayer, 2d,
John W. Thomas,
Abraham Tilton,
Horatio W. Tilton,
Ephraim Tower,
David Turner,
William Tyler,

Messrs. Orison Underwood,
Joel Viles,
George A. Vinton,
Frederic T. Wallace,
Freeland Wallis,
Amasa Walker,
Andrew H. Ward,
Samuel Warner, Jr.,
Asa H. Waters,
Gershom B. Weston,
William F. Wheeler,
Benjamin White,
George White,
Daniel S. Whitney,
James S. Whitney,
J. B. Williams,
Henry Wilson,
Willard Wilson,
Levi M. Winslow,
Charles C. Wood,
Nathaniel Wood,
Otis Wood,
William H. Wood,
Ezekiel Wright.

Mr. Morton, of Taunton, offered an amendment to the amendment of the Committee of the Whole, which, the blanks having been filled, stood as follows:—

That the House of Representatives shall consist of three hundred and twenty members, which shall be divided among the several counties of the Commonwealth, as nearly as possible, according to the number of legal voters by the last preceding decennial census.

As soon as may be after each decennial census, the Senate shall divide each county into as many representative districts as it may deem expedient, so that the basis of each representative shall be as nearly the same number of legal voters as possible without the division of towns, or the wards of cities: *Provided*, no district shall be entitled to more than three representatives, *and provided*, that Nantucket and Dukes Counties shall each form one district, and be entitled to at least one representative.

On motion of Mr. Morton, the yeas and nays were ordered upon the question of adopting this amendment.

On motion of Mr. Phinney, member for Chatham, the rule requiring that an adjournment of the morning session shall take place at one o'clock, was modified so as to change the hour to two o'clock.

But afterwards, on motion of Mr. Hathaway, of Freetown,

At one o'clock, the Convention adjourned.

AFTERNOON SESSION.

Met according to adjournment.

Mr. Briggs, of Pittsfield, moved that when the Convention adjourn this evening, it adjourn to meet again on Wednesday, at nine o'clock.

Mr. Griswold, member for Erving, moved to amend the motion by substituting Tuesday, at ten o'clock,

And the amendment was adopted by a vote of one hundred and twenty-six in the affirmative to fifty-eight in the negative.

The motion, as amended, was then agreed to.

On motion of Mr. Breed, of Lynn, the Convention proceeded to the consideration of the Orders of the Day.

The first subject was the unfinished business of the morning session, viz.: the Resolves on the subject of the House of Representatives; and the pending question was upon the adoption of the amendment of Mr. Morton, of Taunton, to the amendment of the Committee of the Whole.

And the roll being called, one hundred and nineteen members voted in the affirmative, and one hundred and ninety-seven in the negative.

So the amendment was rejected.

Those who voted in the affirmative are:—

Messrs. Alfred A. Abbott,
Benjamin P. Adams,
P. Emory Aldrich,
Joel C. Allen,
Robert Andrews,
William Aspinwall,
David C. Atwood,
George Austin,
Joseph Barrows,
Sidney Bartlett,
Erasmus D. Beach,
William J. A. Bradford,
Milton P. Braman,
Osmyn Brewster,
Francis Brinley,
George N. Briggs,
Asa Bronson,
Rufus Bullock,
Cephas C. Bumpus,
Timothy W. Carter,
Josiah Childs,
J. McKean Churchill,
Nathaniel Cogswell,
Ithamar Conkey,
Henry F. Cooledge,

Messrs. George W. Crockett,
Leander Crosby,
Seth Crowell,
Wilber Curtis,
John Davis,
Robert T. Davis,
Solomon Davis,
James C. Doane,
James Easton, 2d,
Lilley Eaton,
Homer Ely,
Samuel P. Fowler,
Charles H. French,
Henry J. Gardner,
Johnson Gardner,
Joel Giles,
Robert Gould,
Dalton Goulding,
Jason Goulding,
John C. Gray,
Artemas Hale,
Nathan Hale,
A. B. Hammond,
George Haskell,
Elnathan P. Hathaway,

Messrs. Charles Heard,
Henry Hersey,
William H. Hewes,
George S. Hillard,
Thomas Hopkinson,
Samuel Houghton,
William J. Hubbard,
William Hunt,
Asahel Huntington,
Samuel A. Hurlburt,
Samuel Jackson,
William James,
Samuel H. Jenks,
John Johnson,
Giles C. Kellogg,
Martin R. Kellogg,
Joseph Kingman,
George H. Kuhn,
John S. Ladd,
Job G. Lawton, Jr.,
Abishai Lincoln,
Frederic W. Lincoln, Jr.,
Tristram Littlefield,
Isaac Livermore,
Samuel P. Loud,
Seth Miller, Jr.,
Samuel Mixter,
George Morey,
Joseph B. Morss,
Elbridge G. Morton,
Marcus Morton,
Marcus Morton, Jr.,
Joseph E. Ober,
Henry K. Oliver,
John G. Park,

Messrs. Adolphus G. Parker,
Thomas A. Parsons,
William C. Plunkett,
Robert Rantoul,
James Read,
Sampson Reed,
John Sargent,
William Schouler,
Charles Sherman,
John S. Sleeper,
John Souther,
Charles G. Stevens,
Granville Stevens,
J. Thomas Stevenson,
Charles Sumner,
Increase Sumner,
Alanson Swain,
Ralph Taylor,
John W. Thomas,
Edmund P. Tileston,
Charles W. Upham,
Samuel B. Walcott,
Bradford L. Wales,
Samuel Walker,
Cyrus Weeks,
Daniel Wilbur,
Joseph Wilbur,
Joel Wilder,
Ezra Wilkinson,
Henry Williams,
Milo Wilson,
Jonathan B. Winn,
Charles C. Wood,
Josiah B. Woods.

Those who voted in the negative are:—

Messrs. Josiah G. Abbott,
Shubael P. Adams,
Charles Allen,
Parsons Allen,
Josiah Allis,
Samuel Ayres,
Alvah Ballard,
Alpheus Bancroft,
Russel Bartlett,
Eliakim A. Bates,
Moses Bates, Jr.,
John Beal,
William Bennett, Jr.,
Zephaniah Bennett,
Edward B. Bigelow,
Francis W. Bird,

Henry W. Bishop,
William S. Booth,
George S. Boutwell,
Sewell Boutwell,
Hiram N. Breed,
Adolphus F. Brown,
Artemas Brown,
Hammond Brown,
Joseph Brownell,
Asahel Buck,
Anson Burlingame,
Benjamin F. Butler,
Henry Cady,
William Carruthers,
Isaac Case,
Amariah Chandler,

Messrs. Daniel E. Chapin,
Henry Chapin,
Henry Clark,
Ransom Clark,
Alpheus B. Clarke,
Stillman Clarke,
William Cleverly,
Lansing J. Cole,
George B. Crane,
Oliver S. Cressy,
Simeon Crittenden,
Joseph W. Cross,
Henry W. Cushman,
Thomas Cushman,
Simeon N. Cutler,
Richard H. Dana, Jr.,
Charles G. Davis,
Ebenezer Davis,
Isaac Davis,
Gilman Day,
Elijah S. Deming,
Augustus Denton,
Moses Dorman,
Samuel Duncan,
Bradish Dunham,
John M. Durgin,
Philip Eames,
John M. Earle,
Elisha Edwards,
Samuel Edwards,
Sullivan Fay,
James K. Fellows,
Lyman Fisk,
Emery Fiske,
Ezekiel W. Fitch,
Aaron Foster,
Abram Foster,
Samuel Fowle,
James M. Freeman,
Charles A. French,
Rodney French,
Luther Gale,
Elbridge Gates,
Wanton C. Gilbert,
Washington Gilbert,
Charles G. Giles,
Leonard Gooding,
John W. Graves,
Jabez Green,
William B. Greene,
Josiah W. Griswold,
Whiting Griswold,
Samuel P. Hadley,

Messrs. Benjamin F. Hallett,
Lyman W. Hapgood,
Phineas Harmon,
William Haskins,
Stephen E. Hawkes,
Isaac Hayden,
Ezra Heath, 2d,
Samuel Henry,
James Hewes,
William Hinsdale,
Henry Hobart,
Edwin Hobbs,
Nathaniel Holder,
George Hood,
Martin Howard,
Abraham H. Howland,
Charles E. Hunt,
Charles P. Huntington,
Moses C. Hurlbut,
Abijah M. Ide, Jr.,
John Jacobs,
Isaac Kendall,
Joseph Kimball,
Hiram Knight,
Jefferson Knight,
Joseph Knight,
J. S. C. Knowlton,
William H. Knowlton,
Albert Knox,
Gardner P. Ladd,
Wilber C. Langdon,
Luther Lawrence,
Alden Leland,
Otis Little,
Justin E. Loomis,
William P. Marble,
Laban Marcy,
Abijah P. Marvin,
Reuben Meader,
Simeon Merritt,
James L. Monroe,
William S. Morton,
Hiram Nash,
Charles Newman,
William Nichols,
Alfred Norton,
Andrew T. Nute,
Benjamin S. Orne,
E. Wing Packer,
Benjamin Paine,
Jonathan Parris,
John Partridge,
Nathaniel Peabody,

Messrs. Jeremiah Pease, Jr.,
John Penniman,
Daniel A. Perkins,
Jesse Perkins,
Noah C. Perkins,
Charles Phelps,
Silvanus B. Phinney,
Henry Pierce,
James M. Pool,
John A. Putnam,
Silas Rawson,
Luther Richards,
Daniel Richardson,
Nathan Richardson,
Samuel H. Richardson,
Joseph M. Rockwood,
John Rogers,
James C. Royce,
Amasa Sanderson,
Chester Sanderson,
John Sherril,
Chester Sikes,
Perez Simmons,
John W. Simonds,
Matthew Smith,
Melzar Sprague,
Samuel W. Spooner,
William Stevens,
Gideon Stiles,
Alfred L. Strong,

Messrs. Arnold Taft,
Thomas Talbot,
Willard Thayer, 2d,
Abraham Tilton,
Horatio W. Tilton,
Ephraim Tower,
David Turner,
William Tyler,
Orison Underwood,
Joel Viles,
Freeland Wallis,
Amasa Walker,
Andrew H. Ward,
Samuel Warner, Jr.,
Asa H. Waters,
Gershom B. Weston,
William F. Wheeler,
Benjamin White,
George White,
Daniel S. Whitney,
James S. Whitney,
J. B. Williams,
Henry Wilson,
Willard Wilson,
Levi M. Winslow,
Nathaniel Wood,
Otis Wood,
William H. Wood,
Ezekiel Wright.

Mr. Hale, of Boston, moved to amend the amendment of the Committee of the Whole by substituting therefor the Resolve reported by the Minority of the Standing Committee.

Objections being made by Mr. Butler, of Lowell, and Mr. Tyler, of Pawtucket, it was not received.

Mr. Whitney, of Conway, moved the Previous Question, which was ordered.

On motion of Mr. Weeks, of Harwich, the yeas and nays were ordered upon the question of agreeing to the amendment of the Committee of the Whole, as amended.

Mr. Hathaway, of Freetown, called for a division of the Resolves,

And no objection being made, the question was first taken upon the first, second, third and fourth Resolutions.

And the roll being called, two hundred and six members voted for the Resolves, and one hundred and twelve against them.

So they were adopted.

Those who voted in the affirmative are:—

Messrs. Josiah G. Abbott,
Shubael P. Adams,
Charles Allen,
James B. Allen,
Joel C. Allen,
Parsons Allen,
John B. Alley,
Josiah Allis,
D. W. Alvord,
David C. Atwood,
George Austin,
Samuel Ayres,
Alvah Ballard,
George S. Ball,
Russel Bartlett,
Eliakim A. Bates,
Moses Bates, Jr.,
William Bennett, Jr.,
Zephaniah Bennett,
Edward B. Bigelow,
Francis W. Bird,
Henry W. Bishop,
William S. Booth,
George S. Boutwell,
Sewell Boutwell,
Hiram N. Breed,
Asa Bronson,
Adolphus F. Brown,
Alpheus R. Brown,
Artemas Brown,
Hammond Brown,
Joseph Brownell,
Anson Burlingame,
Benjamin F. Butler,
William Carruthers,
Isaac Case,
Amariah Chandler,
Daniel E. Chapin,
Henry Chapin,
Henry Clark,
Ransom Clark,
Alpheus B. Clarke,
William Cleverly,
Jacob Coggin,
Sumner Cole,
Henry F. Cooledge,
George B. Crane,
Oliver S. Cressy,
Simeon Crittenden,
Joseph W. Cross,
Wilber Curtis,

Messrs. Henry W. Cushman,
Thomas Cushman,
Simeon N. Cutler,
Richard H. Dana, Jr.,
Ebenezer Davis,
Isaac Davis,
Gilman Day,
Elijah S. Deming,
Augustus Denton,
Moses Dorman,
Samuel Duncan,
Bradish Dunham,
John M. Durgin,
Philip Eames,
John M. Earle,
James Easton, 2d,
Elisha Edwards,
Samuel Edwards,
Sullivan Fay,
James K. Fellows,
Lyman Fisk,
Emery Fiske,
Ezekiel W. Fitch,
Aaron Foster,
Abram Foster,
Samuel Fowle,
James M. Freeman,
Charles A. French,
Rodney French,
Luther Gale,
Johnson Gardner,
Elbridge Gates,
Wanton C. Gilbert,
Washington Gilbert,
Charles G. Giles,
Joel Giles,
Daniel W. Gooch,
Leonard Gooding,
John W. Graves,
Jabez Green,
William B. Greene,
Josiah W. Griswold,
Whiting Griswold,
Samuel P. Hadley,
Benjamin F. Hallett,
Lyman W. Hapgood,
Phineas Harmon,
George Haskell,
William Haskins,
Stephen E. Hawkes,
Ezra Heath, 2d,

Messrs. Samuel Henry,
James Hewes,
Edwin Hobbs,
Nathaniel Holder,
George Hood,
Martin Howard,
Abraham H. Howland,
Charles E. Hunt,
George H. Huntington,
Moses C. Hurlbut,
Abijah M. Ide, Jr.,
John Jacobs,
Joseph Kimball,
Joseph Kingman,
Hiram Knight,
Jefferson Knight,
Joseph Knight,
J. S. C. Knowlton,
William H. Knowlton,
Albert Knox,
Gardner P. Ladd,
Wilber C. Langdon,
Alden Leland,
Abishai Lincoln,
Otis Little,
Justin E. Loomis,
William P. Marble,
Laban Marcy,
Abijah P. Marvin,
Reuben Meader,
Simeon Merritt,
James L. Monroe,
James M. Moore,
Elbridge G. Morton,
William S. Morton,
Hiram Nash,
Charles Newman,
William Nichols,
Alfred Norton,
Andrew T. Nute,
Benjamin S. Orne,
E. Wing Packer,
Benjamin Paine,
Jonathan Parris,
John Partridge,
Nathaniel Peabody,
Jeremiah Pease, Jr.,
John Penniman,
Daniel A. Perkins,
Jesse Perkins,
Noah C. Perkins,
Charles Phelps,

Messrs. Silvanus B. Phinney,
Henry Pierce,
James M Pool,
John A. Putnam,
Silas Rawson,
Luther Richards,
Daniel Richardson,
Nathan Richardson,
Samuel H. Richardson,
Joseph M. Rockwood,
John Rogers,
James C. Royce,
Amasa Sanderson,
Chester Sanderson,
John Sherril,
Chester Sikes,
Perez Simmons,
John W. Simonds,
Matthew Smith,
Melzar Sprague,
Samuel W. Spooner,
William Stevens,
Gideon Stiles,
Alfred L. Strong,
Alanson Swain,
Isaac C. Taber,
Arnold Taft,
Willard Thayer, 2d,
John W. Thomas,
Abraham Tilton,
Horatio W. Tilton,
Ephraim Tower,
William Tyler,
Orison Underwood,
Joel Viles,
Freeland Wallis,
Andrew H. Ward,
Samuel Warner, Jr.,
Gershom B. Weston,
Benjamin White,
George White,
Daniel S. Whitney,
James S. Whitney,
J. B. Williams,
Henry Wilson,
Willard Wilson,
Levi M. Winslow,
Charles C. Wood,
Nathaniel Wood,
Otis Wood,
William H. Wood,
Ezekiel Wright.

Those who voted in the negative are:—

Messrs. Alfred A. Abbott,
Benjamin P. Adams,
P. Emory Aldrich,
Robert Andrews,
William Aspinwall,
Alpheus Bancroft,
Joseph Barrows,
Sidney Bartlett,
Erasmus D. Beach,
John Beal,
William J. A. Bradford,
Osmyn Brewster,
Francis Brinley,
George N. Briggs,
Asahel Buck,
Rufus Bullock,
Cephas C. Bumpus,
Henry Cady,
Timothy W. Carter,
Chester W. Chapin,
J. McKean Churchill,
Lansing J. Cole,
Ithamar Conkey,
Benjamin F. Copeland,
George W. Crockett,
Leander Crosby,
Seth Crowell,
Joseph Cummings,
Charles G. Davis,
John Davis,
Robert T. Davis,
Solomon Davis,
Hiram S. Denison,
James C. Doane,
Lilley Eaton,
Homer Ely,
William T. Eustis,
A. G. Farwell,
Samuel P. Fowler,
Henry J. Gardner,
Robert Gould,
Dalton Goulding,
Jason Goulding,
John C. Gray,
Artemas Hale,
Nathan Hale,
Elnathan P. Hathaway,
George Hayward,
Charles Heard,
Henry Hersey,
William H. Hewes,

Messrs. George S. Hillard,
Thomas Hopkinson,
Samuel Houghton,
William J. Hubbard,
William Hunt,
Asahel Huntington,
Charles P. Huntington,
Samuel Jackson,
William James,
Samuel H. Jenks,
Giles C. Kellogg,
Martin R. Kellogg,
George H. Kuhn,
John S. Ladd,
Job G. Lawton, Jr.,
Frederic W. Lincoln, Jr.,
Isaac Livermore,
Samuel P. Loud,
Seth Miller, Jr.,
Samuel Mixter,
George Morey,
Joseph B. Morss,
Marcus Morton,
Marcus Morton, Jr.,
Daniel Noyes,
Henry K. Oliver,
Nathan Orcutt,
Adolphus G. Parker,
Thomas A. Parsons,
William C. Plunkett,
Robert Rantoul,
James Read,
Sampson Reed,
John Sargent,
William Schouler,
Charles Sherman,
John S. Sleeper,
Charles G. Stevens,
Granville Stevens,
J. Thomas Stevenson,
Increase Sumner,
Thomas Talbot,
Ralph Taylor,
Charles Thompson,
Edmund P. Tileston,
David Turner,
Charles W. Upham,
Samuel B. Walcott,
Bradford L. Wales,
Samuel Walker,
Cyrus Weeks,

Messrs. Thomas Wetmore,	Messrs. Ezra Wilkinson,
William F. Wheeler,	Henry Williams,
Daniel Wilbur,	Milo Wilson,
Joseph Wilbur,	Jonathan B. Winn,
Joel Wilder,	Josiah B. Woods.

On the question of adopting the fifth Resolution, no objection being made, the calling of the roll was dispensed with; and upon a division, one hundred and eighty-nine members voted for the Resolve, and twenty-seven against it.

So it was adopted.

The Resolves were then ordered to a second reading.

On motion of Mr. Boutwell, member for Berlin, the Resolves were specially assigned for consideration on Wednesday next at half past ten o'clock, and were ordered to be printed.

On motion of Mr. Wilson, of Natick, the Resolves reported by the Committee on the subject of the secretary, treasurer, &c., together with the motion of Mr. Dana, member for Manchester, to reconsider the vote by which they were passed, was taken from the table, and considered.

But without taking the question,

On motion of Mr. Dana, the subject was again laid upon the table.

Mr. Frothingham, of Charlestown, from a Select Committee, submitted a Report and Resolves on the subject of banking,

Referred to the Committee of the Whole and ordered to be printed.

Mr. Fay, of Southborough, from the Committee on Leave of Absence, submitted a Report, granting leave of absence for three weeks to Mr. Houghton, of Sterling.

The Report was considered and accepted.

At a quarter past six o'clock, on motion of Mr. Phinney, member for Chatham,

The Convention adjourned.

TUESDAY, July 5, 1853.

Met according to adjournment. Prayer was offered by the Chaplain. The Journal of Friday last was read.

A communication was received from the Secretary of State, enclosing a list of justices of the supreme judicial court, and of the court of common pleas.

Also, a communication from the same gentleman, enclosing a list of pardons, remissions, restorations, and commutations, from 1843 to 1852, inclusive.

Laid upon the table and ordered to be printed.

On motion of Mr. Wilson, of Natick, the Convention resolved itself into Committee of the Whole, for the purpose of considering the Report of the Committee on the Encouragement of Literature, inexpedient to act upon the subject of an Order of May 20th, and of the Petition of Harriet K. Hunt, on the subject of providing for the education of females; and the President requested Mr. Parker, of Cambridge, to take the chair.

Afterwards, Mr. Parker reported, that it was the opinion of the committee that the Report ought to be accepted.

And it was accordingly accepted.

On motion of Mr. Wilson, of Natick, the Convention resolved itself into Committee of the Whole, for the purpose of considering the Report of the Committee on the Encouragement of Literature, inexpedient to act upon the subject of an Order of May 23d, concerning the expediency of providing that the Board of Education and the Board of Agriculture shall be established as permanent departments of government; and the President requested Mr. Walker, of North Brookfield, to take the chair.

Afterwards, Mr. Walker reported, that it was the opinion of the committee, that the Report ought to be accepted.

And it was acordingly accepted.

On motion of Mr. Wilson, of Natick, the Convention resolved itself into Committee of the Whole, for the purpose of considering the Resolve reported by the Committee on the Encouragement of Literature, on the subject of appropriating moneys for sectarian or denominational schools; and the President requested Mr. Schouler, of Boston, to take the chair.

Afterwards, Mr. Schouler reported, that it was the opinion of the committee, that the Resolve ought to pass.

And it was accordingly ordered to a second reading.

On motion of Mr. Kingman, of West Bridgewater, the rules were suspended, and the Resolve considered, the question being on its final passage.

On motion of Mr. Bird, of Walpole, the yeas and nays were ordered; and then,

On motion of Mr. Warner, of Wrentham, the Resolve was postponed until to-morrow.

On motion of Mr. Bird, of Walpole, the Convention resolved itself into Committee of the Whole, for the purpose of considering the series of Resolutions reported by the Committee on Oaths and Subscriptions, on the subject of oaths, incompatibility of offices, the enacting style, attachment on mesne process, and electing bank officers to office; and the President requested Mr. Sumner, member for Otis, to take the chair.

Afterwards, Mr. SUMNER reported the Resolves to the Convention, with an amendment, viz.: striking from the last line of the first Resolve, the words "the legislature," and inserting instead thereof the word "law."

The amendment was agreed to.

On motion of Mr. WARD, of Newton, the second Resolve was amended by striking out the words "or place," in the third line, and also the words "place or" in the seventh line.

Mr. WHITNEY, of Boylston, moved to amend by striking out the fifth Resolve, and substituting therefor the following:—

Resolved, That it is expedient so to alter the Constitution as to provide that persons conscientiously scrupulous of taking human life, may act in an official capacity under the Constitution without taking the ordinary oath or affirmation.

The amendment was rejected, and the Resolves, as amended, were Ordered to a second reading.

On motion of Mr. WALKER, of North Brookfield, the Convention resolved itself into Committee of the Whole, for the purpose of considering the unfinished business of the session of June 22d, viz.: the Resolves reported by the Committee on the Qualifications of Voters, on the subject of the residence of voters, &c.; and the President requested Mr. Giles, of Boston, to take the chair.

Afterwards, Mr. GILES reported, that the committee had made further progress in the consideration of the subject, but had come to no conclusion, and had instructed him to ask leave to sit again.

And leave was accordingly granted.

At one o'clock, on motion of Mr. OLIVER, of Lawrence,

The Convention adjourned.

AFTERNOON SESSION.

Met according to adjournment.

On motion of Mr. ALLEY, of Lynn, the Convention resolved itself into Committee of the Whole, for the purpose of considering the Resolves on the subject of the residence of voters, &c., and the President requested Mr. Giles, of Boston, to take the chair.

Afterwards, Mr. GILES reported, that the committee had made further progress in the consideration of the subject, but for want of a quorum had been unable to come to any conclusion.

At a quarter before seven o'clock, on motion of Mr. CROWNINSHIELD, of Boston,

The Convention adjourned.

WEDNESDAY, July 6, 1853.

Met according to adjournment. Prayer was offered by the Chaplain. The Journal of yesterday was read.

Mr. WALKER, of North Brookfield, from the Committee on the Qualifications of Voters, submitted a Report, inexpedient to act upon the subject of an Order of May 19th, concerning betting on elections, and the exclusion from the right of suffrage of persons convicted of bribery, &c.; and an Order of June 18th, concerning the expediency of exempting voters, during the time of election, from military duty, attending court, &c.; and an Order of May 31st, concerning the expediency of requiring, in all persons admitted to vote after 1856, an ability to read the Constitution in the English language; and the Petition of Harriet K. Hunt, to be excused from paying taxes; and the Petition of Wendell Phillips and others, that women may be heard before the Convention.

Referred to the Committee of the Whole and ordered to be printed.

On motion of Mr. WILSON, of Natick, the Committee of the Whole having under consideration the Resolves concerning the residence of voters, &c., was discharged from the further consideration of that subject; and

The Resolves were then laid upon the table.

On motion of Mr. WILSON, of Natick, the Convention resolved itself into Committee of the Whole, for the purpose of considering the Resolve reported by the Committee on the Encouragement of Literature, on the subject of the enlargement and preservation of the School Fund; and the President requested Mr. Wood, of Fitchburg, to take the chair.

Afterwards, Mr. WOOD reported, that it was the opinion of the committee that the Resolve ought to pass.

And it was accordingly ordered to a second reading.

On motion of Mr. WILSON, of Natick, the Convention resolved

itself into Committee of the Whole, for the purpose of considering the Resolve reported by the Committee on the Encouragement of Literature, in favor of amending the second section of the fifth chapter of the Constitution; and the President requested Mr. Oliver, of Lawrence, to take the chair.

Afterwards, Mr. OLIVER reported, that it was the opinion of the committee that the Resolve ought to pass.

And it was accordingly ordered to a second reading.

On motion of Mr. STETSON, of Braintree, the Convention resolved itself into Committee of the Whole, for the purpose of considering the Report of the Special Committee, inexpedient to act upon the subject of the loan of the State credit.

Afterwards, on motion of Mr. EAMES, of Washington, the vote was reconsidered, and the Convention refused to go into committee on that subject.

On motion of Mr. WESTON, of Duxbury, the Resolves reported by the Committee on Secretary, Treasurer, &c., with the motion made by Mr. Dana, member for Manchester, to reconsider the vote by which they were finally passed, were taken from the table and considered.

After debate, Mr. MORTON, of Quincy, moved the Previous Question.

Pending the consideration of which,

Mr. STETSON, of Braintree, called for the subject specially assigned for half past ten o'clock to-day, which was the Resolves on the basis of the House of Representatives.

The Resolves were read a second time, and then, on motion of Mr. BOUTWELL, member for Berlin, were

Laid upon the table.

On motion of Mr. BOUTWELL, the Convention resumed the consideration of the subject of the Resolves on the secretary, treasurer, &c., and the motion to reconsider, &c.

The motion for the Previous Question was rejected, by a vote of one hundred and two in the affirmative, to one hundred and seventeen in the negative.

After further debate, Mr. WILSON, of Natick, asked the unanimous consent of the Convention that he might introduce a motion, that the question be taken on the proposition to reconsider at a quarter past twelve o'clock.

Objection being made by Mr. LORD, of Salem,

On motion of Mr. WILSON, the Orders of the Day were laid upon the table, by a vote of one hundred and twelve in the affirmative, to fifty-four in the negative; and then,

On motion of Mr. Wilson,

Ordered, That the question be taken on the motion to reconsider, at seventeen minutes past twelve o'clock.

That time having arrived, the question was called for.

On request of Mr. Bird, of Walpole, the question was divided, and the vote taken separately upon each of the four Resolutions;

And the motion to reconsider the vote on the passage of the first, second and fourth Resolutions, was rejected, without a division.

The motion to reconsider the vote on the passage of the third Resolution, was also rejected, by a vote of eighty-five in the affirmative to one hundred and sixty-six in the negative.

On motion of Mr. Wilson, of Natick, the Convention proceeded to the consideration of the Orders of the Day.

The first subject, being the Resolve on the subject of general laws for corporations, was passed over.

The second subject was the Resolve on the subject of appropriations for sectarian schools.

Mr. Stetson, of Braintree, moved to amend the Resolve by adding, at the close, the words, "or any seminaries of learning;" but afterwards withdrew his motion.

Mr. Blagden, of Boston, moved to amend the Resolve by inserting, before the word "sectarian" in the fourth line, (printed copy,) the words, "any common schools of a," and by inserting at the close, the word "character," instead of the word "schools."

Pending the consideration of this amendment,

At one o'clock, the Convention adjourned.

AFTERNOON SESSION.

Met according to adjournment.

Mr. Hall, of Haverhill, from the Committee on the Secretary, Treasurer, &c., submitted a Report and series of Resolves on the subject of the election of justices of the peace.

Referred to the Committee of the Whole and ordered to be printed.

On motion of Mr. Leland, of Holliston, the Convention proceeded to the consideration of the Orders of the Day.

The first subject was the unfinished business of the morning session, viz.: The Resolve on the subject of appropriations for sectarian schools.

And the pending question was upon the amendment offered by Mr. Blagden, of Boston.

Without taking the question,

On motion of Mr. STETSON, of Braintree, the whole subject was

Laid upon the table.

The next subject in the Orders of the Day was taken up, viz.: the Resolves reported by the Committee on Oaths and Subscriptions, &c., on the subject of oaths, incompatibility of offices, the enacting style, attachment on mesne process, and electing bank officers to office.

Mr. BRINLEY, of Boston, moved to amend the series by striking out the third Resolve.

Mr. HOOPER, of Fall River, moved to amend the amendment, by striking from the Resolve the words "General Court of Massachusetts," and inserting instead thereof the words, "people represented in the general court."

But the amendment to the amendment was rejected, and

The amendment offered by Mr. Brinley was also rejected, by a vote of fifty-two in the affirmative, to one hundred and twenty-five in the negative.

On motion of Mr. HALLETT, member for Wilbraham, the first Resolve was amended by striking out the words, "or before a judge of the supreme court," wherever they occur in the second paragraph.

Also, by striking out the words, "and councillors," in the second and third lines of the same paragraph, (printed copy,) and by inserting the word "and" before the word "lieutenant-governor" in the second line, and by inserting after the word "assembly" in the fourth line, the words "and by councillors before the president of the Senate, and in presence of the Senate."

On motion of Mr. BATES, of Plymouth, the first Resolve was further amended by substituting the words, "in convention," for the words "of assembly" in the fourth line of the second paragraph.

On motion of Mr. EDWARDS, of Southampton, the second Resolve was amended by striking out the words, "or receiver-general" in the fifth and sixth lines of the fourth paragraph.

The Resolves, as amended, were then finally passed, by a vote of one hundred and fifty in the affirmative, to six in the negative; as follow:—

1. *Resolved,* That the first article of the sixth chapter be amended in the last paragraph thereof, by the insertion of the words, "or before a judge of the supreme court" after the word "assembly," and by the

insertion of the same words, after the word "being," so that the paragraph, as amended, shall read as follows :—

"And the said oaths and affirmations shall be taken and subscribed by the governor and lieutenant-governor before the president of the Senate, in presence of the two Houses in convention, and by councillors before the president of the Senate, and in presence of the Senate, and by the senators and representatives before the governor and council for the time being, and by the residue of the officers aforesaid before such persons and in such manner as shall from time to time be prescribed by law."

2. *Resolved*, That the first paragraph of said article ought to be amended by inserting after the word "court" in the second line, "or court of common pleas," and by adding after the last word of said paragraph the following: "Except that they may be appointed to take depositions or acknowledgments of deeds, or other legal instruments, by the authority of any other state or country."

So that the same, amended, shall read as follows, to wit:

No governor, lieutenant-governor, or judge of the supreme judicial court or court of common pleas, shall hold any other office, under the authority of this Commonwealth, except such as by this Constitution they are admitted to hold, saving that the judges of the said courts may hold the offices of justices of the peace through the State; nor shall they hold any other office, or receive any pension or salary from any other state, or government, or power whatever; except that they may be appointed to take depositions, or acknowledgments of deeds, or other legal instruments, by the authority of any other state or country.

Also, that the second, third, and fourth paragraphs, and article eight of the amendments of said article, be stricken out, and the following inserted :—

No person shall hold or exercise at the same time more than one of the following offices, to wit: the office of governor, lieutenant-governor, senator, representative, judge of the supreme judicial court, or court of common pleas, secretary of the Commonwealth, attorney-general, treasurer, auditor, councillor, judge of probate, register of probate, register of deeds, sheriff, or his deputy, clerk of the supreme judicial court, or court of common pleas, clerk of the Senate or House of Representatives; and any person holding either of the above offices shall be deemed to have vacated the same by accepting a seat in the congress of the United States, or any office under the authority of the United States, the office of postmaster excepted; and no person shall be capable of holding at the same time more than two offices which are held by appointment of the governor, or governor and council, or the Senate, or the House of Representatives; military offices, and the offices of justices of the peace, justices of the peace and quorum, and notaries public, excepted; and whenever there shall be a vacancy of any of the above offices, the office of governor and lieutenant-governor excepted, the same may be filled.

That the fifth paragraph of said article ought to be retained without alteration or amendment.

3. *Resolved*, That the eighth article of the sixth chapter be amended by striking out the words, "Senate and House of Representatives in," and the words "assembled, and by authority of the same," and by adding the words "of Massachusetts," so that the article, as amended, shall read:—

ART. 8. The enacting style in making and passing all acts, statutes, and laws, shall be: *Be it enacted by the General Court of Massachusetts.*

4. *Resolved*, That it is inexpedient to make any constitutional provision relative to the subject of the Order exempting a certain amount of property from attachment on mesne process.

5. *Resolved*, That it is inexpedient to provide that any persons may act under the Constitution in an official capacity, without at least an affirmation that they will discharge and perform all the duties incumbent upon them in such capacity, according to the best of their abilities and understanding, agreeably to the rules and regulations of the Constitution and the laws of the Commonwealth.

6. *Resolved*, That it is not expedient, by a provision of the Constitution, to render any officer of a banking company incapable of holding any office to which he may be duly chosen by the votes of the people, or any portion thereof.

On motion of Mr. BOUTWELL, member for Berlin, the Resolves on the subject of the House of Representatives were taken from the table, and

The hour of half past nine o'clock, to-morrow, was specially assigned for their consideration.

Mr. WILSON, of Natick, moved that the hour of half past eleven o'clock on Friday, be assigned for taking the question on the final passage of the Resolves.

Mr. LORD, of Salem, called for the yeas and nays on this motion, but the demand was not sustained by one-fifth of the members voting.

The motion of Mr. Wilson was then agreed to.

Mr. FAY, of Southborough, from the Committee on Leave of Absence, submitted a Report, granting to Mr. Taber, of New Bedford, leave of absence for ten days.

The Report was considered, and leave of absence granted.

On motion of Mr. BIRD, of Walpole, the Convention resolved itself into Committee of the Whole, for the purpose of considering the Resolves on the subject of amendments of the Constitution; and the President requested Mr. Griswold, member for Erving, to take the chair.

Afterwards, Mr. GRISWOLD reported, that the committee had made progress in the consideration of the subject, but had come to no conclusion, and had instructed him to ask leave to sit again.

And leave was accordingly granted.

At a quarter past six o'clock, on motion of Mr. KNIGHT, of Peru,

The Convention adjourned.

THURSDAY, July 7, 1853.

Met according to adjournment. Prayer was offered by the Chaplain. The Journal of yesterday was read.

Mr. CHANDLER, of Greenfield, presented the Petition of C. J. J. Ingersoll and thirty-eight other inhabitants of Greenfield, for a declaration in favor of protection to fugitive slaves.

Referred to the Committee on the Bill of Rights.

Mr. COLE, of Cheshire, offered the following Resolution:—

Resolved, That the Constitution be so amended that a majority of the members of the House shall be necessary to constitute a quorum.

On motion of Mr. WILSON, of Natick, the Convention proceeded to the consideration of the Orders of the Day.

The first subject, being the Resolve on the subject of general laws for corporations, was passed over.

The second subject was the Resolve on the subject of the enlargement and preservation of the School Fund.

Mr. LOTHROP, of Boston, moved to amend the Resolve by inserting after the word "appropriated," in the fifth line, (printed copy,) the words "under the direction of the Board of Education, or such similar agency as may be provided by law;" but the amendment was rejected.

The Resolve was then finally passed, as follows:—

Resolved, That the legislature shall, as soon as may be, provide for the enlargement of the School Fund of this Commonwealth, until it shall amount, at least, to the sum of two millions of dollars; and the said fund shall be preserved inviolate, and the income thereof shall be annually appropriated for the aid and improvement of the common schools of the State, and for no other purpose.

Mr. Boutwell, member for Berlin, called for the special assignment for half-past nine o'clock, viz.: the Resolves on the subject of the House of Representatives.

On motion of Mr. Wood, of Middleborough, the Resolves were amended by striking out the second paragraph of the first Resolve, and substituting therefor the following:—

Any two of such towns may, by a vote of a major part of the legal voters of each, at legal meetings thereof, and held at some time preceding the first election which shall take place under this amendment to the Constitution, and thereafter, at legal meetings, held at some time preceding the first election which shall take place next after each decennial State census, unite together in a district, which shall be entitled to a representative each year, and which shall continue until the next decennial census, excepting the year in which the valuation of estates is settled.

At one o'clock, the Convention adjourned.

AFTERNOON SESSION.

Met according to adjournment.

On motion of Mr. Breed, of Lynn, the Convention proceeded to the consideration of the Orders of the Day; the first subject being the unfinished business specially assigned, viz.: the Resolves on the subject of the House of Representatives.

Mr. Hale, of Boston, moved to amend the Resolves by substituting therefor the following:—

Resolved, That it is expedient so to alter and amend the Constitution, as to provide for a periodical division of the Commonwealth into equal districts on the basis of population, with a view to the establishment of a House of Representatives on the principle of equality, and consisting of such a number of members as may be best entitled to the confidence of the people, and best adapted to the convenient despatch of the legislative business. In order thereto, a census of the inhabitants of each city and town, on the first day of May in the year one thousand eight hundred and fifty-four, and on the first day of May in every tenth year thereafter, shall be taken and returned to the office of the secretary of the Commonwealth, on or before the last day of June next ensuing the dates aforesaid. And it shall be the duty of the general court, which shall be next chosen after the taking of each decennial census, to divide the towns and cities of the Commonwealth into eighty districts, in such manner that each shall contain, as nearly as may be, an equal number of inhabitants; and they shall, in all cases where the same shall be practicable, be formed by the union of towns and cities, or parts of cities, adjoining one another; and in the formation of such districts no town shall be divided. But the cities, when containing a greater number of inhabitants than the average of the districts throughout the Commonwealth, shall be so divided that each district shall, as nearly as may be, contain that number; and any part of the inhabitants exceeding the number required for the entire districts therein, shall be set off to form a part of such adjoining district as the general court shall direct. The division of cities into districts shall be formed, and the inhabitants who may be set off to an adjoining district shall be organized for the purpose of conducting the elections therein, by the municipal authorities of the respective cities, in the same manner as the wards for city purposes are constituted therein. And the inhabitants of each district shall elect three representatives, constituting a House of two hundred and forty members.

On motion of Mr. Hale, the yeas and nays were ordered upon the adoption of the amendment.

Mr. Hallett, member for Wilbraham, moved a reconsideration of the vote by which the Convention, in the morning session, agreed to the amendment offered by Mr. Wood, of Middleborough.

And pending this question,

At six o'clock, on motion of Mr. Briggs, of Pittsfield,

The Convention adjourned.

FRIDAY, July 8, 1853.

Met according to adjournment. Prayer was offered by the Chaplain. The Journal of yesterday was read.

On motion of Mr. James, of South Scituate, the Convention proceeded to the consideration of the Orders of the Day.

The first subject was the unfinished business of yesterday, viz.: the Resolves on the subject of the House of Representatives, and

The pending question was upon the motion of Mr. Hallett, member for Wilbraham, to reconsider the vote by which the amendment of Mr. Wood, of Middleborough, was adopted.

The vote was reconsidered, and the question then recurring upon the adoption of the amendment, it was, on motion of Mr. Hallett, amended by substituting the following:—

Any two of such towns may, by a vote of the majority of the legal voters present at a legal meeting, in each of said towns respectively, called for that purpose, unite together in a district, which shall be entitled to a representative each year; and which shall continue not less than two years, excepting the year in which the valuation of estates is settled.

The amendment, as amended, was then adopted.

On motion of Mr. Abbott, of Lowell, the third Resolve was amended by striking out all after the words "seasonably published," and inserting instead thereof the following:—

And in all apportionments after the first, the number which shall entitle any city or town to two, three, four, or more representatives, shall be increased or decreased, in the same proportion as the population of the whole Commonwealth shall have increased or diminished since the last apportionment.

Mr. Earle, of Worcester, moved to amend the first Resolve by adding at the close of the fourth paragraph the word "and"; striking out the fifth and sixth paragraphs; and striking from the seventh paragraph the words "containing over twelve thousand inhabitants," and also the word "twelve."

But the amendment was rejected.

The question was then stated upon the amendment, offered yesterday by Mr. Hale, of Boston, modified by him, by substituting the words "one thousand eight hundred and fifty-five," for the words "one thousand eight hundred and fifty-four," in the eleventh and twelfth lines.

And the roll being called, one hundred and twenty-two members voted for the amendment, and two hundred and forty-four against it.

So it was rejected.

Those who voted in the affirmative are:—

Messrs. Alfred A. Abbott,
Benjamin P. Adams,
P. Emory Aldrich,
William Appleton,
William Aspinwall,
David C. Atwood,
Joseph Barrows,
Sidney Bartlett,

Messrs. James M. Beebe,
Luther V. Bell,
George W. Blagden,
Ebenezer Bradbury,
William J. A. Bradford,
Milton P. Braman,
Osmyn Brewster,
Francis Brinley,

Messrs. George N. Briggs,
Asa Bronson,
Rufus Bullock,
Cephas C. Bumpus,
Josiah Childs,
J. McKean Churchill,
Nathaniel Cogswell,
Charles E. Cook,
Henry F. Cooledge,
Benjamin F. Copeland,
George W. Crockett,
Leander Crosby,
Seth Crowell,
Francis B. Crowninshield,
Joseph Cummings,
Wilber Curtis,
John Davis,
Solomon Davis,
Henry L. Dawes,
William Dehon,
James C. Doane,
James Easton, 2d,
Lilley Eaton,
Homer Ely,
A. G. Farwell,
Samuel P. Fowler,
Charles H. French,
Henry J. Gardner,
Joel Giles,
Robert Gould,
Dalton Goulding,
Jason Goulding,
John C. Gray,
Simon Greenleaf,
Artemas Hale,
Nathan Hale,
A. B. Hammond,
George Haskell,
Elnathan P. Hathaway,
George Hayward,
Charles Heard,
Henry Hersey,
George S. Hillard,
Thomas Hopkinson,
William J. Hubbard,
Asahel Huntington,
Samuel Jackson,
William James,
John Jenkins,
Samuel H. Jenks,
Giles C. Kellogg,
Martin R. Kellogg,
Henry W. Kinsman,

Messrs. George H. Kuhn,
John S. Ladd,
Frederic W. Lincoln, Jr.,
Tristram Littlefield,
Isaac Livermore,
Otis P. Lord,
Samuel K. Lothrop,
Samuel P. Loud,
John A. Lowell,
Theophilus R. Marvin,
Seth Miller, Jr.,
Marcus Morton,
Marcus Morton, Jr.,
Henry K. Oliver,
Nathan Orcutt,
James W. Paige,
John G. Park,
Joel Parker,
Samuel D. Parker,
George Peabody,
Jonathan C. Perkins,
William C. Plunkett,
Jonathan Preston,
Robert Rantoul,
James Read,
Sampson Reed,
George R. Sampson,
John Sargent,
William Schouler,
John S. Sleeper,
Eben H. Stacy,
Caleb Stetson,
Charles G. Stevens,
Joseph L. Stevens, Jr.,
J. Thomas Stevenson,
Charles Sumner,
Alanson Swain,
Ralph Taylor,
Joseph Thayer,
Edmund P. Tileston,
John S. Tyler,
Charles W. Upham,
George B. Upton,
Samuel B. Walcott,
Samuel Walker,
Cyrus Weeks,
Thomas Wetmore,
Joseph Wilbur,
Joel Wilder,
John H. Wilkins,
Ezra Wilkinson,
Milo Wilson,
Jonathan B. Winn.

Those who voted in the negative are :—

Messrs. Josiah G. Abbott,
Shubael P. Adams,
Charles Allen,
Joel C. Allen,
Parsons Allen,
John B. Alley,
Josiah Allis,
D. W. Alvord,
Samuel Ayres,
Alvah Ballard,
George S. Ball,
Alpheus Bancroft,
Russel Bartlett,
Marcus Barrett,
Eliakim A. Bates,
Moses Bates, Jr.,
John Beal,
William Bennett, Jr.,
Zephaniah Bennett,
Edward B. Bigelow,
Francis W. Bird,
Henry W. Bishop,
Gad O. Bliss,
William S. Booth,
George S. Boutwell,
Sewell Boutwell,
Hiram N. Breed,
Adolphus F. Brown,
Alpheus R. Brown,
Artemas Brown,
Hammond Brown,
Hiram C. Brown,
Frederick Brownell,
Joseph Brownell,
Patrick Bryant,
Asahel Buck,
Anson Burlingame,
Henry Cady,
William Carruthers,
Isaac Case,
Amariah Chandler,
Chester W. Chapin,
Daniel E. Chapin,
Henry Chapin,
Henry Clark,
Ransom Clark,
Alpheus B. Clarke,
Stillman Clarke,
William Cleverly,
Lansing J. Cole,
Sumner Cole,

Messrs. George B. Crane,
Oliver S. Cressy,
Simeon Crittenden,
Joseph W. Cross,
Henry W. Cushman,
Thomas Cushman,
Simeon N. Cutler,
Richard H. Dana, Jr.,
Charles G. Davis,
Ebenezer Davis,
Isaac Davis,
Robert T. Davis,
Gilman Day,
Silas Dean,
Elijah S. Deming,
Augustus Denton,
Alexander De Witt,
Moses Dorman,
Samuel Duncan,
Bradish Dunham,
John M. Durgin,
Philip Eames,
John M. Earle,
Peter Easland,
Calvin D. Eaton,
Elisha Edwards,
Samuel Edwards,
Joseph M. Ely,
Sullivan Fay,
Lyman Fisk,
Emery Fiske,
Ezekiel W. Fitch,
Aaron Foster,
Abram Foster,
Samuel Fowle,
James M. Freeman,
Charles A. French,
Rodney French,
Samuel French,
Richard Frothingham, Jr.,
Luther Gale,
Johnson Gardner,
Elbridge Gates,
Wanton C. Gilbert,
Washington Gilbert,
Charles G. Giles,
Leonard Gooding,
John W. Graves,
Jabez Green,
William B. Greene,
Josiah W. Griswold,

Messrs. Whiting Griswold,
Samuel P. Hadley,
Charles B. Hall,
Benjamin F. Hallett,
Lyman W. Hapgood,
Seth Hapgood,
Phineas Harmon,
William Haskins,
Stephen E. Hawkes,
Isaac Hayden,
Ezra Heath, 2d,
Samuel Henry,
James Hewes,
William H. Hewes,
William Hinsdale,
Aaron Hobart,
Henry Hobart,
Edwin Hobbs,
Nathaniel Holder,
George Hood,
Foster Hooper,
Martin Howard,
Abraham H. Howland,
Henry K. Hoyt,
Charles E. Hunt,
Charles P. Huntington,
Moses C. Hurlbut,
Abijah M. Ide, Jr.,
John Jacobs,
John Johnson,
Edward L. Keyes,
Joseph Kimball,
Joseph Kingman,
Hiram Knight,
Jefferson Knight,
Joseph Knight,
Charles L. Knowlton,
J. S. C. Knowlton,
William H. Knowlton,
Gardner P. Ladd,
Wilber C. Langdon,
Luther Lawrence,
Job G. Lawton, Jr.,
Alden Leland,
Abishai Lincoln,
Otis Little,
Justin E. Loomis,
William P. Marble,
Laban Marcy,
Abijah P. Marvin,
Charles Mason,
Reuben Meader,
Simeon Merritt,

Messrs. James L. Monroe,
James M. Moore,
Joseph B. Morss,
William S. Morton,
Hiram Nash,
Jonathan Nayson,
Charles Newman,
William Nichols,
Alfred Norton,
Daniel Noyes,
Andrew T. Nute,
Benjamin S. Orne,
Charles Osgood,
E. Wing Packer,
Benjamin Paine,
Henry Paine,
Jonathan Parris,
Samuel C. Parsons,
John Partridge,
Nathaniel Peabody,
Jeremiah Pease, Jr.,
John Penniman,
Daniel A. Perkins,
Jesse Perkins,
Noah C. Perkins,
Charles Phelps,
Sylvanus B. Phinney,
Henry Pierce,
Jeremiah Pomroy,
James M. Pool,
Peter Powers,
John A. Putnam,
Silas Rawson,
Luther Richards,
Daniel Richardson,
Nathan Richardson,
Samuel H. Richardson,
Elkanah Ring, Jr.,
Joseph M. Rockwood,
John Rogers,
David S. Ross,
James C. Royce,
Amasa Sanderson,
Chester Sanderson,
Luther Sheldon,
John Sherril,
Chester Sikes,
Perez Simmons,
John W. Simonds,
Matthew Smith,
Melzar Sprague,
Samuel W. Spooner,
Granville Stevens,

Messrs. William Stevens,
Gideon Stiles,
Alfred L. Strong,
Increase Sumner,
Thomas Talbot,
Willard Thayer, 2d,
John W. Thomas,
Abraham Tilton,
Horatio W. Tilton,
David P. Turner,
William Tyler,
Orison Underwood,
Joel Viles,
George A. Vinton,
Frederick T. Wallace,
Freeland Wallis,
Amasa Walker,
Andrew H. Ward,

Messrs. Marshal Warner,
Samuel Warner, Jr.,
Asa H. Waters,
Gershom B. Weston,
William F. Wheeler,
Benjamin White,
George White,
Daniel S. Whitney,
Henry Williams,
J. B. Williams,
Henry Wilson,
Willard Wilson,
Levi M. Winslow,
Charles C. Wood,
Nathaniel Wood,
Otis Wood,
William H. Wood,
Ezekiel Wright.

On motion of Mr. Gray, of Boston, the yeas and nays were ordered on the final passage of the Resolves.

Mr. Wood, of Fitchburg, moved a suspension of the rule requiring that the names of members shall be called in alphabetical order; but the motion was rejected.

The roll was then called, and two hundred and thirty-five members voted for the final passage of the Resolves, and one hundred and thirty-one in opposition.

Those who voted in the affirmative are:—

Messrs. Josiah G. Abbott,
Shubael P. Adams,
Charles Allen,
Joel C. Allen,
Parsons Allen,
John B. Alley,
Josiah Allis,
D. W. Alvord,
George Austin,
Samuel Ayres,
Hillel Baker,
Alvah Ballard,
George S. Ball,
Alpheus Bancroft,
Russel Bartlett,
Marcus Barrett,
Eliakim A. Bates,
Moses Bates, Jr.,
John Beal,
William Bennett, Jr.,
Zephaniah Bennett,
Edward B. Bigelow,

Messrs. Francis W. Bird,
Henry W. Bishop,
Gad O. Bliss,
William S. Booth,
George S. Boutwell,
Sewell Boutwell,
Hiram N. Breed,
Adolphus F. Brown,
Alpheus R. Brown,
Artemas Brown,
Hammond Brown,
Hiram C. Brown,
Frederick Brownell,
Joseph Brownell,
Patrick Bryant,
Asahel Buck,
Anson Burlingame,
Henry Cady,
William Carruthers,
Isaac Case,
Amariah Chandler,
Daniel E. Chapin,

Messrs. Henry Chapin,
Henry Clark,
Ransom Clark,
Alpheus B. Clarke,
Stillman Clarke,
William Cleverly,
Lansing J. Cole,
Sumner Cole,
Henry F. Cooledge,
George B. Crane,
Oliver S. Cressy,
Simeon Crittenden,
Joseph W. Cross,
Wilber Curtis,
Henry W. Cushman,
Thomas Cushman,
Simeon N. Cutler,
Richard H. Dana, Jr.,
Ebenezer Davis,
Isaac Davis,
Gilman Day,
Silas Dean,
Elijah S. Deming,
Augustus Denton,
Alexander De Witt,
Samuel Duncan,
Bradish Dunham,
John M. Durgin,
Philip Eames,
John M. Earle,
Peter Easland,
James Easton, 2d,
Calvin D. Eaton,
Elisha Edwards,
Samuel Edwards,
Joseph M. Ely,
Sullivan Fay,
James K. Fellows,
Lyman Fisk,
Emery Fiske,
Ezekiel W. Fitch,
Aaron Foster,
Abram Foster,
Samuel Fowle,
James M. Freeman,
Charles A. French,
Rodney French,
Samuel French,
Luther Gale,
Johnson Gardner,
Elbridge Gates,
Wanton C. Gilbert,
Washington Gilbert,

Messrs. Charles G. Giles,
Joel Giles,
Daniel W. Gooch,
Leonard Gooding,
John W. Graves,
Jabez Green,
William B. Greene,
Josiah W. Griswold,
Whiting Griswold,
Samuel P. Hadley,
Benjamin F. Hallett,
Seth Hapgood,
Phineas Harmon,
William Haskins,
Stephen E. Hawkes,
Isaac Hayden,
Ezra Heath, 2d,
Samuel Henry,
James Hewes,
William Hinsdale,
Henry Hobart,
Edwin Hobbs,
Nathaniel Holder,
George Hood,
Martin Howard,
Abraham H. Howland,
Henry K. Hoyt,
Charles E. Hunt,
Moses C. Hurlbut,
Abijah M. Ide, Jr.,
John Jacobs,
Isaac Kendall,
Edward L. Keyes,
Joseph Kingman,
Hiram Knight,
Jefferson Knight,
Joseph Knight,
Charles L. Knowlton,
J. S. C. Knowlton,
William H. Knowlton,
Gardner P. Ladd,
Wilber C. Langdon,
Luther Lawrence,
Alden Leland,
Abishai Lincoln,
Otis Little,
Tristram Littlefield,
Justin E. Loomis,
William P. Marble,
Laban Marcy,
Abijah P. Marvin,
Charles Mason,
Reuben Meader,

Messrs. Simeon Merritt,
James L. Monroe,
James M. Moore,
Elbridge G. Morton,
William S. Morton,
Hiram Nash,
Jonathan Nayson,
Charles Newman,
William Nichols,
Alfred Norton,
Andrew T. Nute,
Benjamin S. Orne,
Charles Osgood,
E. Wing Packer,
Benjamin Paine,
Henry Paine,
Jonathan Parris,
Samuel C. Parsons,
John Partridge,
Nathaniel Peabody,
Jeremiah Pease, Jr.,
John Penniman,
Daniel A. Perkins,
Jesse Perkins,
Noah C. Perkins,
Charles Phelps,
Sylvanus B. Phinney,
Henry Pierce,
Jeremiah Pomroy,
James M. Pool,
Peter Powers,
John A. Putnam,
Silas Rawson,
Luther Richards,
Daniel Richardson,
Nathan Richardson,
Samuel H. Richardson,
Elkanah Ring, Jr.,
Joseph M. Rockwood,
John Rogers,
David S. Ross,
James C. Royce,
Amasa Sanderson,

Messrs. Chester Sanderson,
Luther Sheldon,
John Sherril,
Chester Sikes,
John W. Simonds,
Matthew Smith,
Melzar Sprague,
Samuel W. Spooner,
William Stevens,
Gideon Stiles,
Alfred L. Strong,
Charles Sumner,
Increase Sumner,
Alanson Swain,
Willard Thayer, 2d,
John W. Thomas,
Abraham Tilton,
Horatio W. Tilton,
David P. Turner,
William Tyler,
Orison Underwood,
Joel Viles,
George A. Vinton,
Frederick T. Wallace,
Freeland Wallis,
Amasa Walker,
Andrew H. Ward,
Marshal Warner,
Samuel Warner, Jr.,
Gershom B. Weston,
Benjamin White,
George White,
Daniel S. Whitney,
J. B. Williams,
Henry \\ ilson,
Willard Wilson,
Levi M. Winslow,
Charles C. Wood,
Nathaniel Wood,
Otis Wood,
William H. Wood,
Ezekiel Wright.

Those who voted in the negative are:—

Messrs. Alfred A. Abbott,
Benjamin P. Adams,
P. Emory Aldrich,
William Appleton,
William Aspinwall,
David C. Atwood,
Joseph Barrows,

Messrs. Sidney Bartlett,
Erasmus D. Beach,
Luther V. Bell,
George W. Blagden,
Ebenezer Bradbury,
William J. A. Bradford,
Milton P. Braman,

Messrs. Osmyn Brewster,
Francis Brinley,
George N. Briggs,
Asa Bronson,
Rufus Bullock,
Cephas C. Bumpus,
Chester W. Chapin,
Josiah Childs,
J. McKean Churchill,
Nathaniel Cogswell,
Charles E. Cook,
Benjamin F. Copeland,
George W. Crockett,
Leander Crosby,
Seth Crowell,
Francis B. Crowninshield,
Joseph Cummings,
Charles G. Davis,
John Davis,
Robert T. Davis,
Solomon Davis,
Henry L. Dawes,
James C. Doane,
Moses Dorman,
Lilley Eaton,
Homer Ely,
A. G. Farwell,
Samuel P. Fowler,
Charles H. French,
Henry J. Gardner,
Robert Gould,
Dalton Goulding,
Jason Goulding,
John C. Gray,
Simon Greenleaf,
Artemas Hale,
Nathan Hale,
A. B. Hammond,
George Haskell,
Elnathan P. Hathaway,
George Hayward,
Charles Heard,
Henry Hersey,
William H. Hewes,
George S. Hillard,
Foster Hooper,
Thomas Hopkinson,
William J. Hubbard,
Asahel Huntington,
Charles P. Huntington,
Samuel Jackson,
William James,
John Jenkins,

Messrs. Samuel H. Jenks,
Giles C. Kellogg,
Martin R. Kellogg,
Henry W. Kinsman,
George H. Kuhn,
John S. Ladd,
Job G. Lawton, Jr.,
Frederic W. Lincoln, Jr.,
Isaac Livermore,
Samuel K. Lothrop,
Samuel P. Loud,
John A. Lowell,
Theophilus R. Marvin,
Seth Miller, Jr.,
Joseph B. Morss,
Marcus Morton,
Marcus Morton, Jr.,
Daniel Noyes,
Joseph E. Ober,
Henry K. Oliver,
Nathan Orcutt,
James W. Paige,
John G. Park,
Joel Parker,
Samuel D. Parker,
George Peabody,
Jonathan C. Perkins,
William C. Plunkett,
Jonathan Preston,
Robert Rantoul,
James Read,
Sampson Reed,
George R. Sampson,
John Sargent,
William Schouler,
John S. Sleeper,
Eben H. Stacy,
Caleb Stetson,
Charles G. Stevens,
Granville Stevens,
Joseph L. Stevens, Jr.,
J. Thomas Stevenson,
Thomas Talbot,
Ralph Taylor,
Joseph Thayer,
Charles Thompson,
Edmund P. Tileston,
John S. Tyler,
Charles W. Upham,
George B. Upton,
Samuel B. Walcott,
Samuel Walker,
Asa H. Waters,

Messrs. Cyrus Weeks,	Messrs. John H. Wilkins,
Thomas Wetmore,	Ezra Wilkinson,
William F. Wheeler,	Henry Williams,
Daniel Wilbur,	Milo Wilson,
Joseph Wilbur,	Jonathan B. Winn.
Joel Wilder,	

The Resolves, as finally passed, are as follow:—

That the Constitution be so revised, and altered, that the representation of the Commonwealth shall be apportioned as follows:—

Every town, of a less number than one thousand inhabitants, shall be entitled to five representatives, in each ten years, with an additional representative for the year when the valuation of estates shall be settled.

Any two of such towns may, by a vote of a majority of the legal voters present at a legal meeting in each of said towns respectively, called for that purpose, unite together in a district, which shall be entitled to a representative each year, and which shall continue not less than two years, excepting the year in which the valuation of estates shall be settled.

Every town of one thousand inhabitants, and of less than four thousand, shall be entitled to one representative each year.

Every town of four thousand inhabitants, and of less than eight thousand, shall be entitled to two representatives each year.

Every town of eight thousand inhabitants, and of less than twelve thousand, shall be entitled to three representatives each year.

Every city or town of twelve thousand inhabitants, shall be entitled to four representatives each year.

Every city or town containing over twelve thousand inhabitants, shall be entitled to elect one additional representative for every five thousand inhabitants it may contain over twelve thousand.

Resolved, That this apportionment be based upon the census of 1850, until a new census be taken.

Resolved, That the Senate, at its first session after this Constitution shall have been adopted, and at its first session after the next State census shall have been taken, and at its first session next after each decennial State census thereafterwards, shall apportion the number of representatives to which each town and city shall be entitled, and shall cause the same to be seasonably published; and in all apportionments after the first, the number which shall entitle any city or town to two, three, four or more representatives, shall be increased or decreased in the same proportion as the population of the whole

Commonwealth shall have increased or diminished since the last apportionment.

Resolved, That no town hereafter be incorporated with a privilege of representation as such, containing less than fifteen hundred inhabitants.

Resolved, That each city in this Commonwealth shall be divided, by such means as the legislature may provide, into districts of contiguous territory, as nearly equal in population as may be, for the election of representatives, which districts shall not be changed oftener than once in five years: *provided*, *however*, that no one district shall be entitled to elect more than three representatives.

At one o'clock, on motion of Mr. Wilson, of Natick,
The Convention adjourned.

AFTERNOON SESSION.

Met according to adjournment.

Mr. Morton, of Taunton, offered a Resolution, instructing the Committee appointed to Reduce the Amendments to Form, to prepare certain questions to be submitted to the people, on the subject of the House of Representatives.

Referred to the Committee of the Whole and ordered to be printed.

Mr. Sumner, member for Marshfield, from the Committee on the Bill of Rights, submitted a Report and Resolves on that subject.

Referred to the Committee of the Whole and ordered to be printed.

On motion of Mr. Stetson, of Braintree, the Convention resolved itself into Committee of the Whole, for the purpose of considering the Report, inexpedient to act on the subject of the loan of the State credit; and the President requested Mr. Boutwell, member for Berlin, to take the chair.

Afterwards, Mr. Boutwell, reported, that the committee had made further progress in the consideration of the subject, but had come to no conclusion, and had instructed him to ask leave to sit again.

And leave was accordingly granted.

At six o'clock, on motion of Mr. Parsons, of Sandisfield,
The Convention adjourned.

SATURDAY, July 9, 1853.

Met according to adjournment. Prayer was offered by the Chaplain. The Journal of yesterday was read.

Mr. EAMES, of Washington, presented the Petition of Otis F. R. Waite and eleven others, inhabitants of Pittsfield, for the preservation of town representation.

Laid upon the table.

On motion of Mr. GARDNER, of Seekonk,

Ordered, That when the Convention adjourn, it adjourn to meet again on Monday, at ten o'clock.

On motion of Mr. WILSON, of Natick, the Order of the Convention requiring an adjournment of the morning session at one o'clock, was so far modified as to extend the hour, for this day, until two o'clock.

Mr. WHITE, of Quincy, moved a reconsideration of the vote by which the Resolves on the subject of the House of Representatives, were finally passed.

Placed in the Orders of the Day.

On motion of Mr. WALKER, of North Brookfield, the Convention resolved itself into Committee of the Whole, for the purpose of considering the Report of the Committee on the Qualifications of Voters, inexpedient to act upon the subject of various Orders and Petitions committed to them; and the President requested Mr. Aspinwall, of Brookline, to take the chair.

Afterwards, Mr. ASPINWALL reported, that it was the opinion of the committee that the Report ought to be accepted.

And it was accordingly accepted.

On motion of Mr. WHITNEY, of Conway,

Ordered, That debate in Committee of the Whole, on the subject of the loan of the State credit, shall cease in one hour after the Convention goes into committee on that subject.

On motion of Mr. BUTLER, of Lowell, the Convention resolved itself into Committee of the Whole, for the purpose of considering the Report, inexpedient to act upon the subject of the loan of the State credit; and the President requested Mr. Boutwell, member for Berlin, to take the chair.

Afterwards, Mr. BOUTWELL reported, that it was the opinion of the committee that the Report ought to be accepted.

The question being upon concurrence with the Committee of the Whole in accepting the Report,

Mr. BIRD, of Walpole, moved the Previous Question.

Mr. WEEKS, of Harwich, called for the yeas and nays upon this motion; and then, no objection being made,

Mr. BIRD withdrew his motion.

Mr. MORTON, of Taunton, moved to amend the Report, by striking out the words "it is inexpedient to act thereon," and insert instead thereof, the following:—

The Constitution ought to be so amended as to provide, that

1st. The legislature shall not hereafter have power, directly or indirectly, to grant or loan the credit of the State, or create any liability on behalf of the State in aid of any individual, corporation or association. But the legislature may submit to the people a proposition to make any such loan or grant, which, if adopted by a majority of all the legal voters voting thereon, shall authorize the same.

2d. The legislature shall not, hereafter, in any manner, create any debt or debts, which shall singly or in the aggregate, with any pre-existing debts hereafter created, exceed the sum of one million of dollars, except to repel invasion or suppress insurrection.

After debate, on motion of Mr. BUTLER, of Lowell,

Ordered, That debate shall cease on the question at ten minutes before one o'clock.

On motion of Mr. STETSON, of Braintree, the yeas and nays were ordered upon the adoption of the amendment.

The hour having arrived for the debate to close,

The roll was called, and one hundred and four members voted for the amendment, and one hundred and thirty-seven against it.

So it was rejected.

Those who voted in the affirmative are:—

Messrs. Alfred A. Abbott,
Josiah G. Abbott,
Parsons Allen,
George Austin,
Samuel Ayres,
Sidney Bartlett,
Russel Bartlett,
Erasmus D. Beach,
John Beal,
James M. Beebe,
Gad O. Bliss,
Hiram N. Breed,
Osmyn Brewster,
George N. Briggs,
Asa Bronson,
Hiram C. Brown,
Frederick Brownell,

Messrs. Asahel Buck,
Cephas C. Bumpus,
Daniel E. Chapin,
Josiah Childs,
J. McKean Churchill,
Nathaniel Cogswell,
Lansing J. Cole,
Sumner Cole,
Benjamin F. Copeland,
George B. Crane,
Seth Crowell,
Francis B. Crowninshield,
Solomon Davis,
Silas Dean,
Elijah S. Deming,
Augustus Denton,
James C. Doane,

Messrs. Bradish Dunham,
John M. Earle,
Peter Easland,
Ezekiel W. Fitch,
Samuel Fowle,
Henry J. Gardner,
Wanton C. Gilbert,
Daniel W. Gooch,
Leonard Gooding,
Dalton Goulding,
Benjamin F. Hallett,
A. B. Hammond,
Seth Hapgood,
George Haskell,
Elnathan P. Hathaway,
Charles Heard,
Henry Hersey,
Aaron Hobart,
Henry Hobart,
Thomas Hopkinson,
William J. Hubbard,
Samuel Jackson,
William James,
John Jenkins,
John Johnson,
Hiram Knight,
Jefferson Knight,
Job G. Lawton, Jr.,
Alden Leland,
Abishai Lincoln,
Tristram Littlefield,
Samuel Mixter,
Elbridge G. Morton,
Marcus Morton,
Marcus Morton, Jr.,

Messrs. Jonathan Nayson,
Charles Newman,
William Nichols,
Alfred Norton,
Henry K. Oliver,
Nathan Orcutt,
Benjamin S. Orne,
Adolphus G. Parker,
Joel Parker,
Jeremiah Pease, Jr.,
Noah C. Perkins,
Robert Rantoul,
Daniel Richardson,
John Sargent,
Perez Simmons,
John W. Simonds,
Caleb Stetson,
Granville Stevens,
Gideon Stiles,
Thomas Talbot,
Ralph Taylor,
Horatio W. Tilton,
David P. Turner,
William Tyler,
Bradford L. Wales,
Freeland Wallis,
Samuel Walker,
Andrew H. Ward,
Cyrus Weeks,
Daniel Wilbur,
Joseph Wilbur,
Henry Williams,
J. B. Williams,
Willard Wilson,
Otis Wood.

Those who voted in the negative are:—

Messrs. Benjamin P. Adams,
Shubael P. Adams,
P. Emory Aldrich,
John B. Alley,
Josiah Allis,
D. W. Alvord,
William Aspinwall,
Hillel Baker,
Alvah Ballard,
George S. Ball,
Alpheus Bancroft,
Marcus Barrett,
Eliakim A. Bates,
Moses Bates, Jr.,
William Bennett, Jr.,
Edward B. Bigelow,

Messrs. Francis W. Bird,
Henry W. Bishop,
William S. Booth,
George S. Boutwell,
Sewell Boutwell,
Milton P. Braman,
Francis Brinley,
Hammond Brown,
Patrick Bryant,
Benjamin F. Butler,
Henry Cady,
Amariah Chandler,
Henry Chapin,
Ransom Clark,
William Cleverly,
Charles E. Cook,

Messrs. Henry F. Cooledge,
Simeon Crittenden,
Joseph W. Cross,
Joseph Cummings,
Wilber Curtis,
Henry W. Cushman,
Simeon N. Cutler,
Richard H. Dana, Jr.,
Henry L. Dawes,
Gilman Day,
Hiram S. Denison,
Samuel Duncan,
John M. Durgin,
Philip Eames,
Lilley Eaton,
Elisha Edwards,
Samuel Edwards,
Joseph M. Ely,
Sullivan Fay,
Lyman Fisk,
Aaron Foster,
Abram Foster,
James M. Freeman,
Samuel French,
Luther Gale,
Elbridge Gates,
Charles G. Giles,
Joel Giles,
Jason Goulding,
John W. Graves,
John C. Gray,
Jabez Green,
William B. Greene,
Josiah W. Griswold,
Whiting Griswold,
Lyman W. Hapgood,
Phineas Harmon,
Stephen E. Hawkes,
Isaac Hayden,
Ezra Heath, 2d,
William Hinsdale,
Edwin Hobbs,
Nathaniel Holder,
George Hood,
Henry K. Hoyt,
John Jacobs,
Giles C. Kellogg,
Isaac Kendall,
Joseph Kingman,
Joseph Knight,
William H. Knowlton,
John S. Ladd,
Wilber C. Langdon,

Messrs. Luther Lawrence,
Justin E. Loomis,
Abijah P. Marvin,
Charles Mason,
Simeon Merritt,
James L. Monroe,
James M. Moore,
Hiram Nash,
Andrew T. Nute,
Joseph E. Ober,
Charles Osgood,
E. Wing Packer,
Benjamin Paine,
Henry Paine,
John G. Park,
Jonathan Parris,
Samuel C. Parsons,
Charles Phelps,
Henry Pierce,
Jeremiah Pomroy,
James M. Pool,
Sampson Reed,
Nathan Richardson,
Samuel H. Richardson,
Elkanah Ring, Jr.,
Joseph M. Rockwood,
Amasa Sanderson,
Chester Sanderson,
William Schouler,
John Sherril,
Chester Sikes,
John S. Sleeper,
John Souther,
Samuel W. Spooner,
William Stevens,
J. Thomas Stevenson,
Increase Sumner,
John W. Thomas,
Charles Thompson,
Charles R. Train,
Orison Underwood,
Joel Viles,
Gershom B. Weston,
William F. Wheeler,
Benjamin White,
George White,
Daniel S. Whitney,
James S. Whitney,
Joel Wilder,
John H. Wilkins,
Henry Wilson,
Jonathan B. Winn.

Mr. Stetson, of Braintree, moved an adjournment, but the motion was rejected.

Mr. Giles, of Boston, moved to amend the Report by substituting the following Resolution :—

Resolved, That the legislature shall not have power to grant the credit of the State to any individual or corporation, without a two-thirds vote of the House of Representatives and the Senate in its favor.

The amendment was adopted by a vote of one hundred and fourteen in the affirmative to seventy-six in the negative.

And the Resolve was ordered to a second reading.

At half-past one o'clock, on motion of Mr. Thompson, of Charlestown,

The Convention adjourned.

MONDAY, July 11, 1853.

Met according to adjournment. Prayer was offered by Rev. Mr. Cogswell, of Yarmouth, a member of the Convention. The Journal of Saturday was read.

Mr. Hallett, member for Wilbraham, offered the following Resolution, which, on his motion, was referred to a select committee, to consist of five members :—

Resolved, That the Constitution ought to provide, in addition to the remedies now recognized therein for all injuries to person and property, that a remedy shall be given to the legal representatives of any deceased person, whose death was caused by the negligence or misconduct of a railroad corporation, in the same manner as for like injuries resulting in disability and not in death.

Mr. Thompson, of Charlestown, moved a reconsideration of the vote by which the Resolve on the subject of loaning the State credit was ordered to a second reading.

Placed in the Orders of the Day for to-morrow.

On motion of Mr. Earle, of Worcester, the Convention proceeded to the consideration of the Orders of the Day.

The first subject, viz. : the motion of Mr. White, of Quincy, that the vote by which the Resolves on the subject of the House of Representatives were finally passed be reconsidered, was,

On motion of Mr. WHITE,

Laid upon the table.

The second subject, viz.: the Resolve on the subject of general laws for corporations,

And the third subject, viz.: the Resolve in favor of amending section 2, chapter 5, of the Constitution, by striking therefrom the words "University at Cambridge,"

Were passed over.

And then, on motion of Mr. BUTLER, of Lowell,

The Orders of the Day were laid upon the table.

On motion of Mr. BUTLER, of Lowell, the Convention resolved itself into Committee of the Whole, for the purpose of considering the Resolves on the subject of the judiciary, and the President requested Mr. Hallett, member for Wilbraham, to take the chair.

Afterwards, Mr. HALLETT reported, that the committee had made progress in the consideration of the subject, but had come to no conclusion, and had instructed him to ask leave to sit again.

And leave was accordingly granted.

At one o'clock, on motion of Mr. PERKINS, of Malden,

The Convention adjourned.

AFTERNOON SESSION.

Met according to adjournment.

Mr. MARVIN, of Winchendon, moved a reconsideration of the vote by which the Report of the Committee on the Qualifications of Voters, inexpedient to act upon the subject of various orders and petitions, was accepted.

Placed in the Orders of the Day.

On motion of Mr. WHITE, of Quincy, the Convention resolved itself into Committee of the Whole, for the purpose of considering the Resolves on the subject of the judiciary, and the President requested Mr. Hallett, member for Wilbraham, to take the chair.

Afterwards, Mr. HALLETT reported the Resolves to the Convention, with amendments, as follow:—

In the first Resolve, striking out the word "respectively"; inserting the words "and council" after the word "governor," and the words "or either of them" after the word "legislature."

Also, striking out all of the fourth Resolve, after the word "Resolved," and inserting instead thereof the following:—

That it is proper and expedient so to amend the Constitution as to provide that the justices of the supreme judicial court shall be appointed for the term of ten years, and the justices of such inferior courts as are or may be established by law, for the term of seven years; said justices to be eligible to reappointment, but in no case to continue in office after attaining seventy years of age.

The amendments to the first Resolve were concurred in.

Mr. HOOPER, of Fall River, moved to amend the proposed amendment to the third Resolve by striking out the word "appointed," and inserting instead thereof the words "elected by the people of the Commonwealth."

And on this question he called for the yeas and nays; which were ordered.

On motion of Mr. MORTON, of Taunton, the further consideration of the subject was postponed until Wednesday next, at ten o'clock, and assigned for consideration at that time.

On motion of Mr. NAYSON, of Amesbury, the Convention resolved itself into Committee of the Whole, for the purpose of considering the Resolves on the subject of amendments of the Constitution, being the unfinished business of the session of July 6th, and the President requested Mr. Griswold, member for Erving, to take the chair.

Afterwards, Mr. GRISWOLD reported, that the committee had made further progress in the consideration of the subject, but had come to no conclusion, and had instructed him to ask leave to sit again.

And leave was accordingly granted.

At six o'clock, on motion of Mr. PARSONS, of Sandisfield,

The Convention adjourned.

TUESDAY, July 12, 1853.

Met according to adjournment. Prayer was offered by the Chaplain. The Journal of yesterday was read.

Mr. KNOWLTON, of Worcester, from the Committee on the University at Cambridge, submitted a Report, enclosing letters from the Treasurers of Amherst College, Williams College, and Harvard College, giving information in answer to an Order of the Convention of May 19th.

Laid upon the table, and ordered to be printed.

On motion of Mr. GREENE, of Brookfield, the Convention resolved itself into Committee of the Whole, for the purpose of considering the Report of the Committee on the Qualifications of Voters, leave to withdraw to Francis Jackson and others, petitioners that the word "male" may be struck out of the Constitution, and Mrs. Abby B. Alcott and other women of Massachusetts, petitioners that women may be allowed to vote on the amendments of the Constitution; and the President requested Mr. Butler, of Lowell, to take the chair.

Afterwards, Mr. BUTLER reported, that the committee had made progress in the consideration of the subject, but had come to no conclusion, and had instructed him to ask leave to sit again.

And leave was accordingly granted.

Mr. BOUTWELL, member for Berlin, announced the death of Mr. Francis R. Gourgas, Delegate in the Convention from the town of Concord;

And moved that a committee be appointed to consider what notice the Convention ought to take of the event.

The motion was seconded by Mr. WILSON, of Natick.

And after further remarks by Messrs. SCHOULER, of Boston, BURLINGAME, member for Northborough, WALKER, of North Brookfield, HOBBS, of Weston, BROWN, of Medway, BIRD, of Walpole, DURGIN, of Wilmington, CROSS, of West Boylston, BRIGGS, of Pittsfield, and HOPKINSON, of Boston,

The motion was agreed to; and the President appointed the committee, consisting of the following gentlemen, viz.:—Messrs. Boutwell, member for Berlin, Briggs, of Pittsfield, Wilson, of Natick, Schouler, of Boston, Alley, of Lynn, and Bliss, of Longmeadow.

Afterwards, Mr. BOUTWELL, in behalf of the committee, submitted the following Resolves:—

Resolved, That the Convention has heard with regret the death of Mr. FRANCIS R GOURGAS, a Delegate from the town of Concord.

Resolved, That we deeply sympathize with those relatives and friends upon whom this great calamity has fallen.

Resolved, That as a token of our respect for the deceased, a committee of twenty members be appointed to attend his funeral to-morrow at Concord.

Resolved, That a copy of these Resolves be forwarded to the family of the deceased.

Resolved, That these Resolves be entered upon the Journal of the Convention, and that, in sorrow for our loss, this Convention now adjourn until nine o'clock to-morrow morning.

The Resolves were unanimously adopted, and at a quarter before twelve o'clock,

The Convention adjourned.

WEDNESDAY, July 13, 1853.

Met according to adjournment. Prayer was offered by the Chaplain. The Journal of yesterday was read.

Mr. DUNHAM, of Savoy, presented the Petition of James Cain and one hundred and sixteen others, for the preservation of town representation.

Laid upon the table.

The PRESIDENT appointed the following gentlemen to constitute the committee, under the Resolve adopted yesterday, to attend the funeral of Mr. Gourgas, lately a Delegate in the Convention, from Concord:

Messrs. Boutwell, member for Berlin, Briggs, of Pittsfield, Wilson, of Natick, Schouler, of Boston, Bell, of Somerville, Weston, of Duxbury, Morton, of Andover, Upham, of Salem, Earle, of Worcester, Gilbert, of Plainfield, Whitney, of Conway, Stevens, of Clinton, Bliss, of Longmeadow, Ward, of Newton, Bird, of Walpole, Thompson, of Charlestown, Hobbs, of Weston, Ide, of Attleboro', Phinney, member for Chatham, Norton, of Tisbury, and Meader, of Nantucket.

The following communication from the President of the Fitchburg Railroad Company, was read:—

OFFICE OF THE FITCHBURG R. R. CO.,
BOSTON, July 12th, 1853.

Hon. N. P. BANKS, President of the Convention, State House, Boston.

Dear Sir:—I notice, by the newspapers this afternoon, that a Committee of the Convention are to be appointed to-morrow morning, to attend the funeral of the late Hon. F. R. Gourgas, at Concord. I enclose a free pass over the Fitchburg Railroad, to Concord and back, for said Committee, and such other members of the Convention as may wish to attend.

Very respectfully,
JACOB FORSTER,
President of the Fitchburg Railroad Co.

On motion of Mr. THOMPSON, of Charlestown,

Ordered, That the thanks of the Convention be tendered to the President of the Fitchburg Railroad Company, for the invitation contained in his letter.

Mr. HOBBS, of Weston, moved that when the Convention adjourns, it adjourn to meet at nine o'clock, to-morrow; but the motion was rejected.

On motion of Mr. WALKER, of North Brookfield,

Ordered, That in Committee of the Whole, on the subject of the Petitions of Francis Jackson and others, debate shall cease in thirty minutes after going into committee.

On motion of Mr. MORTON, of Andover, the Convention resolved itself into Committee of the Whole, for the purpose of considering the Report, inexpedient to act upon the subject of the Petitions of Francis Jackson and others, and Mrs. A. B. Alcott and others; and the President requested Mr. Butler, of Lowell, to take the chair.

Afterwards, Mr. BUTLER reported, that the Report ought to be accepted, with an amendment,

Striking out all after the word "that" in the eighth line (printed copy,) as far as the words "it is inexpedient" in the last line except one.

On motion of Mr. WHITNEY, of Conway, the Previous Question was ordered.

The amendment was concurred in, and the Report accepted.

Mr. HOOPER, of Fall River, called for the special assignment for ten o'clock, viz.: the Resolves on the subject of the judiciary.

Mr. HOOPER modified his amendment to the amendment of the Committee of the Whole, so as to read as follows:—

Strike out all after the word "court" in the third line, and insert the following:—

Whenever a vacancy shall occur upon that bench, shall be elected by the qualified voters of the Commonwealth for the term of —— years, so arranged that two shall not be elected at the same time for the same term of years.

Without taking the question,

At one o'clock, on motion of Mr. SCHOULER, of Boston,

The Convention adjourned.

AFTERNOON SESSION.

Met according to adjournment.

Mr. KINGMAN, of West Bridgewater, moved a reconsideration of the vote by which the Report, inexpedient, &c., on the Petitions of Francis Jackson and others, and Abby B. Alcott and others, was accepted.

On motion of Mr. HOOD, of Lynn, the Rule of the Convention was suspended, and the motion immediately considered;

And it was rejected.

On motion of Mr. Bates, of Plymouth, the Convention proceeded to the consideration of the unfinished business of the morning session, viz.: the Resolves on the subject of the judiciary.

Mr. Hooper, of Fall River, moved that the further consideration of the subject be postponed until half past nine o'clock, to-morrow;

But the motion was rejected by a vote of sixty-two in the affirmative, to seventy-nine in the negative.

After debate, Mr. Parker, of Cambridge, moved that the further consideration of the subject be postponed until nine o'clock, to-morrow.

Without taking the question,

At half past five o'clock, on motion of Mr. Greene, of Brookfield,

The Convention adjourned.

THURSDAY, July 14, 1853.

Met according to adjournment. Prayer was offered by the Chaplain. The Journal of yesterday was read.

On motion of Mr. Wilson, of Natick,

Ordered, That the Secretary of the Convention give notice to the selectmen of Concord, of the vacancy existing in the Convention, occasioned by the death of Hon. Francis R. Gourgas, Delegate from that town.

Mr. Cushman, of Bernardston, and Mr. Fellows, of Lowell, severally offered Orders providing for a limitation of the time of speaking on any one subject, to half an hour.

Laid over, under the rule.

On motion of Mr. Boutwell, member for Berlin, sustained by a vote of one hundred in the affirmative, to forty-three in the negative,

Ordered, That the question be taken upon the Resolves on the subject of the judiciary, at four o'clock this afternoon.

On motion of Mr. Stevens, of Rehoboth, the Convention proceeded to the consideration of the Orders of the Day; the first subject being the Resolves on the judiciary; and the pending question being upon Mr. Hooper's amendment to the amendment of the Committee of the Whole.

Without taking the question,

At one o'clock, on motion of Mr. Morton, of Taunton,

The Convention adjourned.

AFTERNOON SESSION.

Met according to adjournment.

On motion of Mr. Morton, of Taunton, the Convention resumed the consideration of the Orders of the Day.

At the hour of four, the time assigned for taking the question,

Mr. Morton, of Taunton, moved the reconsideration of the vote making the assignment;

But the motion was rejected.

The question was then stated upon the amendment of Mr. Hooper, to the amendment of the Committee of the Whole,

And the roll being called, one hundred and one members voted for the amendment, and two hundred and twenty-seven against it.

So it was rejected.

Those who voted in the affirmative are:—

Messrs. Shubael P. Adams,
James B. Allen,
Josiah Allis,
D. W. Alvord,
Hillel Baker,
Alpheus Bancroft,
Eliakim A. Bates,
Moses Bates, Jr.,
Edward B. Bigelow,
Francis W. Bird,
William J. A. Bradford,
Hiram N. Breed,
Hammond Brown,
Frederick Brownell,
Joseph Brownell,
Patrick Bryant,
Asahel Buck,
Anson Burlingame,
Benjamin F. Butler,
Isaac Case,
Daniel E. Chapin,
Josiah Childs,
Henry Clark,
Alpheus B. Clarke,
William Cleverly,
Sumner Cole,
George B. Crane,
Henry W. Cushman,
Thomas Cushman,
Ebenezer Davis,
Isaac Davis,
Gilman Day,
Silas Dean,

Messrs. Samuel Duncan,
Lyman Fisk,
Ezekiel W. Fitch,
Abram Foster,
Charles A. French,
Rodney French,
Samuel French,
Richard Frothingham, Jr.,
Leonard Gooding,
Josiah W. Griswold,
Whiting Griswold,
Lyman W. Hapgood,
Stephen E. Hawkes,
Nathaniel Holder,
George Hood,
Foster Hooper,
Henry K. Hoyt,
John Jacobs,
Joseph Kingman,
J. S. C. Knowlton,
William H. Knowlton,
Albert Knox,
Luther Lawrence,
Job G. Lawton, Jr.,
Alden Leland,
Charles Mason,
Simeon Merritt,
Joseph B. Morss,
William S. Morton,
Jonathan Nayson,
William Nichols,
Alfred Norton,
Andrew T. Nute,

Messrs. Benjamin S. Orne,
Charles Osgood,
Jonathan Parris,
John Partridge,
Daniel A. Perkins,
Noah C. Perkins,
Charles Phelps,
James M. Pool,
Silas Rawson,
Daniel Richardson,
John Rogers,
James C. Royce,
Chester Sanderson,
Perez Simmons,
John W. Simonds,
Melzar Sprague,
Samuel W. Spooner,
Eben H. Stacy,

Messrs. Joseph L. Stevens, Jr.,
Charles Sumner,
Arnold Taft,
Willard Thayer, 2d,
Abraham Tilton,
Charles W. Upham,
Gershom B. Weston,
George White,
Daniel S. Whitney,
James S. Whitney,
Joseph Wilbur,
J. B. Williams,
Willard Wilson,
Charles C. Wood,
Otis Wood,
William H. Wood,
Ezekiel Wright.

Those who voted in the negative are :—

Messrs. Josiah G. Abbott,
Benjamin P. Adams,
P. Emory Aldrich,
Joel C. Allen,
John B. Alley,
Robert Andrews,
William Appleton,
William Aspinwall,
David C. Atwood,
George Austin,
Samuel Ayres,
Alvah Ballard,
Joseph Barrows,
John Beal,
William Bennett, Jr.,
Henry W. Bishop,
George W. Blagden,
Gad O. Bliss,
William C. Bliss,
William S. Booth,
George S. Boutwell,
Sewell Boutwell,
Ebenezer Bradbury,
Milton P. Braman,
Osmyn Brewster,
Francis Brinley,
George N. Briggs,
Alpheus R. Brown,
Artemas Brown,
Rufus Bullock,
Cephas C. Bumpus,
Henry Cady,

Messrs. Timothy W. Carter,
William Carruthers,
Amariah Chandler,
Chester W. Chapin,
Rufus Choate,
J. McKean Churchill,
Ransom Clark,
Jacob Coggin,
Nathaniel Cogswell,
Lansing J. Cole,
Ithamar Conkey,
Charles E. Cook,
Henry F. Cooledge,
Benjamin F. Copeland,
Simeon Crittenden,
George W. Crockett,
Joseph W. Cross,
Francis B. Crowninshield,
Joseph Cummings,
Wilber Curtis,
Simeon N. Cutler,
Richard H. Dana, Jr.,
Charles G. Davis,
John Davis,
Solomon Davis,
William Dehon,
Elijah S. Deming,
Hiram S. Denison,
Augustus Denton,
James C. Doane,
Bradish Dunham,
Philip Eames,

Messrs. John M. Earle,
Peter Easland,
Lilley Eaton,
Elisha Edwards,
Samuel Edwards,
Joseph M. Ely,
Homer Ely,
William T. Eustis,
A. G. Farwell,
Sullivan Fay,
James K. Fellows,
Emery Fiske,
Aaron Foster,
Samuel Fowle,
Samuel P. Fowler,
James M. Freeman,
Charles H. French,
Luther Gale,
Johnson Gardner,
Elbridge Gates,
Wanton C. Gilbert,
Washington Gilbert,
Charles G. Giles,
Joel Giles,
Dalton Goulding,
John W. Graves,
John C. Gray,
Jabez Green,
Simon Greenleaf,
Samuel P. Hadley,
Artemas Hale,
Nathan Hale,
Charles B. Hall,
Benjamin F. Hallett,
A. B. Hammond,
Seth Hapgood,
Phineas Harmon,
William Haskins,
Elnathan P. Hathaway,
Isaac Hayden,
George Hayward,
Charles Heard,
Ezra Heath, 2d,
Samuel Henry,
Henry Hersey,
James Hewes,
William H. Hewes,
George S. Hillard,
William Hinsdale,
Aaron Hobart,
Edwin Hobbs,
Martin Howard,
William J. Hubbard,

Messrs. William Hunt,
Asahel Huntington,
Samuel A. Hurlburt,
Moses C. Hurlbut,
William James,
John Jenkins,
John Johnson,
Giles C. Kellogg,
Isaac Kendall,
Joseph Kimball,
Henry W. Kinsman,
Hiram Knight,
Jefferson Knight,
Joseph Knight,
Charles L. Knowlton,
George H. Kuhn,
Gardner P. Ladd,
John S. Ladd,
Abishai Lincoln,
Frederic W. Lincoln, Jr.,
Tristram Littlefield,
Isaac Livermore,
Samuel K. Lothrop,
Samuel P. Loud,
John A. Lowell,
William P. Marble,
Laban Marcy,
Abijah P. Marvin,
Theophilus R. Marvin,
Seth Miller, Jr.,
James M. Moore,
George Morey,
Elbridge G. Morton,
Marcus Morton,
Marcus Morton, Jr.,
Charles Newman,
Daniel Noyes,
Joseph E. Ober,
Henry K. Oliver,
Nathan Orcutt,
James W. Paige,
Benjamin Paine,
Henry Paine,
Adolphus G. Parker,
Joel Parker,
Samuel C. Parsons,
Thomas A. Parsons,
Nathaniel Peabody,
Jeremiah Pease, Jr.,
John Penniman,
Jesse Perkins,
Silvanus B. Phinney,
William C. Plunkett,

Messrs. Jeremiah Pomroy,
Peter Powers,
Jonathan Preston,
F. O. Prince,
George Putnam,
John A. Putnam,
Robert Rantoul,
Sampson Reed,
David Rice,
Nathan Richardson,
Samuel H. Richardson,
Joseph M. Rockwood,
David S. Ross,
Amasa Sanderson,
John Sargent,
William Schouler,
John Sherril,
Chester Sikes,
John S. Sleeper,
Matthew Smith,
Caleb Stetson,
Charles G. Stevens,
Granville Stevens,
William Stevens,
Gideon Stiles,
Charles S. Storrow,
Ralph Taylor,
Joseph Thayer,
Edmund P. Tileston,

Messrs. Horatio W. Tilton,
David Turner,
David P. Turner,
William Tyler,
George B. Upton,
Joel Viles,
George A. Vinton,
Samuel B. Walcott,
Bradford L. Wales,
Freeland Wallis,
Amasa Walker,
Samuel Walker,
Andrew H. Ward,
Marshal Warner,
Samuel Warner, Jr.,
Asa H. Waters,
Cyrus Weeks,
Thomas Wetmore,
William F. Wheeler,
Benjamin White,
Joel Wilder,
John H. Wilkins,
Ezra Wilkinson,
Henry Wilson,
Milo Wilson,
Jonathan B. Winn,
Levi M. Winslow,
Josiah B. Woods.

Mr. Hallett, member for Wilbraham, moved to amend the amendment of the Committee of the Whole, by striking out all after the word "reappointment," viz.: the words, "but in no case to continue in office after attaining seventy years of age."

And the amendment was agreed to by a vote of one hundred and forty-eight in the affirmative, to ninety-eight in the negative.

Mr. Butler, of Lowell, moved to amend by substituting the word "seven" for the word "ten," in the third line, (printed copy); but the motion was rejected by a vote of eighty-eight in the affirmative, to eighty-four in the negative.

Mr. Bates, of Plymouth, moved to amend by striking out the words, "said justices to be eligible to reappointment"; but the motion was rejected.

Mr. Cole, of Cheshire, moved to amend by inserting after the word "appointed" in the third line, (printed copy,) the words, "by the governor of the Commonwealth, with the concurrence of the Senate"; but the motion was rejected.

On motion of Mr. Bird, of Walpole, the yeas and nays were

ordered upon the question of adopting the amendment of the Committee of the Whole, as amended.

And the roll being called, one hundred and fifty-eight members voted for the amendment, and one hundred and sixty against it;

So it was rejected.

Those who voted in the affirmative are:—

Messrs. Josiah G. Abbott,
Benjamin P. Adams,
Shubael P. Adams,
Charles Allen,
James B. Allen,
John B. Alley,
Josiah Allis,
George Austin,
Alpheus Bancroft,
Eliakim A. Bates,
Moses Bates, Jr.,
John Beal,
William Bennett, Jr.,
Edward B. Bigelow,
Francis W. Bird,
Henry W. Bishop,
William S. Booth,
George S. Boutwell,
Sewell Boutwell,
Ebenezer Bradbury,
William J. A. Bradford,
Alpheus R. Brown,
Artemas Brown,
Hammond Brown,
Joseph Brownell,
Patrick Bryant,
Asahel Buck,
Isaac Case,
Daniel E. Chapin,
Josiah Childs,
Henry Clark,
Ransom Clark,
Alpheus B. Clarke,
William Cleverly,
Henry F. Cooledge,
George B. Crane,
Joseph W. Cross,
Henry W. Cushman,
Thomas Cushman,
Charles G. Davis,
Ebenezer Davis,
Isaac Davis,
Gilman Day,
Silas Dean,
Elijah S. Deming,

Messrs. Augustus Denton,
Samuel Duncan,
Bradish Dunham,
John M. Earle,
Peter Easland,
Elisha Edwards,
Joseph M. Ely,
Sullivan Fay,
James K. Fellows,
Lyman Fisk,
Ezekiel W. Fitch,
Abram Foster,
Samuel Fowle,
James M. Freeman,
Rodney French,
Samuel French,
R. Frothingham, Jr.,
Charles G. Giles,
Joel Giles,
John W. Graves,
Jabez Green,
Josiah W. Griswold,
Whiting Griswold,
Samuel P. Hadley,
Benjamin F. Hallett,
Lyman W. Hapgood,
Seth Hapgood,
William Haskins,
Elnathan P. Hathaway,
Isaac Hayden,
Ezra Heath, 2d,
William H. Hewes,
Martin Howard,
Henry K. Hoyt,
Moses C. Hurlbut,
Joseph Kimball,
Joseph Kingman,
Hiram Knight,
Jefferson Knight,
William H. Knowlton,
Albert Knox,
Gardner P. Ladd,
Luther Lawrence,
Job G. Lawton, Jr.,
Alden Leland,

Messrs. Abishai Lincoln,
Tristram Littlefield,
William P. Marble,
Laban Marcy,
Abijah P. Marvin,
Charles Mason,
Simeon Merritt,
James M. Moore,
Elbridge G. Morton,
Marcus Morton, Jr.,
William S. Morton,
Hiram Nash,
Charles Newman,
William Nichols,
Alfred Norton,
Joseph E. Ober,
Benjamin S. Orne,
Charles Osgood,
Benjamin Paine,
Henry Paine,
Samuel C. Parsons,
John Partridge,
John Penniman,
Noah C. Perkins,
Charles Phelps,
Silvanus B. Phinney,
James M. Pool,
Silas Rawson,
David Rice,
Daniel Richardson,
Nathan Richardson,
Samuel H. Richardson,
David S. Ross,
James C. Royce,

Messrs. Amasa Sanderson,
Chester Sanderson,
John Sherril,
John W. Simonds,
Matthew Smith,
Samuel W. Spooner,
Eben H. Stacy,
Granville Stevens,
Joseph L. Stevens, Jr.,
William Stevens,
Gideon Stiles,
Charles Sumner,
Arnold Taft,
Joseph Thayer,
Willard Thayer, 2d,
Horatio W. Tilton,
David P. Turner,
Joel Viles,
George A. Vinton,
Freeland Wallis,
Amasa Walker,
Andrew H. Ward,
Marshal Warner,
Samuel Warner, Jr.,
Asa H. Waters,
Gershom B. Weston,
George White,
Joseph Wilbur,
Henry Wilson,
Willard Wilson,
Levi M. Winslow,
Charles C. Wood,
Otis Wood,
William H. Wood.

Those who voted in the negative are:—

Messrs. P. Emory Aldrich,
Joel C. Allen,
D. W. Alvord,
Robert Andrews,
William Appleton,
William Aspinwall,
Samuel Ayres,
Hillel Baker,
Alvah Ballard,
Joseph Barrows,
Marcus Barrett,
George W. Blagden,
Gad O. Bliss,
William C. Bliss,
Milton P. Braman,
Hiram N. Breed,

Messrs. Osmyn Brewster,
Francis Brinley,
George N. Briggs,
Frederick Brownell,
Rufus Bullock,
Cephas C. Bumpus,
Anson Burlingame,
Benjamin F. Butler,
Henry Cady,
Timothy W. Carter,
William Carruthers,
Amariah Chandler,
Chester W. Chapin,
Rufus Choate,
J. McKean Churchill,
Jacob Coggin,

Messrs. Nathaniel Cogswell,
Lansing J. Cole,
Sumner Cole,
Ithamar Conkey,
Charles E. Cook,
Benjamin F. Copeland,
Simeon Crittenden,
George W. Crockett,
Francis B. Crowninshield,
Joseph Cummings,
Wilber Curtis,
Richard H. Dana, Jr.,
John Davis,
Solomon Davis,
William Dehon,
Hiram S. Denison,
James C. Doane,
Philip Eames,
Lilley Eaton,
Samuel Edwards,
Homer Ely,
William T. Eustis,
A. G. Farwell,
Emery Fiske,
Aaron Foster,
Samuel P. Fowler,
Charles A. French,
Charles H. French,
Luther Gale,
Elbridge Gates,
Wanton C. Gilbert,
Washington Gilbert,
Dalton Goulding,
John C. Gray,
Simon Greenleaf,
Artemas Hale,
Nathan Hale,
A. B. Hammond,
Phineas Harmon,
Stephen E. Hawkes,
George Hayward,
Charles Heard,
Samuel Henry,
Henry Hersey,
James Hewes,
George S. Hillard,
William Hinsdale,
Edwin Hobbs,
Nathaniel Holder,
George Hood,
William J. Hubbard,
William Hunt,
Asahel Huntington,

Messrs. Samuel A. Hurlburt,
William James,
John Jenkins,
John Johnson,
Giles C. Kellogg,
Isaac Kendall,
Henry W. Kinsman,
Joseph Knight,
Charles L. Knowlton,
J. S. C. Knowlton,
George H. Kuhn,
John S. Ladd,
Frederic W. Lincoln, Jr.,
Isaac Livermore,
Otis P. Lord,
Samuel K. Lothrop,
Samuel P. Loud,
John A. Lowell,
Theophilus R. Marvin,
Seth Miller, Jr.,
George Morey,
Joseph B. Morss,
Marcus Morton,
Jonathan Nayson,
Daniel Noyes,
Andrew T. Nute,
Henry K. Oliver,
Nathan Orcutt,
James W. Paige,
Adolphus G. Parker,
Joel Parker,
Thomas A. Parsons,
Nathaniel Peabody,
Jeremiah Pease, Jr.,
Jesse Perkins,
William C. Plunkett,
Jeremiah Pomroy,
Jonathan Preston,
F. O. Prince,
George Putnam,
John A. Putnam,
Robert Rantoul,
Sampson Reed,
Joseph M. Rockwood,
John Rogers,
John Sargent,
William Schouler,
Chester Sikes,
Perez Simmons,
John S. Sleeper,
Melzar Sprague,
Charles G. Stevens,
Charles S. Storrow,

Messrs. Ralph Taylor,	Messrs. William F. Wheeler,
Edmund P. Tileston,	Benjamin White,
David Turner,	James S. Whitney,
William Tyler,	Joel Wilder,
Charles W. Upham,	John H. Wilkins,
George B. Upton,	Ezra Wilkinson,
Samuel B. Walcott,	J. B. Williams,
Bradford L. Wales,	Milo Wilson,
Samuel Walker,	Jonathan B. Winn,
Cyrus Weeks,	Josiah B. Woods,
Thomas Wetmore,	Ezekiel Wright.

The Resolves were then ordered to a second reading, by a vote of one hundred and sixty-seven in the affirmative, to thirty-two in the negative.

By leave of the Convention,

Mr. ALLEY, of Lynn, made a personal explanation in reference to a speech delivered by Mr. Hillard, of Boston, and printed in the *Boston Atlas.*

And, also by leave of the Convention, Mr. HILLARD made a personal explanation in reply.

Mr. OLIVER, of Lawrence, moved an adjournment.

Mr. BIRD, of Walpole, called for the yeas and nays on the question, but the call was not sustained by one-fifth of the members.

The motion for an adjournment was then rejected.

On motion of Mr. BUTLER, of Lowell, the Convention resolved itself into Committee of the Whole, for the purpose of considering the Resolve on the subject of the number which should constitute a quorum to do business in the House of Representatives; and the President requested Mr. Giles, of Boston, to take the chair.

Afterwards, Mr. GILES reported, that it was the opinion of the committee that the Resolve ought to pass, with an amendment, viz.:

Substituting the words "one hundred" for the words "a majority."

On motion of Mr. HALLETT, member for Wilbraham, the Resolve was

Laid upon the table.

And then, on motion of Mr. HALLETT,

The Standing Committee on the House of Representatives were discharged from the further consideration of the subject of a quorum in the House of Representatives.

At half-past six o'clock, on motion of Mr. ELY, of Westfield,

The Convention adjourned.

FRIDAY, July 15, 1853.

Met according to adjournment. Prayer was offered by the Chaplain. The Journal of yesterday was read.

The Order of Mr. Cushman, laid over yesterday, was taken up, and

On motion of Mr. ALLEN, of Worcester, amended by the addition of the following words :—

" Provided, that the chairman of any committee shall be allowed to speak one hour upon the subject of his Report."

It was then adopted, as follows :—

Ordered, That on and after to-morrow, no member of the Convention shall speak in Convention, or in Committee of the Whole, exceeding half an hour on any one subject, provided that the chairman of any committee shall be allowed to speak one hour upon the subject of his Report.

On motion of Mr. WILSON, of Natick, the Convention proceeded to the consideration of the Orders of the Day.

The first subject was the motion of Mr. Thompson, of Charlestown, to reconsider the vote by which the Convention ordered to a second reading, the Resolve on the subject of the loan of the State credit.

After debate, Mr. THOMAS, of Weymouth, moved the Previous Question, which was ordered.

And the motion to reconsider prevailed, by a vote of one hundred and eighty-nine in the affirmative, to eighty-seven in the negative.

The question recurred upon ordering the Resolve to a second reading.

Mr. FREEMAN, of Franklin, moved the Previous Question, which was ordered.

On motion of Mr. CROWNINSHIELD, of Boston, the yeas and nays were ordered.

And the roll being called, one hundred and twelve members voted for the Resolve, and two hundred against it.

So the Resolve was refused a second reading.

Those who voted in the affirmative are :—

Messrs. P. Emory Aldrich,
William Appleton,
George Austin,
Joseph Barrows,
Erasmus D. Beach,
John Beal,
Gad O. Bliss,

Messrs. Sewell Boutwell,
William J. A. Bradford,
Hiram N. Breed,
George N. Briggs,
Hiram C. Brown,
Frederick Brownell,
Henry Cady,

Messrs. Timothy W. Carter,
Isaac Case,
Chester W. Chapin,
Henry Clark,
Nathaniel Cogswell,
Benjamin F. Copeland,
George B. Crane,
Francis B. Crowninshield,
Solomon Davis,
Elijah S. Deming,
Augustus Denton,
James C. Doane,
Bradish Dunham,
John M. Earle,
Lilley Eaton,
Homer Ely,
Ezekiel W. Fitch,
Samuel Fowle,
Henry J. Gardner,
Wanton C. Gilbert,
Joel Giles,
John C. Gray,
Artemas Hale,
Benjamin F. Hallett,
A. B. Hammond,
Seth Hapgood,
George Haskell,
Elnathan P. Hathaway,
George Hayward,
Charles Heard,
Henry Hersey,
Aaron Hobart,
Thomas Hopkinson,
Samuel A. Hurlburt,
Samuel Jackson,
William James,
John Jenkins,
Hiram Knight,
Jefferson Knight,
Job G. Lawton, Jr.,
Abishai Lincoln,
Tristram Littlefield,
John A. Lowell,
Seth Miller, Jr.,
George Morey,
Elbridge G. Morton,
Marcus Morton,
Marcus Morton, Jr.,
Charles Newman,

Messrs. William Nichols,
Alfred Norton,
Henry K. Oliver,
Nathan Orcutt,
Benjamin S. Orne,
Adolphus G. Parker,
Joel Parker,
George Peabody,
Nathaniel Peabody,
Jeremiah Pease, Jr.,
Noah C. Perkins,
Robert Rantoul,
Silas Rawson,
Sampson Reed,
Joseph M. Rockwood,
John Rogers,
David S. Ross,
James C. Royce,
Chester Sikes,
Perez Simmons,
John W. Simonds,
Melzar Sprague,
Granville Stevens,
Joseph L. Stevens, Jr.,
J. Thomas Stevenson,
Gideon Stiles,
Isaac C. Taber,
Arnold Taft,
Thomas Talbot,
Ralph Taylor,
Horatio W. Tilton,
David Turner,
David P. Turner,
Freeland Wallis,
Samuel Walker,
Andrew H. Ward,
Asa H. Waters,
Cyrus Weeks,
Thomas Wetmore,
Daniel Wilbur,
Joseph Wilbur,
Ezra Wilkinson,
Henry Williams,
J. B. Williams,
Willard Wilson,
Levi M. Winslow,
Nathaniel Wood,
Josiah B. Woods,
Otis Wood.

Those who voted in the negative are :—

Messrs. Josiah G. Abbott,
Benjamin P. Adams,
Charles Allen,
James B. Allen,
Joel C. Allen,
John B. Alley,
Josiah Allis,
D. W. Alvord,
Robert Andrews,
William Aspinwall,
David C. Atwood,
Samuel Ayres,
Hillel Baker,
Alvah Ballard,
George S. Ball,
Alpheus Bancroft,
Marcus Barrett,
Moses Bates, Jr.,
Luther V. Bell,
William Bennett, Jr.,
Zephaniah Bennett,
Edward B. Bigelow,
Francis W. Bird,
Henry W. Bishop,
William S. Booth,
George S. Boutwell,
Milton P. Braman,
Francis Brinley,
Asa Bronson,
Alpheus R. Brown,
Artemas Brown,
Hammond Brown,
Joseph Brownell,
Patrick Bryant,
Rufus Bullock,
Cephas C. Bumpus,
Anson Burlingame,
Benjamin F. Butler,
William Carruthers,
Amariah Chandler,
Henry Chapin,
Josiah Childs,
J. McKean Churchill,
Ransom Clark,
Alpheus B. Clarke,
Stillman Clarke,
William Cleverly,
Charles E. Cook,
Henry F. Cooledge,
Oliver S. Cressy,
Simeon Crittenden,

Messrs. Joseph W. Cross,
Joseph Cummings,
Henry W. Cushman,
Thomas Cushman,
Richard H. Dana, Jr.,
Charles G. Davis,
Gilman Day,
Silas Dean,
Hiram S. Denison,
Samuel Duncan,
John M. Durgin,
Philip Eames,
Peter Easland,
Elisha Edwards,
Samuel Edwards,
Joseph M. Ely,
William T. Eustis,
A. G. Farwell,
Sullivan Fay,
James K. Fellows,
Lyman Fisk,
Aaron Foster,
Abram Foster,
Samuel P. Fowler,
James M. Freeman,
Charles A. French,
Rodney French,
Samuel French,
Luther Gale,
Elbridge Gates,
Washington Gilbert,
Charles G. Giles,
Leonard Gooding,
John W. Graves,
Jabez Green,
Josiah W. Griswold,
Whiting Griswold,
Samuel P. Hadley,
Charles B. Hall,
Lyman W. Hapgood,
Phineas Harmon,
William Haskins,
Stephen E. Hawkes,
Isaac Hayden,
Ezra Heath, 2d,
Samuel Henry,
James Hewes,
William H. Hewes,
George S. Hillard,
William Hinsdale,
Nathaniel Holder,

Messrs. George Hood,
Foster Hooper,
Martin Howard,
Henry K. Hoyt,
Charles E. Hunt,
William Hunt,
George H. Huntington,
Moses C. Hurlbut,
Abijah M. Ide, Jr.,
John Jacobs,
Samuel H. Jenks,
Giles C. Kellogg,
Isaac Kendall,
Joseph Kimball,
Joseph Kingman,
Joseph Knight,
Charles L. Knowlton,
J. S. C. Knowlton,
William H. Knowlton,
Albert Knox,
George H. Kuhn,
Gardner P. Ladd,
John S. Ladd,
Luther Lawrence,
Alden Leland,
Frederic W. Lincoln, Jr.,
Isaac Livermore,
William P. Marble,
Laban Marcy,
Abijah P. Marvin,
Charles Mason,
Reuben Meader,
Simeon Merritt,
James M. Moore,
William S. Morton,
Daniel Noyes,
Joseph E. Ober,
Charles Osgood,
Benjamin Paine,
Henry Paine,
John G. Park,
Jonathan Parris,
Samuel C. Parsons,
John Partridge,
John Penniman,
Daniel A. Perkins,
Jesse Perkins,
Charles Phelps,
Silvanus B. Phinney,

Messrs. William C. Plunkett,
Jeremiah Pomroy,
James M. Pool,
F. O. Prince,
John A. Putnam,
James Read,
David Rice,
Luther Richards,
Nathan Richardson,
Samuel H. Richardson,
Amasa Sanderson,
Chester Sanderson,
William Schouler,
Luther Sheldon,
John Sherril,
John S. Sleeper,
John Souther,
Samuel W. Spooner,
Charles G. Stevens,
William Stevens,
Charles Sumner,
Willard Thayer, 2d,
John W. Thomas,
Charles Thompson,
Abraham Tilton,
Ephraim Tower,
Charles R. Train,
William Tyler,
Orison Underwood,
Charles W. Upham,
Joel Viles,
George A. Vinton,
Samuel B. Walcott,
Amasa Walker,
Marshal Warner,
Samuel Warner, Jr.,
Gershom B. Weston,
William F. Wheeler,
Benjamin White,
George White,
Daniel S. Whitney,
James S. Whitney,
Joel Wilder,
John H. Wilkins,
Henry Wilson,
Milo Wilson,
Jonathan B. Winn,
Charles C. Wood,
William H. Wood.

At one o'clock, on motion of Mr. Wilson, of Natick,
The Convention adjourned.

AFTERNOON SESSION.

Met according to adjournment.

The PRESIDENT appointed the committee under the Resolve offered by Mr. Hallett, member for Wilbraham, on the subject of a judicial remedy to the legal representatives of deceased persons whose deaths are caused by negligence or misconduct of a railroad corporation, viz.:—

Messrs. Hallett, member for Wilbraham, Stevenson, of Boston, Haskins, of Medford, Richardson, of Middleton, and Fowler, of Danvers.

Mr. Knowlton, of Worcester, was appointed to take the place of the late Mr. Gourgas, of Concord, upon the Committee on the Reports of Debates.

Mr. Bird, of Walpole, was appointed to fill the vacancy, in place of Mr. Gourgas, upon the Committee on the Preservation of the Records.

On motion of Mr. BROWN, of Medway, the Convention proceeded to the consideration of the Orders of the Day.

The first subject, viz.: the motion of Mr. Marvin, of Winchendon, to reconsider the vote on the acceptance of the Report of the Committee on the Qualifications of Voters, inexpedient to act upon the subject of various Orders and Petitions, was

Laid upon the table.

On motion of Mr. KNOWLTON, of Worcester, the Orders of the Day were laid upon the table.

On motion of Mr. KNOWLTON, the Convention resolved itself into Committee of the Whole, for the purpose of considering the Resolve on the subject of Harvard College; and the President requested Mr. Morton, of Taunton, to take the chair.

Afterwards, Mr. MORTON reported, that the committee had made progress in the consideration of the subject, but had come to no conclusion, and had instructed him to ask leave to sit again.

And leave was accordingly granted.

On motion of Mr. ALLEN, of Worcester, amended at the suggestion of Mr. Hooper, of Fall River,

Ordered, That the rule limiting debate be suspended, so far as it applies to the last member who addressed the Committee of the Whole.

And then, on motion of Mr. BRIGGS, of Pittsfield, the Convention again resolved itself into Committee of the Whole, for the purpose of considering the subject just previously before it; and the President requested Mr. Sumner, member for Marshfield, to take the chair.

Afterwards, Mr. SUMNER reported, that it was the opinion of the committee that the Resolve ought to pass.

Mr. HOPKINSON, of Boston, moved to amend the Resolve by substituting the words, "best interests of the college," for the words, "advancement of learning;" but afterwards withdrew the motion.

The Resolve was then ordered to a second reading.

And at half past six o'clock, on motion of Mr. BREED, of Lynn,

The Convention adjourned.

SATURDAY, July 16, 1853.

Met according to adjournment. Prayer was offered by the Chaplain. The Journal of yesterday was read.

On motion of Mr. KNOWLTON, of Worcester,

Ordered, That be a committee to consider and report at what time the session of the Convention may be brought to a close.

The President appointed the committee under the above Order, as follows:—

Messrs. Knowlton, of Worcester, Schouler, of Boston, Giles, of Boston, Cushman, of Bernardston, Wilson, of Natick, Burlingame, member for Northborough, and Eames, of Washington.

On motion of Mr. CRESSY, of Hamilton,

Ordered, That when the Convention adjourn, it adjourn to meet on Monday, at ten o'clock.

On motion of Mr. WILSON, of Natick, the Order requiring the forenoon session to close at one o'clock, was so far modified as to provide for an adjournment at two o'clock.

On motion of Mr. WHITNEY, of Conway, the Convention proceeded to the consideration of the Orders of the Day.

The first subject was the Resolve concerning general laws for corporations, as amended in accordance with the recommendation of the Committee of the Whole;

And the pending question was upon the amendment proposed by Mr. Davis, of Worcester.

Mr. DE WITT, of Oxford, moved to amend the amendment of Mr. Davis, by inserting before the word "corporations," the words, "manufacturing, mechanical and banking," and by striking out all after the words "special act."

After debate, Mr. DENTON, of Chelsea, moved the Previous Question; which was ordered.

By leave of the Convention, Mr. DE WITT then withdrew his amendment.

The amendment of Mr. Davis was then adopted.

The question recurred upon ordering the Resolve, as amended, to a second reading, and,

On motion of Mr. STETSON, of Braintree, the yeas and nays were ordered.

And the roll being called, one hundred and eighty-eight members voted for the Resolve, and fifty-two against it.

So it was ordered to a second reading.

Those who voted in the affirmative are:—

Messrs. Shubael P. Adams,
P. Emory Aldrich,
James B. Allen,
John B. Alley,
D. W. Alvord,
Robert Andrews,
George Austin,
Hillel Baker,
Alvah Ballard,
Marcus Barrett,
Moses Bates, Jr.,
Edward B. Bigelow,
Francis W. Bird,
Henry W. Bishop,
William S. Booth,
George S. Boutwell,
Sewell Boutwell,
William J. A. Bradford,
Hiram N. Breed,
Asa Bronson,
Artemas Brown,
Hiram C. Brown,
Joseph Brownell,
Patrick Bryant,
Asahel Buck,
Anson Burlingame,
Henry Cady,
William Carruthers,
Isaac Case,
Amariah Chandler,
Daniel E. Chapin,
Josiah Childs,
J. McKean Churchill,

Messrs. Ransom Clark,
Alpheus B. Clarke,
Stillman Clarke,
William Cleverly,
Sumner Cole,
George B. Crane,
Oliver S. Cressy,
Simeon Crittenden,
Henry W. Cushman,
Thomas Cushman,
Simeon N. Cutler,
Ebenezer Davis,
Silas Dean,
Hiram S. Denison,
Augustus Denton,
Alexander De Witt,
Samuel Duncan,
Bradish Dunham,
John M. Durgin,
Philip Eames,
John M. Earle,
Peter Easland,
Elisha Edwards,
Samuel Edwards,
Sullivan Fay,
Lyman Fisk,
Ezekiel W. Fitch,
Abram Foster,
Samuel Fowle,
James M. Freeman,
Charles A. French,
Samuel French,
Richard Frothingham, Jr.,

Messrs. Luther Gale,
Johnson Gardner,
Elbridge Gates,
Charles G. Giles,
Joel Giles,
Daniel W. Gooch,
Leonard Gooding,
Jabez Green,
Josiah W. Griswold,
Whiting Griswold,
Samuel P. Hadley,
Benjamin F. Hallett,
Phineas Harmon,
William Haskins,
Elnathan P. Hathaway,
Stephen E. Hawkes,
Isaac Hayden,
Ezra Heath, 2d,
James Hewes,
William H. Hewes,
Aaron Hobart,
Henry Hobart,
Edwin Hobbs,
George Hood,
Foster Hooper,
Martin Howard,
Henry K. Hoyt,
Charles E. Hunt,
Moses C. Hurlbut,
John Jacobs,
John Johnson,
Joseph Kingman,
Hiram Knight,
Jefferson Knight,
J. S. C. Knowlton,
William H. Knowlton,
Albert Knox,
George H. Kuhn,
Gardner P. Ladd,
Luther Lawrence,
Alden Leland,
Abishai Lincoln,
Tristram Littlefield,
William P. Marble,
Simeon Merritt,
Samuel Mixter,
Elbridge G. Morton,
Marcus Morton,
William S. Morton,
Jonathan Nayson,
Charles Newman,
William Nichols,
Alfred Norton,

Messrs. Joseph E. Ober,
Benjamin S. Orne,
Charles Osgood,
Benjamin Paine,
Henry Paine,
Jonathan Parris,
Samuel C. Parsons,
John Partridge,
Nathaniel Peabody,
Jeremiah Pease, Jr.,
John Penniman,
Daniel A. Perkins,
Jesse Perkins,
Noah C. Perkins,
Charles Phelps,
Jeremiah Pomroy,
James M. Pool,
John A. Putnam,
Robert Rantoul,
Silas Rawson,
David Rice,
Luther Richards,
Daniel Richardson,
Nathan Richardson,
Joseph M. Rockwood,
John Rogers,
David S. Ross,
James C. Royce,
Chester Sanderson,
John Sherril,
Chester Sikes,
Perez Simmons,
John W. Simonds,
Matthew Smith,
John Souther,
Melzar Sprague,
Samuel W. Spooner,
Eben H. Stacy,
Caleb Stetson,
Joseph L. Stevens, Jr.,
Gideon Stiles,
Thomas Talbot,
Willard Thayer, 2d,
John W. Thomas,
Charles Thompson,
Horatio W. Tilton,
David Turner,
David P. Turner,
William Tyler,
Joel Viles,
Freeland Wallis,
Amasa Walker,
Andrew H. Ward,

Messrs. Marshal Warner,
Asa H. Waters,
Gershom B. Weston,
Benjamin White,
George White,
Daniel S. Whitney,
James S. Whitney,
Daniel Wilbur,
Messrs. Joseph Wilbur,
Henry Wilson,
Willard Wilson,
Jonathan B. Winn,
Levi M. Winslow,
Charles C. Wood,
Otis Wood,
William H. Wood.

Those who voted in the negative are :—

Messrs. William Appleton,
William Aspinwall,
David C. Atwood,
Joseph Barrows,
James M. Beebe,
William Bennett, Jr.,
Jacob Bigelow,
Ebenezer Bradbury,
Milton P. Braman,
Osmyn Brewster,
Francis Brinley,
Cephas C. Bumpus,
Henry Chapin,
Nathaniel Cogswell,
Benjamin F. Copeland,
Francis B. Crowninshield,
Henry J. Gardner,
Wanton C. Gilbert,
Robert Gould,
Artemas Hale,
Nathan Hale,
Charles Heard,
Henry Hersey,
William Hinsdale,
William J. Hubbard,
William Hunt,
Messrs. Samuel A. Hurlburt,
Samuel Jackson,
John Jenkins,
Samuel H. Jenks,
Giles C. Kellogg,
Isaac Kendall,
Frederic W. Lincoln, Jr.,
Isaac Livermore,
Samuel P. Loud,
Seth Miller, Jr.,
Nathan Orcutt,
James W. Paige,
John G. Park,
James Read,
Sampson Reed,
John Sargent,
William Schouler,
Edmund P. Tileston,
Ephraim Tower,
John S. Tyler,
Charles W. Upham,
Samuel B. Walcott,
Samuel Walker,
Cyrus Weeks,
William F. Wheeler,
Milo Wilson,

The second subject, was the Resolve in favor of amending section 2, chapter 5, of the Constitution, by striking therefrom the words "University at Cambridge;" the question being upon its final passage.

The Resolve was rejected by a vote of nineteen in the affirmative, to one hundred and eight in the negative.

On motion of Mr. Wilson, of Natick, the Orders of the Day were laid upon the table.

On motion of the same gentleman, the Committee of the Whole was discharged from the consideration of the Resolve on the subject of the incorporation of new towns; and

The rule of the Convention requiring that Orders, and Resolutions, &c., proposing an alteration of the Constitution shall be first considered in Committee of the Whole, was suspended, and the Resolve considered and read.

Mr. Wilson, of Natick, moved that the Resolve be indefinitely postponed.

Mr. Hooper, of Fall River, moved that the Resolve be amended by striking out all after the word "incorporated," and insert instead thereof the words "by a division of a town, leaving less than fifteen hundred inhabitants in the town from which the new town shall be taken."

Pending this question, Mr. Gardner, of Boston, moved an adjournment; but the motion was rejected by a vote of thirty-eight in the affirmative, to fifty-nine in the negative.

A quorum of members not being present,

Mr. Wilson, of Natick, renewed the motion for an adjournment, and,

At half-past one o'clock, the Convention adjourned.

MONDAY, July 18, 1853.

Met according to adjournment. Prayer was offered by Rev. Mr. Foster, of Charlemont, a member of the Convention. The Journal of Saturday was read.

Mr. Brown, of Medway, offered the following Order:—

Ordered, That on and after Monday next, no member of the Convention, except chairmen of the committees, shall speak more than fifteen minutes on one subject, without leave.

Laid over, under the rule.

On motion of Mr. Butler, of Lowell,

Ordered, That the Committee on the Pay Roll be instructed to make up the pay of Mr. Francis R. Gourgas, late Delegate from Concord, to the close of the session.

Mr. Livermore, of Cambridge, from the Committee on the Pay Roll, submitted a Report and Resolve on the subject of the compensation of the officers of the Convention.

Read once, laid upon the table, and ordered to be printed.

Mr. Hallett, member for Wilbraham, from the Special Committee on the subject of remedies to the representatives of persons killed by the negligence or misconduct of railroad corporations, &c., submitted a Report on that subject.

Referred to the Committee of the Whole and ordered to be printed.

The same gentleman, in behalf of a Minority of the Committee on the Bill of Rights, submitted a Report, recommending an addition to the fifteenth article, and an alteration of the second article and the twenty-eighth article.

Referred to the Committee of the Whole and ordered to be printed.

On motion of Mr. Wilson, of Natick, the Convention proceeded to the consideration of the Orders of the Day.

The first subject was the unfinished business of Saturday, viz.: the Resolve on the subject of the incorporation of new towns.

The question was upon the motion of Mr. Wilson, of Natick, that the Resolve be indefinitely postponed;

Pending which, an amendment moved by Mr. Hooper, of Fall River, was first in order.

Mr. Hallett, member for Wilbraham, moved to amend the amendment by adding to it the words, "but the incorporation of any new town shall not thereby increase the whole number of representatives."

The amendment was rejected; and then,

The amendment of Mr. Hooper was also rejected.

Mr. Hoyt, of Deerfield, moved to amend by striking out all after the word "incorporated," and inserting instead thereof the words, "without consent of the town or towns from which the territory shall be taken."

But the amendment was rejected; and then,

The motion to indefinitely postpone the Resolve was agreed to, by a vote of one hundred and thirty-three in the affirmative, to forty-six in the negative.

On motion of Mr. Butler, of Lowell, the Orders of the Day were laid upon the table; and,

On motion of the same gentleman, the Convention resolved itself into Committee of the Whole, for the purpose of considering the Resolves reported by the Special Committee on the subject of elections by plurality and majority; and the President requested Mr. Hillard, of Boston, to take the chair.

Afterwards, Mr. Hillard reported, that the committee had made progress in the consideration of the subject, but had come to no conclusion, and had instructed him to ask leave to sit again.

And leave was accordingly granted.

At one o'clock, the Convention adjourned.

AFTERNOON SESSION.

Met according to adjournment.

Mr. Wilson, of Natick, offered the following Order:—

Ordered, That the Committee on the Pay Roll be instructed to make up the same, including the day of final adjournment, allowing to each member pay only for his actual attendance, except in cases of sickness.

Mr. Knowlton, of Worcester, from a Special Committee "appointed to consider and report at what time the session of the Convention may be brought to a close," submitted a Report, "that in the opinion of the committee the Convention may complete its business and adjourn finally, on Saturday, the 23d inst."

The Report was considered, and adopted.

Mr. Frothingham, of Charlestown, from the Special Committee on the subject of banking, submitted a Report, inexpedient to act upon the subject of an Order of June 20th, on the expediency of providing that the legislature shall have no power to authorize or pass any law sanctioning the suspension of specie payments, by any corporations issuing bank notes.

On motion of Mr. Boutwell, member for Berlin, the Resolves on the subject of the Council were taken from the table, and placed in the Orders of the Day.

Mr. Adams, of Lowell, moved, that in Committee of the Whole on the subject of elections by plurality and majority, debate shall cease in one hour after going into committee.

Mr. Bradbury, of Newton, moved to substitute "three hours," and afterwards "two hours" for "one hour;" but these amendments were successively rejected.

Mr. Butler, of Lowell, moved to amend by substituting "three-quarters of an hour."

The amendment was adopted, and then the motion of Mr. Adams, as amended, was agreed to, by a vote of one hundred and seven in the affirmative, to seventy-three in the negative.

On motion of Mr. Underwood, of Milford, the Convention resolved itself into Committee of the Whole, for the purpose of considering the Resolves on the subject of elections by plurality and majority; and the President requested Mr. Hillard, of Boston, to take the chair.

Afterwards, Mr. Hillard reported the Resolves, with amendments, as follow:—

Striking out the word "whom" in the last line but one of the first Resolve, and insert instead thereof, the word "which," and adding to the Resolve the words "or other officer to be thus elected."

These amendments were concurred in.

Mr. SCHOULER, of Boston, moved that the first Resolve be amended, by striking out all after the word "Resolved," and inserting instead thereof, the following:—

That it is expedient to provide in the Constitution, that in the election of a governor, lieutenant-governor, councillors, secretary, treasurer, auditor, and attorney-general of the Commonwealth, the person having the largest number of votes shall be deemed and taken to be elected.

On motion of Mr. SCHOULER, the yeas and nays were ordered on the adoption of the amendment.

Before taking the question,

On motion of Mr. OLIVER, of Lawrence, the Orders of the Day were laid upon the table.

On motion of Mr. HALLETT, member for Wilbraham, the Convention resolved itself into Committee of the Whole, for the purpose of considering the unfinished business of July 11th, viz.: the Resolves on the subject of amendments of the Constitution; and in the absence of Mr. Griswold, member for Erving, who was chairman of the committee at its last session for the purpose of considering this subject, the President requested Mr. Wood, of Fitchburg, to take the chair.

Afterwards, Mr. WOOD reported, that the Committee had made progress in the consideration of the subject, but had come to no conclusion, and had instructed him to ask leave to sit again.

And leave was accordingly granted.

An amendment offered by Mr. Hallett, member for Wilbraham, in Committee of the Whole, to the Resolves on the subject of amendments of the Constitution; and an amendment, of which notice was given by Mr. Giles, of Boston, were ordered to be printed.

And at ten minutes before seven o'clock, on motion of Mr. BROWN, of Douglas,

The Convention adjourned.

TUESDAY, July 19, 1853.

Met according to adjournment. Prayer was offered by the Chaplain. The Journal of yesterday was read.

Mr. Hobbs, of Weston, presented the Credentials of Mr. Charles C. Hazewell, elected a Delegate from Concord, in place of Mr. Gourgas, deceased; which were received, and the Delegate was admitted.

Mr. Griswold, member for Erving, from the Committee on the House of Representatives, submitted a Report, inexpedient to act upon the subject of an Order of June 25th, on the expediency of providing that towns and districts may have the right to be represented by any citizens of the Commonwealth.

Referred to the Committee of the Whole and ordered to be printed.

The Order offered yesterday by Mr. Wilson, of Natick, on the subject of the pay roll, was taken up and considered.

Mr. Wheeler, of Lincoln, moved to amend the Order, by inserting the words, "and that the members of the Convention be required to certify under oath their attendance."

Pending the question,

On motion of Mr. Hyde, of Sturbridge, the Order was laid upon the table, by a vote of one hundred and thirty-seven in the affirmative to forty-four in the negative.

The Order offered yesterday, by Mr. Brown, of Medway, limiting speeches to fifteen minutes time, was taken up and considered.

Mr. Aspinwall, of Brookline, moved to amend the Order, by striking out the words "except chairmen of the committees."

Pending this question, on motion of Mr. Allen, of Worcester, the Order was

Laid upon the table.

Mr. Briggs, of Pittsfield, moved that the Resolve on the subject of appropriations for sectarian schools, be taken from the table, and placed in the Orders of the Day.

But the motion was rejected, by a vote of seventy-three in the affirmative, to eighty-five in the negative.

On motion of Mr. Butler, of Lowell, the Convention proceeded to the consideration of the Orders of the Day.

The first subject was the Resolves relating to elections by plurality and majority,

And the pending question was upon the amendment offered yesterday, by Mr. Schouler, of Boston.

Mr. Upton, of Boston, moved to amend the first Resolve, by striking out all after the word "the" at the end of the sixth line, (printed copy,) and inserting instead thereof, the words "individual having the highest number of votes shall be declared elected."

But the amendment was rejected.

The question was then stated upon Mr. Schouler's amendment,

And the roll being called, it appeared that one hundred and sixty members voted for the amendment, and one hundred and sixty against it.

The President voted in the negative, and the amendment was rejected.

Afterwards, Mr. Bates, of Plymouth, stated that a mistake had occurred, in placing the name of Mr. Brown, of Tolland, among those who had voted for the amendment.

It appearing that the name of Mr. Brown had been thus recorded, and it also appearing, from the statement of that gentleman, that he did not vote upon the question, it was

Ordered, That the Journal be amended so as to conform to the facts.

Those who voted in the affirmative are:—

Messrs. Benjamin P. Adams,
P. Emory Aldrich,
Robert Andrews,
William Aspinwall,
David C. Atwood,
George Austin,
Samuel Ayres,
Joseph Barrows,
Luther V. Bell,
Henry W. Bishop,
George W. Blagden,
George S. Boutwell,
Ebenezer Bradbury,
Milton P. Braman,
Hiram N. Breed,
Osmyn Brewster,
Francis Brinley,
George N. Briggs,
Adolphus F. Brown,
Rufus Bullock,
Cephas C. Bumpus,
Anson Burlingame,
Timothy W. Carter,
Amariah Chandler,
Chester W. Chapin,
Josiah Childs,
Henry Clark,
Alpheus B. Clarke,

Messrs. Stillman Clarke,
Jacob Coggin,
Nathaniel Cogswell,
Sumner Cole,
Ithamar Conkey,
Charles E. Cook,
Henry F. Cooledge,
Simeon Crittenden,
George W. Crockett,
Leander Crosby,
Seth Crowell,
Henry W. Cushman,
Richard H. Dana, Jr.,
Solomon Davis,
Henry L. Dawes,
Silas Dean,
James C. Doane,
James Easton, 2d,
Lilley Eaton,
Elisha Edwards,
Samuel Edwards,
Homer Ely,
A. G. Farwell,
Aaron Foster,
Charles H. French,
Richard Frothingham, Jr.,
Wanton C. Gilbert,
Robert Gould,

Messrs. Dalton Goulding,
John C. Gray,
Jabez Green,
Josiah W. Griswold,
Whiting Griswold,
Artemas Hale,
Charles B. Hall,
A. B. Hammond,
George Haskell,
Stephen E. Hawkes,
George Hayward,
Charles Heard,
Samuel Henry,
Henry Hersey,
James Hewes,
Levi Heywood,
George S. Hillard,
William Hinsdale,
Aaron Hobart,
Edwin Hobbs,
Foster Hooper,
Thomas Hopkinson,
William J. Hubbard,
William Hunt,
Asahel Huntington,
Charles P. Huntington,
Samuel A. Hurlburt,
Benjamin D. Hyde,
Samuel Jackson,
John Jacobs,
William James,
John Jenkins,
Samuel H. Jenks,
Giles C. Kellogg,
Joseph Kingman,
Henry W. Kinsman,
Hiram Knight,
Jefferson Knight,
Joseph Knight,
Charles L. Knowlton,
George H. Kuhn,
John S. Ladd,
Alden Leland,
Tristram Littlefield,
Isaac Livermore,
Otis P. Lord,
Samuel K. Lothrop,
Samuel P. Loud,
Reuben Meader,
Seth Miller, Jr.,
Samuel Mixter,
George Morey,

Messrs. Joseph B. Morss,
Marcus Morton,
Jonathan Nayson,
Daniel Noyes,
Henry K. Oliver,
Nathan Orcutt,
Charles Osgood,
John G. Park,
Adolphus G. Parker,
Jonathan C. Perkins,
Jeremiah Pomroy,
George Putnam,
John A. Putnam,
Robert Rantoul,
James Reed,
John Sargent,
William Schouler,
Chester Sikes,
John S. Sleeper,
John Souther,
Caleb Stetson,
Charles G. Stevens,
Granville Stevens,
Joseph L. Stevens, Jr.,
J. Thomas Stevenson,
Charles S. Storrow,
Alfred L. Strong,
Increase Sumner,
Thomas Talbot,
Ralph Taylor,
Charles R. Train,
David Turner,
David P. Turner,
Charles W. Upham,
George B. Upton,
Joel Viles,
Samuel B. Walcott,
Bradford L. Wales,
Samuel Walker,
Samuel Warner, Jr.,
Cyrus Weeks,
William F. Wheeler,
Benjamin White,
Daniel Wilbur,
Joel Wilder,
John H. Wilkins,
Ezra Wilkinson,
J. B. Williams,
Milo Wilson,
Jonathan B. Winn,
Nathaniel Wood.

Those who voted in the negative are:—

Messrs. Josiah G. Abbott,
Shubael P. Adams,
Charles Allen,
James B. Allen,
Joel C. Allen,
Parsons Allen,
D. W. Alvord,
Hillel Baker,
Nathaniel P. Banks, Jr.,
Marcus Barrett,
Eliakim A. Bates,
Moses Bates, Jr.,
Zephaniah Bennett,
Edward B. Bigelow,
Francis W. Bird,
William S. Booth,
Sewell Boutwell,
Asa Bronson,
Alpheus R. Brown,
Artemas Brown,
Hammond Brown,
Joseph Brownell,
Patrick Bryant,
Asahel Buck,
Benjamin F. Butler,
William Carruthers,
Isaac Case,
Daniel E. Chapin,
Henry Chapin,
J. McKean Churchill,
Ransom Clark,
William Cleverly,
George B. Crane,
Oliver S. Cressy,
Joseph W. Cross,
Thomas Cushman,
Simeon N. Cutler,
Ebenezer Davis,
Isaac Davis,
Gilman Day,
Elijah S. Deming,
Augustus Denton,
Alexander De Witt,
Samuel Duncan,
Bradish Dunham,
John M. Durgin,
Philip Eames,
John M. Earle,
Peter Easland,
Calvin D. Eaton,
Sullivan Fay,

Messrs. James K. Fellows,
Emery Fiske,
Ezekiel W. Fitch,
Abram Foster,
Samuel Fowle,
Samuel P. Fowler,
James M. Freeman,
Rodney French,
Samuel French,
Luther Gale,
Elbridge Gates,
Washington Gilbert,
Charles G. Giles,
Joel Giles,
Daniel W. Gooch,
Leonard Gooding,
John W. Graves,
William B. Greene,
Benjamin F. Hallett,
Lyman W. Hapgood,
Seth Hapgood,
William Haskins,
Elnathan P. Hathaway,
Isaac Hayden,
Ezra Heath, 2d,
William H. Hewes,
Henry Hobart,
George Hood,
Martin Howard,
Henry K. Hoyt,
Moses C. Hurlbut,
Abijah M. Ide, Jr.,
John Johnson,
Isaac Kendall,
Edward L. Keyes,
Joseph Kimball,
J. S. C. Knowlton,
William H. Knowlton,
Albert Knox,
Gardner P. Ladd,
Luther Lawrence,
Abishai Lincoln,
Otis Little,
William P. Marble,
Laban Marcy,
Abijah P. Marvin,
Charles Mason,
Simeon Merritt,
James M. Moore,
Elbridge G. Morton,
William S. Morton,

Messrs. Charles Newman,
William Nichols,
Alfred Norton,
Andrew T. Nute,
Benjamin S. Orne,
E. Wing Packer,
Benjamin Paine,
Henry Paine,
Jonathan Parris,
Samuel C. Parsons,
John Partridge,
Nathaniel Peabody,
Jeremiah Pease, Jr.,
John Penniman,
Jesse Perkins,
Noah C. Perkins,
Charles Phelps,
Silvanus B. Phinney,
James M. Pool,
Silas Rawson,
David Rice,
Luther Richards,
Daniel Richardson,
Samuel H. Richardson,
John Rogers,
David S. Ross,
Amasa Sanderson,
Chester Sanderson,
Luther Sheldon,
John Sherril,

Messrs. John W. Simonds,
Matthew Smith,
Melzar Sprague,
Samuel W. Spooner,
William Stevens,
Gideon Stiles,
Arnold Taft,
Willard Thayer, 2d,
Charles Thompson,
Abraham Tilton,
Horatio W. Tilton,
William Tyler,
Orison Underwood,
Freeland Wallis,
Amasa Walker,
Andrew H. Ward,
Marshal Warner,
Asa H. Waters,
Gershom B. Weston,
Daniel S. Whitney,
James S. Whitney,
Joseph Wilbur,
Henry Williams,
Henry Wilson,
Willard Wilson,
Levi M. Winslow,
Charles C. Wood,
Otis Wood,
Ezekiel Wright.

One hundred and fifty-nine in the affirmative, and one hundred and sixty-one in the negative.

Mr. Hathaway, of Freetown, moved to amend the third Resolve, by striking out the words "in the election of," in the first line, and also all after the words "general court," and inserting after the words "general court" the words "shall be elected as by law shall be provided."

Mr. Sumner, member for Otis, moved a reconsideration of the vote by which the amendment offered by Mr. Schouler, was rejected.

And upon this question,

On motion of Mr. Wheeler, of Lincoln, the yeas and nays were ordered.

Mr. Train, of Framingham, moved the Previous Question,

And upon this motion,

On motion of Mr. Allen, of Worcester, the yeas and nays were ordered.

At a quarter before one o'clock, on motion of Mr. Lord, of Salem,

The Convention adjourned.

AFTERNOON SESSION.

Met according to adjournment.

Mr. Bird, of Walpole, from the Committee on the Preservation of the Records, submitted a Report and Resolves on that subject.

On motion of Mr. Bird, the Resolves were considered, and they were ordered to a second reading.

Mr. Hooper, of Fall River, moved a reconsideration of the vote by which the Resolve on the subject of the incorporation of new towns, was indefinitely postponed.

And the motion was placed in the Orders of the Day.

Mr. Wilson, of Natick, moved that the hour of ten to-morrow, be assigned for taking the question upon the Resolves on the subject of elections by plurality and majority.

Without taking the question,

On motion of Mr. Lord, of Salem, the Convention proceeded to the consideration of the Orders of the Day.

The first subject was the Resolves relating to elections by plurality and majority,

And the pending question was the motion of Mr. Sumner, member for Otis, that the vote by which Mr. Schouler's amendment was rejected, be reconsidered.

And the roll being called, one hundred and forty-nine members voted for the reconsideration, and one hundred and eighty-nine against it.

So the motion to reconsider was rejected.

Those who voted in the affirmative are:—

Messrs. Benjamin P. Adams,
P. Emory Aldrich,
Robert Andrews,
William Aspinwall,
David C. Atwood,
Samuel Ayres,
Joseph Barrows,
James M. Beebe,
Jacob Bigelow,
Gad O. Bliss,
Ebenezer Bradbury,
Milton P. Braman,
Hiram N. Breed,
Osmyn Brewster,
Francis Brinley,
George N. Briggs,
Rufus Bullock,

Messrs. Cephas C. Bumpus,
Timothy W. Carter,
Amariah Chandler,
Chester W. Chapin,
Rufus Choate,
Jacob Coggin,
Nathaniel Cogswell,
Sumner Cole,
Ithamar Conkey,
Henry F. Cooledge,
Simeon Crittenden,
George W. Crockett,
Leander Crosby,
Seth Crowell,
Joseph Cummings,
Richard H. Dana, Jr.,
John Davis,

Messrs. Solomon Davis,
Henry L. Dawes,
Elijah S. Deming,
James C. Doane,
James Easton, 2d,
Lilley Eaton,
Homer Ely,
William T. Eustis,
A. G. Farwell,
Aaron Foster,
Charles H. French,
Richard Frothingham, Jr.,
Henry J. Gardner,
Wanton C. Gilbert,
Robert Gould,
Dalton Goulding,
Jason Goulding,
John C. Gray,
Jabez Green,
Simon Greenleaf,
Artemas Hale,
Nathan Hale,
A. B. Hammond,
Stephen E. Hawkes,
George Hayward,
Charles Heard,
Samuel Henry,
Henry Hersey,
James Hewes,
Levi Heywood,
George S. Hillard,
William Hinsdale,
Aaron Hobart,
Thomas Hopkinson,
William J. Hubbard,
William Hunt,
Asahel Huntington,
Charles P. Huntington,
Samuel A. Hurlburt,
Benjamin D. Hyde,
Samuel Jackson,
William James,
John Jenkins,
Samuel H. Jenks,
John Johnson,
Giles C. Kellogg,
Joseph Kingman,
Henry W. Kinsman,
Hiram Knight,
Jefferson Knight,
Joseph Knight,
George H. Kuhn,
John S. Ladd,

Messrs. Alden Leland,
Frederic W. Lincoln, Jr.,
Tristram Littlefield,
Isaac Livermore,
Otis P. Lord,
Samuel K. Lothrop,
Samuel P. Loud,
Theophilus R. Marvin,
Seth Miller, Jr.,
Samuel Mixter,
George Morey,
Joseph B. Morss,
Marcus Morton,
Marcus Morton, Jr.,
Daniel Noyes,
Henry K. Oliver,
Nathan Orcutt,
James W. Paige,
John G. Park,
Adolphus G. Parker,
Jonathan C. Perkins,
Jeremiah Pomroy,
Peter Powers,
John A. Putnam,
Robert Rantoul,
James Read,
Sampson Reed,
John Sargent,
William Schouler,
Chester Sikes,
John S. Sleeper,
John Souther,
Caleb Stetson,
Charles G. Stevens,
Granville Stevens,
Joseph L. Stevens, Jr.,
Charles S. Storrow,
Increase Sumner,
Thomas Talbot,
Ralph Taylor,
John W. Thomas,
Edmund P. Tileston,
Charles R. Train,
David Turner,
John S. Tyler,
Charles W. Upham,
George B. Upton,
Joel Viles,
Samuel B. Walcott,
Bradford L. Wales,
Samuel Walker,
Cyrus Weeks,
Thomas Wetmore,

Messrs. William F. Wheeler,
Benjamin White,
Daniel Wilbur,
Joel Wilder,
John H. Wilkins,
Messrs. Ezra Wilkinson,
J. B. Williams,
Milo Wilson,
Nathaniel Wood.

Those who voted in the negative are:—

Messrs. Josiah G. Abbott,
Shubael P. Adams,
Charles Allen,
James B. Allen,
Joel C. Allen,
Parsons Allen,
John B. Alley,
D. W. Alvord,
Hillel Baker,
Alvah Ballard,
George S. Ball,
Marcus Barrett,
Eliakim A. Bates,
Moses Bates, Jr.,
William Bennett, Jr.,
Zephaniah Bennett,
Edward B. Bigelow,
Francis W. Bird,
William S. Booth,
George S. Boutwell,
Sewell Boutwell,
William J. A. Bradford,
Asa Bronson,
Alpheus R. Brown,
Artemas Brown,
Hammond Brown,
Hiram C. Brown,
Joseph Brownell,
Patrick Bryant,
Asahel Buck,
Henry Cady,
William Carruthers,
Isaac Case,
Daniel E. Chapin,
Henry Chapin,
J. McKean Churchill,
Henry Clark,
Ransom Clark,
Alpheus B. Clarke,
Stillman Clarke,
William Cleverly,
George B. Crane,
Joseph W. Cross,
Henry W. Cushman,
Thomas Cushman,
Messrs. Simeon N. Cutler,
Charles G. Davis,
Ebenezer Davis,
Isaac Davis,
Gilman Day,
Silas Dean,
Augustus Denton,
Samuel Duncan,
Bradish Dunham,
John M. Durgin,
Philip Eames,
John M. Earle,
Peter Easland,
Calvin D. Eaton,
Elisha Edwards,
Samuel Edwards,
Sullivan Fay,
James K. Fellows,
Lyman Fisk,
Emery Fiske,
Ezekiel W. Fitch,
Abram Foster,
Samuel Fowle,
Samuel P. Fowler,
James M. Freeman,
Charles A. French,
Samuel French,
Luther Gale,
Johnson Gardner,
Elbridge Gates,
Washington Gilbert,
Charles G. Giles,
Joel Giles,
Leonard Gooding,
John W. Graves,
Josiah W. Griswold,
Whiting Griswold,
Samuel P. Hadley,
Benjamin F. Hallett,
Lyman W. Hapgood,
Seth Hapgood,
William Haskins,
Elnathan P. Hathaway,
Isaac Hayden,
Charles C. Hazewell,

Messrs. Ezra Heath, 2d,
William H. Hewes,
Henry Hobart,
Edwin Hobbs,
George Hood,
Foster Hooper,
Abraham H. Howland,
Henry K. Hoyt,
Charles E. Hunt,
Moses C. Hurlbut,
Abijah M. Ide, Jr.,
John Jacobs,
Isaac Kendall,
Edward L. Keyes,
Joseph Kimball,
J. S. C. Knowlton,
William H. Knowlton,
Albert Knox,
Gardner P. Ladd,
Luther Lawrence,
Abishai Lincoln,
Otis Little,
Justin E. Loomis,
William P. Marble,
Laban Marcy,
Abijah P. Marvin,
Charles Mason,
Reuben Meader,
Simeon Merritt,
James L. Monroe,
James M. Moore,
Elbridge G. Morton,
William S. Morton,
Charles Newman,
William Nichols,
Andrew T. Nute,
Joseph E. Ober,
Benjamin S. Orne,
Charles Osgood,
E. Wing Packer,
Benjamin Paine,
Jonathan Parris,
Samuel C. Parsons,
John Partridge,
Nathaniel Peabody,
Jeremiah Pease, Jr.,
John Penniman,
Jesse Perkins,
Noah C. Perkins,
Charles Phelps,

Messrs. Sylvanus B. Phinney,
Henry Pierce,
James M. Pool,
Silas Rawson,
David Rice,
Luther Richards,
Daniel Richardson,
Nathan Richardson,
Samuel H. Richardson,
John Rogers,
David S. Ross,
James C. Royce,
Amasa Sanderson,
Chester Sanderson,
Luther Sheldon,
John Sherril,
John W. Simonds,
Matthew Smith,
Melzar Sprague,
Samuel W. Spooner,
Eben H. Stacy,
William Stevens,
Gideon Stiles,
Alfred L. Strong,
Arnold Taft,
Willard Thayer, 2d,
Charles Thompson,
Abraham Tilton,
Horatio W. Tilton,
David P. Turner,
Orison Underwood,
George A. Vinton,
Freeland Wallis,
Amasa Walker,
Andrew H. Ward,
Marshal Warner,
Asa H. Waters,
Gershom B. Weston,
Daniel S. Whitney,
James S. Whitney,
Joseph Wilbur,
Henry Williams,
Henry Wilson,
Willard Wilson,
Jonathan B. Winn,
Levi M. Winslow,
Charles C. Wood,
Otis Wood,
Ezekiel Wright.

The question recurred upon the amendment offered by Mr. Hathaway, of Freetown, in the morning session;

And it was rejected.

Mr. WILSON, of Natick, moved to amend by striking out the third and fourth Resolves, and inserting in their place the following:—

Resolved, That the Constitution be so amended as to provide that in all elections of representatives to the general court, when no election is effected on the first trial, the meetings may be adjourned, from time to time, until the meeting of the legislature to which the said representatives are to be chosen, provided that no one adjournment shall be for a longer time than six days.

The amendment was rejected by a vote of fifty-nine in the affirmative, to one hundred and forty-five in the negative.

Mr. ALLEN, of Worcester, moved to amend by striking out the third Resolve.

Mr. STETSON, of Braintree, moved the Previous Question; which was ordered.

Mr. Allen's amendment was then rejected.

The question being upon ordering the Resolves to a second reading, a call was made for a division of the question,

And the first Resolve was adopted by a vote of one hundred and forty in the affirmative, to ninety in the negative.

The second Resolve was then adopted.

Mr. HALLETT, member for Wilbraham, called for the yeas and nays upon the adoption of the third Resolve; but the call was not sustained by one-fifth of the members.

The third, fourth, fifth and sixth Resolves were then adopted;

And so the Resolves were ordered to a second reading.

At six o'clock, on motion of Mr. DUNCAN, of Williamstown,

The Convention adjourned.

WEDNESDAY, July 20, 1853.

Met according to adjournment. Prayer was offered by the Chaplain. The Journal of yesterday was read.

On motion of Mr. BREED, of Lynn, the Convention proceeded to the consideration of the Orders of the Day.

The following subjects were passed over, viz.:—

The motion to reconsider the vote by which the Resolve concerning the incorporation of new towns, was indefinitely postponed.

The Resolves on the subject of the Judiciary ; and

The Resolve on the subject of Harvard College.

The next subject was the Resolve concerning general constitutional provisions for the creation of corporations.

After debate, Mr. Waters, of Millbury, moved the Previous Question, which was ordered.

And the Resolve was finally passed, as follows :—

Resolved, That it is expedient to incorporate into the Constitution a provision, that corporations shall not be created by special act, when the object of the incorporation shall be attainable under general laws.

On motion of Mr. Knowlton, of Worcester, the Convention took up the Resolves on the subject of the judiciary, previously passed over.

Mr. Knowlton offered the following amendment, viz. :—

Strike out all of the last Resolve, after the word "Resolved," and insert the following :—

That it is expedient so to amend the Constitution, that all judicial officers, except those concerning whom a different provision shall be made in the Constitution, shall be nominated and appointed by the Governor, by and with the consent of the Senate, for the term of seven years; that they may be reappointed at the expiration of such term ; and that all such nominations shall be made at least seven days before such appointment.

Mr. Dana, member for Manchester, moved that the amendment be laid upon the table; but afterwards withdrew the motion.

Without taking the question upon the Resolves,

At one o'clock, the Convention adjourned.

AFTERNOON SESSION.

Met according to adjournment.

Mr. Cushman, of Bernardston, offered a Resolve, intended as an amendment to the Resolves on the subject of the election of justices of the peace.

Ordered to be printed.

Mr. Fay, of Southborough, from the Committee on Leave of Absence, submitted a Report, granting leave of absence to Mr. Norton, of Tisbury, for the remainder of the session.

The Report was considered and accepted.

The Convention resumed the consideration of the Orders of the Day.

Mr. HOOPER, of Fall River, moved to amend the amendment of Mr. Knowlton, by striking out all after the word "that" in the second line, and inserting instead thereof, the words :—

All vacancies occasioned by death, resignation, or other cause, among the judges of the supreme judicial court, shall be filled by an election at large throughout the State, for a term of ——— years, so arranged that two shall not be elected at the same time for the same term of years.

Resolved, That it is expedient so to revise the Constitution, as to require that provision shall be made, by law, for the election of all the judges and justices of inferior courts, in districts, for a term of years; and that so long as the court of common pleas shall continue as at present constituted, the judges thereof shall be elected in districts for a term of ——— years, so arranged that only one shall be elected in any one year, unless it shall be to fill a vacancy in an unexpired term, and the judge whose term of service is first to expire, shall be the chief justice of said court, till such expiration, so that each shall in turn be, successively, the chief justice.

After debate, Mr. ADAMS, of Lowell, moved the Previous Question.

On motion of Mr. TRAIN, of Framingham, the yeas and nays were ordered upon the motion for the Previous Question.

Mr. Adams afterwards withdrew his motion.

During the debate upon the motion for the Previous Question,

Mr. LORD, of Salem, asked and obtained leave to make a personal explanation.

On motion of Mr. ADAMS, of Lowell, the Orders of the Day were laid upon the table.

On motion of Mr. FROTHINGHAM, of Charlestown,

Ordered, That the question upon the Resolves on the subject of the judiciary, be taken at eleven o'clock to-morrow.

On motion of Mr. FROTHINGHAM, the Orders of the Day were laid upon the table.

On motion of Mr. BREED, of Lynn, the yeas and nays were ordered upon the adoption of Mr. Hooper's amendment.

At six o'clock, on motion of Mr. SCHOULER, of Boston,

The Convention adjourned.

THURSDAY, July 21, 1853.

Met according to adjournment. In the absence of the President, the Convention was called to order by William S. Robinson, one of the Secretaries. Prayer was offered by the Chaplain.

On motion of Mr. RANTOUL, of Beverly,

Ordered, That the Convention proceed to the election of a President *pro tempore*, by nomination.

Mr. RANTOUL then nominated Mr. Wilson, of Natick, to be President *pro tempore*.

And this motion was unanimously agreed to.

Messrs. Briggs, of Pittsfield, and Boutwell, member for Berlin, were requested to conduct Mr. WILSON to the chair; which they did,

And the President *pro tempore* announced his acceptance of this office, and entered upon its duties.

The Journal of yesterday was then read.

Mr. TYLER, of Pawtucket, offered the following Order, which, pending an amendment offered by Mr. Earle, of Worcester, was laid over:

Ordered, That the Committee on Reporting and Printing, be instructed to append to the published Debates and Proceedings of the Convention, Poole's Statistical View of the Delegates thereof, with such additions and improvements as may be deemed expedient by the committee.

On motion of Mr. BOUTWELL, member for Berlin,

Ordered, That the Committee appointed to reduce amendments to form, have leave to report in print.

On motion of the same gentleman,

Ordered, That the adjournment of the forenoon session hereafter take place at two o'clock.

On motion of the same gentleman, the Convention proceeded to the consideration of the Orders of the Day.

The first subject was the Resolves on the judiciary, and the pending question was upon the amendment of Mr. Hooper to the amendment of Mr. Knowlton.

After debate, on motion of Mr. BARTLETT, of Boston, sustained by a vote of one hundred and twenty-three in the affirmative, to sixty-one in the negative,

The Orders of the Day were laid upon the table.

Mr. Bartlett then moved to amend the Order adopted yesterday, on the subject of closing the debate, by adding thereto the following:

Amendments shall be admitted after debate upon the main question shall cease, and the mover of each amendment shall be allowed ten minutes to explain his amendment, and the same time shall be allowed to members of the Convention who shall obtain the floor to oppose such amendment, when the question thereon shall be taken without further debate.

After debate, Mr. Dana, member for Manchester, moved the Previous Question; which was ordered,

And the amendment of Mr. Bartlett was rejected, by a vote of one hundred and forty in the affirmative, to one hundred and forty-four in the negative.

On motion of Mr. Knowlton, of Worcester, the Orders of the Day were laid upon the table.

By leave of the Convention,

Mr. Knowlton modified his amendment by inserting after the word "years," in the fifth line, the words "and for the purpose of such confirmation, the governor shall have the power to convene the Senate from time to time at his discretion."

Mr. Hooper also modified his amendment by striking out the words "in districts," in the third and fourth lines of the second Resolve, (printed copy,) and by inserting a blank before the word "years," in the fourth line.

The question was then stated upon adopting the amendment of Mr. Hooper, as modified;

And the roll being called, one hundred and fifty members voted for the amendment, and two hundred and thirty-six against it.

So the amendment was rejected.

Those who voted in the affirmative are:—

Messrs. P. Emory Aldrich,
James B. Allen,
Josiah Allis,
D. W. Alvord,
George Austin,
Hillel Baker,
Alpheus Bancroft,
Marcus Barrett,
Moses Bates, Jr.,
Edward B. Bigelow,
Francis W. Bird,
Sewell Boutwell,
Hiram N. Breed,
Asa Bronson,
Adolphus F. Brown,
Hammond Brown,
Frederick Brownell,
Joseph Brownell,
Patrick Bryant,
Asahel Buck,
Anson Burlingame,
Benjamin F. Butler,
Isaac Case,
Josiah Childs,
Henry Clark,
Alpheus B. Clarke,
William Cleverly,
Sumner Cole,

Messrs. George B. Crane,
Oliver S. Cressy,
Henry W. Cushman,
Thomas Cushman,
Isaac Davis,
Robert T. Davis,
Henry L. Dawes,
Gilman Day,
Silas Dean,
Augustus Denton,
Samuel Duncan,
Bradish Dunham,
John M. Durgin,
John M. Earle,
Calvin D. Eaton,
Elisha Edwards,
Joseph M. Ely,
Lyman Fisk,
Emery Fiske,
Ezekiel W. Fitch,
Abram Foster,
James M. Freeman,
Charles A. French,
Rodney French,
Samuel French,
Richard Frothingham, Jr.,
Leonard Gooding,
William B. Greene,
Josiah W. Griswold,
Whiting Griswold,
Lyman W. Hapgood,
Stephen E. Hawkes,
Charles C. Hazewell,
Ezra Heath, 2d,
William H. Hewes,
Nathaniel Holder,
George Hood,
Foster Hooper,
Henry K. Hoyt,
Charles E. Hunt,
Charles P. Huntington,
Benjamin D. Hyde,
Abijah M. Ide, Jr.,
John Jacobs,
Edward L. Keyes,
Joseph Kingman,
J. S. C. Knowlton,
William H. Knowlton,
Albert Knox,
Wilber C. Langdon,
Luther Lawrence,
Job G. Lawton, Jr.,
Alden Leland,

Messrs. Abishai Lincoln,
Otis Little,
Justin E. Loomis,
Charles Mason,
Simeon Merritt,
James L. Monroe,
James M. Moore,
Joseph B. Morss,
William S. Morton,
Hiram Nash,
Jonathan Nayson,
Charles Newman,
Andrew T. Nute,
Benjamin S. Orne,
Charles Osgood,
E. Wing Packer,
Benjamin Paine,
Jonathan Parris,
John Partridge,
Daniel A. Perkins,
Noah C. Perkins,
Charles Phelps,
Henry Pierce,
James M. Pool,
Peter Powers,
Silas Rawson,
Daniel Richardson,
Nathan Richardson,
Elkanah Ring, Jr.,
John Rogers,
David S. Ross,
James C. Royce,
Amasa Sanderson,
Chester Sanderson,
Luther Sheldon,
Perez Simmons,
John W. Simonds,
Melzar Sprague,
Samuel W. Spooner,
Eben H. Stacy,
Granville Stevens,
Joseph L. Stevens, Jr.,
Alfred L. Strong,
Charles Sumner,
Increase Sumner,
Arnold Taft,
Willard Thayer, 2d,
John W. Thomas,
Abraham Tilton,
David P. Turner,
William Tyler,
Orison Underwood,
Charles W. Upham,

Messrs. Amasa Walker,
Andrew H. Ward,
Gershom B. Weston,
George White,
Daniel S. Whitney,
James S. Whitney,
Daniel Wilbur,
Joseph Wilbur,
Messrs. Henry Williams,
J. B. Williams,
Willard Wilson,
Levi M. Winslow,
Charles C. Wood,
Otis Wood,
William H. Wood,
Ezekiel Wright.

Those who voted in the negative are:—

Messrs. Josiah G. Abbott,
Benjamin P. Adams,
Shubael P. Adams,
Charles Allen,
Joel C. Allen,
John B. Alley,
Robert Andrews,
William Aspinwall,
David C. Atwood,
Samuel Ayres,
George S. Ball,
Joseph Barrows,
Sidney Bartlett,
Eliakim A. Bates,
Erasmus D. Beach,
John Beal,
James M. Beebe,
Luther V. Bell,
William Bennett, Jr.,
Zephaniah Bennett,
Jacob Bigelow,
Henry W. Bishop,
George W. Blagden,
Gad O. Bliss,
William S. Booth,
George S. Boutwell,
Milton P. Braman,
Osmyn Brewster,
Francis Brinley,
George N. Briggs,
Alpheus R. Brown,
Artemas Brown,
Hiram C. Brown,
Rufus Bullock,
Cephas C. Bumpus,
Henry Cady,
Timothy W. Carter,
William Carruthers,
Amariah Chandler,
Henry Chapin,
Rufus Choate,
J. McKean Churchill,
Messrs. Ransom Clark,
Stillman Clarke,
Jacob Coggin,
Nathaniel Cogswell,
Ithamar Conkey,
Charles E. Cook,
Henry F. Cooledge,
Benjamin F. Copeland,
Simeon Crittenden,
George W. Crockett,
Leander Crosby,
Joseph W. Cross,
Seth Crowell,
Francis B. Crowninshield,
Joseph Cummings,
Simeon N. Cutler,
Richard H. Dana, Jr.,
Charles G. Davis,
Ebenezer Davis,
John Davis,
Solomon Davis,
William Dehon,
Elijah S. Deming,
Hiram S. Denison,
James C. Doane,
Moses Dorman,
Philip Eames,
Peter Easland,
James Easton, 2d,
Lilley Eaton,
Samuel Edwards,
Homer Ely,
William T. Eustis,
A. G. Farwell,
Sullivan Fay,
James K. Fellows,
Aaron Foster,
Samuel Fowle,
Samuel P. Fowler,
Charles H. French,
Luther Gale,
Henry J. Gardner,

Messrs. Johnson Gardner,
Elbridge Gates,
Wanton C. Gilbert,
Washington Gilbert,
Charles G. Giles,
Joel Giles,
Daniel W. Gooch,
Robert Gould,
Dalton Goulding,
Jason Goulding,
John W. Graves,
John C. Gray,
Jabez Green,
Simon Greenleaf,
Samuel P. Hadley,
Artemas Hale,
Nathan Hale,
Benjamin F. Hallett,
A. B. Hammond,
Seth Hapgood,
William Haskins,
Elnathan P. Hathaway,
Isaac Hayden,
George Hayward,
Charles Heard,
Samuel Henry,
Henry Hersey,
James Hewes,
Levi Heywood,
George S. Hillard,
William Hinsdale,
Aaron Hobart,
Henry Hobart,
Edwin Hobbs,
Thomas Hopkinson,
Samuel Houghton,
Martin Howard,
Abraham H. Howland,
William J. Hubbard,
William Hunt,
Asahel Huntington,
Samuel A. Hurlburt,
Moses C. Hurlbut,
Samuel Jackson,
William James,
John Jenkins,
Samuel H. Jenks,
John Johnson,
Giles C. Kellogg,
Isaac Kendall,
Joseph Kimball,
Henry W. Kinsman,
Hiram Knight,

Messrs. Jefferson Knight,
Joseph Knight,
Charles L. Knowlton,
George H. Kuhn,
Gardner P. Ladd,
John S. Ladd,
Frederic W. Lincoln, Jr.,
Tristram Littlefield,
Isaac Livermore,
Samuel K. Lothrop,
Samuel P. Loud,
John A. Lowell,
William P. Marble,
Laban Marcy,
Abijah P. Marvin,
Theophilus R. Marvin,
Reuben Meader,
Seth Miller, Jr.,
Samuel Mixter,
George Morey,
Elbridge G. Morton,
Marcus Morton,
Marcus Morton, Jr.,
William Nichols,
Alfred Norton,
Daniel Noyes,
Joseph E. Ober,
Henry K. Oliver,
Nathan Orcutt,
James W. Paige,
Henry Paine,
John G. Park,
Adolphus G. Parker,
Joel Parker,
Samuel D. Parker,
Samuel C. Parsons,
Thomas A. Parsons,
George Peabody,
Nathaniel Peabody,
Jeremiah Pease, Jr.,
John Penniman,
Jesse Perkins,
Sylvanus B. Phinney,
William C. Plunkett,
Jeremiah Pomroy,
Jonathan Preston,
George Putnam,
Robert Rantoul,
James Read,
Sampson Reed,
David Rice,
Luther Richards,
Samuel H. Richardson,

Messrs. Julius Rockwell,
Joseph M. Rockwood,
George R. Sampson,
John Sargent,
William Schouler,
John Sherril,
Chester Sikes,
John S. Sleeper,
Matthew Smith,
John Souther,
Caleb Stetson,
Charles G. Stevens,
William Stevens,
J. Thomas Stevenson,
Gideon Stiles,
Charles S. Storrow,
Isaac C. Taber,
Thomas Talbot,
Ralph Taylor,
Joseph Thayer,
Charles Thompson,
Edmund P. Tileston,
Horatio W. Tilton,

Messrs. Charles R. Train,
David Turner,
John S. Tyler,
George B. Upton,
Joel Viles,
George A. Vinton,
Samuel B. Walcott,
Bradford L. Wales,
Freeland Wallis,
Samuel Walker,
Marshal Warner,
Samuel Warner, Jr.,
Asa H. Waters,
Cyrus Weeks,
Thomas Wetmore,
William F. Wheeler,
Benjamin White,
Joel Wilder,
John H. Wilkins,
Henry Wilson,
Milo Wilson,
Jonathan B. Winn,
Nathaniel Wood.

Mr. Davis, of Plymouth, moved to amend the amendment of Mr. Knowlton, by substituting the word "Council" for the word "Senate," and by striking out the words "and for the purpose of such confirmation, the governor shall have the power to convene the Senate, from time to time, at his discretion."

A division of the question was called for, and the question being taken upon substituting the word "Council" for the word "Senate," the amendment was adopted by a vote of two hundred and thirteen in the affirmative, to seventy-eight in the negative.

The second branch of the amendment was then adopted.

On motion of Mr. Alvord, member for Montague, the amendment was further amended by adding the words, "and the judges now in office shall hold their offices according to their commissions."

Mr. Huntington, of Northampton, moved to amend by striking out the word "seven" in the fifth line, (printed copy).

But the amendment was rejected by a vote of one hundred and sixty-four in the affirmative to one hundred and seventy-nine in the negative.

Mr. Hallett, member for Wilbraham, moved to amend by inserting after the word "that," in the first line, (printed copy,) the words, "from and after seven years from the adoption of this Constitution";

But afterwards withdrew his amendment.

Mr. MORTON, of Andover, moved to amend by striking out the word "seven" in the fifth line, and inserting the word "ten."

Mr. BREED, of Lynn, called for the yeas and nays on this question; but the call was not sustained by one-fifth of the members.

Mr. Morton's amendment was then adopted by a vote of one hundred and eighty-six in the affirmative, to one hundred and seventy-three in the negative.

Mr. STEVENSON, of Boston, moved to amend by adding after the word "Constitution," in the third line, (printed copy,) the words, "and the justices of the supreme judicial court"; but the amendment was rejected.

Mr. BUTLER, of Lowell, moved a reconsideration of the vote by which the amendment offered by Mr. Morton was adopted;

And on his motion, the yeas and nays were ordered upon this question.

And the roll being called, one hundred and eighty-nine members voted for the reconsideration, and one hundred and ninety-five against it.

So the motion to reconisder was rejected.

Those who voted in the affirmative are:—

Messrs. Josiah G. Abbott,
Shubael P. Adams,
Charles Allen,
James B. Allen,
Parsons Allen,
Josiah Allis,
D. W. Alvord,
George Austin,
Hillel Baker,
George S. Ball,
Alpheus Bancroft,
Marcus Barrett,
Eliakim A. Bates,
Moses Bates, Jr.,
William Bennett, Jr.,
Edward B. Bigelow,
Francis W. Bird,
Henry W. Bishop,
William S. Booth,
Sewell Boutwell,
William J. A. Bradford,
Hiram N. Breed,
Asa Bronson,
Adolphus F. Brown,
Alpheus R. Brown,
Artemas Brown,
Hammond Brown,

Messrs. Frederick Brownell,
Joseph Brownell,
Patrick Bryant,
Asahel Buck,
Anson Burlingame,
Benjamin F. Butler,
Isaac Case,
Josiah Childs,
Henry Clark,
Ransom Clark,
Alpheus B. Clarke,
Stillman Clarke,
William Cleverly,
Sumner Cole,
George B. Crane,
Oliver S. Cressy,
Joseph W. Cross,
Henry W. Cushman,
Thomas Cushman,
Ebenezer Davis,
Isaac Davis,
Robert T. Davis,
Gilman Day,
Silas Dean,
Augustus Denton,
Samuel Duncan,
Bradish Dunham,

Messrs. John M. Earle,
Peter Easland,
Calvin D. Eaton,
Elisha Edwards,
Joseph M. Ely,
James K. Fellows,
Lyman Fisk,
Ezekiel W. Fitch,
Abram Foster,
James M. Freeman,
Charles A. French,
Rodney French,
Samuel French,
Richard Frothingham, Jr.,
Johnson Gardner,
Charles G. Giles,
Daniel W. Gooch,
Leonard Gooding,
John W. Graves,
Jabez Green,
William B. Greene,
Josiah W. Griswold,
Whiting Griswold,
Samuel P. Hadley,
Benjamin F. Hallett,
Lyman W. Hapgood,
Seth Hapgood,
William Haskins,
Stephen E. Hawkes,
Isaac Hayden,
Charles C. Hazewell,
Ezra Heath, 2d,
William H. Hewes,
Henry Hobart,
Nathaniel Holder,
George Hood,
Foster Hooper,
Martin Howard,
Henry K. Hoyt,
Charles E. Hunt,
Moses C. Hurlbut,
Benjamin D. Hyde,
Abijah M. Ide, Jr.,
John Jacobs,
Edward L. Keyes,
Joseph Kimball,
Joseph Kingman,
Hiram Knight,
Jefferson Knight,
J. S. C. Knowlton,
William H. Knowlton,
Albert Knox,
Gardner P. Ladd,

Messrs. Wilber C. Langdon,
Luther Lawrence,
Alden Leland,
Otis Little,
Justin E. Loomis,
William P. Marble,
Charles Mason,
Simeon Merritt,
James L. Monroe,
James M. Moore,
Elbridge G. Morton,
William S. Morton,
Jonathan Nayson,
Charles Newman,
William Nichols,
Andrew T. Nute,
Charles Osgood,
E. Wing Packer,
Benjamin Paine,
Jonathan Parris,
John Partridge,
Nathaniel Peabody,
John Penniman,
Daniel A. Perkins,
Noah C. Perkins,
Charles Phelps,
Silvanus B. Phinney,
Henry Pierce,
James M. Pool,
Peter Powers,
John A. Putnam,
Silas Rawson,
Daniel Richardson,
Nathan Richardson,
Samuel H. Richardson,
John Rogers,
David S. Ross,
James C. Royce,
Amasa Sanderson,
Chester Sanderson,
Luther Sheldon,
John Sherril,
Perez Simmons,
John W. Simonds,
Matthew Smith,
Melzar Sprague,
Samuel W. Spooner,
Granville Stevens,
Joseph L. Stevens, Jr.,
William Stevens,
Gideon Stiles,
Alfred L. Strong,
Charles Sumner,

Messrs. Arnold Taft,
Joseph Thayer,
Willard Thayer, 2d,
John W. Thomas,
Charles Thompson,
Abraham Tilton,
David P. Turner,
Orison Underwood,
Joel Viles,
George A. Vinton,
Freeland Wallis,
Amasa Walker,
Andrew H. Ward,
Marshal Warner,
Samuel Warner, Jr.,

Messrs. Gershom B. Weston,
George White,
Daniel S. Whitney,
James S. Whitney,
Daniel Wilbur,
Joseph Wilbur,
J. B. Williams,
Willard Wilson,
Levi M. Winslow,
Charles C. Wood,
Nathaniel Wood,
Otis Wood,
William H. Wood,
Ezekiel Wright.

Those who voted in the negative are:—

Messrs. Benjamin P. Adams,
P. Emory Aldrich,
Joel C. Allen,
John B. Alley,
Robert Andrews,
William Aspinwall,
David C. Atwood,
Samuel Ayres,
Joseph Barrows,
Sidney Bartlett,
Erasmus D. Beach,
John Beal,
James M. Beebe,
Luther V. Bell,
Zephaniah Bennett,
Jacob Bigelow,
George W. Blagden,
Gad O. Bliss,
George S. Boutwell,
Milton P. Braman,
Osmyn Brewster,
Francis Brinley,
George N. Briggs,
Hiram C. Brown,
Rufus Bullock,
Cephas C. Bumpus,
Henry Cady,
Timothy W. Carter,
Amariah Chandler,
Chester W. Chapin,
Daniel E. Chapin,
Henry Chapin,
Rufus Choate,
J. McKean Churchill,
Jacob Coggin,

Messrs. Nathaniel Cogswell,
Lansing J. Cole,
Ithamar Conkey,
Charles E. Cook,
Henry F. Cooledge,
Benjamin F. Copeland,
Simeon Crittenden,
George W. Crockett,
Leander Crosby,
Seth Crowell,
Francis B. Crowninshield,
Joseph Cummings,
Simeon N. Cutler,
Richard H. Dana, Jr.,
Charles G. Davis,
John Davis,
Solomon Davis,
Henry L. Dawes,
William Dehon,
Elijah S. Deming,
Hiram S. Denison,
Moses Dorman,
Philip Eames,
James Easton, 2d,
Samuel Edwards,
Homer Ely,
William T. Eustis,
A. G. Farwell,
Sullivan Fay,
Emery Fiske,
Aaron Foster,
Samuel Fowle,
Samuel P. Fowler,
Charles H. French,
Luther Gale,

Messrs. Henry J. Gardner,
Elbridge Gates,
Wanton C. Gilbert,
Washington Gilbert,
Joel Giles,
Robert Gould,
Dalton Goulding,
Jason Goulding,
John C. Gray,
Simon Greenleaf,
Artemas Hale,
Nathan Hale,
A. B. Hammond,
Elnathan P. Hathaway,
George Hayward,
Charles Heard,
Samuel Henry,
Henry Hersey,
James Hewes,
Levi Heywood,
George S. Hillard,
William Hinsdale,
Aaron Hobart,
Edwin Hobbs,
Thomas Hopkinson,
Samuel Houghton,
Abraham H. Howland,
William J. Hubbard,
William Hunt,
Asahel Huntington,
Charles P. Huntington,
Samuel A. Hurlburt,
Samuel Jackson,
William James,
John Jenkins,
Samuel H. Jenks,
John Johnson,
Giles C. Kellogg,
Isaac Kendall,
Henry W. Kinsman,
Joseph Knight,
Charles L. Knowlton,
George H. Kuhn,
John S. Ladd,
Job G. Lawton, Jr.,
Abishai Lincoln,
Frederic W. Lincoln, Jr.,
Tristram Littlefield,
Isaac Livermore,
Otis P. Lord,
Samuel K. Lothrop,
Samuel P. Loud,
John A. Lowell,

Messrs. Laban Marcy,
Abijah P. Marvin,
Theophilus R. Marvin,
Reuben Meader,
Seth Miller, Jr.,
Samuel Mixter,
George Morey,
Joseph B. Morss,
Marcus Morton,
Marcus Morton, Jr.,
Alfred Norton,
Daniel Noyes,
Joseph E. Ober,
Henry K. Oliver,
Nathan Orcutt,
Benjamin S. Orne,
James W. Paige,
John G. Park,
Adolphus G. Parker,
Joel Parker,
Samuel D. Parker,
Samuel C. Parsons,
Thomas A. Parsons,
George Peabody,
Jeremiah Pease, Jr.,
Jesse Perkins,
William C. Plunkett,
Jeremiah Pomroy,
Jonathan Preston,
George Putnam,
Robert Rantoul,
James Read,
Sampson Reed,
David Rice,
Luther Richards,
Elkanah Ring, Jr.,
Julius Rockwell,
Joseph M. Rockwood,
George R. Sampson,
John Sargent,
William Schouler,
Chester Sikes,
John S. Sleeper,
John Souther,
Caleb Stetson,
Charles G. Stevens,
J. Thomas Stevenson,
Charles S. Storrow,
Increase Sumner,
Isaac C. Taber,
Thomas Talbot,
Ralph Taylor,
Edmund P. Tileston,

Messrs. Horatio W. Tilton,
Charles R. Train,
David Turner,
John S. Tyler,
Charles W. Upham,
George B. Upton,
Samuel B. Walcott,
Bradford L. Wales,
Frederick T. Wallace,
Samuel Walker,

Messrs. Cyrus Weeks,
Thomas Wetmore,
William F. Wheeler,
Benjamin White,
Joel Wilder,
John H. Wilkins,
Henry Williams,
Milo Wilson,
Jonathan B. Winn.

Mr. Hooper, of Fall River, moved to amend the amendment, by adding the following words: "*Provided*, That no judge hereafter appointed, shall continue to hold office after he shall have arrived at the age of seventy years."

The amendment was adopted by a vote of one hundred and fifty-eight in the affirmative, to one hundred and fifty-four in the negative.

On motion of Mr. Hallett, member for Wilbraham, the amendment was further amended, by inserting after the word "made," in the seventh line, (printed copy,) the words "and publicly announced."

Mr. Allen, of Worcester, moved a reconsideration of the vote by which the amendment offered by Mr. Hooper, was adopted.

And the vote was reconsidered, by a vote of one hundred and sixty-eight in the affirmative, to one hundred and sixty-two in the negative.

The question then recurring upon the adoption of Mr. Hooper's amendment,

It was rejected, by a vote of one hundred and sixty in the affirmative, to one hundred and sixty-eight in the negative.

Mr. Allen, of Worcester, moved to amend the amendment, by providing that the age of seventy-five should be the limit of the term of service.

Mr. Thomas, of Weymouth, moved to make the age of eighty years the limit; and Mr. Stetson, of Braintree, moved to make the age of seventy-two years the limit; but these amendments were successively rejected.

Mr. Dana, member for Manchester, moved to amend the amendment, by adding the words: "*Provided*, that no judge shall continue to hold office after he shall have arrived at the age of seventy-five years."

But the amendment was rejected, by a vote of one hundred and two in the affirmative, to one hundred and ninety-three in the negative.

Mr. Gooch, of Melrose, moved a reconsideration of the vote by which the amendment offered by Mr. Alvord, member for Montague, was adopted; but the motion to reconsider was rejected.

The question then recurring upon the amendment of Mr. Knowlton, as amended,

The roll was called, and two hundred members voted for the amendment, and one hundred and sixty-four against it.

So it was adopted.

Those who voted in the affirmative are :—

Messrs. Charles Allen,
James B. Allen,
Parsons Allen,
John B. Alley,
Josiah Allis,
George Austin,
George S. Ball,
Marcus Barrett,
Eliakim A. Bates,
Moses Bates, Jr.,
John Beal,
William Bennett, Jr.,
Zephaniah Bennett,
Edward B. Bigelow,
William S. Booth,
George S. Boutwell,
Sewell Boutwell,
William J. A. Bradford,
Asa Bronson,
Adolphus F. Brown,
Artemas Brown,
Hammond Brown,
Frederick Brownell,
Joseph Brownell,
Patrick Bryant,
Asahel Buck,
Henry Cady,
Isaac Case,
Daniel E. Chapin,
Josiah Childs,
Henry Clark,
Ransom Clark,
Stillman Clarke,
William Cleverly,
Henry F. Cooledge,
George B. Crane,
Oliver S. Cressy,
Simeon Crittenden,
Joseph W. Cross,
Henry W. Cushman,
Thomas Cushman,
Simeon N. Cutler,
Charles G. Davis,
Isaac Davis,
Robert T. Davis,

Messrs. Gilman Day,
Silas Dean,
Elijah S. Deming,
Augustus Denton,
Samuel Duncan,
Bradish Dunham,
Philip Eames,
John M. Earle,
Peter Easland,
James Easton, 2d,
Calvin D. Eaton,
Elisha Edwards,
Samuel Edwards,
Joseph M. Ely,
Sullivan Fay,
James K. Fellows,
Lyman Fisk,
Emery Fiske,
Ezekiel W. Fitch,
Aaron Foster,
Abram Foster,
Samuel Fowle,
James M. Freeman,
Rodney French,
Samuel French,
Richard Frothingham, Jr.,
Luther Gale,
Johnson Gradner,
Charles G. Giles,
Joel Giles,
Daniel W. Gooch,
Leonard Gooding,
John W. Graves,
Jabez Green,
William B. Greene,
Josiah W. Griswold,
Whiting Griswold,
Samuel P. Hadley,
Benjamin F. Hallett,
Lyman W. Hapgood,
Seth Hapgood,
William Haskins,
Elnathan P. Hathaway,
Isaac Hayden,
Charles C. Hazewell,

Messrs. Ezra Heath, 2d,
James Hewes,
William H. Hewes,
Aaron Hobart,
Henry Hobart,
Edwin Hobbs,
Foster Hooper,
Martin Howard,
Abraham H. Howland,
Charles E. Hunt,
Charles P. Huntington,
Moses C. Hurlbut,
Benjamin D. Hyde,
Abijah M. Ide, Jr.,
John Jacobs,
John Johnson,
Edward L. Keyes,
Joseph Kimball,
Joseph Kingman,
Hiram Knight,
Jefferson Knight,
Charles L. Knowlton,
J. S. C. Knowlton,
William H. Knowlton,
Albert Knox,
Gardner P. Ladd,
Luther Lawrence,
Job G. Lawton, Jr.,
Alden Leland,
Abishai Lincoln,
Otis Little,
Tristram Littlefield,
Justin E. Loomis,
William P. Marble,
Abijah P. Marvin,
Charles Mason,
Reuben Meader,
Simeon Merritt,
James L. Munroe,
James M. Moore,
Elbridge G. Morton,
Marcus Morton, Jr.,
William S. Morton,
Hiram Nash,
Charles Newman,
William Nichols,
Benjamin S. Orne,
Charles Osgood,
E. Wing Packer,
Benjamin Paine,
Jonathan Parris,
Samuel C. Parsons,
John Partridge,

Messrs. Nathaniel Peabody,
John Penniman,
Daniel A. Perkins,
Noah C. Perkins,
Charles Phelps,
Silvanus B. Phinney,
Henry Pierce,
James M. Pool,
Peter Powers,
John A. Putnam,
David Rice,
Daniel Richardson,
Nathan Richardson,
Samuel H. Richardson,
Elkanah Ring, Jr.,
Joseph M. Rockwood,
John Rogers,
David S. Ross,
Amasa Sanderson,
Luther Sheldon,
John W. Simonds,
Matthew Smith,
Melzar Sprague,
Samuel W. Spooner,
Eben H. Stacy,
Caleb Stetson,
Granville Stevens,
Gideon Stiles,
Charles Sumner,
Increase Sumner,
Arnold Taft,
Joseph Thayer,
Willard Thayer, 2d,
John W. Thomas,
Charles Thompson,
Abraham Tilton,
Horatio W. Tilton,
David P. Turner,
Orison Underwood,
Joel Viles,
George A. Vinton,
Frederick T. Wallace,
Freeland Wallis,
Amasa Walker,
Andrew H. Ward,
Samuel Warner, Jr.,
Asa H. Waters,
Gershom B. Weston,
Daniel S. Whitney,
Daniel Wilbur,
Joseph Wilbur,
J. B. Williams,
Henry Wilson,

Messrs. Willard Wilson,
Jonathan B. Winn,
Levi M. Winslow,
Nathaniel Wood.

Those who voted in the negative are :—

Messrs. Josiah G. Abbott,
Benjamin P. Adams,
Shubael P. Adams,
P. Emory Aldrich,
Joel C. Allen,
D. W. Alvord,
Robert Andrews,
William Aspinwall,
David C. Atwood,
Samuel Ayres,
Joseph Barrows,
Sidney Bartlett,
James M. Beebe,
Luther V. Bell,
Jacob Bigelow,
Francis W. Bird,
George W. Blagden,
Gad O. Bliss,
Milton P. Braman,
Hiram N. Breed,
Osmyn Brewster,
Francis Brinley,
George N. Briggs,
Alpheus R. Brown,
Hiram C. Brown,
Rufus Bullock,
Cephas C. Bumpus,
Anson Burlingame,
Benjamin F. Butler,
Timothy W. Carter,
William Carruthers,
Amariah Chandler,
Henry Chapin,
Rufus Choate,
J. McKean Churchill,
Jacob Coggin,
Nathaniel Cogswell,
Ithamar Conkey,
Charles E. Cook,
Benjamin F. Copeland,
George W. Crockett,
Leander Crosby,
Seth Crowell,
Francis B. Crowninshield,
Joseph Cummings,
Richard H. Dana, Jr.,
Ebenezer Davis,
John Davis,
Solomon Davis,
Henry L. Dawes,
William Dehon,
Hiram S. Denison,
James C. Doane,
Moses Dorman,
Homer Ely,
A. G. Farwell,
Samuel P. Fowler,
Charles H. French,
Henry J. Gardner,
Elbridge Gates,
Wanton C. Gilbert,
Robert Gould,
Dalton Goulding,
Jason Goulding,
John C. Gray,
Simon Greenleaf,
Artemas Hale,
Nathan Hale,
A. B. Hammond,
Stephen E. Hawkes,
George Hayward,
Charles Heard,
Samuel Henry,
Henry Hersey,
George S. Hillard,
William Hinsdale,
Nathaniel Holder,
George Hood,
Thomas Hopkinson,
Samuel Houghton,
Henry K. Hoyt,
William J. Hubbard,
William Hunt,
Asahel Huntington,
Samuel A. Hurlburt,
Samuel Jackson,
William James,
John Jenkins,
Samuel H. Jenks,
Giles C. Kellogg,
Henry W. Kinsman,
Joseph Knight,
John S. Ladd,
Frederic W. Lincoln, Jr.,
Isaac Livermore,
Otis P. Lord,

Messrs. Samuel K. Lothrop,
Samuel P. Loud,
John A. Lowell,
Theophilus R. Marvin,
Seth Miller, Jr.,
Samuel Mixter,
George Morey,
Joseph B. Morss,
Marcus Morton,
Daniel Noyes,
Andrew T. Nute,
Henry K. Oliver,
Nathan Orcutt,
James W. Paige,
John G. Park,
Adolphus G. Parker,
Joel Parker,
Samuel D. Parker,
Thomas A. Parsons,
George Peabody,
Jeremiah Pease, Jr.,
Jesse Perkins,
William C. Plunkett,
Jeremiah Pomroy,
Jonathan Preston,
George Putnam,
Robert Rantoul,
James Read,
Sampson Reed,
Luther Richards,
Julius Rockwell,
James C. Royce,
George R. Sampson,
John Sargent,

Messrs. William Schouler,
John Sherril,
Chester Sikes,
Perez Simmons,
John S. Sleeper,
John Souther,
Charles G. Stevens,
J. Thomas Stevenson,
Charles S. Storrow,
Isaac C. Taber,
Thomas Talbot,
Ralph Taylor,
Edmund P. Tileston,
Charles R. Train,
David Turner,
John S. Tyler,
William Tyler,
Charles W. Upham,
George B. Upton,
Samuel B. Walcott,
Bradford L. Wales,
Samuel Walker,
Cyrus Weeks,
Thomas Wetmore,
William F. Wheeler,
Benjamin White,
George White,
Joel Wilder,
John H. Wilkins,
Henry Williams,
Milo Wilson,
Charles C. Wood,
Otis Wood,
Ezekiel Wright.

Mr. PHINNEY, member for Chatham, moved an adjournment; but the motion was rejected.

The vote was then taken separately, upon the final passage of the Resolves,

And the first, second and third of the series were agreed to.

On motion of Mr. LORD, of Salem, the yeas and nays were ordered upon the passage of the fourth Resolve.

Mr. DENTON, of Chelsea, moved an adjournment.

Mr. KEYES, member for Abington, called for the yeas and nays upon this motion; and they were ordered.

Afterwards, on motion of Mr. SHELDON, of Easton, the vote by which the yeas and nays were ordered, was reconsidered,

And the question recurring upon the demand for the yeas and nays, it was not sustained.

The motion of Mr. Denton was then agreed to.

At two o'clock, the Convention adjourned.

AFTERNOON SESSION.

Met according to adjournment.

On motion of Mr. Schouler, of Boston, the Convention resumed the consideration of the Orders of the Day, the question being upon the passage of the fourth Resolve on the subject of the judiciary.

And the roll being called, two hundred and four members voted in the affirmative, and one hundred and forty-three in the negative.

Those who voted in the affirmative are:—

Messrs. Charles Allen,
James B. Allen,
Parsons Allen,
John B. Alley,
Josiah Allis,
Robert Andrews,
George Austin,
Hillel Baker,
George S. Ball,
Alpheus Bancroft,
Marcus Barrett,
Eliakim A. Bates,
Moses Bates, Jr.,
Erasmus D. Beach,
John Beal,
William Bennett, Jr.,
Zephaniah Bennett,
Edward B. Bigelow,
Francis W. Bird,
Henry W. Bishop,
William S. Booth,
George S. Boutwell,
Sewell Boutwell,
Asa Bronson,
Adolphus F. Brown,
Hammond Brown,
Frederick Brownell,
Joseph Brownell,
Patrick Bryant,
Asahel Buck,
Henry Cady,
Isaac Case,
Daniel E. Chapin,
Josiah Childs,
J. McKean Churchill,

Messrs. Henry Clark,
Alpheus B. Clarke,
Stillman Clarke,
William Cleverly,
Sumner Cole,
Henry F. Cooledge,
George B. Crane,
Oliver S. Cressy,
Simeon Crittenden,
Joseph W. Cross,
Henry W. Cushman,
Thomas Cushman,
Simeon N. Cutler,
Charles G. Davis,
Ebenezer Davis,
Isaac Davis,
Robert T. Davis,
Gilman Day,
Silas Dean,
Elijah S. Deming,
Augustus Denton,
Bradish Dunham,
Philip Eames,
John M. Earle,
Peter Easland,
Calvin D. Eaton,
Elisha Edwards,
Samuel Edwards,
Joseph M. Ely,
Sullivan Fay,
James K. Fellows,
Lyman Fisk,
Emery Fiske,
Ezekiel W. Fitch,
Aaron Foster,

Messrs. Abram Foster,
Samuel Fowle,
James M. Freeman,
Charles A. French,
Samuel French,
R. Frothingham, Jr.,
Luther Gale,
Washington Gilbert,
Charles G. Giles,
Joel Giles,
Leonard Gooding,
John W. Graves,
Jabez Green,
Josiah W. Griswold,
Whiting Griswold,
Samuel P. Hadley,
Benjamin F. Hallett,
Lyman W. Hapgood,
Seth Hapgood,
William Haskins,
Elnathan P. Hathaway,
Isaac Hayden,
Charles C. Hazewell,
Ezra Heath, 2d,
James Hewes,
William H. Hewes,
Levi Heywood,
Henry Hobart,
Edwin Hobbs,
George Hood,
Foster Hooper,
Martin Howard,
Abraham H. Howland,
Charles E. Hunt,
Moses C. Hurlbut,
Benjamin D. Hyde,
Abijah M. Ide, Jr.,
John Jacobs,
Edward L. Keyes,
Joseph Kimball,
Joseph Kingman,
Hiram Knight,
Jefferson Knight,
Charles L. Knowlton,
J. S. C. Knowlton,
William H. Knowlton,
Albert Knox,
Gardner P. Ladd,
Luther Lawrence,
Job G. Lawton, Jr.,
Alden Leland,
Abishai Lincoln,
Tristram Littlefield,

Messrs. Justin E. Loomis,
William P. Marble,
Abijah P. Marvin,
Charles Mason,
Reuben Meader,
Simeon Merritt,
James L. Monroe,
James M. Moore,
Elbridge G. Morton,
Marcus Morton, Jr.,
William S. Morton,
Hiram Nash,
Jonathan Nayson,
Charles Newman,
William Nichols,
Joseph E. Ober,
Benjamin S. Orne,
Charles Osgood,
E. Wing Packer,
Benjamin Paine,
Jonathan Parris,
Samuel C. Parsons,
John Partridge,
Nathaniel Peabody,
John Penniman,
Noah C. Perkins,
Charles Phelps,
Silvanus B. Phinney,
Henry Pierce,
James M. Pool,
Peter Powers,
John A. Putnam,
Silas Rawson,
Daniel Richardson,
Nathan Richardson,
Samuel H. Richardson,
Elkanah Ring, Jr.,
Joseph M. Rockwood,
John Rogers,
David S. Ross,
Amasa Sanderson,
Chester Sanderson,
Luther Sheldon,
Matthew Smith,
Melzar Sprague,
Samuel W. Spooner,
Caleb Stetson,
Granville Stevens,
Joseph L. Stevens, Jr.,
William Stevens,
Gideon Stiles,
Charles Sumner,
Increase Sumner,

Messrs. Arnold Taft,
Joseph Thayer,
John W. Thomas,
Charles Thompson,
Horatio W. Tilton,
David P. Turner,
Orison Underwood,
Joel Viles,
George A. Vinton,
Frederick T. Wallace,
Freeland Wallis,
Amasa Walker,
Andrew H. Ward,
Marshal Warner,

Messrs. Samuel Warner, Jr.,
Asa H. Waters,
Gershom B. Weston,
Daniel S. Whitney,
Daniel Wilbur,
Joseph Wilbur,
J. B. Williams,
Henry Wilson,
Willard Wilson,
Jonathan B. Winn,
Levi M. Winslow,
Charles C. Wood,
Nathaniel Wood,
Otis Wood.

Those who voted in the negative are:—

Messrs. Benjamin P. Adams,
Shubael P. Adams,
Joel C. Allen,
William Aspinwall,
David C. Atwood,
Samuel Ayres,
Joseph Barrows,
Sidney Bartlett,
James M. Beebe,
George W. Blagden,
Gad O. Bliss,
Milton P. Braman,
Hiram N. Breed,
Osmyn Brewster,
Francis Brinley,
George N. Briggs,
Alpheus R. Brown,
Hiram C. Brown,
Rufus Bullock,
Cephas C. Bumpus,
Anson Burlingame,
William Carruthers,
Timothy W. Carter,
Amariah Chandler,
Chester W. Chapin,
Henry Chapin,
Rufus Choate,
Jacob Coggin,
Nathaniel Cogswell,
Ithamar Conkey,
Charles E. Cook,
George W. Crockett,
Leander Crosby,
Seth Crowell,
Francis B. Crowninshield,
Joseph Cummings,
Richard H. Dana, Jr.,

Messrs. John Davis,
Solomon Davis,
Henry L. Dawes,
William Dehon,
Hiram S. Denison,
Moses Dorman,
Homer Ely,
William T. Eustis,
A. G. Farwell,
Samuel P. Fowler,
Charles H. French,
Henry J. Gardner,
Elbridge Gates,
Wanton C. Gilbert,
Robert Gould,
Dalton Goulding,
Jason Goulding,
Simon Greenleaf,
Artemas Hale,
Nathan Hale,
A. B. Hammond,
Stephen E. Hawkes,
George Hayward,
Charles Heard,
Henry Hersey,
George S. Hillard,
Nathaniel Holder,
Samuel Houghton,
Henry K. Hoyt,
William J. Hubbard,
William Hunt,
Asahel Huntington,
Samuel A. Hurlburt,
Samuel Jackson,
William James,
John Jenkins,
Samuel H. Jenks,

Messrs. Giles C. Kellogg,
Isaac Kendall,
Henry W. Kinsman,
Joseph Knight,
George H. Kuhn,
Frederic W. Lincoln, Jr.,
Isaac Livermore,
Otis P. Lord,
Samuel K. Lothrop,
Samuel P. Loud,
John A. Lowell,
Seth Miller, Jr.,
Samuel Mixter,
George Morey,
Joseph B. Morss,
Marcus Morton,
Daniel Noyes,
Andrew T. Nute,
Henry K. Oliver,
Nathan Orcutt,
James W. Paige,
John G. Park,
Adolphus G. Parker,
Joel Parker,
Samuel D. Parker,
Thomas A. Parsons,
George Peabody,
Jeremiah Pease, Jr.,
Jesse Perkins,
William C. Plunkett,
Jeremiah Pomroy,
Jonathan Preston,
George Putnam,
Robert Rantoul,
James Read,

Messrs. Sampson Reed,
Luther Richards,
Julius Rockwell,
James C. Royce,
John Sargent,
William Schouler,
John Sherril,
Chester Sikes,
Perez Simmons,
John W. Simonds,
John S. Sleeper,
Charles G. Stevens,
J. Thomas Stevenson,
Charles S. Storrow,
Isaac C. Tabor,
Thomas Talbot,
Ralph Taylor,
Edmund P. Tileston,
Charles R. Train,
David Turner,
John S. Tyler,
William Tyler,
Charles W. Upham,
George B. Upton,
Samuel B. Walcott,
Bradford L. Wales,
Samuel Walker,
Cyrus Weeks,
William F. Wheeler,
Benjamin White,
George White,
Joel Wilder,
Milo Wilson,
Ezekiel Wright.

So the Resolves were finally passed, as follow:—

Resolved, That it is expedient to amend the Constitution by substituting for the second article of the third chapter, the following:—

The Governor and Council, and the two branches of the legislature, or either of them, shall not hereafter be authorized to propose questions to justices of the supreme judicial court, and require their opinions thereon.

Resolved, That it is expedient to amend the Constitution by substituting for the last two clauses of the thirteenth article of the first section of the second chapter, the following:—

The judicial power of the Commonwealth shall be vested in a supreme judicial court, and such other courts as the legislature may from time to time establish.

The justices of the supreme judicial court, shall receive honorable salaries, which shall not be diminished during their continuance in office.

Resolved, That it is expedient to amend the third chapter of the Constitution by substituting for the fifth article in said chapter, the following:—

The legislature shall have power to make laws regulating marriage, divorce, and alimony, but shall in no case decree a divorce, or hear and determine any causes touching the validity of the marriage contract.

Resolved, That it is expedient so to amend the Constitution that all judicial officers, except those concerning whom a different provision is made in the Constitution, shall be nominated and appointed by the Governor, by and with the consent of the Council, for the term of ten years; that they may be reappointed at the expiration of such term, and that all such nominations shall be made and publicly announced at least seven days before such appointment; and the judges now in office shall hold their offices according to their commissions.

Mr. Frothingham, of Charlestown, moved that the Orders of the Day be laid upon the table; but the motion was rejected.

The second subject in the Orders of the Day, was the motion of Mr. Hooper, of Fall River, that the vote by which the Resolve on the subject of the incorporation of new towns was indefinitely postponed, be reconsidered.

And the vote was reconsidered, one hundred and thirty members voting in the affirmative, and one hundred and fourteen in the negative.

Mr. Keyes, member for Abington, moved that the whole subject be laid upon the table; but the motion was rejected.

Mr. Hooper, of Fall River, and Mr. Hallett, member for Wilbraham, severally offered amendments to the Resolve, which were declared to be not in order.

Mr. Hooper appealed from the decision of the Chair upon his amendment; but afterwards withdrew his appeal.

Mr. Day, of Templeton, moved the Previous Question, but withdrew it by request of Mr. Hallett, who afterwards renewed the motion; and the Previous Question was ordered, and

The Resolve was refused a second reading.

The next subject in the Orders of the Day, was the Resolve in relation to Harvard College.

On motion of Mr. Boutwell, member for Berlin, the yeas and nays were ordered upon the final passage of the Resolve.

Afterwards, on motion of Mr. Livermore, of Cambridge, the vote ordering the yeas and nays was reconsidered.

And the question recurring upon the demand for the yeas and nays, it was sustained by one-fifth of the members.

Mr. Lothrop, of Boston, moved to amend the Resolve, by striking out the words "hereafter granted."

On motion of Mr. Greene, of Brookfield, the Previous Question was ordered.

The amendment was rejected; and

The roll then being called, one hundred and twenty-one members voted for the Resolve, and twenty-eight against it.

Those who voted in the affirmative are:—

Messrs. James B. Allen,
Parsons Allen,
Josiah Allis,
Robert Andrews,
George Austin,
Hillel Baker,
Alpheus Bancroft,
Moses Bates, Jr.,
Erasmus D. Beach,
John Beal,
William Bennett, Jr.,
Gad O. Bliss,
George S. Boutwell,
Hiram N. Breed,
Adolphus F. Brown,
Hammond Brown,
Hiram C. Brown,
Frederick Brownell,
Joseph Brownell,
Asahel Buck,
Timothy W. Carter,
William Carruthers,
Isaac Case,
Chester W. Chapin,
Josiah Childs,
J. McKean Churchill,
Ransom Clark,
Lansing J. Cole,
Sumner Cole,
Ithamar Conkey,
Simeon Crittenden,
Joseph W. Cross,
Joseph Cummings,
Henry W. Cushman,
Thomas Cushman,

Messrs. Richard H. Dana, Jr.,
Gilman Day,
Silas Dean,
Elijah S. Deming,
Augustus Denton,
Samuel Duncan,
Bradish Dunham,
Peter Easland,
Calvin D. Eaton,
Elisha Edwards,
Samuel Edwards,
Lyman Fisk,
Ezekiel W. Fitch,
Aaron Foster,
Rodney French,
Samuel French,
Luther Gale,
Elbridge Gates,
Wanton C. Gilbert,
Charles G. Giles,
Joel Giles,
Jason Goulding,
Jabez Green,
William B. Greene,
Josiah W. Griswold,
Whiting Griswold,
Benjamin F. Hallett,
Seth Hapgood,
Phineas Harmon,
Ezra Heath, 2d,
George Hood,
Abraham H. Howland,
Henry K. Hoyt,
J. S. C. Knowlton,
Albert Knox,

Messrs. Gardner P. Ladd,
Wilber C. Langdon,
Otis Little,
Justin E. Loomis,
William P. Marble,
Simeon Merritt,
James L. Monroe,
Elbridge G. Morton,
William S. Morton,
Hiram Nash,
Jonathan Nayson,
Charles Newman,
Charles Osgood,
E. Wing Packer,
Benjamin Paine,
Adolphus G. Parker,
Samuel C. Parsons,
John Partridge,
John Penniman,
Charles Phelps,
Silvanus B. Phinney,
Henry Pierce,
Jeremiah Pomroy,
Silas Rawson,
David Rice,
Luther Richards,

Messrs. Daniel Richardson,
Samuel H. Richardson,
Elkanah Ring, Jr.,
John Rogers,
David S. Ross,
James C. Royce,
William Schouler,
John W. Simonds,
Matthew Smith,
Melzar Sprague,
Samuel W. Spooner,
Granville Stevens,
Gideon Stiles,
Charles Sumner,
Increase Sumner,
Horatio W. Tilton,
Freeland Wallis,
Amasa Walker,
Andrew H. Ward,
Marshal Warner,
Gershom B. Weston,
Henry Wilson,
Charles C. Wood,
Otis Wood,
Ezekiel Wright.

Those who voted in the negative are:—

Messrs. Benjamin P. Adams,
P. Emory Aldrich,
Joel C. Allen,
George S. Ball,
Francis Brinley,
Rufus Bullock,
Cephas C. Bumpus,
Seth Crowell,
Francis B. Crowninshield,
Philip Eames,
George Hayward,
Thomas Hopkinson,
Samuel Houghton,
William J. Hubbard,

Messrs. Charles P. Huntington,
Giles C. Kellogg,
Isaac Kendall,
Hiram Knight,
Isaac Livermore,
Samuel K. Lothrop,
Joel Parker,
Samuel D. Parker,
George Putnam,
Sampson Reed,
Charles G. Stevens,
William Tyler,
Thomas Wetmore,
George White.

So the Resolve was finally passed, as follows:—

Resolved, That the Constitution ought to be amended by adding to chapter 5, section 1, the following article, to wit:—

The legislature shall forever have full power and authority, as may be judged needful for the advancement of learning, to grant any further powers to, or alter, limit, annul, or restrain, any of the powers now vested in the President and Fellows of Harvard College: *Pro-*

vided, the obligation of contracts shall not be impaired; and shall have the like power and authority over all corporate franchises hereafter granted for the purposes of education in this Commonwealth.

At a quarter before seven o'clock, on motion of Mr. French, of New Bedford,

The Convention adjourned.

FRIDAY, July 22, 1853.

Met according to adjournment. Prayer was offered by the Chaplain. The Journal of yesterday was read.

The Order offered yesterday, by Mr. Tyler, of Pawtucket, and laid over, was, together with the amendment proposed by Mr. Earle, of Worcester,

Referred to the Committee on Reporting and Printing.

The Order offered on the 18th of July, by Mr. Brown, of Medway, was taken from the table.

The amendment of Mr. Aspinwall, of Brookline, striking out the words "except chairmen of committees," was adopted; and then the Order was adopted, as follows:—

Ordered, that on and after Monday next, no member of this Convention shall speak more than fifteen minutes on one subject, without leave.

On motion of Mr. Cushman, of Bernardston, the Convention proceeded to the consideration of the Orders of the Day.

The first subject was the Resolves on the subject of the Council.

Mr. Churchill, of Milton, moved to amend the Resolves by adding the following, as a fourth Resolve:—

Resolved, That it is expedient to amend the Constitution as follows, to wit: The legislature may provide by law, that public notice shall be given of all applications to the Governor and Council, for remission of sentence of persons imprisoned for crime.

The amendment was adopted, by a vote of one hundred and thirty in the affirmative, to one hundred and fifteen in the negative.

Mr. Upton, of Boston, moved to amend by striking out the second Resolve; but the motion was rejected.

The Previous Question was moved, by Mr. Bates, of Plymouth, but withdrawn by him, and afterwards renewed by Mr. Upton, of Boston, and ordered by the Convention.

A division of the question was called for,

And the first, second and third Resolves were agreed to.

The fourth was rejected, by a vote of one hundred and twenty-nine in the affirmative, to one hundred and thirty-five in the negative.

The Resolves, as finally passed, are as follow:—

Resolved, That eight councillors be elected by the people in single districts, each district to consist of five contiguous senatorial districts.

Resolved, That it is expedient so to amend the Constitution, as to provide, that the record of the proceedings of the Council shall always be subject to public examination.

Resolved, That it is expedient so to amend the Constitution, as to provide, that no councillor, during the time for which he shall be elected, shall be appointed on any commission, or to any place, for which he shall receive any compensation whatever, other than that which he receives as councillor.

The second subject was the Resolves on the preservation of the records; which were finally passed, as follow:—

Resolved, That at the close of the session, the Secretaries of the Convention deposit the original Journals, together with the papers of the Convention, in the office of the Secretary of State.

Resolved, That William S. Robinson prepare an Index to the Journal, and procure two thousand copies of the Journal and Index to be printed and bound, on such terms and in such manner as shall be approved by the Committee on the Preservation of the Records, and that he be paid four dollars a day for his services therein.

Resolved, That His Excellency the Governor be requested to draw his warrant on the treasury for such expenses incurred in the execution of the preceding Resolves, as shall be approved by the Committee on the Preservation of the Records.

Resolved, That the Secretary of the Commonwealth be requested to distribute copies of the Journal to each member of the Convention, and to all persons and public bodies mentioned in chapter 2, section 2, of the Revised Statutes, excepting members of the legislature.

The next subject was the Resolves on the subject of elections by plurality and majority.

Mr. Dana, member for Manchester, moved to amend by striking out all after the word "Resolved," and inserting instead thereof, the following:—

That in the election of all officers required by this Constitution to be chosen by the people, except town officers and representatives to the general court, the person having the highest number of votes shall be deemed elected. In the election of town officers and representatives to the general court, a majority of votes shall be required, unless otherwise provided by the legislature.

Mr. BIRD, of Walpole, moved to amend the Resolves, by substituting for the third Resolve, the following:—

Resolved, That it is expedient so to amend the Constitution, as to provide that a majority of the votes shall be necessary for the election of representatives to the general court, until otherwise provided by law.

Mr. GOOCH, of Melrose, moved to amend the amendment of Mr. Bird, by adding to it the words: "*Provided*, that no law on this subject shall take effect until two years after its passage."

Mr. ELY, of Westfield, moved the Previous Question, which was ordered, by a vote of one hundred and sixty-one in the affirmative, to forty-four in the negative.

The amendment of Mr. Gooch was rejected.

On motion of Mr. ABBOTT, of Lowell, the yeas and nays were ordered upon the adoption of Mr. Bird's amendment.

And the roll being called, one hundred and eighty-eight members voted for the amendment, and one hundred and sixty-seven against it.

So it was adopted.

Those who voted in the affirmative are:—

Messrs. Josiah G. Abbott,
Shubael P. Adams,
Joel C. Allen,
Parsons Allen,
Josiah Allis,
D. W. Alvord,
George Austin,
Samuel Ayres,
George S. Ball,
Sidney Bartlett,
Marcus Barrett,
Moses Bates, Jr.,
John Beal,
Zephaniah Bennett,
Jacob Bigelow,
Francis W. Bird,
William S. Booth,
George S. Boutwell,
Sewell Boutwell,

Messrs. William J. A. Bradford,
Asa Bronson,
Artemas Brown,
Hammond Brown,
Hiram C. Brown,
Joseph Brownell,
Patrick Bryant,
Anson Burlingame,
Benjamin F. Butler,
Henry Cady,
William Carruthers,
Isaac Case,
Amariah Chandler,
Henry Chapin,
J. McKean Churchill,
Henry Clark,
Ransom Clark,
Stillman Clarke,
William Cleverly,

Messrs. George B. Crane,
Oliver S. Cressy,
Joseph W. Cross,
Henry W. Cushman,
Thomas Cushman,
Simeon N. Cutler,
Richard H. Dana, Jr.,
Charles G. Davis,
Ebenezer Davis,
Isaac Davis,
Gilman Day,
Silas Dean,
Elijah S. Deming
Augustus Denton,
Alexander De Witt,
Samuel Duncan,
Bradish Dunham,
John M. Durgin,
Philip Eames,
John M. Earle,
Samuel Edwards,
Sullivan Fay,
James K. Fellows,
Emery Fiske,
Lyman Fisk,
Ezekiel W. Fitch,
Aaron Foster,
Abram Foster,
Samuel Fowle,
James M. Freeman,
Charles A. French,
Rodney French,
Samuel French,
Luther Gale,
Johnson Gardner,
Elbridge Gates,
Wanton C. Gilbert,
Washington Gilbert,
Charles G. Giles,
Joel Giles,
Daniel W. Gooch,
Leonard Gooding,
John W. Graves,
William B. Greene,
Josiah W. Griswold,
Samuel P. Hadley,
Lyman W. Hapgood,
Seth Hapgood,
Elnathan P. Hathaway,
Isaac Hayden,
Charles C. Hazewell,
Ezra Heath, 2d,
James Hewes,

Messrs. George S. Hillard,
Martin Howard,
Abraham H. Howland,
Henry K. Hoyt,
Charles E. Hunt,
Charles P. Huntington,
Moses C. Hurlbut,
John Jacobs,
Isaac Kendall,
Joseph Kimball,
Joseph Kingman,
Jefferson Knight,
J. S. C. Knowlton,
William H. Knowlton,
Albert Knox,
Gardner P. Ladd,
Wilber C. Langdon,
Luther Lawrence,
Job G. Lawton, Jr.,
Abishai Lincoln,
Otis Little,
Justin E. Loomis,
William P. Marble,
Abijah P. Marvin,
Charles Mason,
Reuben Meader,
Simeon Merritt,
James M. Moore,
Joseph B. Morss,
Elbridge G. Morton,
Marcus Morton, Jr.,
William S. Morton,
Hiram Nash,
William Nichols,
Andrew T. Nute,
Joseph E. Ober,
Benjamin S. Orne,
E. Wing Packer,
Benjamin Paine,
Henry Paine,
Jonathan Parris,
John Partridge,
Thomas A. Parsons,
Nathaniel Peabody,
Jeremiah Pease, Jr.,
John Penniman,
Jesse Perkins,
Noah C. Perkins,
Charles Phelps,
Silvanus B. Phinney,
Henry Pierce,
James M. Pool,
Peter Powers,

Messrs. Robert Rantoul,
Silas Rawson,
David Rice,
Luther Richards,
Daniel Richardson,
Nathan Richardson,
Samuel H. Richardson,
Elkanah Ring, Jr.,
Joseph M. Rockwood,
David S. Ross,
Amasa Sanderson,
Chester Sanderson,
John Sherril,
Perez Simmons,
John W. Simonds,
Matthew Smith,
Melzar Sprague,
Samuel W. Spooner,
Granville Stevens,
William Stevens,
Gideon Stiles,
Alfred L. Strong,

Messrs. Alanson Swain,
Arnold Taft,
Willard Thayer, 2d,
John W. Thomas,
Charles Thompson,
Abraham Tilton,
David P. Turner,
Orison Underwood,
George A. Vinton,
Frederick T. Wallace,
Freeland Wallis,
Amasa Walker,
Andrew H. Ward,
Gershom B. Weston,
Daniel S. Whitney,
Daniel Wilbur,
Joseph Wilbur,
Henry Wilson,
Levi M. Winslow,
Otis Wood,
William H. Wood,
Ezekiel Wright.

Those who voted in the negative are:—

Messrs. Benjamin P. Adams,
P. Emory Aldrich,
James B. Allen,
John B. Alley,
Robert Andrews,
William Aspinwall,
David C. Atwood,
Alpheus Bancroft,
Joseph Barrows,
Russel Bartlett,
Eliakim A. Bates,
Erasmus D. Beach,
Luther V. Bell,
William Bennett, Jr.,
Edward B. Bigelow,
Gad O. Bliss,
William C. Bliss,
Ebenezer Bradbury,
Milton P. Braman,
Hiram N. Breed,
Osmyn Brewster,
Francis Brinley,
George N. Briggs,
Adolphus F. Brown,
Frederick Brownell,
Rufus Bullock,
Cephas C. Bumpus,
Timothy W. Carter,

Messrs. Chester W. Chapin,
Daniel E. Chapin,
Josiah Childs,
Alpheus B. Clarke,
Jacob Coggin,
Nathaniel Cogswell,
Lansing J. Cole,
Ithamar Conkey,
Charles E. Cook,
Henry F. Cooledge,
Simeon Crittenden,
George W. Crockett,
Leander Crosby,
Seth Crowell,
Francis B. Crowninshield,
Joseph Cummings,
John Davis,
Solomon Davis,
Henry L. Dawes,
Hiram S. Denison,
James C. Doane,
Moses Dorman,
Peter Easland,
Lilley Eaton,
Elisha Edwards,
Joseph M. Ely,
Homer Ely,
William T. Eustis,

Messrs. A. G. Farwell,
Samuel P. Fowler,
Charles H. French,
Richard Frothingham, Jr.,
Robert Gould,
Dalton Goulding,
Jason Goulding,
John C. Gray,
Jabez Green,
Whiting Griswold,
Artemas Hale,
Nathan Hale,
Charles B. Hall,
A. B. Hammond,
Phineas Harmon,
George Haskell,
William Haskins,
Stephen E. Hawkes,
George Hayward,
Charles Heard,
Samuel Henry,
Henry Hersey,
Levi Heywood,
William Hinsdale,
Aaron Hobart,
Henry Hobart,
Nathaniel Holder,
George Hood,
Foster Hooper,
Thomas Hopkinson,
Samuel Houghton,
William J. Hubbard,
William Hunt,
Asahel Huntington,
Samuel Jackson,
William James,
John Jenkins,
Samuel H. Jenks,
Giles C. Kellogg,
Martin R. Kellogg,
Henry W. Kinsman,
Hiram Knight,
Joseph Knight,
George H. Kuhn,
Alden Leland,
Frederic W. Lincoln, Jr.,
Tristram Littlefield,
Isaac Livermore,
Samuel K. Lothrop,
Samuel P. Loud,
John A. Lowell,
Theophilus R. Marvin,
Seth Miller, Jr.,

Messrs. Samuel Mixter,
James L. Monroe,
George Morey,
Marcus Morton,
Charles Newman,
Daniel Noyes,
Henry K. Oliver,
Nathan Orcutt,
Charles Osgood,
James W. Paige,
John G. Park,
Adolphus G. Parker,
Joel Parker,
George Peabody,
Daniel A. Perkins,
Jonathan C. Perkins,
William C. Plunkett,
Jeremiah Pomroy,
Jonathan Preston,
George Putnam,
John A. Putnam,
James Read,
Sampson Reed,
John Rogers,
John Sargent,
William Schouler,
Chester Sikes,
John S. Sleeper,
John Souther,
Eben H. Stacy,
Caleb Stetson,
Joseph L. Stevens, Jr.,
J. Thomas Stevenson,
Thomas Talbot,
Ralph Taylor,
Edmund P. Tileston,
Horatio W. Tilton,
Charles R. Train,
David Turner,
John S. Tyler,
Charles W. Upham,
George B. Upton,
Samuel B. Walcott,
Bradford L. Wales,
Samuel Walker,
Marshal Warner,
Cyrus Weeks,
Thomas Wetmore,
William F. Wheeler,
Benjamin White,
George White,
Joel Wilder,
John H. Wilkins,

Messrs. Henry Williams,
J. B. Williams,
Jonathan B. Winn,
Messrs. Charles C. Wood,
Nathaniel Wood.

On motion of Mr. CROWNINSHIELD, of Boston, the yeas and nays were ordered upon the question of adopting the amendment offered by Mr. Dana.

And the roll being called, one hundred and sixty-nine members voted in the affirmative, and one hundred and eighty-eight in the negative.

So it was rejected.

Those who voted in the affirmative are:—

Messrs. Benjamin P. Adams,
P. Emory Aldrich,
Robert Andrews,
William Aspinwall,
David C. Atwood,
George Austin,
Alpheus Bancroft,
Joseph Barrows,
Russel Bartlett,
Sidney Bartlett,
Erasmus D. Beach,
James M. Beebe,
Luther V. Bell,
William Bennett, Jr.,
Jacob Bigelow,
Gad O. Bliss,
William C. Bliss,
Milton P. Braman,
Hiram N. Breed,
Osmyn Brewster,
Francis Brinley,
George N. Briggs,
Rufus Bullock,
Cephas C. Bumpus,
Anson Burlingame,
Timothy W. Carter,
Amariah Chandler,
Chester W. Chapin,
Josiah Childs,
Alpheus B. Clarke,
Jacob Coggin,
Nathaniel Cogswell,
Lansing J. Cole,
Ithamar Conkey,
Charles E. Cook,
Henry F. Cooledge,
George W. Crockett,
Leander Crosby,
Messrs. Seth Crowell,
Francis B. Crowninshield,
Joseph Cummings,
Richard H. Dana, Jr.,
John Davis,
Solomon Davis,
Henry L. Dawes,
Hiram S. Denison,
James C. Doane,
Moses Dorman,
James Easton, 2d,
Lilley Eaton,
Homer Ely,
William T. Eustis,
A. G. Farwell,
Aaron Foster,
Samuel P. Fowler,
Charles H. French,
Richard Frothingham, Jr.,
Wanton C. Gilbert,
Robert Gould,
Dalton Goulding,
Jason Goulding,
John C. Gray,
Jabez Green,
Whiting Griswold,
Artemas Hale,
Nathan Hale,
Charles B. Hall,
A. B. Hammond,
Phineas Harmon,
George Haskell,
Stephen E. Hawkes,
George Hayward,
Charles Heard,
Samuel Henry,
Henry Hersey,
James Hewes,

Messrs. Levi Heywood,
George S. Hillard,
William Hinsdale,
Aaron Hobart,
Nathaniel Holder,
Foster Hooper,
Thomas Hopkinson,
Samuel Houghton,
William J. Hubbard,
William Hunt,
Asahel Huntington,
Charles P. Huntington,
Samuel Jackson,
William James,
John Jenkins,
Samuel H. Jenks,
Giles C. Kellogg,
Martin R. Kellogg,
Joseph Kingman,
Henry W. Kinsman,
Hiram Knight,
Jefferson Knight,
Joseph Knight,
George H. Kuhn,
John S. Ladd,
Frederic W. Lincoln, Jr.,
Tristram Littlefield,
Isaac Livermore,
Otis P. Lord,
Samuel K. Lothrop,
Samuel P. Loud,
John A. Lowell,
Theophilus R. Marvin,
Reuben Meader,
Seth Miller, Jr.,
Samuel Mixter,
George Morey,
Joseph B. Morss,
Marcus Morton,
Marcus Morton, Jr.,
Daniel Noyes,
Henry K. Oliver,
Nathan Orcutt,
Charles Osgood,
James W. Paige,
John G. Park,
Adolphus G. Parker,

Messrs. Joel Parker,
George Peabody,
Daniel A. Perkins,
Jonathan C. Perkins,
William C. Plunkett,
Jeremiah Pomroy,
Jonathan Preston,
George Putnam,
John A. Putnam,
Robert Rantoul,
James Read,
Sampson Reed,
John Rogers,
George R. Sampson,
John Sargent,
William Schouler,
Chester Sikes,
John S. Sleeper,
John Souther,
Granville Stevens,
Joseph L. Stevens, Jr.,
J. Thomas Stevenson,
Alfred L. Strong,
Thomas Talbot,
Ralph Taylor,
John W. Thomas,
Edmund P. Tileston,
Horatio W. Tilton,
Charles R. Train,
David Turner,
John S. Tyler,
Charles W. Upham,
George B. Upton,
Samuel B. Walcott,
Bradford L. Wales,
Samuel Walker,
Cyrus Weeks,
Thomas Wetmore,
William F. Wheeler,
Benjamin White,
George White,
Daniel Wilbur,
Joel Wilder,
John H. Wilkins,
Henry Williams,
Nathaniel Wood.

Those who voted in the negative are :—

Messrs. Josiah G. Abbott,
Shubael P. Adams,
Joel C. Allen,

Messrs. Parsons Allen,
John B. Alley,
Josiah Allis,

Messrs. D. W. Alvord,
George S. Ball,
Marcus Barrett,
Eliakim A. Bates,
Moses Bates, Jr.,
John Beal,
Zephaniah Bennett,
Edward B. Bigelow,
Francis W. Bird,
William S. Booth,
George S. Boutwell,
Sewell Boutwell,
William J. A. Bradford,
Asa Bronson,
Artemas Brown,
Hammond Brown,
Hiram C. Brown,
Frederick Brownell,
Joseph Brownell,
Patrick Bryant,
Asahel Buck,
Benjamin F. Butler,
Henry Cady,
William Carruthers,
Isaac Case,
Daniel E. Chapin,
Henry Chapin,
J. McKean Churchill,
Henry Clark,
Ransom Clark,
Stillman Clarke,
William Cleverly,
Sumner Cole,
George B. Crane,
Oliver S. Cressy,
Simeon Crittenden,
Joseph W. Cross,
Henry W. Cushman,
Thomas Cushman,
Simeon N. Cutler,
Charles G. Davis,
Ebenezer Davis,
Isaac Davis,
Gilman Day,
Silas Dean,
Elijah S. Deming,
Augustus Denton,
Alexander De Witt,
Samuel Duncan,
Bradish Dunham,
John M. Durgin,
Philip Eames,
John M. Earle,

Messrs. Peter Easland,
Elisha Edwards,
Samuel Edwards,
Joseph M. Ely,
Sullivan Fay,
James K. Fellows,
Lyman Fisk,
Ezekiel W. Fitch,
Abram Foster,
Samuel Fowle,
James M. Freeman,
Charles A. French,
Rodney French,
Samuel French,
Luther Gale,
Johnson Gardner,
Elbridge Gates,
Washington Gilbert,
Charles G. Giles,
Joel Giles,
Daniel W. Gooch,
Leonard Gooding,
John W. Graves,
William B. Greene,
Josiah W. Griswold,
Samuel P. Hadley,
Benjamin F. Hallett,
Lyman W. Hapgood,
Seth Hapgood,
Elnathan P. Hathaway,
Isaac Hayden,
Charles C. Hazewell,
Ezra Heath, 2d,
William H. Hewes,
Henry Hobart,
George Hood,
Martin Howard,
Abraham H. Howland,
Henry K. Hoyt,
Charles E. Hunt,
Moses C. Hurlbut,
John Jacobs,
Isaac Kendall,
Joseph Kimball,
J. S. C. Knowlton,
William H. Knowlton,
Albert Knox,
Gardner P. Ladd,
Wilber C. Langdon,
Luther Lawrence,
Job G. Lawton, Jr.,
Alden Leland,
Abishai Lincoln,

Messrs. Justin E. Loomis,
William P. Marble,
Charles Mason,
Simeon Merritt,
James L. Monroe,
James M. Moore,
Elbridge G. Morton,
William S. Morton,
Hiram Nash,
Charles Newman,
William Nichols,
Andrew T. Nute,
Joseph E. Ober,
Benjamin S. Orne,
E. Wing Packer,
Benjamin Paine,
Henry Paine,
Jonathan Parris,
John Partridge,
Thomas A. Parsons,
Nathaniel Peabody,
Jeremiah Pease, Jr.,
John Penniman,
Jesse Perkins,
Noah C. Perkins,
Charles Phelps,
Silvanus B. Phinney,
Henry Pierce,
James M. Pool,
Peter Powers,
Silas Rawson,
David Rice,
Luther Richards,
Daniel Richardson,
Nathan Richardson,
Samuel H. Richardson,
Elkanah Ring, Jr.,
Joseph M. Rockwood,

Messrs. David S. Ross,
Amasa Sanderson,
John Sherril,
Perez Simmons,
John W. Simonds,
Matthew Smith,
Melzar Sprague,
Samuel W. Spooner,
Eben H. Stacy,
William Stevens,
Gideon Stiles,
Alanson Swain,
Arnold Taft,
Joseph Thayer,
Willard Thayer, 2d,
Charles Thompson,
Abraham Tilton,
David P. Turner,
William Tyler,
Orison Underwood,
Frederick T. Wallace,
Freeland Wallis,
Amasa Walker,
Andrew H. Ward,
Marshal Warner,
Samuel Warner, Jr.,
Asa H. Waters,
Gershom B. Weston,
Daniel S. Whitney,
Joseph Wilbur,
Henry Wilson,
Willard Wilson,
Jonathan B. Winn,
Levi M. Winslow,
Charles C. Wood,
Otis Wood,
William H. Wood,
Ezekiel Wright.

On motion of Mr. Hathaway, of Freetown, the yeas and nays were ordered upon the final passage of the Resolves, as amended,

And the roll being called, one hundred and eighty-one members voted for the Resolves, and one hundred and twenty against them.

Those who voted in the affirmative are:—

Messrs. Josiah G. Abbott,
Shubael P. Adams,
James B. Allen,
Parsons Allen,
Josiah Allis,
D. W. Alvord,
George S. Ball,

Messrs. Alpheus Bancroft,
Marcus Barrett,
Eliakim A. Bates,
Moses Bates, Jr.,
Erasmus D. Beach,
John Beal,
Zephaniah Bennett,

Messrs. Edward B. Bigelow,
Francis W. Bird,
Gad O. Bliss,
William S. Booth,
George S. Boutwell,
Sewell Boutwell,
Asa Bronson,
Adolphus F. Brown,
Artemas Brown,
Hammond Brown,
Frederick Brownell,
Joseph Brownell,
Patrick Bryant,
Benjamin F. Butler,
Henry Cady,
William Carruthers,
Isaac Case,
Amariah Chandler,
Henry Chapin,
J. McKean Churchill,
Henry Clark,
Ransom Clark,
Stillman Clarke,
George B. Crane,
Oliver S. Cressy,
Simeon Crittenden,
Joseph W. Cross,
Thomas Cushman,
Simeon N. Cutler,
Charles G. Davis,
Ebenezer Davis,
Isaac Davis,
Silas Dean,
Augustus Denton,
Alexander De Witt,
Bradish Dunham,
John M. Durgin,
Philip Eames,
John M. Earle,
Peter Easland,
Calvin D. Eaton,
Elisha Edwards,
Samuel Edwards,
Sullivan Fay,
Lyman Fisk,
Aaron Foster,
Samuel Fowle,
James M. Freeman,
Rodney French,
Samuel French,
Luther Gale,
Charles G. Giles,
Daniel W. Gooch,

Messrs. Leonard Gooding,
John W. Graves,
Jabez Green,
William B. Greene,
Josiah W. Griswold,
Whiting Griswold,
Samuel P. Hadley,
Charles B. Hall,
Benjamin F. Hallett,
Lyman W. Hapgood,
Seth Hapgood,
Phineas Harmon,
Stephen E. Hawkes,
Ezra Heath, 2d,
James Hewes,
William H. Hewes,
Henry Hobart,
Nathaniel Holder,
George Hood,
Martin Howard,
Abraham H. Howland,
Henry K. Hoyt,
Charles E. Hunt,
Moses C. Hurlbut,
Isaac Kendall,
Joseph Kimball,
Joseph Kingman,
Jefferson Knight,
J. S. C. Knowlton,
William H. Knowlton,
Albert Knox,
Gardner P. Ladd,
Luther Lawrence,
Alden Leland,
Abishai Lincoln,
Justin E. Loomis,
William P. Marble,
Charles Mason,
Reuben Meader,
Simeon Merritt,
James M. Moore,
Joseph B. Morss,
Elbridge G. Morton,
Marcus Morton, Jr.,
William S. Morton,
Hiram Nash,
Charles Newman,
William Nichols,
Andrew T. Nute,
Joseph E. Ober,
Benjamin S. Orne,
Charles Osgood,
E. Wing Packer,

Messrs. Benjamin Paine,
Jonathan Parris,
John Partridge,
Nathaniel Peabody,
Jeremiah Pease, Jr.,
John Penniman,
Jesse Perkins,
Noah C. Perkins,
Charles Phelps,
Sylvanus B. Phinney,
Henry Pierce,
James M. Pool,
Peter Powers,
Robert Rantoul,
Silas Rawson,
David Rice,
Daniel Richardson,
Nathan Richardson,
Samuel H. Richardson
Elkanah Ring, Jr.,
Joseph M. Rockwood,
David S. Ross,
John Sherril,
Chester Sikes,
Perez Simmons,
John W. Simonds,
Matthew Smith,
Melzar Sprague,
Samuel W. Spooner,
Eben H. Stacy,
Granville Stevens,

Messrs. Joseph L. Stevens, Jr.,
William Stevens,
Gideon Stiles,
Alanson Swain,
Arnold Taft,
Joseph Thayer,
Willard Thayer, 2d,
John W. Thomas,
Abraham Tilton,
Horatio W. Tilton,
David P. Turner,
William Tyler,
Orison Underwood,
Frederick T. Wallace,
Freeland Wallis,
Amasa Walker,
Andrew H. Ward,
Samuel Warner, Jr.,
Asa H. Waters,
Gershom B. Weston,
George White,
Daniel S. Whitney,
Joseph Wilbur,
Henry Wilson,
Willard Wilson,
Jonathan B. Winn,
Levi M. Winslow,
Charles C. Wood,
Nathaniel Wood,
Otis Wood.

Those who voted in the negative are :—

Messrs. Benjamin P. Adams,
P. Emory Aldrich,
Joel C. Allen,
Robert Andrews,
William Aspinwall,
David C. Atwood,
George Austin,
Joseph Barrows,
Russel Bartlett,
James M. Beebe,
Luther V. Bell,
William Bennett, Jr.,
George W. Blagden,
Ebenezer Bradbury,
Milton P. Braman,
Osmyn Brewster,
Francis Brinley,
George N. Briggs,
Rufus Bullock,

Messrs. Cephas C. Bumpus,
Timothy W. Carter,
Chester W. Chapin,
Daniel E. Chapin,
Jacob Coggin,
Nathaniel Cogswell,
Ithamar Conkey,
Charles E. Cook,
Henry F. Cooledge,
Leander Crosby,
Seth Crowell,
Richard H. Dana, Jr.,
John Davis,
Solomon Davis,
Henry L. Dawes,
Hiram S. Denison,
James C. Doane,
Moses Dorman,
James Easton, 2d,

Messrs. Lilley Eaton,
Homer Ely,
A. G. Farwell,
Samuel P. Fowler,
Charles H. French,
Wanton C. Gilbert,
Joel Giles,
Robert Gould,
Dalton Goulding,
Jason Goulding,
Artemas Hale,
Nathan Hale,
A. B. Hammond,
Elnathan P. Hathaway,
Charles C. Hazewell,
Charles Heard,
Samuel Henry,
Henry Hersey,
George S. Hillard,
Aaron Hobart,
Thomas Hopkinson,
Samuel Houghton,
William J. Hubbard,
William Hunt,
Asahel Huntington,
Samuel Jackson,
William James,
John Jenkins,
Samuel H. Jenks,
Giles C. Kellogg,
Henry W. Kinsman,
Hiram Knight,
George H. Kuhn,
John S. Ladd,
Job G. Lawton, Jr.,
Frederic W. Lincoln, Jr.,
Isaac Livermore,
Otis P. Lord,
Samuel K. Lothrop,
Samuel P. Loud,
John A. Lowell,

Messrs. Seth Miller, Jr.,
James L. Monroe,
George Morey,
Marcus Morton,
Daniel Noyes,
Henry K. Oliver,
Nathan Orcutt,
James W. Paige,
John G. Park,
Adolphus G. Parker,
George Peabody,
Daniel A. Perkins,
Jonathan C. Perkins,
William C. Plunkett,
Jeremiah Pomroy,
George Putnam,
John A. Putnam,
James Read,
Sampson Reed,
John Rogers,
George R. Sampson,
Amasa Sanderson,
John Sargent,
William Schouler,
John S. Sleeper,
John Souther,
J. Thomas Stevenson,
Thomas Talbot,
Edmund P. Tileston,
Charles R. Train,
David Turner,
Charles W. Upham,
George B. Upton,
Samuel Walker,
Marshal Warner,
Cyrus Weeks,
Thomas Wetmore,
William F. Wheeler,
Benjamin White,
Joel Wilder,
Ezekiel Wright.

So the Resolves were finally passed, as follow:—

Resolved, That it is expedient to provide in the Constitution that a majority of all the votes given shall be necessary to the election of a governor, lieutenant-governor, secretary, treasurer, auditor, and attorney-general of the Commonwealth: *Provided*, that if at any election of either of the above-named officers, no person shall have a majority of the votes given, the House of Representatives shall, by a majority of *viva voce* votes, elect two out of three persons who had the highest, if so many shall have been voted for, and return the persons so elected to the Senate, from whom the Senate shall, by *viva voce* vote, elect one who shall be governor, or other officer to be thus elected.

Resolved, That in all the elections of senators and councillors, the person having the highest number of votes shall be elected.

Resolved, That it is expedient so to amend the Constitution as to provide that a majority of votes shall be necessary for the election of representatives to the general court, until otherwise provided by law.

Resolved, That in the election of all city and town officers, the same rule shall govern as in case of representatives to the general court.

Resolved, That in the election of all county and district officers, the person having the highest number of votes shall be elected.

Resolved, That in all elections where the person having the highest number of votes may be elected, and there is a failure of election because two persons have an equal number of votes, subsequent trials may be had at such times as may be prescribed by the legislature.

On motion of Mr. Fay, of Southborough, the Orders of the Day were laid upon the table.

The same gentleman, from the Committee on Leave of Absence, submitted a Report, granting leave of absence to Mr. Meader, of Nantucket, and Mr. Cummings, of Ware, for the remainder of the session.

The Report was considered and accepted, and leave of absence granted.

Mr. Griswold, member for Erving, moved that the Committee of the Whole, having under consideration the subject of Amendments of the Constitution, be discharged from the further consideration of that subject.

Without taking the question,

At two o'clock, on motion of Mr. Walker, of Roxbury,

The Convention adjourned.

AFTERNOON SESSION.

Met according to adjournment.

On motion of Mr. Griswold, member for Erving, the Committee of the Whole having under consideration the Report,

Inexpedient to act upon the subject of an Order to consider the expediency of providing that the legislature shall have no power to authorize or pass any law sanctioning the suspension of specie payments by any corporations issuing bank notes;

And the Report,

Inexpedient to act upon the subject of an Order of June 25th, on the expediency of so modifying article 3 of section 3, chapter 1 of the Constitution, that towns and districts may have the right to be represented by any citizens of the Commonwealth,

Were discharged from the consideration of those subjects.

The rule requiring that propositions concerning an amendment of the Constitution shall be considered in Committee of the Whole, was suspended, and these Reports were placed in the Orders of the Day.

On motion of Mr. GRISWOLD, member for Erving, the Resolve on the subject of a quorum in the House of Representatives, and

The Resolve for the payment of the Chaplain and other officers of the Convention, were

Taken from the table, and placed in the Orders of the Day.

Mr. CHAPIN, of Worcester, moved that the Resolve on the subject of appropriations for sectarian schools, be taken from the table; but the motion was rejected.

On motion of Mr. GRISWOLD, member for Erving, the Convention resumed the consideration of the Orders of the Day.

The Resolves on the subject of the lieutenant-governor, were passed, as follow:—

Resolved, That the following be adopted as a part of the Constitution, relating to the lieutenant-governor:—

ARTICLE 1. There shall be annually elected a lieutenant-governor of the Commonwealth of Massachusetts, whose eligibility to the office and qualification therefor, shall be the same as those of the governor; and the day and manner of his election, and the qualifications of the electors, shall be the same as are required in the election of a governor. The return of the votes for this officer, and the declaration of his election, shall be in the same manner; and if no one person shall be found to be elected, the vacancy shall be filled by the Senate and House of Representatives in the same manner as the governor is to be elected, in case no one person shall have been elected by the people, to be governor.

The lieutenant-governor shall hold his office for one year, next following the first Wednesday of January, and until another is chosen and qualified in his stead.

ART. 2. When, by reason of sickness or temporary absence from the Commonwealth, the governor shall be unable to perform his official duties, the lieutenant-governor shall have the power and perform the duties of the governor; and in case of the removal from office, resignation or death of the governor, the lieutenant-governor shall succeed to the office, and be the governor of the Commonwealth.

The Reports, inexpedient to act on the subject of the suspension of specie payments, and the representation of towns and cities by any citizens of the Commonwealth, were accepted.

The Resolve on the subject of a quorum in the House of Representatives, was amended by striking out the words "a majority," and substituting therefor the words "one hundred," and then

Ordered to a second reading.

The Resolve for the payment of the Chaplain and other officers of the Convention, was finally passed, as follows:—

Resolved, That there be paid out of the treasury of the Commonwealth, to the several persons whose names are borne on the accompanying list, for each and every day's service, as follows: to the two Secretaries, ten dollars each; to the Chaplain, three dollars; to the Messenger, five dollars; to the two Assistant Messengers, three dollars each; to the Door-keeper and three Assistant Door-keepers, three dollars each; to the Postmaster, three dollars; to the four Pages, two dollars each; and the Governor, by and with the advice and consent of the Council, is hereby requested to draw his warrant on the treasurer for the same, on an Order of this Convention.

List of officers of the Convention embraced in the Resolve:—

William S. Robinson and James T. Robinson, Secretaries; Warren Burton, Chaplain; Benjamin Stevens, Messenger; Issachar Fuller and Tilson Fuller, Assistant Messengers; Alexis Poole, Door-keeper; David Murphy, William M. Wise, and John A. Sargent, Assistant Door-keepers; William Sayward, Postmaster; Joseph P. Dexter, Jr., Charles A. Murphy, Thaddeus Page, and James N. Tolman, Jr., Pages.

On motion of Mr. Cushman, of Bernardston,

Ordered, That debate in Committee of the Whole on the subject of amendments of the Constitution, cease in one hour after the Convention goes into Committee.

On motion of Mr. Cushman, the Convention resolved itself into Committee of the Whole, for the purpose of considering the Resolves on the subject of amendments of the Constitution; and the President requested Mr. Griswold, member for Erving, to take the chair.

Afterwards, Mr. GRISWOLD reported the Resolves to the Convention, with amendments, as follow:—

First, striking out all of the second Resolution.

Second, striking out all after the word "Resolved" in the first Resolve, and substituting the following for the whole series:—

Resolved, That it is expedient to provide in the Constitution, that a Convention to revise or amend this Constitution, may be called and held in the following manner: At the general election which shall be in the year eighteen hundred and seventy-three, and in each twentieth year thereafter, the qualified voters in State elections shall give in their votes to be received, counted, returned and declared, in the same manner as by law is provided in the choice of general officers at such election, upon the question, "Shall there be a Convention to revise the Constitution, in conformity to the provisions of the Act of 1852, chapter 188, relating to the calling a Convention of Delegates of the people for the purpose of revising the Constitution?" and if it shall appear, by the returns made, that a majority of the qualified voters throughout the State, who shall assemble and vote thereon, are in favor of such revision, the same shall be deemed and taken to be the will of the people of the Commonwealth, that a Convention should meet accordingly; and thereupon delegates shall be chosen on the first Monday of March next succeeding, in conformity with the law then in force for the election of representatives, and such delegates shall meet in Convention in the State House, on the first Wednesday of May succeeding, in the same manner and with the same authority as is provided in the second, third, and fourth sections of said Act.

The general court shall have power and authority in any year other than the year above specified, to submit to the people the same proposition, to be voted on in the same manner, at the next ensuing general election; and if it shall appear by the returns made, that a majority of the qualified voters throughout the State, who shall assemble and vote thereon, are in favor of such revision, the same shall be deemed and taken to be the will of the people of the Commonwealth, that a Convention should meet accordingly; and thereupon the same proceedings, with the same powers and authority, shall be had, as is provided in the foregoing clause of this Constitution.

The foregoing provisions shall in no wise restrain or impair the reserved right of the people, in their sovereign capacity, at all times.

to reform, alter, or totally change their Constitution and frame of government.

The first of the amendments was concurred in.

Mr. BRIGGS, of Pittsfield, moved to amend the second amendment, by striking out all after the word "Constitution," in the tenth line, (printed copy,) as far as the word "and" in the thirteenth line; and also the word "same," in the last line but two of the first paragraph; and also all of the same paragraph after the word "manner" in the same line, and to insert after the word "manner," the words "to be provided by the legislature to be chosen at the said election."

On motion of Mr. BRIGGS, the yeas and nays were ordered upon the question of adopting this amendment.

Without taking the question,

At a quarter past six o'clock, on motion of Mr. BRIGGS, of Pittsfield,

The Convention adjourned.

SATURDAY, July 23, 1853.

Met according to adjournment. Prayer was offered by the Chaplain. The Journal of yesterday was read.

On motion of Mr. CUSHMAN, of Bernardston,

Ordered, That the Committee on Reducing Amendments to the Constitution to a suitable form to be submitted to the people, be requested to prepare an Address to the people to accompany the Revised Constitution.

Mr. FAY, of Southborough, from the Committee on Leave of Absence, submitted a Report, granting leave of absence to Messrs. Bliss, of Hatfield, Taylor, of Great Barrington, and Kellogg, of West Stockbridge, for the remainder of the session.

The Report was considered and accepted, and leave of absence granted.

On motion of Mr. EARLE, of Worcester,

Ordered, That when the Convention adjourn, it adjourn to meet at ten o'clock on Monday.

Mr. BATES, of Plymouth, from the Committee on Reporting and Printing the Debates, submitted a Report and Resolve, granting authority to the committee.

The Resolve was considered and ordered to a second reading.

Mr. DUNCAN, of Williamstown, offered a Resolve on the subject of uniformity in the mode of receiving votes, &c.

Referred to the Committee of the Whole and ordered to be printed.

Mr. PARKER, of Cambridge, offered a Resolve on the subject of the mode in which moneys shall be appropriated for schools.

Laid upon the table, and ordered to be printed.

Mr. HALLETT, member for Wilbraham, moved a reconsideration of the vote of yesterday, by which the Resolves on the subject of the Council were finally passed.

Placed in the Orders of the Day.

Mr. BIRD, of Walpole, moved a reconsideration of the vote by which the Resolves on the subject of elections by plurality and majority were finally passed; and,

On motion of Mr. BIRD,

The motion to reconsider was laid upon the table.

Mr. BUTLER, of Lowell, offered the following Resolve:—

Resolved, That all judicial commissions which shall issue to any person from and after the first day of August, in the year one thousand eight hundred and fifty-three, shall confer no greater tenure of office than the term of ten years.

On motion of Mr. BUTLER, sustained by a vote of one hundred and forty-one in the affirmative, to fifty-two in the negative,

The rule requiring propositions for an amendment of the Constitution to be considered in Committee of the Whole, was suspended, so as to allow the Resolve to be considered in Convention, and

The Resolve was placed in the Orders of the Day for Monday.

Mr. DANA, member for Manchester, declined further service upon the Committee on the Preservation of the Records; and

Mr. HAZEWELL, of Concord, was appointed in his place.

On motion of Mr. GRISWOLD, member for Erving, the Convention proceeded to the consideration of the Orders of the Day.

The first subject, viz.: the Resolves on the subject of amendments of the Constitution, was specially assigned for consideration on Monday, at ten o'clock.

The Resolve on the subject of a quorum in the House of Representatives, was finally passed, as follows:—

Resolved, That the Constitution be so amended, that one hundred of the members of the House of Representatives shall be necessary to constitute a quorum.

On motion of Mr. Griswold, member for Erving, the Convention resolved itself into Committee of the Whole, for the purpose of considering the Resolves on the subject of banking; and the President *pro tempore* requested Mr. Butler, of Lowell, to take the chair.

Afterwards, Mr. Butler reported the Resolves to the Convention, without amendment;

And they were ordered to a second reading.

On motion of Mr. Griswold, member for Erving, the Convention resolved itself into Committee of the Whole, for the purpose of considering the Resolves on the subject of justices of the peace; and the President *pro tempore* requested Mr. Morton, of Andover, to take the chair.

Afterwards, Mr. Morton reported, that the committee had made progress in the consideration of the subject, but had come to no conclusion, and had instructed him to ask leave to sit again.

Upon the question of granting leave, thirty members voted in the affirmative, and sixty-eight in the negative.

There appearing to be no quorum present,

Mr. Briggs, of Pittsfield, moved an adjournment, which was sustained by a vote of fifty-two in the affirmative, to forty-seven in the negative, and

At two o'clock, the Convention adjourned.

MONDAY, July 25, 1853.

Met according to adjournment. Prayer was offered by the Chaplain. The Journal of Friday last was read.

The special assignment, viz.: the Resolves on the subject of the amendments of the Constitution, was taken up.

On motion of Mr. Hallett, member for Wilbraham, the vote by which the yeas and nays were ordered upon the question of adopting the amendment of Mr. Briggs to the amendment of the Committee of the Whole, was reconsidered,

And the question recurring upon the demand for the yeas and nays, it was not sustained.

The question then being upon the amendment of Mr. Briggs, a division was called for, and the first part of the amendment, viz.: the proposition to strike out all after the word "Constitution," in the tenth line, as far as the word "and," in the thirteenth line, was agreed to.

The second part of the amendment, viz.: the proposition to strike out the word "same," in the last line but two of the first paragraph, and also all of the same paragraph after the word "manner," in the same line, and to insert after the word "manner," the words "to be provided by the legislature to be chosen at the said election,"

Was rejected, by a vote of seventy-seven in the affirmative, to one hundred and five in the negative.

Mr. HALLETT, member for Wilbraham, moved to amend the amendment of the Committee of the Whole, by inserting the word "then" after the word "is," in the eighth line; and also, after the word "Constitution," in the tenth line, the words "in conformity to the provisions in the Constitution for holding such Convention"; and also, after the word "succeeding," in the nineteenth line, the words "in conformity with the law then in force for the election of representatives, and upon the then basis for the year when the valuation of estates was settled"; and also after the word "of," in the twenty-third line, the words, "an act relating to the calling a Convention of the people for the purpose of revising the Constitution," approved May 7th, 1852. "And it shall be the duty of the proper officers and persons in authority to perform all acts necessary to carry into effect these provisions;" also by striking out the words, "in the same manner and," in the nineteenth line, the word, "second," in the twentieth line, and the words "said Act," in the twenty-first line.

On motion of Mr. ALLEN, of Worcester, the whole subject was committed to a special committee, consisting of seven members, with instructions to report to-morrow morning.

The President *pro tempore* appointed the committee, consisting, after the filling of the vacancies, of the following members, viz.:—

Messrs. Hallett, member for Wilbraham, Lord, of Salem, Upton, of Boston, Sumner, member for Marshfield, Williams, of Taunton, Alvord, member for Montague, and Simmons, of Hanover.

Afterwards, Mr. DENTON, of Chelsea, moved a reconsideration of the vote by which the subject was committed to a special committee; but the motion was rejected.

On motion of Mr. WESTON, of Duxbury, the Convention proceeded to the consideration of the Orders of the Day.

Leave was granted to the Committee of the Whole to sit for the further consideration of the subject of the election of justices of the peace.

The motion of Mr. HALLETT, member for Wilbraham, to reconsider the vote by which the Resolves on the subject of the Council were finally passed, was rejected.

The Resolves on the subject of banking were taken up.

Mr. Hooper, of Fall River, moved to amend the first Resolve, by adding to it the words "*Provided*, that no note or bill of a less denomination than ten dollars, shall be issued as currency, after the year eighteen hundred and sixty."

Mr. Brown, of Douglas, moved that leave be granted to Mr. Hall, of Haverhill, to speak more than fifteen minutes, but the motion was rejected.

The amendment of Mr. Hooper was rejected.

Mr. Plunkett, of Adams, moved to amend, by striking out the first Resolve;

And upon this motion, he called for the yeas and nays, which were ordered.

On motion of Mr. Duncan, of Williamstown, the Previous Question was ordered.

The roll being called, ninety-nine members voted for the amendment, and one hundred and fifty-eight against it.

So it was rejected.

Those who voted in the affirmative are:—

Messrs. Alfred A. Abbott,
Benjamin P. Adams,
P. Emory Aldrich,
John B. Alley,
William Aspinwall,
David C. Atwood,
Samuel Ayres,
Joseph Barrows,
Russel Bartlett,
John Beal,
Luther V. Bell,
William Bennett, Jr.,
Edward B. Bigelow,
Osmyn Brewster,
Francis Brinley,
George N. Briggs,
Rufus Bullock,
Nathaniel Cogswell,
Ithamar Conkey,
Charles E. Cook,
Benjamin F. Copeland,
George W. Crockett,
Leander Crosby,
Seth Crowell,
Francis B. Crowninshield,
Wilber Curtis,
John Davis,
Solomon Davis,

Messrs. Henry L. Dawes,
Elijah S. Deming,
Hiram S. Denison,
Philip Eames,
Peter Easland,
A. G. Farwell,
Sullivan Fay,
Samuel P. Fowler,
James M. Freeman,
Henry J. Gardner,
Wanton C. Gilbert,
John W. Graves,
Artemas Hale,
Charles B. Hall,
A. B. Hammond,
Isaac Hayden,
George Hayward,
Henry Hersey,
George S. Hillard,
William Hinsdale,
Thomas Hopkinson,
William J. Hubbard,
William Hunt,
Samuel A. Hurlburt,
Samuel Jackson,
John Jenkins,
Samuel H. Jenks,
Giles C. Kellogg,

Messrs. Edward L. Keyes,
Hiram Knight,
Joseph Knight,
George H. Kuhn,
Abishai Lincoln,
Frederic W. Lincoln, Jr.,
Otis P. Lord,
Samuel P. Loud,
Seth Miller, Jr.,
Samuel Mixter,
James M. Moore,
Henry K. Oliver,
Nathan Orcutt,
E. Wing Packer,
John G. Park,
Samuel D. Parker,
Jonathan C. Perkins,
William C. Plunkett,
John A. Putnam,
James Read,
Sampson Reed,
George R. Sampson,

Messrs. John Sargent,
William Schouler,
John W. Simonds,
John Souther,
Granville Stevens,
J. Thomas Stevenson,
Alanson Swain,
Edmund P. Tileston,
Charles R. Train,
Orison Underwood,
Charles W. Upham,
George B. Upton,
Samuel B. Walcott,
Samuel Walker,
Cyrus Weeks,
Thomas Wetmore,
William F. Wheeler,
Benjamin White,
Joel Wilder,
John H. Wilkins,
Jonathan B. Winn.

Those who voted in the negative are:—

Messrs. Shubael P. Adams,
Charles Allen,
James B. Allen,
Josiah Allis,
Alpheus Bancroft,
Marcus Barrett,
Zephaniah Bennett,
Francis W. Bird,
Henry W. Bishop,
Gad O. Bliss,
William S. Booth,
William J. A. Bradford,
Hiram N. Breed,
Asa Bronson,
Adolphus F. Brown,
Artemas Brown,
Hammond Brown,
Hiram C. Brown,
Frederick Brownell,
Joseph Brownell,
Asahel Buck,
Benjamin F. Butler,
Isaac Case,
Amariah Chandler,
Daniel E. Chapin,
Henry Chapin,
Josiah Childs,
Henry Clark,

Messrs. Ransom Clark,
William Cleverly,
Lansing J. Cole,
Sumner Cole,
Henry F. Cooledge,
George B. Crane,
Oliver S. Cressy,
Joseph W. Cross,
Thomas Cushman,
Silas Dean,
Augustus Denton,
Alexander De Witt,
Samuel Duncan,
Bradish Dunham,
John M. Durgin,
John M. Earle,
Elisha Edwards,
Samuel Edwards,
Emery Fiske,
Samuel Fowle,
Charles A. French,
Samuel French,
Richard Frothingham, Jr.,
Johnson Gardner,
Charles G. Giles,
Daniel W. Gooch,
Leonard Gooding,
Jabez Green,

Messrs. Whiting Griswold,
Samuel P. Hadley,
Benjamin F. Hallett,
Lyman W. Hapgood,
Seth Hapgood,
Phineas Harmon,
Elnathan P. Hathaway,
Stephen E. Hawkes,
Charles C. Hazewell,
Ezra Heath, 2d,
James Hewes,
William H. Hewes,
Aaron Hobart,
Henry Hobart,
Nathaniel Holder,
George Hood,
Foster Hooper,
Henry K. Hoyt,
Charles P. Huntington,
Moses C. Hurlbut,
Abijah M. Ide, Jr.,
John Jacobs,
Isaac Kendall,
Joseph Kimball,
Jefferson Knight,
William H. Knowlton,
Albert Knox,
Gardner P. Ladd,
Luther Lawrence,
Job G. Lawton, Jr.,
Alden Leland,
Tristram Littlefield,
Justin E. Loomis,
Abijah P. Marvin,
Simeon Merritt,
James L. Monroe,
Elbridge G. Morton,
Marcus Morton,
Marcus Morton, Jr.,
Hiram Nash,
Jonathan Nayson,
Charles Newman,
William Nichols,
Andrew T. Nute,
Benjamin S. Orne,
Charles Osgood,
Nathaniel Peabody,
Jeremiah Pease, Jr.,
John Penniman,
Daniel A. Perkins,
Jesse Perkins,

Messrs. Noah C. Perkins,
Charles Phelps,
Henry Pierce,
James M. Pool,
Robert Rantoul,
Silas Rawson,
David Rice,
Daniel Richardson,
Samuel H. Richardson,
Elkanah Ring, Jr.,
John Rogers,
James C. Royce,
Amasa Sanderson,
Chester Sanderson,
Luther Sheldon,
John Sherril,
Perez Simmons,
Matthew Smith,
Melzar Sprague,
Samuel W. Spooner,
Caleb Stetson,
Joseph L. Stevens, Jr.,
William Stevens,
Gideon Stiles,
Increase Sumner,
Arnold Taft,
Willard Thayer, 2d,
John W. Thomas,
Horatio W. Tilton,
David Turner,
David P. Turner,
William Tyler,
Joel Viles,
George A. Vinton,
Freeland Wallis,
Amasa Walker,
Andrew H. Ward,
Samuel Warner, Jr.,
Asa H. Waters,
Gershom B. Weston,
George White,
Daniel Wilbur,
Joseph Wilbur,
Henry Williams,
J. B. Williams,
Willard Wilson,
Levi M. Winslow,
Charles C. Wood,
Nathaniel Wood,
Otis Wood,
Ezekiel Wright.

The Resolves were then finally passed, as follow:—

Resolved, That it is expedient to insert into the Constitution articles providing,—

1. That the legislature shall have no power to pass any act granting any special charter for banking purposes, or any special act to increase the capital stock of any charter bank; but corporations may be formed for such purposes, or the capital stock of charter banks may be increased, under general laws.

2. That the legislature shall provide by law for the registry of all notes or bills authorized by general laws to be issued or put in circulation as money; and shall require ample security for the redemption of such notes, in specie.

One hundred and eight members voted for the Resolves, and sixty-eight against them.

On motion of Mr. WESTON, of Duxbury, the Convention resolved itself into Committee of the Whole, for the purpose of considering the Resolves on the subject of justices of the peace; and the President *pro tempore* requested Mr. Morton, of Andover, to take the chair.

Afterwards, Mr. MORTON reported, that the committee had made further progress in the consideration of the subject, but finding themselves without a quorum, had directed him to report that fact to the Convention.

At two o'clock, the Convention adjourned.

AFTERNOON SESSION.

Met according to adjournment.

Mr. FAY, of Southborough, from the Committee on Leave of Absence, submitted a Report, granting leave of absence to Mr. Henry, of Prescott, and Mr. Gale, of Heath, for the remainder of the session

The Report was considered and accepted, and leave granted.

On motion of Mr. BUTLER, of Lowell, the Resolve in relation to the commissions of the judges, was taken up and considered; and, after being amended by substituting the word "tenth" for the word "first," was

Ordered to a second reading.

Mr. LORD, of Salem, moved that the rule limiting speeches to fifteen minutes, be rescinded; but the motion was rejected.

On motion of Mr. WESTON, of Duxbury,

Ordered, That debate upon the Resolves concerning justices of the peace, shall cease at four o'clock.

On motion of Mr. WALKER, of North Brookfield, the Convention resumed the consideration of the Orders of the Day.

The first subject was the Resolves on the subject of justices of the peace.

Mr. MORTON, of Andover, moved to amend, by striking out the first Resolve, and inserting instead thereof, the following:—

Resolved, That it is expedient to amend the Constitution as follows:—

1. Trial Justices shall be elected by the legal voters of the several towns for a term of three years. There shall be one in each town, and one additional for every two thousand inhabitants. They shall have the same jurisdiction, powers, and duties, that are now exercised by justices of the peace, justices of the quorum, and commissioners to qualify civil officers; and such other powers as may be given them by the legislature.

2. Justices of the Peace shall be appointed by the Governor and Council for a term of seven years; and those who now hold that office shall continue as such, according to their respective commissions: *Provided*, that the jurisdiction of justices of the peace shall not extend to the hearing or trial of causes, or the issuing of warrants in criminal cases.

On motion of Mr. GRISWOLD, member for Erving, the amendment was amended, by striking out the words "justices of the quorum, and commissioners to qualify civil officers."

On motion of Mr. DAWES, of Adams, the amendment was further amended, by inserting, after the word "towns," in the second line of the first section, the words, "and cities where no police court is or shall be established by law."

On motion of Mr. ALVORD, member for Montague, the amendment was further amended, by inserting the word "such" before the word "justices," in the fifth line of the second section, and striking out the words, "of the peace," in the same line.

On motion of Mr. CHAPIN, of Worcester, the amendment was further amended by adding an additional section, as follows:—

3d. Justices and clerks of the police courts of the several towns and cities of the Commonwealth, shall be elected by the legal voters of the several towns and cities, for a term of three years.

On motion of Mr. MORTON, of Andover, the amendment was further amended, by striking out the words, "and such other powers as may be given them," and inserting instead thereof, the words "subject to alterations."

On motion of Mr. FROTHINGHAM, of Charlestown, the amendment was further amended, by inserting the words "may be" after the word "and," in the third line of the first section.

On motion of Mr. MORTON, of Andover, the amendment was further amended, by striking out the words "each town," in the third line of the first section, and inserting, instead thereof, the words, "in every such town or city."

On motion of Mr. LELAND, of Holliston, the amendment was further amended, by adding to the first section the words, "*Provided* that no trial justice shall act as such, upon his ceasing to reside in the town in which he was elected."

The amendment of Mr. Morton, as amended, was then adopted.

Mr. LORD, of Salem, moved to amend by adding the following section:—

No trial justice shall have jurisdiction in any civil action in which both parties shall be inhabitants of towns within this Commonwealth, other than the town by which such justice was elected.

But the amendment was rejected.

Mr. STEVENSON, of Boston, moved that the subject be referred to a special committee; but the motion was rejected, by a vote of ninety-seven in the affirmative, to one hundred and nineteen in the negative.

Afterwards, on motion of Mr. CHAPIN, of Worcester, the above vote was reconsidered, by a vote of one hundred and twenty-seven in the affirmative, to eighty-nine in the negative.

Mr. BOUTWELL, member for Berlin, moved that the subject be laid upon the table; but the motion was rejected, by a vote of ninety-four in the affirmative to one hundred and forty in the negative.

The motion to refer to a special committee, was then agreed to, and the committee were instructed to report to-morrow morning.

On motion of Mr. KEYES, member for Abington,

Ordered, That the committee consist of seven members.

The President appointed the committee, as follows:—

Messrs. Stevenson, of Boston, Butler, of Lowell, Chapin, of Worcester, Bartlett, of Boston, Griswold, member for Erving, Dawes, of Adams, and Morton, of Andover.

Mr. CHURCHILL, of Milton, offered Resolutions on the subject of justices of the peace.

Referred to the special committee.

The Resolve granting authority to the Committee on Reporting and Printing, was finally passed, as follows:—

Resolved, That the Committee appointed to superintend the publication of the Reports and Proceedings of this Convention, be authorized, in connection with the President and State Auditor, to allow the accounts for such service, and the Governor is hereby requested to draw his order on the treasury for the payment of the same.

On motion of Mr. Bird, of Walpole, the Convention resolved itself into Committee of the Whole, for the purpose of considering the Resolves reported by the Committee on the Bill of Rights, also the Resolves reported by a minority of the same committee; also the Resolves reported by a special committee on the subject of legal remedies to the representatives of persons killed by the negligence or misconduct of railroad corporations; and the President *pro tempore* requested Mr. Schouler, of Boston, to take the chair.

Afterwards Mr. Schouler reported the Resolves of the committee, with an amendment to the second Resolve, viz.:—

Add the words, "said writ shall be granted as of right in all cases where the legislature shall not specially confer a discretion therein upon the court. But the legislature may prescribe preliminary proceedings to the obtaining of said writ."

Mr. Schouler also reported, that the committee had instructed him to ask leave to sit again, for the consideration of the Resolves reported by the minority of the committee, and the Resolve on the subject of legal remedies, &c.

And leave was accordingly granted.

The amendment to the second Resolve was concurred in.

On motion of Mr. Lord, of Salem, the further consideration of the subject was postponed until ten o'clock to-morrow.

Mr. Stevenson, of Boston, from the Special Committee on the subject of justices of the peace, submitted a Report and Resolves on that subject.

Laid upon the table and ordered to be printed.

At a quarter before seven o'clock, on motion of Mr. Breed, of Lynn,

The Convention adjourned.

TUESDAY, July 26, 1853.

Met according to adjournment. Prayer was offered by the Chaplain. The Journal of yesterday was read.

Mr. MIXTER, of New Braintree, offered the following Order:—

Ordered, That the clerk of each of the towns in this Commonwealth that have not sent a Delegate to this Convention, shall receive, for the use of the town, one copy of the Constitutions of the United States, and one copy of the Debates of the Massachusetts Convention of 1820.

Laid over, under the rule.

Mr. DANA, member for Manchester, offered an Order, which, after being amended, on motion of Mr. BIRD, of Walpole, by substituting an Order to "consider the expediency," was adopted, as follows:—

Ordered, That the Committee on the Judiciary, consider the expediency of reporting upon the following subjects, to wit:—

1. The holding over of officers having authority under the present Constitution, until officers holding under the Revised Constitution shall be qualified.

2. The commissioning by the governor, of certain officers elected by the people.

3. The authority of the governor to suspend or remove officers elected by the people, or the legislature.

4. The time for the first election under the new Constitution, if adopted.

Mr. HALLETT, member for Wilbraham, from the Special Committee to whom was referred the resolves and proposed amendments on the subject of amendments to the Constitution, submitted a Report on that subject.

On motion of Mr. BUTLER, of Lowell, the rule requiring it to be considered in Committee of the Whole, was suspended.

The Resolve was laid upon the table and ordered to be printed.

On motion of Mr. MORTON, of Taunton, the Committee on the Judiciary were authorized to sit during the sessions of the Convention.

On motion of Mr. BUTLER, of Lowell, the Convention proceeded to the consideration of the Orders of the Day.

The first subject, viz.: the Resolve on the subject of the commissions of the judges, was amended, on motion of Mr. WALKER, of North Brookfield, by inserting the words "that the Constitution be so amended," in the first line;

And then finally passed, as follows :—

Resolved, That the Constitution be so amended, that all judicial commissions which shall issue to any person from and after the tenth day of August, in the year one thousand eight hundred and fifty-three, shall confer no greater tenure of office than the term of ten years.

On motion of Mr. BUTLER, of Lowell, the Convention resolved itself into Committee of the Whole, for the purpose of considering the Resolve on the subject of uniformity in the mode of receiving votes, &c.; and the President *pro tempore* requested Mr. Nayson, of Amesbury, to take the chair.

Afterwards, Mr. NAYSON reported, that it was the opinion of the committee that the Resolve ought to pass.

On motion of Mr. ELY, of Westfield, the Resolve was indefinitely postponed.

On motion of Mr. BUTLER, of Lowell, the Resolve reported by the Special Committee, on the subject of justices of the peace, was taken from the table;

And, on motion of the same gentleman, the rule requiring it to be considered in Committee of the Whole, was suspended,

And the Resolve was considered.

On motion of Mr. BUTLER, the fourth section was amended by inserting after the word "officer" in the second line, the words, "clerk or justice aforesaid."

On motion of Mr. WALKER, of North Brookfield,

Ordered, That debate on this subject shall close at a quarter past eleven o'clock.

Mr. DUNCAN, of Williamstown, moved to amend by striking out all after the words "provide that," and insert instead thereof the words, "justices of the peace shall be elected by the legal voters of the several towns and cities, as may be hereafter provided by law."

Mr. HATHAWAY, of Freetown, moved to amend by striking out the words, "or the issuing of warrants in criminal cases;" but the amendment was rejected by a vote of forty-three in the affirmative, to one hundred and forty-four in the negative.

The amendment of Mr. Duncan was then rejected.

The Resolve, as amended, was then ordered to a second reading.

On motion of Mr. BUTLER, of Lowell, the rule was suspended, and the Resolve considered, on the question of its final passage.

Mr. Whitney, of Conway, moved to amend by striking out the words, "or the issuing of warrants in criminal cases;"

Mr. Adams, of Lowell, moved the Previous Question; which was ordered.

Mr. Whitney's amendment was then rejected.

The Resolve was then finally passed, as follows:—

Resolved, That it is expedient to amend the Constitution so as to provide that

1. Trial Justices shall be elected by the legal voters of the several towns and cities where, at the time of such election, there is no police court established by law, who shall hold their offices for a term of three years.

Every such city or town shall elect one such justice, and may elect one additional for each two thousand inhabitants therein, according to the next preceding decennial census.

They shall have the same jurisdiction, powers and duties, as are now exercised by justices of the peace, which jurisdiction, powers and duties, may be changed by the legislature: *Provided*, that every trial justice who shall remove from the town in which he was elected, shall thereby vacate his office.

2. Justices of the peace, justices of the peace and quorum, justices of the peace throughout the Commonwealth, and commissioners to qualify civil officers, may be appointed by the Governor and Council for a term of seven years; and those now in office shall continue therein according to the tenure of their respective commissions: *Provided*, that the jurisdiction of all such justices shall not extend to the hearing or trial of any causes, or the issuing of warrants in criminal cases.

3. Justices and clerks of the police courts of the several cities and towns of the Commonwealth, shall be elected by the legal voters thereof, for a term of three years.

4. In case of vacancy by resignation, or otherwise, of any State, county, or district officer, clerk or justice aforesaid, excepting members of the legislature, whose election is provided for in the Constitution; and whose term of office does not expire at the next annual election, the governor shall issue his warrant to the mayors and aldermen of the several cities, and the selectmen of the several towns, to fill the vacancy at the next annual election after it shall have happened; and the Governor, with the advice and consent of the Council, may appoint suitable persons to fill such vacancies until an election by the people.

Mr. HALLETT, member for Wilbraham, moved a reconsideration of the vote by which the Resolve was finally passed.

The rule was suspended, and, on motion of Mr. FREEMAN, of Franklin, the Previous Question was ordered, and

The motion to reconsider was rejected.

On motion of Mr. LIVERMORE, of Cambridge, the special assignment was taken up, viz.: the Resolves reported by the Committee on the Bill of Rights.

Mr. STRONG, of Easthampton, moved to amend, by adding the following Resolve:—

Resolved, That the Bill of Rights be so amended that no person shall be subject to imprisonment for debt in this Commonwealth, upon any contract, express or implied, unless in cases of fraud.

On motion of Mr. STRONG, the yeas and nays were ordered upon the question of adopting the amendment.

And the roll being called, one hundred and twenty members voted for the amendment, and forty-five against it.

So it was adopted.

Those who voted in the affirmative are:—

Messrs. Charles Allen,
Josiah Allis,
D. W. Alvord,
David C. Atwood,
Hillel Baker,
John Beal,
George W. Blagden,
Sewell Boutwell,
William J. A. Bradford,
Hiram N. Breed,
George N. Briggs,
Asa Bronson,
Joseph Brownell,
Asahel Buck,
Rufus Bullock,
Anson Burlingame,
Benjamin F. Butler,
Henry Cady,
Timothy W. Carter,
Amariah Chandler,
Daniel E. Chapin,
J. McKean Churchill,
Nathaniel Cogswell,
Benjamin F. Copeland,
George B. Crane,
Simeon Crittenden,
Joseph W. Cross,
Richard H. Dana, Jr.,

Messrs. Silas Dean,
Augustus Denton,
John M. Earle,
Lilley Eaton,
Elisha Edwards,
Joseph M. Ely,
Sullivan Fay,
Lyman Fisk,
Emery Fiske,
James M. Freeman,
Charles A. French,
Rodney French,
Richard Frothingham, Jr.,
Wanton C. Gilbert,
Charles G. Giles,
Joel Giles,
Leonard Gooding,
Dalton Goulding,
Jabez Green,
Samuel P. Hadley,
Benjamin F. Hallett,
Phineas Harmon,
Stephen E. Hawkes,
Isaac Hayden,
Charles C. Hazewell,
Henry Hersey,
William H. Hewes,
William Hinsdale,

Messrs. Edwin Hobbs,
Martin Howard,
Henry K. Hoyt,
Charles E. Hunt,
George H. Huntington,
John Jacobs,
Giles C. Kellogg,
Edward L. Keyes,
Joseph Kimball,
Joseph Kingman,
Jefferson Knight,
Joseph Knight,
J. S. C. Knowlton,
William H. Knowlton,
Gardner P. Ladd,
Luther Lawrence,
Job G. Lawton, Jr.,
Alden Leland,
Justin E. Loomis,
Simeon Merritt,
Elbridge G. Morton,
Marcus Morton,
Marcus Morton, Jr.,
William S. Morton,
Charles Newman,
Andrew T. Nute,
Joseph E. Ober,
Henry K. Oliver,
E. Wing Packer,
John Partridge,
Jeremiah Pease, Jr.,
John Penniman,

Messrs. Jesse Perkins,
Charles Phelps,
Henry Pierce,
Jeremiah Pomroy,
James M. Pool,
Luther Richards,
John Rogers,
William Schouler,
Luther Sheldon,
Eben H. Stacy,
Joseph L. Stevens, Jr.,
Gideon Stiles,
Alfred L. Strong,
Charles Sumner,
Increase Sumner,
Isaac C. Taber,
Arnold Taft,
John W. Thomas,
Abraham Tilton,
David Turner,
William Tyler,
Bradford L. Wales,
Frederick T. Wallace,
Samuel Walker,
Andrew H. Ward,
William F. Wheeler,
Benjamin White,
George White,
James S. Whitney,
Daniel Wilbur,
Henry Wilson,
Willard Wilson.

Those who voted in the negative are:—

Messrs. Alfred A. Abbott,
Benjamin P. Adams,
Parsons Allen,
Russel Bartlett,
Zephaniah Bennett,
Edward B. Bigelow,
Francis W. Bird,
William S. Booth,
George S. Boutwell,
Artemas Brown,
Henry F. Cooledge,
Solomon Davis,
Abram Foster,
Samuel Fowle,
Samuel P. Fowler,
Daniel W. Gooch,
Jason Goulding,
George S. Hillard,

Messrs. Thomas Hopkinson,
Samuel Houghton,
William J. Hubbard,
Samuel Jackson,
Isaac Kendall,
Hiram Knight,
Albert Knox,
George H. Kuhn,
Abishai Lincoln,
Seth Miller, Jr.,
George Morey,
John G. Park,
Samuel D. Parker,
Jonathan Parris,
Nathaniel Peabody,
Noah C. Perkins,
Robert Rantoul,
Daniel Richardson,

Messrs. Samuel H. Richardson,	Messrs. Milo Wilson,
David S. Ross,	Levi M. Winslow,
Willard Thayer, 2d,	Nathaniel Wood,
Horatio W. Tilton,	Ezekiel Wright.
Freeland Wallis,	

The Resolves, as amended, were then ordered to a second reading.

And at one o'clock, on motion of Mr. WHEELER, of Lincoln,

The Convention adjourned.

AFTERNOON SESSION.

Met according to adjournment.

On motion of Mr. MORTON, of Andover, the Convention resolved itself into Committee of the Whole, for the purpose of considering the Resolves reported by the minority of the Committee on the Bill of Rights; and the Resolve on the subject of legal remedies, &c.; and the President *pro tempore* requested Mr. Schouler, of Boston, to take the chair.

Afterwards, Mr. SCHOULER reported, that the Committee had instructed him to report that the first Resolve ought not to pass;

And that the second Resolve ought to pass;

And had also instructed him to ask leave to sit again, for the consideration of the third Resolve of the minority of the committee, and the Resolve on the subject of legal remedies, &c.

On motion of Mr. BUTLER, of Lowell, the Committee of the Whole were discharged from the further consideration of these subjects.

The question was stated upon agreeing to the recommendation of the committee, that the first Resolve, which is as follows, ought not to pass.

That the second article of the Bill of Rights ought to be so altered, as to change the words, "for his religious profession or sentiments," to the words "for his profession or sentiments concerning religion." So that it will read, if so amended, "and no subject shall be hurt, molested or restrained in his person, liberty or estate, for worshipping God in the manner and season most agreeable to the dictates of his own conscience, or for his profession or sentiments concerning religion."

On motion of Mr. HOLDER, of Lynn, the yeas and nays were ordered upon the question of concurring with the committee.

And the roll being called, one hundred and thirty-three members voted in favor of concurrence, and one hundred and seven against it.

So the Resolve was rejected.

Those who voted in the affirmative are :—

Messrs. Benjamin P. Adams,
P. Emory Aldrich,
D. W. Alvord,
Robert Andrews,
William Aspinwall,
David C. Atwood,
Samuel Ayres,
Joseph Barrows,
Russel Bartlett,
Sidney Bartlett,
William Bennett, Jr.,
George S. Boutwell,
Ebenezer Bradbury,
Francis Brinley,
George N. Briggs,
Asahel Buck,
Rufus Bullock,
Henry Cady,
Timothy W. Carter,
William Carruthers,
Daniel E. Chapin,
Henry Chapin,
Josiah Childs,
J. McKean Churchill,
Salah Clark,
William Cleverly,
Nathaniel Cogswell,
Lansing J. Cole,
Ithamar Conkey,
Simeon Crittenden,
Leander Crosby,
Joseph W. Cross,
Seth Crowell,
Francis B. Crowninshield,
Thomas Cushman,
Richard H. Dana, Jr.,
Solomon Davis,
Henry L. Dawes,
Silas Dean,
Hiram S. Denison,
Alexander De Witt,
James C. Doane,
John M. Durgin,
Philip Eames,
Elisha Edwards,
Samuel Edwards
Homer Ely,
William T. Eustis,
Aaron Foster,
Abram Foster,
Samuel Fowle,

Messrs. James M. Freeman,
Luther Gale,
Wanton C. Gilbert,
Joel Giles,
Dalton Goulding,
Jason Goulding,
John C. Gray,
Josiah W. Griswold,
Artemas Hale,
Nathan Hale,
A. B. Hammond,
Lyman W. Hapgood,
Phineas Harmon,
William Haskins,
George Hayward,
Henry Hersey,
James Hewes,
William Hinsdale,
Henry Hobart,
Edwin Hobbs,
Samuel Houghton,
Abraham H. Howland,
William Hunt,
Charles P. Huntington,
Samuel A. Hurlburt,
Moses C. Hurlbut,
William James,
John Jenkins,
John Johnson,
Giles C. Kellogg,
Joseph Knight,
George H. Kuhn,
Wilber C. Langdon,
Frederic W. Lincoln, Jr.,
Tristram Littlefield,
Isaac Livermore,
Justin E. Loomis,
Seth Miller, Jr.,
Samuel Mixter,
George Morey,
Marcus Morton, Jr.,
William S. Morton,
Daniel Noyes,
Henry K. Oliver,
Nathan Orcutt,
E. Wing Packer,
Benjamin Paine,
Henry Paine,
Adolphus G. Parker,
Joel Parker,
William C. Plunkett,

Messrs. Jeremiah Pomroy,
Jonathan Preston,
Silas Rawson,
James Read,
Sampson Reed,
Luther Richards,
Daniel Richardson,
Samuel H. Richardson,
James C. Royce,
Amasa Sanderson,
John Sargent,
Chester Sikes,
Matthew Smith,
John Souther,
Caleb Stetson,
Charles G. Stevens,
Messrs. Granville Stevens,
Increase Sumner,
Thomas Talbot,
David Turner,
William Tyler,
Bradford L. Wales,
Asa H. Waters,
Cyrus Weeks,
Thomas Wetmore,
William F. Wheeler,
Benjamin White,
George White,
Joel Wilder,
Milo Wilson,
Jonathan B. Winn.

Those who voted in the negative are:—

Messrs. Josiah G. Abbott,
Shubael P. Adams,
James B. Allen,
Joel C. Allen,
Parsons Allen,
John B. Alley,
George Austin,
Hillel Baker,
Alpheus Bancroft,
Marcus Barrett,
Moses Bates, Jr.,
John Beal,
Francis W. Bird,
William S. Booth,
Sewell Boutwell,
William J. A. Bradford,
Hiram N. Breed,
Hammond Brown,
Hiram C. Brown,
Frederick Brownell,
Joseph Brownell,
Patrick Bryant,
Anson Burlingame,
Benjamin F. Butler,
Isaac Case,
Amariah Chandler,
Ransom Clark,
Alpheus B. Clarke,
Sumner Cole,
Ebenezer Davis,
Gilman Day,
Elijah S. Deming,
Augustus Denton,
Samuel Duncan,
Messrs. Bradish Dunham,
John M. Earle,
James Easton, 2d,
Joseph M. Ely,
Charles A. French,
Samuel French,
Richard Frothingham, Jr.,
Washington Gilbert,
Charles G. Giles,
Daniel W. Gooch,
Jabez Green,
Benjamin F. Hallett,
Stephen E. Hawkes,
Charles C. Hazewell,
George S. Hillard,
Nathaniel Holder,
Thomas Hopkinson,
Martin Howard,
Henry K. Hoyt,
Charles E. Hunt,
Benjamin D. Hyde,
Samuel Jackson,
Isaac Kendall,
Hiram Knight,
Jefferson Knight,
J. S. C. Knowlton,
William H. Knowlton,
Albert Knox,
Gardner P. Ladd,
Otis Little,
William P. Marble,
Charles Mason,
Simeon Merritt,
James L. Munroe,

Messrs. Charles Newman,
William Nichols,
Andrew T. Nute,
Charles Osgood,
John Partridge,
Daniel A. Perkins,
Charles Phelps,
Silvanus B. Phinney,
Henry Pierce,
James M. Pool,
Elkanah Ring, Jr.,
David S. Ross,
William Schouler,
John W. Simonds,
Melzar Sprague,
Samuel W. Spooner,
William Stevens,
Gideon Stiles,
Alfred L. Strong,
Charles Sumner,

Messrs. Alanson Swain,
Arnold Taft,
Joseph Thayer,
Willard Thayer, 2d,
Charles Thompson,
Horatio W. Tilton,
David P. Turner,
Orison Underwood,
Joel Viles,
Frederick T. Wallace,
Freeland Wallis,
Amasa Walker,
Samuel Warner, Jr.,
Gershom B. Weston,
J. B. Williams,
Henry Wilson,
Willard Wilson,
Charles C. Wood,
Otis Wood.

The second Resolve was agreed to, and ordered to a second reading, by a vote of seventy-three in the affirmative, to forty-one in the negative.

At half-past six o'clock, on motion of Mr. PLUNKETT, of Adams,

The Convention adjourned.

WEDNESDAY, July 27, 1853.

Met according to adjournment. The President of the Convention resumed the chair. Prayer was offered by the Chaplain. The Journal of yesterday was read.

The Order offered yesterday, by Mr. Mixter, of New Braintree, and laid over, was taken up, amended and adopted, as follows:—

Ordered, That the Secretary be directed to send to each of the towns in this Commonwealth that have not sent a Delegate to this Convention, one copy of Barnes's Constitutions of the United States, one copy of the Journal of the Massachusetts Convention of 1820, and one copy of the Journal and Debates of this Convention.

On motion of Mr. WILSON, of Natick, the Convention proceeded to the consideration of the Orders of the Day.

The first subject was the Resolve on the right of juries to judge of the law, &c.

After debate, Mr. WALKER, of North Brookfield, moved the Previous Question; which was ordered, by a vote of one hundred and fifty-nine in the affirmative, to seventy-five in the negative.

On motion of Mr. GARDNER, of Seekonk, the yeas and nays were ordered upon the question of agreeing to the Resolve;

And the roll being called, one hundred and ninety-two members voted in the affirmative, and one hundred and forty-six in the negative.

So the Resolve was ordered to a second reading.

Those who voted in the affirmative are:—

Messrs. Josiah G. Abbott,
Shubael P. Adams,
Charles Allen,
James B. Allen,
John B. Alley,
Josiah Allis,
D. W. Alvord,
George Austin,
Hillel Baker,
Alpheus Bancroft,
Marcus Barrett,
Eliakim A. Bates,
Moses Bates, Jr.,
John Beal,
Zephaniah Bennett,
Edward B. Bigelow,
Francis W. Bird,
George S. Boutwell,
Sewell Boutwell,
Hiram N. Breed,
Asa Bronson,
Adolphus F. Brown,
Alpheus R. Brown,
Hammond Brown,
Hiram C. Brown,
Joseph Brownell,
Patrick Bryant,
Anson Burlingame,
William Carruthers,
Isaac Case,
Chester W. Chapin,
Daniel E. Chapin,
Henry Chapin,
J. McKean Churchill,
Henry Clark,
Ransom Clark,
Salah Clark,
William Cleverly,
Sumner Cole,
George B. Crane,

Messrs. Joseph W. Cross,
Thomas Cushman,
Simeon N. Cutler,
Charles G. Davis,
Isaac Davis,
Gilman Day,
Silas Dean,
Augustus Denton,
Samuel Duncan,
Bradish Dunham,
John M. Durgin,
John M. Earle,
Peter Easland,
Elisha Edwards,
Joseph M. Ely,
James K. Fellows,
Lyman Fisk,
Emery Fiske,
Abram Foster,
James M. Freeman,
Charles A. French,
Rodney French,
Samuel French,
Richard Frothingham, Jr.,
Johnson Gardner,
Elbridge Gates,
Washington Gilbert,
Charles G. Giles,
Daniel W. Gooch,
Leonard Gooding,
John W. Graves,
Josiah W. Griswold,
Whiting Griswold,
Samuel P. Hadley,
Benjamin F. Hallett,
Lyman W. Hapgood,
Seth Hapgood,
William Haskins,
Stephen E. Hawkes,
Isaac Hayden,

Messrs. Charles C. Hazewell,
Ezra Heath, 2d,
James Hewes,
William H. Hewes,
Henry Hobart,
Nathaniel Holder,
George Hood,
Foster Hooper,
Martin Howard,
Henry K. Hoyt,
Charles E. Hunt,
Moses C. Hurlbut,
Benjamin D. Hyde,
Abijah M. Ide, Jr.,
John Jacobs,
Edward L. Keyes,
Joseph Kimball,
Joseph Kingman,
Hiram Knight,
Jefferson Knight,
J. S. C. Knowlton,
William H. Knowlton,
Albert Knox,
Gardner P. Ladd,
Wilber C. Langdon,
Luther Lawrence,
Alden Leland,
Justin E. Loomis,
William P. Marble,
Laban Marcy,
Abijah P. Marvin,
Charles Mason,
Simeon Merritt,
James L. Monroe,
James M. Moore,
Joseph B. Morss,
Elbridge G. Morton,
Marcus Morton, Jr.,
William S. Morton,
Hiram Nash,
Charles Newman,
William Nichols,
Andrew T. Nute,
Joseph E. Ober,
Benjamin S. Orne,
Charles Osgood,
E. Wing Packer,
Benjamin Paine,
Henry Paine,
Jonathan Parris,
John Partridge,
Nathaniel Peabody,
Jeremiah Pease, Jr.,

Messrs. John Penniman,
Daniel A. Perkins,
Jesse Perkins,
Noah C. Perkins,
Charles Phelps,
Silvanus B. Phinney,
Henry Pierce,
James M. Pool,
Robert Rantoul,
Silas Rawson,
Luther Richards,
Daniel Richardson,
Nathan Richardson,
Samuel H. Richardson,
Elkanah Ring, Jr.,
John Rogers,
David S. Ross,
Chester Sanderson,
John Sherril,
Perez Simmons,
John W. Simonds,
Melzar Sprague,
Samuel W. Spooner,
Eben H. Stacy,
Joseph L. Stevens, Jr.,
William Stevens,
Gideon Stiles,
Alfred L. Strong,
Charles Sumner,
Alanson Swain,
Isaac C. Taber,
Arnold Taft,
Joseph Thayer,
Willard Thayer, 2d,
John W. Thomas,
Charles Thompson,
Abraham Tilton,
Horatio W. Tilton,
Orison Underwood,
Joel Viles,
George A. Vinton,
Bradford L. Wales,
Freeland Wallis,
Amasa Walker,
Andrew H. Ward,
Samuel Warner, Jr.,
Asa H. Waters,
Gershom B. Weston,
Daniel S. Whitney,
James S. Whitney,
Daniel Wilbur,
Henry Williams,
Henry Wilson,

Messrs. Willard Wilson,
Levi M. Winslow,
Charles C. Wood,
Messrs. Otis Wood,
William H. Wood,
Ezekiel Wright.

Those who voted in the negative are:—

Messrs. Alfred A. Abbott,
Benjamin P. Adams,
P. Emory Aldrich,
Joel C. Allen,
Robert Andrews,
William Aspinwall,
David C. Atwood,
Samuel Ayres,
Joseph Barrows,
Russel Bartlett,
Sidney Bartlett,
Luther V. Bell,
William Bennett, Jr.,
Jacob Bigelow,
Gad O. Bliss,
William S. Booth,
Ebenezer Bradbury,
William J. A. Bradford,
Milton P. Braman,
Osmyn Brewster,
Francis Brinley,
George N. Briggs,
Artemas Brown,
Asahel Buck,
Rufus Bullock,
Timothy W. Carter,
Amariah Chandler,
Josiah Childs,
Stillman Clarke,
Jacob Coggin,
Nathaniel Cogswell,
Lansing J. Cole,
Ithamar Conkey,
Charles E. Cook,
Henry F. Cooledge,
Benjamin F. Copeland,
Simeon Crittenden,
George W. Crockett,
Leander Crosby,
Seth Crowell,
Francis B. Crowninshield,
Wilber Curtis,
Richard H. Dana, Jr.,
Solomon Davis,
Henry L. Dawes,
Elijah S. Deming,
Hiram S. Denison,
Messrs. James C. Doane,
Moses Dorman,
Philip Eames,
Lilley Eaton,
Samuel Edwards,
Homer Ely,
A. G. Farwell,
Sullivan Fay,
Aaron Foster,
Samuel Fowle,
Samuel P. Fowler,
Charles H. French,
Luther Gale,
Henry J. Gardner,
Joel Giles,
Robert Gould,
Dalton Goulding,
Jason Goulding,
John C. Gray,
Jabez Green,
Artemas Hale,
Nathan Hale,
A. B. Hammond,
Phineas Harmon,
George Haskell,
Elnathan P. Hathaway,
Charles Heard,
Samuel Henry,
Henry Hersey,
George S. Hillard,
William Hinsdale,
Aaron Hobart,
Samuel Houghton,
Abraham H. Howland,
William J. Hubbard,
William Hunt,
Asahel Huntington,
Charles P. Huntington,
George H. Huntington,
Samuel A. Hurlburt,
Samuel Jackson,
William James,
John Jenkins,
Samuel H. Jenks,
John Johnson,
Giles C. Kellogg,
Isaac Kendall,

Messrs. Henry W. Kinsman,
Joseph Knight,
George H. Kuhn,
John S. Ladd,
Job G. Lawton, Jr.,
Abishai Lincoln,
Frederic W. Lincoln, Jr.,
Isaac Livermore,
Otis P. Lord,
Samuel K. Lothrop,
Samuel P. Loud,
Seth Miller, Jr.,
Samuel Mixter,
George Morey,
Jonathan Nayson,
Daniel Noyes,
Henry K. Oliver,
Nathan Orcutt,
John G. Park,
Adolphus G. Parker,
Joel Parker,
Jonathan C. Perkins,
William C. Plunkett,
Jeremiah Pomroy,
James Read,
Sampson Reed,

Messrs. George R. Sampson,
John Sargent,
William Schouler,
Chester Sikes,
John S. Sleeper,
Matthew Smith,
John Souther,
Caleb Stetson,
Charles G. Stevens,
Granville Stevens,
Increase Sumner,
Edmund P. Tileston,
Charles R. Train,
David Turner,
George B. Upton,
Samuel B. Walcott,
Samuel Walker,
Cyrus Weeks,
William F. Wheeler,
Benjamin White,
Joel Wilder,
John H. Wilkins,
J. B. Williams,
Milo Wilson,
Jonathan B. Winn,
Josiah B. Woods.

The Resolve on the subject of legal remedies to the representatives of persons killed by the negligence or misconduct of railroad corporations, was, on motion of Mr. Davis, of Plymouth,

Laid upon the table.

The Resolve on the subject of the law martial, was, on motion of Mr. Churchill, of Milton, by a vote of seventy-seven in the affirmative, to fifty-seven in the negative,

Laid upon the table.

Mr. Bird, of Walpole, called for the yeas and nays upon the question of laying the Resolve upon the table; but the call was not sustained by one-fifth of the members.

On motion of Mr. Schouler, of Boston, the Orders of the Day were laid upon the table;

And at a quarter before two o'clock, on motion of Mr. Schouler,

The Convention adjourned.

AFTERNOON SESSION.

Met according to adjournment.

Leave of absence was granted to Mr. Huntington, of Becket, for the remainder of the session.

On motion of Mr. Wilson, of Natick, the Resolves of the Special Committee on the subject of Amendments of the Constitution, were taken from the table.

On motion of Mr. Wilson, the rule requiring them to be considered in Committee of the Whole, was suspended, and they were placed in the Orders of the Day.

On motion of Mr. Parker, of Cambridge, the Resolve on the subject of appropriations for sectarian schools,

And the Resolve introduced by him on the same subject, were

Taken from the table, and considered.

On motion of Mr. Parker, the Resolve reported by the committee was amended, by substituting the Resolve introduced by him; and as thus amended, the Resolve was finally passed, as follows:—

Resolved, That all moneys raised by taxation in the towns and cities for the support of Public Schools, and all moneys which may be appropriated by the State for the support of Common Schools, shall be applied to and expended in no other schools than those which are conducted according to law, under the order and superintendence of the authorities of the town or city in which the money is to be expended; and such moneys shall never be appropriated to any religious sect for the maintenance, exclusively, of its own schools.

Mr. White, of Quincy, moved a reconsideration of the vote by which the Resolve was finally passed;

And the motion was placed in the Orders of the Day for to-morrow.

On motion of Mr. Morton, of Taunton, the Committee of the Whole were discharged from the consideration of the Resolve on the mode of submitting the question of representation to the people; and

The rule requiring the subject to be considered in committee, was suspended, and the Resolve was specially assigned for consideration on Thursday, at ten o'clock.

On motion of Mr. Wilson, of Natick, the Convention proceeded to the consideration of the Orders of the Day.

The first subject was the Resolves of the Committee on the Bill of Rights, as amended.

Mr. Hallett, member for Wilbraham, moved to amend the second Resolve, by striking from the article proposed to be inserted, the words which were adopted as an amendment at a former stage of the Resolve, viz.:—

Said writ shall be granted as of right, in all cases where the legislature shall not especially confer a discretion upon the court. But the legislature may prescribe preliminary proceedings to the obtaining of said writ.

A division of the Resolves was called for, and the question was stated to be upon adopting the first and second Resolves.

On motion of Mr. ADAMS, of Lowell, the Previous Question was ordered.

Mr. WALES, of Randolph, called for the yeas and nays upon the amendment of Mr. Hallett; but the call was not sustained by one-fifth of the members voting.

The amendment was then rejected, by a vote of thirty-seven in the affirmative, to one hundred and seventy-six in the negative.

The first and second Resolves were then finally passed, as follow:

Resolved, That the Bill of Rights be amended by adding to the eleventh article, as part of the same, the following words:—

And every person having a claim against the Commonwealth, ought to have a judicial remedy therefor.

Resolved, That the Bill of Rights be amended by inserting, between the eleventh and twelfth articles, the following additional article, being identical with one now in another chapter of the Constitution, and which more appropriately belongs to the Bill of Rights, viz.:—

VII. The privilege and benefit of the writ of habeas corpus shall be enjoyed in this Commonwealth in the most free, easy, cheap, expeditious and ample manner, and shall not be suspended by the legislature, except upon the most urgent and pressing occasions, and for a limited time, not exceeding twelve months. Said writ shall be granted as of right, in all cases where the legislature shall not especially confer a discretion upon the court. But the legislature may prescribe preliminary proceedings to the obtaining of said writ.

The third Resolve was also finally passed, as follows:—

Resolved, That the Bill of Rights be amended, in the last sentence of the twenty-ninth article, by striking out the words "so long as they behave themselves well, and that they," and inserting "by tenures established by the Constitution, and;" also by striking out the words, "ascertained and established by standing laws," and inserting "which shall not be diminished during their continuance in office;" so that the whole sentence, as amended, shall read as follows:—

It is, therefore, not only the best policy, but for the security of the rights of the people, and of every citizen, that the judges of the supreme judicial court should hold their offices by tenures established by the Constitution, and should have honorable salaries, which shall not be diminished during their continuance in office.

The question being upon the passage of the fourth Resolve, which is as follows:—

Resolved, That the Bill of Rights be amended, by inserting between the twenty-ninth and thirtieth article, the following additional article:

This enumeration of rights shall not impair others retained by the people, and no powers shall ever be assumed by the legislature, that are not granted in this Constitution.

Mr. Davis, of Worcester, moved to amend, by striking out after the word "people."

Mr. Morton, of Quincy, moved the Previous Question; which was ordered.

Mr. Briggs, of Pittsfield, called for the yeas and nays upon the amendment; but the call was not sustained by one-fifth of the members voting.

The amendment was adopted, by a vote of one hundred and thirty-five in the affirmative, to sixty in the negative.

And the Resolve was then rejected, by a vote of one hundred and sixteen in the affirmative, to one hundred and eighteen in the negative.

The question being upon the passage of the fifth Resolve,

Mr. Miller, of Wareham, called for the yeas and nays; but the call was not sustained by one-fifth of the members voting.

Mr. Lord, of Salem, moved to amend the amendment, by adding the words, " or upon any judgment hereafter recovered, in any civil suit."

Mr. Huntington, of Northampton, moved to amend, by inserting after the word "debt," the words "hereafter contracted."

Mr. Davis, of Plymouth, moved that the subject be laid upon the table.

On motion of Mr. Schouler, of Boston, the yeas and nays were ordered upon this question.

Afterwards, on motion of Mr. Keyes, member for Abington, the vote ordering the yeas and nays was reconsidered;

And the question recurring upon the call for the yeas and nays, it was not sustained by one-fifth of the members voting.

The motion of Mr. Davis was then rejected.

Mr. BIRD, of Walpole, moved the Previous Question; which was ordered.

Mr. Lord's amendment was then rejected, and

Mr. Huntington's amendment was adopted.

The Resolve, as amended, was then finally passed, as follows:—

Resolved, That the Bill of Rights be so amended, that no person shall be subjected to imprisonment for debt hereafter contracted in this Commonwealth, founded upon any contract, express or implied, unless in cases of fraud.

The Resolves of the special committee on the subject of amendments of the Constitution, were next in order.

On motion of Mr. HALLETT, member for Wilbraham, the first Resolve was amended, by striking out the words, "in the newspapers in which the laws are then published," in the twelfth and thirteenth lines, (printed copy,) and by inserting the word "officially" before the word "publish" in the twelfth line.

On motion of Mr. GRISWOLD, member for Erving, the first Resolve was further amended, by striking out the word "and" in the twenty-second line, and by inserting after the word "cities" in the same line, the words "and districts;" and also by inserting, after the word "elect" in the line succeeding, the words "in any year of that decennial period;" also by substituting the word "Wednesday" for the word "Monday," in the line next following.

Mr. LORD, of Salem, moved further to amend the first Resolve, by inserting after the word "affirmative," in the fifteenth line, the words, "and such majority shall be at least equal to one-half of the votes given for governor at such election.

Mr. BATES, of Plymouth, moved the Previous Question.

On motion of Mr. LORD, of Salem, the yeas and nays were ordered upon this motion.

Mr. GARDNER, of Boston, moved an adjournment, but the motion was rejected, by a vote of sixty-six in the affirmative, to ninety in the negative.

The question was stated on the demand for the Previous Question,

And the roll being called, one hundred and six members voted in the affirmative, and thirty-three in the negative.

So the Previous Question was ordered.

Those who voted in the affirmative are:—

Messrs. Parsons Allen,
Josiah Allis,
D. W. Alvord,
Messrs. George Austin,
Hillel Baker,
Alpheus Bancroft,

Messrs. Moses Bates, Jr.,
John Beal,
William Bennett, Jr.,
Francis W. Bird,
George S. Boutwell,
Hiram N. Breed,
Hammond Brown,
Hiram C. Brown,
Joseph Brownell,
Patrick Bryant,
Cephas C. Bumpus,
Isaac Case,
J. McKean Churchill,
Ransom Clark,
Salah Clark,
Sumner Cole,
Charles G. Davis,
Isaac Davis,
Gilman Day,
Silas Dean,
Augustus Denton,
Samuel Duncan,
Philip Eames,
Peter Easland,
James Easton, 2d,
Calvin D. Eaton,
Samuel Edwards,
Joseph M. Ely,
Sullivan Fay,
Lyman Fisk,
Charles A. French,
Richard Frothingham, Jr.,
Luther Gale,
Henry J. Gardner,
Johnson Gardner,
Elbridge Gates,
Wanton C. Gilbert,
Charles G. Giles,
Jason Goulding,
Jabez Green,
Josiah W. Griswold,
Whiting Griswold,
Benjamin F. Hallett,
Lyman W. Hapgood,
Seth Hapgood,
Phineas Harmon,
Stephen E. Hawkes,
Isaac Hayden,
Ezra Heath, 2d,
George Hood,

Messrs. Martin Howard,
Abraham H. Howland,
Henry K. Hoyt,
George H. Huntington,
Moses C. Hurlbut,
Benjamin D. Hyde,
John Jacobs,
Jefferson Knight,
Albert Knox,
Gardner P. Ladd,
Wilber C. Langdon,
Alden Leland,
Justin E. Loomis,
Simeon Merritt,
James L. Monroe,
Elbridge G. Morton,
William S. Morton,
Hiram Nash,
Charles Newman,
Charles Osgood,
E. Wing Packer,
Benjamin Paine,
John Partridge,
John Penniman,
Charles Phelps,
Henry Pierce,
Robert Rantoul,
Silas Rawson,
Samuel H. Richardson,
Elkanah Ring, Jr.,
David S. Ross,
James C. Royce,
Melzar Sprague,
Samuel W. Spooner,
Charles G. Stevens,
Granville Stevens,
Gideon Stiles,
Charles Sumner,
Increase Sumner,
Alanson Swain,
Charles Thompson,
Horatio W. Tilton,
Freeland Wallis,
Amasa Walker,
Andrew H. Ward,
Gershom B. Weston,
Daniel S. Whitney,
James S. Whitney,
Charles C. Wood,
Otis Wood.

Those who voted in the negative are:—

Messrs. Benjamin P. Adams,
Robert Andrews,
Sidney Bartlett,
Ebenezer Bradbury,
William J. A. Bradford,
Francis Brinley,
George N. Briggs,
Asahel Buck,
Rufus Bullock,
Timothy W. Carter,
Nathaniel Cogswell,
Charles E. Cook,
Elijah S. Deming,
Homer Ely,
Joel Giles,
Nathan Hale,
Charles Heard,

Messrs. Samuel Houghton,
John Jenkins,
Giles C. Kellogg,
Isaac Kendall,
Joseph Knight,
Frederic W. Lincoln, Jr.,
Otis P. Lord,
Seth Miller, Jr.,
Samuel Mixter,
George Morey,
William C. Plunkett,
Jeremiah Pomroy,
Jonathan Preston,
Chester Sikes,
Perez Simmons,
Benjamin White.

Mr. Lord's amendment was then rejected,

And the Resolves were ordered to a second reading.

At seven o'clock, on motion of Mr. Eames, of Washington,

The Convention adjourned.

THURSDAY, July 28, 1853.

Met according to adjournment. Prayer was offered by the Chaplain. The Journal of yesterday was read.

Mr. Wheeler, of Lincoln, moved a reconsideration of the vote by which the Resolve on the subject of imprisonment for debt was finally passed.

On motion of Mr. Wilson, of Natick, the rule of the Convention was suspended, and the motion was placed at the foot of the calendar, in the Orders of the Day for to-day.

On motion of Mr. Wilson, the Convention proceeded to the consideration of the Orders of the Day.

The first subject, viz.: the motion of Mr. White, of Quincy, to reconsider the vote on the final passage of the Resolve on the subject of appropriations for sectarian schools, was passed over.

The Resolve reported by the minority of the Committee on the Bill of Rights, on the subject of the right of the jury to judge of the law, &c., was next in order.

Mr. Huntington, of Northampton, moved to amend the Resolve, by the addition of the following words:—

But it shall be the duty of the court to superintend the course of the trial, to decide upon the admission and rejection of evidence, and upon all questions of law raised during the trial, and upon all collateral and incidental proceedings, and also to allow bills of exceptions, and the court may grant a new trial in case of conviction.

Mr. DAY, of Templeton, moved the Previous Question.

Mr. DANA, member for Manchester, moved that the Resolve be laid upon the table.

On motion of Mr. EARLE, of Worcester, the yeas and nays were ordered upon this question,

And the roll being called, one hundred and fifty-four members voted in the affirmative, and one hundred and eighty-two in the negative.

So the motion to lay upon the table was rejected.

Those who voted in the affirmative are:—

Messrs. Benjamin P. Adams,
P. Emory Aldrich,
Joel C. Allen,
Parsons Allen,
John B. Alley,
Robert Andrews,
William Aspinwall,
David C. Atwood,
Samuel Ayres,
George S. Ball,
Joseph Barrows,
Russel Bartlett,
Sidney Bartlett,
Eliakim A. Bates,
Luther V. Bell,
William Bennett, Jr.,
Jacob Bigelow,
Gad O. Bliss,
Ebenezer Bradbury,
William J. A. Bradford,
Milton P. Braman,
Osmyn Brewster,
Francis Brinley,
George N. Briggs,
Asahel Buck,
Rufus Bullock,
Cephas C. Bumpus,
Timothy W. Carter,
Amariah Chandler,
Chester W. Chapin,
Daniel E. Chapin,
Josiah Childs,
Jacob Coggin,
Nathaniel Cogswell,

Messrs. Lansing J. Cole,
Ithamar Conkey,
Henry F. Cooledge,
Benjamin F. Copeland,
Simeon Crittenden,
George W. Crockett,
Leander Crosby,
Seth Crowell,
Wilber Curtis,
Richard H. Dana, Jr.,
Solomon Davis,
Henry L. Dawes,
Elijah S. Deming,
Hiram S. Denison,
Moses Dorman,
Philip Eames,
Lilley Eaton,
Samuel Edwards,
Homer Ely,
William T. Eustis,
A. G. Farwell,
Sullivan Fay,
Aaron Foster,
Samuel Fowle,
Samuel P. Fowler,
Charles H. French,
Luther Gale,
Henry J. Gardner,
Wanton C. Gilbert,
Joel Giles,
Robert Gould,
Dalton Goulding,
Jason Goulding,
John C. Gray,

Messrs. Artemas Hale,
A. B. Hammond,
Phineas Harmon,
George Haskell,
Elnathan P. Hathaway,
George Hayward,
Charles Heard,
Samuel Henry,
Henry Hersey,
George S. Hillard,
William Hinsdale,
Aaron Hobart,
Edwin Hobbs,
Thomas Hopkinson,
Samuel Houghton,
Abraham H. Howland,
William J. Hubbard,
William Hunt,
Asahel Huntington,
Samuel A. Hurlburt,
Samuel Jackson,
William James,
John Jenkins,
Samuel H. Jenks,
Giles C. Kellogg,
Isaac Kendall,
Henry W. Kinsman,
Joseph Knight,
Charles L. Knowlton,
George H. Kuhn,
John S. Ladd,
Tristram Littlefield,
Isaac Livermore,
Otis P. Lord,
Samuel K. Lothrop,
Samuel P. Loud,
John A. Lowell,
Theophilus R. Marvin,
Seth Miller, Jr.,
Samuel Mixter,
George Morey,
Elbridge G. Morton,
Marcus Morton,

Messrs. Daniel Noyes,
Nathan Orcutt,
John G. Park,
Adolphus G. Parker,
Thomas A. Parsons
George Peabody,
Jonathan C. Perkins,
William C. Plunkett,
Jeremiah Pomroy,
John A. Putnam,
James Read,
Sampson Reed,
Julius Rockwell,
George R. Sampson,
Chester Sanderson,
John Sargent,
William Schouler,
Chester Sikes,
John S. Sleeper,
Matthew Smith,
John Souther,
Caleb Stetson,
Charles G. Stevens,
Granville Stevens,
Increase Sumner,
Thomas Talbot,
Edmund P. Tileston,
Charles R. Train,
David Turner,
Charles W. Upham,
Samuel B. Walcott,
Frederick T. Wallace,
Samuel Walker,
Cyrus Weeks,
Thomas Wetmore,
William F. Wheeler,
Benjamin White,
Joseph Wilbur,
Joel Wilder,
John H. Wilkins,
Milo Wilson,
Jonathan B. Winn,
Josiah B. Woods.

Those who voted in the negative are:—

Messrs. Josiah G. Abbott,
Shubael P. Adams,
James B. Allen,
Josiah Allis,
D. W. Alvord,
George Austin,
Hillel Baker,

Messrs. Moses Bates, Jr.,
John Beal,
Zephaniah Bennett,
Edward B. Bigelow,
Francis W. Bird,
George S. Boutwell,
Sewell Boutwell,

Messrs. Hiram N. Breed,
Asa Bronson,
Adolphus F. Brown,
Alpheus R. Brown,
Artemas Brown,
Hammond Brown,
Frederick Brownell,
Joseph Brownell,
Patrick Bryant,
Anson Burlingame,
William Carruthers,
Isaac Case,
Henry Clark,
Ransom Clark,
Salah Clark,
Alpheus B. Clarke,
Stillman Clarke,
William Cleverly,
Sumner Cole,
George B. Crane,
Oliver S. Cressy,
Thomas Cushman,
Simeon N. Cutler,
Charles G. Davis,
Ebenezer Davis,
Robert T. Davis,
Gilman Day,
Silas Dean,
Augustus Denton,
Bradish Dunham,
John M. Earle,
James Easton, 2d,
Calvin D. Eaton,
Elisha Edwards,
Joseph M. Ely,
James K. Fellows,
Lyman Fisk,
Abram Foster,
James M. Freeman,
Charles A. French,
Rodney French,
Samuel French,
Richard Frothingham, Jr.,
Johnson Gardner,
Elbridge Gates,
Washington Gilbert,
Charles G. Giles,
Leonard Gooding,
John W. Graves,
Jabez Green,
William B. Greene,
Josiah W. Griswold,
Whiting Griswold,

Messrs. Samuel P. Hadley,
Benjamin F. Hallett,
Lyman W. Hapgood,
Seth Hapgood,
William Haskins,
Stephen E. Hawkes,
Isaac Hayden,
Charles C. Hazewell,
Ezra Heath, 2d,
James Hewes,
William H. Hewes,
Henry Hobart,
George Hood,
Foster Hooper,
Martin Howard,
Henry K. Hoyt,
Charles E. Hunt,
Charles P. Huntington,
Moses C. Hurlbut,
Benjamin D. Hyde,
Abijah M. Ide, Jr.,
John Jacobs,
John Johnson,
Edward L. Keyes,
Joseph Kimball,
Joseph Kingman,
Hiram Knight,
Jefferson Knight,
J. S. C. Knowlton,
William H. Knowlton,
Albert Knox,
Gardner P. Ladd,
Wilber C. Langdon,
Luther Lawrence,
Alden Leland,
Justin E. Loomis,
Laban Marcy,
Abijah P. Marvin,
Charles Mason,
Simeon Merritt,
James L. Monroe,
James M. Moore,
Joseph B. Morss,
Marcus Morton, Jr.,
William S. Morton,
Hiram Nash,
William Nichols,
Andrew T. Nute,
Benjamin S. Orne,
Charles Osgood,
E. Wing Packer,
Benjamin Paine,
Henry Paine,

Messrs. Jonathan Parris,
John Partridge,
Jeremiah Pease, Jr.,
John Penniman,
Daniel A. Perkins,
Jesse Perkins,
Noah C. Perkins,
Charles Phelps,
Henry Pierce,
James M. Pool,
Peter Powers,
Robert Rantoul,
Silas Rawson,
David Rice,
Luther Richards,
Daniel Richardson,
Nathan Richardson,
Samuel H. Richardson,
Elkanah Ring, Jr.,
John Rogers,
David S. Ross,
James C. Royce,
Amasa Sanderson,
John Sherril,
Perez Simmons,
John W. Simonds,
Samuel W. Spooner,
Melzar Sprague,
Eben H. Stacy,
Joseph L. Stevens, Jr.,
William Stevens,

Messrs. Gideon Stiles,
Alfred L. Strong,
Charles Sumner,
Alanson Swain,
Arnold Taft,
Joseph Thayer,
Willard Thayer, 2d,
John W. Thomas,
Charles Thompson,
Abraham Tilton,
Horatio W. Tilton,
Orison Underwood,
Joel Viles,
George A. Vinton,
Freeland Wallis,
Amasa Walker,
Andrew H. Ward,
Samuel Warner, Jr.,
Asa H. Waters,
Gershom B. Weston,
George White,
Daniel S. Whitney,
Daniel Wilbur,
Henry Williams,
J. B. Williams,
Henry Wilson,
Willard Wilson,
Charles C. Wood,
Otis Wood,
William H. Wood,
Ezekiel Wright.

The demand for the Previous Question was sustained.

Mr. Huntington's amendment was then agreed to,

And the Resolve was finally passed, as follows:—

That there should be added to the 15th Article of the Bill of Rights the following clause:—

In all trials for criminal offences, the jury, after having received the instruction of the court, shall have the right, in their verdict of guilty or not guilty, to determine the law and the facts of the case. But it shall be the duty of the court to superintend the course of the trial, to decide upon the admission and rejection of evidence, and upon all questions of law raised during the trial, and upon all collateral and incidental proceedings, and also to allow bills of exceptions, and the court may grant a new trial in case of conviction.

The Resolves on the subject of future amendments of the Constitution, were next in order.

Mr. Jenkins, of Falmouth, moved to amend the first Resolve, by striking out all after the word "ensuing" in the eighteenth line, (printed copy,) and inserting instead thereof, the following:—

The qualified voters of each senatorial district in the Commonwealth shall elect, in the same manner as they shall elect senators to the general court, —— delegates.

Mr. Bradford, of Essex, moved to amend the amendment, by striking out all after the word "chosen" in the nineteenth line, as far as, and including, the word "elect" in the twenty-third line, and inserting instead thereof, the following:—

In the same manner as the senators shall by law be chosen, in the proportion of —— to each senator, to be elected by general ticket in each senatorial district, unless before that time the State shall be by law divided into single districts for that purpose, or for the election of Representatives; in which case one delegate shall be chosen for each district thus constituted.

Mr. Bradford's amendment was rejected.

Jenkins afterwards modified his amendment, as follows:—

Insert after the word "and" at the end of the eighteenth line, the following: "the legal voters of each senatorial district shall, by general ticket, in the manner then provided by law for the election of senators, choose —— delegates."

On motion of Mr. Jenkins, the yeas and nays were ordered upon this amendment.

On motion of Mr. Alvord, member for Montague, the Orders of the Day were laid upon the table.

The same gentleman moved, that debate on the subject of amendments of the Constitution close at a quarter past one o'clock.

On motion of Mr. Aspinwall, of Brookline, the yeas and nays were ordered upon this motion.

On motion of Mr. Griswold, member for Erving, Mr. Alvord's motion was laid upon the table,

And then, on motion of Mr. Griswold, sustained by a vote of one hundred and six in the affirmative, to ninety-nine in the negative, it was

Ordered, That the session be extended until eight o'clock this evening.

The motion of Mr. Alvord was then taken from the table and considered.

And the roll being called, one hundred and sixty-seven members voted in the affirmative, and ninety-six in the negative.

So it was adopted.

Those who voted in the affirmative are:—

Messrs. Josiah G. Abbott,
Shubael P. Adams,
Charles Allen,
James B. Allen,
Joel C. Allen,
Parsons Allen,
John B. Alley,
D. W. Alvord,
Hillel Baker,
George S. Ball,
Alpheus Bancroft,
Marcus Barrett,
Moses Bates, Jr.,
William Bennett, Jr.,
Zephaniah Bennett,
Edward B. Bigelow,
Francis W. Bird,
William S. Booth,
Sewell Boutwell,
Hiram N. Breed,
Asa Bronson,
Adolphus F. Brown,
Artemas Brown,
Hammond Brown,
Joseph Brownell,
Patrick Bryant,
Anson Burlingame,
Henry Cady,
William Carruthers,
Isaac Case,
Daniel E. Chapin,
J. McKean Churchill,
Henry Clark,
Ransom Clark,
Salah Clark,
Sumner Cole,
George B. Crane,
Oliver S. Cressy,
Thomas Cushman,
Simeon N. Cutler,
Charles G. Davis,
Isaac Davis,
Robert T. Davis,
Silas Dean,
William Dehon,
Augustus Denton,
Samuel Duncan,

Messrs. Bradish Dunham,
Philip Eames,
John M. Earle,
Calvin D. Eaton,
Elisha Edwards,
Samuel Edwards,
Joseph M. Ely,
Sullivan Fay,
James K. Fellows,
Lyman Fisk,
Emery Fiske,
Aaron Foster,
Abram Foster,
James M. Freeman,
Charles A. French,
Rodney French,
Samuel French,
Richard Frothingham, Jr.,
Luther Gale,
Washington Gilbert,
Charles G. Giles,
Leonard Gooding,
John W. Graves,
Jabez Green,
William B. Greene,
Whiting Griswold,
Benjamin F. Hallett,
Lyman W. Hapgood,
Seth Hapgood,
Stephen E. Hawkes,
Isaac Hayden,
Charles C. Hazewell,
Ezra Heath, 2d,
James Hewes,
William H. Hewes,
Henry Hobart,
Edwin Hobbs,
George Hood,
Martin Howard,
Abraham H. Howland,
Henry K. Hoyt,
Charles P. Huntington,
George H. Huntington,
Abijah M. Ide, Jr.,
Isaac Kendall,
Edward L. Keyes,
Joseph Kimball,

Messrs. Jefferson Knight,
J. S. C. Knowlton,
William H. Knowlton,
Albert Knox,
Gardner P. Ladd,
Luther Lawrence,
Justin E. Loomis,
Charles Mason,
Simeon Merritt,
Samuel Mixter,
James L. Monroe,
James M. Moore,
Elbridge G. Morton,
Marcus Morton, Jr.,
Hiram Nash,
Jonathan Nayson,
William Nichols,
Andrew T. Nute,
Benjamin S. Orne,
Charles Osgood,
E. Wing Packer,
Benjamin Paine,
Jonathan Parris,
John Partridge,
Jeremiah Pease, Jr.,
John Penniman,
Charles Phelps,
Henry Pierce,
James M. Pool,
Peter Powers,
Robert Rantoul,
Silas Rawson,
David Rice,
Luther Richards,
Daniel Richardson,
Nathan Richardson,
Samuel H. Richardson,

Messrs. Elkanah Ring, Jr.,
John Rogers,
James C. Royce,
Amasa Sanderson,
John Sherril,
John W. Simonds,
Matthew Smith,
Samuel W. Spooner,
Eben H. Stacy,
Joseph L. Stevens, Jr.,
William Stevens,
Gideon Stiles,
Alfred L. Strong,
Isaac C. Taber,
Arnold Taft,
Willard Thayer, 2d,
John W. Thomas,
Abraham Tilton,
Horatio W. Tilton,
David P. Turner,
Joel Viles,
George A. Vinton,
Frederick T. Wallace,
Freeland Wallis,
Andrew H. Ward,
Samuel Warner, Jr.,
George White,
Daniel S. Whitney,
James S. Whitney,
Daniel Wilbur,
Henry Wilson,
Willard Wilson,
Levi M. Winslow,
Charles C. Wood,
Otis Wood,
Ezekiel Wright.

Those who voted in the negative are :—

Messrs. Benjamin P. Adams,
P. Emory Aldrich,
Robert Andrews,
William Aspinwall,
David C. Atwood,
Sidney Bartlett,
John Beal,
Luther V. Bell,
Jacob Bigelow,
Ebenezer Bradbury,
William J. A. Bradford,
Milton P. Braman,
Osmyn Brewster,

Messrs. Francis Brinley,
George N. Briggs,
Frederick Brownell,
Timothy W. Carter,
Chester W. Chapin,
Jacob Coggin,
Nathaniel Cogswell,
Henry F. Cooledge,
Benjamin F. Copeland,
Leander Crosby,
Seth Crowell,
Wilber Curtis,
John Davis,

Messrs. Solomon Davis,
Henry L. Dawes,
Hiram S. Denison,
Lilley Eaton,
Homer Ely,
Samuel P. Fowler,
Henry J. Gardner,
Wanton C. Gilbert,
Joel Giles,
Robert Gould,
Jason Goulding,
John C. Gray,
Artemas Hale,
George Haskell,
Elnathan P. Hathaway,
George Hayward,
Charles Heard,
Henry Hersey,
George S. Hillard,
William Hinsdale,
Thomas Hopkinson,
Samuel Houghton,
William J. Hubbard,
William Hunt,
Asahel Huntington,
Samuel A. Hurlburt,
Samuel Jackson,
William James,
John Jenkins,
Giles C. Kellogg,
Henry W. Kinsman,
Joseph Knight,
Job G. Lawton, Jr.,
Frederic W. Lincoln, Jr.,
Otis P. Lord,

Messrs. Samuel P. Loud,
John A. Lowell,
Seth Miller, Jr.,
George Morey,
Marcus Morton,
Henry K. Oliver,
Nathan Orcutt,
John G. Park,
Adolphus G. Parker,
Joel Parker,
Samuel D. Parker,
George Peabody,
Daniel A. Perkins,
Jesse Perkins,
Noah C. Perkins,
William C. Plunkett,
Jeremiah Pomroy,
James Read,
Sampson Reed,
John Sargent,
William Schouler,
Thomas Talbot,
Charles Thompson,
Edmund P. Tileston,
Charles R. Train,
Charles W. Upham,
George B. Upton,
Samuel B. Walcott,
Bradford L. Wales,
Samuel Walker,
Thomas Wetmore,
William F. Wheeler,
Benjamin White,
John H. Wilkins,
Henry Williams.

The Orders of the Day were then taken from the table,

And the question being upon the amendment offered by Mr. Jenkins,

The roll was called, and ninety members voted in the affirmative, and one hundred and sixty-three in the negative.

So the amendment was rejected.

Those who voted in the affirmative are:—

Messrs. P. Emory Aldrich,
Robert Andrews,
David C. Atwood,
Joseph Barrows,
Sidney Bartlett,
Jacob Bigelow,
Ebenezer Bradbury,
Milton P. Braman,

Messrs. Asa Bronson,
Frederick Brownell,
Timothy W. Carter,
Nathaniel Cogswell,
Henry F. Cooledge,
Benjamin F. Copeland,
Leander Crosby,
Seth Crowell,

Messrs. Wilber Curtis,
Charles G. Davis,
Solomon Davis,
Henry L. Dawes,
Hiram S. Denison,
Moses Dorman,
Lilley Eaton,
Homer Ely,
Emery Fiske,
Samuel P. Fowler,
Richard Frothingham, Jr.,
Henry J. Gardner,
Wanton C. Gilbert,
Joel Giles,
Robert Gould,
John C. Gray,
Artemas Hale,
Nathan Hale,
George Haskell,
Elnathan P. Hathaway,
Charles Heard,
Henry Hersey,
George S. Hillard,
William Hinsdale,
Foster Hooper,
Thomas Hopkinson,
William J. Hubbard,
William Hunt,
Asahel Huntington,
Samuel A. Hurlburt,
Samuel Jackson,
William James,
John Jenkins,
Giles C. Kellogg,
Henry W. Kinsman,
George H. Kuhn,
John S. Ladd,
Messrs. Job G. Lawton, Jr.,
Frederic W. Lincoln, Jr.,
Tristram Littlefield,
Isaac Livermore,
Otis P. Lord,
Samuel K. Lothrop,
John A. Lowell,
Seth Miller, Jr.,
George Morey,
Marcus Morton,
Daniel Noyes,
Henry K. Oliver,
Benjamin S. Orne,
John G. Park,
Samuel D. Parker,
George Peabody,
Daniel A. Perkins,
William C. Plunkett,
Robert Rantoul,
James Read,
Sampson Reed,
John Sargent,
Charles G. Stevens,
Thomas Talbot,
Charles Thompson,
Edmund P. Tileston,
Charles R. Train,
Charles W. Upham,
George B. Upton,
Bradford L. Wales,
Samuel Walker,
Cyrus Weeks,
Thomas Wetmore,
William F. Wheeler,
John H. Wilkins,
Henry Williams,
Milo Wilson.

Those who voted in the negative are :—

Messrs. Josiah G. Abbott,
Shubael P. Adams,
Charles Allen,
James B. Allen,
Joel C. Allen,
Parsons Allen,
D. W. Alvord,
Hillel Baker,
George S. Ball,
Alpheus Bancroft,
Marcus Barrett,
Eliakim A. Bates,
Moses Bates, Jr.,
Messrs. William Bennett, Jr.,
Zephaniah Bennett,
Edward B. Bigelow,
Francis W. Bird,
William S. Booth,
Sewell Boutwell,
Hiram N. Breed,
Francis Brinley,
George N. Briggs,
Artemas Brown,
Joseph Brownell,
Patrick Bryant,
Henry Cady,

Messrs. Isaac Case,
Daniel E. Chapin,
J. McKean Churchill,
Henry Clark,
Ransom Clark,
Salah Clark,
Stillman Clarke,
George B. Crane,
Oliver S. Cressy,
Simeon N. Cutler,
Isaac Davis,
Silas Dean,
Augustus Denton,
Bradish Dunham,
Philip Eames,
John M. Earle,
Calvin D. Eaton,
Elisha Edwards,
Samuel Edwards,
Joseph M. Ely,
Sullivan Fay,
James K. Fellows,
Lyman Fisk,
Aaron Foster,
Abram Foster,
James M. Freeman,
Charles A. French,
Rodney French,
Samuel French,
Luther Gale,
Charles G. Giles,
Leonard Gooding,
Dalton Goulding,
John W. Graves,
Jabez Green,
Josiah W. Griswold,
Whiting Griswold,
Benjamin F. Hallett,
Lyman W. Hapgood,
Seth Hapgood,
Phineas Harmon,
Stephen E. Hawkes,
Isaac Hayden,
Ezra Heath, 2d,
James Hewes,
William H. Hewes,
Henry Hobart,
Edwin Hobbs,
George Hood,
Martin Howard,
Abraham H. Howland,
Henry K. Hoyt,
Charles P. Huntington,

Messrs. George H. Huntington,
Moses C. Hurlbut,
Abijah M. Ide, Jr.,
John Jacobs,
Isaac Kendall,
Edward L. Keyes,
Joseph Kimball,
Joseph Kingman,
Jefferson Knight,
J. S. C. Knowlton,
William H. Knowlton,
Albert Knox,
Gardner P. Ladd,
Luther Lawrence,
Alden Leland,
Abishai Lincoln,
Justin E. Loomis,
Simeon Merritt,
James L. Monroe,
James M. Moore,
Elbridge G. Morton,
Marcus Morton, Jr.,
Hiram Nash,
Jonathan Nayson,
William Nichols,
Andrew T. Nute,
Charles Osgood,
E. Wing Packer,
Benjamin Paine,
Jonathan Parris,
John Partridge,
Jeremiah Pease, Jr.,
John Penniman,
Jesse Perkins,
Noah C. Perkins,
Charles Phelps,
Henry Pierce,
Jeremiah Pomroy,
James M. Pool,
Peter Powers,
Silas Rawson,
David Rice,
Luther Richards,
Daniel Richardson,
Nathan Richardson,
Samuel H. Richardson,
Elkanah Ring, Jr.,
Joseph M. Rockwood,
John Rogers,
David S. Ross,
James C. Royce,
Amasa Sanderson,
John Sherril,

Messrs. John W. Simonds,
Matthew Smith,
Samuel W. Spooner,
Eben H. Stacy,
William Stevens,
Gideon Stiles,
Arnold Taft,
Willard Thayer, 2d,
John W. Thomas,
Abraham Tilton,
Horatio W. Tilton,
David Turner,
David P. Turner,
Joel Viles,
George A. Vinton,
Frederick T. Wallace,

Messrs. Freeland Wallis,
Andrew H. Ward,
Samuel Warner, Jr.,
Benjamin White,
George White,
Daniel S. Whitney,
James S. Whitney,
Henry Wilson,
Willard Wilson,
Levi M. Winslow,
Charles C. Wood,
Otis Wood,
William H. Wood,
Josiah B. Woods,
Ezekiel Wright.

At ten minutes past two o'clock, the Convention adjourned.

AFTERNOON SESSION.

Met according to adjournment.

The result of the vote upon Mr. Jenkins's amendment, was announced.

The Convention resumed the consideration of the unfinished business of the morning session, viz.: the Resolves on the subject of future amendments of the Constitution.

Mr. Hooper, of Fall River, moved to amend the first Resolve by substituting the words "one thousand eight hundred and seventy-six," instead of "one thousand eight hundred and seventy-three;" but the amendment was rejected.

Mr. Lord, of Salem, moved to amend the first Resolve by inserting, after the word "affirmative" in the thirteenth line, the words "and such majority shall be equal to two-fifths of the votes given for governor at such election;" but the amendment was rejected, by a vote of thirty in the affirmative, to one hundred and thirty-six in the negative.

Mr. Alvord, member for Montague, moved to amend by striking out the last Resolve, which is as follows:—

Resolved, The foregoing provisions shall in no wise restrain or impair the reserved right of the people, in their sovereign capacity, and by such mode of proceeding as shall fully and fairly collect and ascertain the will of the majority, at all times, to reform, alter, or totally change their Constitution and Frame of Government.

But the motion was rejected, by a vote of twenty-five in the affirmative, to one hundred and forty-three in the negative.

Mr. GILES, of Boston, moved to amend, by striking out the words "and by such mode of proceeding as shall fully and fairly collect and ascertain the will of the majority," and inserting instead thereof, the words, "according to their will legally expressed."

But the amendment was rejected.

Mr. LORD, of Salem, moved to amend the first Resolve, by inserting after the word "affirmative," in the thirteenth line, the words "and such majority shall be equal to one-third of the votes given for governor at such election;" but the amendment was rejected.

The first and second Resolves were then finally passed, without a division.

And the third Resolve was passed, by a vote of one hundred and forty-two in the affirmative, to sixty-four in the negative.

Mr. SCHOULER, of Boston, moved a reconsideration of the vote; and the rule was suspended, and the motion immediately considered.

After debate, Mr. KINGMAN, of West Bridgewater, moved the Previous Question; which was ordered.

And the motion to reconsider was agreed to, by a vote of one hundred and ninety-five in the affirmative, to thirty-three in the negative.

Mr. ALLEN, of Worcester, moved a reconsideration of the vote by which the motion of Mr. Alvord, member for Montague, to strike out the third Resolve, was rejected.

After debate, Mr. WHITNEY, of Boylston, moved the Previous Question; which was ordered.

And the motion to reconsider prevailed.

The question recurring on the motion to strike out the third Resolve,

Mr. HALLETT, member for Wilbraham, moved to amend the Resolve by striking out the words, "and by such mode of proceeding as shall fully and fairly collect and ascertain the will of the majority."

Mr. BIRD, of Walpole, moved the Previous Question; which was ordered.

Mr. Hallett's amendment was then adopted, by a vote of one hundred and fifty-nine in the affirmative, to fifty-eight in the negative.

The question recurring upon the motion to strike out the third Resolve, it was agreed to by a vote of one hundred and fifty-eight in the affirmative, to eighty-nine in the negative.

Mr. HUBBARD, of Boston, called for a division of the questions.

On motion of Mr. LORD, of Salem, the yeas and nays were ordered upon the passage of the first and second Resolves.

It was here stated, that the motion of Mr. Schouler to reconsider embraced only the third Resolve; and the Chair considered this to be the state of the question.

So the first and second Resolves remained finally passed, as follow:

1. *Resolved*, That it is expedient to provide in the Constitution that—

A Convention to revise or amend this Constitution, may be called and held in the following manner: At the general election in the year 1873, and in each twentieth year thereafter, the qualified voters in State elections shall give in their votes upon the question, "Shall there be a Convention to revise the Constitution?" which votes shall be received, counted, recorded and declared, in the same manner as in the election of governor; and a copy of the record thereof, shall, within one month, be returned to the office of the Secretary of State, who shall, thereupon, examine the same, and shall officially publish the number of yeas and nays given upon said question, in each town and city, and if a majority of said votes shall be in the affirmative, it shall be deemed and taken to be the will of the people that a Convention should meet accordingly; and thereafter, on the first Monday of March ensuing, meetings shall be held, and delegates shall be chosen, in all the towns, cities, and districts in the Commonwealth, in the manner and number then provided by law for the election of the largest number of representatives, which the towns, cities and districts shall then be entitled to elect in any year of that decennial period. And such delegates shall meet in Convention at the State House on the first Wednesday of May next ensuing, and when organized, shall have all the powers necessary to execute the purpose for which such Convention was called; and may establish the compensation of its officers and members, and the expense of its session, for which the Governor, with the advice and consent of the Council, shall draw his warrant on the treasury. And if such alterations and amendments as shall be proposed by the Convention, shall be adopted by the people voting thereon in such manner as the Convention shall direct, the Constitution shall be deemed and taken to be altered or amended accordingly. And it shall be the duty of the proper officers and persons in authority, to perform all acts necessary to carry into effect the foregoing provisions.

2. *Resolved*, That whenever towns or cities containing not less than one-third of the qualified voters of the Commonwealth, shall at any meeting for the election of State officers, request that a Convention be called to revise the Constitution, it shall be the duty of the legislature, at its next session, to pass an act for the calling of the

same, and submit the question to the qualified voters of the Commonwealth, whether a Convention shall be called accordingly: *Provided*, that nothing herein contained shall impair the power of the legislature to take action for calling a Convention, without such request, as heretofore practised in this Commonwealth.

On motion of Mr. WILSON, of Natick, the Orders of the Day were laid upon the table.

Mr. MORTON, of Taunton, from the Committee on the Judiciary, submitted a series of Resolves.

Laid upon the table, and ordered to be printed.

On motion of Mr. WILSON, the motion of Mr. Bird, of Walpole, to reconsider the vote by which the Resolves on the subject of elections by plurality and majority, were finally passed, was taken from the table, and considered.

And the motion to reconsider was rejected, by a vote of one hundred and twelve in the affirmative, to one hundred and eighteen in the negative.

After the vote had been declared, its correctness was doubted by several members; but upon a re-examination of the returns of the Monitors, the President announced the result to be correct.

Another count was called for, but the President remarked that it could only be taken by unanimous consent.

Objections were made, and then Mr. DAVIS, of Plymouth, called for the yeas and nays upon the question,

And the Chair decided that the motion was in order.

Mr. STEVENSON, of Boston, appealed from the decision of the chair.

On motion of Mr. LORD, of Salem, the yeas and nays were ordered upon the question of the appeal.

Mr. WILSON, of Natick, moved that the appeal be laid upon the table.

Mr. GRAY, of Boston, raised the question whether it was competent to lay an appeal upon the table,

And the President decided that the motion was in order.

On motion of Mr. GRAY, the yeas and nays were ordered upon the motion that the appeal be laid upon the table.

The motion, to lay upon the table, was then withdrawn.

Mr. WATERS, of Millbury, moved the Previous Question; which was ordered.

And the question being stated, "shall the decision of the Chair stand?"

The roll was called, and one hundred and sixty-eight members voted in the affirmative, and sixty-two in the negative.

So the decision of the Chair stood as the decision of the Convention.

Those who voted in the affirmative are :—

Messrs. Josiah G. Abbott,
Benjamin P. Adams,
Shubael P. Adams,
James B. Allen,
Joel C. Allen,
Parsons Allen,
John B. Alley,
Josiah Allis,
D. W. Alvord,
George Austin,
Hillel Baker,
George S. Ball,
Alpheus Bancroft,
Moses Bates, Jr.,
William Bennett, Jr.,
Zephaniah Bennett,
Francis W. Bird,
William S. Booth,
George S. Boutwell,
Sewell Boutwell,
Hiram N. Breed,
Adolphus F. Brown,
Hammond Brown,
Hiram C. Brown,
Frederick Brownell,
Joseph Brownell,
Patrick Bryant,
Rufus Bullock,
Cephas C. Bumpus,
Anson Burlingame,
Benjamin F. Butler,
Henry Cady,
William Carruthers,
Isaac Case,
Chester W. Chapin,
Josiah Childs,
J. McKean Churchill,
Alpheus B. Clarke,
William Cleverly,
Sumner Cole,
Henry F. Cooledge,
Simeon Crittenden,
Joseph W. Cross,
Richard H. Dana, Jr.,
Charles G. Davis,
Robert T. Davis,
Silas Dean,
Elijah S. Deming,
Augustus Denton,

Messrs. Samuel Duncan,
Bradish Dunham,
John M. Durgin,
Philip Eames,
John M. Earle,
Peter Easland,
James Easton, 2d,
Calvin D. Eaton,
Elisha Edwards,
Samuel Edwards,
Joseph M. Ely,
Sullivan Fay,
James K. Fellows,
Lyman Fisk,
Aaron Foster,
Abram Foster,
Samuel Fowle,
James M. Freeman,
Charles A. French,
Rodney French,
Samuel French,
Richard Frothingham, Jr.,
Luther Gale,
Elbridge Gates,
Washington Gilbert,
Charles G. Giles,
Joel Giles,
Jabez Green,
William B. Greene,
Josiah W. Griswold,
Whiting Griswold,
Lyman W. Hapgood,
Phineas Harmon,
William Haskins,
Stephen E. Hawkes,
Ezra Heath, 2d,
James Hewes,
Henry Hobart,
George Hood,
Martin Howard,
Abraham H. Howland,
Henry K. Hoyt,
Charles E. Hunt,
George H. Huntington,
Benjamin D. Hyde,
Abijah M. Ide, Jr.,
John Jacobs,
Isaac Kendall,
Joseph Kingman,

Messrs. Hiram Knight,
Charles L. Knowlton,
William H. Knowlton,
Albert Knox,
Wilber C. Langdon,
Job G. Lawton, Jr.,
Otis Little,
Justin E. Loomis,
Abijah P. Marvin,
Charles Mason,
Simeon Merritt,
James L. Monroe,
Elbridge G. Morton,
Marcus Morton,
Marcus Morton, Jr.,
William S. Morton,
Hiram Nash,
Jonathan Nayson,
William Nichols,
Andrew T. Nute,
Charles Osgood,
E. Wing Packer,
Benjamin Paine,
Adolphus G. Parker,
Jonathan Parris,
John Partridge,
John Penniman,
Daniel A. Perkins,
Charles Phelps,
Sylvanus B. Phinney,
Henry Pierce,
Jeremiah Pomroy,
Silas Rawson,
Luther Richards,
Samuel H. Richardson,

Messrs. Elkanah Ring, Jr.,
James C. Royce,
Amasa Sanderson,
Chester Sanderson,
John Sherril,
Chester Sikes,
Perez Simmons,
John W. Simonds,
Melzar Sprague,
Samuel W. Spooner,
Granville Stevens,
William Stevens,
Alfred L. Strong,
Increase Sumner,
Alanson Swain,
Charles Thompson,
Horatio W. Tilton,
David P. Turner,
William Tyler,
Frederick T. Wallace,
Freeland Wallis,
Amasa Walker,
Andrew H. Ward,
Samuel Warner, Jr.,
Asa H. Waters,
Gershom B. Weston,
George White,
James S. Whitney,
J. B. Williams,
Henry Wilson,
Levi M. Winslow,
Charles C. Wood,
Otis Wood,
William H. Wood,
Ezekiel Wright.

Those who voted in the negative are:—

Messrs. P. Emory Aldrich,
Robert Andrews,
William Aspinwall,
Samuel Ayres,
Russel Bartlett,
Sidney Bartlett,
Ebenezer Bradbury,
Osmyn Brewster,
Francis Brinley,
George N. Briggs,
Nathaniel Cogswell,
Ithamar Conkey,
Wilber Curtis,
Henry L. Dawes,
Homer Ely,

Messrs. Henry J. Gardner,
Wanton C. Gilbert,
Jason Goulding,
John C. Gray,
Artemas Hale,
Nathan Hale,
Benjamin F. Hallett,
Seth Hapgood,
Charles Heard,
Samuel Henry,
George S. Hillard,
Samuel Houghton,
William J. Hubbard,
William Hunt,
Asahel Huntington,

Messrs. Samuel A. Hurlburt,
John Jenkins,
Giles C. Kellogg,
Henry W. Kinsman,
J. S. C. Knowlton,
Frederic W. Lincoln, Jr.,
Isaac Livermore,
Otis P. Lord,
Samuel K. Lothrop,
Samuel P. Loud,
Theophilus R. Marvin,
Seth Miller, Jr.,
Samuel Mixter,
George Morey,
Henry K. Oliver,
Nathan Orcutt,

Messrs. James W. Paige,
Samuel D. Parker,
William C. Plunkett,
Jonathan Preston,
Julius Rockwell,
William Schouler,
J. Thomas Stevenson,
Gideon Stiles,
Charles R. Train,
Charles W. Upham,
George B. Upton,
Samuel B. Walcott,
Cyrus Weeks,
Ezra Wilkinson,
Milo Wilson,
Josiah B. Woods.

The question then being upon the motion to reconsider the vote upon the final passage of the Resolves,

The roll was called, and one hundred and thirty-seven members voted in the affirmative, and forty-eight in the negative.

So the motion to reconsider was agreed to.

Those who voted in the affirmative are :—

Messrs. Benjamin P. Adams,
Shubael P. Adams,
P. Emory Aldrich,
James B. Allen,
Parsons Allen,
D. W. Alvord,
Alpheus Bancroft,
Moses Bates, Jr.,
John Beal,
Zephaniah Bennett,
Jacob Bigelow,
Francis W. Bird,
George S. Boutwell,
Ebenezer Bradbury,
Hiram N. Breed,
Francis Brinley,
George N. Briggs,
Adolphus F. Brown,
Hammond Brown,
Hiram C. Brown,
Frederick Brownell,
Joseph Brownell,
Patrick Bryant,
Rufus Bullock,
Anson Burlingame,
Benjamin F. Butler,
Henry Cady,
William Carruthers,

Messrs. Isaac Case,
Chester W. Chapin,
Josiah Childs,
J. McKean Churchill,
Salah Clark,
Alpheus B. Clarke,
William Cleverly,
Lansing J. Cole,
Thomas Cushman,
Richard H. Dana, Jr.,
Charles G. Davis,
Elijah S. Deming,
Samuel Duncan,
Bradish Dunham,
Philip Eames,
John M. Earle,
Peter Easland,
James Easton, 2d,
Elisha Edwards,
Samuel Edwards,
Joseph M. Ely,
Homer Ely,
James K. Fellows,
Abram Foster,
James M. Freeman,
Charles A. French,
Rodney French,
Richard Frothingham, Jr.,

Messrs. Luther Gale,
Elbridge Gates,
Wanton C. Gilbert,
Joel Giles,
William B. Greene,
Josiah W. Griswold,
Whiting Griswold,
Nathan Hale,
Benjamin F. Hallett,
Lyman W. Hapgood,
Seth Hapgood,
Phineas Harmon,
Stephen E. Hawkes,
Ezra Heath, 2d,
James Hewes,
George S. Hillard,
Henry Hobart,
George Hood,
Abraham H. Howland,
William J. Hubbard,
William Hunt,
Giles C. Kellogg,
Isaac Kendall,
Joseph Kingman,
Hiram Knight,
Joseph Knight,
Charles L. Knowlton,
J. S. C. Knowlton,
Wilber C. Langdon,
Otis Little,
Isaac Livermore,
Justin E. Loomis,
Samuel K. Lothrop,
Abijah P. Marvin,
Theophilus R. Marvin,
Charles Mason,
Simeon Merritt,
George Morey,
Elbridge G. Morton,
Marcus Morton,
Marcus Morton, Jr.,

Messrs. William S. Morton,
Jonathan Nayson,
Andrew T. Nute,
Joseph E. Ober,
Henry K. Oliver,
Nathan Orcutt,
Charles Osgood,
Adolphus G. Parker,
Samuel D. Parker,
Jonathan Parris,
John Partridge,
Silvanus B. Phinney,
Jeremiah Pomroy,
Luther Richards,
Elkanah Ring, Jr.,
Joseph M. Rockwood,
David S. Ross,
Amasa Sanderson,
William Schouler,
Perez Simmons,
Melzar Sprague,
Samuel W. Spooner,
Charles G. Stevens,
J. Thomas Stevenson,
Alfred L. Strong,
Alanson Swain,
Charles R. Train,
William Tyler,
Orison Underwood,
George B. Upton,
Amasa Walker,
Andrew H. Ward,
Samuel Warner, Jr.,
Asa H. Waters,
Gershom B. Weston,
Benjamin White,
James S. Whitney,
Ezra Wilkinson,
Henry Wilson,
Charles C. Wood.

Those who voted in the negative are:—

Messrs. Joel C. Allen,
John B. Alley,
Josiah Allis,
Hillel Baker,
Russel Bartlett,
William S. Booth,
Sewell Boutwell,
Asahel Buck,
Cephas C. Bumpus,

Messrs. Ransom Clark,
Simeon Crittenden,
Silas Dean,
Augustus Denton,
Calvin D. Eaton,
Sullivan Fay,
Samuel French,
Henry J. Gardner,
Washington Gilbert,

Messrs. Charles G. Giles,
Jabez Green,
Artemas Hale,
William Haskins,
Elnathan P. Hathaway,
William Hinsdale,
Henry K. Hoyt,
John Jenkins,
William H. Knowlton,
Albert Knox,
Gardner P. Ladd,
Job G. Lawton, Jr.,
Laban Marcy,
Seth Miller, Jr.,
John Penniman,

Messrs. Daniel A. Perkins,
Henry Pierce,
Silas Rawson,
David Rice,
James C. Royce,
John Sherril,
John W. Simonds,
Gideon Stiles,
Charles Thompson,
Horatio W. Tilton,
David P. Turner,
Frederick T. Wallace,
Freeland Wallis,
Joel Wilder,
Levi M. Winslow.

Mr. Bird, of Walpole, moved an amendment to the first Resolve.

Mr. Schouler, of Boston, moved an amendment to the amendment; which was accepted by Mr. Bird.

Mr. Davis, of Plymouth, moved another amendment.

Afterwards, Mr. Bird modified his amendment, so as to read as follows:—

Insert after the word "Commonwealth" in the fourth line, (printed copy,) the words "until otherwise provided by law, but no such law providing that the Governor, Lieutenant-Governor, Secretary, Treasurer, Auditor, Attorney-General and Representatives to the General Court, or either of them, shall be elected by plurality instead of a majority of votes given in, shall take effect until one year after its passage; and if at any time after the enactment of any such law, and the same shall have taken effect, such law shall be repealed, such repeal shall not become a law until one year after the passage of the repealing act; and in default of any such law, if at any election of either of the above-named officers, except the Representatives to the General Court;"

Also, strike out the words "provided, that if at any election of either of the above-named officers."

Mr. Bird also moved to amend the fourth Resolve, by striking out all after the word "Resolved," and inserting the following:—

That in the election of all city or town officers, such rule of election shall govern as the legislature may by law prescribe.

Mr. Alvord, member for Montague, moved the Previous Question.

Mr. Gardner, of Boston, called for the yeas and nays upon this motion; and they were ordered.

Mr. Lord, of Salem, moved an adjournment; which motion was declared rejected.

On motion of Mr. LORD, the yeas and nays were then ordered upon the question of adjournment,

And the roll being called, fifty-six members voted in the affirmative, and one hundred and forty-four in the negative.

So the motion to adjourn was rejected.

Those who voted in the affirmative are:—

Messrs. Benjamin P. Adams,
P. Emory Aldrich,
Robert Andrews,
William Aspinwall,
Joseph Barrows,
Luther V. Bell,
Gad O. Bliss,
Ebenezer Bradbury,
Francis Brinley,
Asahel Buck,
Nathaniel Cogswell,
Ithamar Conkey,
Simeon Crittenden,
Leander Crosby,
Seth Crowell,
Solomon Davis,
Henry L. Dawes,
Hiram S. Denison,
Elisha Edwards,
William T. Eustis,
Henry J. Gardner,
Wanton C. Gilbert,
Jason Goulding,
John C. Gray,
Artemas Hale,
Nathan Hale,
Phineas Harmon,
George S. Hillard,

Messrs. William Hinsdale,
Samuel Houghton,
William J. Hubbard,
William Hunt,
William James,
John Jenkins,
Giles C. Kellogg,
Frederic W. Lincoln, Jr.,
Isaac Livermore,
Otis P. Lord,
Theophilus R. Marvin,
Seth Miller, Jr.,
George Morey,
Daniel Noyes,
Henry K. Oliver,
Nathan Orcutt,
Samuel D. Parker,
Daniel A. Perkins,
William C. Plunkett,
John Sherril,
J. Thomas Stevenson,
Charles Thompson,
Charles R. Train,
Cyrus Weeks,
Benjamin White,
Joel Wilder,
Ezra Wilkinson,
Milo Wilson.

Those who voted in the negative are:—

Messrs. Shubael P. Adams,
James B. Allen,
Parsons Allen,
Josiah Allis,
D. W. Alvord,
George Austin,
Hillel Baker,
George S. Ball,
Alpheus Bancroft,
Moses Bates, Jr.,
John Beal,
William Bennett, Jr.,
Francis W. Bird,
William S. Booth,

Messrs. George S. Boutwell,
Sewell Boutwell,
Hiram N. Breed,
Adolphus F. Brown,
Hammond Brown,
Hiram C. Brown,
Joseph Brownell,
Patrick Bryant,
Cephas C. Bumpus,
Anson Burlingame,
Benjamin F. Butler,
Henry Cady,
William Carruthers,
Isaac Case,

Messrs. Chester W. Chapin,
J. McKean Churchill,
Ransom Clark,
Alpheus B. Clarke,
Sumner Cole,
Thomas Cushman,
Richard H. Dana, Jr.,
Charles G. Davis,
Robert T. Davis,
Gilman Day,
Silas Dean,
Elijah S. Deming,
Augustus Denton,
John M. Earle,
Peter Easland,
James Easton, 2d,
Calvin D. Eaton,
Samuel Edwards,
Joseph M. Ely,
Sullivan Fay,
James K. Fellows,
Lyman Fisk,
James M. Freeman,
Charles A. French,
Rodney French,
Luther Gale,
Johnson Gardner,
Elbridge Gates,
Washington Gilbert,
Charles G. Giles,
Jabez Green,
William B. Greene,
Josiah W. Griswold,
Whiting Griswold,
Benjamin F. Hallett,
A. B. Hammond,
Lyman W. Hapgood,
Seth Hapgood,
Elnathan P. Hathaway,
Ezra Heath, 2d,
James Hewes,
Levi Heywood,
Henry Hobart,
George Hood,
Martin Howard,
Abraham H. Howland,
Henry K. Hoyt,
George H. Huntington,
Samuel A. Hurlburt,
Abijah M. Ide, Jr.,
Isaac Kendall,
Joseph Kingman,
J. S. C. Knowlton,

Messrs. William H. Knowlton,
Albert Knox,
Gardner P. Ladd,
Wilber C. Langdon,
Otis Little,
Justin E. Loomis,
Laban Marcy,
Abijah P. Marvin,
Charles Mason,
Simeon Merritt,
James L. Monroe,
Elbridge G. Morton,
Marcus Morton,
Marcus Morton, Jr.,
William S. Morton,
Hiram Nash,
Andrew T. Nute,
Joseph E. Ober,
Charles Osgood,
E. Wing Packer,
Jonathan Parris,
John Partridge,
John Penniman,
Charles Phelps,
Silvanus B. Phinney,
Henry Pierce,
Silas Rawson,
David Rice,
Luther Richards,
Daniel Richardson,
Samuel H. Richardson,
Joseph M. Rockwood,
David S. Ross,
James C. Royce,
Amasa Sanderson,
William Schouler,
Chester Sikes,
Perez Simmons,
John W. Simonds,
Melzar Sprague,
Samuel W. Spooner,
Charles G. Stevens,
Granville Stevens,
Alfred L. Strong,
Charles Sumner,
Alanson Swain,
Joseph Thayer,
Horatio W. Tilton,
David Turner,
David P. Turner,
William Tyler,
George B. Upton,
Frederick T. Wallace,

Messrs. Freeland Wallis,
Andrew H. Ward,
Samuel Warner, Jr.,
Asa H. Waters,
Gershom B. Weston,

Messrs. James S. Whitney,
Henry Wilson,
Charles C. Wood,
Otis Wood,
William H. Wood.

At eight o'clock, Mr. Hale, of Bridgewater, raised the question, whether, under the rule adopted in the morning session, on motion of Mr. Griswold, the Convention was not under the necessity of adjourning at eight o'clock.

The President, (Mr. Wilson, of Natick, in the chair,) decided, that by the terms of that vote he was not authorized to declare the Convention adjourned at that time.

Mr. Schouler, of Boston, appealed from this decision.

Mr. Lord, of Salem, moved an adjournment; but the motion was rejected, by a vote of sixty-eight in the affirmative, to one hundred and thirteen in the negative.

The question being upon the appeal taken by Mr. Schouler, it was not sustained by the Convention.

So the decision of the Chair stood as the judgment of the Convention.

Mr. Alvord then withdrew his motion for the Previous Question.

On motion of Mr. Butler, of Lowell, the Orders of the Day were laid upon the table.

Mr. Butler then moved that debate upon the pending question cease at ten o'clock; but afterwards withdrew the motion.

On motion of Mr. Walker, of North Brookfield, the Orders of the Day were again taken up.

Mr. Weeks, of Harwich, called for the yeas and nays upon the amendment of Mr. Bird to the first Resolve;

But the motion was not sustained by one-fifth of the members voting.

Mr. Bird's amendment to the first Resolve was then adopted, by a vote of seventy-seven in the affirmative, to sixty-two in the negative.

Mr. Ely, of Westfield, moved an adjournment; but the motion was rejected.

Mr. Bird's amendment to the fourth Resolve was then adopted.

The first and fourth Resolves, as amended, were then, on motion of Mr. Butler, of Lowell, passed over, and it was

Ordered, That the question upon their final passage be taken at ten o'clock on Friday, without debate.

The second, third, fifth and sixth Resolves were then finally passed, as follow:—

Resolved, That in all elections of senators and councillors, the person having the highest number of votes shall be elected.

Resolved, That it is expedient so to amend the Constitution as to provide, that a majority of votes shall be necessary for the election of representatives to the general court, until otherwise provided by law.

Resolved, That in the election of all county and district officers, the person having the highest number of votes shall be elected.

Resolved, That in all elections where the person having the highest number of votes, may be elected, and there is a failure of election because two persons have an equal number of votes, subsequent trials may be had, at such times as may be prescribed by the legislature.

On motion of Mr. Lord, of Salem, the first and fourth Resolves, as amended, were ordered to be printed.

Mr. Bates, of Plymouth, from the Committee on Reporting and Printing, submitted two Reports on that subject.

Placed in the Orders of the Day for Friday.

At twenty minutes before one o'clock A. M. on Friday,

On motion of Mr. Oliver, of Lawrence,

The Convention adjourned.

FRIDAY, July 29, 1853.

Met according to adjournment. Prayer was offered by the Chaplain. The Journal of yesterday was read.

Leave of absence for the remainder of the session, was granted to Mr. Crowell, of Dennis, on account of the illness of his son.

Mr. Livermore, of Cambridge, offered the following Order:—

Ordered, That the pay of members for attendance and travel, be made up by the Committee on the Pay Roll, including Monday, the first day of August next.

On motion of Mr. Bates, of Plymouth, the Order was amended by the addition of the following words:—

And no member shall be entitled to pay beyond that time.

The Order was then adopted.

The special assignment for Thursday at ten o'clock, viz.: the Resolves offered by Mr. Morton, of Taunton, upon the mode of submitting the question of representation to the people, was taken up.

After debate, the Resolves were laid upon the table.

The special assignment for this day, at ten o'clock, viz.: the first and fourth Resolves on the subject of elections by plurality, was taken up.

Mr. TRAIN, of Framingham, moved to amend the first Resolve, by striking out the word "majority" in the second line, and inserting instead thereof, the word "plurality," and by striking out the word "all" in the same line.

But the motion was rejected, by a vote of one hundred and twenty in the affirmative, to one hundred and sixty-four in the negative.

On motion of Mr. BUTLER, of Lowell, the yeas and nays were ordered upon the final passage of the Resolves.

And the Roll being called, one hundred and eighty-five members voted in the affirmative, and one hundred and fifty-nine in the negative.

So the Resolves were finally passed, as follow:—

1. *Resolved*, That it is expedient to provide in the Constitution, that a *majority* of all the votes given shall be necessary to the election of a Governor, Lieutenant-Governor, Secretary, Treasurer, Auditor, and Attorney-General of the Commonwealth, until otherwise provided by law, but no such law providing that the Governor, Lieutenant-Governor, Secretary, Treasurer, Auditor, Attorney-General, and Representatives to the General Court, or either of them, shall be elected by plurality, instead of a majority of votes given in, shall take effect until one year after its passage; and if at any time after the enactment of any such law, and the same shall have taken effect, such law shall be repealed, such repeal shall not become a law until one year after the passage of the repealing act; and in default of any such law, if at any election of either of the above-named officers, except the Representatives to the General Court, no person shall have a majority of the votes given, the House of Representatives shall, by a majority of *viva voce* votes, elect two out of three persons who had the highest, if so many shall have been voted for, and return the persons so elected to the Senate, from which the Senate shall, by *viva voce* vote, elect one who shall be Governor.

4. *Resolved*, That in the election of all city or town officers, such rule of election shall govern as the legislature may by law prescribe.

Those who voted in the affirmative are:—

Messrs. Josiah G. Abbott,
Shubael P. Adams,
James B. Allen,
Josiah Allis,
D. W. Alvord,

Messrs. George Austin,
Hillel Baker,
Marcus Barrett,
Eliakim A. Bates,
Moses Bates, Jr.,

Messrs. John Beal,
Zephaniah Bennett,
Edward B. Bigelow,
Francis W. Bird,
Gad O. Bliss,
William S. Booth,
George S. Boutwell,
Sewell Boutwell,
William J. A. Bradford,
Hiram N. Breed,
Asa Bronson,
Adolphus F. Brown,
Artemas Brown,
Hammond Brown,
Frederick Brownell,
Joseph Brownell,
Patrick Bryant,
Anson Burlingame,
Benjamin F. Butler,
Henry Cady,
William Carruthers,
Isaac Case,
Daniel E. Chapin,
Henry Chapin,
Josiah Childs,
J. McKean Churchill,
Henry Clark,
Salah Clark,
Stillman Clarke,
William Cleverly,
George B. Crane,
Oliver S. Cressy,
Joseph W. Cross,
Henry W. Cushman,
Thomas Cushman,
Simeon N. Cutler,
Richard H. Dana, Jr.,
Charles G. Davis,
Isaac Davis,
Robert T. Davis,
Gilman Day,
Elijah S. Deming,
Augustus Denton,
Samuel Duncan,
Bradish Dunham,
John M. Durgin,
Philip Eames,
John M. Earle,
Peter Easland,
Elisha Edwards,
Sullivan Fay,
James K. Fellows,
Lyman Fisk,

Messrs. Emery Fiske,
Aaron Foster,
Abram Foster,
Samuel Fowle,
James M. Freeman,
Charles A. French,
Rodney French,
Samuel French,
Luther Gale,
Charles G. Giles,
Daniel W. Gooch,
Leonard Gooding,
Jabez Green,
Josiah W. Griswold,
Whiting Griswold,
Samuel P. Hadley,
Lyman W. Hapgood,
Seth Hapgood,
William Haskins,
Stephen E. Hawkes,
Isaac Hayden,
Ezra Heath, 2d,
James Hewes,
William H. Hewes,
Henry Hobart,
Nathaniel Holder,
George Hood,
Foster Hooper,
Martin Howard,
Charles E. Hunt,
Charles P. Huntington,
George H. Huntington,
Moses C. Hurlbut,
Benjamin D. Hyde,
Abijah M. Ide, Jr.,
John Jacobs,
John Johnson,
Isaac Kendall,
Joseph Kimball,
Hiram Knight,
Jefferson Knight,
Charles L. Knowlton,
William H. Knowlton,
Albert Knox,
Wilber C. Langdon,
Luther Lawrence,
Job G. Lawton, Jr.,
Alden Leland,
Abishai Lincoln,
Otis Little,
Tristram Littlefield,
Justin E. Loomis,
William P. Marble,

Messrs. Laban Marcy,
Abijah P. Marvin,
Simeon Merritt,
James M. Moore,
Marcus Morton, Jr.,
William S. Morton,
Hiram Nash,
Jonathan Nayson,
William Nichols,
Andrew T. Nute,
Joseph E. Ober,
Benjamin S. Orne,
Charles Osgood,
E. Wing Packer,
Benjamin Paine,
Henry Paine,
Jonathan Parris,
John Partridge,
Nathaniel Peabody,
John Penniman,
Noah C. Perkins,
Charles Phelps,
Silvanus B. Phinney,
James M. Pool,
John A. Putnam,
Robert Rantoul,
Luther Richards,
Daniel Richardson,
Nathan Richardson,
Samuel H. Richardson,
Elkanah Ring, Jr.,
Joseph M. Rockwood,
John Rogers,
David S. Ross,
Amasa Sanderson,

Messrs. Chester Sanderson,
Perez Simmons,
John W. Simonds,
Melzar Sprague,
Samuel W. Spooner,
Joseph L. Stevens, Jr.,
William Stevens,
Gideon Stiles,
Alfred L. Strong,
Joseph Thayer,
Willard Thayer, 2d,
Abraham Tilton,
David P. Turner,
William Tyler,
Orison Underwood,
George A. Vinton,
Amasa Walker,
Andrew H. Ward,
Samuel Warner, Jr.,
Asa H. Waters,
Gershom B. Weston,
George White,
Daniel S. Whitney,
James S. Whitney,
Daniel Wilbur,
Joseph Wilbur,
J. B. Williams,
Henry Wilson,
Jonathan B. Winn,
Levi M. Winslow,
Charles C. Wood,
Nathaniel Wood,
Otis Wood,
Ezekiel Wright.

Those who voted in the negative are:—

Messrs. Benjamin P. Adams,
P. Emory Aldrich,
Charles Allen,
Joel C. Allen,
Parsons Allen,
Robert Andrews,
William Aspinwall,
David C. Atwood,
Samuel Ayres,
George S. Ball,
Alpheus Bancroft,
Joseph Barrows,
Russel Bartlett,
Sidney Bartlett,
James M. Beebe,

Messrs. Luther V. Bell,
William Bennett, Jr.,
Jacob Bigelow,
Ebenezer Bradbury,
Osmyn Brewster,
Francis Brinley,
George N. Briggs,
Asahel Buck,
Rufus Bullock,
Cephas C. Bumpus,
Amariah Chandler,
Chester W. Chapin,
Ransom Clark,
Alpheus B. Clarke,
Jacob Coggin,

Messrs. Lansing J. Cole,
Sumner Cole,
Ithamar Conkey,
Charles E. Cook,
Henry F. Cooledge,
Benjamin F. Copeland,
Simeon Crittenden,
George W. Crockett,
Leander Crosby,
Ebenezer Davis,
John Davis,
Solomon Davis,
Henry L. Dawes,
Silas Dean,
William Dehon,
Hiram S. Denison,
James C. Doane,
Moses Dorman,
Lilley Eaton,
Homer Ely,
A. G. Farwell,
Samuel P. Fowler,
Charles H. French,
Richard Frothingham, Jr.,
Henry J. Gardner,
Johnson Gardner,
Elbridge Gates,
Wanton C. Gilbert,
Washington Gilbert,
Joel Giles,
Robert Gould,
Dalton Goulding,
Jason Goulding,
John C. Gray,
Artemas Hale,
Nathan Hale,
Benjamin F. Hallett,
A. B. Hammond,
Phineas Harmon,
Elnathan P. Hathaway,
George Hayward,
Charles C. Hazewell,
Charles Heard,
Samuel Henry,
Henry Hersey,
Levi Heywood,
William Hinsdale,
Aaron Hobart,
Thomas Hopkinson,
Samuel Houghton,
Abraham H. Howland,
Henry K. Hoyt,
William Hunt,

Messrs. Asahel Huntington,
Samuel A. Hurlburt,
William James,
John Jenkins,
Giles C. Kellogg,
Henry W. Kinsman,
Joseph Knight,
J. S. C. Knowlton,
George H. Kuhn,
Gardner P. Ladd,
Frederic W. Lincoln, Jr.,
Isaac Livermore,
Otis P. Lord,
Samuel K. Lothrop,
Samuel P. Loud,
John A. Lowell,
Theophilus R. Marvin,
Seth Miller, Jr.,
Samuel Mixter,
James L. Munroe,
George Morey,
Joseph B. Morss,
Marcus Morton,
Daniel Noyes,
Henry K. Oliver,
Nathan Orcutt,
John G. Park,
Adolphus G. Parker,
Jeremiah Pease, Jr.,
Daniel A. Perkins,
Jesse Perkins,
Henry Pierce,
William C. Plunkett,
Jeremiah Pomroy,
Silas Rawson,
James Read,
Sampson Reed,
David Rice,
Julius Rockwell,
James C. Royce,
John Sargent,
William Schouler,
John Sherril,
Chester Sikes,
John S. Sleeper,
Matthew Smith,
John Souther,
Caleb Stetson,
Charles G. Stevens,
Granville Stevens,
Increase Sumner,
Arnold Taft,
John W. Thomas,

Messrs. Charles Thompson,
Edmund P. Tileston,
Horatio W. Tilton,
Charles R. Train,
David Turner,
Charles W. Upham,
George B. Upton,
Joel Viles,
Samuel B. Walcott,
Bradford L. Wales,
Frederick T. Wallace,
Freeland Wallis,

Messrs. Samuel Walker,
Cyrus Weeks,
Thomas Wetmore,
William F. Wheeler,
Benjamin White,
Joel Wilder,
Ezra Wilkinson,
Henry Williams,
Milo Wilson,
Willard Wilson,
Josiah B. Woods.

On motion of Mr. Wilson, of Natick, the Convention resumed the consideration of the Resolves introduced by Mr. Morton, of Taunton, on the subject of the mode of submitting the question of representation to the people.

After debate, on motion of Mr. Fay, of Southborough, the Resolves were laid upon the table.

Mr. Fay then submitted a Report from the Committee on Leave of Absence, granting leave of absence, for the remainder of the session, to the following members, viz.:—

Messrs. Marble, of Charlton, Hoyt of Deerfield, Knowlton, of Holden, Warner, of Stockbridge, Marcy, of Greenwich, Atwood, of Eastham, Cady, of Monson, Tilton, of Chilmark, Allen, of Brimfield, Swain, of Nantucket, Easton, of Nantucket, Turner, of South Hadley, and Hapgood, of Athol.

The Report was considered and accepted, and leave of absence granted.

At two o'clock, on motion of Mr. Hathaway, of Freetown,
The Convention adjourned.

AFTERNOON SESSION.

Met according to adjournment.
On motion of Mr. Brown, of Medway,

Ordered, That debate upon the question under consideration previous to the adjournment in the forenoon, shall cease at four o'clock.

The Convention resumed the consideration of the Resolve introduced by Mr. Morton, on the subject of the mode of submitting the question of representation to the people.

Mr. Wilson, of Natick, moved to amend the proposition of Mr. Morton, by striking out all after the word "Resolved," and inserting instead thereof, the following:—

That it is expedient so to amend the Constitution as to provide, that the legislature which shall be chosen at the general election in November, 1855, shall be required to divide the State into forty single districts for the choice of senators, such districts to be of contiguous territory, and as equal in the number of qualified voters contained in each district as may be; and also to divide the State into single or double districts for the choice of not less than two hundred and forty, nor more than three hundred and twenty representatives, such districts to be of contiguous territory, and as equal in the number of qualified voters contained in each district as may be, with proper provisions for the redistricting of the State as aforesaid, in the year 1866, and every tenth year thereafter, and with all other provisions necessary for carrying such system of districts into operation; and to submit the same to the people at the general election to be held in the year 1856 for their ratification; and if the same shall be ratified by the people, it shall become part of this Constitution, in place of the provision herein contained for the apportioning of senators and representatives.

On motion of Mr. Morton, of Taunton, the yeas and nays were ordered on the question of adopting the amendment;

And the roll being called, two hundred and nine members voted in the affirmative, and one hundred and thirty-eight in the negative.

So the amendment was adopted.

Those who voted in the affirmative are:—

Messrs. Shubael P. Adams,
James B. Allen,
Joel C. Allen,
Parsons Allen,
John B. Alley,
Josiah Allis,
D. W. Alvord,
George Austin,
Hillel Baker,
George S. Ball,
Marcus Barrett,
Eliakim A. Bates,
Moses Bates, Jr.,
John Beal,
Zephaniah Bennett,
Edward B. Bigelow,
Francis W. Bird,
Henry W. Bishop,
Gad O. Bliss,
George S. Boutwell,
Sewell Boutwell,
Hiram N. Breed,

Messrs. Asa Bronson,
Adolphus F. Brown,
Alpheus R. Brown,
Artemas Brown,
Hammond Brown,
Hiram C. Brown,
Frederick Brownell,
Joseph Brownell,
Asahel Buck,
Anson Burlingame,
Benjamin F. Butler,
Henry Cady,
William Carruthers,
Isaac Case,
Amariah Chandler,
Chester W. Chapin,
Daniel E. Chapin,
Henry Chapin,
Josiah Childs,
J. McKean Churchill,
Henry Clark,
Ransom Clark,

Messrs. Salah Clark,
Alpheus B. Clarke,
William Cleverly,
Sumner Cole,
George B. Crane,
Joseph W. Cross,
Henry W. Cushman,
Thomas Cushman,
Simeon N. Cutler,
Charles G. Davis,
Ebenezer Davis,
Isaac Davis,
Robert T. Davis,
Gilman Day,
Silas Dean,
Elijah S. Deming,
Augustus Denton,
Alexander De Witt,
Samuel Duncan,
Bradish Dunham,
John M. Durgin,
Philip Eames,
John M. Earle,
Peter Easland,
James Easton, 2d,
Elisha Edwards,
Samuel Edwards,
Joseph M. Ely,
Sullivan Fay,
James K. Fellows,
Lyman Fisk,
Emery Fiske,
Aaron Foster,
Samuel Fowle,
James M. Freeman,
Charles A. French,
Rodney French,
Samuel French,
Richard Frothingham, Jr.,
Luther Gale,
Johnson Gardner,
Elbridge Gates,
Washington Gilbert,
Charles G. Giles,
Leonard Gooding,
Dalton Goulding,
John W. Graves,
Jabez Green,
William B. Greene,
Josiah W. Griswold,
Whiting Griswold,
Samuel P. Hadley,
Benjamin F. Hallett,

Messrs. Lyman W. Hapgood,
Seth Hapgood,
Phineas Harmon,
William Haskins,
Isaac Hayden,
Charles C. Hazewell,
Ezra Heath, 2d,
James Hewes,
William H. Hewes,
Henry Hobart,
Edwin Hobbs,
Nathaniel Holder,
George Hood,
Martin Howard,
Abraham H. Howland,
Henry K. Hoyt,
Charles E. Hunt,
Charles P. Huntington,
George H. Huntington,
Moses C. Hurlbut,
John Johnson,
Isaac Kendall,
Edward L. Keyes,
Joseph Kimball,
Joseph Kingman,
Hiram Knight,
Jefferson Knight,
Joseph Knight,
Charles L. Knowlton,
William H. Knowlton,
Albert Knox,
Gardner P. Ladd,
Wilber C. Langdon,
Alden Leland,
Otis Little,
Justin E. Loomis,
William P. Marble,
Laban Marcy,
Charles Mason,
Simeon Merritt,
James L. Monroe,
James M. Moore,
Elbridge G. Morton,
Marcus Morton, Jr.,
William S. Morton,
Hiram Nash,
William Nichols,
Andrew T. Nute,
Joseph E. Ober,
Benjamin S. Orne,
Charles Osgood,
Benjamin Paine,
Henry Paine,

Messrs. Jonathan Parris,
John Partridge,
Nathaniel Peabody,
Jeremiah Pease, Jr.,
John Penniman,
Jesse Perkins,
Silvanus B. Phinney,
James M. Pool,
Peter Powers,
John A. Putnam,
Silas Rawson,
Luther Richards,
Samuel H. Richardson,
Joseph M. Rockwood,
John Rogers,
James C. Royce,
Amasa Sanderson,
Chester Sanderson,
Chester Sikes,
Perez Simmons,
John W. Simonds,
Matthew Smith,
Melzar Sprague,
Samuel W. Spooner,
Eben H. Stacy,
Granville Stevens,
William Stevens,
Alfred L. Strong,
Charles Sumner,
Increase Sumner,

Messrs. Alanson Swain,
Arnold Taft,
Willard Thayer, 2d,
John W. Thomas,
Charles Thompson,
Abraham Tilton,
Horatio W. Tilton,
David Turner,
David P. Turner,
William Tyler,
Orison Underwood,
Joel Viles,
George A. Vinton,
Frederick T. Wallace,
Freeland Wallis,
Amasa Walker,
Andrew H. Ward,
Samuel Warner, Jr.,
Asa H. Waters,
Gershom B. Weston,
Daniel S. Whitney,
James S. Whitney,
J. B. Williams,
Henry Wilson,
Jonathan B. Winn,
Levi M. Winslow,
Nathaniel Wood,
Otis Wood,
Ezekiel Wright.

Those who voted in the negative are :—

Messrs. Benjamin P. Adams,
P. Emory Aldrich,
Robert Andrews,
William Aspinwall,
David C. Atwood,
Samuel Ayres,
Alpheus Bancroft,
Joseph Barrows,
Sidney Bartlett,
James M. Beebe,
Luther V. Bell,
William Bennett, Jr.,
Jacob Bigelow,
William S. Booth,
Ebenezer Bradbury,
William J. A. Bradford,
Osmyn Brewster,
Francis Brinley,
George N. Briggs,
Patrick Bryant,

Messrs. Rufus Bullock,
Rufus Choate,
Jacob Coggin,
Nathaniel Cogswell,
Lansing J. Cole,
Ithamar Conkey,
Charles E. Cook,
Henry F. Cooledge,
Simeon Crittenden,
George W. Crockett,
Leander Crosby,
John Davis,
Solomon Davis,
Henry L. Dawes,
Hiram S. Denison,
James C. Doane,
Moses Dorman,
Lilley Eaton,
Homer Ely,
William T. Eustis,

Messrs. A. G. Farwell,
Samuel P. Fowler,
Charles H. French,
Henry J. Gardner,
Wanton C. Gilbert,
Joel Giles,
Robert Gould,
Jason Goulding,
John C. Gray,
Artemas Hale,
Nathan Hale,
A. B. Hammond,
Elnathan P. Hathaway,
Stephen E. Hawkes,
George Hayward,
Charles Heard,
Henry Hersey,
Levi Heywood,
George S. Hillard,
William Hinsdale,
Aaron Hobart,
Foster Hooper,
Thomas Hopkinson,
Samuel Houghton,
William J. Hubbard,
William Hunt,
Samuel A. Hurlburt,
Benjamin D. Hyde,
Samuel Jackson,
William James,
John Jenkins,
Samuel H. Jenks,
Giles C. Kellogg,
George H. Kuhn,
John S. Ladd,
Job G. Lawton, Jr.,
Frederic W. Lincoln, Jr.,
Tristram Littlefield,
Isaac Livermore,
Samuel K. Lothrop,
Samuel P. Loud,
John A. Lowell,
Seth Miller, Jr.,
Samuel Mixter,
George Morey,
Marcus Morton,
Daniel Noyes,
Nathan Orcutt,
James W. Paige,

Messrs. Adolphus G. Parker,
Joel Parker,
George Peabody,
Daniel A. Perkins,
Jonathan C. Perkins,
Charles Phelps,
William C. Plunkett,
Jeremiah Pomroy,
F. O. Prince,
George Putnam,
Robert Rantoul,
James Read,
Sampson Reed,
David Rice,
Daniel Richardson,
Elkanah Ring, Jr.,
David S. Ross,
John Sargent,
William Schouler,
John Sherril,
John S. Sleeper,
John Souther,
Caleb Stetson,
Charles G. Stevens,
Joseph L. Stevens, Jr.,
J. Thomas Stevenson,
Gideon Stiles,
Thomas Talbot,
Joseph Thayer,
Edmund P. Tileston,
Charles R. Train,
John S. Tyler,
Charles W. Upham,
George B. Upton,
Samuel B. Walcott,
Bradford L. Wales,
Samuel Walker,
Cyrus Weeks,
Thomas Wetmore,
William F. Wheeler,
Benjamin White,
Daniel Wilbur,
Joseph Wilbur,
Joel Wilder,
Ezra Wilkinson,
Henry Williams,
Milo Wilson,
Charles C. Wood,
Josiah B. Woods.

The question being upon ordering the Resolve, as amended, to a second reading,

Mr. Earle, of Worcester, called for the yeas and nays; but the call was not sustained by one-fifth of the members voting.

The Resolve, as amended, was then ordered to a second reading, by a vote of one hundred and eighty-three in the affirmative, to ninety in the negative.

On motion of Mr. Griswold, member for Erving, the rule was suspended, and the Resolve considered, the question being on its final passage.

Mr. Gardner, of Boston, moved to amend, by substituting the words "eighteen hundred and fifty-three" for the words "eighteen hundred and fifty-five."

Mr. Plunkett, of Adams, called for the yeas and nays upon this motion; but the call was not sustained by one-fifth of the members voting.

The amendment was then rejected,

And the Resolve was finally passed, by a vote of one hundred and eighty-nine in the affirmative, to eighty-two in the negative, as follows:—

Resolved, That it is expedient so to amend the Constitution, as to provide—

That the legislature which shall be chosen at the general election in November, 1855, shall be required to divide the State into forty single districts for the choice of senators, such districts to be of contiguous territory, and as equal in the number of qualified voters contained in each district as may be; and also to divide the State into single or double districts, for the choice of not less than two hundred and forty nor more than three hundred and twenty representatives, each district to be of contiguous territory, and as equal in the number of qualified voters contained in each district, as may be; with proper provisions for the redistricting of the State as aforesaid, in the year 1866, and every tenth year thereafter, and with all other provisions necessary for carrying such system of districts into operation, and to submit the same to the people at the general election to be held in the year 1856, for their ratification; and if the same shall be ratified by the people it shall become a part of this Constitution, in place of the provision herein contained, for the apportioning of senators and representatives.

On motion of Mr. Wilson, of Natick, the Convention proceeded to the consideration of the Orders of the Day.

The first subject was the motion of Mr. White, of Quincy, that the vote by which the Convention finally passed the Resolve on the subject of appropriations for sectarian schools, be reconsidered.

Mr. White called for the yeas and nays upon this motion; but the call was not sustained by one-fifth of the members voting.

After debate, Mr. Perkins, of Malden, moved the Previous Question; which was ordered.

And the motion to reconsider was rejected, by a vote of eighty-seven in the affirmative, to one hundred and three in the negative.

On motion of Mr. Wilson, of Natick, the Orders of the Day were laid upon the table.

On motion of Mr. Dana, member for Manchester, the Resolves reported by the Committee on the Judiciary, were taken from the table and considered.

Mr. Wilson, of Natick, moved a suspension of the rule, requiring that propositions to amend the Constitution shall be first considered in Committee of the Whole.

On this question the vote was seventy-eight in the affirmative, and seven in the negative.

There appearing to be no quorum present, the question was again put, and the vote stood eighty-three in the affirmative, to ten in the negative.

There still appearing to be no quorum,

Mr. Lothrop, of Boston, moved an adjournment; but the motion was rejected, by a vote of twenty-three in the affirmative, to seventy-seven in the negative.

The motion to suspend the rule was agreed to, by a vote of ninety-five in the affirmative, to six in the negative.

Mr. Dana, member for Manchester, offered an amendment to the third Resolve; but afterwards withdrew it.

And the Resolves were then ordered to a second reading.

On motion of Mr. Train, of Framingham, the Orders of the Day were again taken up.

The first subject was the motion of Mr. Wheeler, of Lincoln, that the vote by which the Resolve on the subject of imprisonment for debt was finally passed, be reconsidered.

On motion of Mr. Schouler, of Boston, the motion to reconsider was

Laid upon the table.

The question was raised, whether the Resolve on the subject of imprisonment for debt had ever been considered in Committee of the Whole previous to being considered in Convention,

And it appearing that it had not been so considered,

Mr. Schouler, of Boston, moved a suspension of the rule,

And the motion was agreed to.

The first subject was the Resolves reported by the Committee on Reporting and Printing.

The Resolves were read a second time, and finally passed, as follow:—

Resolved, That the chairman of the Committee on Reporting and Printing be authorized, under the direction and sanction of said committee, to superintend the Reporting, Indexing, Printing and Publication of the Debates and Proceedings of the Convention, until the same are completed, and that he be paid therefor the sum of four dollars per day, and travel.

Resolved, That said committee be authorized to pay to the Secretary of the Commonwealth such expenses, not exceeding six hundred dollars, as may have been incurred for extra services performed by order of this Convention, and that the Order of May 18th, be so far altered as that said committee shall have the direction of all matters relative to the sale or distribution of the Reports and Proceedings of this Convention.

Resolved, That a copy of the Debates and Proceedings of this Convention, when completed, be furnished by the committee to each of the Reporters to the Convention.

The Report, inexpedient to act upon the subject of an Order of July 21st, relative to appending to the published debates, "Poole's Statistical View of the Members," and "the pay for attendance and travel of the members,"

Was accepted.

Mr. Bird, of Walpole, from the Committee on the Preservation of the Records, reported a Resolve, which was read, and then finally passed, as follows:—

Resolved, That the Journal of the Proceedings in Committee of the Whole, with an Index, be printed, under the supervision of the Committee on the Preservation of the Records, in the same volume with the Journal of the Convention, and on the same terms as provided for in the Resolves relating to the preservation of the Records, with the same provision for the payment of the expense thereof.

At half past seven o'clock, on motion of Mr. Wood, of Fitchburg,
The Convention adjourned.

SATURDAY, July 30, 1853.

Met according to adjournment. Prayer was offered by the Chaplain. The Journal of yesterday was read.

On motion of Mr. BATES, of Plymouth,

Ordered, That each member of the Convention who has ordered copies of the Debates and Proceedings of this Convention, be entitled to complete files of those Debates, the address and order of each member to be left with the Messenger of the Convention.

On motion of Mr. WALKER, of North Brookfield,

Ordered, That one hundred thousand copies of the new Constitution to be submitted to the people, be published in the same manner as the General Laws and Resolves; and one copy be distributed to each family in the Commonwealth.

Mr. WALKER, of North Brookfield, offered the following Order:—

Ordered, That the Committee on Reporting and Printing be instructed to employ some suitable person to receive and distribute all the documents ordered by this Convention, in the manner and form which has been heretofore directed.

On motion of Mr. BIRD, of Walpole, the Order was referred to a Select Committee.

The President appointed the committee, consisting of the following members, viz.: Messrs. Walker, of North Brookfield, Williams, of Taunton, Schouler, of Boston, White, of Quincy, Phinney, member for Chatham, Parsons, of Lawrence, and Bird, of Walpole.

Mr. EARLE, of Worcester, offered the following Order; which was referred to the same Committee:—

Ordered, That such members of the Convention as elected to take one or more copies of the Official Reports of the Debates and Proceedings of the Convention, instead of papers to which they were entitled under the Order of this body, but who are unable to procure the same in consequence of the deficiency in the number provided, be entitled to receive in lieu thereof the same number of copies of the octavo edition of the Reports, not to exceed three copies in the whole to any one member. And the Messenger is hereby directed to furnish said copies from those already ordered to be published by the Convention.

On motion of Mr. DANA, member for Manchester, the Convention proceeded to the consideration of the Orders of the Day.

The first subject was the Resolves from the Committee on the Judiciary.

On motion of Mr. Dana, the third Resolve was amended by inserting after the word "for" in the third line, the words "incapacity, misconduct, or maladministration in their offices;" and also by striking out all after the word "provided" in the same Resolve, and inserting the following: "That the cause be entered upon the records of the Council, and a copy thereof be furnished to the party to be removed, and a reasonable opportunity be given him for defence. And the Governor may at any time, if the public exigency demand it, either before or after such entry and notice, suspend any of said officers, and appoint substitutes who shall hold office until the final action upon the question of removal."

On motion of Mr. Morton, of Taunton, the Resolves were further amended by the addition of the following Resolve:—

Resolved, That the terms of all elective officers not otherwise provided for in this Constitution, shall commence on the first Wednesday in January next after their election.

The Resolves, as amended, were then finally passed, as follow:—

Resolved, That persons holding office by election or appointment under the present Constitution, shall continue to discharge the duties thereof until their term of office shall expire, or officers authorized to perform their duties, or any part thereof, shall be elected and qualified, pursuant to the provisions of this amended Constitution; when all powers not reserved to them by the provisions of this amended Constitution shall cease: *Provided, however,* that justices of the peace, justices of the peace and of the quorum, and commissioners of insolvency, shall be authorized to finish and complete all proceedings pending before them at the time, when their powers and duties shall cease, or be altered as aforesaid.

Resolved, That the legislature shall provide, from time to time, the mode in which commissions or certificates of election shall be issued to all officers elected pursuant to the Constitution, except in case where provision shall be made therein.

Resolved, That the Governor, by and with the consent of the Council, may at any time for incapacity, misconduct, or maladministration in their offices, cause shown, remove from office, clerks of courts, commissioners of insolvency, judges and registers of probate, district-attorneys, registers of deeds, county treasurers, county commissioners, sheriffs, trial justices, and justices of police courts: *Provided,* that the cause be entered upon the records of the Council, and a copy thereof be furnished to the party to be removed, and a reasonable opportunity be given him for defence. And the Governor may, at any time, if the public exigency demand it, either before or after such entry and notice, suspend any of said officers, and appoint substitutes, who shall hold office until the final action upon the question of removal.

Resolved, That whenever a vacancy shall occur in any elective office provided for in this Constitution, except that of governor, lieutenant-governor, councillor, senator, member of the House of Representatives, and town and city officers, the Governor for the time being, by and with the advice and consent of the Council, may appoint some suitable person to fill such vacancy until the next annual election, when the same shall be filled by a new election, in the manner to be provided by law: *Provided, however*, trial justices shall not be deemed to be town officers for this purpose.

Resolved, That all elections provided to be had under this amended Constitution shall, unless otherwise provided, be first held on the Tuesday next after the first Monday of November, A. D. 1854.

Resolved, That the terms of all elective officers, not otherwise provided for in this Constitution, shall commence on the first Wednesday in January next after their election.

Mr. DAVIS, of Plymouth, moved that the Committee on the Frame of Government be instructed to report upon the subject of an Order on the subject of the governor's appointing members of the legislature to offices created, or the emoluments of which have been increased during their term of office.

On motion of Mr. HUNTINGTON, of Northampton, the motion was Laid upon the table.

Mr. STETSON, of Braintree, moved that the Resolve on the subject of the law martial, be taken from the table; but the motion was rejected.

Mr. BOUTWELL, member for Berlin, from the Committee on Revision, submitted a Report, asking that the Committee be discharged from the further consideration of a Resolve referred to them, adopted by the Convention on the 30th of May, on the mode in which the governor shall be chosen by the legislature, in case of the non-election of that officer by the people.

The Report was accepted, and the committee discharged.

Mr. LORD, of Salem, moved a suspension of the rule, so as to allow a motion to reconsider the vote by which the Resolve referred to in the above Report was passed.

But the motion was ruled to be not in order.

Mr. Hillard, of Boston, being in the chair,

Mr. Briggs, of Pittsfield, offered the following Resolution, which was unanimously adopted:—

Resolved, That the thanks of this Convention be given to Hon. Nathaniel P. Banks, Jr., for the dignified, fair, and able manner in which he has presided over its deliberations.

On motion of Mr. Lord, of Salem, the Committee on the Pay Roll were instructed to make up the pay of Mr. Wilson, of Natick, at the rate of three dollars per day additional to his pay as a member, for the time during which he was President *pro tempore* of the Convention.

Mr. Wilson, of Natick, moved that the Convention adjourn until three o'clock; but afterwards withdrew the motion.

On motion of Mr. Butler, of Lowell,

Ordered, That when the Convention adjourn, it adjourn to meet on Monday, at ten o'clock.

Mr. Butler then moved an adjournment; but the motion was ed.

Mr. Livermore, of Cambridge, then moved a reconsideration of the vote by which the Convention agreed to the Order offered by Mr. Butler.

And the vote was reconsidered.

The question then recurred upon the Order of Mr. Butler, and it was rejected.

On motion of Mr. Livermore, of Cambridge,

The Convention adjourned.

AFTERNOON SESSION.

Met according to adjournment.

Mr. Wilson, of Natick, moved that the Convention adjourn until Monday, at ten o'clock;

But afterwards withdrew the motion,

And moved that when the Convention adjourn, it adjourn to meet on Monday, at ten o'clock.

The motion was agreed to.

Mr. Wilson then moved an adjournment,

And this motion was agreed to, by a vote of ninety-four in the affirmative, to sixty-seven in the negative.

And at ten minutes past three o'clock,

The Convention adjourned.

MONDAY, August 1, 1853.

Met according to adjournment. Prayer was offered by the Chaplain. The Journal of Saturday was read.

Mr. OLIVER, of Lawrence, by leave of the Convention, made a personal explanation in relation to his vote upon the Resolve providing that ballots shall be enclosed in sealed envelopes.

Mr. KEYES, member for Abington, presented the Protest of William C. Nell and others, against the action of the Convention on the subject of the Petition of the colored citizens, who asked that they should not be prohibited from serving in the militia;

And moved that the paper be entered upon the Journal of the Convention.

The motion was agreed to by a vote of ninety-seven in the affirmative, to sixty-six in the negative.

Mr. LIVERMORE, of Cambridge, from the Committee on the Pay Roll, submitted a Report and Order on that subject; which, on motion of Mr. GRISWOLD, member for Erving, were

Laid upon the table.

Mr. WALKER, of North Brookfield, from the Special Committee on the subject of the distribution of documents, &c., submitted a Report and Resolves, which were considered; and

Pending an amendment offered by Mr. Earle, of Worcester,

On motion of Mr. BUTLER, of Lowell, the subject was laid upon the table.

Mr. BOUTWELL, member for Berlin, from the committee appointed to reduce the amendments to form, submitted a Report, accompanied by Resolves, and a series of Constitutional Propositions, to be submitted to the people.

No objection being made, the question was stated upon the final passage of the Resolves.

And the Resolves were read.

On motion of Mr. BOUTWELL, member for Berlin, and no objection being made,

The first Proposition, comprising the proposed Preamble, Declaration of Rights and Frame of Government, was read and considered by chapters;

And that portion which contained the Preamble and Declaration of Rights, was first read.

Mr. SCHOULER, of Boston, moved to amend, by inserting at the close of article 27th, the words standing as the fifth Proposition, on page 39th, viz.: the words—

No person shall be imprisoned for any debt hereafter contracted, unless in cases of fraud.

The motion was rejected.

Mr. KELLOGG, of Hadley, moved to amend, by striking from the fourth article of the Declaration of Rights, the words "in Congress assembled."

The President decided the motion to be not in order, being an amendment of the substance of the Constitution and not merely of the form.

Mr. JENKS, of Boston, offered an amendment; which was also ruled to be not in order for the same reason.

Mr. PLUNKETT, of Adams, moved to amend, by inserting at the end of the thirteenth article of the Declaration of Rights, the words standing as the third Proposition, viz.:—

In all trials for criminal offences, the jury, after having received the instruction of the court, shall have the right, in their verdict of guilty or not guilty, to determine the law and the facts of the case; but it shall be the duty of the court to superintend the course of the trials, to decide upon the admission and rejection of evidence, and upon all questions of law raised during the trials, and upon all collateral and incidental proceedings; and also to allow bills of exceptions. And the court may grant a new trial in case of conviction.

Chapter first of the proposed Frame of Government, relating to the General Court, was then read.

Mr. UPTON, of Boston, moved to amend, by inserting in the chapter on the general court the words standing as the seventh and eighth Propositions, viz.:—

The legislature shall not create corporations by special act, when the object of the incorporation is attainable by general laws.

The legislature shall have no power to pass any act granting any special charter for banking purposes, or any special act to increase the capital stock of any chartered bank; but corporations may be formed for such purposes, or the capital stock of chartered banks may be increased, under general laws.

The legislature shall provide by law for the registry of all notes or bills authorized by general laws to be issued or put in circulation as money; and shall require ample security for the redemption of such notes in specie.

The motion was rejected.

Mr. LIVERMORE, of Cambridge, moved to amend, by striking out the words contained in the last sentence of the second article, viz.:—

But nothing herein contained shall prevent the general court from assembling at such other times as they shall judge necessary, or when called together by the governor.

The President ruled the motion to be not in order.

Mr. ALLEN, of Worcester, afterwards asked the general consent of the Convention that such an amendment might be introduced.

But objection was made.

Mr. LORD, of Salem, moved to amend, by striking out the word "present" from the thirteenth line of the fourth article; but the mo- was rejected, by a vote of sixty-three in the affirmative, to one hundred and sixty-two in the negative.

Mr. OLIVER, of Lawrence, moved to amend, by taking from its place in the first chapter, the words standing as article third, viz.: "The compensation of members of the general court shall be established by standing laws; but no act increasing the compensation shall apply to the general court which passes such act; and no compensation shall be allowed for attendance of members at any one session for a longer time than one hundred days;" and placing them among the Propositions to be submitted separately.

But the motion was rejected.

Mr. OLIVER also moved to amend, by taking from its place in the first chapter, the words standing as article thirteenth, viz.: "In all elections by the general court, or either branch thereof, a majority of votes shall be required, and the members shall vote *viva voce;*" and placing them among the Propositions to be submitted separately.

But the motion was rejected.

Chapter second, relating to the Senate, was then read.

No amendments being offered,

Chapter third, relating to the House of Representatives, was read.

Mr. EARLE, of Worcester, moved to amend, by striking from the second article, the words, "every town containing eight thousand inhabitants and less than twelve thousand, may elect three representatives. Every city or town containing twelve thousand inhabitants, may elect four representatives." And by striking out the word "twelve" in the fifteenth line, and inserting instead thereof, the word "four."

But the amendment was rejected.

Mr. MORTON, of Taunton, moved to amend the eighth article, by adding to it the words: "and he shall cease to represent the said town immediately on his ceasing to be qualified as aforesaid."

Mr. LORD, of Salem, raised the question whether this language was not a part of the present Constitution, and therefore, not having been struck out by the action of the Convention, it must remain a part of the revised instrument.

In reply, the President stated that the committee, by their Report, had given the opinion that these words are not a part of the present Constitution.

Mr. WILKINSON, of Dedham, moved a reconsideration of the vote by which Mr. Morton's amendment was rejected.

On this motion, Mr. GRAY, of Boston, called for the yeas and nays; which were ordered.

At two o'clock, the Convention adjourned.

AFTERNOON SESSION.

Met according to adjournment.

The Convention resumed the consideration of the Report of the Committee on Revision.

On motion of Mr. GRAY, of Boston, the vote by which the yeas and nays were ordered upon the question of reconsidering the vote by which Mr. Morton's amendment was rejected,

Was reconsidered; and Mr. GRAY then withdrew his demand for the yeas and nays.

The question being upon the motion to reconsider,

It was rejected, by a vote of thirty-nine in the affirmative, to one hundred and three in the negative.

Mr. LORD, of Salem, moved to amend, by providing that the second, third, fourth and fifth articles, viz.:—

ART. 2. And in order to provide for a representation of the citizens of this Commonwealth, founded upon the principle of equality, every corporate town, containing less than one thousand inhabitants, may elect one representative in the year when the valuation of estates shall be settled, and, in addition thereto, one representative five years in every ten years. Every town containing one thousand inhabitants and less than four thousand, may elect one representative. Every town containing four thousand inhabitants and less than eight thousand, may elect two representatives. Every town containing eight thousand inhabitants and less than twelve thousand, may elect three representatives. Every city or town containing twelve thousand inhabitants, may elect four representatives. Every city or town containing over twelve thousand inhabitants, may elect one additional representative for every four thousand inhabitants it shall contain, over twelve thousand. Any two towns, each containing less than one thousand inhabitants, may, by consent of a majority of the legal voters present at a legal meeting, in each of said towns respectively, called for that purpose, form themselves into a representative district, to continue for the term of not less than two years; and such district shall have all the rights, in regard to representation, which belong to a town having one thousand inhabitants. And this apportionment shall be based upon the census of the year one thousand eight hundred and fifty, until a new census shall be taken.

ART. 3. The Senate, at its first session after this Constitution shall have been adopted, and at its first session after the next State census shall have been taken, and at its first session next after each decennial State census thereafterwards, shall apportion the number of representatives to which each town and city shall be entitled, and shall cause the same to be seasonably published; and in all apportionments after the first, the numbers which shall entitle any town or city, to two, three, four, or more representatives, shall be increased or diminished in the same proportion as the population of the whole Commonwealth shall have increased or decreased since the last preceding apportionment.

ART. 4. No town hereafter incorporated, containing less than fifteen hundred inhabitants, shall be entitled to choose a representative.

ART. 5. Each city, in this Commonwealth, shall be divided, by such means as the legislature may provide, into districts of contiguous territory, as nearly equal in population as may be, for the election of representatives, which districts shall not be changed oftener than once in five years: *Provided, however*, that no one district shall be entitled to elect more than three representatives,

Be struck out of their place in the third chapter, and placed among the Propositions to be submitted separately.

And upon his motion, the yeas and nays were ordered upon this question.

And the roll being called, ninety-one members voted in the affirmative, and two hundred and five in the negative.

So the amendment was rejected.

Those who voted in the affirmative are:—

Messrs. Alfred A. Abbott,
Benjamin P. Adams,
P. Emory Aldrich,
William Aspinwall,
Samuel Ayres,
Messrs. Sidney Bartlett,
Erasmus D. Beach,
Jacob Bigelow,
Ebenezer Bradbury,
William J. A. Bradford,

Messrs. Milton P. Braman,
Rufus Bullock,
Rufus Choate,
Nathaniel Cogswell,
Charles E. Cook,
Henry F. Cooledge,
Benjamin F. Copeland,
John Davis,
Solomon Davis,
Hiram S. Denison,
Lilley Eaton,
Homer Ely,
A. G. Farwell,
Samuel P. Fowler,
Charles H. French,
Henry J. Gardner,
Robert Gould,
Dalton Goulding,
John C. Gray,
Artemas Hale,
A. B. Hammond,
George Haskell,
Elnathan P. Hathaway,
Stephen E. Hawkes,
George Hayward,
Charles Heard,
Henry Hersey,
James Hewes,
George S. Hillard,
Foster Hooper,
Thomas Hopkinson,
Samuel Houghton,
William J. Hubbard,
William Hunt,
Samuel A. Hurlburt,
Samuel Jackson,
John Jenkins,
Samuel H. Jenks,
Giles C. Kellogg,
George H. Kuhn,
Abishai Lincoln,

Messrs. Tristram Littlefield,
Isaac Livermore,
Otis P. Lord,
Samuel K. Lothrop,
Samuel P. Loud,
John A. Lowell,
Seth Miller, Jr.,
George Morey,
Joseph B. Morss,
Marcus Morton,
Daniel Noyes,
Henry K. Oliver,
James W. Paige,
John G. Park,
Adolphus G. Parker,
Joel Parker,
Daniel A. Perkins,
Jonathan C. Perkins,
William C. Plunkett,
Jeremiah Pomroy,
George Putnam,
Robert Rantoul,
James Read,
Sampson Reed,
John Sargent,
John Souther,
Caleb Stetson,
Charles G. Stevens,
J. Thomas Stevenson,
Thomas Talbot,
Charles Thompson,
John S. Tyler,
George B. Upton,
Samuel B. Walcott,
William F. Wheeler,
Joseph Wilbur,
Joel Wilder,
Ezra Wilkinson,
Henry Williams,
Milo Wilson.

Those who voted in the negative are :—

Messrs. Shubael P. Adams,
Charles Allen,
James B. Allen,
Joel C. Allen,
John B. Alley,
Josiah Allis,
D. W. Alvord,
George Austin,
Hillel Baker,

Messrs. George S. Ball,
Alpheus Bancroft,
Russel Bartlett,
Marcus Barrett,
Eliakim A. Bates,
John Beal,
William Bennett, Jr.,
Zephaniah Bennett,
Edward B. Bigelow,

Messrs. Francis W. Bird,
William S. Booth,
George S. Boutwell,
Sewell Boutwell,
Hiram N. Breed,
Asa Bronson,
Adolphus F. Brown,
Alpheus R. Brown,
Artemas Brown,
Hammond Brown,
Hiram C. Brown,
Frederick Brownell,
Joseph Brownell,
Patrick Bryant,
Asahel Buck,
Amos H. Bullen,
Anson Burlingame,
Benjamin F. Butler,
William Carruthers,
Isaac Case,
Amariah Chandler,
Chester W. Chapin,
Daniel E. Chapin,
Henry Chapin,
Josiah Childs,
Henry Clark,
Ransom Clark,
Salah Clark,
Alpheus B. Clarke,
Stillman Clarke,
Lansing J. Cole,
Sumner Cole,
George B. Crane,
Oliver S. Cressy,
Simeon Crittenden,
Joseph W. Cross,
Henry W. Cushman,
Thomas Cushman,
Simeon N. Cutler,
Richard H. Dana, Jr.,
Ebenezer Davis,
Isaac Davis,
Robert T. Davis,
Silas Dean,
Elijah S. Deming,
Augustus Denton,
Samuel Duncan,
Bradish Dunham,
John M. Durgin,
Philip Eames,
John M. Earle,
Peter Easland,
Calvin D. Eaton,

Messrs. Elisha Edwards,
Samuel Edwards,
Sullivan Fay,
James K. Fellows,
Lyman Fisk,
Emery Fiske,
Samuel Fowle,
James M. Freeman,
Charles A. French,
Rodney French,
Samuel French,
Johnson Gardner,
Elbridge Gates,
Wanton C. Gilbert,
Washington Gilbert,
Charles G. Giles,
Daniel W. Gooch,
Leonard Gooding,
John W. Graves,
Jabez Green,
William B. Greene,
Josiah W. Griswold,
Whiting Griswold,
Samuel P. Hadley,
Benjamin F. Hallett,
Seth Hapgood,
Phineas Harmon,
Isaac Hayden,
Charles C. Hazewell,
Ezra Heath, 2d,
William H. Hewes,
Levi Heywood,
Henry Hobart,
Edwin Hobbs,
Nathaniel Holder,
George Hood,
Martin Howard,
Abraham H. Howland,
Henry K. Hoyt,
Moses C. Hurlbut,
Abijah M. Ide, Jr.,
John Jacobs,
John Johnson,
Isaac Kendall,
Edward L. Keyes,
Joseph Kimball,
Joseph Kingman,
Hiram Knight,
Jefferson Knight,
Joseph Knight,
J. S. C. Knowlton,
William H. Knowlton,
Albert Knox,

Messrs. Gardner P. Ladd,
Wilber C. Langdon,
Luther Lawrence,
Alden Leland,
Otis Little,
William P. Marble,
Abijah P. Marvin,
Charles Mason,
Simeon Merritt,
James L. Monroe,
James M. Moore,
Elbridge G. Morton,
Marcus Morton, Jr.,
William S. Morton,
Hiram Nash,
Jonathan Nayson,
William Nichols,
Andrew T. Nute,
Benjamin S. Orne,
Charles Osgood,
E. Wing Packer,
Benjamin Paine,
Henry Paine,
Jonathan Parris,
John Partridge,
Nathaniel Peabody,
John Penniman,
Jesse Perkins,
Noah C. Perkins,
Silvanus B. Phinney,
Henry Pierce,
John A. Putnam,
Silas Rawson,
David Rice,
Luther Richards,
Daniel Richardson,
Nathan Richardson,
Samuel H. Richardson,
Elkanah Ring, Jr.,
John Rogers,
David S. Ross,

Messrs. James C. Royce,
Amasa Sanderson,
Chester Sanderson,
John Sherril,
Perez Simmons,
John W. Simonds,
Matthew Smith,
Melzar Sprague,
Samuel W. Spooner,
Eben H. Stacy,
Granville Stevens,
William Stevens,
Gideon Stiles,
Isaac C. Taber,
Arnold Taft,
Willard Thayer, 2d,
John W. Thomas,
Abraham Tilton,
William Tyler,
Orison Underwood,
Joel Viles,
George A. Vinton,
Frederick T. Wallace,
Freeland Wallis,
Amasa Walker,
Andrew H. Ward,
Gershom B. Weston,
Benjamin White,
George White,
Daniel S. Whitney,
James S. Whitney,
Daniel Wilbur,
J. B. Williams,
Henry Wilson,
Willard Wilson,
Levi M. Winslow,
Charles C. Wood,
Nathaniel Wood,
Otis Wood,
Ezekiel Wright.

Mr. GARDNER, of Boston, moved to amend the first article of the third chapter, by striking out the word "people" and inserting instead thereof the words, "several towns," and also by striking out the word "equality" and inserting instead thereof the words "prerogative rights."

But the amendment was ruled to be not in order, being an amendment of substance, and not merely of form.

The fourth chapter, relating to the Governor, was then read.

On motion of Mr. BOUTWELL, member for Berlin, the second article was amended by adding at the close, the words: "And no person shall be eligible to this office, unless, at the time of his election, he shall have been an inhabitant of this Commonwealth for seven years next preceding."

The fifth chapter, relating to the Lieutenant-Governor, was then read.

The sixth chapter, relating to the Council, was also read.

Mr. WILSON, of Natick, moved to amend the second article by inserting after the words "General Court" the words "holden next after the adoption of the Constitution, and next after each decennial census thereafter."

But the amendment was ruled to be not in order, being an amendment of substance, and not merely of form.

Mr. HALE, of Boston, moved to amend the word "Councillor," wherever it occurs in the chapter, by substituting for it the word, as spelled "Counsellor."

But the amendment was rejected.

The seventh chapter, relating to the Secretary, Treasurer, &c., was then read.

On motion of Mr. BOUTWELL, member for Berlin, the title of the chapter was amended by adding the words, "District-Attorney and County Officers."

The eighth chapter, relating to the Judiciary, was then read.

Mr. CHOATE, of Boston, moved to amend by striking from their place in the chapter, the words:

All judicial officers, duly appointed, commissioned and sworn, shall hold their offices for the term of ten years, excepting such concerning whom there is different provision made in this Constitution. And upon the expiration of such term they may be reappointed.

Also the words standing as the third article, viz.:—

The present justices of the Supreme Judicial Court shall hold their offices according to their respective commissions; and the present justices of the Court of Common Pleas shall hold their offices by the same tenure, while the law establishing the said Court of Common Pleas shall continue. All nominations of judicial officers, whose term of office is by this Constitution limited to ten years, shall be publicly announced at least seven days before their appointment: and no person who shall have been commissioned after the tenth day of August, in the year one thousand eight hundred and fifty-three, shall hold by any longer tenure of office than the term of ten years.

Also, to strike from the Declaration of Rights the words contained in the 30th article, viz.:—

It is essential to the preservation of the rights of every individual, his life, liberty, property and character, that there be an impartial interpretation of the laws, and administration of justice. It is the right of every citizen to be tried by judges as free, impartial and independent, as the lot of humanity will admit. It is therefore not only the best policy, but for the security of the rights of the people, and of every citizen, that the Judges of the Supreme Judicial Court should hold their offices by tenures established by the Constitution, and should have honorable salaries, which shall not be diminished during their continuance in office.

And to place these provisions of the Constitution among the Propositions to be separately submitted to the people.

But the amendment was rejected, by a vote of seventy-two in the affirmative, to one hundred and sixty-eight in the negative.

On motion of Mr. HALLETT, member for Wilbraham, the second paragraph of the second article was amended, by striking out the word "any" in the fourth line.

On motion of Mr. BOUTWELL, member for Berlin, the same paragraph was amended by the addition of the following words after the words "judicial officers," in the fifth line: "for whose appointment a different provision is not made in this Constitution, shall be nominated and appointed by the governor, by and with the advice and consent of the council, and they."

The ninth chapter, relating to the Qualifications of Voters, was then read.

Mr. PARKER, of Cambridge, moved an adjournment; but the motion was rejected, by a vote of fifty-one in the affirmative, to one hundred and thirty-two in the negative.

On motion of Mr. BOUTWELL, member for Berlin, article first was amended, by inserting the word "State" after the word "any," in the sixth line.

Mr. HALLETT, member for Wilbraham, moved further to amend, by adding the words "or other" after the word "State."

But the amendment was ruled to be not in order, being an amendment of substance, and not merely of form.

Mr. HALLETT then asked unanimous consent to enable him to introduce the amendment; but objection was made by Mr. Aspinwall, of Brookline, and the amendment was not received.

The tenth chapter, relating to Oaths and Subscriptions, was then read.

The eleventh chapter, relating to the Militia, was also read.

At five minutes before seven o'clock, on motion of Mr. BUTLER, of Lowell,

The Convention took a recess for one hour.

EVENING SESSION.

At eight o'clock, the Convention reassembled,

And the consideration of the Report of the Committee on Revision, was resumed.

No amendment being proposed to the chapter relating to the Militia,

The twelfth chapter, relating to the University at Cambridge, &c., was read,

And also the thirteenth chapter, containing miscellaneous provisions.

On motion of Mr. BOUTWELL, member for Berlin, the first article of thirteenth chapter, was amended, by substituting the words "one thousand eight hundred and fifty-five," for the words "eighteen hundred and fifty-five,"

And the sixth article was amended, by striking out the word "amended," in the second line.

On motion of Mr. CHAPIN, of Worcester, the fourth article was amended, by inserting the words "and clerks" after the word "justices," in the seventh line.

On motion of Mr. HILLARD, of Boston, the fifth article was amended, by the insertion of the word "that," before the words "Trial Justices," in the ninth line.

On motion of Mr. MASON, of Fitchburg, the sixth article was amended, by inserting the words "in the year," after the word "November."

The fourteenth chapter, relating to Revision and Amendments of the Constitution, was then read.

On motion of Mr. WILSON, of Natick, the fourth article was amended, by substituting the word "into" for the word "in," in the eighth line, and also, by inserting the word "the" before the word "Commonwealth," in the thirteenth line.

Mr. MORTON, of Taunton, moved to amend, by striking the words standing as the fourth article, from their place in the chapter, and placing them among the Propositions to be separately submitted.

Mr. WILLIAMS, of Taunton, called for the yeas and nays upon this question; but the call was not sustained by one-fifth of the members voting.

Mr. Morton's amendment was then rejected, by a vote of fifty-three in the affirmative, to one hundred and sixty-nine in the negative.

The question being upon the passage of the first Proposition, containing the Preamble, the Declaration of Rights, and the Frame of Government,

Mr. WILKINSON, of Dedham, moved to recommit the Resolves, with instructions to report the several amendments agreed upon by the Convention, in such form and with such references to the parts of the existing Constitution proposed to be altered or annulled, that each of said amendments may be separately submitted to the people for their adoption or rejection.

On this motion, Mr. WILKINSON called for the yeas and nays, and they were ordered by a vote of fifty-one in the affirmative, to one hundred and eighty-one in the negative.

And the roll being called, seventy-three members voted in the affirmative, and one hundred and seventy in the negative.

So the motion was rejected.

Those who voted in the affirmative are:—

Messrs. Benjamin P. Adams,
P. Emory Aldrich,
William Aspinwall,
Joseph Barrows,
Erasmus D. Beach,
James M. Beebe,
Jacob Bigelow,
Ebenezer Bradbury,
Osmyn Brewster,
Rufus Bullock,
Timothy W. Carter,
Rufus Choate,
Nathaniel Cogswell,
Lansing J. Cole,
Charles E. Cook,
George W. Crockett,
Leander Crosby,
Solomon Davis,
Hiram S. Denison,
Homer Ely,
William T. Eustis,
A. G. Farwell,
Wanton C. Gilbert,
Joel Giles,
Nathan Hale,
A. B. Hammond,
Elnathan P. Hathaway,
Stephen E. Hawkes,
George Hayward,
George S. Hillard,
William Hinsdale,
Samuel Houghton,

Messrs. William Hunt,
John Jenkins,
Samuel H. Jenks,
Giles C. Kellogg,
Joseph Knight,
John S. Ladd,
Job G. Lawton, Jr.,
Frederic W. Lincoln, Jr.,
Isaac Livermore,
Samuel K. Lothrop,
Theophilus R. Marvin,
Seth Miller, Jr.,
George Morey,
Marcus Morton,
Henry K. Oliver,
Nathan Orcutt,
James W. Paige,
Adolphus G. Parker
Samuel D. Parker,
Daniel A. Perkins,
William C. Plunkett,
Jeremiah Pomroy,
Jonathan Preston,
James Read,
Sampson Reed,
John Sargent,
Charles Sherman,
John S. Sleeper,
John Souther,
Caleb Stetson,
Charles G. Stevens,
Charles Thompson,

Messrs. Edmund P. Tileston,
Cyrus Weeks,
Thomas Wetmore,
Benjamin White,
Joel Wilder,
Messrs. Ezra Wilkinson,
Henry Williams,
Milo Wilson,
Nathaniel Wood.

Those who voted in the negative are:—

Messrs. Shubael P. Adams,
James B. Allen,
Joel C. Allen,
John B. Alley,
Josiah Allis,
D. W. Alvord,
Hillel Baker,
George S. Ball,
Alpheus Bancroft,
Marcus Barrett,
Moses Bates, Jr.,
John Beal,
Francis W. Bird,
Henry W. Bishop,
William S. Booth,
George S. Boutwell,
Sewell Boutwell,
Hiram N. Breed,
Asa Bronson,
Adolphus F. Brown,
Hammond Brown,
Hiram C. Brown,
Frederick Brownell,
Joseph Brownell,
Patrick Bryant,
Asahel Buck,
Amos H. Bullen,
Anson Burlingame,
Benjamin F. Butler,
William Carruthers,
Isaac Case,
Amariah Chandler,
Chester W. Chapin,
Daniel E. Chapin,
Henry Chapin,
Josiah Childs,
Salah Clark,
Alpheus B. Clarke,
Sumner Cole,
George B. Crane,
Simeon Crittenden,
Joseph W. Cross,
Henry W. Cushman,
Thomas Cushman,
Richard H. Dana, Jr.,
Messrs. Isaac Davis,
Robert T. Davis,
Silas Dean,
Elijah S. Deming,
Augustus Denton,
Bradish Dunham,
John M. Durgin,
Philip Eames,
John M. Earle,
Peter Easland,
Calvin D. Eaton,
Elisha Edwards,
Sullivan Fay,
James K. Fellows,
Lyman Fisk,
Aaron Foster,
Abram Foster,
Samuel Fowle,
James M. Freeman,
Charles A. French,
Rodney French,
Samuel French,
Richard Frothingham, Jr.,
Johnson Gardner,
Elbridge Gates,
Washington Gilbert,
Charles G. Giles,
Leonard Gooding,
John W. Graves,
Jabez Green,
William B. Greene,
Josiah W. Griswold,
Whiting Griswold,
Samuel P. Hadley,
Charles B. Hall,
Benjamin F. Hallett,
Seth Hapgood,
Phineas Harmon,
William Haskins,
Ezra Heath, 2d,
William H. Hewes,
Henry Hobart,
George Hood,
Martin Howard,
Henry K. Hoyt,

Messrs. Moses C. Hurlbut,
Abijah M. Ide, Jr.,
John Jacobs,
Isaac Kendall,
Hiram Knight,
J. S. C. Knowlton,
William H. Knowlton,
Albert Knox,
Gardner P. Ladd,
Wilber C. Langdon,
Alden Leland,
Otis Little,
William P. Marble,
Charles Mason,
Simeon Merritt,
James L. Monroe,
Elbridge G. Morton,
Marcus Morton, Jr.,
William S. Morton,
Hiram Nash,
Jonathan Nayson,
Andrew T. Nute,
Charles Osgood,
E. Wing Packer,
Benjamin Paine,
Henry Paine,
Jonathan Parris,
John Partridge,
John Penniman,
Noah C. Perkins,
Sylvanus B. Phinney,
Henry Pierce,
James M. Pool,
Peter Powers,
John A. Putnam,
Robert Rantoul,
Silas Rawson,
David Rice,
Luther Richards,
Daniel Richardson,

Messrs. Nathan Richardson,
Samuel H. Richardson,
Elkanah Ring, Jr.,
John Rogers,
David S. Ross,
James C. Royce,
Amasa Sanderson,
Chester Sanderson,
William Schouler,
John Sherril,
Chester Sikes,
Perez Simmons,
John W. Simonds,
Matthew Smith,
Melzar Sprague,
Samuel W. Spooner,
Granville Stevens,
Gideon Stiles,
Alfred L. Strong,
Arnold Taft,
Abraham Tilton,
William Tyler,
Orison Underwood,
George A. Vinton,
Frederick T. Wallace,
Freeland Wallis,
Amasa Walker,
Asa H. Waters,
Gershom B. Weston,
Daniel S. Whitney,
James S. Whitney,
Daniel Wilbur,
J. B. Williams,
Henry Wilson,
Willard Wilson,
Jonathan B. Winn,
Levi M. Winslow,
Charles C. Wood,
Otis Wood,
Ezekiel Wright.

Mr. OLIVER, of Lawrence, moved to strike from its place, the chapter relating to the Militia, and place it among the Propositions to be separately submitted.

But the motion was rejected.

On motion of Mr. DANA, member for Manchester, the first Resolve was amended, by striking out the words "Auditor and" in the eighth line, and inserting after the words "Attorney-General," in the ninth line, the words "Auditor, District-Attorney, and County Officers."

On motion of Mr. MASON, of Fitchburg, article first of chapter second, relating to the Senate, was amended by striking out the words "to be."

On motion of Mr. BOUTWELL, member for Berlin, the yeas and nays were ordered upon the passage of the first Proposition of the first Resolve.

And the roll being called, one hundred and seventy-four members voted in the affirmative, and fifty-eight in the negative.

So the Proposition was agreed to.

Those who voted in the affirmative are:—

Messrs. Shubael P. Adams,
James B. Allen,
Joel C. Allen,
John B. Alley,
Josiah Allis,
D. W. Alvord,
George Austin,
Hillel Baker,
George S. Ball,
Alpheus Bancroft,
Marcus Barrett,
Moses Bates, Jr.,
Erasmus D. Beach,
John Beal,
Francis W. Bird,
Henry W. Bishop,
William S. Booth,
George S. Boutwell,
Sewell Boutwell,
Hiram N. Breed,
Asa Bronson,
Adolphus F. Brown,
Hammond Brown,
Hiram C. Brown,
Frederick Brownell,
Joseph Brownell,
Patrick Bryant,
Amos H. Bullen,
Anson Burlingame,
Benjamin F. Butler,
William Carruthers,
Isaac Case,
Amariah Chandler,
Chester W. Chapin,
Daniel E. Chapin,
Henry Chapin,
Josiah Childs,
Ransom Clark,
Salah Clark,
Alpheus B. Clarke,
Lansing J. Cole,

Messrs. Sumner Cole,
George B. Crane,
Simeon Crittenden,
Joseph W. Cross,
Henry W. Cushman,
Richard H. Dana, Jr.,
Isaac Davis,
Robert T. Davis,
Silas Dean,
Augustus Denton,
Bradish Dunham,
John M. Durgin,
Philip Eames,
John M. Earle,
Peter Easland,
Calvin D. Eaton,
Elisha Edwards,
Sullivan Fay,
James K. Fellows,
Lyman Fisk,
Aaron Foster,
Abram Foster,
Samuel Fowle,
Charles A. French,
Rodney French,
Samuel French,
Richard Frothingham, Jr.,
Johnson Gardner,
Elbridge Gates,
Washington Gilbert,
Charles G. Giles,
Leonard Gooding,
John W. Graves,
Jabez Green,
William B. Greene,
Josiah W. Griswold,
Whiting Griswold,
Samuel P. Hadley,
Charles B. Hall,
Benjamin F. Hallett,
Seth Hapgood,

Messrs. Phineas Harmon,
Elnathan P. Hathaway,
Stephen E. Hawkes,
Isaac Hayden,
Ezra Heath, 2d,
William H. Hewes,
Henry Hobart,
George Hood,
Martin Howard,
Henry K. Hoyt,
Moses C. Hurlbut,
Benjamin D. Hyde,
Abijah M. Ide, Jr.,
John Jacobs,
Isaac Kendall,
Hiram Knight,
Joseph Knight,
J. S. C. Knowlton,
William H. Knowlton,
Albert Knox,
Gardner P. Ladd,
Wilber C. Langdon,
Job G. Lawton, Jr.,
Alden Leland,
Otis Little,
William P. Marble,
Charles Mason,
Simeon Merritt,
James L. Monroe,
Elbridge G. Morton,
Marcus Morton, Jr.,
William S. Morton,
Hiram Nash,
Jonathan Nayson,
Andrew T. Nute,
Charles Osgood,
E. Wing Packer,
Benjamin Paine,
Henry Paine,
Jonathan Parris,
John Partridge,
John Penniman,
Daniel A. Perkins,
Noah C. Perkins,
Sylvanus B. Phinney,
Henry Pierce,

Messrs. James M. Pool,
Peter Powers,
John A. Putnam,
Robert Rantoul,
David Rice,
Luther Richards,
Daniel Richardson,
Nathan Richardson,
Samuel H. Richardson,
Elkanah Ring, Jr.,
John Rogers,
David S. Ross,
James C. Royce,
Amasa Sanderson,
John Sherril,
Perez Simmons,
John W. Simonds,
Matthew Smith,
Melzar Sprague,
Samuel W. Spooner,
Granville Stevens,
Gideon Stiles,
Alfred L. Strong,
Arnold Taft,
Abraham Tilton,
William Tyler,
Orison Underwood,
George A. Vinton,
Frederick T. Wallace,
Freeland Wallis,
Amasa Walker,
Asa H. Waters,
Gershom B. Weston,
George White,
Daniel S. Whitney,
James S. Whitney,
Daniel Wilbur,
J. B. Williams,
Henry Wilson,
Willard Wilson,
Jonathan B. Winn,
Levi M. Winslow,
Charles C. Wood,
Nathaniel Wood,
Otis Wood,
Ezekiel Wright.

Those who voted in the negative are :—

Messrs. Benjamin P. Adams,
P. Emory Aldrich,
William Aspinwall,
Joseph Barrows,

Messrs. Russel Bartlett,
James M. Beebe,
Jacob Bigelow,
Ebenezer Bradbury,

Messrs. Osmyn Brewster,
Timothy W. Carter,
Rufus Choate,
George W. Crockett,
Leander Crosby,
Solomon Davis,
Hiram S. Denison,
Homer Ely,
A. G. Farwell,
Wanton C. Gilbert,
Joel Giles,
Nathan Hale,
A. B. Hammond,
George Hayward,
George S. Hillard,
William Hinsdale,
Samuel Houghton,
William Hunt,
Samuel A. Hurlburt,
John Jenkins,
Samuel H. Jenks,
Giles C. Kellogg,
John S. Ladd,
Frederic W. Lincoln, Jr.,
Isaac Livermore,

Messrs. Samuel K. Lothrop,
Theophilus R. Marvin,
Seth Miller, Jr.,
George Morey,
Marcus Morton,
Henry K. Oliver,
Nathan Orcutt,
James W. Paige,
Adolphus G. Parker,
William C. Plunkett,
Jonathan Preston,
James Read,
Sampson Reed,
John Sargent,
Chester Sikes,
John S. Sleeper,
John Souther,
Charles G. Stevens,
Edmund P. Tileston,
Cyrus Weeks,
Benjamin White,
Joel Wilder,
Ezra Wilkinson,
Henry Williams,
Milo Wilson.

The second Proposition, viz.: that relating to the Writ of Habeas Corpus, was agreed to, by a vote of one hundred and sixty-nine in the affirmative, to seventeen in the negative.

The third Proposition, viz.: that relating to the Rights of Juries, was agreed to, by a vote of one hundred and forty-nine in the affirmative, to fifty-six in the negative.

The fourth Proposition, viz.: that relating to Claims against the Commonwealth, was agreed to, by a vote of one hundred and eighty-three in the affirmative, to six in the negative.

The fifth Proposition, viz.: that relating to Imprisonment for Debt, was agreed to by a vote of one hundred and fifty-three in the affirmative, to sixteen in the negative.

The sixth Proposition of the first Resolve was amended, on motion of Mr. Dana, member for Manchester, by substituting the words "then Proposition numbered six" for the word "it," in the last line but one.

The sixth Proposition, viz.: that relating to Sectarian Schools, was agreed to, by a vote of one hundred and fifty-nine in the affirmative, to twenty-four in the negative.

The seventh Proposition, viz.: that relating to General Laws for Corporations, was agreed to, by a vote of one hundred and sixty-nine in the affirmative, to sixteen in the negative.

The eighth Proposition, viz.: that relating to Banking, was agreed to, by a vote of one hundred and fifty-three in the affirmative, to thirty-six in the negative.

The first Resolve, and the accompanying Propositions, having been passed,

On motion of Mr. BOUTWELL, member for Berlin, the second Resolve was amended, by substituting the words "sealed envelopes" for the words "a sealed envelope" in the seventh line.

The Resolve was then agreed to.

The third Resolve was then considered, and the blank in it was, on motion of Mr. DANA, member for Manchester, filled with the words "the President of the Convention, and twenty other members, to be by him designated."

The Resolve was then agreed to.

The fourth Resolve was then considered.

On motion of Mr. FROTHINGHAM, of Charlestown, the Resolve was amended, by striking out all after the word "whole," in the third line, and inserting instead thereof, the following:—

And every voter shall vote on each Proposition by its appropriate number, indicating upon his ballot the subject of the Proposition, and expressing in writing or printing opposite to each Proposition the word YES or NO; but the Propositions shall all be written or printed on one ballot, in substance as follows:—

CONSTITUTIONAL PROPOSITIONS.

Shall Proposition *Number One*, containing the Preamble, Declaration of Rights and Frame of Government, stand as the Constitution of the Commonwealth of Massachusetts? . . . Yes or No.

Shall Proposition *Number Two*, respecting the Habeas Corpus, stand as part of the Constitution? . . . . Yes or No.

Shall Proposition *Number Three*, respecting the Rights of Juries, stand as part of the Constitution? . . . Yes or No.

Shall proposition *Number Four*, respecting Claims against the Commonwealth, stand as part of the Constitution? . Yes or No.

Shall Proposition *Number Five*, respecting Imprisonment for Debt, stand as part of the Constitution? . . . Yes or No.

Shall Proposition *Number Six*, respecting Sectarian Schools, stand as part of the Constitution? . . . . . Yes or No.

Shall Proposition *Number Seven*, respecting the Creation of Corporations, stand as part of the Constitution? . . Yes or No.

Shall Proposition *Number Eight*, respecting the Formation of Banks, and requiring Security for Bank Bills, stand as part of the Constitution? . . . . Yes or No.

The Resolve was then agreed to.

The fifth Resolve was then considered, and was amended, by inserting the words, "The President and" before the word "Secretaries," in the third line.

The Resolve was then agreed to.

And so the Resolves and the accompanying Propositions were finally adopted, in the following form:—

Commonwealth of Massachusetts.

IN THE YEAR ONE THOUSAND EIGHT HUNDRED AND FIFTY-THREE.

RESOLVES.

In the Convention of the Delegates of the People assembled in Boston, on the first Wednesday of May, in the year one thousand eight hundred and fifty-three, for the purpose of Revising and Amending the Constitution of this Commonwealth.

Resolved, That the Revised Constitution, proposed by said Convention, be submitted to the people of the Commonwealth for their ratification and adoption, in the manner following, viz.:—

I. The Preamble; A Declaration of the Rights of the Inhabitants of the Commonwealth of Massachusetts; The Frame of Government, with its Preamble and Chapters numbered One, Two, Three, Four, Five, Six, Seven, Eight, Nine, Ten, Eleven, Twelve, Thirteen, and Fourteen, entitled, respectively, General Court,—Senate,—House of Representatives,— Governor,— Lieutenant-Governor,— Council,— Secretary, Treasurer, Attorney-General, Auditor, District-Attorney, and County Officers,—Judiciary Power,—Qualifications of Voters and Elections,—Oaths and Subscriptions,—Militia,—The University at Cambridge, The School Fund and the Encouragement of Literature,— Miscellaneous Provisions,—Revisions and Amendments of the Constitution—as a distinct Proposition, numbered "One."

If this Proposition, so submitted, shall be ratified and adopted by a majority of the legal voters of the Commonwealth, present and voting thereon, at meetings duly called, then the same shall be the Constitution of the Commonwealth of Massachusetts.

II. The provision respecting the granting of the Writ of Habeas Corpus, as a Proposition, numbered "Two."

If this Proposition be ratified and adopted, it shall be an addition to the provision respecting the Habeas Corpus.

III. The provision respecting the Rights of Juries in criminal trials as a Proposition, numbered "Three."

If this Proposition be ratified and adopted, it shall be an addition to the article in the Declaration of Rights, respecting the rights of persons charged with crimes.

IV. The provision respecting Claims against the Commonwealth, as a Proposition, numbered "Four."

If this Proposition be ratified and adopted, it shall be an addition to Article XI., of the Declaration of Rights.

V. The provision respecting Imprisonment for Debt, as a Proposition, "numbered Five."

If this Proposition be adopted, it shall be an addition to the Article in the Declaration of Rights respecting excessive bail and fines.

VI. The provision respecting Sectarian Schools, as a Proposition, numbered "Six."

If this Proposition be ratified and adopted, it shall be an addition to Article IV. of Chapter XII., entitled, "The University at Cambridge, The School Fund, and the Encouragement of Literature." If Proposition numbered "One" shall not be adopted, then Proposition numbered "Six" shall be added as an amendment to the Constitution.

VII. The provision respecting Corporations, as a Proposition, numbered "Seven."

VIII. The Proposition respecting Banks and Banking, as a Proposition, numbered "Eight."

If the Propositions numbered "Seven" and "Eight" be ratified and confirmed, they shall be added as separate articles, or if either of them be ratified and confirmed, as an article in Chapter XIII., entitled, "Miscellaneous Provisions."

If Proposition numbered "One" be not ratified and confirmed, they shall be added as amendments to the Constitution.

Resolved, That at the meetings for the election of Governor, Senators and Representatives to the General Court, to be holden on the second Monday in November, in the year one thousand eight hundred and fifty-three, the qualified voters of the several towns and cities shall vote by ballot upon each of the Propositions aforesaid, for or against the same, which ballots shall be enclosed within sealed envelopes, according to the provisions of an Act of this Commonwealth, passed on the twenty-second day of May, in the year eighteen hundred and fifty-one, and an Act passed the twentieth day of May, in the year eighteen hundred and fifty-two, and no ballots not so enclosed shall be received. And said votes shall be received, sorted, counted, declared, and recorded, in open meeting, in the same manner as is by law provided in reference to votes for governor, and a true copy of the record of said votes, attested by the selectmen and town clerk of each of the several towns, and the mayor and aldermen, and city clerk of each of the several cities, shall be sealed up by said selectmen and mayor and aldermen, and directed to the Secretary of the Commonwealth, with a superscription expressing the purport of the contents thereof, and delivered to the sheriff of the county within fifteen days after said meetings, to be by him transmitted to the secretary's office, on or before the third Monday of December next; or, the said selectmen and mayor and aldermen shall themselves transmit the same to the secretary's office, on or before the day last aforesaid.

Resolved, That the Secretary shall deliver said copies, so transmitted to him, to a Committee of this Convention, consisting of the President of the Convention, and twenty other members, to be by him designated, who shall assemble at the State House, on the third Monday of December next, and open the same, and examine and count the votes so returned; and if it shall appear that either of said Propositions has been adopted by a majority of votes, then the Proposition so adopted shall become and be either the whole or a portion of the Constitution of this Commonwealth, as hereinbefore provided, and the said Committee shall promulgate the results of said votes upon each of said Propositions, by causing the same to be published in those newspapers in which the laws are now published; and shall also notify the Governor and Legislature, as soon as may be, of the said results; and the Governor shall forthwith make public proclamation of the fact of the adoption of either or all of said Propositions, as the whole or as parts of the Constitution of this Commonwealth.

Resolved, That each of said Propositions shall be considered as a whole by itself, to be adopted in the whole, or rejected in the whole. And every voter shall vote on each Proposition by its appropriate number, indicating upon his ballot the subject of the Proposition, and expressing in writing or printing opposite to each Proposition the word YES or NO; but the Propositions shall be written or printed on one ballot, in substance as follows:

CONSTITUTIONAL PROPOSITIONS.

Shall Proposition *Number One*, containing the Preamble, Declaration of Rights and Frame of Government, stand as the Constitution of the Commonwealth of Massachusetts? . . Yes or No.

Shall proposition *Number Two*, respecting the Habeas Corpus, stand as part of the Constitution? . . . . . . Yes or No.

Shall Proposition *Number Three*, respecting the Rights of Juries, stand as part of the Constitution? . . . . . . Yes or No.

Shall Proposition *Number Four*, respecting Claims against the Commonwealth, stand as part of the Constitution? . Yes or No.

Shall Proposition *Number Five*, respecting Imprisonment for Debt, stand as part of the Constitution? . . . Yes or No.

Shall Proposition *Number Six*, respecting Sectarian Schools, stand as part of the Constitution? . . . . . . Yes or No.

Shall Proposition *Number Seven*, respecting the Creation of Corporations, stand as part of the Constitution? . . Yes or No.

Shall Proposition *Number Eight*, respecting the Formation of Banks, and requiring Security for Bank Bills, stand as part of the Constitution? . . . . Yes or No.

Resolved, That a printed copy of these Resolutions, with the several Constitutional Propositions annexed, shall be attested by the President and Secretaries of the Convention, and transmitted by them, as soon as may be, to the selectmen of each town, and the mayor and aldermen of each city, in the Commonwealth, whose duty it shall be to insert a proper article in reference to the voting upon said Propositions, in the warrant calling the meetings aforesaid, on the second Monday of November next.

PROPOSITION NUMBER ONE.

CONSTITUTION, OR FORM OF GOVERNMENT OF THE COMMONWEALTH OF MASSACHUSETTS.

Preamble.

The end of the institution, maintenance, and administration of government, is to secure the existence of the body politic; to protect it; and to furnish the individuals who compose it, with the power of enjoying, in safety and tranquillity, their natural rights and the blessings of life; and whenever these great objects are not obtained, the people have a right to alter the government, and to take measures necessary for their safety, prosperity, and happiness.

The body politic is formed by a voluntary association of individuals; it is a social compact, by which the whole people covenants with each citizen, and each citizen with the whole people, that all shall be governed by certain laws for the common good. It is the duty of the people, therefore, in framing a constitution of government, to provide for an equitable mode of making laws, as well as for an impartial interpretation, and a faithful execution of them; that every man may, at all times, find his security in them.

We, therefore, the People of Massachusetts, acknowledging with grateful hearts, the great Legislator of the universe, in affording us, in the course of his providence, an opportunity, deliberately and peaceably, without fraud, violence, or surprise, of entering into an original, explicit, and solemn compact with each other; and of forming a new constitution of civil government for ourselves and posterity; and devoutly imploring his direction in so interesting a design, do agree upon, ordain, and establish the following, *Declaration of Rights, and Frame of Government*, as the Constitution of the Commonwealth of Massachusetts.

A Declaration

Of the Rights of the Inhabitants of the Commonwealth of Massachusetts.

Article 1. All men are born free and equal, and have certain natural, essential, and unalienable rights; among which may be reckoned the right of enjoying and defending their lives and liberties; that of acquiring, possessing and protecting property; in fine, that of seeking and obtaining their safety and happiness.

Art. 2. It is the right as well as the duty of all men in society, publicly, and at stated seasons, to worship the Supreme Being, the great Creator and Preserver of the Universe. And no subject shall be hurt, molested, or restrained, in his person, liberty, or estate, for worshipping God in the manner and season most agreeable to the dictates of his own conscience; or for his religious profession or sentiments; provided he doth not disturb the public peace, or obstruct others in their religious worship.

Art. 3. As the public worship of God, and instructions in piety, religion, and morality, promote the happiness and prosperity of a people, and the security of a republican government; therefore, the several religious societies of this Commonwealth, whether corporate or unincorporate, at any meeting legally warned and holden for that purpose, shall ever have the right to elect their pastors or religious teachers, to contract with them for their support, to raise money for erecting and repairing houses for public worship, for the maintenance of religious instruction, and for the payment of necessary expenses: And all persons belonging to any religious society shall be taken and held to be members, until they shall file with the clerk of such society a written notice declaring the dissolution of their membership, and thenceforth shall not be liable for any grant or contract which may be thereafter made or entered into by such society: And all religious sects and denominations, demeaning themselves peaceably, and as good citizens of the Commonwealth, shall be equally under the protection of the law; and no subordination of any one sect or denomination to another shall ever be established by law.

Art. 4. The people of this Commonwealth have the sole and exclusive right of governing themselves, as a free, sovereign and independent State; and do, and forever hereafter shall, exercise and enjoy every power, jurisdiction, and right, which is not, or may not hereafter, be by them expressly delegated to the United States of America, in Congress assembled.

Art. 5. All power residing originally in the people, and being derived from them, the several magistrates and officers of government vested with authority, whether legislative, executive, or judicial, are their substitutes and agents, and are at all times accountable to them.

Art. 6. No man, nor corporation, or association of men, have any other title to obtain advantages, or particular and exclusive privileges, distinct from those of the community, than what arises from the consideration of services rendered to the public; and this title being in nature neither hereditary, nor transmissible to children, or descendants, or relations by blood, the idea of a man being born a magistrate, lawgiver, or judge, is absurd and unnatural.

Art. 7. Government is instituted for the common good; for the protection, safety, prosperity, and happiness of the people; and not for the profit, honor, or private interest of any one man, family, or class of men: Therefore the people alone have an incontestible, unalienable, and indefeasible right to institute government; and to reform, alter, or totally change the same, when their protection, safety, prosperity, and happiness require it.

Art. 8. In order to prevent those who are vested with authority, from becoming oppressors, the people have a right, at such periods, and in such manner, as they shall establish by their frame of government, to cause their public officers to return to private life; and to fill up vacant places by certain and regular elections and appointments.

Art. 9. All elections ought to be free; and all the inhabitants of this Commonwealth, having such qualifications as they shall establish by their frame of government, have an equal right to elect officers, and to be elected, for public employments.

Art. 10. Each individual of the society has a right to be protected by it in the enjoyment of his life, liberty, and property, according to standing laws. He is obliged, consequently, to contribute his share to the expense of this protection; to give his personal service, or an equivalent, when necessary; but no part of the property of any individual can, with justice, be taken from him, or applied to public uses, without his own consent, or that of the representative body of the people. In fine, the people of this Commonwealth are not controllable by any other laws, than those to which their constitutional representative body have given their consent. And whenever the public exigencies require that the property of any individual should be appropriated to public uses, he shall receive a reasonable compensation therefor.

Art. 11. Every subject of the Commonwealth ought to find a certain remedy, by having recourse to the laws, for all injuries or wrongs which he may receive in his person, property, or character. He ought to obtain right and justice freely, and without being obliged to purchase it; completely, and without any denial; promptly, and without delay; conformably to the laws.

Art. 12. The privilege and benefit of the writ of *habeas corpus* shall be enjoyed, in this Commonwealth, in the most free, easy, cheap, expeditious, and ample manner; and shall not be suspended by the Legislature, except upon the most urgent and pressing occasions, and for a limited time, not exceeding twelve months.

ART. 13. No subject shall be held to answer for any crimes or offence, until the same is fully and plainly, substantially and formally, described to him; or be compelled to accuse, or furnish evidence against himself; and every subject shall have a right to produce all proofs, that may be favorable to him; to meet the witnesses against him face to face, and to be fully heard in his defence by himself, or his counsel, at his election: and no subject shall be arrested, imprisoned, despoiled, or deprived of his property, immunities, or privileges, put out of the protection of the law, exiled, or deprived of his life, liberty, or estate, but by the judgment of his peers, or the law of the land. And the Legislature shall not make any law that shall subject any person to a capital or infamous punishment, excepting for the government of the army and navy, without trial by jury.

ART. 14. In criminal prosecutions, the verification of facts in the vicinity where they happen, is one of the greatest securities of the life, liberty, and property of the citizen.

ART. 15. Every subject has a right to be secure from all unreasonable searches and seizures of his person, his houses, his papers, and all his possessions. All warrants, therefore, are contrary to this right, if the cause or foundation of them be not previously supported by oath or affirmation; and if the order in the warrant to a civil officer, to make search in suspected places, or to arrest one or more suspected persons, or to seize their property, be not accompanied with a special designation of the persons or objects of search, arrest, or seizure; and no warrant ought to be issued but in cases, and with the formalities, prescribed by the laws.

ART. 16. In all controversies concerning property, and in all suits between two or more persons, except in cases in which it has heretofore been otherways used and practised, the parties have a right to a trial by jury; and this method of procedure shall be held sacred, unless, in causes arising on the high seas, and such as relate to mariners' wages, the Legislature shall hereafter find it necessary to alter it.

ART. 17. The liberty of the press is essential to the security of freedom in a state: it ought not, therefore, to be restrained in this Commonwealth.

Art. 18. The people have a right to keep and to bear arms for the common defence; and, as in time of peace, armies are dangerous to liberty, they ought not to be maintained without the consent of the Legislature; and the military power shall always be held in an exact subordination to the civil authority, and be governed by it.

Art. 19. A frequent recurrence to the fundamental principles of the Constitution, and a constant adherence to those of piety, justice, moderation, temperance, industry and frugality, are absolutely necessary to preserve the advantages of liberty, and to maintain a free government. The people ought, consequently, to have a particular attention to all those principles, in the choice of their officers and representatives; and they have a right to require of their lawgivers and magistrates, an exact and constant observance of them, in the formation and execution of the laws necessary for the good administration of the Commonwealth.

Art. 20. The people have a right, in an orderly and peaceable manner, to assemble to consult upon the common good; give instructions to their representatives; and to request of the legislative body, by the way of addresses, petitions, or remonstrances, redress of the wrongs done them, and the grievances they suffer.

Art. 21. The power of suspending the laws, or the execution of the laws, ought never to be exercised but by the Legislature, or by authority derived from it, to be exercised in such particular cases only as the Legislature shall expressly provide for.

Art. 22. The freedom of deliberation, speech and debate, in either House of the Legislature, is so essential to the rights of the people, that it cannot be the foundation of any accusation or prosecution, action or complaint, in any other court or place whatsoever.

Art. 23. The Legislature ought frequently to assemble for the redress of grievances, for correcting, strengthening, and confirming the laws, and for making new laws, as the common good may require.

Art. 24. No subsidy, charge, tax, impost, or duties, ought to be established, fixed, laid, or levied, under any pretext whatsoever, without the consent of the people, or their representatives in the Legislature.

Art. 25. Laws made to punish for actions done before the existence of such laws, and which have not been declared crimes by preceding laws, are unjust, oppressive, and inconsistent with the fundamental principles of a free government.

Art. 26. No subject ought, in any case, or in any time, to be declared guilty of treason or felony by the Legislature.

Art. 27. No magistrate or court of law shall demand excessive bail or sureties, impose excessive fines, or inflict cruel or unusual punishments.

Art. 28. In time of peace, no soldier ought to be quartered in any house without the consent of the owner; and in time of war, such quarters ought not to be made but by the civil magistrate, in a manner ordained by the Legislature.

Art. 29. No person can in any case be subjected to law martial, or to any penalties or pains, by virtue of that law, except those employed in the army or navy, and except the militia in actual service, but by authority of the Legislature.

Art. 30. It is essential to the preservation of the rights of every individual, his life, liberty, property and character, that there be an impartial interpretation of the laws, and administration of justice. It is the right of every citizen to be tried by judges as free, impartial and independent, as the lot of humanity will admit. It is therefore not only the best policy, but for the security of the rights of the people, and of every citizen, that the judges of the Supreme Judicial Court should hold their offices by tenures established by the Constitution, and should have honorable salaries, which shall not be diminished during their continuance in office.

Art. 31. In the government of this Commonwealth, the legislative department shall never exercise the executive and judicial powers, or either of them: the executive shall never exercise the legislative and judicial powers, or either of them: the judicial shall never exercise the legislative and executive powers, or either of them: to the end it may be a government of laws and not of men.

THE FRAME OF GOVERNMENT.

The people, inhabiting the territory formerly called the Province of Massachusetts Bay, do hereby solemnly and mutually agree with each other, to form themselves into a free, sovereign, and independent body politic or state, by the name of The Commonwealth of Massachusetts.

CHAPTER I.

General Court.

Article 1. The department of legislation shall be styled the General Court of Massachusetts. It shall consist of two branches, a Senate and a House of Representatives, each of which shall have a negative upon the other.

Art. 2. The political year shall begin on the first Wednesday in January; and the General Court shall assemble every year on the said first Wednesday in January, and shall be dissolved on the day next preceding the first Wednesday in January following, without any proclamation or other act of the governor. But nothing herein contained shall prevent the General Court from assembling at such other times as they shall judge necessary, or when called together by the governor.

Art. 3. The compensation of members of the General Court shall be established by standing laws; but no act increasing the compensation shall apply to the General Court which passes such act; and no compensation shall be allowed for attendance of members at any one session for a longer time than one hundred days.

Art. 4. No bill or resolve of the Senate or House of Representatives shall become a law, and have force as such, until it shall have been laid before the governor for his revisal; and if he, upon such revision, approve thereof, he shall signify his approbation by signing the same. But if he have any objection to the passing of such bill or resolve, he shall return the same, together with his objections thereto, in writing, to the Senate or House of Representatives, in whichsoever the same shall have originated; who shall enter the objections sent down by the governor, at large, on their records, and proceed to reconsider the said bill or resolve: but if, after such reconsideration, two-thirds of the said Senate or House of Representatives, present, shall, notwithstanding the said objections, agree to pass the same, it shall, together with the objections, be sent to the other branch of the Legislature, where it shall also be reconsidered, and if approved by two-thirds of the members present, shall have the force of a law: but, in all such cases, the votes of both Houses shall be determined by yeas and nays; and the names of the persons voting for, or against, the said bill or resolve, shall be entered upon the public records of the Commonwealth.

And in order to prevent unnecessary delays, if any bill or resolve shall not be returned by the governor, within five days after it shall have been presented to him, the same shall have the force of a law.

But if any bill or resolve shall be objected to and not approved by the governor, and if the General Court shall adjourn within five days after the same shall have been laid before the governor for his approbation, and thereby prevent his returning it, with his objections, as provided by the Constitution, such bill or resolve shall not become a law, nor have force as such.

Art. 5. The General Court shall forever have full power and authority to erect and constitute judicatories and courts of record, or other courts, to be held in the name of the Commonwealth, for the hearing, trying, and determining of all manner of crimes, offences, pleas, processes, plaints, actions, matters, causes and things, whatsoever, arising or happening within the Commonwealth, or between or concerning persons inhabiting, or residing, or brought within the same; whether the same be criminal or civil, or whether the said crimes be capital or not capital, and whether the said pleas be real, personal, or mixt; and for the awarding and making out of execution thereupon: to which courts and judicatories are hereby given and granted full power and authority, from time to time, to administer oaths or affirmations, for the better discovery of truth in any matter in controversy, or depending before them.

Art. 6. The General Court shall have power to make laws regulating marriage, divorce and alimony, but shall in no case decree a divorce, or hear and determine any causes touching the validity of the marriage contract.

Art. 7. And further, full power and authority are hereby given and granted to the said General Court, from time to time, to make, ordain, and establish, all manner of wholesome and reasonable orders, laws, statutes, and ordinances, directions and instructions, either with penalties or without; so as the same be not repugnant or contrary to this Constitution, as they shall judge to be for the good and welfare of this Commonwealth, and for the government and ordering thereof, and of the subjects of the same, and for the necessary support and defence of the government thereof; and to name and settle annually, or provide, by fixed laws, for the naming and settling all civil officers within the said Commonwealth, the election and constitution of whom are not hereafter in this form of government otherwise provided for; and to set forth the several duties, powers, and limits, of the several civil and military officers of this Commonwealth, and the forms of such oaths or affirmations as shall be respectively administered unto them for the execution of their several offices and places, so as the same be not repugnant or contrary to this Constitution; and to impose and levy proportional and reasonable assessments, rates, and taxes, upon all the inhabitants of, and persons resident, and estates lying within the said Commonwealth; and also to impose and levy reasonable duties and excises upon any produce, goods, wares, merchandise, and commodities, whatsoever, brought into, produced, manufactured, or being within the same; to be issued and disposed of by warrant, under the hand of the governor of this Commonwealth for the time being, with the advice and consent of the council for the public service, in the necessary defence and support of the government of the said Commonwealth, and the protection and preservation of the subjects thereof, according to such acts as are or shall be in force within the same.

Art. 8. The General Court shall have full power and authority to erect and constitute municipal or city governments in any corporate town or towns in this Commonwealth, and to grant to the inhabitants thereof, such powers, privileges and immunities, not repugnant to the Constitution, as the General Court shall deem necessary or expedient for the regulation and government thereof, and to prescribe the manner of calling and holding public meetings of the inhabitants in wards, or otherwise, for the election of officers under the Constitution, and the manner of returning the votes given at such meetings: *provided*, that no such government shall be erected or constituted in any town not containing twelve thousand inhabitants; nor unless it be with the consent and on the application of a majority of the inhabitants of such town, present and voting thereon, pursuant to a vote at a meeting duly warned and holden for that purpose: *and provided, also*, that all by-laws, made by such municipal or city government, shall be subject, at all times, to be annulled by the General Court.

Art. 9. Each branch of the General Court shall have authority to punish, by imprisonment, every person, not one of its members, who shall be guilty of disrespect thereto, by any disorderly or contemptuous behavior, in its presence; or who, in the town or city where the General Court is sitting, and during the time of its sitting, shall threaten harm to the body or estate of any of its members, or assault any of them for any thing said or done in its session; or shall assault, or arrest, any witness, or other person, ordered to attend it, in his way in going, or returning; or who shall rescue any person arrested by its order; provided, that no imprisonment, on its warrant or order, for either of the above described offences, shall be for a term exceeding thirty days; and the governor and council shall have the same authority to punish in like cases. And no member, during his going to, returning from, or attending the General Court, shall be arrested, or held to bail, on mesne process.

Art. 10. Each branch of the General Court may try, and determine all cases where their rights and privileges are concerned, and which, by the Constitution, they have authority to try and determine, by committees of their own members, or in any such other way as they may respectively think best.

Art. 11. Each branch shall be the final judge of the elections, returns, and qualifications, of its members, as pointed out in the Constitution; shall choose a presiding officer from among its members; appoint its other officers; and settle its rules and orders of proceeding, and shall have power to adjourn, *provided* such adjournment shall not exceed three days at a time.

Art. 12. And whereas the elections appointed to be made by this Constitution, on the first Wednesday in January, annually, by the two Houses of the Legislature, may not be completed on that day, the said elections may be adjourned from day to day until the same shall be completed.

Art. 13. In all elections by the General Court, or either branch thereof, a majority of votes shall be required, and the members shall vote *viva voce.*

Art. 14. The enacting style, in making and passing all acts, statutes and laws, shall be: *Be it enacted by the General Court of Massachusetts.*

CHAPTER II.

Senate.

Art. 1. There shall be annually elected by the inhabitants of this Commonwealth, qualified as in this Constitution is provided, forty persons to be senators, for the year ensuing their election; and the Senate shall be the first branch of the General Court. For this purpose the General Court holden next after the adoption of this Constitution, and next after each decennial census thereafter, shall divide the Commonwealth into forty districts, composed of contiguous territory, and as nearly equal in population as may be: *provided,* that no town or ward of a city be divided therefor. Each district shall be entitled to elect one senator, who shall have been an inhabitant of this Commonwealth for five years immediately preceding his election, and at the time of his election shall be an inhabitant of the district for which he is chosen.

Art. 2. There shall be a meeting on the Tuesday next after the first Monday in November, annually, forever, of the inhabitants of each town and city in this Commonwealth, to be called and warned in due course of law, at least seven days before the day of such meeting, for the purpose of electing senators; and at such meetings every qualified voter shall have a right to give in his vote for a senator for the district of which he is an inhabitant.

The selectmen of the several towns shall preside at the town meetings impartially; and shall receive the votes of all the inhabitants of such towns present and qualified to vote for a senator, and shall sort and count them in open town meeting, and in presence of the town clerk, who shall make a fair record, in presence of the selectmen, and, in open town meeting, of the name of every person voted for, and of the number of votes against his name; and a fair copy of this record shall be attested by the selectmen and the town clerk, and shall be sealed up, directed to the secretary of the Commonwealth, for the time being, with a superscription, expressing the purport of the contents thereof, and delivered by the town clerk of said towns, to the sheriff of the county in which such town lies, thirty days at least before the first Wednesday in January annually; or it shall be delivered into the secretary's office seventeen days at least before the said first Wednesday in January; and the sheriff of each county shall deliver all such certificates, by him received, into the secretary's office, seventeen days before the said first Wednesday in January.

And the inhabitants of plantations unincorporated, qualified as this Constitution provides, shall have the same privilege of voting for a senator, in the plantations where they reside, as town inhabitants have in their respective towns; and the plantation meetings for that purpose shall be held annually on the same Tuesday next after the first Monday, in November, at such place in the plantations respectively as the assessors thereof shall direct; which assessors shall have like authority for notifying the voters, collecting and returning the votes, as the selectmen and town clerks have in their several towns, by this Constitution. And all other persons living in places unincorporated, (qualified as aforesaid,) shall have the privilege of giving in their votes for a senator, in the town where the inhabitants of such unincorporated places shall be assessed, and be notified of the place of meeting by the selectmen of the said town for that purpose, accordingly.

Art. 3. The governor and council shall, as soon as may be, exämine the returned copies of the record, provided for in article second of this chapter, and ascertain who shall have received the largest number of votes in each of the several senatorial districts, and the person who has so received the largest number of votes in each of said districts shall be a senator for the following political year; and the governor shall cause each of said persons, so appearing to be elected, to be notified at least fourteen days before the first Wednesday in January of each year, to attend on that day, and take his seat accordingly.

Art. 4. Not less than twenty-one members shall constitute a quorum, for doing business; but a less number may organize, adjourn from day to day, and compel the attendance of absent members.

Art. 5. The Senate shall be a court with full authority to hear and determine all impeachments made by the House of Representatives, against any officer or officers of the Commonwealth, for misconduct and maladministration in their offices; but previous to the trial of every impeachment, the members of the Senate shall respectively be sworn, truly and impartially to try and determine the charge in question, according to evidence. Their judgment, however, shall not extend further than to removal from office and disqualification to hold or enjoy any place of honor, trust, or profit, under this Commonwealth; but the party so convicted, shall be, nevertheless, liable to indictment, trial, judgment and punishment, according to the laws of the land.

CHAPTER III.

House of Representatives.

Article 1. There shall be, in the Legislature of this Commonwealth, a representation of the people, annually elected, and founded upon the principle of equality.

Art. 2. And in order to provide for a representation of the citizens of this Commonwealth, founded upon the principle of equality, every corporate town, containing less than one thousand inhabitants, may elect one representative in the year when the valuation of estates shall be settled, and, in addition thereto, one representative five years in every ten years. Every town containing one thousand inhabitants and less than four thousand, may elect one representative. Every town containing four thousand inhabitants and less than eight thousand, may elect two representatives. Every town containing eight thousand inhabitants and less than twelve thousand, may elect three representatives. Every city or town containing twelve thousand inhabitants, may elect four representatives. Every city or town containing over twelve thousand inhabitants, may elect one additional representative for every four thousand inhabitants it shall contain, over twelve thousand. Any two towns, each containing less than one thousand inhabitants, may, by consent of a majority of the legal voters present at a legal meeting, in each of said towns respectively, called for that purpose, form themselves into a representative district, to continue for the term of not less than two years; and such district shall have all the rights, in regard to representation, which belong to a town having one thousand inhabitants. And this apportionment shall be based upon the census of the year one thousand eight hundred and fifty, until a new census shall be taken.

Art. 3. The Senate, at its first session after this Constitution shall have been adopted, and at its first session after the next State census shall have been taken, and at its first session next after each decennial State census thereafterwards, shall apportion the number of representatives to which each town and city shall be entitled, and shall cause the same to be seasonably published; and in all apportionments after the first, the numbers which shall entitle any town or city, to two, three, four, or more representatives, shall be increased or diminished in the same proportion as the population of the whole Commonwealth shall have increased or decreased since the last preceding apportionment.

Art. 4. No town hereafter incorporated, containing less than fifteen hundred inhabitants, shall be entitled to choose a representative.

Art. 5. Each city in this Commonwealth shall be divided, by such means as the Legislature may provide, into districts of contiguous territory, as nearly equal in population as may be, for the election of representatives, which districts shall not be changed oftener than once in five years: *provided, however*, that no one district shall be entitled to elect more than three representatives.

Art. 6. The members of the House of Representatives shall be chosen on the Tuesday next after the first Monday in November, annually; but meetings may be adjourned, if necessary, for the choice of representatives, to the next day, and again to the next succeeding day, but no further: but in case a second meeting shall be necessary for the choice of representatives, such meetings shall be held on the fourth Monday of the same month of November.

Art. 7. The House of Representatives shall have power, from time to time, to impose fines upon such towns as shall neglect to choose and return members to the same, agreeably to this Constitution.

Art. 8. Every member of the House of Representatives shall have been, for one year at least, next preceding his election, an inhabitant of the town he shall be chosen to represent.

Art. 9. The House of Representatives shall be the grand inquest of this Commonwealth; and all impeachments made by them shall be heard and tried by the Senate.

Art. 10. All money bills shall originate in the House of Representatives; but the Senate may propose or concur with amendments, as on other bills.

Art. 11. Not less than one hundred members of the House of Representatives shall constitute a quorum for doing business.

CHAPTER IV.

Governor.

Art. 1. There shall be a supreme executive magistrate, who shall be styled, The Governor of the Commonwealth of Massachusetts.

Art. 2. The governor shall be a citizen of Massachusetts, and shall be chosen annually, by the inhabitants of the towns and cities of this Commonwealth, on the Tuesday next after the first Monday in November. He shall hold his office for one year next following the first Wednesday of January, and until another is chosen and qualified in his stead. And no person shall be eligible to this office, unless, at the time of his election, he shall have been an inhabitant of this Commonwealth for seven years next preceding.

Art. 3. Those persons who shall be qualified to vote for senators and representatives, within the several towns of this Commonwealth, shall, at a meeting to be called for that purpose, on the Tuesday next after the first Monday in November, annually, give in their votes for a governor, to the selectmen, who shall preside at such meeting; and the town clerk, in the presence and with the assistance of the selectmen, shall, in open town meeting, sort and count the votes, and form a list of the persons voted for, with the number of votes for each person against his name; and shall make a fair record of the same in the town books, and a public declaration thereof in the said meeting; and shall, in the presence of the inhabitants, seal up copies of the said list, attested by him and the selectmen, and transmit the same to the sheriff of the county, thirty days at least before the first Wednesday in January; and the sheriff shall transmit the same to the secretary's office seventeen days at least before the said first Wednesday in January; or the selectmen may cause returns of the same to be made to the office of the secretary of the Commonwealth seventeen days at least before the said day; and the secretary shall lay the same before the Senate and the House of Representatives, on the first Wednesday in January, to be by them examined; and in case of an election, the choice shall be by them declared and published.

ART. 4. The governor shall have authority, from time to time, at his discretion, to assemble and call together the councillors of this Commonwealth for the time being; and the governor, with the said councillors, or five of them at least, shall, and may, from time to time, hold and keep a Council, for the ordering and directing the affairs of the Commonwealth, agreeably to the Constitution and the laws of the land.

ART. 5. The governor, with advice of council, shall have full power and authority, during the session of the General Court, to adjourn or prorogue the same to any time the two Houses shall desire; and in the recess of the said Court, to prorogue the same from time to time, not exceeding ninety days in any one recess; and to call it together sooner than the time to which it may be adjourned or prorogued, if the welfare of the Commonwealth shall require the same; and in case of any infectious distemper prevailing in the place where the said Court is next at any time to convene, or any other cause happening, whereby danger may arise to the health or lives of the members from their attendance, he may direct the session to be held at some other the most convenient place within the State.

ART. 6. In cases of disagreement between the two Houses, with regard to the necessity, expediency, or time of adjournment, or prorogation, the governor, with advice of the council, shall have a right to adjourn or prorogue the General Court, not exceeding ninety days, as he shall determine the public good shall require.

ART. 7. The power of pardoning offences, except such as persons may be convicted of before the Senate, by an impeachment of the House, shall be in the governor, by and with the advice of council: but no charter of pardon, granted by the governor, with advice of the council, before conviction, shall avail the party pleading the same, notwithstanding any general or particular expressions contained therein, descriptive of the offence, or offences intended to be pardoned.

Art. 8. Notaries public shall be appointed by the governor, in the same manner as judicial officers are appointed, and shall hold their offices during seven years, unless sooner removed by the governor, with the consent of the council, upon the address of both Houses of the General Court.

Art. 9. Coroners shall be nominated and appointed by the governor, by and with the advice and consent of the council; and every such nomination shall be made by the governor, and made at least seven days prior to such appointment.

Art. 10. No moneys shall be issued out of the treasury of this Commonwealth, and disposed of (except such sums as may be appropriated for the redemption of bills of credit or treasurer's notes, or for the payment of interest arising thereon) but by warrant under the hand of the governor for the time being, with the advice and consent of the council, for the necessary defence and support of the Commonwealth; and for the protection and preservation of the inhabitants thereof, agreeably to the acts and resolves of the General Court.

Art. 11. All public boards, the commissary-general, all superintending officers of public magazines and stores, belonging to this Commonwealth, and all commanding officers of forts and garrisons within the same, shall, once in every three months, officially, and without requisition, and at other times, when required by the governor, deliver to him an account of all goods, stores, provisions, ammunition, cannon with their appendages, and small arms with their accoutrements, and of all other public property whatever under their care, respectively; distinguishing the quantity, number, quality and kind of each, as particularly as may be; together with the condition of such forts and garrisons; and the said commanding officer shall exhibit to the governor, when required by him, true and exact plans of such forts, and of the land and sea, or harbor or harbors, adjacent.

And the said boards, and all public officers, shall communicate to the governor, as soon as may be after receiving the same, all letters, despatches, and intelligences of a public nature, which shall be directed to them respectively.

Art. 12. As the public good requires that the governor should not be under the undue influence of any of the members of the General

Court, by a dependence on them for his support—that he should, in all cases, act with freedom for the benefit of the public—that he should not have his attention necessarily diverted from that object to his private concerns—and that he should maintain the dignity of the Commonwealth in the character of its chief magistrate—it is necessary that he should have an honorable stated salary, of a fixed and permanent value, amply sufficient for those purposes, and established by standing laws: and it shall be among the first acts of the General Court, after the commencement of this Constitution, to establish such salary by law accordingly.

CHAPTER V.

Lieutenant-Governor.

ARTICLE 1. There shall be annually elected a Lieutenant-Governor of the Commonwealth of Massachusetts, who shall be qualified in the same manner with the governor; and the day and manner of his election, the qualifications of the voters, the return of the votes, and the declaration of the election, shall be the same as in the election of a governor.

And the lieutenant-governor shall hold his office for one year next following the first Wednesday of January, and until another is chosen and qualified in his stead.

ART. 2. The governor, and in his absence, the lieutenant-governor, shall be president of the council, but shall have no vote in council; and the lieutenant-governor shall always be a member of the council, except when the chair of the governor shall be vacant.

ART. 3. Whenever, by reason of sickness or absence from the Commonwealth, or otherwise, the governor shall be unable to perform his official duties, the lieutenant-governor, for the time being, shall have and exercise all the powers and authorities, and perform all the duties of governor; and whenever the chair of the governor shall be vacant, by reason of his resignation, death, or removal from office, the lieutenant-governor shall be governor of the Commonwealth.

CHAPTER VI.

Council.

ARTICLE 1. There shall be a Council for advising the governor in the executive part of the government, to consist of eight persons besides the lieutenant-governor, whom the governor for the time being, shall have full power and authority, from time to time, at his discretion, to assemble and call together; and the governor, with the said councillors, or five of them at least, shall and may, from time to time, hold and keep a Council, for the ordering and directing the affairs of the Commonwealth, according to the laws of the land.

Art. 2. Eight councillors shall be annually chosen by the people; and for that purpose the State shall be divided by the General Court into eight districts, each district to consist of five contiguous senatorial districts, and entitled to elect one councillor, who shall hold his office for one year next following the first Wednesday in January, and until a successor is chosen and qualified in his stead.

Art. 3. No person shall be elected a councillor who has not been an inhabitant of this Commonwealth for the term of five years immediately preceding his election.

Art. 4. The day and manner of the election of councillors, the qualifications of the voters, the return of the votes, and the declaration of the elections, shall be the same as are required in the election of senators; and the person having the highest number of votes shall be declared to be elected.

Art. 5. No councillor, during the time for which he is elected, shall be appointed on any commission or to any place and receive compensation therefor.

Art. 6. The councillors, in the civil arrangements of the Commonwealth, shall have rank next after the lieutenant-governor.

Art. 7. The resolutions and advice of the council shall be recorded in a register, and signed by the members present; and any member of the council may insert his opinion contrary to the resolution of the majority. This record shall always be subject to public examination, and may be called for by either House of the Legislature.

Art. 8. Whenever the office of the governor and lieutenant-governor shall be vacant, by reason of death, absence, or otherwise, then the council, or the major part of them, shall, during such vacancy, have full power and authority, to do, and execute all and every such acts, matters and things, as the governor, or the lieutenant-governor might or could, by virtue of this Constitution, do or execute, if they, or either of them, were personally present.

CHAPTER VII.

Secretary, Treasurer, Attorney-General, Auditor, District-Attorney, and County Officers.

ARTICLE 1. The secretary, treasurer, auditor, and attorney-general, shall be chosen by the people, annually, on the Tuesday next after the first Monday in November; and they shall hold their offices, respectively, for one year next following the first Wednesday in the succeeding January, and until their successors are chosen and qualified in their stead.

The day and manner of their election, the qualifications of the voters, the return of the votes, and the declaration of the elections, shall be the same as are required in the election of governor.

ART. 2. No man shall be eligible as treasurer more than five years successively.

ART. 3. The records of the Commonwealth shall be kept in the office of the secretary, who may appoint his deputies, for whose conduct he shall be accountable; and he shall attend the governor and Council, the Senate and House of Representatives, in person, or by his deputies, as they shall respectively require.

ART. 4. Judges of probate, registers of probate, sheriffs, clerks of the courts, commissioners of insolvency, district-attorneys, registers of deeds, county treasurers, and county commissioners, shall be elected triennially by the people of their respective counties and districts, on the Tuesday next after the first Monday in November, and shall hold their offices, respectively, for three years next following the first Wednesday in the succeeding January, and until their respective successors are chosen and qualified in their stead.

The manner of their election, the qualifications of the voters, the return of the votes, and the declaration of the elections, shall be the same as are required in the election of senators, and the person having the highest number of votes shall be elected.

CHAPTER VIII.

Judiciary Power.

ARTICLE 1. The judicial power of the Commonwealth shall be vested in a Supreme Judicial Court, and such other courts as the Legislature may from time to time establish.

ART. 2. The tenure that all commission officers shall by law have in their offices, shall be expressed in their respective commissions.

All judicial officers, duly appointed, commissioned and sworn, shall hold their offices for the term of ten years, excepting such concerning whom there is different provision made in this Constitution. And upon the expiration of such term they may be reappointed; and all judicial officers for whose appointment a different provision is not made in this Constitution, shall be nominated and appointed by the governor, by and with the advice and consent of the Council, and they may be removed by the governor, with consent of the Council, upon the address of both Houses of the Legislature.

ART. 3. The present justices of the Supreme Judicial Court shall hold their offices according to their respective commissions; and the present justices of the Court of Common Pleas shall hold their offices by the same tenure, while the law establishing the said Court of Common Pleas shall continue. All nominations of judicial officers, whose term of office is by this Constitution limited to ten years, shall be publicly announced at least seven days before their appointment; and no person who shall have been commissioned after the tenth day of August, in the year one thousand eight hundred and fifty-three, shall hold by any longer tenure of office than the term of ten years.

ART. 4. Neither the governor and Council, nor the two branches of the Legislature, or either of them, shall hereafter propose questions to justices of the Supreme Judicial Court, and require their opinions thereon.

ART. 5. The judges of probate of wills, and for granting letters of administration, shall hold their courts at such place or places, on fixed days, as the convenience of the people shall require; and the Legislature shall from time to time, hereafter, appoint such times and places; until which appointments, the said courts shall be holden at the times and places which the respective judges shall direct.

ART. 6. Justices of the peace, justices of the peace and quorum, justices of the peace throughout the Commonwealth, and commissioners to qualify civil officers, may be appointed by the governor and Council for a term of seven years; and upon the expiration of any commission, the same may be renewed; and those now in office shall continue therein according to the tenure of their respective commissions: *provided*, that the jurisdiction of the justices named in this article, shall not extend to the hearing or trial of any causes, or the issuing of warrants in criminal cases.

ART. 7. Trial justices shall be elected by the legal voters of the several towns and cities, where, at the time of such election there is no Police Court established by law, who shall hold their offices for a term of three years, and have the same jurisdiction, powers, and duties, as are now exercised by justices of the peace, or such as may hereafter be established by law. Every city or town, authorized as herein provided, shall elect a trial justice, and may elect one additional, for each two thousand inhabitants therein, according to the next preceding decennial census: *provided*, however, that any trial justice who shall remove from the city or town in which he was elected shall thereby vacate his office.

Art. 8. Justices and clerks of the Police Courts of the several cities and towns of the Commonwealth, shall be elected by the legal voters thereof, respectively, for a term of three years.

CHAPTER IX.

Qualifications of Voters, and Elections.

Article 1. Every male citizen, of twenty-one years of age and upwards, (excepting paupers and persons under guardianship,) who shall have resided within the Commonwealth one year, and within the town or district, in which he may claim a right to vote, six calendar months next preceding any election of any national officer, or any state officer required by this Constitution to be elected by the people, shall have a right to vote in such election; and no other person shall have such right.

Art. 2. All ballots required by law to be given at any national, state, county, district, or city election, including elections for representatives and trial justices, justices and clerks of police courts, shall be deposited in sealed envelopes of uniform size and appearance, to be furnished by the Commonwealth.

Art. 3. Lists of the names of qualified voters shall be used at all elections required by this Constitution. They shall be made out and used in such manner as shall be by law provided. The presiding officers at such elections shall receive the votes of all persons whose names are borne on such lists, and shall not be held answerable for refusing the votes of any persons whose names are not borne thereon.

Art. 4. All meetings for the choice of national, state, county, or district officers, including representatives, trial justices, clerks and justices of police courts, by the people, shall be held on the Tuesday next after the first Monday in November, annually; and they shall be called by the mayor and aldermen of the cities, and the selectmen of the towns, and warned in due course of law. The manner of calling and holding public meetings in cities, for the election of officers under this Constitution, and the manner of returning the votes given at such meetings shall be as now prescribed, or as shall hereafter be prescribed by the Legislature.

ART. 5. A majority of all the votes given shall be necessary to the election of governor, lieutenant-governor, secretary, treasurer, auditor, and attorney-general, of the Commonwealth, until otherwise provided by law; but no such law providing that such officers, or either of them, or representatives to the General Court, shall be elected by plurality, instead of a majority of votes given, shall take effect until one year after its passage; and if at any time after any such law shall have taken effect, it shall be repealed, such repeal shall not become a law until one year after the passage of the repealing act; and in the absence of any such law, if at any election of either of the above-named officers, except the representatives to the General Court, no person shall have a majority of the votes given, the House of Representatives shall elect two out of three persons then eligible, who had the highest number of votes, if so many shall have been voted for, and return the persons so elected to the Senate, from whom the Senate shall choose one who shall be the officer thus to be elected.

ART. 6. A majority of votes shall be required in all elections of representatives to the General Court, until otherwise provided by law.

ART. 7. In the election of all city or town officers, such rule of election shall govern as the Legislature may by law prescribe.

ART. 8. In all elections of councillors and senators, and in all elections of county or district officers, the person having the highest number of votes shall be elected.

ART. 9. Whenever, in any election, where the person having the highest number of votes may be elected, there is a failure of election because two persons have an equal number of votes, subsequent trials may be had at such times as may be prescribed by the Legislature.

CHAPTER X.

Oaths and Subscriptions; Incompatibility of and Exclusion from Offices; Continuation of Officers; Commissions; Writs; Confirmation of Laws.

ARTICLE 1. The following oaths shall be taken and subscribed by every person chosen or appointed to any office, civil or military, under the government of the Commonwealth, before he shall enter upon the duties of his office, to wit:

"I, A. B., do solemnly swear that I will bear true faith and allegiance to the Commonwealth of Massachusetts, and will support the Constitution thereof; and that I will faithfully and impartially discharge and perform all the duties incumbent on me as [here insert the office], according to the best of my abilities and understanding, agreeably to the Constitution and laws of the Commonwealth. So help me God."

Provided, that when any person, chosen or appointed as aforesaid, shall be conscientiously scrupulous of taking and subscribing an oath, and shall for that reason decline taking the above oath, he shall make and subscribe his affirmation in the foregoing form, omitting the word "swear," and substituting the word "affirm;" and omitting the words "So help me God," and subjoining instead thereof the words "And this I do under the pains and penalties of perjury."

And the said oaths or affirmations shall be taken and subscribed, by the governor and lieutenant-governor before the president of the Senate, in presence of the two Houses in convention; and by councillors before the president of the Senate and in presence of the Senate; and by the senators and representatives before the governor and Council for the time being; and by the residue of the officers aforesaid before such persons, and in such manner, as shall from time to time be prescribed by law.

Art. 2. No governor, lieutenant-governor, or judge of the Supreme Judicial Court or Court of Common Pleai, shall hold any other office under the authority of this Commonwealth, except such as by this Constitution they are admitted to hold, saving that the judges of the said courts may hold the offices of justices of the peace through the State; nor shall they hold any other office, or receive any pension or salary from any other state, or government, or power whatever, except that they may be appointed to take depositions, or acknowledgments of deeds, or other legal instruments, by the authority of other states or countries.

No person shall hold or exercise, at the same time, more than one of the following offices, to wit: the office of governor, lieutenant-governor, senator, representative, judge of the Supreme Judicial Court, or Court of Common Pleas, secretary of the Commonwealth, attorney-general, treasurer, auditor, councillor, judge of probate, register of probate, register of deeds, sheriff or his deputy, clerk of the Supreme Judicial Court, or Court of Common Pleas, clerk of the Senate or House of Representatives; and any person holding either of the above offices shall be deemed to have vacated the same by accepting a seat in the

Congress of the United States, or any office under the authority of the United States, the office of postmaster excepted. And no person shall be capable of holding at the same time more than two offices, which are held by appointment of the governor, or governor and Council, or the Senate, or the House of Representatives, military offices, and the offices of justices of the peace, justices of the peace and quorum, notaries public, and commissioners to qualify civil officers, excepted.

ART. 3. And no person shall ever be admitted to hold a seat in the Legislature, or any office of trust or importance under the government of this Commonwealth, who shall, in the due course of law, have been convicted of bribery or corruption, in obtaining an election or appointment.

ART. 4. All commissions shall be in the name of the Commonwealth of Massachusetts, signed by the governor, and attested by the secretary or his deputy, and have the great seal of the Commonwealth affixed thereto.

ART. 5. All writs, issuing out of the clerk's office in any of the courts of law, shall be in the name of the Commonwealth of Massachusetts; they shall be under the seal of the court from whence they issue, and be signed by the clerk of such court.

ART. 6. All the laws, which have heretofore been adopted, used, and approved in the Province, Colony, State or Commonwealth of Massachusetts, and usually practised on in the courts of law, shall still remain and be in full force, until altered or repealed by the Legislature; such parts only excepted as are repugnant to the rights and liberties contained in this Constitution.

CHAPTER XI.

Militia.

ARTICLE 1. The governor shall be the commander-in-chief of the army and navy of the Commonwealth, and of the militia thereof, excepting when these forces shall be actually in the service of the United States; and shall have power to call out any part of the military force to aid in the execution of the laws, to suppress insurrection, and to repel invasion.

ART. 2. All citizens of this Commonwealth liable to military service, except such as may by law be exempted, shall be enrolled in the militia, and held to perform such military duty as by law may be required.

Art. 3. The militia may be divided into convenient divisions, brigades, regiments, squadrons, battalions, and companies; and officers with appropriate rank and titles may be elected to command the same. And the discipline of the militia shall be made to conform, as nearly as practicable, to the discipline of the army of the United States.

Art. 4. The governor shall appoint an adjutant-general, a quartermaster-general, and such other general staff-officers as shall be designated by law; who shall be commissioned by him for the term of one year, and until their successors shall be commissioned and qualified. And the adjutant-general and quartermaster-general shall have salaries fixed by law, which shall be in full for all services rendered by them in their several offices.

Art. 5. The major-generals shall be elected by the votes of the brigadier-generals and field-officers of the brigades, regiments, squadrons, and battalions of the respective divisions.

Art. 6. The brigadier-generals shall be elected by the votes of the field-officers of the regiments, squadrons, and battalions, and captains of companies, of the respective brigades.

Art. 7. The field-officers of regiments, squadrons, and battalions, shall be elected by the votes of the captains and subalterns of companies of the respective regiments, squadrons, and battalions.

Art. 8. The captains and subalterns shall be elected by the members of the respective companies.

Art. 9. All elections of military officers shall be by a majority of the written votes of those present and voting, and no person, within the description of a voter as hereinbefore specified, shall be disqualified by reason of his being a minor.

Art. 10. The Legislature shall prescribe the time and manner of convening the electors hereinbefore named, of conducting the elections, and of certifying to the governor the names of the officers elected.

Art. 11. The several officers elected shall be forthwith commissioned by the governor for the term of three years from the dates of their respective commissions, and until their successors shall be commissioned and qualified.

Art. 12. If the electors of the several officers before-named shall refuse or neglect to make an election, for the space of three months after legal notice of a meeting for that purpose, the governor shall appoint and commission for three years a suitable person to fill the vacant office, with the advice of the Council if the vacancy be that of a major-general, or with the advice of the major-general of the division in which the appointment is to be made, if the vacancy be of an inferior grade.

Art. 13. Major-generals, brigadier-generals, and commandants of regiments, squadrons, and battalions, shall severally appoint such staff-officers as shall be designated by law in their respective commands.

Art. 14. All non-commissioned officers, whether of staff or company, and all musicians, shall be appointed in such manner as may be prescribed by law.

Art. 15. All officers of the militia may be removed from office by sentence of court-martial, or by such other modes as may be prescribed by law.

CHAPTER XII.

The University at Cambridge; The School Fund; and the Encouragement of Literature.

Article 1. Whereas our wise and pious ancestors, so early as the year one thousand six hundred and thirty-six, laid the foundation of Harvard College, in which university many persons of great eminence have, by the blessing of God, been initiated in those arts and sciences, which qualified them for public employments, both in church and state; and whereas the encouragement of arts and sciences, and all good literature, tends to the honor of God, the advantage of the Christian religion, and the great benefit of this, and the other United States of America—it is declared, that the President and Fellows of Harvard College, in their corporate capacity, and their successors in that capacity, their officers and servants, shall have, hold, use, exercise and enjoy, all the powers, authorities, rights, liberties, privileges, immunities and franchises, which they now have, or are entitled to have, hold, use, exercise and enjoy; and the same are hereby ratified and confirmed unto them, the said President and Fellows of Harvard College, and to their successors, and to their officers and servants, respectively, forever. But the Legislature shall always have full power and authority, as may be judged needful for the advancement of learning, to grant any further powers to the President and Fellows of Harvard

College, or to alter, limit, annul, or restrain, any of the powers now vested in them: *provided*, the obligation of contracts shall not be impaired; and shall have the like power and authority over all corporate franchises hereafter granted, for the purposes of education, in this Commonwealth.

ART. 2. And whereas there have been, at sundry times, by divers persons, gifts, grants, devises of houses, lands, tenements, goods, chattels, legacies and conveyances, heretofore made, either to Harvard College in Cambridge, in New England, or to the President and Fellows of Harvard College, or to the said college by some other description, under several charters successively; it is declared, that all the said gifts, grants, devises, legacies and conveyances, are hereby forever confirmed unto the President and Fellows of Harvard College, and to their successors, in the capacity aforesaid, according to the true intent and meaning of the donor or donors, grantor or grantors, devisor or devisors.

ART. 3. And whereas by an Act of the General Court of the Colony of Massashusetts Bay, passed in the year one thousand six hundred and forty-two, the governor and deputy-governor, for the time being, and all the magistrates of that jurisdiction, were, with the president, and a number of the clergy in the said Act described, constituted the Overseers of Harvard College; and it being necessary, in this new constitution of government, to ascertain who shall be deemed successors to the said governor, deputy-governor, and magistrates; it is declared, that the governor, lieutenant-governor, Council and Senate of this Commonwealth, are, and shall be deemed, their successors; who, with the president of Harvard College, for the time being, together with the ministers of the congregational churches in the towns of Cambridge, Watertown, Charlestown, Boston, Roxbury, and Dorchester, mentioned in the said Act, shall be, and hereby are, vested with all the powers and authority belonging, or in any way appertaining, to the Overseers of Harvard College: *provided*, that nothing herein shall be construed to prevent the Legislature of this Commonwealth from making such alterations in the government of the said University, as shall be conducive to its advantage, and the interest of the republic of letters, in as full a manner as might have been done by the Legislature of the late Province of the Massachusetts Bay.

ART. 4. It shall be the duty of the Legislature, as soon as may be, to provide for the enlargement of the School Fund of the Commonwealth, until it shall amount to a sum not less than two millions of dollars; and the said fund shall be preserved inviolate, and the income thereof shall be annually appropriated for the aid and improvement of the common schools of the State, and for no other purpose.

Art. 5. Wisdom, and knowledge, as well as virtue, diffused generally among the body of the people, being necessary for the preservation of their rights and liberties; and as these depend on spreading the opportunities and advantages of education in the various parts of the country, and among the different orders of the people, it shall be the duty of legislatures and magistrates, in all future periods of this Commonwealth, to cherish the interests of literature and the sciences, and all seminaries of them; especially the University at Cambridge, public schools, and grammar schools in the towns; to encourage private societies, and public institutions, rewards and immunities, for the promotion of agriculture, arts, sciences, commerce, trades, manufactures, and a natural history of the country; to countenance and inculcate the principles of humanity and general benevolence, public and private charity, industry and frugality, honesty and punctuality in their dealings; sincerity, good humor, and all social affections, and generous sentiments among the people.

CHAPTER XIII.

Miscellaneous Provisions.

Article 1. A census of the inhabitants of each city and town in the Commonwealth, on the first day of May in the year one thousand eight hundred and fifty-five, and on the first day of May of each tenth year thereafter, shall be taken and returned into the secretary's office, on or before the last day of the June following the said first day of May in each of said years; and while the public charges of government, or any part thereof, shall be assessed on polls and estates, in the manner that has hitherto been practised, in order that such assessments may be made with equality, there shall be a valuation of estates within the Commonwealth taken anew once in every ten years at least, and as much oftener as the General Court shall order.

Art. 2. Persons holding office by election or appointment, when this Constitution takes effect, shall continue to discharge the duties thereof until their term of office shall expire, or officers authorized to perform their duties, or any part thereof, shall be elected and qualified, pursuant to the provisions of this Constitution; when all powers not reserved to them by the provisions of this Constitution shall cease: *provided, however*, that justices of the peace, justices of the peace and of the quorum, and commissioners of insolvency, shall be authorized to finish and complete all proceedings pending before them at the time, when their powers and duties shall cease, or be altered as aforesaid. All laws in force when this Constitution goes into effect, not inconsistent therewith, shall continue in force until amended or repealed.

ART. 3. The Legislature shall provide, from time to time, the mode in which commissions or certificates of election shall be issued to all officers elected pursuant to the Constitution, except in cases where provision is made therein.

ART. 4. The governor, by and with the consent of the Council, may at any time, for incapacity, misconduct or maladministration in their offices, remove from office, clerks of courts, commissioners of insolvency, judges and registers of probate, district-attorneys, registers of deeds, county treasurers, county commissioners, sheriffs, trial justices and justices and clerks of police Courts: *provided*, that the cause of their removal be entered upon the records of the Council, and a copy thereof be furnished to the party to be removed, and a reasonable opportunity be given him for defence. And the governor may at any time, if the public exigency demand it, either before or after such entry and notice, suspend any of said officers, and appoint substitutes, who shall hold office until the final action upon the question of removal.

ART. 5. Whenever a vacancy shall occur in any elective office, provided for in this Constitution, except that of governor, lieutenant-governor, councillor, senator, member of the House of Representatives, and town and city officers, the governor for the time being, by and with the advice and consent of the Council, may appoint some suitable person to fill such vacancy, until the next annual election, when the same shall be filled by a new election, in the manner to be provided by law: *provided*, *however*, that trial justices shall not be deemed to be town officers for this purpose.

ART. 6. All elections provided to be had under this Constitution shall, unless otherwise provided, be first held on the Tuesday next after the first Monday of November, in the year one thousand eight hundred and fifty-four.

ART. 7. This Constitution shall go into operation on the first Monday in February, in the year one thousand eight hundred and fifty-four.

ART. 8. The terms of all elective officers, not otherwise provided for in this Constitution, shall commence on the first Wednesday in January next after their election.

Art. 9. In order to remove all doubt of the meaning of the word "inhabitant," in this Constitution, every person shall be considered as an inhabitant, for the purpose of electing and being elected into any office or place within this State, in that town, district, or plantation, where he dwelleth, or hath his home.

Art. 10. This form of government shall be enrolled on parchment, and deposited in the secretary's office, and be a part of the laws of the land; and printed copies thereof shall be prefixed to the book containing the laws of this Commonwealth, in all future editions of the said laws.

CHAPTER XIV.

Revision and Amendments of the Constitution.

Article 1. A Convention to revise or amend this Constitution may be called and held in the following manner: At the general election in the year one thousand eight hundred and seventy-three, and in each twentieth year thereafter, the qualified voters in State elections shall give in their votes upon the question, "Shall there be a Convention to revise the Constitution?" which votes shall be received, counted, recorded, and declared, in the same manner as in the election of governor; and a copy of the record thereof shall, within one month, be returned to the office of the secretary of State, who shall, thereupon, examine the same, and shall officially publish the number of yeas and nays, given upon said question, in each town and city; and if a majority of said votes shall be in the affirmative, it shall be deemed and taken to be the will of the people that a Convention shall meet accordingly; and thereafter, on the first Monday of March, ensuing, meetings shall be held, and delegates shall be chosen, in all the towns, cities, and districts, in the Commonwealth, in the manner and number then provided by law for the election of the largest number of representatives, which the towns, cities, and districts shall then be entitled to elect in any year of that decennial period. And such delegates shall meet in Convention at the State House, on the first Wednesday of May next ensuing, and when organized, shall have all the powers necessary to execute the purpose for which such Convention was called; and may establish the compensation of its officers and members, and the expense of its session, for which the governor, with the advice and consent of the Council, shall draw his warrant on the treasury. And if such alterations and amendments, as shall be proposed by the Convention, shall be adopted by the people voting theron in such manner as the Convention shall direct, the Constitution shall be deemed and taken to be altered or amended accordingly. And it shall be the duty of the proper officers, and persons in authority, to perform all acts necessary to carry into effect the foregoing provisions.

ART. 2. Whenever towns or cities containing not less than one-third of the qualified voters of the Commonwealth, shall at any meeting for the election of State officers, request that a Convention be called to revise the Constitution, it shall be the duty of the Legislature, at its next session, to pass an Act for calling of the same, and submit the question to the qualified voters of the Commonwealth, whether a Convention shall be called accordingly: *provided*, that nothing herein contained shall impair the power of the Legislature to take action for calling a Convention, without such request, as heretofore practised in this Commonwealth.

ART. 3. If, at any time hereafter, any specific and particular amendment or amendments to the Constitution be proposed in the General Court, and agreed to by a majority of the senators and two-thirds of the members of the House of Representatives, present and voting thereon, such proposed amendment or amendments shall be entered on the Journals of the two Houses, with the yeas and nays taken thereon, and referred to the General Court then next to be chosen, and shall be published; and if, in the General Court next chosen, as aforesaid, such proposed amendment or amendments shall be agreed to by a majority of the senators and two-thirds of the members of the House of Representatives, present and voting thereon; then it shall be the duty of the General Court to submit such proposed amendment or amendments to the people; and if they shall be approved and ratified by a majority of the qualified voters, voting thereon, at meetings legally warned and holden for that purpose, they shall become part of the Constitution of this Commonwealth.

ART. 4. The Legislature which shall be chosen at the general election on the Tuesday next after the first Monday in November, in the year one thousand eight hundred and fifty-five, shall divide the State into forty single districts for the choice of senators, such districts to be of contiguous territory, and as nearly equal as may be in the number of qualified voters resident in each; and shall also divide the State into single or double districts, to be of contiguous territory, and as nearly equal as may be in the number of qualified voters resident in each, for the choice of not less than two hundred and forty, nor more than three hundred and twenty representatives; with proper provisions for districting the Commonwealth as aforesaid, in the year one thousand eight hundred and sixty-six, and every tenth year thereafter; and with all other provisions necessary for carrying such system of districts into operation; and shall submit the same to the people at the general election to be held in the year one thousand eight hundred and fifty-six, for their ratification; and if the same shall be ratified and adopted by the people, it shall become a part of this Constitution in place of the provisions contained in this Constitution for the apportionment of senators and representatives.

PROPOSITION NUMBER TWO.

The writ of *habeas corpus* shall be granted as of right in all cases in which a discretion is not especially conferred upon the court by the Legislature; but the Legislature may prescribe forms of proceeding preliminary to the obtaining of the writ.

PROPOSITION NUMBER THREE.

In all trials for criminal offences, the jury, after having received the instruction of the court, shall have the right, in their verdict of guilty or not guilty, to determine the law and the facts of the case, but it shall be the duty of the court to superintend the course of the trials, to decide upon the admission and rejection of evidence, and upon all questions of law raised during the trials, and upon all collateral and incidental proceedings; and also to allow bills of exceptions. And the court may grant a new trial in case of conviction.

PROPOSITION NUMBER FOUR.

Every person having a claim against the Commonwealth, ought to have a judicial remedy therefor.

PROPOSITION NUMBER FIVE.

No person shall be imprisoned for any debt hereafter contracted, unless in cases of fraud.

PROPOSITION NUMBER SIX.

All moneys raised by taxation in the towns and cities, for the support of public schools, and all moneys which may be appropriated by the State for the support of common schools, shall be applied to and expended in no other schools than those which are conducted according to law, under the order and superintendence of the authorities of the town or city in which the money is to be expended; and such moneys shall never be appropriated to any religious sect, for the maintenance, exclusively, of its own schools.

PROPOSITION NUMBER SEVEN.

The Legislature shall not create corporations by special act, when the object of the incorporation is attainable by general laws.

PROPOSITION NUMBER EIGHT.

The Legislature shall have no power to pass any act granting any special charter for banking purposes, or any special act to increase the capital stock of any chartered bank; but corporations may be formed for such purposes, or the capital stock of chartered banks may be increased, under general laws.

The Legislature shall provide by law for the registry of all notes or bills authorized by general laws to be issued or put in circulation as money; and shall require ample security for the redemption of such notes in specie.

On motion of Mr. MARVIN, of Boston,

Ordered, That the official copy of the Constitution, to be distributed in the Commonwealth, shall be prepared in such form as shall, so far as possible, distinguish the amendments from the text.

Mr. BOUTWELL, member for Berlin, from the Committee on Revision, submitted the following Address to the people; which was read, and adopted by the Convention.

To the People of Massachusetts:—

The Convention of Delegates, assembled by your authority and directed to revise the Constitution of this Commonwealth, has now closed its labors; and it seeks only to commend and commit the result to your consideration and final judgment. The necessity for the Convention was great, and its labors have been arduous and protracted. As your delegates, we have sought for the principles of freedom in the ancient institutions of the State; but we have thought it wise also to accept the teachings and experience of nearly a century of independent existence.

It has then been our purpose to unite in one system of organic law, the principles of American republican institutions, and the experiences of other free States, all contemplated in the light derived from the history and usages of Massachusetts.

And first of all, we think it proper to present for your consideration a complete system of organic law. The present Constitution was adopted in 1780, and there have since been added thirteen important amendments. By these amendments much of the original text is already annulled, and it is only by a careful and critical analysis and comparison, that the existing provisions can be determined. This ought not to be. Constitutional laws should be plain, that they may be impartially interpreted and faithfully executed, "that every man may at all times find his security in them." We have not then thought it wise, or even proper, to preserve, as a part of the Constitution, provisions which have long since been annulled; nor do we feel justified in proposing new specific amendments, whose adoption will render the fundamental law of the Commonwealth more difficult to be understood, and less certain in its requirements.

We have, therefore, taken what remains unchanged of the Constitution of 1780, and the subsequent amendments, preserving the original language wherever it appeared practicable, as the basis of a new Constitution; and incorporated therewith, such of the resolutions of this Convention as are necessary to give to the whole, at once, a comprehensive and concise character. This has been our purpose; and if our view of duty is correct, we are entirely justified in submitting so much of our work as will give to the people of Massachusetts a complete system of organic law, as one proposition for your adoption and ratification. It is undoubtedly true, that when amendments are specific and not numerous, they should be separately submitted to the judgment of the people; but this mode becomes impracticable in the formation of a new government, or the thorough revision of an old one. Our attention has been necessarily directed to every provision of the Constitution, and but one chapter is preserved in its original form. It only remained for us, either to submit our work, to be added to the old Constitution, as specific amendments, with the conviction that their ratification would render your form of government more complicated than it now is, or else, to embody all of the old and the new that appears necessary to the safe and harmonious action of the system, and present it as *The Constitution of Massachusetts.*

This we now do; and we invite you to consider, that while government is essential to the safety and happiness of each individual, it must necessarily happen that it cannot be in every part alike acceptable to all.

"We may not expect," said the founders of the Commonwealth, "to agree in a perfect system of government: this is not the lot of mankind. The great end of government is to promote the supreme good of human society." We commend the new Constitution to you; not as being perfect, but as greatly to be preferred to the existing frame of government. It declares the rights and liberties essential to the freedom of the people; it contains, as we believe, a framework arranged according to reason and correct analysis, and it embodies all the fundamental provisions necessary to a just administration of every department of the government.

You will naturally examine, with care, the character of the changes we have proposed.

We have thought it necessary to make a provision for the purpose of limiting the sessions of the General Court to one hundred days; and to require that the pay of its members shall be fixed by standing laws.

At present, the members of the Senate are chosen by the several counties, which elect from one to six senators, upon a general ticket. We have provided for the division of the State into forty districts, of equal population, and each entitled to elect one senator.

The basis of the House of Representatives has been a subject of careful and anxious deliberation. Differences of opinion existed among us; but a majority of more than one hundred members determined to preserve the system of town representation under which Massachusetts has existed so long and prospered so well. We have then based the House of Representatives upon the municipal institutions of the State, having reference, so far as practicable, to their relative population. By the proposed system, towns containing less than one thousand inhabitants, are entitled to elect a representative for the year when the valuation of estates is settled, and one in addition, annually, for five years, out of every decennial period. Towns having a population of one thousand, and not more than four thousand inhabitants, are entitled to elect a representative every year; towns of more than four thousand, and less than eight, will elect two representatives; towns of eight thousand, and less than twelve, will elect three representatives; while towns and cities of twelve thousand inhabitants, will elect four representatives, and one additional representative for each addition of four thousand to their population. We do not claim that this system, separately considered, is precisely equal; but if it is in some degree favorable to the rural districts, the loss sustained by the large towns and cities is in a fair measure compensated by the manifest advantages accorded to them in the constitution of the Council and the Senate. The inequality of representation between particular towns, when tested solely by population, may, in some cases, apparently be great; but when the rights of different interests and different sections of the Commonwealth are considered in connection with the whole system of elective government, the basis of the House cannot be deemed unequal or unjust. The Senate and Council are based upon population rather than voters, by which the inhabitants of the cities and large towns have influence in these two important departments of the government, quite disproportionate to their just elective power. No human government can attain to theoretic accuracy; and in a state where pursuits, habits and interests are various, it certainly is not the part of wisdom to place unlimited power in the hands of any. We invite you to consider that the governor represents the voters of the State; that the Council and Senate represent population, without any reference to voters, and, as a consequence, that these two departments of the government will eventually be in the control of the cities and chief towns; and finally, that we have sought only to secure to the rural districts, and to the agricultural and mechanical population and interests, a reasonable share of power in one branch of the Legislature. This influence gives to this portion of the people, power to assent to, but never to dictate, the policy of the government. The Convention of 1780 declared that "an exact representation would be impracticable, even in a system of government arising from the state of nature, and much more so in a State already divided into nearly three hundred corporations." We have encountered the same difficulty, and hope we have overcome it, in our day, as well as they overcame it, in their day.

But our deliberations have not been confined to the proposed system. Many of your delegates are of opinion that the State should be divided into districts, for the election of representatives, according to the number of voters in each. In this opinion a large majority of the Convention do not concur; but we think it our duty, first, to interpret the people's will, and then to give a fair opportunity for its expression upon all questions of importance, whenever such a course is practicable. We have therefore made a constitutional provision, that the Legislature of 1856, under the census to be taken in 1855, shall present a district system, which may be then substituted for the one recommended by the Convention, if, in the judgment of the whole people, it is wise to make the change.

We have also provided that the cities and large towns shall be so districted for the choice of representatives, that no district shall be entitled to elect more than three members.

In the judgment of the Convention, the election of many officers on a single general ticket, is not compatible with the freedom and purity of the representative system.

The property qualification of the governor and lieutenant-governor has been abolished.

The Council has been made elective by the people in single districts, and the records of that body are hereafter to be subject to public examination.

We have provided that the attorney-general, the secretary of the Commonwealth, the auditor, and the treasurer, officers now appointed by the governor or chosen by the Legislature, shall hereafter be elected annually by the people; and that judges of probate, registers of probate, sheriffs, clerks of the courts, commissioners of insolvency, and district-attorneys, officers now appointed by the executive or the courts, shall also be elected by the people for terms of three years.

We have also provided that the justices of the Supreme Judicial Court, and the Court of Common Pleas hereafter appointed, shall hold their offices for the term of ten years.

In a free government the people should be relieved in a reasonable time, and by the ordinary course of affairs, from the weight of incompetent or unfaithful public servants. Under the present Constitution a judge can only be removed by the difficult and unpleasant process of impeachment or of address. Such remedies will be resorted to only in the most aggravated cases.

Under the proposed system we have no apprehension but that faithful and competent judges will be retained in the public service, while those whose places can be better filled by other men, will retire to private life, without violence or ungracious circumstances, and scarcely with observation.

It is proposed that justices of the peace shall be divided into two classes. Those whose duties are chiefly ministerial, will be, as heretofore, appointed by the Governor and Council, while those intrusted with judicial authority are to be elected by the people, and to hold by a tenure of three years.

Under the original Constitution, voters and public officers were required to possess property qualifications. These have heretofore been removed in part, and we now recommend the entire abolition of the property qualification in the voter for all national and all state officers mentioned in the Constitution. The obligations of citizens to contribute to the public expenses by assessment of taxes are not in any degree changed.

Provision is also made for the secrecy of the ballot. By the ballot the citizen, at the same time, declares his opinion on public affairs, and asserts his equality with every other citizen. Freedom of opinion and freedom in the expression of opinion, are individual rights, to be limited or controlled only by a public necessity. We see no public necessity which ought to deprive the citizen of these rights, and we have therefore made provision for their protection.

We also provide absolutely that, in many elections, persons having the highest number of votes shall be chosen. This rule has been applied principally to the elections in counties and districts, where the trouble of frequent trials is great.

The governor, lieutenant-governor, secretary of the Commonwealth, attorney-general, treasurer, auditor, representatives to the General Court, and town officers, are exceptions to the rule.

In case of a failure to elect either of the first six named, the election is referred to the General Court, while subsequent trials may be had for the choice of representatives and municipal officers. We have, therefore, as we think, retained the majority rule where its application will be least burdensome to the people. At the same time, we have provided that the legislature may substitute the plurality rule, whenever the public will shall demand it, with a condition, that no act for that purpose, shall take effect until one year after its passage,

Thus, we have given an opportunity to test the wisdom of the plurality system by experience, and power to apply it to every popular election in the Commonwealth, whenever the deliberate judgment of the people shall require it.

The various provisions relating to the militia have been revised, some important changes have been made, and that department of the government will rest more firmly than ever on a constitutional basis.

Changes are proposed concerning the University at Cambridge, and the General Court is instructed to provide means for the enlargement of the School Fund, until it shall amount to a sum not less than two million of dollars.

Although the Constitution has always asserted, in the strongest terms, the right of the people, at all times, to alter, reform, or totally change, their frame of government, yet it has been contended by some, that the operation and effect of the specific provisions for amendments, contained therein, have been such as practically to impair or render doubtful, this great right. We have, therefore, thought it wise, while we recognize and retain the mode of exercising this right, practiced hitherto in this Commonwealth, to introduce additional provisions, to meet possible future exigencies, and to enable the people, without controversy, to hold periodical Conventions, that shall not be subject to, or restricted by, any previous or subsequent act of the Legislature.

Trusting that you will examine with care, the proceedings of the Convention, and the result to which it has come, we deem it unnecessary to explain several less prominent changes proposed in the Constitution of this Commonwealth.

We also submit seven distinct amendments, which are presented separately for your ratification. Some of them are new, and all of them are independent of the framework of the government, and may either be adopted or rejected, without disturbing the system or harmony of the Constitution. They have all, however, been sustained by decisive majorities of your delegates, and embrace important and essential principles in popular government.

The formation or the revision of a popular constitution is an epoch in the history of a free people.

We are sensible of the magnitude of the trust which you have confided in us; but it is not more important than the just decision of the questions which we submit to you.

We have no doubt that your decision will secure a result beneficial to Massachusetts, and, under Divine Providence, will render more and more illustrious our ancient Commonwealth.

On motion of Mr. Bird, of Walpole,

Ordered, That the Resolves contained in Document No. 128, and the Address to the people, signed by the President and Secretaries, be printed, in connection with the copies of the Revised Constitution ordered to be printed for distribution; and that thirty-five thousand additional copies of said Constitution, with the Resolves and Address, be printed for distribution, in accordance with the Orders already adopted.

On motion of Mr. Cushman, of Bernardston, the Report of the Committee on the Pay Roll was taken from the table, and adopted, as follows:—

COMMONWEALTH OF MASSACHUSETTS.

In Convention, August 1, 1853.

The Committee on the Pay Roll, in compliance with an Order of the Convention, directing them to make up the pay roll, have attended to that duty, in accordance with a Resolve passed on the 28th day of June last, and report the sum herewith, amounting to $114,092, and also report the accompanying Order.

For the Committee,

ISAAC LIVERMORE, *Chairman.*

Ordered, That the Pay Roll of the Convention, as reported by the Committee, in accordance with the Resolve of the 28th of June last, and the Order of July 29th, be transmitted by the Secretary to the Auditor of Accounts, and that he be requested to obtain from the Governor a warrant upon the treasury of the Commonwealth, to authorize the payment thereof, and notify the Convention when the warrant has been drawn.

The Resolves reported by the special committee to whom were referred several Orders concerning the Documents and Debates, &c.,

Were taken up, and amended, on motions of Mr. Earle, of Worcester, and Mr. Paige, of Boston,

And then finally passed, as follow :—

1. *Resolved,* That White & Potter be instructed to deliver, without additional charge, the remaining numbers of the quarto edition of the Journal of Debates, at such places in Boston as the members shall respectively order.

2. *Resolved,* That each member of this Convention be furnished with one copy of the Journal of the Debates, of the octavo edition, additional, to the one heretofore ordered.

3. *Resolved,* That the Messenger be directed to deliver, without additional cost, the copies of the Debates aforesaid, together with the Journals of the Convention, heretofore ordered, and the completed file of the Documents belonging to each member, at such place in Boston as the members shall respectively order; and also to send, in the usual manner, the copies of the Journals and Debates to the towns, cities, and public bodies, as ordered by the Convention, and also send to each town or city, its quota, in proportion to population, of the copies of the new Constitution, heretofore ordered to be published.

On motion of Mr. STETSON, of Braintree, the vote by which the Protest of William C. Nell and others, was ordered to be placed upon the Journal of the Convention,

Was reconsidered, and

The Protest was laid upon the table.

The President announced the Committee, under the third Resolve, for the purpose of counting the votes given for and against the Constitutional Propositions, consisting of the following gentlemen:—

Messrs. Boutwell, member for Berlin; Dana, member for Manchester; Giles, of Boston; Morton, of Andover; Upham, of Salem; Butler, of Lowell; Wilson, of Natick; Griswold, member for Erving; Frothingham, of Charlestown; Wood, of Middleborough; Hillard, of Boston; Aspinwall, of Brookline; Chapin, of Springfield; Sleeper, of Roxbury; Allen, of Worcester; French, of New Bedford; Oliver, of Lawrence; Eames, of Washington; Phinney, member for Chatham, and White, of Quincy.

The business of the Convention having been completed,

Remarks were made by Messrs. Lothrop, of Boston; Eames, of Washington; Hillard, of Boston; Hallett, member for Wilbraham; and Marvin, of Boston.

And on suggestion of Mr. Wilson, of Natick, and by invitation of the President,

The Rev. Mr. Lothrop, of Boston, a member of the Convention, offered a prayer.

Mr. Walker, of North Brookfield, then moved that the Convention adjourn without day.

The question was put and declared to be carried.

The President then addressed the Convention, and at the close of his remarks declared the Convention adjourned, without day;

And at six minutes before two o'clock on Tuesday morning, August 2d, the members separated.

JOURNAL

OF THE

COMMITTEE OF THE WHOLE.

COMMITTEE OF THE WHOLE.

THURSDAY, May 19, 1853.

Mr. MORTON, of Taunton, in the chair.

The Convention having resolved itself into Committee of the Whole, the Committee proceeded to the consideration of the first subject referred to them, being the Report from the Standing Committee on the Senate.

After remarks by Mr. Wilson, of Natick,

Mr. Bradford, of Essex, moved to amend the Report, by striking out after the word "Resolved," in the first line thereof, and inserting as follows:—"That the second section of chapter one of part two, be amended as follows, viz.: by striking out the first, third, and fourth paragraphs of said section; also, by striking out the word 'inhabitants,' and inserting the words 'ratable polls,' in the first line of the second paragraph of said section;" also, that said section be amended, further, by inserting, article second and third, of printed Document Number Two.

After debate by Messrs. Bradford, of Essex, Wilson, of Natick, Hooper, of Fall River, Simonds, of Bedford, Butler, of Lowell, Gardner, of Seekonk, Hillard, of Boston, Giles, of Boston, Earle, of Worcester, Hathaway, of Freetown, Greene, of Brookfield, Bates, of Plymouth, and Holder, of Lynn,

On motion of Mr. Kinsman, of Newburyport, it was

Voted, That the Committee rise, report progress, and ask leave to sit again.

And the Committee accordingly rose.

FRIDAY, May 20, 1853.

Mr. Morton, of Taunton, in the chair.

By direction of the Convention, the Committee resumed the consideration of the Report from the Committee on the Senate,—the pending question being upon the amendment offered by Mr. Bradford, of Essex.

After debate by Messrs. Kinsman, of Newburyport, Wallace, of Palmer, Schouler, of Boston, Simonds, of Bedford, Wilson, of Natick, and Bradford, of Essex,

Mr. Earle, of Worcester, asked for a division of the question, so that the sense of the Committee might first be taken upon the proposition to insert the words "legal voters," instead of the word "inhabitants," whenever that word occurs.

The question being so taken, that amendment was rejected.

The question then being taken upon the residue of the amendments, they were rejected.

When, on motion of Mr. Bates, of Plymouth, it was

Voted, That the Committee rise, and report to the Convention that the Resolutions ought to pass without amendment.

And the Committee accordingly rose.

TUESDAY, May 24, 1853

Mr. Sumner, member for Marshfield, in the chair.

The Committee proceeded to the consideration of the Report of the Special Committee on Elections by Plurality, recommending that the Constitution be so revised, that in all elections, by the people, of officers named therein, the person receiving the highest number of votes, shall be deemed and declared to be elected.

After debate by Messrs. Hooper, of Fall River, Parsons, of Lawrence, Schouler, of Boston, Ball, of Upton, French, of Berkley, Bates, of Plymouth, Churchill, of Milton, Keyes, member for Abington, Holder, of Lynn, Hyde, of Sturbridge, and Walker, of N. Brookfield,

On motion of Mr. Ward, of Newton, it was

Voted, That the Committee rise, report progress, and ask leave to sit again.

And the Committee accordingly rose.

THURSDAY, May 26, 1853.

Mr. SUMNER, member for Marshfield, in the chair.

By direction of the Convention, the Committee resumed the consideration of the Report of the Special Committee, recommending the adoption of the plurality rule, in all elections.

After debate by Messrs. Ward, of Newton, Hall, of Haverhill, Gray, of Boston, Durgin, of Wilmington, Sargent, of Cambridge, Morton, of Taunton, Allen, of Worcester, and Griswold, member for Erving,

Mr. Bates, of Plymouth, moved to amend the Resolution, by inserting after the word "it," in the second line, the following words: "excepting the governor, lieutenant-governor, secretary, treasurer, attorney-general, and auditor of the Commonwealth; provided, those officers shall be made elective."

The same gentleman then moved that the Committee rise, report progress, and ask leave to sit again.

The question was then taken upon the motion of Mr. Bates, and decided in the affirmative.

And the Committee accordingly rose.

FRIDAY, May 27, 1853.

Mr. SUMNER, member for Marshfield, in the chair.

By direction of the Convention, the Committee resumed the consideration of the Report and Resolves concerning the Plurality Rule in all Elections; the immediate question being upon the amendment offered by Mr. Bates, of Plymouth.

After debate by Messrs. Bates, of Plymouth, Butler, of Lowell, Morton, of Taunton, Hale, of Boston, and Hillard, of Boston,

Mr. Knowlton, of Worcester, moved the following as an amendment to the amendment:—

"In the election of governor and lieutenant-governor, senators and representatives, a majority of all the votes cast shall be necessary for a choice; and the election of all other officers shall be by a majority or a plurality of the votes, as the legislature shall determine, unless otherwise specially provided for in the Constitution."

The Chairman decided it not in order at that time.

The debate was then renewed by Messrs. Hooper, of Fall River, Briggs, of Pittsfield, Allen, of Worcester, Hall, of Haverhill, Abbott, of Lowell, Schouler, of Boston, Hallett, member for Wilbraham, Davis, of Worcester, Aspinwall, of Brookline, Gray, of Boston, and Holder, of Lynn,

When, without taking the question, on motion of Mr. Noyes, of Newbury, it was

Voted, That the Committee rise, report progress, and ask leave to sit again.

And the Committee accordingly rose.

Afterwards, Mr. SUMNER, member for Marshfield, in the chair,

The Committee resumed the consideration of the Report and Resolves concerning Elections by Plurality; the pending question being on the amendment of Mr. Bates, of Plymouth.

After debate by Messrs. Gray, of Boston, Simonds, of Bedford, Perkins, of Malden, Griswold, member for Erving, Hubbard, of Boston, and Schouler, of Boston,

The amendment was rejected.

Mr. Walker, of North Brookfield, then moved to amend the Resolution by inserting, in the second line, after the word "that," the following:—

"In the election of governor and lieutenant-governor, senators and representatives, a majority of all the votes cast shall be necessary for a choice; and the election of all other officers shall be by a majority or a plurality of the votes, as the legislature shall determine, unless otherwise specially provided for in the Constitution."

After debate by Messrs. Walker, of North Brookfield, Davis, of Plymouth, Hallett, member for Wilbraham, Aspinwall, of Brookline, Gray, of Boston, Keyes, member for Abington, and Butler, of Lowell,

Mr. Lawton, of Fall River, moved that the Committee rise, report progress, and ask leave to sit again; but the motion was rejected.

After further debate, by Messrs. Train, of Framingham, Wilson, of Natick, Schouler, of Boston, and Keyes, member for Abington,

Mr. Morton, of Quincy, moved that the Committee rise, report progress, and ask leave to sit again; and the motion was adopted—one hundred and thirty-five members voting in the affirmative, and forty-one in the negative.

And the Committee accordingly rose.

SATURDAY, May 28, 1853.

Mr. Hooper, of Fall River, in the chair.

By direction of the Convention, the Committee proceeded to the consideration of the Report and Resolves, from the standing committee, upon the subject of the Governor.

After debate by Messrs. Davis, of Worcester, Wilson, of Natick, Hathaway, of Freetown, Miller, of Wareham, Bradbury, of Newton, Sumner, member for Otis, Briggs, of Pittsfield, and Sargent, of Cambridge,

Mr. Bradford, of Essex, moved to strike out all after the word "Resolved," in the first Resolution, and insert the following:—

"That it is expedient to alter and amend the Constitution so as to provide that every legal voter shall be eligible to the office of governor."

After debate by Messrs. Wilson, of Natick, and Bradford, of Essex,

The amendment was rejected.

Mr. Davis, of Plymouth, then moved to amend the first Resolution, by striking out the words, "except a citizen of the United States," and by adding the words, "and no person of foreign birth shall be eligible to the office of governor, unless he is a naturalized citizen."

After debate by Messrs. Davis, of Plymouth, Aspinwall, of Brookline, Davis, of Fall River, Wilson, of Natick, Hubbard, of Boston, and Morton, of Taunton,

Mr. Davis—accepting a modification suggested by Mr. Morton, of Taunton—withdrew his amendment, and moved to strike out, in the first Resolution, the words "United States," and insert in place thereof the word "Massachusetts."

After debate by Messrs. Hubbard, of Boston, Keyes, member for Abington, Hopkinson, of Boston, Bird, of Walpole, Livermore, of Cambridge, Butler, of Lowell, Hallett, member for Wilbraham, Morton, of Taunton, Briggs, of Pittsfield, Whitney, of Boylston, Hood, of Lynn, Gooch, of Melrose, Wilson, of Natick, and Davis, of Plymouth,

The amendment was adopted.

The question recurring upon the adoption of the Resolutions, as amended,

Mr. Sumner, member for Otis, moved to strike out all after the word "governor," in the third line of the first Resolution, and the motion was adopted.

Mr. Churchill, of Milton, moved to amend the first Resolution, by adding the words, "nor shall any person be eligible to that office who shall not have attained to the age of twenty-five years;" but the motion was rejected.

Mr. Hood, of Lynn, moved to substitute the word "inexpedient" for the word "expedient," in the second Resolution; but the motion was rejected.

The question then recurring upon the Resolve, as amended, it was agreed to.

The remaining Resolves were then adopted.

Mr. Wilson, of Natick, proposed to offer a Resolve; but the Chairman decided it to be not in order.

On motion of Mr. Butler, of Lowell, it was

Voted, That the Committee rise and report to the Convention, that the Resolves, as amended, ought to pass.

And the Committee accordingly rose.

MONDAY, May 30, 1853.

Mr. Thompson, of Charlestown, in the chair.

By direction of the Convention, the Committee proceeded to the consideration of the Report of the Committee on the Frame of Government, that the name, "Commonwealth of Massachusetts," be retained.

The Report was adopted, without debate:

When, on motion of Mr. Hall, of Haverhill, it was

Voted, That the Committee rise, and report to the Convention that the Resolution ought to pass.

And the Committee accordingly rose.

Afterwards, Mr. Butler, of Lowell, in the chair,

The Committee proceeded to the consideration of the Report of the Committee on the Frame of Government, relating to the time of holding State and County Elections.

On motion of Mr. Allen, of Worcester, the Report was adopted, without debate.

On motion of Mr. Earle, of Worcester, it was

Voted, That the Committee rise and report to the Convention that the Resolve ought to pass.

And the Committee accordingly rose.

Afterwards, Mr. CROWNINSHIELD, of Boston, in the chair.

By direction of the Convention, the Committee proceeded to consider the Report and Resolves upon the subject of the Lieutenant-Governor, (printed Document No. 9.)

Mr. Butler, of Lowell, moved to amend the first article, by striking out, in the second and third lines, (printed copy,) the words "whose title shall be His Honor."

After debate by Messrs. Butler, of Lowell, Wilson, of Natick, Train, of Framingham, Wilkins, of Boston, Keyes, member for Abington, Eames, of Washington, and Frothingham, of Charlestown,

The amendment was adopted.

On motion of Mr. Wilkins, of Boston, the words, "have a majority of all the votes returned," in the ninth and tenth lines of the same article, (printed copy,) were stricken out, and the words "be elected," were inserted in their place.

Also, on motion of the same gentleman, the words "a majority of," in the thirteenth line, (same article,) were stricken out, and the words "been elected by," were inserted in their place.

Mr. Wilson, of Natick, then moved to strike out the second article of the Resolves.

After debate by Messrs. Hallett, member for Wilbraham, Sargent, of Cambridge, Wilson, of Natick, Hubbard, of Boston, Butler, of Lowell, Frothingham, of Charlestown, and Gray, of Boston,

Mr. Wilson withdrew his amendment.

When, on motion of Mr. Butler, of Lowell, it was

Voted, That the Committee rise and report to the Convention the Resolutions, as amended.

And the Committee accordingly rose.

Afterwards, Mr. GRAY, of Boston, in the chair.

By direction of the Convention, the Committee proceeded to the consideration of the Report and Resolves from the Committee on Oaths and Subscriptions, (printed Document No. 16.)

After debate by Messrs. Butler, of Lowell, Hubbard, of Boston, and Dana, member for Manchester,

Mr. Hallett, member for Wilbraham, moved to amend the second Resolve, by adding the following:—

I, A. B., do solemnly swear to support the Constitution of the United States.

Also, by striking out, in the sixth line of the second Resolve, (printed copy,) the words "there shall be but one."

Also, the word "which," and inserting the word "the" after the word "that," in the same line.

Also, to substitute the word "oaths" for the word "oath."

After debate by Messrs. Crowninshield, of Boston, Hallett, member for Wilbraham, and Kellogg, of Hadley,

Mr. Frothingham, of Charlestown, moved that the Committee rise, report progress, and ask leave to sit again, which motion was adopted.

And the Committee accordingly rose.

TUESDAY, May 31, 1853.

Mr. Gray, of Boston, in the chair.

By direction of the Convention, the Committee resumed the consideration of the unfinished business of yesterday, being the Report of the Committee upon the subject of Oaths and Subscriptions, the pending question being upon the amendment of Mr. Hallett, member for Wilbraham.

After debate by Messrs. Hallett, member for Wilbraham, Butler, of Lowell, Bird, of Walpole, Keyes, member for Abington, French, of New Bedford, and Gooch, of Melrose,

The amendment was rejected.

Mr. Whitney, of Boylston, then moved to amend the Report by striking out all after the word "Resolved," and inserting the following:

"That it is expedient to amend and alter the existing Constitution by leaving out all oaths and subscriptions."

After remarks by Mr. Whitney, the amendment was rejected.

Mr. Hopkinson, of Boston, moved to strike out from the Resolutions, all except the fourth article of the third Resolve, and the fourth Resolve; but the motion was rejected.

On motion of Mr. Wilson, of Natick, it was

Voted, That the Committee rise, and report that the Resolves ought to pass.

And the Committee accordingly rose.

Afterwards, Mr. SUMNER, member for Marshfield, in the chair.

By direction of the Convention, the Committee resumed the consideration of the Report from the Special Committee on Elections, relating to Elections by Plurality; the pending question being no the amendment previously offered by Mr. Walker, of North Brookfield.

After debate by Messrs. Morton, of Taunton, Kinsman, of Newburyport, and Aspinwall, of Brookline,

Mr. Oliver of Lawrence, moved to amend the amendment of Mr. Walker, by inserting the word "civil" between the words "of" and "officers."

Pending this motion, Mr. Dana, member for Manchester, moved that the Committee rise, report progress, and ask leave to sit again.

The motion was agreed to.

And the Committee accordingly rose.

Afterwards, Mr. SUMNER, member for Marshfield, in the chair.

The Committee resumed the consideration of the subject of Elections by Plurality, the pending question being on the amendment of Mr. Oliver, of Lawrence, to the amendment of Mr. Walker, of North Brookfield.

Mr. Walker accepted the amendment of Mr. Oliver.

After debate by Messrs. Dana, member for Manchester, Adams, of Lowell, Keyes, member for Abington, Hurlbut, of Sudbury, White, of Quincy, Walker, of North Brookfield, and Hathaway, of Freetown,

Mr. Butler, of Lowell, moved that the Committee rise, report progress, and ask leave to sit again.

The motion was agreed to.

And the Committee accordingly rose.

WEDNESDAY, June 1, 1853.

Mr. SUMNER, member for Marshfield, in the chair.

By direction of the Convention, the Committee resumed the consideration of the subject of Elections by Plurality, the pending question being on the amendment offered by Mr. Walker, of North Brookfield.

Mr. Walker withdrew his amendment.

The question then recurring on the adoption of the original Resolution reported by the Committee,

Mr. Hubbard, of Boston, moved to amend the Resolve by striking out all after the word "Resolved," and inserting the following:—

That it is expedient so to amend the Constitution as to provide that the persons respectively having the highest number of votes, for governor and lieutenant-governor, shall be elected: but in case two or more shall have an equal and the highest number of votes for governor or lieutenant-governor, the Senate and House of Representatives shall meet in convention and choose one of the said persons so having an equal and the highest number of votes for governor or lieutenant-governor, and the person having the highest number of votes in the convention of the two houses shall be elected.

Resolved, That it is expedient so to amend the Constitution as to provide that, in the election of senators, the person having the highest number of votes in each district shall be elected; but in case two or more shall have an equal and the highest number of votes in any district, the Senate and House of Representatives shall meet in convention and choose one of the persons so having an equal and the highest number of votes for senator of said district, and the person having the highest number of votes in the convention of the two houses shall be elected.

After debate by Messrs. Hubbard, of Boston, Churchill, of Milton, and Hillard, of Boston,

Mr. Hale, of Bridgewater, moved to amend the amendment offered by Mr. Hubbard, by adding the following:—

Also, That in all elections of representatives to the general court, where there shall be a failure to elect by a majority of all the votes given in on the first meeting for that purpose, the person or persons, when more than one is to be chosen, having the highest number of votes at a meeting for that purpose on any subsequent day when such meetings may be constitutionally holden, shall be elected.

After debate by Messrs. Wilson, of Natick, Butler, of Lowell, French, of Berkley, and Hooper, of Fall River,

The amendment of Mr. Hale was rejected.

The question then recurred upon the amendment of Mr. Hubbard, which was also rejected.

The question recurred on the original Resolve reported by the Committee.

Mr. Hooper, of Fall River, moved to amend the Resolve by striking out, in the second line, (printed copy,) the words "officers named in it," and inserting the following: "governor and lieutenant-governor, senators in the state senate, representatives in the general court, all county officers and all municipal officers." Mr. Allen, of Worcester, moved to amend the amendment offered by Mr. Hooper, by striking out the words "governor and lieutenant-governor, senators and representatives."

After debate by Messrs. Hubbard, of Boston, Bradbury, of Newton, Banks, of Waltham, and Gray, of Boston,

Mr. Allen modified his amendment by moving to strike out the word "governor."

After debate by Messrs. Parker, of Cambridge, and Crowninshield, of Boston,

The amendment offered by Mr. Allen was rejected;—one hundred and seventy-five gentlemen voting in the affirmative, and one hundred and seventy-six voting in the negative.

Mr. Allen then moved to amend the amendment by striking out the word "lieutenant-governor," and the motion was adopted;—one hundred and eighty-three gentlemen voting in the affirmative, and one hundred and eighty-one in the negative.

Mr. Allen, of Worcester, moved to reconsider the vote by which the Committee refused to strike out the word "governor" from the amendment offered by Mr. Hooper, and the motion was adopted;—one hundred and ninety-four gentlemen voting in the affirmative, and one hundred and sixty-seven voting in the negative.

The question then recurred upon the motion of Mr. Allen, to amend the amendment by striking out the word "governor."

On this question, one hundred and eighty-six gentlemen voted in the affirmative, and one hundred and seventy-three in the negative.

So the motion of Mr. Allen was adopted.

Mr. Allen then moved to amend the amendment by striking out the words "senators in the state senate;" but the motion was rejected;—one hundred and sixty-seven gentlemen voting in the affirmative, and one hundred and ninety-three in the negative.

Mr. Allen further moved to amend the amendment, by striking out the words "representatives in the general court," which motion was adopted;—one hundred and eighty-six gentlemen voting in the affirmative, and one hundred and seventy-one in the negative.

Mr. Thompson, of Charlestown, moved to amend the amendment

by striking out the words "all county officers;" but the motion was rejected;—ninety gentlemen voting in the affirmative, and two hundred and three in the negative.

Mr. Spooner, of Warwick, moved to amend the amendment, by striking out the words "and all municipal officers;" but the motion was rejected;—one hundred and fifty-three gentlemen voting in the affirmative, and one hundred and fifty-four in the negative.

Mr. Spooner then moved a reconsideration of the last vote, which motion was agreed to by a vote of one hundred and eighty-three in the affirmative, and one hundred and fifty-seven in the negative.

The question then recurring on the motion of Mr. Spooner, to strike out the words "and all municipal officers," one hundred and ninety-eight gentlemen voted in the affirmative, and one hundred and sixty-four in the negative. So the amendment was adopted.

Mr. Churchill, of Milton, moved to reconsider the vote by which the Committee refused to strike from the amendment of Mr. Hooper the words "senators in the state senate;" but the motion was rejected, by a vote of one hundred and sixteen in the affirmative, and two hundred in the negative.

Mr. Lawton, of Fall River, moved to reconsider the vote by which the Committee refused to strike from the amendment offered by Mr. Hooper the words "all county officers;" but the motion was rejected, by a vote of twenty-six in the affirmative, and one hundred and seventy-six in the negative.

The question recurring on the amendment offered by Mr. Hooper, as amended, it was adopted, by a vote of one hundred and fifty-nine in the affirmative, and one hundred and thirty in the negative.

Mr. Hale, of Bridgewater, moved to reconsider the last vote, but the motion was rejected.

Mr. Wilson, of Natick, moved to amend the Resolution, as amended, by inserting, after the word "receiving," the words, "at the second trial;" but the motion was rejected, by a vote of one hundred and fifty-six in the affirmative, and one hundred and seventy-six in the negative.

Mr. Hallett, member for Wilbraham, moved to amend the original Resolve of the Committee, as amended, by adding the following:—

But in all elections of representatives to the general court, and of town and municipal officers, a majority of votes shall be required.

Mr. Gardner, of Seekonk, moved that the Committee rise, report progress, and ask leave to sit again; but the motion was rejected.

Mr. Hathaway, of Freetown, moved to amend the amendment

offered by Mr. Hallett, by striking out the words, "and of town and municipal officers;" but the motion was rejected.

The question recurring on the amendment, one hundred and fifty-four gentlemen voted in the affirmative, and one hundred and fifty-nine in the negative.

So the amendment of Mr. Hallett was rejected.

The question then recurred upon the adoption of the original Resolve as amended.

The question being taken, one hundred and seventy-five gentlemen voted in the affirmative, and one hundred and seventy-six in the negative.

So the Resolve of the Committee, as amended, was rejected.

Mr. Bates, of Plymouth, moved that the Committee rise, and report to the Convention, that the Resolve, as amended, ought not to pass.

After debate by Messrs. Banks, of Waltham, Kinsman, of Newburyport, Allen, of Worcester, Morton, of Taunton, Crowninshield, of Boston, and Briggs, of Pittsfield,

The motion of Mr. Bates was adopted,

And the Committee accordingly rose.

Afterwards, Mr. Briggs, of Pittsfield, in the chair.

By direction of the Convention, the Committee proceeded to consider the Resolves on the subject of the Council, (printed Document, No. 19.) Also the Resolve on the subject of the Lieutenant-Governor, (printed Document No. 9.)

The Resolves concerning the Council, were first taken up and considered.

Mr. Hallett, member for Wilbraham, addressed the Committee at length.

When, on motion of Mr. Gourgas, of Concord, it was

Voted, That the Committee rise, report progress, and ask leave to sit again.

And the Committee accordingly rose.

THURSDAY, June 2, 1853.

Mr. Briggs, of Pittsfield, in the chair.

By direction of the Convention, the Committee resumed the consideration of the unfinished business of yesterday—the Resolves on the subject of the Council.

After debate by Messrs. Gourgas, of Concord, Keyes, member for Abington, Upton, of Boston, and Durgin, of Wilmington,

Mr. Boutwell, member for Berlin, moved to amend the Resolves of the Committee, by striking out all after the word "Resolved," and inserting, instead thereof, the following:—

Resolved, That eight councillors be elected by the people, in single districts, each district to consist of five contiguous senatorial districts.

Resolved, That it is expedient so to amend the Constitution, as to provide that the record of the Proceedings of the Council shall always be subject to public examination.

After remarks by Mr. Boutwell,

Mr. Schouler, of Boston, moved that the Committee rise, report progress, and ask leave to sit again.

The motion was agreed to,

And the Committee accordingly rose.

Afterwards, Mr. Briggs, of Pittsfield, in the chair.

The Committee resumed the consideration of the Resolves on the subject of the Council, the pending question being on the amendment offered by Mr. Boutwell, member for Berlin.

After debate by Messrs. Boutwell, member for Berlin, Adams, of Lowell, Frothingham, of Charlestown, and Hubbard, of Boston,

Mr. Walker, of North Brookfield, moved to amend the amendment, by striking out the word "eight," in the first line of the first Resolve, and inserting in place thereof, the word "five," and striking out the word "five," in the last line, and inserting the word "eight."

After debate by Messrs. Gardner, of Seekonk, Walcott, of Salem, Kingman, of West Bridgewater, Wilson, of Natick, Cole, of Cheshire, Butler, of Lowell, and Bird, of Walpole,

Mr. Hallett, member for Wilbraham, moved that the Committee rise, report progress, and ask leave to sit again.

The motion was agreed to,

And the Committee accordingly rose.

FRIDAY, June 3, 1853.

Mr. Briggs, of Pittsfield, in the chair.

The Committee resumed the consideration of the unfinished business of yesterday—the Resolves on the subject of the Council; the pending question being on the amendment of Mr. Walker, to the amendment moved by Mr. Boutwell, to the original Resolves of the Committee.

After debate by Messrs. Hallett, member for Wilbraham, Upton, of Boston, and Giles, of Boston,

Mr. Hopkinson, of Boston, moved that the Committee rise, report progress, and ask leave to sit again.

The motion was adopted,

And the Committee accordingly rose.

Afterwards, Mr. Briggs, of Pittsfield, in the chair.

By direction of the Convention, the Committee resumed the consideration of the Resolves relating to the Council, the pending question being upon the amendment of Mr. Walker to the amendment moved by Mr. Boutwell, to the original Resolves.

After debate by Messrs. Giles, of Boston, and Morey, of Boston,

Mr. Walker, of North Brookfield, withdrew his amendment. The question then recurring upon the amendment of Mr. Boutwell, it was adopted by a vote of one hundred and forty-one in the affirmative, and one hundred and twenty-three in the negative.

Mr. Wilson, of Natick, moved to amend the Resolves as amended, by adding the following:—

Resolved, That it is expedient so to amend the Constitution, as to provide that no councillor, during the time for which he shall be elected, shall be appointed on any commission, or to any place, for which he shall receive any compensation whatever, other than that which he receives as councillor.

The amendment was agreed to.

The question was then taken upon the Resolves, as amended, and they were adopted by a vote of one hundred and fifty-eight in the affirmative, and eighty-three in the negative.

The Committee then proceeded to consider the next subject referred, viz.: the Resolves relating to the Lieutenant-Governor.

After remarks by Mr. Cushman, of Bernardston,

Mr. Wilkins, of Boston, moved to amend the second article of the Resolves, by striking out in the last line, (printed copy,) the words, "the Senate is equally divided," and inserting the following: "his vote may affect the decision of a question."

Debate followed between Messrs. Wilkins, of Boston, Wilson, of Natick, Cushman, of Bernardston, and Sargent, of Cambridge,

When Mr. Schouler, of Boston, moved that the Committee rise, and report to the Convention the Resolves, relating to the Council, as amended; and on the Resolves relating to the Lieutenant-Governor, report progress, and ask leave to sit again.

The motion was agreed to,

And the Committee accordingly rose.

SATURDAY, June 4, 1853.

Mr. GRISWOLD, member for Erving, in the chair.

The Committee resumed the consideration of the Resolves on the subject of the Lieutenant-Governor, the immediate question being upon the amendment of Mr. Wilkins, of Boston.

After debate by Messrs. Bates, of Plymouth, Wilkins, of Boston, Bird, of Walpole, Hooper, of Fall River, Morton, of Quincy, Cushman, of Bernardston, Wilson, of Natick, Sargent, of Cambridge, and Cole, of Cheshire,

The amendment was rejected.

Mr. Wilson, of Natick, moved to amend the Report of the Committee, by striking out the second article of the Resolve.

And the motion was adopted.

Mr. Hubbard, of Boston, moved to amend the Resolve, as amended, by adding to the first article, the following:—

The governor, and, in his absence, the lieutenant-governor, shall be president of the Council, but shall have no vote in the Council; and the lieutenant-governor shall always be a member of the Council, except when the chair of the governor shall be vacant.

After remarks by Mr. Hubbard, the motion was adopted.

Mr. Knowlton, of Worcester, moved to amend the Resolve, as amended, by striking out all after the word "Resolved," and adding the following:—

That it is expedient to strike from the Constitution, as much thereof as relates to the office of Lieutenant-Governor.

After debate by Messrs. Bradbury, of Newton, Bates, of Plymouth, Hooper, of Fall River, and Earle, of Worcester,

The amendment was rejected.

Mr. Wilkinson, of Dedham, then moved that the Committee rise, and report to the Convention, that the Resolutions, as amended, ought to pass.

The motion was agreed to,

And the Committee accordingly rose.

MONDAY, June 6, 1853.

Mr. Hood, of Lynn, in the chair.

By direction of the Convention, the Committee proceeded to the consideration of the Report, respecting the originating of Bills and Resolves in the House of Representatives, (printed Document No. 21.)

The Report was accepted, without debate.

When, upon motion of Mr. Wilson, of Natick, it was

Voted, That the Committee rise, and report to the Convention, that the Report of the Standing Committee ought to be accepted.

And the Committee accordingly rose.

Afterwards, Mr. Frothingham, of Charlestown, in the chair.

By direction of the Convention, the Committee proceeded to the consideration of the Report from the Committee on the Frame of Government, in favor of the *viva voce* mode of Elections in the Legislature, (printed Document No. 23.)

After remarks by Mr. Allen, of Worcester, the Resolve was adopted.

On motion of Mr. Earle, of Worcester, it was

Voted, That the Committee rise, and report to the Convention that the Resolve ought to pass.

And the Committee accordingly rose.

Afterwards, Mr. Bates, of Plymouth, in the chair.

By direction of the Convention, the Committee proceeded to the consideration of the Report from the Committee on the Frame of Government:—

"Inexpedient to act on an Order, relating to the permanent establishment of the Seat of Government at Boston."

The Report was accepted, without debate,

When, on motion of Mr. Earle, of Worcester, it was

Voted, That the Committee rise, and report to the Convention, that the Report of the Standing Committee ought to pass,

And the Committee accordingly rose.

Afterwards, Mr. WHITNEY, of Conway, in the chair.

The Committee proceeded to the consideration of the Report from the Committee on the Frame of Government, concerning a limitation of the time for the reception of Petitions by the Legislature, (printed Document No. 22.)

After debate by Messrs. Gardner, of Seekonk, Allen, of Worcester, Earle, of Worcester, and Bird, of Walpole,

The Report was accepted.

On motion of Mr. Allen, of Worcester, it was

Voted, That the Committee rise, and report to the Convention that the Report of the Standing Committee ought to pass,

And the Committee accordingly rose.

Afterwards, Mr. DANA, member for Manchester, in the chair.

The Committee, by direction of the Convention, proceeded to the consideration of the Report from the Committee on the Qualifications of Voters, (printed Document No. 10.)

After debate by Messrs. Williams, of Taunton, and Cady, of Monson,

Mr. Durgin, of Wilmington, moved that the Committee rise, report progress, and ask leave to sit again; but the motion was rejected, by a vote of forty-six in the affirmative, and seventy-five in the negative.

Mr. Clark, of Holyoke, moved to amend the first Resolve, by striking out, in the third and fourth lines, (printed copy,) the words, "of governor, lieutenant-governor, senators, and representatives of."

After debate by Messrs. Cady, of Monson, Tyler, of Pawtucket, Hooper, of Fall River, Edwards, of Southampton, Bird, of Walpole, and Hood, of Lynn,

Mr. Churchill, of Milton, moved to amend the first Resolve, by striking out the word "not," in the second line.

Debate followed between Messrs. Tyler, of Pawtucket, Simonds, of Bedford, and Hooper, of Fall River,

When Mr. Churchill withdrew his amendment.

After further debate by Messrs. Hubbard, of Boston, and Hood, of Lynn,

Mr. Bird, of Walpole, moved that the Committee rise, report progress, and ask leave to sit again, which motion was adopted,

And the Committee accordingly rose.

Afterwards, Mr. Dana, member for Manchester, in the chair.

The Committee resumed the consideration of the Report of the Committee on the Qualifications of Voters;

The immediate question being upon the amendment offered by Mr. Clark, of Holyoke.

After remarks by Mr. Walker, of North Brookfield,

Mr. Leland, of Holliston, moved to strike out in the third line of the first Resolve, the words, "any election," and insert after the word "Commonwealth," the words, "except in parish affairs."

After debate by Messrs. Bates, of Plymouth, Earle of Worcester, Morey, of Boston, Morton, of Quincy, Simonds, of Bedford, Perkins, of Malden, French, of Berkley, Childs, of Westborough, Eames, of Washington, and Hallett, member for Wilbraham,

Mr. Clark accepted the amendment offered by Mr. Leland.

The debate was continued by Messrs. Keyes, member for Abington, Hood, of Lynn, and Houghton, of Stirling.

When Mr. Schouler, of Boston, moved that the Committee rise, report progress, and ask leave to sit again.

The motion was adopted by a vote of one hundred and twenty-two in the affirmative, and twenty-three in the negative.

And the Committee accordingly rose.

TUESDAY, June 7, 1853.

Mr. Dana, member for Manchester, in the chair.

The Committee resumed the consideration of the Report of the Committee on the Qualifications of Voters, the pending question being on the amendment moved by Mr. Clark, of Holyoke.

Mr. Clark withdrew his amendment.

After debate by Messrs. Whitney, of Boylston, Lord, of Salem, Wilson, of Natick, and Burlingame, member for Northborough,

Mr. Lord, of Salem, moved that the Committee rise, report progress, and ask leave to sit again;

But the motion was rejected.

Mr. Burlingame resumed his remarks; at the conclusion of which,

On motion of Mr. Hooper, of Fall River, it was

Voted, That the Committee rise, report progress, and ask leave to sit again,

And the Committee accordingly rose.

Afterwards, Mr. DANA, member for Manchester, in the chair.

The Committee resumed the consideration of the Report of the Committee on the Qualifications of Voters.

After debate by Messrs. Hooper, of Fall River, Walker, of North Brookfield, Hubbard, of Boston, French, of Berkley, Morss, of Newburyport, Frothingham, of Charlestown, and Houghton, of Stirling,

Mr. Cummings, of Ware, renewed the motion of Mr. Clark to amend the first Resolve, by striking out, in the third and fourth lines the words, "of governor, lieutenant-governor, senators, and representatives of," and inserting in place thereof, the word "in."

After debate by Messrs. Hubbard, of Boston, and Hooper, of Fall River,

Mr. Cummings withdrew his amendment.

The debate was continued by Messrs. Hooper, of Fall River, and Hallett, member for Wilbraham.

Pending the question, Mr. French, of New Bedford, moved that the Committee rise, report progress, and ask leave to sit again,

Which motion was adopted,

And the Committee accordingly rose.

WEDNESDAY, June 8, 1853.

Mr. DANA, member for Manchester, in the chair.

By direction of the Convention, the Committee resumed the consideration of the Report of the Committee upon the Qualifications of Voters.

After debate by Messrs. French, of New Bedford, Hillard, of Boston, Dawes, of Adams, Oliver, of Lawrence, and Schouler, of Boston,

Mr. Upton, of Boston, moved to amend the first Resolution, by striking out all after the word "vote," in the second line, (printed copy.)

Mr. Bradbury, of Newton, moved to amend the amendment, by adding the words, "in any election."

But the motion of Mr. Bradbury was rejected.

The question then recurring upon the amendment moved by Mr. Upton,

It was rejected.

Mr. Aldrich, of Barre, moved to amend the first Resolve, by striking out all after the word "Resolved," and inserting the following:—

That all persons exempted by law, or under any provision of law, from taxation, and who are otherwise qualified, as the Constitution requires now, shall be allowed to vote in all elections;

But the motion was rejected.

Mr. Hood, of Lynn, moved that when the vote is taken upon the acceptance of the first Resolve, it be taken by yeas and nays, but the Chairman decided that the motion could not be entertained in Committee of the Whole.

Mr. Hathaway, of Freetown, moved to amend the first Resolve, by striking out all after the word "Resolved," and inserting the following:—

Every male citizen, of twenty-one years of age and upwards, (excepting paupers and persons under guardianship,) who shall have resided within the Commonwealth one year, and within the town or district in which he may claim a right to vote, three calendar months next preceding any election of governor, lieutenant-governor, senators, or representatives, and who shall have paid by himself or his parent, master or guardian, any state or county tax, which shall, within two years next preceding such election, have been assessed upon him, in any town or district of this Commonwealth. And also every citizen who shall be by law exempted from taxation, and who shall be, in all other respects, qualified as above mentioned, shall have a right to vote in such election of governor, lieutenant-governor, senators, and representatives; and no other person shall be entitled to vote in such elections.

The question being taken on the amendment, it was rejected by a vote of one hundred and eighteen in the affirmative, and one hundred and eighty-five in the negative.

The question then recurring upon the first Resolution, as reported by the Committee, it was agreed to.

Mr. Lord, of Salem, moved that the Committee rise, report progress, and ask leave to sit again;

But the motion was rejected.

Mr. Davis, of Plymouth, moved to strike out the second Resolve,

And the motion was adopted.

Mr. Walker, of North Brookfield, moved to amend the third Resolve, by striking out, in the fifth line, (printed copy,) the word "member," and inserting the word "student;" which motion was adopted.

Mr. Hathaway, of Freetown, moved to strike out the third Resolve,

But the motion was rejected.

The third Resolve, as amended, was then agreed to by the Committee.

Mr. Edwards, of Southampton, moved to amend the fourth Resolve, by striking out the word "municipal," in the second line, (printed copy,) and inserting the word "or," before the word "county," in the same line,

But the motion was rejected.

Mr. Schouler, of Boston, moved to amend the fourth Resolve, by striking out all after the word "Resolved," and inserting the following:—

That all votes required by law to be given at any national, state, county, or municipal election, shall be by secret ballot,

But the motion was rejected.

Mr. Oliver, of Lawrence, moved to amend the same Resolve, by striking out in the second line, (printed copy,) the word "shall," and inserting in place thereof the word "may,"

But the motion was rejected.

Mr. Upton, of Boston, moved further to amend the Resolve, by inserting the word "town," after the word "county," in the second line,

But the motion was rejected.

Mr. Lord, of Salem, moved to amend the Resolve, by striking out in the second line, the words, "national, state, county, or municipal,"

But the motion was rejected.

Mr. Davis, of Plymouth, moved to amend the Resolve, by inserting in the second line, after the word "county," the word "district,"

But the motion was rejected.

Mr. Lawton, of Fall River, moved to reconsider the vote by which the Committee refused to insert the word "town," after the word "county," in the second line,

But the motion was rejected.

On motion of Mr. Bates, of Plymouth, it was

Voted, That the Committee rise, and report to the Convention, that the Resolves, as amended, ought to pass.

And the Committee accordingly rose.

THURSDAY, June 9, 1853.

Mr. Thompson, of Charlestown, in the chair.

By direction of the Convention, the Committee proceeded to the consideration of the Report of the Committee on the Frame of Government, that it is inexpedient to act upon an Order of May 20th, concerning Special Privileges and Immunities, (printed Document No. 35.)

After remarks by Mr. Allen, of Worcester,

The Report was accepted.

When, on motion of Mr. Briggs, of Pittsfield, it was

Voted, That the Committee rise, and report that the Report of the Standing Committee ought to be accepted by the Convention.

And the Committee accordingly rose.

Afterwards, Mr. Morton, of Fairhaven, in the chair.

The Committee proceeded to the consideration of the Report of the Committee on the Frame of Government, that it is inexpedient to act upon an Order of May 24th, respecting the Purchase of Books, &c., by the Legislature.

The Report was accepted, without debate.

On motion of Mr. Thompson, of Charlestown, it was

Voted, That the Committee rise and report to the Convention, that the Report of the Standing Committee ought to be accepted.

And the Committee accordingly rose.

Afterwards, Mr. HALL, of Haverhill, in the chair.

The Committee proceeded to the consideration of the Report of the Committee on the Frame of Government, that it is inexpedient to act upon an Order of the 18th of May, concerning Biennial Elections, and Biennial Sessions of the Legislature.

The Report was accepted, without debate.

On motion of Mr. Cushman, of Barnardston, it was

Voted, That the Committee rise, and report that the Report of the Standing Committee ought to be accepted by the Convention.

And the Committee accordingly rose.

Afterwards, Mr. ALVORD, member for Montague, in the chair.

The Committee proceeded to consider the Report of the Committee on the Frame of Government, that it is inexpedient to act upon an Order of the 13th of May, relative to the expediency of requiring the votes of a majority of all the members elected to the Legislature, to the enactment of a law, or passage of a Resolve, (printed Document No. 34.)

The Report was accepted, without debate.

It was then

Voted, That the Committee rise, and report to the Convention, that the Report of the Standing Committee ought to be accepted.

And the Committee accordingly rose.

FRIDAY, June 10, 1853.

Mr. GRISWOLD, member for Erving, in the chair.

By direction of the Convention, the Committee proceeded to the consideration of the Report and Resolves from the Standing Committee, on so much of the Constitution as relates to the Secretary, Treasurer, Attorney-General, and Solicitor-General, (printed Document No. 30.)

After debate by Messrs. Bishop, of Lenox, and Davis, of Plymouth,

Mr. Davis, of Plymouth, moved that the several Resolves reported by the Committee, be considered separately.

This motion was discussed by Messrs. Aspinwall, of Brookline, and Davis, of Plymouth, when it was adopted.

The question then recurred on the Resolves of the Committee.

After debate by Messrs. Hooper, of Fall River, and Bishop, of Lenox, the first Resolve was adopted.

The second Resolve was then adopted, without debate.

Mr. Dana, member for Manchester, moved to amend the third Resolve, by striking out of the first line, (printed copy,) the words, "judges of probate."

After debate by Messrs. Dana, member for Manchester, Bates, of Plymouth, Hooper, of Fall River, Thompson, of Charlestown, and Schouler, of Boston,

Mr. Wilson, of Natick, moved to amend the amendment, by inserting, after the word "Probate," in the first line, the words, "be elected every six years, and."

Debate followed between Messrs. Schouler, of Boston, Bishop, of Lenox, and Morton, of Quincy,

When Mr. Wilson withdrew his amendment.

Mr. Hooper, of Fall River, moved that the Committee rise, report progress, and ask leave to sit again.

The motion was adopted.

And the Committee accordingly rose.

Afterwards, Mr. Griswold, member for Erving, in the chair.

The Committee resumed the consideration of the unfinished business of its last session, being the Report of the Standing Committee on so much of the Constitution as relates to the Secretary, Treasurer, &c., the pending question being upon the amendment offered by Mr. Dana, member for Manchester.

Mr. Dana withdrew his amendment, and moved to amend the third Resolve, by inserting, after the word "probate," the following words,—"be elected once in six years, and."

After debate by Messrs. Dana, member for Manchester, Bishop, of Lenox, Brinley, of Boston, Bates, of Plymouth Chapin, of Worcester, Bird, of Walpole, and Phinney, member for Chatham,

Mr. Hallett, member for Wilbraham, moved, that when the Committee rise, it recommend to the Convention that it recommit to the Standing Committee, that part of the third Resolve relating to Judges of Probate.

After debate by Messrs. Nayson, of Amesbury, and Hooper, of Fall River,

The motion was rejected.

The question then recurred on the amendment of Mr. Dana, which was adopted by a vote of one hundred and twenty in the affirmative, and ninety-three in the negative.

The question then recurred upon the adoption of the third Resolve, as amended.

After debate by Messrs. Aspinwall, of Brookline, Bishop, of Lenox, and Bates, of Plymouth,

Mr. Aspinwall, of Brookline, moved to amend the Resolution by striking out the words "county treasurers," in the third line, and inserting the words "county treasurers, annually" after the word "triennially," in the fourth line.

Debate followed between Messrs. Hooper, of Fall River, Miller, of Wareham, French, of Berkley, and Bishop, of Lenox,

When the amendment was adopted, by a vote of one hundred and three in the affirmative, and seventy-five in the negative.

The question recurring upon the Resolve, as amended,

Mr. Miller, of Wareham, moved to strike out the words "clerks of the courts," in the first line.

After debate by Messrs. Bates, of Plymouth, Churchill, of Milton, Whitney, of Conway, Hubbard, of Boston, and Davis, of Worcester,

The motion was rejected.

Mr. Hubbard, of Boston, moved to amend the Resolve, by inserting after the word "treasurer," in the third line, (printed copy,) the words "except the treasurer of the county of Suffolk,"

But the motion was rejected.

The third Resolve, as amended, was then adopted.

After remarks by Mr. Wilson, of Natick, the fourth Resolve was adopted.

On motion of Mr. Wilson, of Natick, it was

Voted, That the Committee rise and report to the Convention that the Resolves, as amended, ought to be adopted.

And the Committee accordingly rose.

MONDAY, June 13, 1853.

Mr. Livermore, of Cambridge, in the chair.

By direction of the Convention, the Committee proceeded to the consideration of a Resolve on the Legislative Department of the Government, reported by the Committee on the Frame of Government, (printed Document No. 38.)

Mr. Brinley, of Boston, moved to amend the Resolve, by striking out the last paragraph of article first, commencing with the word "provided."

Mr. Eames, of Washington, moved to amend the amendment, by striking out all after the word "governor," in the eighth line of article 1st.

After debate by Messrs. Allen, of Worcester, Brinley, of Boston, Eames, of Washington, Schouler, of Boston, Parsons, of Lawrence, Wilson, of Natick, Hallett, member for Wilbraham, French, of Berkley, Davis, of Plymouth, Chapin, of Webster, Walker, of North Brookfield, and Chapin, of Worcester,

Mr. Brinley called for a division of the question, and the Chairman decided the motion of Mr. Brinley first in order.

The question being taken, the amendment was rejected.

Mr. Hallett, member for Wilbraham, then moved to amend the amendment of Mr. Eames, of Washington, by adding the following:

The Legislature which shall assemble next after the adoption of this article in the Constitution, shall fix the compensation of members, which may be changed at any subsequent session; but no act affecting the pay of members, passed after the year 1854, shall take effect until the session next after its passage; and no compensation or pay shall hereafter be allowed for the attendance of members, longer than one hundred days, at any one session.

Debate followed between Messrs. Hallett, member for Wilbraham, Allen, of Worcester, Bradbury, of Newton, Wilson, of Natick, Kingman, of West Bridgewater, Davis, of Plymouth, and Morton, of Fairhaven,

When Mr. Bates, of Plymouth, moved that the Committee rise, report progress, and ask leave to sit again. The motion was adopted,

And the Committee accordingly rose.

TUESDAY, June 14, 1853.

Mr. Livermore, of Cambridge, in the chair.

By direction of the Convention, the Committee resumed the consideration of the Resolve on the Legislative Department of the Government, the pending question being upon the amendment offered by Mr. Hallett, member for Wilbraham, to the amendment of Mr. Eames, of Washington.

After debate by Messrs. Wilkins, of Boston, Gray, of Boston, Foster, of Charlemont, Morton, of Taunton, Frothingham, of Charlestown, Whitney, of Boylston, and Sumner, member for Otis,

The question was taken on the amendment of Mr. Eames, and it was rejected.

The question then recurred upon the amendment moved by Mr. Hallett.

After debate by Messrs. Upton, of Boston, and Stetson, of Braintree,

Mr. Morton, of Taunton, moved to amend the amendment, by striking out the first part, as far as and including the word "passage," and inserting instead thereof, the words :—

The Legislature shall, by law, establish the compensation of the members thereof, which shall, in no case, be increased or diminished during their continuance in office.

Debate followed between Messrs. Frothingham, of Charlestown, Nayson, of Amesbury, and Morton, of Taunton,

When Mr. Morton modified his amendment, upon the suggestion of Mr. Bradbury, of Newton, by striking out the words "or diminished."

Mr. Allen, of Worcester, addressed the Committee.

The question then being taken, the amendment of Mr. Morton was rejected, by a vote of fifty-five in the affirmative, and one hundred and thirteen in the negative.

Mr. Whitney, of Conway, moved to reconsider the last vote, but the motion was rejected.

The question then recurring upon the amendment of Mr. Hallett, it was adopted, by a vote of one hundred and thirty-five in the affirmative, and sixty-eight in the negative.

The question then recurred upon the Resolve, as amended. The question being taken, it was adopted.

On motion of Mr. Weston, of Duxbury, it was

Voted, That the Committee rise, and report that the Resolve, as amended, ought to pass.

And the Committee accordingly rose.

Afterwards, Mr. Wilson, of Natick, in the chair.

By direction of the Convention, the Committee proceeded to the consideration of the Resolves reported from the Committee on the House of Representatives, (printed Document No. 18.)

After remarks by Mr. Griswold, member for Erving,

Mr. Knowlton, of Worcester, moved that the Committee rise, report progress, and ask leave to sit again. The motion was agreed to,

And the Committee accordingly rose.

Afterwards, Mr. WILSON, of Natick, in the chair.

The Committee resumed the consideration of the unfinished business of its last session, being the Resolves on the subject of the House of Representatives.

Mr. Griswold, member for Erving, resumed and concluded his remarks, when

Mr. Hale, of Boston, moved to amend the Resolves, by striking out all after the word Resolved, and inserting instead thereof, the Resolve reported from the Minority of the Committee, (printed Document No. 18.)

Mr. Gray, of Boston, moved that the Committee rise, report progress, and ask leave to sit again.

But the motion was rejected.

After debate by Messrs. Hale, of Boston, and Schouler, of Boston, on motion of Mr. Bird, of Walpole, it was

Voted, That the Committee rise, report progress, and ask leave to sit again.

And the Committee accordingly rose.

WEDNESDAY, June 15, 1853.

Mr. WILSON, of Natick, in the chair.

By direction of the Convention, the Committee resumed the consideration of the Report of the Committee on the House of Representatives, the pending question being upon the amendment moved by Mr. Hale, of Boston.

After debate by Messrs. Rantoul, of Beverly, Schouler, of Boston, and Wood, of Middleborough,

Mr. Sargent, of Cambridge, moved that the Committee rise, report progress, and ask leave to sit again. The motion was adopted,

And the Committee accordingly rose.

Afterwards, Mr. Wilson, of Natick, in the chair.

The Committee, by direction of the Convention, resumed the consideration of the unfinished business of its last session—the Report on the House of Representatives, the pending question being on the amendment of Mr. Hale, of Boston.

After debate by Messrs. Sargent, of Cambridge, and Gray, of Boston,

Mr. Kinsman, of Newburyport, moved that the Committee rise, report progress, and ask leave to sit again. The motion was adopted, by a vote of eighty-nine in the affirmative, and fifty-six in the negative.

And the Committee accordingly rose.

THURSDAY, June 16, 1853.

Mr. Wilson, of Natick, in the chair.

The Committee resumed the consideration of the unfinished business of yesterday—the Report on the subject of the House of Representatives, the pending question being on the amendment of Mr. Hale, of Boston.

After remarks by Mr. Choate, of Boston,

Mr. Mixter, of New Braintree, moved that the Committee rise, report progress, and ask leave to sit again. The motion was adopted,

And the Committee accordingly rose.

Afterwards, Mr. Wilson, of Natick, in the chair.

The Committee proceeded to the consideration of the unfinished business of its last session—the Report on the subject of the House of Representatives.

After debate by Messrs. Boutwell, member for Berlin, Walker, of North Brookfield, Keyes, member for Abington, and French, of Berkley,

Mr. Simonds, of Bedford, moved that the Committee rise, report progress, and ask leave to sit again. The motion was adopted, by a vote of ninety-one in the affirmative, and eighty-two in the negative,

And the Committee accordingly rose.

FRIDAY, June 17, 1853.

Mr. Wilson, of Natick, in the chair.

The Committee resumed the consideration of the Report on the subject of the House of Representatives, the immediate question being upon the amendment offered by Mr. Hale, of Boston.

After debate by Messrs. Hallett, member for Wilbraham, and Wood, of Fitchburg,

Mr. Parker, of Cambridge, moved that the Committee rise, report progress, and ask leave to sit again; which motion was adopted.

And the Committee accordingly rose.

Afterwards, Mr. Wilson, of Natick, in the chair.

The Committee resumed the consideration of the unfinished business of its last session—the Report on the subject of the House of Representatives.

After debate by Messrs. Parker, of Cambridge, Hallett, member for Wilbraham, Bird, of Walpole, and Dana, member for Manchester,

On motion of Mr. Dawes, of Adams, it was

Voted, That the Committee rise, report progress, and ask leave to sit again.

And the Committee accordingly rose.

SATURDAY, June 18, 1853.

Mr. Nayson, of Amesbury, in the chair.

By direction of the Convention, the Committee proceeded to the consideration of the Report from the Committee on the Frame of Government:—

"Inexpedient to act upon an Order of June 3d, concerning the Compensation of Commissioners."

The Report was accepted, without debate.

On motion of Mr. Wilson, of Natick, it was

Voted, That the Committee rise, and report to the Convention that the Report of the Standing Committee ought to be accepted.

And the Committee accordingly rose.

Afterwards, Mr. Bradbury, of Newton, in the chair.

The Committee proceeded to the consideration of the Report from the Committee on the subject of the Governor:—

"Inexpedient to act upon an Order of June 3d, relative to the Pardoning Power."

Mr. Churchill, of Milton, moved that it be recommended to the Convention, that the Report be recommitted to the Standing Committee.

After debate by Messrs. Churchill, of Milton, Choate, of Boston, Bird, of Walpole, and Huntington, of Northampton,

Mr. Schouler, of Boston, moved that the Committee rise, report progress, and ask leave to sit again; which motion was adopted.

And the Committee accordingly rose.

MONDAY, June 20, 1853.

Mr. Bradbury, of Newton, in the chair.

By direction of the Convention, the Committee resumed the consideration of the unfinished business of its last session—the Report on the Pardoning Power, the pending question being on the amendment offered by Mr. Churchill, of Milton.

Mr. Davis, of Worcester, addressed the Committee.

Mr. Sumner, member for Otis, moved to amend the motion of Mr. Churchill, by substituting the following:—

That it be recommended that the Report be recommitted, with instructions to report a resolve, that the legislature may provide by law, regulations relative to the manner of applying to the executive for pardons.

After remarks by Mr. Thompson, of Charlestown,

Mr. Churchill withdrew his motion, and moved to amend the Report of the Committee by striking out the words "inexpedient to act thereon," and inserting the following:—

Expedient, that in all applications to the executive to remit a portion of the sentence of a person still under confinement, or to commute, notice shall be given to the attorney for the Commonwealth, of the time and place of such hearing.

After debate by Messrs. Hallett, member for Wilbraham, Briggs, of Pittsfield, Whitney, of Boylston, Keyes, member for Abington, Churchill, of Milton, Crowninshield, of Boston, Wood, of Fitchburg, and Upton, of Boston,

The amendment was rejected.

The question then recurring upon the Report of the Committee, it was accepted.

Mr. Earle, of Worcester, then moved that the Committee rise and report to the Convention that the Report of the Standing Committee ought to be accepted.

The motion was adopted.

And the Committee accordingly rose.

Afterwards, Mr. WOOD, of Fitchburg, in the chair.

The Committee proceeded to consider the following Resolve, reported from the Committee on the subject of the Governor:—

Resolved, That it is expedient to amend the Constitution by abolishing the title of "His Excellency."

The Resolve was adopted, without debate.

On motion of Mr. Earle, of Worcester, it was

Voted, That the Committee rise and report to the Convention that the Resolve ought to pass.

And the Committee accordingly rose.

Afterwards, Mr. ALLEN, of Worcester, in the chair.

The Committee proceeded to consider the Resolves concerning the Militia, reported from the Standing Committee on that subject, (printed Document No. 47.)

After remarks by Mr. Oliver, of Lawrence,

Mr. Wilkins, of Boston, moved to amend the Resolve by striking out the words "written votes," in the third, fourth, fifth and sixth paragraphs, and inserting instead thereof the word "ballot;" but, upon suggestion of Mr. Hathaway, of Freetown, withdrew his motion.

Mr. Oliver, of Lawrence, moved to amend the sixth paragraph of the Resolve, by inserting after the word "by," in the first line, the words, "a majority of."

And the motion was adopted.

Mr. Hallett, member for Wilbraham, moved to amend the twelfth paragraph of the Resolve, by striking out the words "three years," in the second line, and inserting the words "one year," and by striking out all after the word "qualified," in the fourth line.

On motion of Mr. Earle, of Worcester, it was

Voted, That the Committee rise, report progress, and ask leave to sit again.

And the Committee accordingly rose.

Afterwards, Mr. ALLEN, of Worcester, in the chair.

The Committee resumed the consideration of the unfinished business of its last session—the Report and Resolves concerning the Militia, the immediate question being upon the amendment offered by Mr. Hallett to the twelfth paragraph of the Resolve.

The question being taken upon the amendment,

It was rejected.

Mr. Oliver, of Lawrence, moved to amend the tenth paragraph, by inserting, after the word "appoint," in the first line, the words "and commission for one year, or until their successors shall be commissioned and qualified;"

Which motion was adopted.

The same gentleman moved to amend the twelfth paragraph by inserting, after the word "several," in the first line, the word "elective," and striking out all after the word "qualified," in the fourth line;

Which motion was also adopted.

Mr. Bradford, of Essex, moved to amend the seventh paragraph, by adding thereto the following words:—

Provided, that the said governor shall not, at any time hereafter, by virtue of any power by this Constitution granted, or hereafter to be granted to him by the legislature, transport any of the inhabitants of this Commonwealth, or oblige them to march out of the limits of the same, without their free and voluntary consent, or the consent of the general court; except so far as may be necessary to march or transport them, by land or water, for the defence of such part of the State, to which they cannot otherwise conveniently have access.

After debate by Messrs. Wilson, of Natick, Parsons, of Lawrence, Davis, of Fall River, Oliver, of Lawrence, Bird, of Walpole, Hopkinson of Boston, Banks, of Waltham, Briggs, of Pittsfield, Keyes, member for Abington, Walker, of North Brookfield, Hallett, member for Wilbraham, Butler, of Lowell, Frothingham, of Charlestown, Ball, of Upton, and Bradford, of Essex,

The amendment was rejected.

Mr. Hopkinson, of Boston, moved to amend the seventh paragraph by adding the words, "to be exercised according to the laws of the land."

The same gentleman moved that the Committee rise, report progress, and ask leave to sit again;

But the motion was rejected.

Mr. Hopkinson then withdrew his motion.

Mr. Keyes, member for Abington, addressed the Committee, when,

On motion of Mr. Wilson, of Natick, it was

Voted, That the Committee rise, and report that the Resolve, as amended, ought to pass.

And the Committee accordingly rose.

TUESDAY, June 21, 1853.

Mr. Wilson, of Natick, in the chair.

By direction of the Convention, the Committee resumed the consideration of the Report of the Committee on the House of Representatives; the immediate question being upon the motion of Mr. Hale, of Boston, to amend by substituting the Minority Report of the Committee.

After remarks by Mr. Dawes, of Adams,

Mr. Durgin, of Wilmington, moved that the Committee rise, report progress, and ask leave to sit again.

The motion was adopted.

And the Committee accordingly rose.

Afterwards, Mr. Wilson, of Natick, in the chair.

The Committee resumed the consideration of the unfinished business of its last session—the Report concerning the House of Representatives, the pending question being on the motion of Mr. Hale, to substitute the Minority Report of the Committee.

After debate by Messrs. Durgin, of Wilmington, and Walker, of North Brookfield,

The question was taken upon the amendment offered by Mr. Hale, and it was rejected, by a vote of sixty-one in the affirmative, and one hundred and fifty-six in the negative.

Mr. Brinley, of Boston, moved that the Committee rise, report progress, and ask leave to sit again.

The motion was adopted, by a vote of eighty-eight in the affirmative, and eighty-one in the negative.

And the Committee accordingly rose.

WEDNESDAY, June 22, 1853.

Mr. Schouler, of Boston, in the chair.

By direction of the Convention, the Committee proceeded to consider the Report from the Committee on the Militia,

"Inexpedient to act upon the Petition of John P. Coburn, 'That the laws may be so modified, that no able-bodied male citizen may be forbidden or prevented, from serving or holding office or commission in the Militia, on account of color.'"

Mr. Whitney, of Boylston, addressed the Committee.

Mr. Wilson of Natick, moved to amend the Report, by striking out all after the word "That," in the first line, as far as, and including the word "but," in the fifth line, (printed copy.)

Debate followed between Messrs. Wilson, of Natick, and Churchill, of Milton.

Mr. Briggs, of Pittsfield, moved to amend the amendment, by striking out all after the word "Report," in the first line, as far as, and including the word "that," in the last line.

After remarks by Mr. Banks, of Waltham,

Mr. Wilson accepted the amendment.

Mr. Keyes, member for Abington, addressed the Committee,

When, the question being taken, the amendment was rejected.

Mr. Whitney, of Boylston, moved to amend, by inserting after the words "just named," in the sixteenth line, (printed copy,) the words, "but no distinction shall ever be made, in the enrolment of persons to serve in the voluntary militia of Massachusetts, on account of difference of color."

After debate by Messrs. Wilson, of Natick, and Keyes, member for Abington,

Mr. Whitney modified his motion, so as to strike out all after the word "Report," in the first line, and insert the following:—

That in the enrolment of the voluntary militia of the Commonwealth, no distinction shall ever be made on account of color.

The question then being taken, the amendment was rejected, by a vote of seventy-four in the affirmative, and ninety-nine in the negative.

The question then recurred on the adoption of the Report of the Committee, and being taken, it was, without a division, decided in the affirmative.

Mr. Bàtes, of Plymouth, moved that the Committee rise, and report to the Convention that the Report of the Standing Committee ought to be accepted.

The motion was agreed to,

And the Committee accordingly rose.

Afterwards, Mr. Boutwell, member for Berlin, in the chair.

The Committee proceeded to consider the Report of the Specia Committee, to whom was referred the subject of the Loan of the State Credit to any individual or corporation, and the several Orders of May 17th, 18th, and 27th, (printed Document No. 48.)

After debate by Messrs. Keyes, member for Abington, and Wilson, of Shelburne,

Mr. Stetson, of Braintree, moved to amend the Report, by striking out all after the word " Report," in the fourth line, (printed copy,) and inserting the following:—

Resolved, That the Constitution be so amended that, hereafter no loan of the State Credit shall be given to any corporation or individual, unless the question is first submitted to the people.

Mr. Bradford, of Essex, moved that the Committee rise, report progress, and ask leave to sit again.

The motion was adopted,

And the Committee accordingly rose.

Afterwards, Mr. Cushman, of Bernardston, in the chair.

The Committee proceeded to consider the Report from the Committee on the Frame of Government:—

" Inexpedient to act upon an Order of May 31st, concerning the election of Senators in the Congress of the United States, by joint ballot of the two Houses of the Legislature," (printed Document No. 39.)

The Report was accepted, without debate.

On motion of Mr. Wilson, of Natick, it was

Voted, That the Committee rise, and report to the Convention that the Report of the Standing Committee ought to be accepted.

And the Committee accordingly rose.

Afterwards, Mr. Briggs, of Pittsfield, in the chair.

The Committee proceeded to consider the Resolves reported from the Committee on the Qualifications of Voters, to whom was re-committed the third Resolve of that Committee, reported on the 19th of May, together with an amendment prepared thereto, (printed Document No. 55.)

After debate by Messrs. Churchill, of Milton, Aldrich, of Barre, and Houghton, of Sterling,

Mr. Hopkinson, of Boston, moved to amend the second Resolve, by striking out the words "and State," in the fourth line, (printed copy,) and inserting after the word "officers," in the last line, the words, "or for any officer to be chosen, or upon any question to be decided by the vote of the people of the whole State."

After remarks by Messrs. French, of Berkley, and Morton, of Quincy, the amendment was adopted, by a vote of seventy-four in the affirmative, and forty-seven in the negative.

Mr. Stevens, of Clinton, moved to amend the first Resolve, by striking out all after the word "seas," in the fifth line.

Mr. Stevens addressed the Committee upon his motion.

Mr. Duncan, of Williamstown, moved that the Committee rise, report progress, and ask leave to sit again.

The motion was adopted, by a vote of fifty-nine in the affirmative, and fifty-one in the negative.

And the Committee accordingly rose.

THURSDAY, June 23, 1853.

Mr. Sumner, member for Otis, in the chair.

By direction of the Convention, the Committee proceeded to consider the following Resolve, reported from a Special Committee:—

Resolved, That it is expedient to incorporate into the Constitution a provision, that corporations may be formed under general laws, but shall not be created by special act, except for banking or municipal purposes, or where the object of the incorporation shall not be attainable under general laws.

After remarks by Mr. Whitney, of Conway,

Mr. French, of Berkley, moved to amend the Resolve, by striking out all after the word "act," in the third line, (printed copy.)

Remarks were made by Mr. Bradford, of Essex, when the motion was rejected.

Mr. Stetson, of Braintree, moved to amend, by striking out the words "banking or," in the fourth line.

Mr. Nayson, of Amesbury, moved that the Committee rise, report progress, and ask leave to sit again.

But after remarks by Mr. Whitney, of Conway, the motion was rejected.

After debate by Messrs. Earle, of Worcester, and Whitney, of Conway,

Mr. Cole, of Cheshire, moved to amend the amendment of Mr. Stetson, by striking out all after the word "purposes," in the fourth line.

Mr. Chapin, of Springfield, then moved that the Committee rise, report progress, and ask leave to sit again.

The motion was adopted, by a vote of eighty-four in the affirmative, and sixty-five in the negative.

And the Committee accordingly rose.

Afterwards, Mr. Wilson, of Natick, in the chair.

By direction of the Convention, the Committee resumed the consideration of the Majority Report, from the Committee on the House of Representatives.

After debate by Messrs. Hillard, of Boston, Dana, member for Manchester, Schouler, of Boston, Hooper, of Fall River, and Bradford, of Essex,

On motion of Mr. Alley, of Lynn, it was

Voted, That the Committee rise, report progress, and ask leave to sit again.

And the Committee accordingly rose.

Afterwards, Mr. Wilson, of Natick, in the chair.

The Committee resumed the consideration of the unfinished business of its last session—the Report on the House of Representatives.

After remarks by Messrs. Alley, of Lynn, and Butler, of Lowell,

Mr. Butler, of Lowell, moved to amend the Report of the Committee, by striking out all after the word "Resolved," and inserting what is printed as Document No. 65.

Mr. Brinley, of Boston, moved to amend the amendment, by striking out all after the word "Resolved," and inserting what is printed as Document No. 42.

Debate followed between Messrs. Brinley, of Boston, Edwards, of Southampton, Stevens, of Clinton, and Bradbury, of Newton,

When, on motion of Mr. Foster, of Charlemont, it was

Voted, That the Committee rise, report progress, and ask leave to sit again.

And the Committee accordingly rose.

FRIDAY, June 24, 1853.

Mr. WALKER, of North Brookfield, in the chair.

By direction of the Convention, the Committee resumed the consideration of the Report on the House of Representatives, the pending question being upon the amendment of Mr. Brinley, of Boston, to the amendment offered by Mr. Butler, of Lowell.

After debate by Messrs. Foster, of Charlemont, Morss, of Newburyport, Kinsman, of Newburyport, Upham, of Salem, and Holder, of Lynn,

The amendment of Mr. Brinley was rejected.

The question then recurred on the amendment of Mr. Butler.

Mr. Gray, of Boston, moved that the Committee rise, report progress, and ask leave to sit again, but the motion was rejected.

Mr. Butler, of Lowell, modified his amendment by striking out, in the seventh paragraph of the first Resolve, the words, "and of less than fifteen thousand;" also, by striking out, in the eighth paragraph of the same Resolve, the word "fifteen," and inserting the words "over twelve;" and striking out, in the first and second lines, the words, "and upwards," and in the second line, the words, "one representative and," and inserting, after the word "additional," in the third line, the word "representative," and substituting the word "additional" for the word "whole," in the fourth line.

After remarks by Mr. Gray, of Boston,

Mr. Stetson, of Braintree, moved an amendment to the amendment, which is printed as Document No. 70.

After remarks by Mr. Huntington, of Northampton,

On motion of Mr. Butler, of Lowell, it was

Voted, That the Committee rise, report progress, and ask leave to sit again.

And the Committee accordingly rose.

Afterwards, Mr. Wilson, of Natick, in the chair.

The Committee resumed the consideration of the Report on the House of Representatives; the pending question being on the amendment of Mr. Stetson to the amendment of Mr. Butler.

The question being taken upon the amendment of Mr. Stetson, it was rejected.

The question recurred on the amendment of Mr. Butler.

Mr. Earle, of Worcester, moved to amend the amendment, by striking out all after the word "follows," in the first paragraph of the first Resolve, and inserting what is printed as Document No. 71.

After debate by Messrs. Brown, of Dracut, Earle, of Worcester, and Adams, of Lowell,

The amendment was rejected.

The question then recurred on the amendment of Mr. Butler.

Mr. Gardner, of Seekonk, moved to amend the amendment by striking out, in the fourth Resolve, the words "fifteen hundred," and inserting the words "one thousand;" but after debate by Messrs. Gardner, of Seekonk, and Butler, of Lowell,

The motion was rejected.

Mr. Adams, of Lowell, moved to amend the amendment, by striking out all after the word "published," in the seventh line of the third Resolve.

Debate followed between Messrs. Bird, of Walpole, Griswold, member for Erving, Earle, of Worcester, Bradbury, of Newton, Walker, of North Brookfield, Butler, of Lowell, Whitney, of Conway, Adams, of Lowell, Banks, of Waltham, Frothingham, of Charlestown, Hood, of Lynn, and Bates, of Plymouth,

When the amendment was rejected by a vote of thirty-four in the affirmative, and one hundred and seven in the negative.

The question recurring upon the amendment of Mr. Butler,

Mr. Griswold, member for Erving, moved to amend the amendment, by inserting after the word "inhabitants," in the twelfth line of the third Resolve, (printed copy,) the words following: "and of the towns which shall hereafter be created, with power to send one representative."

After remarks by Messrs. Walker, of North Brookfield, and Griswold, member for Erving,

On motion of Mr. Greene, of Brookfield, it was

Voted, That the Committee rise, report progress, and ask leave to sit again.

And the Committee accordingly rose.

SATURDAY, June 25, 1853.

Mr. Wilson, of Natick, in the chair.

By direction of the Convention, the Committee resumed the consideration of the Report from the Committee on the House of Representatives, the immediate question being upon the amendment moved by Mr. Griswold, member for Erving, to the amendment of Mr. Butler.

The question being taken, the amendment was adopted, by a vote of one hundred and eight in the affirmative, and seventeen in the negative.

The question then recurred upon the amendment as amended.

After debate by Messrs. Sargent, of Cambridge, Whitney, of Boylston, Rockwell, of Pittsfield, Spooner, of Warwick, Chapin, of Worcester, Eames, of Washington, Alley, of Lynn, Bradbury, of Newton, Waters, of Millbury, and Churchill, of Milton,

Mr. Gardner, of Seekonk, moved to amend the amendment by substituting what is printed as Document No. 68.

Mr. Gardner addressed the Committee, when

The motion was rejected.

After further debate by Messrs. Hubbard, of Boston, Gardner, of Boston, and Chapin, of Springfield,

Mr. Crowell, of Dennis, moved that the Committee rise, report progress, and ask leave to sit again.

The motion was adopted,

And the Committee accordingly rose.

MONDAY, June 27, 1853.

Mr. Huntington, of Northampton, in the chair.

By direction of the Convention, the Committee proceeded to consider the Report from the Committee on the Militia (printed Document No. 60):—

"Inexpedient to act upon an Order of June 15th, instructing them to consider the expediency of so amending the Constitution, as to strike out whatever relates to the militia, and instead thereof provide for the registration of all citizens between twenty-one and fifty years of age, as a standing police of the Commonwealth, to render such assistance as may be necessary for the preservation of the peace and the faithful and efficient execution of the laws of the Commonwealth."

After debate by Messrs. Oliver, of Lawrence, and Whitney, of Boylston,

Mr. Hall, of Haverhill, moved that the Committee rise, and report to the Convention, that the Report of the Standing Committee ought to be accepted.

The motion was adopted,

And the Committee accordingly rose.

Afterwards, Mr. Griswold, member for Erving, in the chair.

The Committee proceeded to consider the Report from the Committee on the Qualifications of Voters:—

"Inexpedient to act upon an Order of the 30th of May, in relation to the expediency of providing, that ability to read and write shall be an indispensable requisite for the exercise of the elective franchise; and also an Order of same date, in relation to a forfeiture of the right to vote in case of voluntary neglect to exercise that right." (Printed Document No. 67.)

Mr. Lothrop, of Boston, moved to amend the Report by striking out all after the word "Report," in the eighth line, (printed copy,) and inserting the following:—

"That, in every election, every voter born in this Commonwealth, shall be able to read the printed ballots out of which he selects one to deposit as his vote."

Mr. Lothrop addressed the Committee upon his motion.

Mr. Churchill, of Milton, moved to amend the amendment by inserting, after the word "Commonwealth," the words, "after the adoption of this Constitution;" which was accepted by Mr. Lothrop.

Mr. Marvin, of Winchendon, then moved that the Committee rise, report progress, and ask leave to sit again.

But the motion was rejected.

After remarks by Mr. Phelps, of Munroe, the question was taken upon the amendment as amended, and decided in the negative.

Mr. Wilson, of Natick, then moved that the Committee rise, and report to the Convention that the Report of the Standing Committee ought to be accepted.

The motion was adopted,

And the Committee accordingly rose.

Afterwards, Mr. STETSON, of Braintree, in the chair.

The Committee proceeded to consider the following Resolve, reported from the Committee on the Qualifications of Voters:—

Resolved, That the Constitution be so amended as to require a voting list or registry, and to protect presiding officers in adhering thereto.

On motion of Mr. Adams, of Lowell, the Resolve was adopted.

It was then

Voted, That the Committee rise, and report to the Convention that the Resolve ought to pass.

And the Committee accordingly rose.

Afterwards, Mr. KEYES, member for Abington, in the chair.

The Committee resumed the consideration of the following Resolve, reported from a special committee:—

Resolved, That it is expedient to incorporate into the Constitution a provision, that corporations may be formed under general laws, but shall not be created by special act, except for banking or municipal purposes, or where the object of the incorporation shall not be attainable under general laws.

The pending question being upon the amendment of Mr. Cole, of Cheshire, to the amendment offered by Mr. Stetson, of Braintree.

After remarks by Messrs. Stetson, of Braintree, and Whitney, of Conway,

The question was taken upon the amendment of Mr. Stetson, and it was rejected.

The question then recurred upon the amendment of Mr. Cole.

After further debate by Messrs. French of Berkley, Cole, of Cheshire, and Huntington, of Northampton,

Mr. Cole modified his amendment so as to move to strike out all after the word "shall," in the last line of the Resolve, and insert the words "be for literary or charitable purposes."

Mr. Frothingham, of Charlestown, addressed the Committee upon the question.

Mr. Stetson, of Braintree, moved that the Committee rise, report progress, and ask leave to sit again;

But the motion was rejected, by a vote of twenty in the affirmative, and eighty-one in the negative.

After debate by Messrs. Bradford, of Essex, Whitney, of Conway, Huntington, of Northampton, Bartlett, of Boston, Bird of Walpole, Wilson, of Natick, Lord, of Salem, Stetson, of Braintree, Alley, of Lynn, Nayson, of Amesbury, and Cole, of Cheshire,

The amendment of Mr. Cole was rejected.

The question then recurred upon the Resolve, as reported by the Committee.

Mr. Wilson, of Natick, moved to amend by inserting the word "railway," after the word "banking," in the fourth line,

Which motion was adopted, by a vote of ninety-one in the affirmative, and thirty-two in the negative.

Mr. Bird, of Walpole, moved to amend by inserting, after the word "railway," the word "manufacturing;"

But the motion was rejected.

Mr. Nayson, of Amesbury, moved further to amend by striking out all after the word "laws," in the third line, and inserting the words, "in all cases where the object of such corporation is attainable under the same, and where provision is thus made by general laws, no corporation shall be formed by special act."

On motion of Mr. Butler, of Lowell, it was

Voted, That the Committee rise, report progress, and ask leave to sit again.

And the Committee accordingly rose.

Afterwards, Mr. WILSON, of Natick, in the chair.

By direction of the Convention, the Committee resumed the consideration of the Report of the Committee on the House of Representatives; the immediate question being upon the amendment of Mr. Butler, of Lowell, as amended.

After debate by Messrs. Boutwell, member for Berlin, Wilkins, of Boston, and Keyes, member for Abington,

On motion of Mr. Keyes, it was

Voted, That the Committee rise, report progress, and ask leave to sit again.

And the Committee accordingly rose.

Afterwards, Mr. KEYES, member for Abington, in the chair.

The Committee resumed the consideration of the Resolve, reported from a special committee, concerning General Laws for Corporations, the pending question being upon the amendment moved by Mr. Nayson, of Amesbury.

After debate by Messrs. Nayson, of Amesbury, and Upton, of Boston,

The question being taken upon the amendment, it was adopted, by a vote of ninety-six in the affirmative, and twenty-seven in the negative.

Mr. Morton, of Quincy, moved that the Committee rise and report that the Resolve, as amended, ought not to pass;

But the motion was rejected, by a vote of sixty-one in the affirmative, and one hundred and nineteen in the negative.

The question then recurring upon the Resolve, as amended, it was adopted.

On motion of Mr. Wilson, of Natick, it was

Voted, That the Committee rise, and report that the Resolve, as amended, ought to pass.

And the Committee accordingly rose.

Afterwards, Mr. Frothingham, of Charlestown, in the chair.

The Committee proceeded to consider the Resolves (printed Document No. 61) reported from the Committee on the Qualifications of Voters, to whom was referred an Order of 16th of June, respecting loss of residence in consequence of absence while on the business of this State, or of the United States; and also respecting idiots, insane persons, and persons convicted of infamous crimes.

After debate by Messrs. Hooper, of Fall River, Aldrich, of Barre, and Bates, of Plymouth,

Mr. Morton, of Andover, moved that the Committee rise, and report that the Resolves ought not to pass.

The motion was adopted,

And the Committee accordingly rose.

Afterwards, Mr. Boutwell, member for Berlin, in the chair.

The Committee resumed the consideration of the Report of the Special Committee on the subject of Loaning the State Credit, the pending question being upon the amendment moved by Mr. Stetson, of Braintree.

After remarks by Mr. Cole, of Cheshire,

On motion of Mr. Durgin, of Wilmington, it was

Voted, That the Committee rise, report progress, and ask leave to sit again.

And the Committee accordingly rose.

TUESDAY, June 28, 1853.

Mr. BOUTWELL, member for Berlin, in the chair.

By direction of the Convention, the Committee resumed the consideration of the unfinished business of yesterday—the Report on the subject of Loaning the State Credit, the pending question being upon the amendment of Mr. Stetson, of Braintree.

After debate by Messrs. Cole, of Cheshire, Weeks, of Harwich, Stetson, of Braintree, French, of Berkley, Foster, of Charlemont, Sargent, of Cambridge, Wilson, of Natick, and Duncan, of Williamstown,

Mr. Hurlbut, of Sudbury, moved to amend the amendment of Mr. Stetson, by striking out all after the word "that," and inserting the following: "from and after the first day of May, which will be in the year eighteen hundred and fifty-five, the credit or moneys of the State be not loaned to the prosecution of any private enterprise, unless first submitted to, and accepted by, the people."

After debate by Messrs. Hurlbut, of Sudbury, Hooper, of Fall River, Keyes, member for Abington, Hillard, of Boston, Wilson, of Natick, Davis, of Plymouth, Phinney, member for Chatham, Weeks, of Harwich, Morton, of Taunton, Walker, of North Brookfield, and Whitney, of Boylston,

The question was taken, and the amendment was rejected.

The question then recurring upon the amendment of Mr. Stetson,

It was rejected, by a vote of one hundred and forty-four in the affirmative, and one hundred and forty-five in the negative.

The question then recurred upon agreeing to the Report of the Committee.

Mr. Tyler, of Pawtucket, moved to amend the Report by striking out all after the word "Report," and inserting the following:—

That it is expedient so to amend the Constitution, as to provide that every bill for loaning the credit of the State to private corporations, shall be framed by one legislature, and be referred to a succeeding legislature, before it shall become a law.

Mr. Cole, of Cheshire, moved that the Committee rise, report progress, and ask leave to sit again;

But the motion was rejected.

Mr. Tyler addressed the Committee upon his motion.

Mr. Miller, of Wareham, renewed the motion of Mr. Cole, that the Committee rise, report progress, and ask leave to sit again;

But the motion was rejected.

The question being taken upon the amendment of Mr. Tyler, it was rejected.

After remarks by Mr. James, of South Scituate,

Mr. Cogswell, of Yarmouth, moved to amend the Report, by striking out all after the word "Report," and inserting the following Resolve:—

Resolved, That the legislature shall have no power, unless by vote of two-thirds of the members elected to either branch thereof, to loan money or otherwise involve the State in debt, except in case of war, invasion or insurrection.

But the motion was rejected.

The question then recurred upon the Report of the Committee.

Pending this question,

On motion of Mr. Hall, of Haverhill, it was

Voted, That the Committee rise, report progress, and ask leave to sit again.

And the Committee accordingly rose.

Afterwards, Mr. Wilson, of Natick, in the chair.

By direction of the Convention, the Committee resumed the consideration of the Report from the Committee on the House of Representatives, the pending question being upon the amendment moved by Mr. Butler, of Lowell.

After debate by Messrs. Weston, of Duxbury, Keyes, member for Abington, Upton, of Boston, Kingman, of West Bridgewater, Wilkins, of Boston, and Wilkinson, of Dedham,

The question was taken upon the amendment of Mr. Butler,

And it was adopted, by a vote of one hundred and fifty-five in the affirmative, and one hundred and thirteen in the negative.

On motion of Mr. Bird, of Walpole, it was

Voted, That the Committee rise, and report to the Convention the Resolves, with the amendment.

And the Committee accordingly rose.

THURSDAY, June 30, 1853.

Mr. LORD, of Salem, in the chair.

By direction of the Convention, the Committee proceeded to consider the Report from the Committee on the Frame of Government:

"Inexpedient to act upon an Order of May 17th, respecting the reference by the legislature to the people, of legislative acts for approval or rejection," (printed Document No. 82.)

The Report was accepted, without debate,

And on motion of Mr. Davis, of Plymouth, it was

Voted, That the Committee rise, and report to the Convention that the Report of the Standing Committee ought to be accepted.

And the Committee accordingly rose.

Afterwards, Mr. EARLE, of Worcester, in the chair.

The Committee proceeded to consider the Report (printed Document No. 81) from the Committee on the Frame of Government:—

"Inexpedient to act upon an Order of June 3d, instructing them to consider the expediency of securing to women, by constitutional provision, their property, acquired by devise, inheritance or otherwise, and an Order of May 20th, on the same subject."

The Report was accepted, without debate.

It was then

Voted, That the Committee rise, and report to the Convention that the Report of the Standing Committee ought to be accepted.

And the Committee accordingly rose.

Afterwards, Mr. Whitney, of Boylston, in the chair.

The Committee proceeded to consider the Report from the Committee on the Frame of Government:—

"Inexpedient to act upon an Order of June 9th, relative to the remuneration of persons tried for offences against the State and acquitted."

The Report was accepted, without debate,

When it was

Voted, That the Committee rise, and report to the Convention that the Report of the Standing Committee ought to be accepted.

And the Committee accordingly rose.

Afterwards, Mr. Wood, of Middleborough, in the chair.

The Committee proceeded to consider the Report from the Committee on the Frame of Government:—

"Inexpedient to act upon the Petition of Silas Lamson and forty-four others."

The Report was accepted, without debate,

And, on motion of Mr. Davis, of Worcester, it was

Voted, That the Committee rise, and report to the Convention that the Report of the Standing Committee ought to be accepted.

And the Committee accordingly rose.

Afterwards, Mr. James, of South Scituate, in the chair.

The Committee proceeded to consider the Report from the Committee on the Judiciary:—

"Inexpedient to act upon an Order of June 6th, relative to granting the subject 'a certain remedy in law, prompt and without delay,' and an Order of same date, relating to the codification of the laws."

The Report was accepted, without debate.

When, on motion of Mr. Hall, of Haverhill, it was

Voted, That the Committee rise, and report that the Report of the Standing Committee ought to be accepted.

And the Committee accordingly rose.

Afterwards, Mr. Davis, of Plymouth, in the chair.

The Committee proceeded to consider the following Resolve, reported from the Committee on the Secretary, Treasurer, &c.

Resolved, That it is inexpedient so to amend the Constitution, as to require that "every person holding an office in or under the State government, shall retire therefrom at the expiration of six years' service."

The Resolve was adopted, without debate.

When, on motion of Mr. James, of South Scituate, it was

Voted, That the Committee rise, and report to the Convention that the Resolve ought to pass.

And the Committee accordingly rose.

Afterwards, Mr. Sargent, of Cambridge, in the chair.

The Committee proceeded to consider the following Resolve, reported from the Committee on the Governor.

Resolved, That it is expedient to amend the Constitution, by striking out the whole of article 7th in section 1st, chapter 2d.

The Resolve was agreed to, and

On motion of Mr. Davis, of Worcester, it was

Voted, That the Committee rise, and report to the Convention that the Resolve ought to pass.

And the Committee accordingly rose.

Afterwards, Mr. Hooper, of Fall River, in the chair.

The Committee proceeded to consider the following Resolve, reported from the Committee on the Frame of Government:—

Resolved, That the Constitution be so amended, as to require that a census of the State be taken in the year eighteen hundred and fifty-five, and on every tenth year from and after that period.

Mr. Earle, of Worcester, moved to amend the Resolve, by inserting after the word "the," in the second line, the words "whole population of the."

The question was debated by Messrs. Earle, of Worcester, Livermore, of Cambridge, Griswold, member for Erving, Walker, of North

Brookfield, Briggs, of Pittsfield, Wilkins, of Boston, Banks, of Waltham, Hale, of Bridgewater, and Allen, of Worcester,

When the question was taken, and the amendment was adopted.

Mr. Allen, of Worcester, moved further to amend the Resolve, by adding the following words: "instead of the decennial census now required by the Constitution."

The question was taken, and the amendment was adopted.

The question then recurred upon the adoption of the Resolve, as amended.

After debate by Messrs. Briggs, of Pittsfield, Earle, of Worcester, and Gray, of Boston,

The Resolve, as amended, was adopted.

On motion of Mr. Hale, of Bridgewater, it was

Voted, That the Committee rise, and report to the Convention the Resolve, with the amendments.

And the Committee accordingly rose.

TUESDAY, July 5, 1853.

Mr. Parker, of Cambridge, in the chair.

By direction of the Convention, the Committee proceeded to consider the following Resolve, reported from the Committee on the Encouragement of Literature:—

Resolved, That it is not expedient to alter the Constitution, so as to confer any additional powers upon the Legislature in relation to the education of females.

The Resolve was agreed to, without debate.

When, on motion of Mr. Davis, of Worcester, it was

Voted, That the Committee rise, and report to the Convention that the Resolve ought to pass.

And the Committee accordingly rose.

Afterwards, Mr. Walker, of North Brookfield, in the chair.

The Committee proceeded to consider the following Resolve, reported from the Committee on the Encouragement of Literature:—

Resolved, That it is not expedient, so to alter the Constitution as to provide that a Board of Education and a Board of Agriculture shall be established as permanent departments of the government.

Mr. Thompson, of Charlestown, moved that the Resolve be adopted.

After remarks by Mr. Cogswell, of Yarmouth, the motion was agreed to.

It was then voted that the Committee rise, and report to the Convention that the Resolve ought to pass.

And the Committee accordingly rose.

Afterwards, Mr. SCHOULER, of Boston, in the chair.

The Committee proceeded to consider the following Resolve, reported from the Committee on the Encouragement of Literature:—

Resolved, That it is expedient so to amend the Constitution, as to provide that no public money in this Commonwealth, whether accruing from funds, or raised by taxation, shall ever be appropriated for the support of sectarian or denominational schools.

The Resolve was agreed to, without debate.

When, on motion of Mr. Knight, of Peru, it was

Voted, That the Committee rise, and report to the Convention that the Resolve ought to pass.

And the Committee accordingly rose.

Afterwards, Mr. SUMNER, member for Otis, in the chair.

By direction of the Convention, the Committee proceeded to consider a series of Resolves reported from the Committee on Oaths and Subscriptions, which are printed as Document No. 76.

On motion of Mr. Hooper, of Fall River, it was

Voted, To strike out the word "legislature," in the last line of the first Resolve, and insert instead thereof, the word "law."

Mr. Brinley, of Boston, moved to strike out the third Resolve.

The question was debated by Messrs. Stetson, of Braintree, Kingman, of West Bridgewater, Upton, of Boston, and Wilson, of Natick,

Mr. Earle, of Worcester, moved to amend the amendment, by striking out the words "of Massachusetts."

After remarks by Mr. Brinley, of Boston, the motion was rejected.

The question then recurred upon the amendment of Mr. Brinley.

After further debate by Messrs. Earle, of Worcester, Walker, of North Brookfield, and Wilson, of Natick,

Mr. Hooper, of Fall River, moved to amend the amendment, by striking out, in the seventh line of the third Resolve, all after the word "the," and inserting the words "people represented in the general court."

Debate followed between Messrs. Frothingham, of Charlestown, Upton, of Boston, Schouler, of Boston, Hooper, of Fall River, and Kingman, of West Bridgewater,

When the motion was rejected.

The question recurring upon the amendment of Mr. Brinley,

Mr. Earle, of Worcester, moved to amend the amendment, by inserting after the word "of," in the last line, the words, "the Commonwealth of."

After debate by Messrs. Earle, of Worcester, and Oliver, of Lawrence, Mr. Earle withdrew his motion.

The question then recurring upon the amendment of Mr. Brinley, it was withdrawn by the mover.

Mr. Cressy, of Hamilton, moved that the Committee rise, report progress, and ask leave to sit again; but the motion was rejected.

The question was then taken on agreeing to the Resolves, as amended, and decided in the affirmative.

On motion of Mr. Wilson, of Natick, it was

Voted, That the Committee rise, and report to the Convention that the Resolves ought to pass, with an amendment.

And the Committee accordingly rose.

Afterwards, Mr. GILES, of Boston, in the chair.

By direction of the Convention, the Committee resumed the consideration of the series of Resolves reported from the Committee on the Qualifications of Voters, to whom was recommitted the third Resolve of that Committee, reported on the 19th of May, together with an amendment prepared thereto.

The pending question being upon the motion of Mr. Stevens, of Clinton, to amend the first Resolution, by striking out all after the word "seas," in the fifth line.

After debate by Messrs. Duncan, of Williamstown, Walker, of North Brookfield, Sargent, of Cambridge, and Morton, of Taunton,

On motion of Mr. Bird, of Walpole, it was

Voted, That the Committee rise, report progress, and ask leave to sit again.

And the Committee accordingly rose.

Afterwards, Mr. Giles, of Boston, in the chair.

The Committee resumed the consideration of the unfinished business of its last session—the Report of the Committee on the Qualifications of Voters; the pending question being on the amendment of Mr. Stevens, of Clinton.

The question was debated by Messrs. Sumner, member for Otis, Chapin, of Worcester, Bishop, of Lenox, Sargent, of Cambridge, Parker, of Cambridge, Morton, of Taunton, Huntington, of Salem, and Wood, of Fitchburg.

Mr. Wilkinson, of Dedham, moved to amend the amendment, by adding to the words proposed to be stricken out, the following: "or while engaged in any other temporary business or employment."

After debate by Messrs. Walker, of North Brookfield, Stevens, of Clinton, Parker, of Cambridge, Huntington, of Northampton, Huntington, of Salem, Dana, member for Manchester, Wilson, of Natick, Wilkinson, of Dedham, and Duncan, of Williamstown, the question was taken, and the motion was adopted.

The question then recurring upon the amendment of Mr. Stevens, as amended, it was rejected.

The question was then taken upon the Resolves, as amended, when it was found that a quorum was not present.

On motion of Mr. Crowninshield, of Boston, it was then

Voted, That the Committee rise, and report that a quorum was not present.

And the Committee accordingly rose.

WEDNESDAY, July 6, 1853.

Mr. Wood, of Fitchburg, in the chair.

By direction of the Convention, the Committee proceeded to consider the following Resolve, from the Committee on the Encouragement of Literature:—

Resolved, That the legislature shall, as soon as may be, provide for the enlargement of the School Fund of this Commonwealth, until it shall amount, at least, to the sum of two millions of dollars; and the said fund shall be preserved inviolate, and the income thereof shall be annually appropriated for the aid and improvement of the common schools of the State, and for no other purpose.

The Resolve was agreed to, without debate.

And, on motion of Mr. Wilson, of Natick, it was

Voted, That the Committee rise, and report to the Convention that the Resolve ought to pass.

And the Committee accordingly rose.

Afterwards, Mr. Oliver, of Lawrence, in the chair.

The Committee proceeded to consider the following Resolve, reported from the Committee on the Encouragement of Literature:—

Resolved, That it is expedient to amend the second section of the fifth chapter of the Constitution, by striking out therefrom the words "University at Cambridge."

After debate by Messrs. Walker, of North Brookfield, Wood, of Fitchburg, Wilson, of Natick, and Earle, of Worcester,

The Resolve was agreed to.

When, on motion of Mr. Wilson, of Natick, it was

Voted, That the Committee rise, and report to the Convention that the Resolve ought to pass.

And the Committee accordingly rose.

Afterwards, Mr. Griswold, member for Erving, in the chair.

The Committee proceeded to consider a series of Resolves, reported from the Committee on Amendments and Enrolment (printed Document No. 75.)

The Committee was addressed by Messrs. Nayson, of Amesbury, and Boutwell, member for Berlin.

Mr. Walker, of North Brookfield, moved to amend the first Resolve, by striking out the words "seventy-three," in the third line, (printed copy,) and inserting, instead thereof, the words "sixty-five."

After debate by Messrs. Bates, of Plymouth, and Nayson, of Amesbury,

The motion was rejected.

After further debate by Messrs. Bird, of Walpole, Nayson, of Amesbury, and Boutwell, member for Berlin,

Mr. Hale, of Bridgewater, moved to amend the Resolves, by striking out the second Resolve.

Debate followed between Messrs. Nayson, of Amesbury, Hale, of Bridgewater, Boutwell, member for Berlin, Bartlett, of Boston, Cole, of Cheshire, and Simmons of Hanover.

When, on motion of Mr. Thompson, of Charlestown, it was

Voted, That the Committee rise, report progress, and ask leave to sit again.

And the Committee accordingly rose.

FRIDAY, July 8, 1853.

Mr. BOUTWELL, member for Berlin, in the chair.

By direction of the Convention, the Committee resumed the consideration of the Report of the Special Committee, to whom was referred the Order of May 11th, concerning the Loan of the State Credit, and the several Orders of 17th, 18th and 19th of May.

Mr. Stetson, of Braintree, moved to amend the Report by substituting therefor the following:—

Resolved, That the Constitution be so amended, that hereafter the State shall not loan its credit to any corporation, association or individuals, unless the question shall first be submitted to the people, and a decided majority voting thereon, shall sanction the act.

A question of order being raised by Mr. Alvord, member for Montague, the Chairman decided the amendment not in order, the Committee having rejected a similar amendment at a former session.

Mr. Stetson moved to reconsider the vote by which the former amendment was rejected;

But the Chairman decided that the time had passed within which the vote could be reconsidered.

Mr. Stetson then addressed the Committee.

Mr. Morton, of Taunton, moved to amend by striking out the four last lines of the Report, and inserting the following:—

That it is expedient, so to amend the Constitution, as to provide that—

1st. The legislature shall not have power, directly or indirectly, to grant or loan the credit of the State, or create any liability on behalf of the State, in aid of any individual, corporation or association. But the legislature may submit to the people any such loan or grant, which, if adopted by a majority of all the legal voters voting thereon, shall authorize the same.

2d. The legislature shall not, in any manner, create any debt or debts, which shall, singly or in the aggregate with any previous debt, exceed the sum of one million of dollars, except to repel invasion or suppress insurrection.

Mr. Alvord, member for Montague, inquired whether this amendment was not identical with the one offered by the gentleman from Braintree, and therefore out of order?

The Chairman decided the motion to be in order.

After debate by Messrs. Alvord, member for Montague, Durgin, of Wilmington, Cole, of Cheshire, Dawes, of Adams, and Hopkinson, of Boston,

On motion of Mr. Beach, of Springfield, it was

Voted, That the Committee rise, report progress, and ask leave to sit again.

And the Committee accordingly rose.

SATURDAY, July 9, 1853.

Mr. ASPINWALL, of Brookline, in the chair.

By direction of the Convention, the Committee proceeded to consider the Report from the Committee on the Qualifications of Voters, (printed Document No. 105.)

After remarks by Mr. Walker, of North Brookfield,

On motion of Mr. Whitney, of Conway, it was

Voted, That the Committee rise, and report to the Convention that the Report of the Standing Committee ought to pass.

And the Committee accordingly rose.

Afterwards, Mr. BOUTWELL, member for Berlin, in the chair.

By direction of the Convention, the Committee resumed the consideration of the unfinished business of July the 8th, being the subject of Loaning the State Credit to any individuals or corporations, the pending question being upon the amendment moved by Mr. Morton, of Taunton.

After debate by Messrs. Hopkinson, of Boston, and Sumner, member for Otis,

Mr. Morton modified the second Resolve of his amendment by inserting, after the word "not," in the first line, the word "hereafter."

Mr. Buck, of Lanesborough, called for a division. The question was first taken upon the first Resolve,

And it was rejected.

The second Resolve was also rejected.

The question then recurring upon the acceptance of the Report of the Committee,

It was accepted, by a vote of one hundred and fifty-three in the affirmative, and sixty in the negative.

On motion of Mr. Cushman, of Bernardston, it was then

Voted, That the Committee rise, and report that the Report of the Special Committee ought to be accepted.

And the Committee accordingly rose.

MONDAY, July 11, 1853.

Mr. HALLETT, member for Wilbraham, in the chair.

By direction of the Convention, the Committee proceeded to consider a series of Resolves, reported from the Standing Committee on the Judiciary, (printed Document No. 28.)

Mr. Morton, of Taunton, and Mr. French, of Berkley, addressed the Committee.

Mr. Warner, of Wrentham, moved to amend, by striking out the first Resolve; but afterwards withdrew the motion.

The debate was continued by Messrs. Hooper, of Fall River, Lord, of Salem, and Gray, of Boston.

Mr. Earle, of Worcester, moved to amend the first Resolve, by striking out the words "substituting for," in the second line, and inserting the words "striking out;" also, by striking out all after the word "chapter," in the same line, and inserting the word "thereof."

The subject was debated by Messrs. Frothingham, of Charlestown, Sumner, member for Otis, and Briggs, of Pittsfield,

When Mr. Davis, of Worcester, moved to amend the first Resolve, by striking out all after the word "following," in the third line, (printed copy,) and inserting the following:—

Each branch of the legislature, as well as the governor and council, shall have authority to require the opinion of the attorney-general upon important questions of law, and upon solemn occasions.

But the Chairman decided the motion not in order.

After further debate, by Messrs. Earle, of Worcester, Butler, of Lowell, Hooper, of Fall River, Morton, of Taunton, Hathaway, of Freetown, and Warner, of Wrentham,

Mr. Earle withdrew his amendment.

Mr. Morton, of Taunton, moved to amend the first Resolve, by inserting, after the word "and," in the fourth line, (printed copy,) the word "council;" also, by striking out the word "respectively," in the fifth line, and inserting the words "or either of them."

After remarks by Mr. Gardner, of Seekonk,

The motion was adopted.

The question then recurring upon the first Resolve, as amended,

It was adopted.

Mr. Gardner then moved to amend the second Resolve, by inserting, after the word "receive," in the sixth line, (printed copy,) the words "ample and;"

But the motion was rejected.

The question then recurred upon the second Resolve.

After remarks by Mr. Morton of Taunton,

The Resolve was adopted.

The third Resolve was then adopted, without debate.

Mr. Wilson, of Natick, then moved to amend the fourth Resolve, by striking out all after the word "Resolved," and inserting the following (printed Document No. 63):—

Resolved, That it is proper and expedient so to amend the Constitution, as to provide that the justices of the supreme judicial court shall be appointed for the term of ten years, and the justices of such inferior courts as are or may be established by law, for the term of seven years; said justices to be eligible to reappointment, but in no case to continue in office after attaining seventy years of age.

Mr. Wood, of Middleborough, moved to amend the amendment, by striking out the word "appointed," in the third line, (printed copy,) and inserting the following words: "chosen by the qualified voters of the Commonwealth."

Also by striking out the word "reappointment," in the sixth line, and inserting the word reëlection."

After debate by Messrs. Wood, of Middleborough, and Hooper, of Fall River,

Mr. Bird, of Walpole, moved that the Committee rise, report progress, and ask leave to sit again; but the motion was rejected.

Afterwards, on motion of Mr. Dana, member for Manchester, it was

Voted, That the Committee rise, report progress, and ask leave to sit again.

And the Committee accordingly rose.

Afterwards, Mr. HALLETT, member for Wilbraham, in the chair.

The Committee resumed the consideration of the unfinished business of the last session—the Resolves reported from the Committee on the Judiciary, the pending question being upon the amendment of Mr. Wood, of Middleborough, to the amendment of Mr. Wilson, of Natick.

The question being taken upon the pending amendment, it was rejected, by a vote of seventy-five in the affirmative, to one hundred and two in the negative.

The question then recurring upon the amendment of Mr. Wilson,

Mr. Bradford, of Essex, moved to amend the same by striking out the word "eligible," and inserting instead thereof, the word "ineligible;" but the motion was rejected.

Mr. Kingman, of West Bridgewater, moved to amend the amendment, by substituting the word "seven" for the word "ten," also by substituting the word "five" for the word "seven."

After debate by Messrs. Wilson, of Natick, Kingman, of West Bridgewater, and Keyes, member for Abington,

Mr. Kingman modified his amendment, by withdrawing the last clause, to strike out the word "seven" and insert the word "five."

The question then being taken upon the amendment, it was rejected.

Mr. Dana, member for Manchester, moved that the Committee rise, report progress, and ask leave to sit again.

After debate by Messrs. Dana, member for Manchester, and Keyes, member for Abington, the motion was rejected.

The question then recurred upon the adoption of Mr. Wilson's amendment, and being taken, it was decided in the affirmative.

When, on motion of Mr. Wilson, of Natick, it was

Voted, That the Committee rise, and report to the Convention that the Resolves ought to pass, with the amendments.

And the Committee accordingly rose.

Afterwards, Mr. GRISWOLD, member for Erving, in the chair.

By direction of the Convention, the Committee resumed the consideration of the Resolves reported from the Committee on Amendments and Enrolment, concerning Constitutional Conventions; the pending question being upon the motion of Mr. Hale, of Bridgewater, to strike out the second Resolve.

After remarks by Mr. Hale,

Mr. Nayson, of Amesbury, moved to amend the second Resolve, by adding thereto the following words:—

The said delegates to be chosen in the same manner and proportion as the representatives in the general court are, by this Constitution, to be chosen.

The question being taken, the amendment was adopted.

The question then recurred upon the motion of Mr. Hale.

After debate by Messrs. Wheeler, of Lincoln, Wilson, of Natick, Nayson, of Amesbury, Hallett, member for Wilbraham, Hale, of Bridgewater, Whitney, of Conway, and Giles, of Boston,

On motion of Mr. Hale, of Bridgewater, it was

Voted, That the Committee rise, report progress, and ask leave to sit again.

And the Committee accordingly rose.

TUESDAY, July 12, 1853.

Mr. BUTLER, of Lowell, in the chair.

By direction of the Convention, the Committee proceeded to consider the Report from the Committee on the Qualifications of Voters, to whom was referred the petitions of Francis Jackson and others, that the word male may be stricken from the Constitution, and also of Abby B. Alcott and other women of Massachusetts, that they may be allowed to vote on amendments that may be made to the Constitution, (printed Document No. 97.)

After debate by Messrs. Walker, of North Brookfield, Greene, of Brookfield, and Keyes, member for Abington,

Mr. Cressy, of Hamilton, moved that the Committee rise and report to the Convention that the Report of the Standing Committee ought to pass.

Pending this motion, Mr. Whitney, of Boylston, moved to amend the Report, by striking out all after the word "that," in the first line, and inserting instead thereof, the following: "the prayer of the petitioners ought to be granted."

On motion of Mr. Marvin, of Winchendon, it was then

Voted, That the Committee rise, report progress, and ask leave to sit again.

And the Committee accordingly rose.

WEDNESDAY, July 13, 1853.

Mr. Butler, of Lowell, in the chair.

By direction of the Convention, the Committee resumed the consideration of the unfinished business of the last session—the Report from the Committee on the Qualifications of Voters, on the petitions of Francis Jackson and others, that the word "male" may be stricken out; and also of Abby B. Alcott and other women of Massachusetts, that they may be allowed to vote on the amendments that may be made to the Constitution, the pending question being upon the amendment of Mr. Whitney, of Boylston.

Mr. Marvin, of Winchendon, moved to amend the Report, by striking out all after the word "withdraw," in the first line.

But the Chairman decided the motion not in order.

After remarks by Messrs. Kingman, of West Bridgewater, and Marvin, of Winchendon,

The question was taken upon the amendment of Mr. Whitney, and it was rejected.

Mr. Marvin, of Winchendon, then moved to amend the Report, by striking out all after the word "That," in the first line, as far as, and including the word "and," in the last line but one.

The question being taken, the amendment was adopted, by a

32

vote of one hundred and eight in the affirmative, and forty-four in the negative.

On motion of Mr. Bates, of Plymouth, it was then

Voted, That the Committee rise, and report to the Convention that the Report of the Standing Committee ought to pass, with the amendment.

And the Committee accordingly rose.

THURSDAY, July 14, 1853.

Mr. GILES, of Boston, in the chair.

By direction of the Convention, the Committee proceeded to consider the following Resolve, submitted by Mr. Cole, of Cheshire:—

Resolved, That the Constitution be so amended, that a majority of the members of the House of Representatives shall be necessary to constitute a Quorum.

Mr. Griswold, member for Erving, addressed the Committee.

Mr. Butler, of Lowell, moved that the Committee rise, and report to the Convention the Resolve, with a recommendation that it be referred to the Committee on the House of Representatives.

Mr. Hallett, member for Wilbraham, moved to amend the Resolve, by striking out the words "a majority," and inserting the words "one hundred."

After debate by Messrs. Griswold, member for Erving, Butler, of Lowell, Schouler, of Boston, Briggs, of Pittsfield, Whitney, of Conway, Cole, of Cheshire, and Hallett, member for Wilbraham,

The amendment was adopted, by a vote of sixty-three in the affirmative, and fifty-five in the negative.

When, on motion of Mr. Hallett, it was

Voted, That the Committee rise and report to the Convention that the Resolve ought to pass, with the amendment.

And the Committee accordingly rose.

FRIDAY, July 15, 1853.

Mr. MORTON, of Taunton, in the chair.

By direction of the Convention, the Committee proceeded to consider a Resolve (printed Document No. 72) reported from the Committee on the University at Cambridge.

After debate by Messrs. Knowlton, of Worcester, and Braman, of Danvers,

Mr. Hooper, of Fall River, moved that the Committee rise, report progress, and ask leave to sit again.

The motion was agreed to, by a vote of one hundred and six in the affirmative, and eighty-six in the negative.

And the Committee accordingly rose.

Afterwards, Mr. SUMNER, member for Marshfield, in the chair.

The Committee resumed the consideration of the unfinished business of the last session—the Resolve relating to the University at Cambridge.

After debate by Messrs. Braman, of Danvers, Wilson, of Natick, Boutwell, member for Berlin, Briggs, of Pittsfield, Parker, of Cambridge, and French, of New Bedford,

The Resolve was agreed to by a vote of one hundred and twenty-five in the affirmative, and thirty-one in the negative.

When, on motion of Mr. Boutwell, member for Berlin, it was

Voted, That the Committee rise, and report that the Resolve ought to pass.

And the Committee accordingly rose.

MONDAY, July 18, 1853.

Mr. HILLARD, of Boston, in the chair.

By direction of the Convention, the Committee proceeded to consider a series of Rèsolves concerning Elections by Plurality, reported from the Special Committee "to whom was referred the several Orders of the Convention concerning the rules by which the number of votes necessary to the election of the various officers of the Commonwealth may be ascertained; and also a Report of a committee of the Convention upon the same subject," (printed Document No. 77.)

Mr. Butler, of Lowell, moved to amend the first Resolve, by adding thereto the words, "or other officer to be thus elected."

After remarks by Mr. Wheeler, of Lincoln,

The motion was adopted.

On motion of Mr. Butler, of Lowell, the word "which," in the tenth line of the first Resolve, (printed copy,) was stricken out, and the word "whòm" was inserted in its place.

After debate by Messrs. Butler, of Lowell, Wheeler, of Lincoln, and Stevenson, of Boston,

Mr. Davis, of Plymouth, moved to amend the third Resolve, by striking out all after the word "election," in the third line.

Debate followed between Messrs. Davis, of Plymouth, Edwards, of Southampton, and Frothingham, of Charlestown.

Mr. Schouler, of Boston, moved to amend the first Resolve, by striking out all after the word "Resolved," and inserting the following:

That it is expedient to provide in the Constitution, that in the election of a governor, lieutenant-governor, secretary, treasurer, auditor, and attorney-general of the Commonwealth, the person having the highest number of votes shall be deemed and taken to be elected.

After debate by Messrs. Schouler, of Boston, Hallett, member for Wilbraham, Foster, of Charlemont, and Stetson, of Braintree,

On motion of Mr. Cressy, of Hamilton, it was

Voted, That the Committee rise, report progress, and ask leave to sit again.

And the Committee accordingly rose.

Afterwards, Mr. Hillard, of Boston, in the chair.

The Committee resumed the consideration of the unfinished business of the last session—the Resolves concerning Elections by Plurality.

The Chairman stated the pending question to be upon the amendment offered by Mr. Davis, of Plymouth.

After debate by Messrs. Ladd, of Cambridge, Morey, of Boston, Griswold, member for Erving, Gooch, of Melrose, and Butler, of Lowell,

The question was taken, and the amendment was rejected, by a vote of seventy in the affirmative, and one hundred and sixty-four in the negative.

Mr. Ladd, of Cambridge, then moved to amend the third Resolve, by striking out all after the word "Resolved," and inserting the following:—

That in all elections of representatives to the general court, the person having the highest number of votes shall be elected.

But the amendment was rejected, without debate, by a vote of eighty-two in the affirmative, and one hundred and sixty-three in the negative.

The question then recurred upon the amendment to the first Resolve, moved by Mr. Schouler, of Boston, at the last session.

Mr. Hubbard, of Boston, moved to amend the amendment by inserting, after the word "lieutenant-governor," the word "councillors," and the amendment was accepted by Mr. Schouler.

The question then being taken upon the amendment, as modified, it was rejected, by a vote of eighty-five in the affirmative, and one hundred and fifty-six in the negative.

Mr. Hathaway, of Freetown, moved to amend the third Resolve, by striking out all after the word "Resolved," and inserting the following:—

That representatives to the general court, and all county, district, city, and town officers, shall be elected, as by law shall be provided.

But the amendment was rejected.

Mr. Gardner, of Seekonk, moved to reconsider the vote by which the amendment offered by Mr. Davis, of Plymouth, was rejected.

After remarks by Mr. Denton, of Chelsea, the motion was rejected.

When, on motion of Mr. Adams, of Lowell, it was

Voted, That the Committee rise, and report to the Convention, that the Resolves ought to pass, with the amendments.

And the Committee accordingly rose.

Afterwards, Mr. Wood, of Fitchburg, in the chair.

By direction of the Convention, the Committee resumed the consideration of the Resolves (printed Document No. 75) reported from the Committee on Amendments and Enrolment; the pending question being the motion of Mr. Hale, of Bridgewater, to strike out the second Resolve.

Mr. Hallett, member for Wilbraham, moved to amend the Resolves by striking out all after the word "Resolved," and inserting instead thereof the following, to wit: what is printed as Document No. 117.

But the Chairman decided the motion not in order.

Mr. Hale, of Bridgewater, moved that the Committee rise, report progress, and ask leave to sit again.

After debate by Messrs. Hallett, member for Wilbraham, and Hale, of Bridgewater,

The motion was rejected by a vote of twenty-eight in the affirmative, and seventy-six in the negative.

The question then recurred upon the amendment of Mr. Hale, and It was adopted.

Mr. Hallett, member for Wilbraham, then renewed his motion to amend the Resolves, by striking out all after the word "Resolved," and inserting the following:—

That it is expedient to provide in the Constitution, that a Convention to revise or amend this Constitution, may be called and held in the following manner: At the general election which shall be in the year eighteen hundred and seventy-three, and in each twentieth year thereafter, the qualified voters in State election shall give in their votes, to be received, counted, returned and declared, in the same manner as by law is provided in the choice of general officers at such election, upon the question, "Shall there be a Convention to revise the Constitution, in conformity to the provisions of the Act of eighteen hundred and fifty-two, chapter one hundred and eighty-eight, relating to the calling a Convention of Delegates of the people for the purpose of revising the Constitution?" and if it shall appear, by the returns made, that a majority of the qualified voters throughout the State, who shall assemble and vote thereon, are in favor of such revision, the same shall be deemed and taken to be the will of the people of the Commonwealth that a Convention should meet accordingly; and thereupon delegates shall be chosen on the first Monday of March next succeeding, and such delegates shall meet in Convention, in the State House, on the first Wednesday of May succeeding, in the same manner, and with the same authority, as is provided in the second, third and fourth sections of said act.

The general court shall have power and authority in any year other than the year above specified, to submit to the people the same proposition, to be voted on in the same manner, at the next ensuing general election; and if it shall appear by the returns made, that a majority of the qualified voters throughout the State, who shall assemble and vote thereon, are in favor of such revision, the same shall be deemed and taken to be the will of the people of the Commonwealth that a Convention should meet accordingly; and thereupon the same proceedings, with the same powers and authority, shall be had, as is provided in the foregoing clause of this Constitution.

The foregoing provisions shall in no wise restrain or impair the reserved right of the people, in their sovereign capacity, at all times to reform, alter, or totally change their Constitution and Frame of Government.

Mr. Hallett addressed the Committee upon his motion.

Mr. Giles, of Boston, gave notice of an amendment he should offer, when in order.

After remarks by Messrs. Giles, of Boston, and Churchill, of Milton,

Mr. Churchill moved that the whole subject be indefinitely postponed;

But the Chairman decided the motion not in order.

Mr. Wilson addressed the Committee,

When, on motion of Mr. Breed, of Lynn, it was

Voted, That the Committee rise, report progress, and ask leave to sit again.

And the Committee accordingly rose.

FRIDAY, July 22, 1853.

Mr. Griswold, member for Erving, in the chair.

By direction of the Convention, the Committee resumed the consideration of the unfinished business of the session of July 18th—the Resolves (printed Document No. 75) concerning Constitutional Conventions, reported from the Committee on Amendments and Enrolment, the pending question being on the amendment moved by Mr. Hallett, member for Wilbraham.

The Committee was addressed by Messrs. Hallett, member for Wilbraham, and Burlingame, member for Northborough.

Mr. Hale, of Bridgewater, moved that the Committee rise, report progress, and ask leave to sit again;

But the motion was rejected.

Mr. Hale of Bridgewater, then moved to amend the third Resolve, reported by the Committee, by striking out, in the seventh line, (printed copy,) the following words, "representatives elected," and inserting the following: "two-thirds of the whole number of representatives elected;" and also, by inserting, after the word "and," in the twelfth line, the words "two-thirds of."

After remarks by Mr. Briggs, of Pittsfield, the motion was rejected.

Mr. Hallett modified his amendment (printed Document No. 117) by inserting, after the word "succeeding," in the nineteenth line, (printed copy,) the following words: "in conformity with the law then in force for the election of representatives."

Mr. Simmons, of Hanover, moved to amend the amendment, by adding thereto the following:—

It shall be the duty of all magistrates and persons in authority, to verify and recognize the proceedings of all meetings of the people holden for that purpose, to the end that the will of the majority may be ascertained and obeyed by the constituted authorities.

But the motion was rejected.

The question then recurring upon the amendment of Mr. Hallett,

Mr. Upton, of Boston, moved to amend the amendment, by striking out the words "seventy-three," in the fifth line, (printed copy,) and inserting, instead thereof, the words "fifty-eight;" also, by striking out the word "twentieth," in the same line, and inserting instead thereof the word "fifth."

The question being taken upon this amendment,

It was rejected.

Mr. Sargent, of Cambridge, moved to amend the amendment, by striking out, in the fifth line, (printed copy,) the words "seventy-three, and in each twentieth," and inserting, instead thereof, the following: "sixty, and in each tenth;"

But the motion was rejected by a vote of forty-eight in the affirmative, and one hundred and seventy-eight in the negative.

Mr. Cole, of Cheshire, moved further to amend the amendment by striking out, after the word "Constitution," in the tenth line, (printed copy,) the following words: "in conformity to the provisions of the Act of eighteen hundred and fifty-two, chapter one hundred and eighty-eight, relating to the calling a Convention of Delegates of the people for the purpose of revising the Constitution."

The question being taken upon the amendment,

It was rejected.

Mr. Hale, of Bridgewater, then moved to amend the amendment, by striking out the last paragraph thereof, and inserting the following:

And the right of the people, at all times, to amend their Constitution of Government, by Convention, or otherwise, according to their will, legally expressed, shall never be restrained or obstructed in this Commonwealth.

After remarks by Mr. Parker, of Cambridge,

The amendment was rejected.

The question then recurred upon the amendment moved by Mr. Hallett.

The question being taken, the amendment was agreed to, by a vote of one hundred and fifty-nine in the affirmative, and one hundred and one in the negative.

When, on motion of Mr. Butler, of Lowell, it was

Voted, That the Committee rise, and report to the Convention that the Resolves ought to pass, with the amendments.

And the Committee accordingly rose.

SATURDAY, July 23, 1853.

Mr. BUTLER, of Lowell, in the chair.

By direction of the Convention, the Committee proceeded to consider the following Resolve, reported from a special committee:—

Resolved, That it is expedient to insert into the Constitution, articles providing—

1. That the legislature shall have no power to pass any act, granting any special charter for banking purposes, or any special act to increase the capital stock of any charter bank; but corporations may be formed for such purposes, or the capital stock of charter banks may be increased, under general laws.

2. That the legislature shall provide by law for the registry of all notes or bills authorized by general laws to be issued or put in circulation as money; and shall require ample security for the redemption of such notes in specie.

After debate by Messrs. Frothingham, of Charlestown, and Schouler, of Boston,

Mr. Hooper, of Fall River, moved to amend the Resolve by adding to the second paragraph the following:—

Provided, that no note or bill of a less denomination than ten dollars shall be issued as currency after the year eighteen hundred and sixty.

After debate by Messrs. Hooper, of Fall River, French, of Berkley, Walker, of North Brookfield, Stetson, of Braintree, Frothingham, of Charlestown, and Livermore, of Cambridge,

The amendment was rejected, by a vote of twenty-seven in the affirmative, and eighty-five in the negative.

The question then recurred upon the adoption of the Resolve as reported,

And it was decided in the affirmative, by a vote of one hundred and thirty in the affirmative, and twenty-eight in the negative.

On motion of Mr. Davis, of Worcester, it was

Voted, That the Committee rise, and report to the Convention that the Resolve ought to pass.

And the Committee accordingly rose.

Afterwards, Mr. Morton, of Andover, in the chair.

By direction of the Convention, the Committee proceeded to consider a series of Resolves (printed Document No. 104) reported from the Committee on Secretary, Treasurer, etc., concerning Justices of the Peace.

Mr. Cushman, of Bernardston, moved to amend the first Resolve, by striking out all after the word "Resolved," and inserting the following:—

That it is expedient to amend the Constitution as follows.

There shall be two classes of justices of the peace, viz.:—

1st. Trial Justices, who shall be elected by the legal voters of the several towns, for a term of three years. There shall be one in each town, and one additional for every two thousand inhabitants. They shall have the same jurisdictions, powers and duties that are now exercised by justices of the peace, justices of the quorum, and commissioners to qualify civil officers; and such other powers as may be given them by the legislature.

2d. Justices of the Peace, who shall be appointed by the governor and council, for a term of seven years; and those who now hold that office, shall continue as such according to the tenure of their respective commissions: *provided,* that the jurisdiction of justices of the peace shall extend only to the acknowledgment of deeds, the administration of oaths, the issuing of subpœnas, and the solemnization of marriages.

After debate by Messrs. Cushman, of Bernardston, and Hathaway, of Freetown,

Mr. Hathaway moved that the Committee rise, report progress, and ask leave to sit again; but afterwards withdrew the motion.

Mr. Hallett, member for Wilbraham, moved to amend the amendment, by striking out all after the word "extend," in the second paragraph thereof, and inserting the following: "to the hearing or trial of any causes or issuing of warrants;" and also by inserting the word "not," before the word "extend."

At the suggestion of Mr. Morton, of Taunton, Mr. Cushman modified his amendment, by inserting, after the word "deeds," in the second paragraph, the following: "the taking of depositions."

After debate by Messrs. Cushman, of Bernardston, and Butler, of Lowell,

Mr. Weston, of Duxbury, moved that the Committee rise, report progress, and ask leave to sit again.

The motion was adopted by a vote of seventy in the affirmative, and thirty in the negative.

And the Committee accordingly rose.

MONDAY, July 25, 1853.

Mr. MORTON, of Andover, in the chair.

By direction of the Convention, the Committee resumed the consideration of the unfinished business of the last session—the Resolves concerning Justices of the Peace, the pending question being upon the amendment of Mr. Hallett, member for Wilbraham, to the amendment of Mr. Cushman, of Bernardston.

Mr. Hallett modified his amendment, by adding to the words to be inserted, the following words: "in criminal cases."

The amendment as modified, was then adopted.

The question then recurring upon the amendment, as amended, Mr. Hallett further moved to amend the amendment, by striking out, in the third line, (printed copy,) of the Resolve, the following words: "There shall be two classes of justices of the peace, viz.:" and also the word "who," in the first line of the first paragraph; also the word "who," in the first line of the second paragraph.

After remarks by Mr. Bishop, of Lenox,

The amendment was adopted.

Mr. Hallett moved further to amend the amendment, by inserting, after the words "justices of the peace," in the fifth line, (printed copy,) of the second paragraph, the following words: "and justices of the peace and of the quorum, and justices throughout the Commonwealth, and commissioners to qualify civil officers."

After debate by Messrs. Chapin, of Worcester, Davis, of Plymouth, Lord of Salem, and Griswold, member for Erving,

The question was taken upon the amendment, and seventy-four gentlemen voted in the affirmative, and thirteen in the negative.

A quorum not having voted,

On motion of Mr. Earle, of Worcester, it was

Voted, That the Committee rise, and report to the Convention that a quorum was not present.

And the Committee accordingly rose.

Afterwards, Mr. SCHOULER, of Boston, in the chair.

By direction of the Convention, the Committee proceeded to consider a series of Resolves, reported from the Standing Committee on the Preamble and Declaration of Rights, (printed Document No. 107.)

Also, a Report from the Committee to whom was referred the Order relating to remedies to the representatives of persons killed by the negligence or misconduct of Railroad Corporations, (printed Document No. 114.)

Also, a Report from a Minority of the Committee on the Preamble and Declaration of Rights, (printed Document No. 115.)

The Resolves relating to the Bill of Rights were first taken up and considered.

Mr. Sumner, member for Marshfield, proceeded to address the Committee, until his time had expired under the rule adopted by the Convention, limiting debate to fifteen minutes,

When Mr. Wilson, of Natick, moved that leave be granted to Mr. Sumner to proceed.

Mr. Lord, of Salem, inquired whether it was competent for the Committee to change a rule of the Convention?

The Chairman decided that it was in the power of the Committee to rescind the rule.

After remarks by Messrs. Boutwell, member for Berlin, Briggs, of Pittsfield, Aspinwall, of Brookline, and Wilson, of Natick,

Mr. Lord, of Salem, moved to amend the motion of Mr. Wilson, by adding thereto the following words: "and to any other gentleman who chooses."

After remarks by Mr. Briggs, of Pittsfield, the Chairman decided the amendment not in order.

Further debate followed between Messrs. Hallett, member for Wilbraham, Dana, member for Manchester, Bird, of Walpole, and Gardner, of Seekonk,

When the motion of Mr. Wilson was agreed to, by a vote of ninety-two in the affirmative, and eighty-seven in the negative.

Mr. Boutwell, member for Berlin, moved a reconsideration of the last vote.

Mr. Sumner then waived his right to speak under the vote last taken.

After debate by Messrs. Hopkinson, of Boston, and Gardner, of Seekonk,

The question was taken, and the motion of Mr. Boutwell was adopted by a vote of eighty-four in the affirmative, and eighty-two in the negative.

The question then recurred upon the motion of Mr. Wilson.

Mr. Sumner again signified his intention to waive all privilege or right to speak,

When Mr. Wilson withdrew his motion.

Mr. Hallett, member for Wilbraham, moved that the several subjects referred to the Committee be considered separately.

Mr. Thompson, of Charlestown, addressed the Committee.

The question then being taken, the motion of Mr. Hallett was rejected.

The question then recurred upon the Resolves relating to the Bill of Rights.

After remarks by Messrs. Briggs, of Pittsfield, Sumner, member for Marshfield, and Hopkinson, of Boston,

The first Resolve was adopted.

Mr. Dana, member for Manchester, moved to amend the second Resolve, by adding thereto the following:—

Said writ shall be granted as of right in all cases where the legislature shall not especially confer a discretion upon the court; but the legislature may prescribe preliminary proceedings to the obtaining of said writ.

After debate by Messrs. Dana, member for Manchester, and Hallett, member for Wilbraham,

The question was taken, and the amendment was agreed to, by a vote of eighty-five in the affirmative, and twenty-two in the negative.

The question then recurring upon the Resolve, as amended,

It was adopted.

The third Resolve was then agreed to, without debate.

Mr. Hallett moved to amend the fourth Resolve, by inserting the word "expressly," after the word "not," in the last line.

After debate by Messrs. Sumner, member for Marshfield, Hallett, member for Wilbraham, Lord, of Salem, Wilson, of Natick, and Bradford, of Essex,

Mr. Hallett withdrew his amendment.

Mr. Newman, of Bolton, then moved to strike out the last paragraph of the fourth Resolve, and insert the following words:—

We declare every thing in this Bill of Rights is excepted out of the general powers of government, and shall ever remain inviolate.

But the motion was rejected.

The question then recurred upon the fourth Resolve.

Mr. Bradford, of Essex, calling for a division,

The question was taken upon the first part, as far as and including the word "people," in the fifth line, (printed copy,) and it was agreed to.

The remaining part of the Resolve was then agreed to.

When, on motion of Mr. Wilson, of Natick, it was

Voted, That the Committee rise, and report that the Resolves relating to the Bill of Rights ought to pass, with the amendment; and upon the other subjects referred to the Committee, ask leave to sit again.

And the Committee accordingly rose.

TUESDAY, July 26, 1853.

Mr. Nayson, of Amesbury, in the chair.

By direction of the Convention, the Committee proceeded to consider the following Resolve:—

Resolved, That the Constitution ought to be amended so as to make the provisions for receiving, assorting, counting and recording of votes, uniform in the election of all officers whose election is provided for in the Constitution.

After remarks by Mr. Duncan, of Williamstown,

The Resolve was adopted, by a vote of one hundred and seventeen in the affirmative, and thirty-five in the negative.

On motion of Mr. Earle of Worcester, it was

Voted, That the Committee rise, and report to the Convention, that the Resolve ought to pass.

And the Committee accordingly rose.

Afterwards, Mr. SCHOULER, of Boston, in the chair.

By direction of the Convention, the Committee resumed the consideration of the unfinished business of the session of July 25th.

The first subject considered was the following Report, from the Minority of the Committee on the Bill of Rights, (printed Document No. 115) :—

That the second article of the Bill of Rights ought to be so altered as to change the words, "for his religious profession or sentiments," to the words "for his profession or sentiments concerning religion;" so that it will read, if so amended,—

And no subject shall be hurt, molested, or restrained in his person, liberty, or estate, for worshipping God in the manner and season most agreeable to the dictates of his own conscience, or for his profession or sentiments concerning religion.

Mr. Chandler, of Greenfield, moved to amend the Report, by striking out the word "subject," in the first line, and inserting the word "person;" and also, by adding the following at the close: "*provided*, it does not interfere with the rights and privileges of other worshippers."

After debate by Messrs. Allen, of Worcester, Lord, of Salem, and Sumner, member for Marshfield,

Mr. Chandler withdrew the second part of his amendment.

After further debate by Messrs. Sumner, member for Marshfield, and Lord, of Salem,

Mr. Chapin, of Webster, moved to amend the Report, by striking out, in the second paragraph thereof, the words "or restrained," and inserting before the word "molested," the word "or."

At the suggestion of Mr. Sumner, member for Marshfield, Mr. Chandler modified his amendment, by substituting the word "man," for the word "person."

Debate followed between Messrs. Sumner, member for Marshfield,

Briggs, of Pittsfield, Keyes, member for Abington, Dana, member for Manchester, Chapin, of Webster, Bird, of Walpole, Hillard, of Boston, Chandler, of Greenfield, French, of New Bedford, Hallett, member for Wilbraham, and Whitney, of Boylston,

The question was then taken upon the amendment of Mr. Chandler,

And it was rejected.

Mr. Butler, of Lowell, moved to amend the Report by substituting the word "one," for the word "subject."

After debate by Messrs. Butler, of Lowell, Foster, of Charlemont, Chapin, of Webster, Briggs, of Pittsfield, Holder, of Lynn, Jenks, of Boston, Gardner, of Seekonk, and Parker, of Cambridge,

The motion was agreed to by a vote of one hundred and fifty in the affirmative, and one hundred and seven in the negative.

The question then recurred upon the amendment of Mr. Chapin, of Webster,

And it was rejected.

Mr. Spooner, of Warwick, moved to amend the Report by adding, at the close, the following words: "or any other subject."

After remarks by Mr. Spooner,

The amendment was rejected.

The question then recurred upon the Report, as amended.

The Committee was addressed by Messrs. Lord, of Salem, Hallett, member for Wilbraham, Keyes, member for Abington, Kingman, of West Bridgewater, and Chapin, of Webster.

Mr. Walker, of North Brookfield, moved that debate cease at ten minutes past five o'clock;

But the Chairman decided the motion not in order.

The subject was further debated by Messrs. Hallett, member for Wilbraham, Plunkett, of Adams, and Abbott, of Lowell,

When, the question being taken upon the Report, as amended,

It was rejected, by a vote of one hundred and twenty-one in the affirmative, and one hundred and sixty-eight in the negative.

Mr. Hallett, member for Wilbraham, moved a reconsideration of the last vote.

After remarks by Mr. Lord, of Salem,

The question being taken,

The motion was rejected.

The Committee then proceeded to consider the Minority Report (printed Document No. 115) of the same committee, on the subject of Law Martial, to strike out from the twenty-eighth article of the Bill of Rights the words "by the authority of the legislature." So it will read, if amended:—

No person can, in any case, be subjected to law martial, or to any penalties or pains by virtue of that law, except those employed in the army or navy, and except the militia in actual service.

After remarks by Mr. Hallett, member for Wilbraham,

The question was taken on agreeing to the Report, and decided in the affirmative.

So the Report was accepted.

The Committee then proceeded to consider the Report, from the Minority of the same committee, (printed Document No. 115,) concerning the Rights of Juries, that there should be added to the fifteenth article of the Bill of Rights, the following clause:—

In all trials for criminal offences, the jury, after having received the instruction of the court, shall have the right, in their verdict of guilty or not guilty, to determine the law and the facts of the case.

After remarks by Mr. Hillard, of Boston,

Mr. Wilson, of Natick, moved that the Committee rise, report progress, and ask leave to sit again.

The motion was agreed to, by a vote of one hundred and eighteen in the affirmative, and thirty-nine in the negative.

And the Committee accordingly rose.

34

APPENDIX.

JOURNAL

OF THE

Committee of the Constitutional Convention.

SENATE CHAMBER, STATE HOUSE,
December 19, 1853.

The Committee of the Constitutional Convention appointed under the third Resolution adopted by that body on the first day of August, in the year 1853, assembled this day.

Hon. N. P. BANKS, Jr., Chairman, called the Committee to order.

The names of the members were called by William S. Robinson, Secretary of the Convention, and it appeared that the following named members were present, viz.:—

Messrs. BANKS, of Waltham; BOUTWELL, member for Berlin; DANA, member for Manchester; GILES, of Boston; MORTON, of Andover; UPHAM, of Salem; BUTLER, of Lowell; GRISWOLD, member for Erving; FROTHINGHAM, of Charlestown; WOOD, of Middleborough; HILLARD, of Boston; ASPINWALL, of Brookline; SLEEPER, of Roxbury; FRENCH, of New Bedford; OLIVER, of Lawrence; EAMES, of Washington; PHINNEY, member for Chatham; and WHITE, of Quincy.

On motion of Mr. Butler,

W. S. Robinson, senior Secretary of the Convention, was requested to act as Secretary of the Committee.

On motion of Mr. Giles,

The Secretary of the Committee was directed to notify the Secretary of the Commonwealth that the Committee is in session, and ready to receive such returns of votes on the Constitutional Propositions as may have been transmitted to him.

Afterwards, the Chairman of the Committee announced that the following communication had been received from the Secretary of the Commonwealth:—

COMMONWEALTH OF MASSACHUSETTS.

Secretary's Office, Boston, Dec. 19, 1853.

SIR,—I herewith transmit the returns received at this office, purporting to be the returns of votes for and against the adoption of the Constitution of August 1st, 1853. Returns have been received from all the towns in the State, except the town of Grafton, in Worcester County.

Respectfully, your most obedient servant,

E. M. WRIGHT.

To the Committee of the Convention, assembled at the State House.

On motion of Mr. Boutwell,

Ordered, That the returns of votes from the several counties be referred to six sub-committees, each to consist of three members, to be appointed by the Chairman.

The Chairman appointed the sub-committees, as follows:—

To examine the votes of the towns in Suffolk, Essex, and Plymouth Counties—

Messrs. Boutwell, Oliver, and Morton.

To examine the votes of the towns in Middlesex, Dukes, and Nantucket Counties—

Messrs. Dana, Aspinwall, and White.

To examine the votes of the towns in Worcester County—

Messrs. Hillard, Upham, and Wilson.

To examine the votes of the towns in Hampshire and Hampden Counties—

Messrs. Griswold, Giles, and Phinney.

To examine the votes of the towns in Franklin, Norfolk, and Barnstable Counties—

Messrs. Frothingham, Eames, and Aspinwall.

To examine the votes of the towns in Berkshire and Bristol Counties—

Messrs. Sleeper, Butler, and French.

On motion of Mr. Oliver,

Ordered, That when the Committee adjourns, it adjourn to meet to-morrow, at twelve o'clock.

On motion of Mr. Oliver,

Ordered, That the Messenger of the Convention be requested to serve as Messenger of the Committee.

On motion of Mr. Dana,

Ordered, That the rules of the Convention, so far as applicable, be the rules of this Committee.

At one o'clock, on motion of Mr. Butler,
The Committee adjourned.

TUESDAY, December 20, 1853.

The Committee met at twelve o'clock, according to adjournment and the Journal of yesterday's proceedings was read.

Mr. Frothingham, from the Sub-Committee charged with counting the votes from the towns in Franklin, Norfolk, and Barnstable Counties, submitted the following Report, accompanied by a schedule of the result:—

December 20, 1853.

The Sub-Committee to whom were referred the returns of the votes given in for the Constitutional Propositions in the counties of Franklin, Norfolk, and Barnstable, have examined the same, and Report:—

That they find returns, duly signed by the selectmen of the towns or mayor and aldermen of the cities, and attested by the town clerks, and marked on the envelopes as having been received in due time from the several towns in the counties of Franklin, Norfolk, and Barnstable, to wit: from twenty-six towns from the county of Franklin, twenty-three towns from the county of Norfolk, and thirteen towns from the county of Barnstable; and that the number of votes of the several towns is according to the accompanying schedules for each county. There were duplicate returns from the towns of Charlemont and Rowe, which were alike.

For the Committee,

R. FROTHINGHAM, Jr., *Chairman.*

Laid on the table.

Mr. Sleeper, from the Sub-Committee charged with counting the votes from the towns in Berkshire and Bristol Counties, stated that Mr. Butler and Mr. French, his associates upon the committee, were necessarily absent, and he requested that some other members might be appointed to supply their places.

The Chairman appointed Mr. Frothingham to take the place of Mr. Butler, and Mr. Chapin, of Springfield, to take the place of Mr. French.

The Chairman announced that he had received a communication from the Secretary of the Commonwealth, accompanied by the return of votes from the town of Grafton.

The return was referred to the Sub-Committee charged with counting the votes from the towns in the county of Worcester.

Mr. Hillard, from the Sub-Committee charged with counting the votes from the towns in the county of Worcester, submitted the following Report, accompanied by a schedule of the result:—

December 20, 1853.

The Sub-Committee charged with the duty of counting and reporting the votes of the county of Worcester, have attended to the same, and Report:—

That they have examined the returns from one city and fifty-six towns in the said county. The return from Grafton was not counted, not having been received till after the day fixed by law for receiving returns.

The result of the votes of the said county appears by the schedule hereto annexed and returned.

G. S. Hillard.
C. W. Upham.
Henry Wilson.

Laid on the table.

On motion of Mr. Wilson,

Ordered, That a committee be appointed to whom shall be referred the Reports of the several Sub-Committees, with instructions to prepare a tabular statement of the vote by counties, and the result of the whole vote.

The Chairman appointed the committee, as follows:—

Messrs. Wilson, Chapin, Upham, Giles, Griswold, Oliver, Aspinwall, and Morton.

Mr. Griswold, from the Sub-Committee charged with counting the votes from the towns in the counties of Hampshire and Hampden, submitted the following Report, accompanied by a schedule of the result:—

December 20, 1853.

The Sub-Committee to whom were referred the returns of votes upon the several Constitutional Propositions in the counties of Hampshire and Hampden, have attended to the duty assigned them, and ask leave to submit the subjoined Report:—

The Committee find the returns from the several towns in the counties of Hampshire and Hampden duly made out, signed by the selectmen of the several towns or the mayor and aldermen of the cities, or a majority of the same, and attested by the town clerks of the several towns or the city clerks of the cities, and duly sealed, superscribed and returned to the Secretary of the Commonwealth, with the exception of two towns. The return from Williamsburg, in the county of Hampshire, had the signature of only one selectman in the proper place; but over the signature of the town clerk and opposite the printed word attest, was the signature, Caleb L. Thayer. The Committee being of opinion that said Thayer was one of the selectmen and intended to sign the return as such, considered the return as substantially correct, and counted the same. The return from the town of Ludlow, in the county of Hampden, was unsealed. It appeared from a memorandum on said return made by the Secretary of the Commonwealth, that said return was received by the Secretary in a sealed envelope, with other returns, superscribed "Votes for State Officers—Yeas and Nays." The Committee, considering the return substantially in compliance with the Resolves accompanying the Constitutional Propositions, counted the same.

The result of the votes upon the several Constitutional Propositions in the several towns and cities in the counties of Hampshire and Hampden, will appear by the schedules accompanying this Report.

For the Committee,

W. GRISWOLD, *Chairman.*

Mr. Oliver, from the Sub-Committee charged with counting the votes from the towns in the counties of Suffolk, Essex, and Plymouth, submitted the following Report, accompanied by a schedule of the result:—

December 20, 1853.

The Sub-Committee to whom were referred the returns of the votes given for and against the Constitutional Propositions submitted to the people in November last, for the several cities and towns in the counties of Suffolk, Essex, and Plymouth, have examined the same, and beg leave to Report:—

That they find said returns duly signed by the mayors and aldermen of cities and by the selectmen of towns, and duly attested by the city and town clerks of the several cities and towns in said counties, and marked on the envelopes as returned in due season, and that said returns were received as follows, to wit: from one city and three towns in Suffolk County; from four cities and twenty-eight towns in

Essex County; from twenty-two towns in Plymouth County. That in the county of Plymouth, the voters of the town of Marion were by law to vote in the town of Rochester, and the voters of the town of Lakeville were by law to vote in the town of Middleborough.

The Committee further report, that the votes of the several cities and towns in said counties are recorded in the accompanying schedules of the counties.

Duplicate returns were received from the towns of Marblehead and Beverly, and that opposite to the signatures of the selectmen of the several towns of Rowley, Danvers, and Haverhill, in the county of Essex, and of the towns of Plympton and Bridgewater, in the county of Plymouth, and of Winthrop, in the county of Suffolk, at the foot of said returns, the names of the towns were not written; but inasmuch as in each of these cases the name of the town was duly and fully written in the appropriate place in the heading of the return, the Committee considered each of said returns to be authentic.

HENRY K. OLIVER,
MARCUS MORTON, Jr.,
A majority of the Committee.

Mr. Dana, from the Sub-Committee charged with counting the votes from the towns in the counties of Middlesex, Nantucket, and Dukes, submitted the following Report, accompanied by a schedule of the result:

December 20, 1853.

The Sub-Committee, to whom were referred the returns from the several towns and cities in the counties of Middlesex, Nantucket, and Dukes, have examined the same, and Report:—

That they find returns duly signed by the selectmen of the several towns, or mayors and aldermen of the several cities, and attested by the several town or city clerks, and marked on the envelopes as having been received in due time, from the several towns or cities in the counties of Middlesex, Nantucket, and Dukes, to wit: from forty-eight towns and three cities in the county of Middlesex, from one town in the county of Nantucket, and from three towns in the county of Dukes; and that the number of votes in the several towns and cities is according to the accompanying schedules for each county.

That the return from the town of Concord, in the county of Middlesex, encloses a vote on all the Propositions, which was both *Yes* and *No* on each Proposition, and the return does not show whether said vote was counted or not.

That the return from the town of Dracut, in said county, states the vote in the negative on the Proposition number "eight" to have been "one and seven." As all the other votes in the negative on the other Propositions in that town, are between one hundred and six and one hundred and eleven, the Committee are of opinion that the vote actually given was one hundred and seven. But in the schedule appended to their Report, they have not counted the said vote at all.

Richard H. Dana, Jr.
William Aspinwall.
George White.

Mr. Sleeper, from the Sub-Committee charged with counting the votes from the towns in the counties of Berkshire and Bristol, submitted the following Report, accompanied by a schedule of the result:—

December 20, 1853.

The Sub-Committee appointed to examine the returns and report the number of votes given in the counties of Bristol and Berkshire, for and against the proposed amendments to the Constitution, at the late election, have attended to their duty, and Report:—

That the number of votes in the different towns in those counties viz.: thirty-one in Berkshire, and nineteen in Bristol, according to the returns received at the office of the Secretary of State, is contained in the schedules which accompany this Report.

The Committee further state that the returns from the different towns in those counties appear to be regular and in conformity to law, with the exception of the town of New Ashford, in Berkshire County, where the signature of the town clerk, attesting the correctness of the returns from that town, is wanting.

John S. Sleeper, *Chairman.*

These Reports were severally referred to the Committee charged with making a tabular statement of the result by counties, etc.

The Reports from the Sub-Committees charged with counting the votes from the towns in Franklin, Norfolk, and Barnstable Counties, and in Worcester County, were taken from the table and referred to the same committee.

Mr. Hillard offered the following Order:—

Ordered, That the Secretaries of the late Convention return into the hands of this Committee the Journals of the said Convention, together with its papers and files, and its final Report.

Laid upon the table.
On motion of Mr. Hillard,

Ordered, That when the Committee adjourns, it adjourn to meet at 12 o'clock to-morrow.

On motion of Mr. Phinney, at a quarter past two o'clock,
The Committee adjourned.

WEDNESDAY, December 21, 1853.

The Committee met at 12 o'clock, according to adjournment.
The reading of the Journal was dispensed with.
Mr. Wilson, from the Committee appointed to prepare a Tabular Statement of the Result of the Voting, from the Reports of the Sub-Committees, submitted the following Report:—

December 21, 1853.

The Sub-Committee to whom was referred the duty of the summing up of the several county aggregates of the votes given for and against the several Constitutional Propositions submitted to the people by the late Constitutional Convention, and acted upon by them on the second Monday of November last, have attended to that duty, and Report:—

That they decided that the votes of the town of Grafton, in the county of Worcester, upon the several Propositions, should be included in the summing up of the votes of that county; and that the vote of the town of Dracut, in the county of Middlesex, cast in the negative of the Eighth Proposition, should likewise be included in the summing up of the votes of that county; and that the entire aggregate of all the votes of the several counties, for and against the several Constitutional Propositions submitted to the people, is presented in the schedule accompanying this Report.

HENRY WILSON.
C. W. CHAPIN.
C. W. UPHAM.
WHITING GRISWOLD.
HENRY K. OLIVER.
WILL. ASPINWALL.
MARCUS MORTON, Jr.

On motion of Mr. Phinney,

The Report was accepted.

On motion of Mr. Hillard,

The Secretary was instructed to prepare the papers necessary for an official notification to the governor and the legislature and to the people, of the result of the vote.

And, on motion of the same gentleman, a sub-committee was appointed to superintend the preparation of the papers.

The President appointed Messrs. Hillard, Butler, Wood, White, and Morton, to compose the committee.

On motion of Mr. Butler,

The Secretary was instructed to publish in the Journal of the Convention the result of the vote, *in extenso*, and also the Journal of the Proceedings of the Committee.

On motion of Mr. Oliver,

Ordered, That the vote be also published in the Debates.

Mr. Hillard, from the Committee appointed to superintend the preparation of the official notification of the result of the votes, submitted a Report, that duplicate papers had been prepared and signed by the members of the Committee.

On motion of Mr. Hillard,

The Chairman was requested to execute the trust reposed in the Committee by the Convention, relative to the notification of the governor, legislature, and people.

On motion of Mr. Oliver,

The Secretary was directed to make up the pay roll of the Committee.

The Chairman announced that he had received a communication from the Auditor, expressing his readiness to pay the members as soon as the pay roll should be prepared.

The pay roll having been made ready and certified,

On motion of Mr. Oliver,

At $2\frac{1}{2}$ o'clock, the Committee adjourned, without day.

ABSTRACT

Of the Returns of Votes on the several Constitutional Propositions submitted to the People, Nov. 14, 1853, as declared by the Committee appointed by the Convention to examine the same.

SUFFOLK COUNTY.

TOWNS.	No. 1.		No. 2.		No. 3.		No. 4.		No. 5.		No. 6.		No. 7.		No. 8.	
	Yes.	No.	Yes.	No.	Yes.	No.	Yes.	No.	Yes.	No.	Yes.	No.	Yes.	No.	Yes.	No.
Boston,	3,248	9,033	3,154	8,548	3,084	8,468	3,239	8,455	3,248	8,340	3,562	8,234	3,178	8,322	3,210	8,388
Chelsea,	380	483	415	448	383	480	399	466	478	440	436	432	397	466	394	469
North Chelsea,	14	62	14	62	14	62	14	62	16	60	15	61	14	62	15	61
Winthrop,	31	10	30	11	31	10	32	9	32	9	38	2	30	11	31	10
4 Towns,	3,673	9,588	3,613	9,069	3,512	9,020	3,684	8,992	3,774	8,849	4,051	8,729	3,619	8,861	3,650	8,928

COUNTY OF ESSEX.

TOWNS.	No. 1. Yes.	No. 1. No.	No. 2. Yes.	No. 2. No.	No. 3. Yes.	No. 3. No.	No. 4. Yes.	No. 4. No.	No. 5. Yes.	No. 5. No.	No. 6. Yes.	No. 6. No.	No. 7. Yes.	No. 7. No.	No. 8. Yes.	No. 8. No.
Amesbury,	255	255	257	252	255	254	258	251	264	241	278	230	258	251	257	251
Andover,	341	381	342	381	329	391	345	377	349	373	352	370	344	378	343	380

Beverly,	387	423	391	420	383	428	395	419	402	410	402	411	392	419	393	418
Boxford,	25	110	37	108	25	110	27	108	26	109	27	108	25	110	25	110
Bradford,	96	100	96	100	94	100	94	100	93	101	94	101	94	101	94	101
Danvers,	519	719	523	719	510	728	524	715	529	709	529	709	520	709	520	719
Essex,	137	85	137	85	136	86	137	85	138	84	138	84	137	85	137	85
Georgetown,	188	143	188	142	185	145	187	143	187	143	188	142	188	143	186	143
Gloucester,	444	392	442	394	441	395	444	392	454	382	449	387	446	391	452	385
Groveland,	133	101	134	100	130	103	136	99	138	97	138	97	134	101	136	100
Hamilton,	75	75	77	73	74	75	77	73	76	74	76	74	76	74	76	74
Haverhill,	530	497	537	491	525	503	538	489	537	490	550	478	535	494	539	489
Ipswich,	237	214	233	214	228	216	234	213	229	216	234	212	234	212	235	212
Lawrence,	567	622	567	624	549	640	583	607	609	580	602	587	568	621	571	617
Lynn,	1,173	975	1,180	966	1,147	987	1,188	960	1,213	930	1,180	961	1,183	966	1,194	952
Lynnfield,	56	42	55	43	55	43	56	42	56	42	56	42	56	42	56	42
Manchester,	100	82	101	81	93	88	101	80	101	82	102	79	100	81	99	81
Marblehead,	504	333	495	332	487	339	497	329	498	327	500	330	501	329	500	330
Methuen,	184	195	185	195	184	197	185	195	184	195	190	191	182	197	182	197
Middleton,	78	44	76	44	73	47	76	45	75	45	76	44	73	47	73	47

COUNTY OF ESSEX—Continued.

TOWNS.	No. 1.		No. 2.		No. 3.		No. 4.		No. 5.		No. 6.		No. 7.		No. 8.	
	Yes.	No.	Yes.	No.	Yes.	No.	Yes.	No.	Yes.	No.	Yes.	No.	Yes.	No.	Yes.	No.
Nahant,	5	34	5	34	4	35	5	34	5	34	5	34	5	34	6	34
Newbury,	67	103	67	102	67	102	67	102	67	102	66	102	66	102	66	102
Newburyport,	400	848	405	844	426	855	407	841	454	837	469	825	450	841	452	840
Rockport,	226	167	225	167	220	172	225	167	227	165	228	164	223	169	224	168
Rowley,	68	97	68	98	67	97	68	97	68	97	68	96	68	97	68	97
Salem,	581	1,446	576	1,440	580	1,454	583	1,433	598	1,418	596	1,420	577	1,436	583	1,430
Salisbury,	186	148	188	146	183	151	191	144	191	143	194	141	187	147	188	147
Saugus,	137	57	137	57	134	57	137	57	136	56	137	57	137	57	137	57
Swampscott,	84	45	84	45	84	45	84	45	84	45	84	45	84	45	84	45
Topsfield,	32	135	33	136	33	136	32	136	31	136	33	136	32	136	32	137
Wenham,	90	100	90	99	90	99	90	99	90	99	90	99	90	99	90	99
West Newbury,	93	131	93	129	84	131	94	129	94	129	96	128	95	128	97	128
32 Towns,	7,998	9,099	8,024	9,061	7,875	9,209	8,065	9,006	8,203	8,891	8,227	8,884	8,060	9,042	8,095	9,017

COUNTY OF MIDDLESEX.

Acton,	142	81	134	80	135	80	141	81	126	93	142	81	142	77	142	77
Ashby,	105	124	104	125	101	127	104	125	104	125	105	124	104	125	103	126
Ashland,	119	65	118	64	108	74	119	64	119	63	118	64	112	71	117	67
Bedford,	121	43	121	42	115	46	122	41	123	41	123	41	121	42	121	42
Billerica,	149	147	150	144	149	145	150	143	150	143	163	130	150	143	150	143
Boxborough,	55	22	55	22	52	22	55	21	55	22	55	21	55	22	55	22
Brighton,	20	267	22	266	20	267	21	266		266	27	260	20	268	21	267
Burlington,	56	16	55	16	54	17	55	16	56	15	55	16	55	16	55	16
Cambridge,	441	1,421	462	1,404	433	1,429	479	1,385	501	1,362	521	1,346	465	1,399	463	1,398
Carlisle,	74	26	74	26	73	27	74	26	75	25	75	25	74	26	74	26
Charlestown,	791	1,317	809	1,298	795	1,310	831	1,278	869	1,238	877	1,231	822	1,284	818	1,287
Chelmsford,	122	186	125	185	103	203	125	182	128	182	174	135	124	186	126	184
Concord,	172	125	179	116	151	144	180	114	175	120	182	114	174	120	173	122
Dracut,	128	110	129	109	126	111	130	108	127	110	132	106	131	107	131	107
Dunstable,	57	55	57	55	57	55	57	55	57	55	57	55	57	55	57	55
Framingham,	207	353	211	349	194	363	215	348	200	347	224	335	213	345	213	344

COUNTY OF MIDDLESEX—Continued.

TOWNS.	No. 1.		No. 2.		No. 3.		No. 4.		No. 5.		No. 6.		No. 7.		No. 8.	
	Yes.	No.	Yes.	No.	Yes.	No.	Yes.	No.	Yes.	No.	Yes.	No.	Yes.	No.	Yes.	No.
Groton,	207	167	208	166	207	166	207	166	208	166	211	163	207	167	207	167
Holliston,	237	137	237	136	230	141	240	134	234	137	239	134	235	136	236	136
Hopkinton,	254	89	254	89	247	94	254	89	256	88	251	93	254	89	254	89
Lexington,	128	203	128	202	127	204	129	203	131	200	131	200	128	202	128	202
Lincoln,	39	66	40	65	39	66	40	65	41	64	40	65	40	65	40	65
Littleton,	95	75	96	75	94	77	97	74	99	72	100	70	96	74	97	73
Lowell,	2,004	2,151	2,026	2,130	1,941	2,182	2,045	2,111	2,054	2,074	2,201	1,915	2,005	2,146	2,015	2,139
Malden,	242	288	250	279	236	293	256	277	249	277	259	272	245	286	249	286
Marlborough,	261	120	264	117	254	126	266	115	262	118	266	114	264	116	264	116
Medford,	338	351	339	352	334	356	342	349	346	346	355	345	340	351	341	347
Melrose,	160	85	161	84	159	86	161	84	165	81	166	80	161	84	163	84
Natick,	319	276	320	275	308	282	323	274	322	271	339	267	321	271	315	280
Newton,	277	425	289	422	260	441	287	415	286	416	291	412	277	424	281	420
North Reading,	41	113	41	113	38	115	41	113	41	113	41	113	41	113	41	113
Pepperell,	150	126	150	126	150	129	153	127	152	127	152	126	151	127	152	127

Reading, . . .	185	228	188	224	182	230	185	227	192	223	190	224	188	226	188	226
Sherborn, . . .	42	110	42	109	29	119	41	110	41	110	43	109	40	111	42	110
Shirley, ...	99	113	100	112	97	115	99	112	100	111	107	105	98	114	103	109
Somerville, . . .	172	316	171	316	172	316	173	315	171	316	174	314	172	315	173	315
South Reading, . .	174	227	179	223	169	233	181	222	195	208	190	214	180	224	180	223
Stoneham, . . .	296	108	293	109	288	114	299	105	299	104	301	103	297	107	298	106
Stowe, ...	102	75	102	74	94	80	102	74	103	73	104	72	103	74	102	74
Sudbury, . . .	130	98	128	98	127	98	132	96	130	97	134	94	131	96	131	96
Tewksbury, . . .	93	93	94	93	93	93	94	93	94	93	97	88	94	93	94	93
Townsend, . . .	159	84	159	84	157	84	159	84	158	84	158	84	159	84	159	84
Tyngsborough, . .	77	66	77	66	76	66	77	66	76	66	77	66	77	66	76	66
Waltham, . . .	329	366	328	365	322	371	331	364	333	357	308	376	330	365	327	367
Watertown, . . .	104	275	107	272	94	275	108	274	106	275	116	266	108	272	108	272
Wayland, . . .	107	104	108	101	104	107	108	101	108	102	108	101	107	103	106	105
West Cambridge, . .	96	236	100	232	90	244	106	227	111	223	113	221	97	235	99	236
Westford, . . .	137	112	136	112	130	115	135	112	135	113	138	110	136	112	137	111
Weston, . . .	73	91	74	89	73	90	73	89	74	89	75	89	75	89	75	89
Wilmington, . . .	56	61	57	60	55	61	59	60	58	60	59	58	56	61	56	61

COUNTY OF MIDDLESEX—Continued.

TOWNS.	No. 1.		No. 2.		No. 3.		No. 4.		No. 5.		No. 6.		No. 7.		No. 8.	
	Yes.	No.	Yes.	No.	Yes.	No.	Yes.	No.	Yes.	No.	Yes.	No.	Yes.	No.	Yes.	No.
Winchester,	123	152	127	149	119	156	131	145	138	136	138	138	124	152	124	152
Woburn,	274	233	274	232	266	238	279	230	283	225	280	229	276	231	275	232
51 Towns,	10,339	12,178	10,452	12,052	10,027	12,383	10,571	11,955	10,637	11,822	10,982	11,514	10,432	12,067	10,455	12,054

COUNTY OF WORCESTER.

TOWNS.	No. 1.		No. 2.		No. 3.		No. 4.		No. 5.		No. 6.		No. 7.		No. 8.	
	Yes.	No.	Yes.	No.	Yes.	No.	Yes.	No.	Yes.	No.	Yes.	No.	Yes.	No.	Yes.	No.
Ashburnham,	203	146	203	146	201	146	203	146	203	144	203	146	202	146	202	146
Athol,	168	161	169	160	167	162	169	159	164	165	170	159	169	160	169	161
Auburn,	119	13	120	12	120	12	120	12	120	12	120	12	120	12	120	12
Barre,	266	262	266	262	261	264	266	262	261	264	267	261	266	262	267	261
Berlin,	100	46	100	46	100	46	100	46	99	46	100	46	100	46	100	46
Blackstone,	220	171	221	170	220	171	220	171	271	169	221	169	218	121	218	171
Bolton,	91	95	92	95	89	97	91	94	91	94	92	94	91	93	91	93
Boylston,	94	38	94	38	92	39	94	38	94	38	94	38	94	38	94	38
Brookfield,	219	79	216	78	213	78	216	78	222	72	223	68	216	76	218	74

Charlton, . . .	263	41	264	41	263	41	264	41	253	52	264	40	263	42	263	42
Clinton, . . .	136	228	137	226	134	230	136	228	135	228	138	225	135	229	134	229
Dana, ...	83	47	83	47	72	58	85	45	79	51	86	44	84	46	84	46
Douglas, . . .	208	98	208	98	207	99	208	98	209	97	210	96	208	98	208	98
Dudley, . . .	138	68	141	64	127	76	141	63	142	64	144	62	148	66	142	63
Fitchburg, . . .	554	329	547	335	534	341	551	326	548	329	545	328	541	329	540	343
Gardner, . . .	214	81	216	80	216	80	216	80	216	80	216	80	215	81	215	81
Grafton, . . .	301	173	302	172	296	178	302	172	300	174	302	172	300	174	299	175
Hardwick, . . .	137	160	139	158	136	161	140	157	140	157	140	157	138	159	140	157
Harvard, . . .	143	83	143	83	132	84	143	83	140	84	144	81	142	83	142	84
Holden, . . .	180	126	181	126	180	126	181	126	179	127	181	126	179	127	179	127
Hubbardston, . .	240	66	240	67	236	70	239	67	238	68	239	67	239	67	239	67
Lancaster, . . .	70	170	71	168	69	170	73	168	72	167	74	164	71	168	71	168
Leicester, . . .	229	126	232	123	231	123	233	123	231	123	231	124	232	123	233	123
Leominster, . . .	306	205	305	204	301	208	305	205	307	204	309	202	307	204	308	203
Lunenburg, . . .	135	80	134	80	133	81	135	80	136	79	135	79	134	80	134	81
Mendon, . . .	155	55	154	55	141	69	154	55	145	64	158	50	154	55	153	55
Milford, . . .	368	258	366	254	347	275	367	251	365	237	358	250	364	253	364	250

COUNTY OF WORCESTER—Continued.

TOWNS.	No. 1.		No. 2.		No. 3.		No. 4.		No. 5.		No. 6.		No. 7.		No. 8.	
	Yes.	No.	Yes.	No.	Yes.	No.	Yes.	No.	Yes.	No.	Yes.	No.	Yes.	No.	Yes.	No.
Millbury,	246	160	249	156	247	159	249	156	247	160	250	156	249	158	249	158
New Braintree,	62	56	62	56	60	58	62	55	61	56	62	55	60	57	60	57
Northborough,	165	107	165	107	165	107	165	107	158	113	165	107	165	107	165	107
Northbridge,	147	155	147	155	144	155	147	155	157	143	156	127	148	154	148	154
North Brookfield,	228	105	229	104	222	111	227	106	226	107	229	104	228	105	226	107
Oakham,	112	48	113	47	111	50	113	47	113	47	113	47	113	47	113	47
Oxford,	293	119	295	116	284	127	296	116	295	117	296	116	292	119	293	119
Paxton,	112	44	112	44	104	49	112	44	111	44	115	41	112	44	112	44
Petersham,	175	108	176	108	172	111	176	108	177	107	176	108	176	108	176	108
Phillipston,	36	98	35	98	35	98	35	98	35	98	35	98	35	98	35	98
Princeton,	142	76	142	76	138	78	142	76	141	77	142	76	142	76	142	76
Royalston,	87	171	88	170	83	175	88	170	87	172	89	169	87	171	87	171
Rutland,	124	26	124	26	124	26	124	26	124	26	124	26	124	26	123	26
Shrewsbury,	202	80	203	80	203	80	203	80	201	81	204	79	201	82	201	82
Southborough,	97	51	97	51	91	57	98	51	97	51	98	50	97	51	96	52

Southbridge,	301	121	305	120	300	124	311	115	284	139	327	101	303	120	302	120
Spencer,	228	187	228	187	227	189	229	187	230	187	231	186	228	188	228	188
Sterling,	152	186	153	183	147	191	153	183	155	183	154	184	150	187	151	187
Sturbridge,	201	109	201	107	191	116	200	109	170	134	199	110	198	111	199	111
Sutton,	300	74	300	73	294	75	296	73	299	74	300	73	300	73	300	73
Templeton,	222	138	224	137	212	144	225	135	218	140	227	133	224	136	223	137
Upton,	225	144	226	143	224	145	227	142	230	138	229	140	227	141	227	141
Uxbridge,	200	140	198	139	200	140	201	138	201	138	203	136	199	139	199	139
Warren,	143	109	143	109	143	110	143	109	143	109	143	108	143	109	143	109
Webster,	188	112	191	109	189	111	194	106	195	104	203	95	190	110	189	111
Westborough,	219	201	228	193	214	207	230	191	227	194	234	187	222	199	222	197
West Boylston,	238	66	238	66	235	69	238	66	239	65	239	65	238	66	238	66
West Brookfield,	149	93	150	92	148	93	149	92	148	92	149	92	149	93	150	92
Westminster,	206	154	206	154	206	154	206	154	206	153	206	153	206	153	206	153
Winchendon,	213	142	216	139	216	139	218	136	214	138	217	136	214	139	214	140
Worcester,	2,182	939	2,203	917	2,162	947	2,212	908	2,191	921	2,219	898	2,184	928	2,187	924
58 Towns,	12,935	7,724	12,994	7,450	12,609	7,880	13,021	7,611	12,940	7,697	13,098	7,496	12,934	7,633	12,931	7,688

COUNTY OF HAMPSHIRE.

TOWNS.	No. 1.		No. 2.		No. 3.		No. 4.		No. 5.		No. 6.		No. 7.		No. 8.	
	Yes.	No.	Yes.	No.	Yes.	No.	Yes.	No.	Yes.	No.	Yes.	No.	Yes.	No.	Yes.	No.
Amherst,	187	271	186	270	182	271	186	270	188	267	189	278	186	271	186	271
Belchertown,	223	194	223	194	222	195	223	194	222	195	233	184	223	194	223	194
Chesterfield,	120	83	120	83	120	83	120	83	120	83	120	83	120	83	120	83
Cummington,	132	111	132	111	132	111	132	111	133	110	133	110	132	111	132	111
Easthampton,	89	111	90	110	87	113	90	110	91	109	91	109	89	111	89	111
Enfield,	40	147	38	147	38	147	38	147	39	146	40	147	38	147	38	147
Goshen,	34	75	34	75	34	75	34	75	34	75	34	75	34	75	34	75
Granby,	53	94	53	93	48	98	53	93	54	92	54	92	52	94	52	94
Greenwich,	96	61	96	61	93	61	96	61	96	61	96	61	96	61	96	61
Hadley,	59	246	59	246	58	247	59	246	59	244	59	246	59	246	59	246
Hatfield,	83	97	83	97	80	100	81	99	83	97	83	97	83	97	83	97
Middlefield,	55	60	53	62	52	63	53	62	53	62	53	62	53	62	52	61
Northampton,	443	374	444	373	423	386	443	372	442	369	446	368	444	372	444	373
Norwich,	77	47	77	47	77	47	77	47	75	48	78	46	77	47	77	47
Pelham,	97	47	96	47	96	46	97	47	95	48	97	47	97	47	97	47

Plainfield,	88	21	76	33	35	74	78	31	88	21	90	19	39	70	38	71
Prescott,	47	56	47	56	47	56	47	56	47	56	52	51	47	56	47	56
South Hadley,	99	177	98	176	97	176	99	175	99	175	99	175	99	175	99	175
Southampton,	114	107	115	106	110	110	115	106	115	106	116	105	114	107	113	107
Ware,	260	230	260	228	257	233	261	228	261	228	260	228	260	229	261	228
Westhampton,	50	74	50	74	47	74	50	74	50	74	50	74	50	74	50	74
Williamsburg,	157	125	158	124	156	126	157	125	158	124	157	125	156	126	154	127
Worthington,	95	127	95	127	94	128	95	127	94	128	96	126	94	128	95	127
23 Towns,	2,698	2,935	2,683	2,940	2,585	3,020	2,684	2,939	2,696	2,918	2,726	2,908	2,642	2,983	2,639	2,983

COUNTY OF HAMPDEN.

Blandford,	126	82	125	82	114	88	125	82	117	83	125	82	125	82	125	83
Brimfield,	112	119	112	119	108	122	112	119	112	119	113	118	112	119	112	119
Chester,	84	120	84	117	81	120	84	117	84	117	84	117	84	120	84	120
Chicopee,	326	397	332	390	318	403	337	388	342	391	338	387	336	390	332	393
Granville,	140	97	140	97	140	97	140	97	140	97	140	97	140	97	140	97
Holland,	40	37	40	37	40	37	40	37	40	37	40	37	40	35	40	35

COUNTY OF HAMPDEN—Continued.

TOWNS.	No. 1.		No. 2.		No. 3.		No. 4.		No. 5.		No. 6.		No. 7.		No. 8.	
	Yes.	No.	Yes.	No.	Yes.	No.	Yes.	No.	Yes.	No.	Yes.	No.	Yes.	No.	Yes.	No.
Holyoke,	195	174	195	173	190	178	197	172	195	173	197	170	197	172	199	171
Longmeadow,	96	45	93	48	78	62	93	48	94	47	95	46	91	51	91	50
Ludlow,	128	73	128	73	128	73	128	73	128	73	128	73	128	73	129	73
Monson,	169	177	169	177	167	179	169	177	169	176	171	175	169	177	169	177
Montgomery,	63	10	63	10	63	10	63	10	63	10	63	10	63	10	63	10
Palmer,	250	153	249	154	240	161	251	152	248	154	253	151	252	152	252	152
Russell,	82	13	81	14	81	14	81	14	81	14	82	13	81	14	81	14
Southwick,	131	61	130	61	130	61	131	61	131	61	131	61	131	61	131	60
Springfield,	933	805	940	801	927	803	945	795	944	793	948	786	942	796	947	791
Tolland,	81	2	79	4	74	8	78	4	79	4	79	4	79	4	79	4
Wales,	45	63	45	63	44	64	45	63	44	61	63	40	45	63	46	63
Westfield,	469	220	476	214	466	221	485	207	482	207	535	157	471	220	471	219
West Springfield,	173	220	174	219	173	219	174	219	172	219	173	220	173	220	173	219
Wilbraham,	149	110	150	109	149	110	150	109	149	110	150	109	149	110	149	110
20 Towns,	3,792	2,978	3,805	2,962	3,711	3,030	3,828	2,944	3,814	2,946	3,908	2,853	3,808	2,966	3,813	2.960

COUNTY OF FRANKLIN.

Ashfield,	171	115	171	114	162	121	171	114	171	113	171	114	171	115	171	115
Bernardston,	103	90	105	88	103	90	106	87	103	90	107	85	105	88	105	88
Buckland,	165	79	166	78	161	78	165	79	167	77	165	78	165	79	166	78
Charlemont,	121	92	121	92	121	92	121	92	121	92	121	92	121	92	121	92
Coleraine,	175	161	175	161	173	161	175	161	174	161	175	161	175	161	175	161
Conway,	206	189	208	187	205	189	208	187	208	187	209	187	207	188	207	188
Deerfield,	223	190	224	190	221	192	224	190	224	190	224	190	224	190	224	191
Erving,	52	12	52	12	52	12	52	12	51	12	52	12	52	12	53	12
Gill,	46	61	46	61	46	61	46	61	44	63	46	61	46	61	47	60
Greenfield,	255	263	259	259	255	263	259	260	262	258	259	260	257	262	256	262
Hawley,	52	80	51	80	41	87	51	80	50	80	51	80	51	80	51	80
Heath,	72	58	71	59	69	61	71	59	71	59	71	59	72	58	72	58
Leverett,	112	56	112	56	111	56	111	56	111	56	111	56	112	56	112	56
Leyden,	78	29	78	29	77	29	77	29	77	29	77	29	77	29	77	29
Monroe,	25	5	25	5	20	10	25	5	25	5	25	5	25	5	25	5
Montague,	159	108	139	108	139	108	139	108	138	109	141	106	139	108	141	106
New Salem,	116	111	116	111	116	111	116	111	116	111	119	108	117	111	116	111

COUNTY OF FRANKLIN—Continued.

TOWNS.	No. 1.		No. 2.		No. 3.		No. 4.		No. 5.		No. 6.		No. 7.		No. 8.	
	Yes.	No.	Yes.	No.	Yes.	No.	Yes.	No.	Yes.	No.	Yes.	No.	Yes.	No.	Yes.	No.
Northfield,	170	98	169	97	169	97	169	97	168	99	169	97	169	97	169	98
Orange,	157	120	157	120	155	122	157	120	157	120	157	120	157	120	157	120
Rowe,	41	68	41	68	38	71	41	68	41	68	40	68	41	68	41	68
Shelburne,	107	155	107	155	92	162	107	155	105	155	108	153	107	155	103	159
Shutesbury,	104	46	103	46	100	49	104	45	103	47	104	45	105	45	103	46
Sunderland,	97	101	97	100	93	101	97	100	99	98	99	98	97	99	98	99
Warwick,	107	66	106	66	106	66	106	66	106	66	107	65	106	66	107	65
Wendell,	81	26	77	28	74	29	80	26	80	26	80	26	80	26	80	26
Whately,	138	135	138	135	136	136	138	135	139	133	138	135	136	136	136	136
26 Towns,	3,133	2,514	3,114	2,505	3,035	2,554	3,116	2,503	3,111	2,504	3,126	2,490	3,112	2,507	3,113	2,509

COUNTY OF BERKSHIRE.

TOWNS.	No. 1. Yes.	No. 1. No.	No. 2. Yes.	No. 2. No.	No. 3. Yes.	No. 3. No.	No. 4. Yes.	No. 4. No.	No. 5. Yes.	No. 5. No.	No. 6. Yes.	No. 6. No.	No. 7. Yes.	No. 7. No.	No. 8. Yes.	No. 8. No.
Adams,	352	420	352	420	349	422	351	421	350	422	359	418	352	420	352	420
Alford,	63	22	63	21	61	21	63	21	63	21	64	20	63	21	63	21

Becket,	100	91	101	90	101	91	100	91	101	90	101	90	100	91	101	90
Cheshire,	202	13	200	15	196	19	202	13	199	16	201	14	202	13	202	13
Clarksburg,	42	20	41	21	40	22	41	21	40	22	41	21	40	22	40	22
Dalton,	84	73	84	73	84	73	84	73	75	82	84	73	84	73	84	73
Egremont,	106	107	107	106	106	107	106	107	107	106	107	106	106	107	106	107
Florida,	46	36	46	36	45	37	46	36	46	36	46	36	46	36	45	37
Great Barrington,	163	236	163	236	162	237	163	236	163	236	165	234	163	236	163	235
Hancock,	62	58	62	58	61	58	62	58	62	58	62	58	62	58	62	58
Hinsdale,	68	95	61	102	53	110	64	99	59	104	64	99	64	99	65	98
Lanesborough,	122	96	120	97	118	97	120	97	120	97	120	96	120	97	117	97
Lee,	234	271	235	270	233	273	236	269	236	269	236	269	236	269	236	269
Lenox,	128	116	128	116	126	116	128	116	127	116	127	114	128	116	128	116
Monterey,	95	31	95	31	94	32	95	31	95	31	94	32	95	31	94	32
Mount Washington,	26	3	29	–	29	–	29	–	28	1	29	–	29	–	29	–
New Ashford,	31	7	30	7	31	7	31	7	31	7	31	7	31	7	31	7
New Marlborough,	118	136	119	136	113	139	119	136	117	138	119	136	120	135	121	135
Otis,	91	57	90	57	89	58	90	57	90	57	90	56	90	57	90	57
Peru,	28	61	28	61	25	64	27	62	29	60	28	61	28	61	26	63

COUNTY OF BERKSHIRE—Continued.

Towns.	No. 1.		No. 2.		No. 3.		No. 4.		No. 5.		No. 6.		No. 7.		No. 8.	
	Yes.	No.	Yes.	No.	Yes.	No.	Yes.	No.	Yes.	No.	Yes.	No.	Yes.	No.	Yes.	No.
Pittsfield,	440	469	444	464	435	470	451	457	442	462	449	458	443	465	442	466
Richmond,	70	28	69	29	69	29	69	29	69	29	69	29	69	29	69	29
Sandisfield,	141	69	138	69	138	69	138	69	139	65	139	65	140	65	140	65
Savoy,	160	12	160	12	159	12	160	12	157	14	161	11	160	12	160	12
Sheffield,	147	114	146	115	144	117	146	115	144	117	146	115	146	115	147	114
Stockbridge,	164	114	165	113	164	114	166	113	164	113	166	113	165	113	165	113
Tyringham,	68	30	66	29	66	29	66	29	66	29	66	29	66	29	66	29
Washington,	52	32	45	39	45	39	49	35	44	40	48	36	45	39	45	39
West Stockbridge,	59	99	57	96	53	100	57	96	57	96	57	96	57	96	56	95
Williamstown,	240	175	240	175	240	175	240	175	240	175	240	175	240	175	240	176
Windsor,	83	70	83	68	81	70	83	68	83	67	83	68	83	68	83	68
31 Towns,	3,785	3,161	3,767	3,162	3,710	3,207	3,782	3,149	3,743	3,163	3,792	3,135	3,773	3,155	3,768	3,156

COUNTY OF NORFOLK.

Bellingham,	136	42	135	44	131	48	136	42	137	41	136	42	136	42	136	42
Braintree,	155	243	157	243	152	245	158	240	158	240	169	230	158	241	158	241
Brookline,	75	269	73	272	57	287	78	267	79	266	80	265	73	272	74	271
Canton,	154	201	160	198	155	202	162	195	160	196	163	192	157	196	154	198
Cohasset,	50	101	50	100	50	101	56	96	61	96	55	96	50	101	50	101
Dedham,	237	416	242	407	229	419	249	401	247	444	251	397	243	407	238	409
Dorchester,	410	634	417	626	403	639	425	639	433	611	439	601	415	631	414	631
Dover,	36	59	36	59	36	60	43	52	36	58	43	52	36	59	36	59
Foxborough,	125	148	126	147	122	147	126	147	130	143	129	143	126	147	126	147
Franklin,	155	148	157	145	146	155	159	144	151	152	159	144	157	146	158	145
Medfield,	49	112	50	111	40	121	50	111	50	111	52	109	49	112	48	113
Medway,	215	202	218	198	209	206	222	194	213	202	229	185	216	200	215	200
Milton,	97	165	101	161	95	167	102	160	102	160	109	153	99	163	97	165
Needham,	117	117	117	117	113	118	117	117	117	116	117	116	117	117	117	116
Quincy,	238	358	239	357	230	364	239	356	250	345	256	338	237	358	234	359
Randolph,	211	444	216	439	212	443	221	436	239	418	241	416	219	438	228	435
Roxbury,	434	1,085	438	1,077	428	1,083	433	1,071	451	1,001	458	996	437	1,065	438	1,077

COUNTY OF NORFOLK—Continued.

TOWNS.	No. 1.		No. 2.		No. 3.		No. 4.		No. 5.		No. 6.		No. 7.		No. 8.	
	Yes.	No.	Yes.	No.	Yes.	No.	Yes.	No.	Yes.	No.	Yes.	No.	Yes.	No.	Yes.	No.
Sharon, . . .	114	111	113	111	114	111	117	108	116	109	115	109	112	110	112	111
Stoughton, . . .	309	264	312	254	300	260	316	259	324	244	340	231	313	258	299	262
Walpole, . . .	139	208	139	208	128	215	140	207	143	205	140	208	139	208	141	209
West Roxbury, . .	66	373	70	370	66	374	68	372	72	368	79	361	68	372	68	372
Weymouth, . . .	391	424	400	416	380	433	401	415	417	399	410	406	399	417	400	416
Wrentham, . . .	174	262	175	262	170	266	176	261	175	263	178	260	176	262	176	261
23 Towns, . .	4,087	6,386	4,141	6,322	3,966	6,464	4,194	6,290	4,261	6,188	4,348	6,050	4,132	6,322	4,117	6,340

COUNTY OF BRISTOL.

TOWNS.	No. 1.		No. 2.		No. 3.		No. 4.		No. 5.		No. 6.		No. 7.		No. 8.	
	Yes.	No.	Yes.	No.	Yes.	No.	Yes.	No.	Yes.	No.	Yes.	No.	Yes.	No.	Yes.	No.
Attleborough, . .	367	339	344	358	327	376	370	338	341	363	350	359	368	340	368	339
Berkley, . . .	68	48	70	45	70	46	73	44	72	43	72	44	70	46	70	46
Dartmouth, . . .	240	217	240	217	240	217	240	217	240	217	240	217	240	217	240	172
Dighton, . . .	103	106	104	105	102	107	103	105	103	105	105	104	103	105	103	106
Easton, . . .	224	200	226	198	223	201	224	200	230	193	233	191	224	201	225	200

Fairhaven,	310	317	309	317	308	318	310	317	310	317	310	317	310	317	310	317
Fall River,	566	498	571	495	570	495	570	495	566	495	538	526	568	496	567	503
Freetown,	57	64	57	64	56	65	58	63	56	65	58	63	58	63	58	63
Mansfield,	203	35	201	32	200	35	202	32	201	32	191	43	202	33	199	34
New Bedford,	1,195	1,317	1,195	1,316	1,185	1,317	1,199	1,314	1,204	1,308	1,195	1,310	1,198	1,314	1,193	1,315
Norton,	156	116	160	115	159	116	160	115	158	115	158	116	159	114	159	114
Pawtucket,	179	184	179	184	178	185	179	184	178	184	181	183	179	183	179	183
Raynham,	149	82	149	82	145	83	148	82	146	82	149	82	149	82	149	82
Rehoboth,	147	137	147	137	148	136	147	137	147	137	148	136	147	137	147	137
Seekonk,	141	87	141	87	127	100	141	87	137	90	143	85	141	87	141	87
Somerset,	111	134	111	134	111	134	111	134	111	134	111	134	111	134	111	134
Swanzey,	93	112	93	112	92	112	93	112	93	112	93	112	93	112	93	112
Taunton,	549	888	549	889	531	901	552	887	544	890	544	886	547	888	546	891
Westport,	151	97	153	97	154	97	154	97	151	99	154	97	153	97	153	97
19 Towns,	5,009	4,978	4,999	4,984	4,926	5,041	5,034	4,960	4,988	4,981	4,973	5,005	5,020	4,966	5,011	4,977

38

COUNTY OF PLYMOUTH.

TOWNS.	No. 1.		No. 2.		No. 3.		No. 4.		No. 5.		No. 6.		No. 7.		No. 8.	
	Yes.	No.	Yes.	No.	Yes.	No.	Yes.	No.	Yes.	No.	Yes.	No.	Yes.	No.	Yes.	No.
Abington,	525	344	533	337	522	346	534	332	544	322	543	325	530	338	530	337
Bridgewater,	166	296	168	295	165	298	170	293	167	296	171	293	169	294	168	295
Carver,	104	120	105	119	104	119	104	119	104	119	104	119	104	119	104	119
Duxbury,	246	175	246	174	246	175	247	174	247	174	249	172	248	173	248	173
East Bridgewater,	260	230	260	230	260	230	264	226	263	228	263	227	262	228	264	226
Halifax,	73	70	70	72	70	72	70	71	72	68	71	71	70	70	70	71
Hanover,	148	80	148	79	148	79	148	78	145	81	150	77	148	79	149	78
Hanson,	132	50	133	51	128	54	131	49	133	51	132	52	133	49	134	49
Hingham,	207	398	209	397	207	399	209	394	212	394	209	396	209	397	208	398
Hull,	7	16	7	16	7	16	7	16	7	16	7	16	7	16	7	16
Kingston,	123	165	124	164	121	166	135	153	129	160	135	154	136	153	136	153
Marshfield,	146	93	146	93	145	94	146	93	144	95	146	93	146	93	146	93
Middleborough,	361	315	360	315	361	316	363	313	362	314	363	314	361	315	362	315
North Bridgewater,	391	407	393	401	389	405	394	401	394	399	396	399	392	403	392	405
Pembroke,	119	109	119	109	119	109	119	109	119	109	120	108	119	109	119	109

Plymouth, . . .	412	419	420	410	414	415	428	403	432	398	425	405	419	412	419	411
Plympton, . . .	34	115	34	115	34	115	34	115	34	115	34	115	34	115	34	115
Rochester, . . .	135	251	135	250	126	259	135	250	136	249	146	239	136	248	135	249
Scituate, . . .	166	83	166	83	165	84	166	83	163	84	166	83	166	83	166	83
South Scituate, . .	87	191	86	191	84	193	91	186	93	187	96	182	89	189	90	187
Wareham, . . .	101	244	100	243	99	242	100	243	100	242	101	242	101	242	101	243
West Bridgewater, .	131	156	121	127	128	154	122	152	136	148	136	147	129	154	129	154
24 Towns, . . .	4,074	4,327	4,083	4,271	4,042	4,340	4,117	4,253	4,136	4,249	4,163	4,229	4,008	4,279	4,111	4,279

COUNTY OF BARNSTABLE.

Barnstable, . . .	249	151	249	151	249	151	249	151	249	151	249	151	249	151	248	151
Brewster, . . .	69	61	70	61	69	61	70	61	70	61	70	61	70	61	70	61
Chatham, . . .	84	112	84	112	84	112	84	112	84	112	84	112	84	112	84	112
Dennis, ...	90	117	91	116	89	118	92	115	89	118	91	116	90	117	90	117
Eastham, . . .	31	46	30	46	32	45	32	45	32	45	32	45	32	45	32	45
Falmouth, . . .	122	210	122	210	122	210	122	210	122	210	122	210	122	210	122	210
Harwich, . . .	84	139	84	139	84	139	84	139	84	139	84	139	84	139	84	139

COUNTY OF BARNSTABLE—Continued.

TOWNS.	No. 1.		No. 2.		No. 3.		No. 4.		No. 5.		No. 6.		No. 7.		No. 8.	
	Yes.	No.	Yes.	No.	Yes.	No.	Yes.	No.	Yes.	No.	Yes.	No.	Yes.	No.	Yes.	No.
Orleans,	54	73	54	73	54	73	54	73	54	73	54	73	54	73	54	73
Provincetown,	124	132	125	131	123	133	124	131	125	131	125	131	124	132	124	132
Sandwich,	157	264	158	265	158	265	158	265	158	265	159	264	158	265	158	264
Truro,	84	41	85	40	85	40	85	40	85	40	85	40	84	41	84	41
Wellfleet,	111	109	111	109	111	109	111	109	111	109	111	109	111	109	111	109
Yarmouth,	35	148	35	148	35	148	35	147	35	147	35	147	35	147	35	147
13 Towns,	1,294	1,650	1,298	1,601	1,295	1,604	1,300	1,598	1,298	1,601	1,301	1,598	1,297	1,602	1,296	1,601

NANTUCKET COUNTY.

TOWNS.	No. 1. Yes.	No. 1. No.	No. 2. Yes.	No. 2. No.	No. 3. Yes.	No. 3. No.	No. 4. Yes.	No. 4. No.	No. 5. Yes.	No. 5. No.	No. 6. Yes.	No. 6. No.	No. 7. Yes.	No. 7. No.	No. 8. Yes.	No. 8. No.
Nantucket,	273	394	273	393	272	395	273	394	275	392	275	392	273	394	274	393

COUNTY OF DUKES COUNTY.

TOWNS.	No. 1. Yes.	No. 1. No.	No. 2. Yes.	No. 2. No.	No. 3. Yes.	No. 3. No.	No. 4. Yes.	No. 4. No.	No. 5. Yes.	No. 5. No.	No. 6. Yes.	No. 6. No.	No. 7. Yes.	No. 7. No.	No. 8. Yes.	No. 8. No.
Chilmark,	32	16	35	13	35	13	35	13	36	12	41	7	36	12	39	12
Edgartown,	44	159	45	158	43	159	45	158	47	156	44	159	44	159	44	149
Tisbury,	56	63	56	63	56	63	56	63	56	63	56	63	56	63	56	63
3 Towns,	132	238	136	234	134	235	136	234	139	231	141	229	136	234	139	224

RECAPITULATION.

COUNTIES.																
Suffolk,	3,673	9,588	3,613	9,069	3,512	9,020	3,684	8,992	3,774	8,849	4,051	8,729	3,619	8,861	3,650	8,928
Essex,	7,998	9,099	8,024	9,061	7,875	9,209	8,065	9,006	8,203	8,891	8,227	8,884	8,060	9,042	8,095	9,017
Middlesex,	10,339	12,178	10,452	12,052	10,027	12,383	10,571	11,955	10,637	11,822	10,982	11,514	10,432	12,067	10,455	12,054
Worcester,	12,935	7,724	12,994	7,450	12,609	7,880	13,021	7,611	12,940	7,697	13,098	7,496	12,934	7,633	12,931	7,688
Hampshire,	2,698	2,935	2,683	2,940	2,585	3,020	2,684	2,939	2,696	2,918	2,726	2,908	2,642	2,983	2,639	2,983
Hampden,	3,792	2,978	3,805	2,962	3,711	3,030	3,828	2,944	3,814	2,946	3,908	2,853	3,808	2,966	3,813	2,960
Franklin,	3,133	2,514	3,114	2,505	3,035	2,554	3,116	2,503	3,111	2,504	3,126	2,490	3,112	2,507	3,113	2,509
Berkshire,	3,785	3,161	3,767	3,162	3,710	3,207	3,782	3,149	3,743	3,163	3,792	3,135	3,773	3,155	3,768	3,156
Norfolk,	4,087	6,386	4,141	6,322	3,966	6,464	4,194	6,290	4,261	6,188	4,348	6,050	4,132	6,322	4,117	6,340
Bristol,	5,009	4,978	4,999	4,984	4,926	5,041	5,034	4,960	4,988	4,981	4,973	5,005	5,020	4,966	5,011	4,977
Plymouth,	4,074	4,327	4,083	4,271	4,042	4,340	4,117	4,253	4,136	4,249	4,163	4,229	4,008	4,279	4,111	4,279
Barnstable,	1,294	1,650	1,298	1,601	1,295	1,604	1,300	1,598	1,298	1,601	1,301	1,598	1,297	1,602	1,296	1,601
Nantucket,	273	394	273	393	272	395	273	394	275	392	275	392	273	394	274	393
Dukes County,	132	238	136	234	134	235	136	234	139	231	141	229	136	234	139	224
14 Counties,	63,222	68,150	63,382	67,006	61,699	68,382	63,805	66,828	64,015	66,432	65,111	65,512	63,246	67,011	63,412	67,109

INDEX.

INDEX OF SUBJECTS

CONSIDERED IN

COMMITTEE OF THE WHOLE.

CONTENTS OF THE APPENDIX.

NOTE.—The Constitutional Propositions agreed to by the Convention and submitted to the People, may be found on pages 383 to 415, inclusive.

www.ingramcontent.com/pod-product-compliance
Lightning Source LLC
LaVergne TN
LVHW021239110826
84515OLV00002B/352

* 9 7 8 1 4 2 5 5 6 2 6 2 5